INTERNATIONAL BUSINESS MANAGEMENT ■

SECOND EDITION

INTERNATIONAL BUSINESS MANAGEMENT

A GUIDE TO DECISION MAKING

RICHARD D. ROBINSON

Alfred P. Sloan School of Management,
Massachusetts Institute of Technology

THE DRYDEN PRESS
HINSDALE, ILLINOIS

TO HAMLIN ROBINSON

Older brother by blood and friendship, guide by word
and example, whose counsel has frequently brought new
reality into view, some of which may be reflected here.

THE DRYDEN PRESS
SERIES IN MANAGEMENT

William F. Glueck, Consulting Editor

Burack
ORGANIZATION ANALYSIS: Theory and Applications

Duncan
ESSENTIALS OF MANAGEMENT, 2d ed.

Gellerman
MANAGEMENT OF HUMAN RELATIONS

Gellerman
MANAGEMENT OF HUMAN RESOURCES

Gellerman
MANAGERS AND SUBORDINATES

Glans, Grad, Holstein, Meyers & Schmidt
MANAGEMENT SYSTEMS

Glueck
MANAGEMENT

Glueck & Jauch
THE MANAGERIAL EXPERIENCE: Cases, Exercises and Readings

McFarlan, Nolan & Norton
INFORMATION SYSTEMS ADMINISTRATION

Robinson
INTERNATIONAL BUSINESS MANAGEMENT, 2d ed.

PREFACE

This volume is designed as a complete text and teaching vehicle for a basic graduate course in international management. It will be noted that it follows the strategy decisions with which a firm operating internationally is faced and of the variables relevant to each set of choices. This volume, as did the first edition, includes examples of how the variables may influence decision outcomes and a discussion of research findings pertaining to each decision option. The attempt has been to make this, in a very real sense, a state-of-the-art report that should be of value to student, researcher, and practitioner of international business of whatever nationality. A number of appendices are included to enhance the value of the volume as a reference book.

In this, the second edition, has been added summaries of many recent research findings and an entire new strategy area, public affairs. Of the 13 cases included in the second edition, seven are new. And all statistical data have been updated to the most recent.

Admittedly, only English-language sources—with but minor exceptions—have been used in the theory that significant research reported initially in other languages would be listed and commented upon in one or more of the English language periodicals dealing with management and originating in Western Europe, Latin America, Southeast Asia, and Japan and the Soviet Union. These periodicals have been scanned systematically. The reader should appreciate that this volume focuses on international management, not international economics; hence the limited reference to research and works in the area.

It would be a grave oversight not to acknowledge the valuable contributions made by many individuals to the organization and content of the pages that follow. Over the intervening years since the publication of the first edition, literally dozens of people all over the world have offered constructive criticism, much of which has been used to improve this present edition. Nonetheless, the most direct contribution has been made, as before, by students and colleagues at the Sloan School through specific research, literature search, and personal discussion. The list of those contributing significantly to the compilation of this study has simply grown too long to name them individually. But collectively they are my creditor, and I acknowledge a vast indebtedness. But I do wish to express my special appreciation to Ms. Joan Wyatt for her tireless efforts in preparing this volume for publication. Also, a special indebtedness to Donald Lessard must be acknowledged for his valuable critique of various portions of the text.

R.D.R.

Cambridge, Mass.
January 1978

CONTENTS

Introduction
NATIONALISM, WORLD WELFARE, AND THE NATURE OF INTERNATIONAL BUSINESS

NATIONALISM

It is extremely unlikely that one can come to grips effectively with the pressures and conflicts inherent in the international movement of capital, skills, technology, and goods without an appreciation of the essential nature of nationalism and the cluster of interests represented in that notion.

Nationalism is not a mystical, ethereal, will-o'-the-wisp sort of idea, nor is it irrational within the context of contemporary society. On the contrary, it probably represents a way station in the evolution of an individual's identification from tribe to humanity. In other times and places, nationalism has been defined differently from the contemporary idea of a geographically defined state that claims the loyalty of its residents as against other geographically defined states. A nation could be—and has been—identified primarily on a racial or religious basis, even though its citizens were widely dispersed in terms of residence. It is even possible to conceive of a nationalism built upon primary loyalty to a profession or to a global corporation.

The geographically defined nation-state is a product of a unique geopolitical position, a unique historical input, a unique ethnic mix, and a unique demographic record. For a state so defined to survive more than a fleeting historical moment it must enjoy the loyalty of most of its residents. Or, stated in another way, most of its residents must identify their interests more with the preservation of the sovereignty of the state in which they reside than with any other, however the other might be defined. Some would call this personal identification or loyalty "nationalism"; others, "patriotism."

National allocational priorities

The basic cement of such loyalty or identification is a degree of consensus among residents in respect to the allocation of the nation's resources, which is the tangible expression of a shared priority of values. A useful and concrete way to describe this national ranking of priorities is to plot a nation's allocation profile along a series of continua, each of which represents a possible allocation between two extreme points. For example, a nation may give priority in resource allocation:

> To investment in the wherewithal of future production and consumption or of present production and consumption;
>
> To a military establishment or to the civilian sector;
>
> To the private (that is, market) sector or to the public sector;
>
> To human resource development or to the development of physical assets;
>
> To the achievement of full employment or to achievement of technical efficiency;
>
> To the achievement of international integration or of national autarky;
>
> To the achievement of maximum efficiency of resource use or of decentralization of economic power by forced competition;
>
> To the achievement of maximum efficiency or of a more even level of development (that is, from one part of the country to another);
>
> To a reward system based on the market value of one's product (laissez faire) or to the assurance of a given level of consumption to all (that is, welfare);
>
> To the preservation of environmental integrity or to the unrestrained exploitation of the environment.

Each of these choices represents polar points. Under some circumstances these polar points may be very close or, indeed, may converge to a point at which both objectives may be achieved without conflict. But such circumstances are probably rare. There appear to be no self-evident, universally valid, *right* points—that is, no objective function, specifying the way a nation *should* allocate its resources, with the possible exception of that listed last (the environmental choice). Implied in any set of choices, of course, are underlying cultural differences that activate differing governmental policies relevant to the allocation of resources. Culture—that is, the way of looking at the world, the values, the traditions, and the institutions that interact to establish allocational priorities—is a function of a people's unique history (including its level of economic and political development), geography, demographic-ethnic mix, and is another way of describing a people's shared experience.

Characteristically, in a lesser developed country (LDC) there is a need perceived by the political elite to allocate more resources into investment than into consumption, in order to generate a catch-up growth rate. But once economic incentive erupts there is great political pressure in the opposite direction; that is, to consume. For a society just moving away from a near subsistence level of living and newly motivated by economic incentive, the propensity to consume added output is almost universal.

Allocation as between military and civilian status is largely a function of history and geopolitical position, although the need to justify isolating a society from external consumption models may well lead to antagonism, perceived threat, and a high level of "defense spending." Whether the military contributes significantly to economic development depends upon its role. In some instances, it may be very effective in mobilizing manpower for productive uses. No valid generalizations are possible, although it seems quite clear that the global armaments expenditures in 1976 of an estimated $350 billion far exceeded their contribution to useful production.[1]

Allocation between the private and public sectors depends substantially on the perceived effectiveness of the market in allocating resources in such a manner as to support national objectives, whether they be maximum production, maximum consumption, maximum employment, regional development, welfare, or protection of the environment. The imperfections of the market mechanism in the typical less developed country, plus its small market size, render many more industries natural monopolies in the sense of making them decreasing-cost industries by reason of the restraint on output imposed by the small size of the relevant market. One upshot is that many less developed countries have less faith in the capacity of private business to satisfy national objectives than do the more developed countries. Other forces that push resources into the public sector are the historical disrepute of private business (because of the identification with either foreign interests or with ethnic or religious minorities, coupled with the natural tendency toward monopoly in small insulated markets); the greater importance of externalities where industry is imbued with an important educational function and is viewed as a lever for long-term national or regional development; the ineffectiveness of commercial law (thereby rendering unlikely anything other than family-size corporations); and the many market imperfections that generate high entry barriers and make possible the extraction of monopoly profits.

In newer states, where the need to develop popular support (legitimacy) for the political regime is critical, the objective of full employment may be compelling, even at the expense of efficiency. Because of the commercial policies of the more developed countries and the hostility often felt toward the developed countries by reason of past "exploitation," a less developed country may be more enamored of the idea of achieving a greater degree of national autarky than might otherwise be the case. Forced competition has little relevance to small markets. Therefore, pressure in the direction of permitting concentration of resources to maximize efficiency under governmental controls is predictable. Efforts to even out the level of development from one region of the country to another may be given high priority in countries troubled by problems of establishing the legitimacy of relatively new political regimes. Moreover, the sociopolitical problems attending the mass movement of population

---

[1]Figure quoted by Robert S. McNamara in a speech at the Massachusetts Institute of Technology, April 28, 1977.

into one or two metropolitan centers may warrant considerable "noneconomic" investment in order to create employment elsewhere and thus stem the demographic tide somewhat. Finally, in many less developed countries higher levels of pollution and of resource utilization have been considered as measures of success rather than of impending disaster. It is quite obvious on the basis of this discussion, that the self-perceived interests of one nation may lead it to opt for one pattern of resource allocation; another nation, for quite another pattern.

One must also understand the role of ideology in justifying whatever pattern of resource allocation is selected. For example, a national elite may perceive that a high level of investment is required to sustain a high rate of long-run economic and manpower development. This commitment to development may become psychologically compelling for an elite that has seized upon external models. Yet, the national elite may recognize that to remain in power it must provide incentives and rewards for a higher level of productive effort on the part of the people. Since the propensity to consume added output is very high—particularly if external consumption models become pervasive—the elite must make those models less appealing and opt for some variety of nonmaterial award. Control of external communications and promotion of an ideology are likely responses. The ideological appeal must promise in a sense the realization of some nonmaterial reward for present effort, whether it be the pride of being a member of a superior "race," religion (secular or otherwise), or nation-state, or all three. Social distinction may be bestowed for performing well and, at the same time, adhering to approved models of behavior (that is, high productivity and minimum consumption). Those who find it impossible to fit into this scheme of things—to be so programmed, that is—are ruthlessly eliminated. The result may well be a new variety of Puritan ideology that equates a high level of personal consumption with sin (that is, something ideologically and socially—hence morally—reprehensible). One derives pleasure and distinction from performing well under the system, which is ideologically defined. Work, that is, extra effort, comes to have its own intrinsic nonmaterial reward.

The danger, of course, is that an ideology embodying these values is very likely to breed hostility toward systems offering immediate material rewards and equating wealth with social esteem. And the latter see the former as a threat. Indeed, both systems view each other as possibly subversive, hence the need to build defenses by blocking easy communication. Furthermore, an ideology may well outlive its utility and, in fact, constitute a serious obstacle to changing the system even when change is indicated. The ideologically motivated states inevitably face this problem eventually with more intensity than do the market-motivated states.

The notion of economic development is fairly clear; it can be measured fairly easily, either in terms of per-capita consumption or production, or both.

But the level of political development of a society, another important variable influencing resource allocation choices—and, hence, national identity and characteristics—is more difficult of precise definition. The term *political* refers, of course, to the influencing, manipulating, or control of groups (often national in size, but not necessarily) in order to advance group national interests—in other words, the struggle for power in the broad Morganthau sense.[2] The totality of coherent political activity represents a political culture, which is more precisely defined as the manner in which a society is organized about, reacts to, and uses political authority. Political authority, in turn, is equated with the power to make and enforce decisions relating to the integration and adaption of a society in respect to either internal or external variables.[3] As very succinctly spelled out by Gabriel Almond, and simplified and somewhat modified here, a political culture may be analyzed in terms of eight differentiated political functions:

Input Functions

1. Political socialization: the manner and degree to which the members of a society identify with a political culture.

2. Political recruitment: the manner and degree to which a society participates in legitimizing the exercise of political authority.

3. Articulation of interest: the manner and degree to which a population makes known its demands for the exercise of political authority.

4. Aggregation of interest: the manner and degree to which interests relating to political authority are aggregated.

5. Communication of interest: the manner and degree to which political interests are communicated to the political authority.

Output Functions

6. Rule making: the manner in which decisions are made by the political authority and the degree of their inclusiveness (i.e., geographical, social, temporal, content).

7. Rule enforcement: the manner in which political decisions are enforced and the degree to which enforcement is achieved.

8. Rule adjudication: the manner in which conflicts among rules and between rules and enforcement are resolved, and the degree to which judgments are enforced.

The development of a political culture from primitive to modern may be traced in terms of these eight functions. The idealized modern political culture is presumed to be one in which all political functions are (1) affectively neutral (that is, are governed by expected results, not by immediate impulses or emotion); (2) individual-oriented (tend to value the individual rather than the collectivity); (3) universalistic (affect all members of the political culture simi-

[2]See Hans Morganthau, *Politics among Nations* (New York: Alfred A. Knopf, 1950), chap. 1; and Quincy Wright, *The Study of International Relations* (New York: Appleton-Century-Crofts, 1955), chap. 13.

[3]This typology of political culture and political change is adapted from Gabriel A. Almond, "A Functional Approach to Comparative Politics," in *The Politics of Developing Areas* (Princeton: Princeton University Press, 1960), pp. 3–64.

larly); (4) specific (are differentiated, not diffuse); and (5) achievement-oriented (treat persons or objects on the basis of ability to accomplish a given end, not on the basis of qualities unrelated to this ability).

For example, one of the earliest moves toward the modern is perhaps the differentiation of the political culture itself from the religious. Generally, a somewhat later development is the relating of the dominant political culture to all individuals within a given geographical area; that is, the establishment of a universal political authority admitting of no racial or religious bars. Following such expansion and intensification of the political socialization process may be a movement to extend the political culture impartially to all citizens and to define political roles on the basis of ability rather than various ascriptive norms. Often accompanying these developments is a broadening of the process of political recruitment, which tends to generate a different manner and intensity of interest articulation. Another characteristic of political development is the formation of specialized interest-aggregating and communicating functions and of differentiated rule-enforcing and rule-adjudicating agencies; that is, differentiated from the rule-making. At some point during this whole process a differentiation of the economic or business culture from the political will usually appear. There is possibly a tendency for the two to remain largely undifferentiated until the business culture becomes so highly specialized and professionalized as to adopt substantially different values and roles from those associated with the political. Business then tends to be blocked from the performance of any significant political function other than aggregating and communicating its own interests, or at least it generates criticism when it attempts to do more.

There may be further stages of political development in which the collectivity again becomes of paramount concern, albeit defined in different ideological terms than before. Also, it is possible that as market imperfections multiply in the modern technological state, the differentiation between the political and economic functions will tend to fade. Possibly we already are confronted with these developments, although American ideology tends to hide them from being perceived in the United States.

Quite apart from the manner or style in which these various political functions operate, but likewise relevant to the level of political development, is the degree to which they are effective; that is, as political modernization proceeds, the process of political socialization tends to deepen, political recruitment to broaden, interest articulation to increase, interest aggregation to intensify, interest communication to diversify, and the political output functions to expand. The degree to which a political function operates may thus be quite distinct from its manner. For example, one may conceive of a political culture in which political socialization results in a high degree of identification with the political authority by all those within the society, but the manner in which that identification is expressed may be highly affective. An example might be a nomadic tribe.

The firm in a nationalistic world

The point of this discussion of nationalism is that penetration by an alien enterprise always requires the commitment of local resources, even if it simply be labor and the expenditure of personal income on certain products not otherwise available. No contemporary nation-state will tolerate unlimited penetration by an alien enterprise in which control is vested in a management headquartered in another nation-state and making decisions possibly insensitive to the allocational priorities of the host country. It is perhaps unfortunate that the development of rapid transport and communication—the necessary preconditions for the multinational and transnational corporation—has come at a time when many national communities have just begun to find their national identities, perhaps a necessary historical step before people can reach for larger, universal identity with mankind. A by-product of a growing national identity—sometimes a deliberately contrived device—is a strengthened feeling of "we" and "they" across national frontiers even to the extent of perceiving that "they" constitute a threat, whether real or concocted. The threat may be perceived simply in terms of subversion of national priorities, for example, the appeal of external models in respect to the allocation of resources between investment and consumption or between the public and private sectors. Hence, in some parts of the world we are witness to efforts to block the appeal of such external models by cutting off the movement of certain goods and even of communication across frontiers.

For the firm operating internationally, all of this poses two fundamental problems. First, it requires a level of expertise and sophistication in environmental analysis not present in the managements of many firms. Secondly, these differing sets of allocational priorities among nations require a rare flexibility of policy on the part of the firm. The point is that a firm operating across frontiers must fit into the national identity in a tolerable fashion wherever it does business. It must not permit itself to be seen as disturbing national priorities in an important manner. When one says "must not," what is meant is that the firm cannot do so without pushing the level of political risk (manifest in loss of control either of assets, sales, or earnings) to an intolerable level.

WORLD WELFARE   0.2

Given the expanding volume of resources moving internationally through essentially commercial channels, the decisions undertaken by the international business managers are obviously of growing importance to world welfare, however that term might be understood.

The widening gaps

The validity of international business as the prime mover of resources—technology, finance, personnel—from the rich to the poor is under serious challenge, whether one speaks of wealth and income distribution within nations or among them. Internationally, the increasing unevenness of aggregate economic growth may be summarized thus:

The major oil-exporting countries, with less than 4 percent of the population, enjoyed a GNP growth rate not of 5 percent, but 8.4 percent during the First Development Decade. Per capita income in these countries grew 5.2 percent annually.

Countries experiencing a per capita GNP exceeding $500—with 9 percent of the population—had a growth rate of 6.2 percent. Per capita income grew annually by 2.4 percent.

In countries with a per capita GNP between $200 and $500—with 20 percent of the population—the growth rate was 5.4 percent. Per capita income grew annually by 4.2 percent.

The poorest countries, those comprising 67 percent of the population, had a per capita GNP of less than $200. With a growth rate of only 3.9 percent, per capita income grew by similarly slower annual increments—only 1.5 percent.[4]

And Grant writes in 1977,

... the poorest billion—three quarters of whom live in low income countries having a per capita GNP below $300—has benefited all too little as the world has moved from $1 trillion global production in the late 1940s to about three times that today.

All indications are that, in the absence of a very special effort, the numbers below the line of absolute poverty will increase substantially during the next generation, although total global output will probably be more than tenfold that of a generation ago.[5]

It is thus very misleading to assume that an increase in per capita GNP signals healthy economic growth, for such change tells one nothing about wealth and income distribution within a country.[6] In fact, there is considerable evidence leading to the conclusion that as the gap in economic well-being widens between rich and poor countries, so it is within many countries. For example, though Brazil's growth in GNP has been significant, the poorest 40 percent of the population benefited only marginally in that their share of national income dropped from 10 percent in 1960 to 8 percent in 1970, while the share going to the richest 5 percent of the populace grew from 29 to 38 percent. The same

---

[4]Address by Robert S. McNamara (President, International Bank for Reconstruction and Development), *Survey of International Development*, vol. 9, no. 4, April 1972, p. 1.

[5]James P. Grant, "Meeting the Basic Needs of the Poorest Billion," *Development Forum*, vol. 5, no. 3, April 1977, p. 1. Grant is President of the Overseas Development Council and formerly Assistant Administrator of the U.S. Agency for International Development and a Deputy Assistant Secretary of State.

[6]For other doubts relating to the international GNP comparisons, see the "Note on National Income—Product Accounting and International Comparability" at the end of chap. 1.

sort of thing happened in Mexico and India. In the latter case, the poorest 10 percent may have actually grown poorer in absolute terms.[7] There seems to be no evidence signaling a change in these trends. The "New International Order" proposed in 1975 by the so-called Group of 77[8] is specifically designed to effect a reversal.

That these gaps should widen at a time when international trade and investment are bounding upward suggests that the mutually beneficial transfer of resources is taking place principally among the more developed (richer) countries and that the transfers between the more developed and less developed (poorer) countries are biased in favor of the former.

Data from several sources seem to confirm the thesis that private foreign investment may have resulted in a net transfer of scarce resources *from* the poor *to* the rich countries; that is, repatriated earnings, dividends, and royalties of the rich countries have exceeded the outflow to the poor countries and apparently continue to increase rapidly.[9]

For a variety of reasons the international equalization of the marginal return on capital (technology, skills, finance, machines) does not lead to a capital movement in the direction of the poorer countries such as to begin closing the gap of per capita economic well-being between the rich and poor countries. Theoretically, productive resources should flow from the relatively capital-rich, developed country to the relatively capital-poor, less developed country where the marginal return on capital should be very much higher than in the richer countries. Something is wrong.

Consider the classical equilibrium formula:

$$MC_K = MR_K = r$$

in which:

MC_K = marginal cost of capital. (In the absence of risk, MC_K is equal to the interest rate. With risk, it includes a risk premium.)

MR_K = marginal return on capital, defined as the discount rate which equates the future cash returns (R) of an investment with the investment outlay (I), as in the following equation:

$$I = \frac{R_1}{(1+r)} + \frac{R_2}{(1+r)^2} + \cdots + \frac{R_n}{(1+r)^n}$$

Presumably one invests until the stream of anticipated earnings—appropriately discounted—equals the investment outlay. Obviously, to bring about an equalization of MC_K and MC_R internationally, several conditions would have to obtain:

1. No significant cost should accrue to the international movement of capital. That

[7]McNamara, *Survey*, p. 2.

[8]The "Group of 77" is composed of most of the developing countries. Although its membership currently exceeds 100, it is still known as the Group of 77.

[9]Heinrich Rattner, "The Control of Technology Transfer to Developing Countries," unpublished paper, Massachusetts Institute of Technology, SPURS, 1972, p. 22.

is, the MC_K of a unit of capital in one set of countries (say, the rich) should equal the MC_K for the same unit in a second set (the poorer) for projects of similar risk.

2. The objective risks in the poor countries should be no higher than in the rich, i.e., MC_K for the poor should be no greater than the MC_K for the rich.

3. The expected flow of returns (R) must be foreseen with roughly the same degree of accuracy in the poor as in the rich countries.

4. The investor must seek, with similar zeal and competence, to maximize returns in each country.

5. The gestation period—the time between investment and the onset of a flow of returns—must be roughly of the same duration.

6. The last period considered relevant (n) must coincide.

The point is that, in balance, if there is a *consistent* bias against the poor countries (that is, significant capital transfer cost, higher risk, less perfect vision of expected returns, less concern for maximizing returns—or ability to do so—a longer gestation period, and a shorter time horizon), then the perceived marginal return on the investment (MR_K) would be lower than in the richer countries even under the same objective conditions. Hence, less capital would flow from rich to poor country in order to achieve an equalization of marginal cost with marginal return. Indeed, a reverse flow might even occur, which may in fact be the case in some circumstances.

Actually, there are many reasons for suspecting a consistent bias of the sort described.

1. Market imperfections and direct transfer costs probably do increase the cost of capital as it moves from rich to poor countries, for in a sense many of the richer countries are participating in a common capital market (in respect to technology, financial, and skill transfer).

2. The expected flow of returns, given the admitted political and economic uncertainties in many poor countries (at least, as perceived by the foreign investor), are probably believed to be consistently lower than reality.

3. For a variety of reasons internal to the investing firm, many firms do not act so as to maximize returns. For example, it will be shown that very few firms consider seriously all of the strategy options open to them and consequently obviously could not be maximizing the flow of returns.

4. The discount rate includes a risk factor, which is consistently higher for the poorer countries than that used by investors in respect to investments in the richer countries. (Furthermore, there is reason to believe that the investors' perception of risk in the poor countries is consistently higher than subsequent developments justify.) Risk is defined here as the probability of the imposition of an unforeseen cost or a block in profit repatriation. Note that what might be called "obscene" profit may be realized by a corporation if the investment decision is predicated upon the assumption of a significant probability that its assets (that is, its income stream) will be expropriated in whole or in part at some point in the future. Such an assumption means that the firm discounts future earnings by a greater factor than it would otherwise. If it nonetheless invests, it can only mean that expected

future earnings must be high enough to cover the additional risk factor. Now assume that, in fact, the expropriation does not take place. It is all very well to argue that for the firm the realized earnings will be averaged with zero or reduced earnings on investments elsewhere where expropriations have taken place. But, *from the point of view of a single country*, that earnings flow may easily be seen as unjustifiably high, thereby justifying the expropriation of all or some part of that flow. Thus it is that a high political risk discounting factor can be self-fulfilling. Application of the risk factor itself enhances the risk against which one is hedging by insisting on a higher level of earnings.

5.　A longer gestation period is reported generally for the poorer countries by reason of lower levels of motivation, skills, governmental efficiency, and infrastructure.

6.　It is often true that the typical firm would cut off projections within a poor country at five years because of environmental uncertainties. It is hoped that a flow of returns can be maintained thereafter, but the investment equation does not assume it. Indeed, the discount rate is typically so high that any return more than ten years out is likely to be perceived as insignificant.

In short, it would appear that all factors probably combine consistently to the disadvantage of the relatively poor countries; hence, capital does not flow to the extent needed to close the gap of per-capita economic well-being. One might suggest that if private international business does not bring about a change in this situation, it will be seen increasingly as running counter to world welfare and, hence, as dispensable.

Division of earnings

Note that the objective of the multinational firm, by definition, is optimum allocation of the firm's resources on a worldwide basis—optimum either in the sense of generating the highest return on investment over the effective planning horizon (rarely longer than ten years, if that long) or of maximizing managerial power. The former is an internal, financial measure over a relatively short time horizon, certainly short relative to the pay-out of such public sector investment as opening up new land; developing new energy sources; space exploration; national defense; public health, education, and manpower development; and achieving ecological balance. The second objective, maximizing corporate power, takes a firm on a direct collision course with both host and parent country political authorities. Since most international executives will not admit to this second motive, we shall not treat it elaborately in this discussion, but it should not be dismissed from mind. Given the tendency for many corporations to follow strategies internationally that would not appear to generate the highest return on investment but do tend to maximize power—such as a strategy to grow internationally *only* through 100 percent–owned subsidiaries—those who question the operation of the pure profit motive are not without some support. In any event, if the corporation is to achieve its profit-maximizing objective it must act to minimize externally imposed costs and to resist internally generated frictions and conflict that might lead to the suboptimal use of its resources.

Consider the latter first—the internal frictions. The maximization of profit by, say, a Brazilian subsidiary of a United States–based multinational firm, does not necessarily lead to the maximization of profit for the entire corporate family. A few examples follow:

The Brazilian subsidiary may maximize its profit by purchasing relatively low-cost material from an independent Mexican source outside of the corporate family, thereby contributing to excess capacity in an associated firm in the United States or elsewhere.

The Brazilian subsidiary may expand production or facilities so as to include a new product line for the Brazilian market or to supply more of old products to export markets, thereby increasing its profit. Meanwhile, associated firms elsewhere, which may already have adequate capacity to produce for these markets, are forced to produce at lower levels at higher unit costs.

The Brazilian subsidiary may borrow locally to modernize its facilities, thereby reducing the credit line of the parent and its subsidiaries elsewhere—that is, making marginal credit more expensive—even though the parent perceives more profitable investment opportunities than the modernization or expansion of the Brazilian plant. Again, the Brazilian subsidiary may profit but at the expense of the rest of the corporate family that forewent more profit elsewhere.

That is, any time a subsidiary utilizes a resource from which a larger profit (or more power?) could be extracted by an associated firm elsewhere, it does so at the expense of the corporate family.

Therefore, as a firm becomes truly multinational, which means that it deliberately restrains the play of national bias in allocating its resources, it must centralize control. Otherwise, it runs into the sub-optimization problem.[10] The firm must try to equalize worldwide the marginal return on its resources, whether these resources be technology, skilled people, an information system, machines, materials, or money.

Furthermore, because of the plethora of taxes, subsidies, and regulations, which vary from one national scene to another, and the differential inflation rates and changes in foreign exchange rates, the multinational firm will attempt to build up activity and/or profits in one country and hold them down in another, thereby minimizing externally imposed costs. It can do this through intersubsidiary discounts and premiums on the services and goods and funds moving from one national subsidiary to another. Meanwhile, each government is trying to maximize the resources made available to it through its tax and subsidy schemes, sometimes by outright protection through quotas and other restraints, sometimes by grants and protection. There is some reason to believe that the less developed country characteristically loses in the corporate alloca-

---

[10]See Glossary.

tion of earnings, thereby causing its tax base to be eroded. Why? Because corporate headquarters is inclined to identify many less developed countries with high rates of internal inflation, unstable foreign exchange rates, uncertainty of foreign exchange availability at any price, and political instability (translatable into possible loss of control over assets). Hence, even though domestic taxes in many LDCs may be relatively low, the typical multinational corporation probably transfers earnings (and such cash flows as those generated by depreciation) to a more stable environment at the earliest possible moment through transfer pricing or cost allocation techniques. Furthermore, the bureaucrats of less developed countries may well be less sophisticated generally and more susceptible to corporate influence in analyzing the realism of intersubsidiary pricing than their brethren in the more developed countries. In any event, the information resources at the disposal of the latter are surely greater. On average, therefore, it is probably a safe bet that the less developed countries are discriminated against in aggregate in this regard; reported and taxable profits generated by the local subsidiaries of foreign-owned firms are probably unduly low.

It is quite obvious that the leadership of many of the LDCs and some of the more developed countries (for example, Canada) are questioning the division of earnings from foreign direct investment,[11] and corresponding pressure is mounting on foreign owners to relinquish an increasing share of their ownership and, hence, of earnings. Additionally, specific limits are infrequently placed on the repatriation of dividends, royalties, and fees and upon the allocation of general overhead burden to subsidiaries.

Although operationally difficult to implement, the argument is that profits should be divided according to the relative value of the domestic and foreign inputs—that is, various mixes of the land, natural resources, labor, technical skills, management, technology, public services, and capital utilized in producing the final good, whatever it may be. The source of these inputs (local and foreign) may be known at a point in time. But there are at least three important difficulties: (1) determining the relative contribution of each factor to final product where market imperfections are gross—and, hence, where prices are a very imperfect measure of economic value; (2) accounting for changes in these relative contributions over time in that a certain amount of substitutability among factors (capital for labor) is possible as the relative costs of the factors change; (3) ascertaining objectively when it is feasible to develop a local factor comparable in cost/quality with an imported factor (such as management, technical skills, and technology) and, hence, substitutable for these imported factors.

Assume that it is consistently true in the LDC case that the price of foreign capital, technology, technical skills, and management is relatively higher than

---

[11]See Glossary.

the value of their respective contributions to final product, and that the price paid for locally provided land, resources, labor and public service is relatively lower. In such a case, earnings would be inequitably divided in favor of the foreign owners of capital, managerial and technical skills, and technology.

In view of what has been said above about capital flows, it is possible that foreign capital, particularly in the form of direct investment, is consistently overpriced. Also, it may well be that frequently local public sector inputs are underpriced, given the generally lower level of taxes in LDCs and relatively high cost of capital. But even if the division of earnings generated by an enterprise in year one as between owners and host country were equitable, division would become inequitable as managerial skills and technology were transferred over time. Such an enterprise can anticipate increasing pressure to change the division of earnings in favor of the host country. Many developed country firms equate such pressure with "unreasonable nationalism" and, as a result, increase the risk factor by which they discount future earnings. The result is a relatively low level of investment. It should be borne in mind that we are dealing more with the perceptions of foreign investors and host country decision-makers than with objective reality.

International investment theory

The notion of the product life cycle relates to this process. The idea is that, initially, because of the relatively low cost of capital and large domestic market, new technology is developed in the richer countries (particularly in the U.S. because of its superiority in aggregate wealth). This relationship holds because industrial research and development is a highly capital-intensive activity for both the firm and the surrounding society and, hence, should flourish where capital is relatively cheap. Initially, the new technology is used in commercial production for local sale, but sooner or later an export market develops. The theory of comparative advantage in international trade suggests that a relatively rich country tends to export capital-intensive goods. Let it be noted that goods embodying large amounts of high-level skills (that is, new technology) are the most capital intensive of all.

If the pace of the relevant technological development eventually slows, and the protection offered the firm by patents and secrecy is eroded, entry barriers for competitors are reduced. Tariffs, freight costs, unfavorable exchange rates, and many forms of nontariff barriers—plus the threat of foreign competition—tend to push the firm into investment in overseas production. Over time, the firm loses proprietory claim to the necessary skills and know-how; the value of new technology becomes marginal; the market is developed; and uncertainties and risks,[12] reduced—all of which add up to a shift in the direction of

---

[12]See Glossary.

increasing labor intensity. Hence, advantages accrue to firms producing in lower labor cost countries, not only for the local market but for import into the home market as well. The more "mature" the product or technology, the more labor intensive it is likely to become in that less capital is consumed per unit of output, and production shifts to still cheaper labor countries—to Spain, South Korea, Taiwan, the Philippines, India. Meanwhile, the special contribution of the developed country corporation may be reduced. Little new capital flows; the technology and skills have been transferred; markets have been developed. In such case, at some point the foreign corporation is likely to come under considerable pressure to redistribute earnings in favor of the local society. Faced with such pressure, the corporation may resist by strengthening its legal defenses, investing heavily in promotion and advertising in order to build and maintain a differentiated product (even if differentiated only in the consumer's mind), or increase its flow of extra legal payments to buy special treatment. Such strategies tend to restrict entry by others and to bring the firm into conflict with the host government; hence, enhanced political risk. On the other hand, the firm may react by spinning off ownership and control and retreating essentially to a contractual relationship in which the corporation supplies only those inputs not available elsewhere at comparable cost and quality—very frequently, new technology and access to an international distribution system. This strategy is likely to be a less risky one in these circumstances, and more profitable as well. That so many foreign corporations do not easily consider this strategy is strongly suggestive of a power-maximizing objective rather than profit-maximizing.

But the product life cycle theory is not a complete explanation of direct foreign investment. It would not, for example, explain Volkswagen's recent decision to invest in the United States. The automobile is a mature product. Production has been, and theoretically should be, moving *out* of the United States, not in. The more general explanation is, of course, that direct foreign investment moves in the presence of perceived market imperfections. Control of a superior technology (or product) and gradual loss of same, is central to the product life cycle, but this relates to only one kind of market imperfection, albeit an important one. The point is that direct foreign investment may take place whenever the foreign firm has some competitive advantage over local firms, such as access at lower cost to finance, technology, technical skills, managerial talent, labor, materials, markets, and information systems. Additionally, competitive advantage may rest on reduced perceived risk and uncertainty.[13]

Market access may be a function of established brand name and company image. Volkswagen vehicles compete in the U.S. market because of a unique product image, an image based in part on low price and economy in use and

---

[13]See Glossary.

in part on styling and massive promotion and advertising. When its position in the market was threatened by price increases induced by a shift in exchange rates and an increase in fixed labor costs in Germany, management decided to make the move rather than abandon the market. The product life cycle does not explain this decision, but the more general market imperfection theory does. In this case, the imperfection was the carefully nurtured Volkswagen image and the production cost differential between Germany and the U.S., the latter arising in part out of international labor market imperfections. Both elements were undoubtedly crucial to the decision.

If all markets were perfect—for finance, technology, skills, product, labor (that is, if all comers had access at the same price)—then little direct investment would flow. The condition of a perfect market implies, of course, the absence of any unique market appeal of a product associated with any one firm and the same risk and uncertainty for all, conditions which are never satisfied.

Take risk and uncertainty. The size and degree of diversification of a firm will affect the risk and uncertainty it faces. If a given project is a single investment for Investor A, but merely one out of a hundred for Investor B, the latter enjoys a lower risk. B can tolerate failure of the project; A cannot. And the more diversified is B's investment portfolio (that is, one in which the results of his investments are not closely related), the lower his risk will be. This diversification may be measured either in geographical terms, function, and/or product. Similarly, if Investor A must sell the fruits of the project in which he has invested to an external market over which he has no control, and Investor B, being in command of a vertically-integrated operation (but possibly geographically diversified), can sell at least in part to himself, market uncertainty is likely to be reduced for B. At the very least, short-term variations in the market may be more easily smoothed, thereby reducing costs.

The point is that if risk and uncertainty are lower for B than for A, B should discount anticipated future earnings by a lower rate and will thus be in a position to invest in projects promising a lower flow of returns than can A. Indeed, one hears many charges of exploitation directed against the relatively small local firms in the LDCs. And one of the reasons advanced by MNC managers against entering into joint ventures with local interests is the latter's demand for a much higher pay-out than the MNC feels wise. Not infrequently, MNC managers complain that no local partners are available at all, which is simply another way of saying that the expected pay-out is too low to attract local investors.

Ultimately, of course, a countervailing political risk may arise precisely because of the great size and diversified nature of the foreign firm. It comes to be viewed by political decision-makers in both parent and host countries as threatening, and political action is taken to restrain its growth; that is, to make growth more costly via either antitrust enforcement by parent government or the introduction of restrictive entry agreements and post-entry monitoring by host governments.

When the notion of market imperfection is expanded to include differential risks and uncertainties, the theory can possibly explain all direct foreign investment (other than that undertaken simply on the basis of some executive's personal whim, which is really another form of market imperfection), and the product life cycle theory is seen only as a special case. In that market imperfections often lead to the appearance of oligopolies, one also hears reference to the oligopoly theory of direct foreign investment. It would seem more accurate, however, to refer to the underlying causal conditions—that is, to the market imperfections—than to the institutional response.

It should be pointed out that even where market imperfections could and do exist, no direct foreign investment may move. The reason has already been suggested; political risk and market uncertainty may appear so high as to swamp any advantages accruing to the firm by reason of one or more market imperfections. One normally does not invest in a hostile country during a state of war regardless of market imperfection. Nor does one normally invest at a time when the relevant market seems to be collapsing, whatever advantages one might enjoy. These are possibly the extreme cases. Hence, by adding political risk and market uncertainty to the enlarged notion of market imperfection, one has a complete general theory of private direct foreign investment.

This theory suggests that in our world of grossly imperfect markets the internal market provided by the large corporation operating internationally may generate·the lowest cost transfer of resources. If it becomes a political objective to restrain corporate growth, governments should pursue policies designed to improve international capital, technology, skill, labor, and goods markets and to reduce the political risk and market uncertainty faced by local firms. Then the smaller national firms would be in a position to compete more effectively. If it is a political objective to increase the flows of direct foreign investment to such levels as to reverse the present gap-widening tendency in material well-being between rich and poor countries as rapidly as possible, then emphasis on reducing risk and uncertainty faced by the foreign investor is called for. The problem is that governments do not seem to be pursuing either strategy in any systematic fashion. Indeed, many public measures seem to render markets even less perfect and to exaggerate risk and uncertainty in the eyes of the potential investor, both local and foreign.

THE NATURE OF INTERNATIONAL BUSINESS 0.3

Differences

International business as a field of study and practice encompasses that public and private business activity affecting the persons or institutions of more than one national state, territory, or colony. The effect may be in terms of their economic well-being, political status, convictions, skills, or knowledge. The term "business" itself relates to organized human effort directed toward achieving some human satisfaction through the transfer of goods and services from one condition to another, or from one person or group to another, for a mutual profit stated in explicit terms on a *quid pro quo* basis; that is, the production and sale of goods by a government-owned entity for an internal financial profit is a business activity, but payment of social security benefits or foreign aid is not.

It follows that organizational problems of a large corporation operating internationally, as well as the operational problems of a local branch of an alien firm, both fall within the field, as likewise do the contractual relations between entities operating in different nations—from simple sale and purchase to licensing and management contracting—that is, they fall within the field of international business so long as these problems or activities relate to both domestic and foreign persons or institutions.

For example, a domestic business problem generated by reason of a feedback from an overseas activity is included. So likewise is an overseas organizational problem, the resolution of which is ultimately the responsibility of a domestically based management, or which affects that domestic management in some respect. Also, variables introduced from outside the international business field, such as government policy, but which affect business entities in more than one nation, lie within the compass of international business. Such externally generated variables may be considered environmental factors influencing the flow or structure of business relations across an international, territorial, or colonial frontier.

As the web of international business relationships is woven ever more finely among nations, the distinction between domestic and international business becomes fuzzy. Indeed, in the final analysis domestic business is simply subsumed under international business, as some of our larger corporations are now doing in their organizational structure. In these firms, domestic operating companies merely constitute one regional or national group within an internationally oriented corporate structure. This relationship reflects a very different mentality from that present in a firm in which the "international division" is on the same level as the domestic operating divisions, all being subordinated to a domestically oriented corporate headquarters.

Instantaneous communication, rapid transportation, the increasing complexity of industrial production, and the multiplication of goods and services (with the resulting pressure toward specialization) combine to push irresistibly in the direction of making all business international in character. One day virtually all management decisions will have to be viewed internationally if optimum policies are to be maintained. A labor contract entered into in the U.S. will be communicated immediately to labor groups with which the company or its associates are dealing around the world. A draw-down on the company's credit line in the U.S. will become known immediately to all financial institutions worldwide, thereby affecting the credit lines of its associated foreign companies. Given the limited resources available to any one firm, a decision to try for deeper penetration in one national market must necessarily lead to a decision not to do so elsewhere. A promotion of Mr. Smith, a U.S. national, to a top executive position, may discourage Mr. Yamamoto, a Japanese national presently moving up in an associated Japanese firm. Thus, almost any decision is likely to have international implications. Only a few corporations have reached this point as yet, but the dynamics of international business push in this direction with compelling pressure. Therefore, it has become the view of the leading graduate schools of business management that *all* students should be exposed to the international dimensions of business.

International business differs from the purely domestic (the uninational) because it involves operating effectively within different national sovereignties; under widely disparate economic conditions; with peoples living within different value systems and institutions; as part of an industrial revolution set in the contemporary world, often over greater geographical distance; and in national markets varying greatly in population and area. Figure 0.1 tracks some of the more important implications for management generated by these six variables. To take an example: Different national sovereignties generate different legal, monetary, and political systems. Each legal system implies a unique set of relevant rights and obligations in relation to property, taxation, control of monopoly, business organization, and contract. These in turn require the firm to consider new organizational relationships, acquire new skills, and adopt new accounting and control procedures; new, that is, in the sense of being different from that required in a purely domestic setting.

Strategies

A wide range of considerations not relevant for domestic business become relevant variables in management decisions once the international dimension of business is seen as significant. Perhaps this distinction is best seen in the range of alternative strategies for building and maintaining an international business, for none of these alternative strategies lies within the range of vision of domestic management. Nor is there any reason why they should.[14] For example, the strategies implied in cooperative export or participating debt, such as the *partes beneficiares* in Brazil, are not present in a domestic setting within, for example, the U.S. Other strategies are not seen as relevant, for instance, the sale of equity or debt in a *local* operation or the asymmetry in parent-foreign subsidiary relationships implicit in the distinction as to the legal nature of the parent and associated firm arising out of the interposition of different political regimes representing differing interests.

The permutations and combinations of strategies we must consider are

---

[14]The catalogue of strategies appears as the Table of Contents of this book. Each capital letter set identifies a functional area of decision.

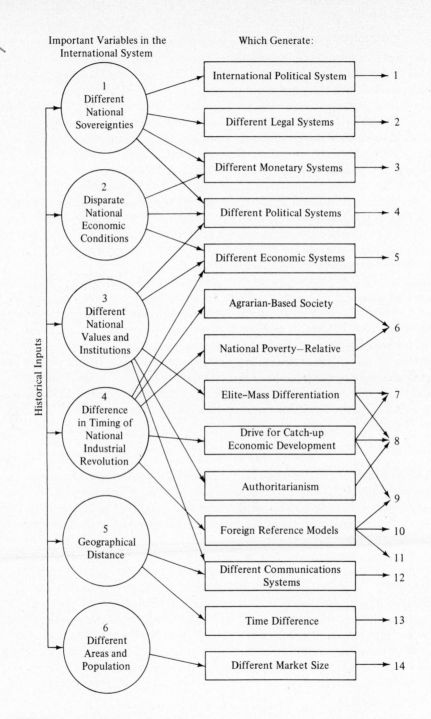

Figure 0.1
VARIABLES IN THE INTERNATIONAL SYSTEM

Leading to Differences in:

Distinctions
Which Require the Firm to:

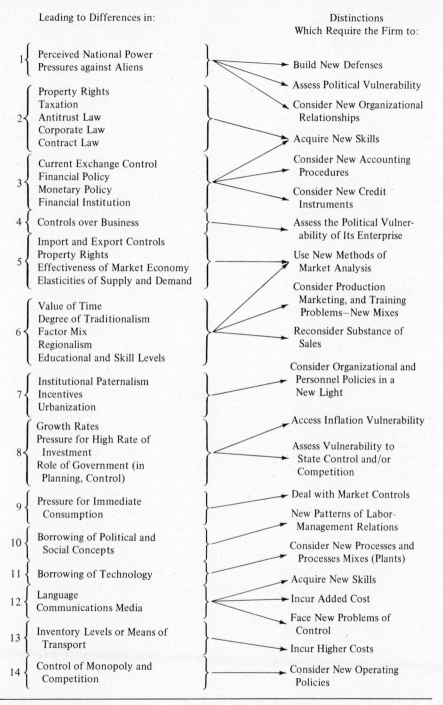

1 { Perceived National Power
Pressures against Aliens

Build New Defenses

Assess Political Vulnerability

2 { Property Rights
Taxation
Antitrust Law
Corporate Law
Contract Law

Consider New Organizational
Relationships

Acquire New Skills

3 { Current Exchange Control
Financial Policy
Monetary Policy
Financial Institution

Consider New Accounting
Procedures

Consider New Credit
Instruments

4 { Controls over Business

Assess the Political Vulnerability of Its Enterprise

5 { Import and Export Controls
Property Rights
Effectiveness of Market Economy
Elasticities of Supply and Demand

Use New Methods of
Market Analysis

Consider Production
Marketing, and Training
Problems–New Mixes

6 { Value of Time
Degree of Traditionalism
Factor Mix
Regionalism
Educational and Skill Levels

Reconsider Substance of
Sales

Consider Organizational and
Personnel Policies in a
New Light

7 { Institutional Paternalism
Incentives
Urbanization

Access Inflation Vulnerability

8 { Growth Rates
Pressure for High Rate of
Investment
Role of Government (in
Planning, Control)

Assess Vulnerability to
State Control and/or
Competition

9 { Pressure for Immediate
Consumption

Deal with Market Controls

New Patterns of Labor-
Management Relations

10 { Borrowing of Political and
Social Concepts

Consider New Processes and
Processes Mixes (Plants)

11 { Borrowing of Technology

Acquire New Skills

12 { Language
Communications Media

Incur Added Cost

Face New Problems of
Control

13 { Inventory Levels or Means of
Transport

Incur Higher Costs

14 { Control of Monopoly and
Competition

Consider New Operating
Policies

Note: Many important relationships are not charted here. This scheme is presented only as an illustration.

almost infinite because the alternatives fall into many diffferent and non-exclusive categories, and even those within a single category are not necessarily mutually exclusive. Very few managements ever consider the full range of alternative strategies vis-à-vis a given foreign opportunity. Why this is so will become apparent as we go along.

The student will note that for purposes of analysis in this volume the field has been broken into nine sets of strategies: sales, supply, labor, management, ownership, financial, legal, control, and public affairs.[15]

The problem for international management is essentially to relate these strategies to sets of relevant variables. What should management consider in selecting an optimum set of strategies? What makes the orderly analysis of these strategy sets difficult is the intricate feedback system arising out of the interdependence of these nine sets. One reaches a first approximation in regard to the first strategy set, moves on into the decision called for by a second strategy set, the results of which may call for revision of one's first decision. Constant adjustment is required. (See Figure 0.2.)

Decision-making

A great many of these decisions are not in fact made consciously and explicitly by firms involved in international business. For example, choice of sales strategy is often simply an extension of a domestic strategy proven successful over the years. The question of whether it is the optimum strategy for achieving international corporate objectives is not really examined. Therefore, often in researching the strategies followed by U.S. firms one finally comes up against such a statement as "We do not have partners in our domestic operations, so why should we abroad?"

A reasonable business approach to the selection of strategies for the exploitation of overseas opportunities is posed by this query (see Figure 0.3): Given (1) the domestic environment, (2) the socioeconomic environment of the host nation, (3) the structure of the international economic and political system—all three of which generate legal restraints—and (4) company resources, what is the most effective strategy for achieving corporate goals?

Considerable rigidity or noise—that is, inability to communicate accurately and to respond in an appropriate manner—is generated in this ideal system by at least four other variables: (1) past company experience (the historical input), (2) existing company structure (structural rigidities), (3) the quality of the communications system (the linkages), and (4) personal likes and biases (partly chance occurrence; for example, the degree of sensitivity to social responsibility). These variables are, of course, closely interrelated. Company

---

[15]A strategy is defined as a policy choice that, once having been made, tends to be institutionalized and thereby resists change in the short run. A tactic is an operational decision that sets up little or no institutionalized resistance to making a different operational decision in the near future.

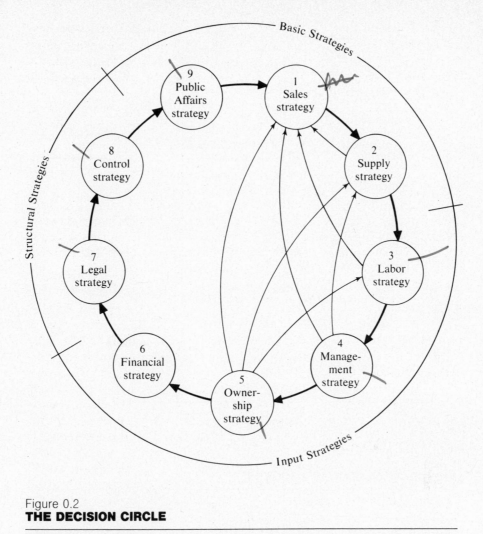

Figure 0.2
THE DECISION CIRCLE

Each strategy area contains a number of subsidiary strategy options. The decision process, which normally starts in the sales strategy area, is an iterative one. As the decision maker proceeds around the decision circle, previously selected strategies must be readjusted. Only a portion of the possible feedback adjustment loops are shown here. The numbers refer to the chapter sequence of this book.

structure and personal likes and biases in part determine the quality of the communications system. And the quality of communications and personal likes and biases has the impact of altering the management's perception of external and internal environments.

Also, the four variables enumerated above, *in interaction with the other variables as perceived by management* (that is, the international environment, the national environment, the domestic environment, and company re-

Inputs   Outputs

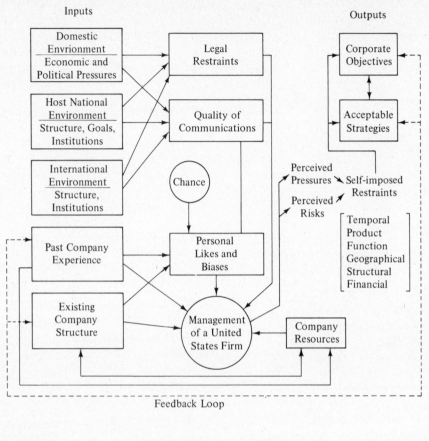

Figure 0.3
THE DECISION-MAKING PROCESS

sources), produce a set of perceived pressures and perceived risks. This system very commonly generates a set of self-imposed restraints, most common of which are:

1. A time dimension in thinking—that is, those strategies are deemed to be optimum that most nearly achieve corporate objectives within *a given period of time*—one year, two years, five years. Profit, however and wherever determined, is maximized over that period. This dimension varies remarkably from company to company. It is probably safe to say that a longer time dimension is required for success in international business than in the purely domestic one because of the growth factor and associated restrictions on monetary movement.

2. A limitation on the products to be sold and/or produced overseas (for example, a product unchanged from the firm's domestic product).

3. A functional limitation (selling, assembly, manufacture, construction, engineering, consulting, licensing).

4. A limitation on the geographical scope of operations (such as within Latin America or the European Community). Such a limitation is often related to the development of export sales by the firm; that is, investment in productive facilities abroad tends to follow the development of export sales. But export sales may be greater precisely for those products in which the home country (such as the U.S.) has some distinct advantage and are, therefore, not necessarily a measure of the advantages of local manufacture. (The advantage may be in cost or in national identity.) In fact, imports may be a more convincing indication of advantages accruing to overseas production.

5. Structural restraints (that is, refusal to consider other than certain types of relationships, such as an agency, 100 percent ownership, license).

6. Financial restraints (such as refusal to seek external debt or equity capital). For a company to face a growth situation requiring expansion precisely at the rate that can be financed out of earnings would be a rare coincidence. The point, of course, is that a firm operating under a policy of expanding only at the rate permitted by retained earnings is disciplined to reject investment opportunities once that growth rate is approached, hence, the apparent coincidence of rates.

It is within the parameters of these six self-imposed restraints, many of which may be entirely reasonable, that management defines corporate objectives, recognizes the alternative strategies, and perceives the relevant variables.

Perhaps of greatest impact is management's time horizon, whether determined implicitly or explicitly. It is of particular relevance in the international area because of the greater time lag between decision and implementation than in the typical domestic case and the greater range of long-run strategies, for example, the multinational option (the strategy of acquiring and allocating resources without regard to national boundaries except as they affect cost or return). Relevant variables in setting an appropriate time horizon include the firm's available resources, its present geographical spread, nature of the product, and growth conditions within markets where the firm is presently operating (particularly in the domestic market). If one or more of these factors do not rule out a time horizon longer than the current fiscal period, then management should probably not impose such a time restraint on its foreign market strategists. Figure 1.5 (in Chapter 1) suggests some of the relationships that may exist between selection of time horizon and acceptable strategies but is not meant to be definitive in any sense. The point is that it is wasteful of time and effort, and therefore costly, to permit analysts to consider strategies that management will not accept, particularly in the international field, because of the greater time and cost involved in investigating and implementing many projects. Bear in mind that there is a significant difference between what management *can* and *is willing to* accept. This difference should be made explicit after careful study of company resources and the company's commitment to present markets.

A word about company structure as it relates to the selection of corporate objectives and acceptable strategies for accomplishing them is appropriate here. By "structure" is meant those organizational rigidities difficult to alter significantly in the short run, such elements as ownership, independence, divisional basis (product, region, function, process, customer, composite), size of company, contractual relationships or interdependence in respect to other firms (for example, as supplier or buyer). Indeed, if this last relationship is very important, management may be prone to enter overseas markets only in concert, say, joint ventures, with the associated firms of the same nationality, thereby limiting its ownership strategy to minority participation with other domestic firms. This is the so-called piggy-back operation. Also, great size may limit consideration of overseas opportunities to international regional or multinational markets, thereby ruling out production for a single national market. Great size may also render product and process modification difficult, thereby eliminating market-oriented modifications of either.[16] On the other hand, small size may limit overseas commitments to one or two national markets, thereby ruling out geographical dispersion and resulting in increased risk.

By company resources, one refers to such variables as financial resources, personnel, technical knowledge, goodwill, intangibles (patents, copyrights, trademarks, trade secrets), distribution system, political leverage. Management may perceive different trade-off values in its portfolio of resources. For example, a management may not be willing to trade its goodwill for external financing or for a stream of earnings (through license contract). Past experience or company structure or personal likes and biases may rule out the use of this resource for such purposes, thereby possibly requiring wholly owned ventures as the vehicle for overseas expansion, if indeed it causes management to feel able to do more than select some form of exporting. In any event, the rate of expansion overseas is thus curtailed, and geographically limited involvement overseas can heighten risk.

A few words about corporate objectives are necessary, otherwise our concern about optimum strategy becomes meaningless. Optimum for what?[17] First, let us all agree that the primary objective is to maximize profit, but to maximize profit where? for whom? over what length or period of time? Profit maximization is meaningless unless management first defines these parameters. If it does not, the system may be irrational in that management is not doing what it set out to do, to maximize profit. There are, of course, a

---

[16]A Ford executive once commented privately that, after all, Ford could not build cars in mud huts, nor could it turn out a specially designed truck for use on the Arabian Peninsula. A small firm, specializing in trucks, could and did design a special truck for Arabia, though admittedly it was not produced in mud huts. Currently both Ford and General Motors are experimenting with the production of very simple, low cost vehicles for LDC markets.

[17]Some have objected to the word "optimum" because, with nine strategy sets and all their feedback loops and complexities, a management can never truly select, or know that is has selected, the *optimum* of anything. Granted. Optimum is used here to refer to an objective toward which a management moves but never really achieves.

number of perfectly valid reasons for limiting the international scope of the firm. One reason would be financial and personnel inadequacies. It should be made quite explicit, however, that these inadequacies are not caused by some unnecessary self-imposed restraint (stemming, for example, from limitations on ownership and salaries, from an incompetent and insecure management, or from imperfections of communications) but are genuine, externally imposed inadequacies. These self-imposed restraints may sometimes flow from management's fear of losing control by moving into unfamiliar areas (such as an international or new functional area) or of the employment of new people with unfamiliar expertise. (This latter comment suggests that power maximizing and profit satisfying on the part of management may in fact be the driving motives for selecting certain strategies.)

Profit-maximization for an international firm suggests long-run planning to achieve a geographically and functionally diversified international association of complementary enterprises. Long-run, profitable survival rests directly upon the selection of appropriate strategies under a given set of circumstances. This policy demands a high degree of flexibility in choice of strategy, which means elimination of as many rigidities in the system as possible, such rigidities as the casual extension of domestic policy, domination by the personal likes or biases of key personnel, management fear of the unfamiliar, or unchallenged projection of past experience into different places and times.

Decision-making

Empirical research would indicate that decisions by which a firm commits resources to a foreign market differ from comparable domestic decisions in several important respects:[18]

1. They are more expensive in that more variables are involved. It is more difficult to apply familiar measures; special legal and financial and area skills are required; the amount of time-consuming communication and travel is greater.

2. They are less likely to be stimulated by an internal company market survey and more likely to be the result of external pressure on the firm.

3. They are more likely to be the result of *selective* analysis of market opportunities, rather than universal and comparative analysis.

4. They are less subject to quantitative analysis because of the application of a subjectively derived discount rate to anticipated earnings, a rate that may be someone's guess as to political risk (that is, continuity of relevant law—contract, tax, exchange control, labor, property).

A study of Figure 0.4 provides some insight into what is involved in these decisions. First, the source of *initial pressure* on the firm to investigate a

---

[18]For more detailed discussion see Richard D. Robinson, *International Business Policy* (New York: Holt, Rinehart, and Winston, 1964), chaps. 4 and 5.

foreign market is very likely to be exogenous to the firm, more so than in the domestic situation. Possible agents of that pressure are shown in the cluster of circles at the top of Figure 0.4, from each of which stem various motives. Second, company organization and policy may act as a check on this initial pressure, because the structure was designed with the needs of the domestic environment in mind, not those of the relevant foreign environment. Third, throughout the decision-making process personal interest on the part of key members of management is likely to play a larger role than in the domestic case precisely because of the greater number of imponderables in assessing a foreign-market opportunity. Once sufficient interest is generated in a firm in a given foreign market, an *evaluative process* begins that may be highly subjective, depending on the size of the firm, its past experience, and the time available. The *decision to investigate* a foreign project is not to be taken lightly, for such a decision in itself may mean the investment of a substantial amount of company resources. This decision may be subdivided into decisions relating to the level at which the investigation is to be made and the nature of that investigation. How the *actual investigation* proceeds is likely to be strongly influenced by personal interest in the foreign case. And again, whether the investigation actually leads to an *investment decision* is likely to be conditioned strongly by the existence of personal interest at the appropriate level within the firm. Strong negative convictions may mean a negative decision simply by default. And, finally, the investment decision itself is in reality a two-fold decision: (1) where to invest (within the target market, in a third market, or domestically as a source of stepped-up and perhaps modified exports), and (2) investment in what sort of facilities (assembly, manufacturing, technical, or managerial assistance).

The organizational implications of this decision-making process are legion. It is sufficient to say here that among the organizational hallmarks of the successful international firm are:

1. Direct exposure of the firm to its foreign markets for market analysis, rather than dependence upon intermediaries, whose interests may not coincide with those of the firm.

2. A centralized, globally oriented market research team that periodically looks at every likely market.

3. A central clearing house for overseas projects, whether generated by internal or external pressures, so as to assure that company assets, including personnel, are assigned to the highest priority markets and enterprises.

4. Employment of, or access to, individuals possessing the necessary international legal, financial, marketing, political, and economic skills to evaluate overseas market opportunities and thereby reduce risk.

5. Intracompany credits to domestic operating divisions assisting in the penetration of overseas markets so as to make such participation attractive to division executives.

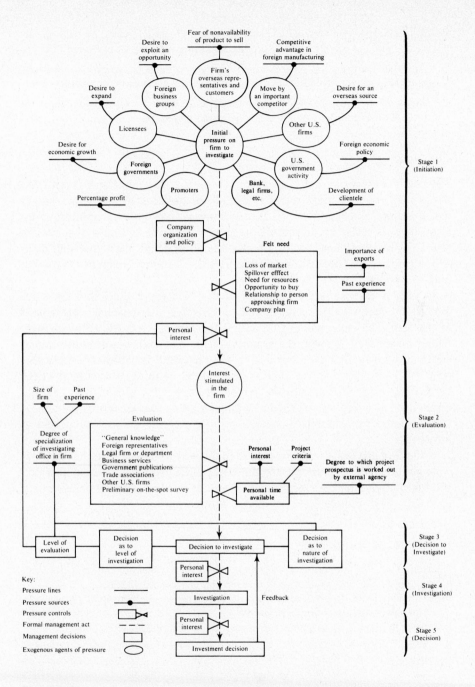

Figure 0.4
PROCESS BY WHICH A FIRM REACHES A DECISION TO COMMIT RESOURCES TO OVERSEAS PROJECTS

6. A specialized research and development group primarily concerned with the development and modification of products and processes vis-à-vis foreign markets.

7. An equal hearing at the level at which relevant decisions are made for spokesmen in favor of foreign projects, whether involving sales, purchasing, or manufacturing.

8. An understanding that successful international experience is a plus factor for promotion in respect to both technicians and management.

Conclusion

The need for these comments grows out of the casual assumption by many that nationalism is "irrational"; that international business by definition serves world welfare, and that the division of earnings is "equitable"; that international business is really no different from purely domestic business; that certain strategies have universal validity regardless of time and place; and that decision-making in the international firm is a purely "rational" response to foreign market opportunities.

In only one sense is the idea correct that strategy choices and decision-making processes need not be altered for effective international involvement of the firm. The statement is true only if the firm is internationally oriented, which means that it possesses a management that makes no culture-bound assumptions (implicitly or explicitly), that relevant variables are constants simply because they happen to be so in the single cultural environment where the firm developed historically and happens to be headquartered. International orientation also implies a decision-making structure that facilitates the allocation of company resources into high priority projects without geographical limitation.

If the firm is internationally oriented in this way, then international business is no different from domestic, for the latter is simply a special case in which the relevant variables are weighted in a unique manner. The variables remain the same, even though some be assigned zero values.

Recommended references:

Aharoni, Yair. *The Foreign Investment Decision Process.* Boston: Harvard Graduate School of Business Administration, Division of Research, 1966.
Fayerweather, John. *International Business Management, A Conceptual Framework.* New York: McGraw-Hill, 1969.
Robinson, Richard D. *International Business Policy.* Cambridge, Massachusetts: Hamlin Publications, 1964.

Discussion questions:

1. How might it be possible to demonstrate that a corporation is power maximizing rather than profit maximizing in respect to its international operations?

2. Other than the examples listed in the text, how might a foreign subsidiary lead a suboptimal allocation of corporate resources? (Assume that the subsidiary is a profit *center.*)

3. Give some examples of how a corporation may move profits from one subsidiary to another or between parent and subsidiary other than via dividends.

4. Relate the product life cycle, oligopoly and market imperfection theory of direct foreign investment.

5. In what sense can the personal biases of corporate decision-makers be considered a form of market imperfection?

6. In your judgment does private business tend to narrow or widen per-capita GNP's between rich and poor nations? Why?

Case A
THE STITCHER COMPANY

Historically, the Stitcher Company had gone into foreign projects as opportunities presented themselves. Decisions had been made on each project as it came up, management being guided by intuition rather than by formalized policies or objectives. The burden on top management became unwieldly, and it was decided to make a formal analysis of (1) what the company was then doing abroad and (2) the strengths and weaknesses of the company in respect to overseas activities. The purpose of the study would be to define company policy in respect to what it should be doing.

To undertake this study, a committee was set up called the Overseas Policy and Planning Committee (OPPC). This group sent "task forces" into each country where the company was then operating and where it might consider operations in the near future. In each case, the initial question was: should the company be in this country? The studies of the task force groups were based on two premises: (1) that the company might consider going into any country and any industry and (2) that the company had complete freedom of action in changing the nature of its investment in respect to either country or industry, or both. Furthermore, no time limit was stipulated during which investment was to be shifted. In other words, in making their studies and forming their recommendations, the task forces were given almost complete flexibility. The OPPC directed that detailed reports be made on 12 African, Asian, and Latin American countries in which Stitcher had interests or projects, plus "less penetrating analysis" of five others in which it had potential interests. The upshot was that on the basis of the task force country reports the OPPC reached certain conclusions as to the outlook for growth in each of these 17 countries relative to opportunities and risks. And in each, the growth industries were singled out for special study. Consideration was given to the company's position in each of the countries, and then related to those industries considered to be especially attractive from the point of view of growth potential. The study finally came down to a recommendation of investment by industry and by country. These recommendations became the criteria against which projects were to be measured. A section of the OPPC report detailed the criteria used in measuring the various "lines of endeavor" of possible interest to the company. It is reproduced in part below:

Summary of OPPC report. From the basic and secondary characteristics of the economics of the seventeen countries, we arrive at definite conclusions as to the criteria by which to determine the right lines of endeavor. If our criteria are correct (and they were one of the first orders of business of the committee when it was formed and have been distilled from all the knowledge that the committee has developed), we have thus a clearly systematic approach to planning for overseas development in Asia, Africa, and Latin America.

Where then do they lead us? What are the guideposts for selecting lines of endeavor?

Primary specifications

1. As we have already mentioned, as a basic fundamental, ventures should be considered only if they *cut broadly through the urbanization and industrialization* trends in the economy. These are the deep and sweeping internal movements that will carry all else before them.

2. Investment policy must contribute to overcoming one of the great dangers in all the economies in which we would have serious interest, namely, the stringency of foreign exchange, meaning that lines of endeavor selected should either be *foreign exchange* earners or help meet the exchange problem by substituting local production for imports.

3. There should be low *vulnerability to currency depreciation* with profitability anticipation commensurately higher as the vulnerability increases as in the case with investments involving higher proportions of working capital.

Secondary specifications

4. The lines of endeavor selected must have the characteristic of filling highly strategic "gap" *opportunities*. It must be in an industry in which consumption is very low compared with what it should be considering the state of the country. It must at the same time have a long range growth potential higher than the rate of growth of economy generally and of personal incomes.

5. There must be long term *growth potential* at a rate greater than the "growth curve" of the economy.

6. "Unique opportunities" that fit into the strategic gaps are especially desirable— those that give an advantage in a market, especially smaller ones. Investments not having this characteristic in small markets would almost certainly be questionable.

7. There must be an *adequate* existing or clearly foreseeable local *market*, a gap opportunity or extraordinary growth, or there should be already an expanding world market.

8. Availability of *local raw materials* is a primary requisite in view of the foreign exchange problems. If imported materials are used they must be a small fraction of the final value of the ultimately finished product. Can-sealing compounds are a good example.

9. *Foreign entrepreneurship* should be a necessity; i.e., the line of endeavor must still be beyond the possibilities of local nationals now (e.g., due to technology or capital requirements or both), but capable of attracting first-rate foreign personnel.

10. In the absence of a local capital market it must be *capable of financing its own growth* through retained earnings, particularly when further investment from abroad is not attractive or costly.

11. Finally, there is the desirability of *low political exposure*. For instance, the investment should not occupy a strategic position in respect to resources that have high emotional appeal in underdeveloped countries.

We have not mentioned minimum profitability or rate of return here. This is a factor in determining investment policy that can only be considered in relation to the company as a whole and its parts. It cannot be set in accordance with country economic characteristics except that it should be obvious that if the lines of endeavor are selected in accordance with the criteria set forth here, the investment policy requirements for long range profitability will be easier to meet. Whatever minimum base is set on company-wide consideration should, however, be adjusted upward in varying amounts, country-by-country, depending on local risk factors and the specific rationale and expectations for the individual business.

Ranking lines of endeavor

The criteria were applied to a wide list of possible industries, particularly those that our surveys in each country brought out as industries that are considered "attractive"; that is, industries that should grow rapidly during the next ten years because of population growth, increases in total and per capita incomes and, most of all, which should tend to move up faster than these indicators. Actually, the industries considered included almost every possible line of endeavor. We put them all through the successive screens of our criteria (basic and secondary) to come up finally with the following main "lines of endeavor" that we concluded were the "opportunity industries":

First we isolated three lines of endeavor that can be considered as having this "opportunity" character without reservation. These are first

1. Economic intermediates of manufacturing.
2. Economic intermediates of distribution.
3. Economic intermediates of construction.

We should explain what we mean by the term "economic intermediates," as it is a term we had to coin. We mean thereby products that in themselves might be considered "finished products" but whose primary use is in making possible manufacturing, distribution, or construction and that are destroyed, absorbed, or used up in the process. An example of the typical "economic intermediate of manufacturing" would be the hermetically sealed motors produced in Mexico. An example of "economic intermediates of distribution" are packaging materials. Without such materials distribution would be impossible. Yet they are absorbed and used up in the process. Typical examples of "economic intermediates of construction" would be wallboard, paint, structural steel forms, sheet glass, and piping.

The characteristic about economic intermediates that makes them particularly attractive is that their own value is a relatively small part of the total finished product into which they are integrated. A secondary characteristic is that there is a relatively low labor content in their making. They have high capital intensity and they can be produced ordinarily in a fairly continuous flow process. (This, incidentally, is the outstanding characteristic of most of the chemical industry and, therefore—although the products among economic intermediates may be highly diversified—their production will not be entirely unfamiliar to us.) The management requirements are similar in manufacturing where scheduling or raw materials, factory flow, and the overhead to total cost relationships are magnitudinally close.

It is a further characteristic that without the intermediate the final product, whether a building, mine, or a piece of communications equipment, is not capable of being produced. In other words, the "economic intermediates" occupy strategic positions in respect to their essential nature for a whole process, while at the same time negligible in the total cost-structure of the process itself.

We next isolated four "lines of endeavor," which are much more doubtful or which can be considered "opportunity lines" for our company only with reservations and restrictions. These are:

1. Export industries producing primary commodities. We call these "mining" for short even though the production of pulp would belong in this category.

   This category, however, applies only to "minor" extractive industries. "Major" extractive industries such as those mining major materials (rather than rare earths which would be "minor") or producing petroleum do not satisfy the "opportunity criteria" in important aspects.

2. A major "opportunity line" is the building up of a "*distribution* system" (provided it can be organized). By this we mean the actual apparatus needed to distribute goods from the manufacturer to the consumer and any part thereof, warehousing, transporting, financing, and, finally, selling, whether wholesale or retail.

   There is no doubt that the development of streamlined and economical distribution systems is one of the greatest needs of many of these countries. It is doubtful, however, whether such a system can be built without undesirable financial characteristics, though the belief that this is primarily a working-capital investment is perhaps no longer quite valid. There is need for further study here.

3. *Economic intermediates of agriculture.* As we have seen, there is need, and encouragement can be expected to be given to increased agricultural productivity in almost all the countries. This means farm mechanization, fertilizers, insecticides, etc. More rapid introduction of agricultural improvements of this nature is being assisted by developed country assistance and by the economic policies of the respective governments. We should not, therefore, leave out of our thinking an agricultural sector, in at least one aspect of which, fertilizers, the company has

expertness. Food imports, as we have seen in the previous chapter, constitute a sizeable drain on the foreign exchange positions of a number of countries. Efforts to substitute local production can be expected to be given emphasis and official encouragement. In relation to the results that can be attained, expenditures for agricultural intermediates represent a fairly small portion of the final product.

4. As a further area that might, with reservations, satisfy the "opportunity character-istics" we list *certain consumer goods, namely those that provide "necessities of status"* rather than "necessities of life" or even "cheap luxuries."

   Consumer goods industries, providing necessities, for example, textiles, clearly do not have the growth potential needed in view of the risk many of these countries pose.

   The situation of "cheap luxuries" consumer goods (packaged foods or biscuits for instance) is much better in that their growth potential is certainly very high, perhaps the highest.

   Such "necessities of status" as durable consumer goods, home appliances, and so on enjoy a growth potential probably as large as that of the "cheap luxuries," though they have greater risks in bad times. At the same time they may be vulnerable in that they depend very much more heavily on the availability of foreign exchange for imports.

The following chart illustrates a checklist method for analyzing lines of endeavor. It is presented only as an approach and to focus the analysis.

Discussion questions

1. What is your reaction to the OPPC report?
2. Does it conflict in any way with international trade and investment theory?
3. What do you think of the rating system?

RATING OF LINES OF ENDEAVOR AGAINST CRITERIA

(Illustrative only—not to be used reaching conclusions on lines of endeavor for specific countries)

CODE   + Line of Endeavor
Rates Favorably
− Line of Endeavor
Rates Unfavorably
0 Line of Endeavor
Rating Neutral

	Lines of endeavor								
Criteria	A	B	C	D	E	F	G	H	I
Basic Criteria									
Urbanization and Industrialization (Broad cut through)	+	+	+	0	+	0	+	+	0
Foreign Exchange (Earner or Saver)	+	−	−	−	0	+	+	+	+
Maintenance of Values in Face of Inflation & Currency Depreciation	+	+	+	+	−	−	−	−	+
Secondary Criteria									
Dynamic Growth of Potential	+	+	+	+	+	0	+	0	0
Strategic Gap Opportunities	+	+	+	0	+	0	0	0	0
Unique Opportunity Possibilities	+	+	+	0	+	+	0	0	0
Adequate Local or Export Markets	+	+	+	+	+	+	0	+	+
Available Raw Materials	+	+	0	0	0	+	0	+	+
Foreign Management and Capital Desirable	+	+	+	+	+	+	+	−	0
Capable of Self-financing	+	+	+	0	+	0	+	0	+
Political Exposure	+	+	0	−	+	−	−	−	−

A = Economic Intermediates of Manufacturing
B = Economic Intermediates of Distribution
C = Construction
D = "Mining"—Including Pulp
E = Distribution Systems
F = Economic Intermediates of Agriculture
G = Consumer Necessities of Status
H = Some Existing Businesses: Textiles
I = Sugar

Chapter 1
SALES STRATEGY

The initial set of decisions any firm must make before committing resources to a foreign market consists of what it is going to sell, to whom, for how much, over what period of time, through which channels, to be serviced by whom, to be promoted by whom, and to be supplied from where. (Supply, or sourcing, is considered here only from the customer's point of view, not from that of the supplier. The latter will be treated in Chapter 2.) In addition, two restraints may or may not be permitted to operate—intracompany and intercompany agreements, implicit or explicit. Obviously, each element in this set is closely related to all others. Decisions cannot be made in splendid isolation, which fact has obvious organizational implications for the firm. At what level within the firm, and whether on a centralized or decentralized basis, such decisions are made are questions more appropriately considered under control. (See Chapter 8.)

Although the "reduction of diversity is usually a necessary goal of the international marketer,"[1] much diversity necessarily remains. In an often-quoted article, Buzzell developed a list of environmental factors rendering the standardization of international marketing strategies exceedingly difficult.[2] These included climate, income level, customer mobility and density, customer preferences, intensity of competition, distribution system and legal restrictions. In the latter category should go rules and regulations regarding labelling, advertising content, product liability, even the capacity of the alien firm to sell at all. In several countries, retailing has been nationalized; that is, limited to citizens or to firms owned predominantly by local citizens. The Philippines passed such a restrictive law in 1964, but not until 1975 was it operationally defined.[3] As Thorelli wrote:

---

[1] Vern Terpstra, *International Marketing* (New York: Holt, Rinehart and Winston, 1972), p. 150.

[2] Robert D. Buzzell, "Can You Standardize Multinational Marketing?" *Harvard Business Review* (November–December 1968), pp. 108–9.

[3] Excluded are sales by manufacturers or processors to individuals and commercial users who use the products to render services to the public and/or produce goods for sale to the public; sales by hotels operating restaurants, sales by manufacturers or processors to the general public provided that the capital does not exceed 5,000 pesos; sales by farmers of their farm products.

The special challenge in international marketing is that strategy design must take into account all three layers of the environment: market structure, local marketing environment, and the international interface. Indeed, merely identifying all of the environmental factors of relevance and their relative importance in a given business is in itself a task of entrepreneurial rank.[4]

It seems quite evident that one global marketing strategy, except in a very general sense, is a meaningless notion.

A 1971 study based on responses from executives in 136 U.S. firms on *Fortune*'s list of the top 500 reported that integration of international marketing into the worldwide corporate effort was most frequently listed as a major marketing problem (24 percent), followed by lack of marketing data (16 percent), unsuitable distribution channels (12 percent), trade barriers (10 percent), unfair competition (9 percent), legal and political complications (8 percent), scarcity of personnel (8 percent), nationalism (4 percent), product adaptation (4 percent). Only 13 percent perceived no significant difference between domestic and international marketing.[5]

Nonetheless, there is some evidence to believe that at least decision-makers of small and medium-sized U.S. firms do not act directly to enter international markets, that they are moved to act only under the pressure of some external stimuli, most frequently unsolicited orders from foreign customers.[6] In addition, perceptions of profit, risk, and cost associated with exports seemed to differ significantly between decision-makers in exporting and nonexporting firms. The general conclusion was that executives did not systematically initiate investigations of foreign markets. Rather, "exporting came about much more frequently as the result of fortuitous circumstances; that is, it has been a reactive strategy."[7]

1.1 SUBSTANCE OF SALES

Unless it has been service oriented in its previous operations (for example, research, engineering, architecture, construction, finance, insurance, transport, communications, management consulting, advertising, franchising), a management is very likely to look at foreign markets only in terms of merchandise. And, unless the firm has hitherto operated in sufficiently different markets as to induce a feedback into the design of products, the chances are that

---

[4]H. B. Thorelli (ed.), *International Marketing Strategy* (Middlesex, England: Penguin Books, 1973), p. 39.

[5]A. Kapoor and R. McKay, *Managing International Markets* (Princeton, N.J.: Darwin Press, 1971), pp. 7–8.

[6]Claude L. Simpson, "The Export Decision: An Interview Study of the Decision Process in Tennessee Manufacturing Firms" (Atlanta: Georgia State University School of Business Administration, unpublished Ph.D. dissertation, 1973).

[7]Simpson, "Export Decision," p. 105.

management will see a foreign market only in terms of the goods that the firm has been producing domestically. The greater the regional variation in product design in the domestic market (that is, the more market-sensitive), the better prepared is a management likely to be to analyze overseas market opportunities in terms of the most appropriate product, within the capability range of the firm, for that particular market.

In fact, very few international divisions possess their own research and development sections. The result is that many firms—particularly North American ones—seem to export products designed for the domestic market with little thought as to whether design might be altered so as to be more appropriate overseas or, indeed, to invent a new or significantly different product. The probable reasons for the U.S. deficiency in this respect are (1) the size and relative sophistication of the North American market; (2) the lower exposure of those controlling product and process design to the facts of life in Asia, Africa, and Latin America; (3) the greater wealth disparity between the U.S. and the less developed world; and (4) the continental isolation of the North American market. Some U. S. firms have, however, demonstrated unusual ingenuity. Among these specially designed products have been a hand-operated washing machine for villages and poorer city dwellers in Mexico, a hand-operated grain thresher for Asian markets, a cheap kerosene stove for Latin America, a hand-cranked cash register and a simplified truck for Turkey. Recently General Motors has introduced its basic motor transport vehicle concept in a number of low-income Asian countries, an idea that was seriously proposed by an independent automotive engineer in the 1950s. Ford has paralleled this move with a specially designed vehicle for the less developed countries (LDC), for example, the Ford "Fiera" in the Philippines. Reportedly, the People's Republic of China has come up with such devices as a rice transplanter, an electric cultivator, and a kerosene lamp that produces electricity to run a radio. India has invented the bullock-powered generator and the Philippines, a bamboo pump for irrigation.

Directly related to product modification is a firm's concept of quality. Does it see quality as an absolute or as relative to consumer need? An internationally minded management examines deliberately and systematically the products it intends to market within the target area from the point of view of the environment of that country. Major factors to be considered in relation to design are shown below:

Level of technical skills	→ **Product simplification**
Level of labor cost	→ **Automation or manualization of product**
Level of literacy	→ **Remarking and simplification of product**
Level of income	→ **Quality and price change; size**

Level of interest rates	→ Quality and price change
Level of maintenance	→ Change in product tolerances
Climatic differences	→ Product adaptation
Isolation	→ Product simplification and reliability improvement
Differences in standards or number system	→ Recalibration of product and resizing (see also Chapter 2)
Availability of other products	→ Greater or lesser product integration
Availability of materials	→ Change in product structure and fuel
Power availability	→ Resizing of product
Special considerations	→ Product redesign or invention

This list is by no means all-inclusive; for example, there is the possibility of national political pressures generated by environmental concern to restrict or make more costly the manufacture of disposable products, or those which are short-lived. One can expect differences in national sensitivities.

But perhaps no *product* is really optimum as an export product if we distinguish product from services, including financing.

Because of their domestic concentration on the manufacture of merchandise and history of export of the same, most nonservice organizations do not see themselves in the business of selling services. Yet, every manufacturer has a number of valuable services he could sell if he chose, specifically, management skills, marketing skills, production skills, construction skills ("turn-key operation"),[8] and research skills. In addition, many manufacturers have valuable rights that are marketable: process and product patents, copyrights, trademarks, agencies, established brand names, and production secrets. Also, from time to time, a firm may find obsolete, but very usable, machinery on its hands or surplus cash for which an investment opportunity is needed. There is reason to believe that in many foreign markets the return to be realized from the sale of services, valuable rights, used machinery, and investable funds (for debt or equity in the portfolio sense) may be substantially greater than the profit to be earned on the export of goods or the return that would be generated by direct investment in foreign-based productive enterprise. Two general reasons may be cited for this conclusion: political vulnerability and comparative cost advantages. Consider the first.

For a variety of reasons (which will be explored later), alien ownership[9] of overseas productive facilities almost always heightens risk. Particularly is this

---

[8]See Glossary.
[9]Ownership is equated with management control arising through equity investment.

true where (1) the enterprise represents an obvious and relatively large feature on the national economic landscape and (2) the owners are identified with a national state very much more affluent than the host state. Also, the movement of goods into a national state is often more easily subject to immediate control than are services. Sale and purchase agreements are relatively short term, often 30 to 90 days. On the other hand, those skills and valuable rights listed above typically move into a national market under the umbrella of relatively long-term contracts, often five to ten years. Very few instances of deliberate breaching of such contracts by either individuals or governments have been reported. Rather than risk international harassment, a state is more likely to wait out the term of the contract and then refuse to approve its renewal, in which case the firm may be forewarned several years in advance and thus have time to shift its strategy with a minimum of loss. The point is that a contract does not bestow a vested interest unlimited in time, as does the ownership of tangible property. Yet a contract does more or less assure a market for a given period of time, which a simple sale (that is export of a product or right) does not.

The second reason for giving careful consideration to the export of skills (which are embodied in people) and valuable rights lies in their possible competitive advantage, and here we turn to the theory of comparative advantage in international trade. Given the widening disparity in material well-being between the richer and poorer nations, the emergence of many new sovereign states (each increasingly sensitive to its own well-being) and the acceptance of rapid economic growth (sustained increase in real product per capita) almost as part of national ideology, one can anticipate growing pressure for maximum use of local resources, including labor. Under these circumstances the theory of comparative advantage in international trade may well become progressively less theoretical, more realistic. Otherwise, the economic disparity grows and, one suspects, political disparity grows as well. Eventually, something gives way as aspirations, based on the accomplishments of the more affluent societies, become completely out of touch with capability for most of the world's population. That "something" might well be increasing inability of the wealthier countries to restrain immigration. In 1977, it was estimated that there were 12 million illegal aliens residing within the United States, and the number appeared to be growing rapidly.

Stated in its simplest form, the theory of comparative advantage holds that a nation should produce those goods and services that embody relatively more of the cheaper factors of production; that is, those that are more abundant within the nation relative to other factors as compared to factor ratios in other nations. For example, if capital in country X were cheaper compared to labor than in country Y, then it would be to the advantage of both countries if X concentrated on producing those products using a lot of capital and country Y, on producing products demanding quantities of labor. The fact that X could produce both the capital- and labor-intensive goods[10] more cheaply than Y is not important. The trade-off between X's capital-intensive goods and Y's labor-intensive goods would be beneficial to both. But a two-factor model is unrealistic. For our purposes it is useful to think of six factors, or production inputs:

1. *Available natural resources*, including arable land.

2. *Capital:* The ability of a people to produce more goods and services than they consume, past and present.

3. *Unskilled labor:* That labor requiring very little capital investment other than that needed to keep a person alive at near subsistence level until the age of productive labor, which typically is not very long.

4. *Skilled labor:* That labor requiring substantial capital investment in education and training before a return is realized.

5. *Entrepreneurship:* The psychological set that generates creativity and a propensity to carry risk, which in turn seems to be a function of heightened expectations, assurance of a socially acceptable minimum level of income, and high-level skill of economic value.

6. *Government:* Public services such as law and order, development of a currency system, enforcement of commercial law, maintenance of services including health, education, agricultural extension, and the like, all of which tend to generate an integrated national market and a long-lived, educated population.

In the absence of certain aspects of the last factor, risk—hence, cost—is increased for an enterprise. Cost is further increased to the extent that an enterprise has to provide certain of these services for itself (for instance, a training function expanded downward to elementary skills and basic education). In addition, the absence of law and order, a currency system, transport and communication services, and effective commercial law renders an integrated national market impossible and, hence, likewise many economies of scale.[11] Furthermore, investment in education and training for high-level skill is uneconomic if public health conditions limit longevity to what might otherwise be considered middle-age. An adequate return is then not possible.

To varying degrees, capital is embodied in consumer goods, production equipment, development of resources, government services, and the preparation of people for productive roles (unskilled labor, skilled labor, entrepreneurship). Least capital intensive are consumer goods; most capital intensive, skilled people. The other factors lie in between in a generally ascending order. The reason for this ordering of capital intensity lies in the time between investment and return, the so-called gestation period of capital investment. Before an individual generates any return on the investment made in him, he must have at least reached a productive age. If high-level skills are involved,

---

[10]See Glossary.
[11]See Glossary.

the time required may be two to three times as long, or more. In the contemporary society, a total investment of well over $100,000 is probably needed to produce top-level professional competence in an individual. This investment may be multiplied in the case of those involved in major research over many years, because the pay-off in enhanced production is so long delayed.

It could be argued that there are only three factors—resources, people, and capital—in that government services, skills, and entrepreneurships are produced by capital. And even the stock of *available* resources often may be altered by capital and people. So perhaps we should talk in terms of two factors. However, even as the *stock* of people and capital may be changed significantly only in the very long run, so likewise the quantity of *skilled* personnel and the public infrastructure of a nation may be altered only quite slowly; that is, the capital embodied and frozen in skills and government cannot be shifted easily as the result of market pressures operating within the time horizon of most business decisions. The same is true for much resource development. Commitments of capital are made long in advance of actual production. The number of entrepreneurs (the innovators and risk-takers) does not shift dramatically in the short run, for such a shift is probably related to changes in the social environment, which in turn generate changes in psychological needs and personality. Therefore, these factors of production are really constants within the time we are concerned with in business decisions, and should be considered as distinct.

The United States, having possessed a relatively high capital/unskilled labor ratio for many years (relative to most other nations), has developed a cost advantage in those goods and services incorporating large amounts of capital relative to unskilled labor. It has also had relatively high resource/unskilled labor, skilled labor/unskilled labor, government/unskilled labor, and entrepreneurship/unskilled labor ratios. Generally, therefore, it possesses an international advantage in the goods and services that are relatively rich in resources, skilled labor, entrepreneurship, and government services—all of which are a function at least in part of the relative capital wealth of the United States over many decades. This means that in the long run, the greatest markets for U.S. business relate to those goods, rights, and services relatively rich in these factors. (We speak of exports here; that is, goods and services produced within the U.S., not those produced in foreign-based plants where the factor relationships may be very different.) Examples are capital goods for capital goods industries (for example, plant construction in the steel, cement, basic chemicals, pulp industries), agricultural products, and technical and managerial assistance.

This argument would tend to rule out the long-run export from the U.S. of many consumer products and would suggest, rather, that the trend will push in the direction of exporting those products rich in resources, capital, high-level skills, and public services. Most intensive in these factors are the resources, the capital, and the skills themselves. Government services per se do not generally move through private business, so we may eliminate that item from our discussion, although such services as defense, basic education, and preventative medicine may sometimes be relevant. Curiously, in its export encouragement programs, the U.S. government has not seen education and health services as export industries. Yet, they are. Perhaps they are invisible because the consumer rather than the product or service moves. To the extent that the foreign student or foreign patient pays out of foreign savings for the services consumed domestically, these industries are foreign exchange earners.

For these two reasons then, political vulnerability and comparative cost, many firms would do well to consider carefully the export of skills, valuable rights (which are produced by high-level skills), and capital in the form of debt or portfolio equity rather than thinking only in terms of merchandise and/or direct investment.[12]

Statistics as to the international traffic in services are very inadequate. It has been estimated, however, that one dollar of U.S. sales abroad in every five is earned by a provider of services rather than a seller of goods.[13]

It should be pointed out that as nations become more sensitive to the requirements of economic development, to their own economic interests, and to comparative costs, pressure will mount to limit imports from the more developed nations (that is, those relatively affluent in skills and capital) to those that are rich in skills and capital. The poorer nations will then be in a position to employ more of their own resources. This pressure, in turn, may well heighten the political vulnerability of firms relying upon the export to these markets of consumer goods which tend to be relatively labor-intensive[14] and of capital in the form of direct investment. Domestic experience and a history of successful export of merchandise and direct investment overseas may not be adequate guidelines for the future.

We are already witnessing such pressure through the many entry control restrictions in LDCs, which place a time limit on foreign property rights unless a continuing beneficial transfer of skills and other assets is perceived. In some cases disinvestment by foreign firms is forced when it is perceived to be in the interest of the host countries. Elsewhere, local governments have turned to service contracts after forcing out alien owners through expropriations and buy-outs. One suspects that these moves constitute a worldwide pattern on the part of the less developed countries to force the greater employment of their own resources in fashioning the goods and services demanded by their people. A few of the richer countries have become equally sensitive, particularly Canada and Australia.

Unfortunately, some of the LDCs have made the costly error of attempting to stimulate industrialization through import substitution, that is, by offering

---

[12]See Glossary.
[13]*Commerce America*, April 11, 1977, p. 8.
[14]See Glossary.

various inducements to both foreign and local firms to manufacture locally what had previously been imported. The object has been to conserve scarce foreign exchange and to generate local employment. The problem is that those goods or services for which a domestic market exists are not necessarily those that a country is best suited to produce. The reverse is likewise true. Those goods and services that a country is best able to produce are often ones which have little or no local market. A government can easily promote import substituting industry by imposing barriers to entry, thereby engaging the defensive investment strategy of foreign firms designed to protect markets. A government can thus sometimes attract foreign investment and technology by creating a protected market, but this attraction is more difficult to generate for export-oriented investment, for in that case the market is independent (i.e., external) and existing sources of supply may be deeply entrenched. Also, a country's comparative advantage may not be obvious.

Having thus determined what the firm should sell, management must then decide where it should attempt to sell it; that is, the sales target. Otherwise, it will not know on which geographical areas to focus its selling effort.

SALES TARGET (GEOGRAPHICAL) 1.2

It should be recognized that the use of historical export sales to predict future trends of exports is hazardous. Although possibly valid in the short run, such sales are subject to discontinuities.[15] A discontinuity may arise because of the collapse of a competitive position (such as appearance of local production), imposition of import controls at the other end of the pipeline for revenue or consumption-control purposes, imposition or release of export controls by one's home government, or an official decision to compel local production. In the longer run, imports into one's domestic market comparable products may be a better guideline to overseas markets, though possibly not to be supplied from a domestic plant. But even imports have a serious flaw as a guide. A product may enjoy a substantial demand in a given foreign market but none in the home market due to disparate income and wealth levels, values and institutions, climate, geography, and style of living. In addition, there are many services produced domestically that have not been pushed into the export stream, but which *theoretically* should enjoy substantial overseas markets. Because of their generally capital-intensive[16] nature they would not show up as imports into the home market. Therefore, the present flow of international trade in many cases provides only a first, short-run

---

[15]See Glossary.
[16]See Glossary.

approximation of foreign market opportunities, which is not to deny its importance.[17]

Logically, a firm should look periodically at every potential market in order to allocate its resources in an optimum fashion. Given the limited managerial, production, marketing, and financial resources at the disposal of a firm, a policy of exerting equal energy in developing each national market is obviously not optimum. Stripped to its essence, the decision then is a determination of those markets on which the firm should concentrate its efforts, *forgetting for the moment the source from which that market will be supplied.* Does a sufficient demand exist for a product or a valuable right or service within the capability of the firm to supply make that market more attractive than others? Securing a convincing answer to that question requires more imagination, greater cost, and encompasses a larger margin of error than the purely domestic decision. Herein lies a major obstacle to the successful conduct of international business.

A flow of detailed studies of virtually every national market is available to the businessman,[18] lists of which are published periodically by the U.S.

---

[17]The United Nations, the U.S. Department of Commerce, the Organization for European Economic Cooperation, and various common market and trade-bloc organizations publish historical series of trade by commodities. Three classification systems being used are the Standard International Trade Classification (SITC) by the United Nations and by governments of countries accounting for about 80 percent of world trade, the Standard Industrial Classification (SIC) by the U.S. Department of Commerce, and the Brussels Tariff Nomenclature (BTN) by roughly 100 nations plus several of the regional trade groups. The BTN is sometimes referred to as the International Customs Cooperation Council Nomenclature (ICCC). In January 1968, the United States shifted its international trade classification to an equivalent of the SITC so as to permit comparison of U.S. trade statistics with those of other countries. The classification ("Schedule B"), a modification of the SITC, is used to identify items for export reported on the Shipper's Export Declaration. As of 1978, it was similar—but not identical—to the Tariff Schedule of the U.S., or TSUS. Cross indices between the SITC and BTN are available. The relationship between these two systems and the SIC is more difficult in that the latter is a classification by industry or economic function, not by commodity as are the other two systems. There is likewise an International Standard Industrial Classification (ISIC), which is similar to the SIC. The SITC consists of 10 sections, 56 divisions, 177 groups, 625 subgroups, 944 subsidiary headings. In the SITC code, the first digit determines the section; the first two digits, the division; the first three, the group; the first four, the subgroup; the first five, the subsidiary breakdown. Countries can and do code further subdivisions for national purposes by adding a sixth or more digits. The Eastern European Council for Mutual Economic Assistance (CMEA) has its own commodity classification system for which a key has been developed by the Statistical Commission of the United Nations. A word of caution in using international trade statistics: the money value may be significantly distorted in some cases by intracorporate (transfer) pricing policies. (See Section 1.12.)

[18]Some standard sources in English are: the Country Area Handbooks published by the U.S. government, *Business International, London Economist Intelligence Unit Reports, International Reports, Inc., The International Executive* (bibliography), *Overseas Business Reports* (U.S. Department of Commerce), the *OECD Country Studies and Main Economic Indicators,* the UN annual regional economic summaries, the *UN Demographic Yearbook* and the *UN Statistical Yearbook.* Several works give sets of the more significant national indicators, country by country: B. M. Russett et al., *World Handbook of Political and Social Indicators* (New Haven: Yale University Press, 1964); A. S. Banks (ed.), *Cross-Polity Time-Series Data* (Cambridge: M.I.T. Press, 1971); Charles L. Taylor and Michael C. Hudson, *World Handbook of Political and Social Indicators* (New Haven: Yale University Press; 1975), *World Tables, 1976* (Baltimore: Johns Hopkins University Press, 1976). A commercial enterprise in New York, Marketing Control Incorporated, maintains a world data bank containing over 300 socioeconomic and demographic descriptors of 45 major countries, which can be used to provide country profiles, forecast sales, and group countries in terms of a set of market factors. The computerized data banks maintained by the *New York Times* and the World Trade Center of New York are also exceedingly useful sources of data. The European Communities Processed Data Network, Euronet, was expected to be operational by the end of 1977 and would be available to commercial users. The first phase called for plugging in all existing data banks, specifically, CELEX (which contains information on all legislation in EC member countries), SDIM (which consists of metallurgical information), SDS (a space documentation service operated by the European Space Agency), DIMDE (a German medical service being expanded for European use), AGREP (which covers

Department of Commerce and comparable government agencies elsewhere, including the United Nations, the General Agreement on Trade and Tariffs (GATT), and the Organization of Economic Cooperation and Development (OECD). But one needs to have a fairly precise notion of wherein his market lies before this mass of information is of much value.

Eliminated immediately from the list of potential markets for firms controlled by U.S. nationals or legal entities are those closed by U.S. government action through export control, which operates for capital equipment, technical information, and skills, as well as merchandise. The Export Control Act of 1949 regulates exports to all countries other than Canada in order to provide support for U.S. foreign policy, national security interests, and the domestic economy (for short-supply reasons). Most goods can move to noncommunist bloc countries through a general license, which requires no formal application. Validated licenses are required for certain types of strategic goods regardless of destination and, in almost all cases, for strategic goods destined for bloc countries. Over the years, the number of items on the control list has been decreased steadily and the definition of strategic goods narrowed to include only militarily strategic goods and not the economically strategic.

Transactions of United States–controlled foreign enterprise are similarly restrained in respect to the transfer of unpublished American-origin technical data, or to the selling of commodities included on the Coordinating Committee (COCOM; see below) list. The so-called Battle Act (Mutual Defense Control Act of 1951) authorized the president to deny aid to any nation which knowingly permits the export of specified strategic goods or data. Such goods and data are generally those agreed upon by the members of the COCOM, including Japan and all NATO countries. This list is subject to annual review and has been pared periodically. It is limited currently to those things likely to be used even in peacetime for military-industrial production and similar purposes. Technical data that are published or would be freely disclosed to the general public upon request may be exported under a general license to any destination other than one subjected to a complete embargo.

From 1949 until mid-1971, there was a virtually complete embargo on U.S. trade with the People's Republic of China, North Korea, North Vietnam, and Cuba. Transactions of U.S.-controlled foreign enterprise were similarly restrained. However, as of December 1969, foreign subsidiaries of U.S. firms were allowed to conduct nonstrategic trade with China so long as the goods did not originate or end up in the U.S. In April 1970, trade was permitted in

all agricultural projects), AGRIS (an agricultural and agri-economic system managed by the United Nations Food and Agricultural Organization). In a second phase, a data bank will be added to provide statistical information on industries and labor agreements. Headquartered in Brussels, Euronet will be available to clients in the six community languages. Also worthy of mention is Project LINK, an internationally supported program at the University of Pennsylvania to construct an econometric model of world trade through the simultaneous projection of 13 large econometric models of major industrial countries and regional models of developing countries and centrally planned economies.

American-made components of foreign-manufactured, nonstrategic goods. And in 1971 direct trade (in designated imports and certain nonstrategic exports) with China was permitted for the first time since 1950. At the same time the control on the use of dollars in current transactions was relaxed.

Periodically, certain national markets may be closed by reason of national or international sanctions, such as Southern Rhodesia, Republic of South Africa, and the United Arab Republic, to cite a few recent cases. A persistent example is the blacklisting by certain Arab states of firms operating or providing goods and services to Israel (or doing business with such firms), also by China of firms doing business directly in Taiwan. In 1976–77 both the U.S. federal government and the governments of several of the states enacted laws and regulations making it difficult for U.S. companies to comply with the Arab boycott regulations, thereby causing some loss of sales in the Arab states. The U.S. has been particularly sticky about permitting U.S. exports to Cuba. In 1974, U.S. business won a modest breakthrough when the government granted U.S. subsidiaries in Argentina permission to export motor vehicles to Cuba. The Argentine government had brought strong pressure to bear on these subsidiaries to respond to Cuban orders. It appeared by 1977 to be a general rule that the foreign subsidiary of a U.S. company could sell to Cuba if under host government pressure to do so.

In order to determine opportunities and restraints within the centrally controlled economies of the Sino-Soviet bloc, it is essential that the businessman know something of the national economic plan. In the Soviet case, the State Planning Commission ("Gosplan") coordinates the activities of all economic organizations in the country and translates the general goals and policies set forth by the Central Committee of the Communist party into a detailed realizable national plan, including import priorities. The details of the plan are closely guarded secrets and uncovering them even partially may require the development of high-level connections both in the appropriate industrial ministries and the various associated technical institutes. Attendance at the relevant trade fairs in Eastern Europe is one of the best ways of getting clues as to the types of goods to which the various foreign ministries are giving priority and for which they have most likely established hard currency allocation.

Quite apart from the centrally controlled economies of the Sino-Soviet bloc countries, many nations (for example, France, the United Kingdom, India, Turkey, the Republic of Korea) periodically develop national development plans, generally with annual revisions. Not infrequently, a careful reading of such plans, which are generally made public, will reveal where special emphasis is to be placed and, hence, will identify sales opportunities. Particularly in less developed countries, the plan will reveal priorities in regard to foreign exchange allocations for the purchase of foreign goods and services. In general, the more centrally controlled is an economy and the more restricted are its foreign exchange earning capacity and reserves vis-à-vis demand for same, the more critical is the national economic plan in assessing market opportunity.

There have been a number of efforts to rank or classify national markets in general terms.[19] Vogel hypothesized the justification for the clustering of countries in the statement, "one source of strength of the multinational corporation (MNC) is that it sells its products in a number of countries. Capitalizing on this, the MNC can transfer useful information from one market to another.... If several countries are similar for marketing purposes, standardization of the planning process may be feasible. With one country serving as a test market, it may be possible to standardize in a number of countries various aspects of the marketing program such as advertising and the product."[20] He correctly pointed out that the problem lies in identifying the relevant variables and then measuring them. He suggested that identification may best be achieved by utilizing the perceptions of corporate managers. Vogel then proceeded to query 55 managers in three MNCs in seven countries, plus the United States. Judgments were requested in respect to 12 countries from the point of view of overall marketing similarities. "The primary question of interest was whether or not countries would be perceived similarly by both headquarters and subsidiary managers. If there weren't a difference in the perceptions by the two groups, there would be greater acceptance of grouping countries based on these perceptions."[21] But, in fact, the study demonstrated that there were significant differences in perceptions, thereby casting doubt on the whole notion of clustering countries by this method. In order to determine the accuracy of the managers' perceptions, Vogel correlated them with objective measures of the variables used. It turned out that the perceptions of 23 students in an international marketing graduate class were more accurate and that headquarters managers were generally more accurate than subsidiary managers.

Efforts to cluster countries notwithstanding, the fact remains that the sale of the products and services of each firm is related to a specific, and often unique, set of variables. Thus, it is of doubtful value to start with the general

---

[19]For example, see A. A. Sherbini, "Classifying and Comparing Countries," in *Comparative Analysis for International Marketing* (Boston: Allyn and Bacon, 1967), part 2, pp. 55–145; I. A. Litvak and P. M. Banting, "A Conceptual Framework for International Business Arrangements," in Robert L. King (ed.), *Marketing and the New Science of Planning* (Chicago: American Marketing Association, 1968 Fall Conference Proceedings), pp. 466–67; S. Prakash Sethi and David Curry, "Variable and Object Clustering of Cross-Cultural Data: Some Implications for Comparative Research and Policy Formulation," in Prakash Sethi and Jagdish M. Sheth (eds.), *Multinational Business Operations, Marketing Management* (Pacific Palisades: Goodyear Publishing Company, 1973), pp. 31–61; and Eugene D. Jaffe, *Grouping: A Strategy for International Marketing* (New York: American Management Association, 1974). The last named publication illustrates the use of factor and cluster analysis. In factor analysis, the international market researcher has as an objective the classification of countries grouped according to some measures of similarity. With this technique, a large number of variables can be reduced to a smaller number that summarize the differences and similarities equally well as the larger number. By using cluster analysis, the researcher can identify groups of countries with a set of common attributes. However, one gets the distinct impression from many of these analyses that the researchers are more enamored of the eloquence of their statistical method than of producing results of real value to the international market researcher.

[20]Ronald H. Vogel, "Uses of Managerial Perceptions in Clustering Countries," *Journal of International Business Studies*, vol. 7, no. 1, Spring 1976, p. 91.

[21]Vogel, "Managerial Perceptions," p. 95.

classifications of national markets by such variables as literacy, education, occupational breakdown (such as farming-nonfarming, industry, service, private-government, technical-nontechnical), gross national product (GNP), GNP per capita, source of GNP by sector (industry, agriculture, services), income distribution, power consumption per capita, occupation, levels and directions of foreign trade, degree of urbanization. Rather, one would best start with those environmental variables known in the domestic market (or in other markets in which the firm has had experience) to be associated with the level of sales of the firm's product or service. What may be misleading, of course, is the fact that the variables may shift significantly in value from one market to another. It is known, for example, that the United States farmer on average buys fewer cameras than the nonfarm population. Therefore the farming-nonfarming occupational breakdown becomes important in constructing a consumption function for the United States. But can one make the same assumption, say, in the case of the Japanese farmer? One cannot be certain. Or, in the United States and Western Europe the consumption of margarine may be related significantly to the level of urbanization. Therefore, can one assume that the market for margarine is limited to the urban centers in Turkey? (In fact, it turned out that it was not.) Hence, one takes those variables known from experience and/or analysis to be linked to demand in familiar markets, then re-examines them critically in the context of an unfamiliar market. Variables given a zero rating (that is, those seen as constant) in the former, may be found to swamp the estimates in the latter. An example might be the imposition of government restrictions on the import of goods seen as nonessential in order to conserve foreign exchange reserves in the face of persistent balance-of-payments crises.

A useful way of looking at a foreign market is to think in terms of six levels of research and analysis: (1) *potential need* (which is a constant over the relevant time horizon and is physically determined), (2) *felt need* (which is culturally determined and may be stimulated if the potential need is there, albeit slowly), (3) *potential demand* (which is economically determined), (4) *effective demand* (which may be equated with potential demand modified by political considerations), (5) *market demand* (which is commercially determined, such as by cost of selling), and (6) *sales* (which is determined by competitive conditions). One may think of these levels as a six-tiered filtering process, as illustrated in Figure 1.1. Consider the sorts of information required at each level to justify the added investment in the commitment of company resources (executive time and cash expense) to research the more important at the next level (see Table 1.1).

From Table 1.1 it is apparent that an expensive overseas junket is unnecessary until one establishes a reasonable presumption that there exists a specific demand for a particular product or service of sufficient size to be attractive within the target market. A short circuit to this level of inquiry may be provided by international trade statistics *if* the product has been sold actively

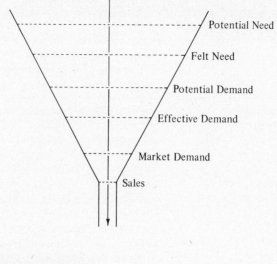

Figure 1.1
THE MARKET RESEARCH FILTER

in international trade for a number of years; that is, if it is a relatively mature product.

Some firms set out the range of goods, rights, and services within their capability and attempt to relate the market of each to certain aggregate national statistical measures, although one should be wary when the macro approach is used to analyze micro markets. The world is then scanned periodically for variables by which to rank potential national markets (sometimes called a multiple factor index). Some of the variables most commonly included:

1. Per-capita income (PCI; bear in mind that comparisons across currency frontiers are very tricky. To secure comparable purchasing powers, dollar figures derived by use of official exchange rates for the poorer countries must be multiplied by a factor of two or three. Also, an average such as PCI may disguise a very skewed distribution).

   Growth in per-capita income tends to be associated with the growth and decline of certain industries. "Knowing trends in manufacturing aids market demand analysis in several ways. First, besides inventory changes and net imports or exports, goods produced are goods consumed. Thus production patterns generally reveal consumption patterns, and knowing them helps exporters to assess market opportunities. Moreover, knowing trends in manufacturing production is useful because these industries represent potential markets for . . . exporters of inputs."[22] Figure 1.2 plots the characteristic shift in production as a nation's per capita

---

[22]R. Moyer, "International Market Analysis," *Journal of Marketing Research,*" vol. 5, 1968, p. 355.

Table 1.1
**DATA REQUIRED BEFORE ENTERING OR EXPANDING
IN A FOREIGN MARKET**

Level	Major Categories of Data (dependent upon nature of product of service)
1. Potential need (physically determined)	Climate, natural resources, land use, population (size), occupational breakdown, life expectancy, topography, overall level of wealth. *Key question:* Is there a potential need?
2. Felt need (culturally determined)	Existence of linking products and services,* values and institutions (for example, class structure, influence of elite, life style), market exposure (means of communication and transport, literacy, mobility, urbanization). *Key question:* What effort (cost) is required to transform a potential need into a felt need of significant intensity and aggregate size to be attractive (profitable)?
3. Potential demand (economically determined)	Disposable income level, income distribution, consumption as a function of income, family budget studies, traditional trading patterns (external and internal). *Key question:* Are there economic and organizational factors beyond the firm's influence that will block the development of a felt need into a potential demand?
4. Effective demand (politically determined)	"Buy national" restrictions, foreign exchange restrictions, import duties, import quotas, imposition of national law regarding standards (such as public health, sanitation, safety, security, pollution), conflict with locally owned rights (patents, copyrights, trademarks), taxation, rationing, subsidy programs, price and wage controls, special external trade relations (such as bilateral trade treaties), effectiveness of commercial law, extent of law and order, relative importance of the government sector in terms of total consumption, government control over communications, state planning. *Key question:* To what extent are market factors permitted to operate? (And, to what extent can the firm circumvent or change politically imposed restraints?)

Table 1.1 (Continued)

5. Market demand (commercially determined)	Cost – or availability – of internal distribution (degree of market dispersion, market organization, credit facilities, insurance, transport costs, special storage and handling facilities), service and maintenance facilities, advertising and promotion facilities and effectiveness. *Key question:* Can the firm get its product or service to the customer at reasonable cost relative to other products and services for which there is a likewise effective demand?
6. Specific demand (sales potential; competitively determined)	Appropriateness of own and competitors' product or service in terms of quality, design, sizing, packaging, and pricing; credit terms; currency accepted (source of product); delivery time; service and warranties offered. *Key question:* Can the firm meet the terms offered by competitors in the supply of the same or similar products and services (what is its likely market share)?

*For example, a felt need for gasoline requires vehicles; a felt need for transmission lines, electric power; and so on. A very real danger is the use of what some have dubbed "self-reference criteria," which refers to a tendency to ascribe to others our own preferences and reactions. An example would be the promotion of filtered cigarettes on the basis that they reduce tar and nicotine content, hence promoting longer life expectancy, in a country where the average life expectancy is, say, 30 years.

income moves up. Similarly, the pattern of a nation's imports shifts as the country becomes more industrialized. Table 1.2 shows such a change.

2. Distribution of personal income (rarely available except for the more developed countries, but can be estimated).

3. Class structure (may be estimated from educational and occupational breakdowns, also by rural-urban split).

4. Degree of industrialization (may be estimated from sectoral breakdown of GNP).

5. Degree of urbanization (population statistics, rural and urban, are generally available).

6. Gross national product (a measure of aggregate market size, but which may hide division of virtually unrelated subnational markets).

7. Degree of national integration (may be estimated from cargo and passenger-miles by land transport as a ratio to total estimated tonnage of marketable goods and total population, respectively, also by internal transport and insurance rates).

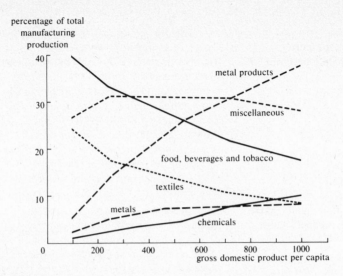

Figure 1.2
TYPICAL PATTERNS OF GROWTH IN MANUFACTURING INDUSTRIES*

Source: R. Moyer, "International Market Analysis," *Journal of Marketing Research*, vol. 5, 1968, p. 355.

*Based on a time series analysis for selected years, 1899–1957 for seven to ten countries, depending upon the industry. Gross domestic product per capita is stated in 1955 dollars.

8. Existence of specific industries, services, or agricultural activity (input-output tables are increasingly available, but even in their absence crude approximations may be derived from general economic surveys of the sort developed by the World Bank).

9. Literacy (local definitions may be misleading; what constitutes literacy?).

10. Age distribution (a decreasing or increasing trend may signal important changes in the market).

11. Climate.

12. Certain natural resources, including water and power.

13. Legal requirements (for example, restraints on the introduction of certain products, such as pharmaceuticals; imposition of different standards; prohibitive import barriers).

Two unresolved questions are (1) the presence of an attractive regional (subnational) or segmented market and (2) projected trends for each of these factors. In respect to the first, an attractive subnational market may be well hidden by aggregate statistics. The poverty of India, considered in the aggregate, does not alert one to the existence of a large subnational market for many

Table 1.2

IMPORTS OF MAJOR COMMODITY GROUPS BY REPRESENTATIVE COUNTRIES CLASSIFIED BY STAGE OF INDUSTRIALIZATION AND EXPRESSED AS PERCENTAGES OF TOTAL IMPORTS, 1965

Stage	Food	Fuels	Industrial materials	Manu-factures
Industrial countries*	19.2%	10.9%	16.1%	53.8%
Semi-industrial countries*†	15.7	6.5	8.3	69.5
Non-industrial countries‡§	17.4	5.1	4.5	73.0

* Belgium-Luxembourg, France, West Germany, Italy, Netherlands, Sweden, Norway, Switzerland, United Kingdom, United States, Canada, Japan.

† Australia, New Zealand, Republic of South Africa, India, Pakistan, Argentina, Brazil, Chile, Colombia, Mexico, Israel, Turkey, Yugoslavia.

‡ Congo, U.A.R., French Morocco, Nigeria, Southern Rhodesia, Indonesia, Iran, Philippines, Cuba, Peru, Venezuela.

§ For Chile 1963 data were used; for several of the nonindustrialized countries 1962, 1963, or 1964 data were used.

Source: Yearbook of International Trade Statistics, United Nations, 1965.

sophisticated products. The set of cultural variables constituting a market for a given product should not be equated necessarily with a national market. Even though a given national market may not appear large enough to warrant more than a reading of the statistics, one may combine segments of different national markets lying within a convenient geographical or cultural area,[23] thereby justifying the commitment of company resources to further exploration, at least to a study of the more detailed literature.

Trying to plot the dynamics of a market is always hazardous. Given the inertia of traditional or near-traditional society, changes may appear as discontinuities; that is, they could not be predicted on the basis of a historical series. For over 3,000 years, the Anatolian Turk used a solid-wheeled ox cart. Between 1955 and 1965, these carts almost disappeared from large areas. Rural society may be under great economic pressure for many years but resist urbanization. Then, almost without warning, the dam bursts. It requires a social anthropologist to predict such shifts with any degree of accuracy.

The importance of coming to grips with the dynamics of a market is reflected in the notion of income elasticity of demand, which describes the relationship between the amount consumed and level of income (that is, level of

---

[23]Of particular importance in this regard are the many trade blocs, tariff unions, free-trade areas, common markets, and arrangements in relation to specific industries or commodities. But one should be alert to the fact that "natural" pressures for or against such market integration (for example, factor complementarity, or absence thereof) may well outlive or redirect politically-inspired integration.

economic development). It answers the question, what difference in consumption is triggered by a change in income, both being represented in percentages?
Thus:

$$\frac{\Delta C_A}{C_A} \bigg/ \frac{\Delta Y}{Y},$$

where C_A and Y represent initial values (quantity of Good A consumed
and personal income), and ΔC_A and ΔY represent the change in values
as of some later time.

If this ratio is greater than one (that is, has an elasticity greater than unity),
it means that proportionately more of Good A is consumed as income moves
up. It is a "superior good." If the ratio is less than one, then proportionately
less of Good A is consumed as income moves up. It is an "inferior good." In
the first case, Good A is income elastic; in the second case, income inelastic.
This concept aids the researcher concerned with predicting growth in demand
for particular goods in international markets, provided he can approximate
their income elasticities. Bear in mind that an income elasticity can be calculated either by looking at consumption preferences for people with different
incomes at one point in time (cross sectional analysis) or by charting changes
in consumption over time as incomes increase (time series). The two approaches may produce different results. Table 1.3 gives an example of some
demand income elasticities. But market projections based on income elasticities assume (a) that one can plot income change and (b) past relationships will
hold in the future.

At this phase, management should become concerned about its potential
competitive position in the market under study. (See levels 5 and 6 in Table
1.1.) A rough demand schedule may be constructed, but what of the supply
side? And where would the firm fit in? Relevant variables to be considered are:

1.   Entry barriers[24]

Displacement of local business and/or present third-country suppliers and their
anticipated responses.

Import restrictions, whether in reference to merchandise, services (that is, visas
and official approvals), valuable rights, or finance.

Need for special permits or franchises.

Degree of cartelization.

Economies of scale.

Control of the distribution systems.

Existence of established brand names.

Control by others of relevant patents, trademarks, copyrights.

---

[24]See Joe S. Bain, *Barriers to New Competition* (Cambridge: Harvard University Press, 1956).

Table 1.3
INCOME ELASTICITY MEASUREMENTS

Commodity	Cross section	Time series
Food and beverages, excluding alcoholic beverages	0·54†, 0·53‡	0·8*
Alcoholic beverages	0·77†	
Tobacco	0·88†	
Clothing	0·8,* 0·9* 0·84, 0·89*	0·7,* 0·8*
Textiles	0·5*	0·8*
Household and personal services	1·19†	
Communication services	2·03†	
Recreation	1·15†	
Health	1·80†	
Durable consumer goods		2·7*
Furniture	1·61‡	
Appliances	1·40‡	
Metals	1·52‡	
Chemicals		2·1‡
Machinery and transportation equipment, except passenger cars		1·5–2·0*

Sources:
† M. Gilbert et al, *Comparative National Products and Price Levels* (Paris: Organization for Economic Cooperation, 1958).

‡ R. Moyer, "International Market Analysis," *Journal of Marketing Research*, vol. 5, 1968.

* M. L. Kastens, "Organizing, Planning and Staffing Market Research Activities in an International Corporation," *Market Research in International Operations* (New York: American Management Association, 1960).

2. Exit barriers

   Repatriation of profits and/or capital.

   Legal protection for valuable rights.

   Personal safety of aliens and their personal property.

   Export of goods, services, rights, and finance.

3. Competitive barriers[25]

   Operating margin of potential competitors; that is, sales price less materials cost.

   Involuntary expense: unavoidable costs in manufacture and, in the case of off-shore supply, transport and entry charges.

   Discretionary expense (cost of goods sold less involuntary costs): that which is available for promotion, development, research, marketing, and profit.

---

[25]See Raphael W. Hodgson and Hugo E. R. Uyterhoeven, "Analyzing Foreign Opportunities," *Harvard Business Review* (March–April 1962), pp. 60–79.

In respect to the third point above, the operating margin may not necessarily reflect either tight or loose competitive conditions. Relevant variables are (1) scale of production (if large scale, generous profits may appear even if operating margins are low), (2) organization of distribution channels (for example, if distribution channels are limited, a high level of discretionary cost may be required and hence, low profit results), (3) structure of an industry (if one large company enjoys maximum economies of scale, the operating margin may be wide and competitive conditions tight), (4) importance of price in creating demand (if price dominates, a narrow operating margin probably means tight competitive conditions). The point is, as Hodgson and Uyterhoeven pointed out:

> The most important condition of entry is that the company's initial marketing objectives create discretionary margins which are large enough to sustain its growth objectives. Recognizing the importance of maintaining the venture's position relative to industry leaders, management may see that it is not sufficient merely to match their discretionary expenses; it may be necessary to exceed the other firm's expenses substantially. For example, if there is a shortage of distribution channels, the capture of which is critical to achieve success, management may have to spend more than competitors on the product lines, services, or promotion needed to secure these channels.[26]

Hodgson and Uyterhoeven admonish against duplicating the programs of industry leaders and urge the new entrant to select his own battleground. In doing so, they warn that the nonrecognition of essential differences in industry or market conditions as between the United States and a foreign market may be costly. "Failure to do so may lead to incorrect assumptions as to a venture's (or a market's permissible) discretionary margin. . . .";[27] that is, a careful examination of the involuntary expenses must be made. Some of those differing from those incurred in the United States are:

1. *Labor.* In many countries the cost of legally-imposed fringe benefits (social welfare taxes, the "13th month" bonus, payments into a publicly administered pension plan, and termination pay) may add up to a significant percentage of the direct payroll, to which must be added the cost to the firm of accounting for these payments. Also, the true cost of labor includes training costs, which may be aggravated by an unexpectedly high turnover rate and an inadequate educational system, vocational and basic. In addition, U.S.-based assumptions as to the number of employees required may not be justified if productivity is substantially different. Finally, given the labor codes operative in many countries, labor is more in the nature of a fixed cost in that termination may be both difficult and expensive. Labor cost may sometimes be made more variable by taking advantage of various escape clauses relating to "temporary labor." Such practices may, however, accelerate the turnover rate, thereby adding to training costs. A relevant variable here is how much internal training has to be undertaken. (See Section 3.4.) In situations

---

[26]Hodgson and Uyterhoeven, "Foreign Opportunities," pp. 68–69.
[27]Hodgson and Uyterhoeven, "Foreign Opportunities," p. 76.

where internal training is of vital importance, manning tables should be constructed, rates of disappearance calculated, and projections of needed labor of various skills set up. Unless explicit policy to the contrary has been announced by the firm, graduates of company training schools and courses tend to feel that the firm is obligated to employ them upon "graduation." If the firm does not do so, and it constitutes an important employer in the local economy, an awkward political situation may be created, further adding to costs.

2. *Materials and power.* An inadequate supply may force an enterprise into an integration with which it is not familiar in the United States, thereby adding to cost. Also, given the economies of scale in power production, power plants serving only a single enterprise may be high cost.

3. *Finance.* Given local inflation and foreign exchange controls, local finance may be required. However, interest rates and local profit expectations may be such as to add significantly to cost. (Possible hedging devices are outlined in Section 6.6.) Differences in taxation, depreciation requirements, working-capital needs, and utilization of debt leverage should, likewise, be considered. All may differ from U.S. practice. For example, distance may mean either high inventories and/or expensive transport (air freight), thereby setting up higher working capital requirements.

4. *Management.* If American management is deemed necessary for reasons of control and/or inadequacy of local nationals, management may be significantly more costly than that in the U.S. due to special bonuses typically paid to expatriate American managers. Chapter 4 deals in greater detail with this problem.

5. *Control.* Distance means added cost in terms of communications, travel, misunderstandings, and tardy handling of problems. A generous allowance is required to cover this item. If management is local and does not use English fluently, a further cost in translation and delay may be incurred.

6. *Production.* Given a smaller market, unused capacity and/or more general purpose machines may be inevitable. In the first case, fixed charges per unit of production are higher; in the latter, more extensive training and supervision are needed. Also, if production depends on imported supplies or components, an uneven allocation of foreign exchange may be anticipated in some cases, thereby causing fluctuation in production and, hence, added cost.

7. *Distribution.* Control of existing channels by others may compel opening new channels that may be costly due to low volume, or organized channels may be wholly absent, which may lead to heavy start-up costs.

If management has gone this far in studying a given geographical sales target and has satisfied itself as to the existence of a relatively attractive demand, competitive conditions with which it can live, and apparently feasible costs, the next step is an on-the-spot survey. Inasmuch as this is a costly procedure, management is well advised to be relatively certain of its ground before dispatching such a group.

Various methods for in-place market surveys are (1) measuring response to exhibition at local trade fairs, professional meetings, and world trade centers (greatly facilitating this initial market contact by small U.S. firms is a program inaugurated by the U.S. Department of Commerce in 1976, the Product Marketing Service. For a very modest fee, the department rents to U.S. businessmen office space abroad and areas in which marketing displays may be set up); (2) sampling of customer response by questioning (mailed, telephoned, or face-to-face); (3) pretesting of the market through free samples or a concerted sales effort for a given period of time without regard for profit; and (4) consulting social anthropologists familiar with the area.

The choice of survey method depends upon several variables: the nature of the market (industrial, professional, or consumer), size and homogeneity of market, geographical concentration of expected consumers, literacy, number of markets being surveyed, customer reaction to the questionnaire approach, availability of dependable surveyors, reliability of mail and telephone services, resources of the firm, and availability of competent social anthropologists in the area. One should be forewarned about making unconsciously a number of culturally conditioned assumptions, such as the (1) use of the product being tested and hence the general identity of the potential customers (one firm did not expect its margarine to be eaten like cheese and thereby overlooked that part of the population not using butter on its bread), (2) propensity of people to buy a given type of product (such as pills in the absence of medical advice), (3) probability that people will respond to a market survey honestly or at all, (4) the location of the buy-or-not-buy decision-making authority, (5) relationship between enthusiasm for a free sample and a willingness to buy, (6) generalization from a sample (overlooking significant bias in a sample because of the presence, in undue numbers, of a religious, racial, class, caste, educational, or occupational group not recognized as relevant by the marketeer or not statistically identified).

There is another dimension to market analysis—time. To justify a heavy marketing investment, a firm needs to assure itself of a reasonable probability that the market will grow or, at least, not shrink. Long-range forecasting of international markets is obviously difficult unless one has had long experience within those markets. Basically, two approaches, or models, may be used: a so-called naive model, which involves a simple projection of historical sale data into the future, or a causal model.

Characteristic of the "naive" approach to market prediction is regression analysis. In its international application, this technique involves studying the relationship between gross economic indicators and demand for a specific good in countries where relevant time series data is available and, by analogy, transferring this relationship to countries in which the data is not available. Very commonly a simple linear regression equation is used of the $P = a + bY$ type, where P is the amount of the product used per thousand of the population, a is some minimum value, b is a constant (a coefficient), and Y is the gross economic indicator, such as GNP per capita. One can test the results to ascertain how much of the variation in the dependent variable (in this case, the amount of product used per thousand of the population) is explained by a shift in the independent variable (GNP per capita), and the chance that such a result could have occurred randomly. The problem with this sort of analysis is that it assumes that roughly the same relationship holds from one country to another and from one time to another, also that there are no intervening variables that will cause a shift in relationship. We might determine, for example, that an increase of $100 per capita in GNP is associated with an increase of ten refrigerators per 1,000 population in Country A. But differences in climatic conditions might swamp these relationships in Country B. And, over time, the relationship even in Country A will break down as the saturation point is reached, or as an entirely new technology for food preservation enters the market. Even a shift in the cost of energy might produce a change in the relationship between demand and income. One may then be led to utilize multiple linear regression techniques where more than a single independent variable is used. The equation might be of the type $P - a + bX + cY$, such that the amount of the product used per thousand of the population is related to both X and Y. The point is that if one can establish a set of consistent relationships between the demand for a product and some measurable market characteristics in one market, at least a first approximation of demand can be made for a second market in which one has had no experience, *provided* one has data for these same market characteristics in that second market and some notion as to how rapidly they are changing and in what direction. Bear in mind that such relationships do not establish a *causal* relationship.

A causal model, as opposed to the naive, attempts to specify the factors that *determine* the demand for a product rather than factors merely *associated* with demand. An example is given in Figure 1.3.

Figure 1.4 illustrates a successful attempt to establish the greater accuracy of a causal model as opposed to a naive model for projecting camera sales in 19 countries. It will be noted that unit sales by country is assumed to be a function of market penetration and market size. Market size is specified as a function of population, the proportion of literacy, the proportion of adults, and the proportion of nonagricultural employment. Market penetration is set up as a function of sales per potential buyer, a constant representing the effective quality of change, personal consumption expenditure per capita, and the retail price index for camera goods. The latter, in turn, is seen as a function of present camera price index, a constant representing technology change, change in relevant taxes, change in resale price maintenance index, and change in non-tariff trade controls. Obviously, the construction of some of these indices poses special problems, also the estimation of the most appropriate coefficients. This same study conservatively estimated the potential savings from improved forecasts to be in excess of 1 percent of annual sales.[28]

---

[28]For a full analysis of this example, see Scott Armstrong, *Long-Run Sales Forecasting for a Consumer Durable in an International Market* (Cambridge, Mass.: unpublished Ph.D. dissertation, Sloan School of Management, Massachusetts Institute of Technology, 1968).

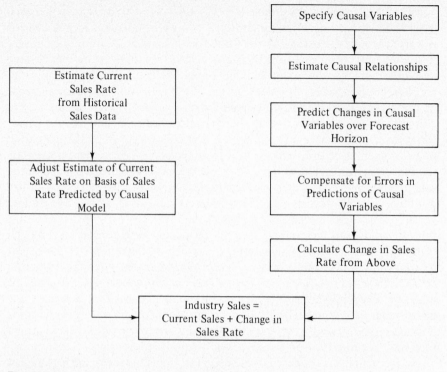

Figure 1.3
DEVELOPMENT OF A CAUSAL MODEL

Source: J. Scott Armstrong, "Long-Range Forecasting for International Markets: The Use of Causal Models" (mimeo, paper presented at the American Marketing Association, Denver, 1968), p. 5.

It is useful to note that financial assistance may be forthcoming from a firm's parent government—the United States included—in making initial market studies and in the systematic development of specific export markets. Not infrequently this public contribution is limited to 50 percent of the total research cost. In some cases the amount thus advanced must be repaid to the government from the proceeds of sales thus generated if, indeed, the study leads to sales.

A 1969 survey of 490 U.S. firms active internationally[29] revealed that only one out of six had an international research director. And one out of six had *never* conducted *any* form of marketing research or economic analysis in any

[29]International Research Associates, Inc., "A Survey of International Research Practices by American International Corporations," New York, mimeo only, 1969, p. 3.

$$P_{t+n} = (P_t)(0.984)^n \left(\frac{T_{t+n}}{T_t}\right)^{0.8} \left(\frac{C_{t+n}}{C_t}\right)^{1.5} \left(\frac{Q_{t+n}}{Q_t}\right)^{0.5}$$

where: P_t is the current retail camera price index as measured by survey and the 0.984 is a constant representing the effects of technological change;
T is a taxation index (tariffs x imports + sales taxes);
C is resale price maintenance index;
Q is non-tariff trade controls index;
W represents some specified future time.

Stage I
Prediction of camera prices

$$R_{t+n} = (R_t)(1.02)^n \left(\frac{E_{t+n}}{E_t}\right)^{1.0} \left(\frac{P_{t+n}}{P_t}\right)^{-1.0}$$

where: R_t is current sales rate per potential buyer (a weighted average of an estimate based on trade and production figures and a prediction from a causal model explaining sales levels in each country.
The 1.02 is a constant representing the effects of quality change;
E is personal consumption expenditure per capita;
P is retail price index for camera goods.

Stage II
Market penetration

$$M_{t+n} = (T_{t+n})(L_{t+n})(A_{t+n})(N_{t+n})^{0.3}$$

where: M is the number of potential buyers;
T is the total population;
L is the literacy proportion of people 15-64;
A is the proportion of the population 15-64;
N is the proportion of nonagricultural employment.

Stage III
Market size

$$L_{t+n} = (R_{t+n})(M_{t+n})$$

where: L is the "long-run" rate of unit camera sales.

Stage IV
Unit camera sales by country

Figure 1.4
A CAUSAL MODEL TO PROVIDE COUNTRY FORECASTS

Source: Same as Figure 1.3.
Note: t = current year; n = forecast horizon.

foreign market, and most of those that had done such work had done very little. "Sales forecasting and general economic analysis are the only forms of systematic analysis practiced in more than half of the international companies. Specific, goal-oriented research, or research to aid tactical marketing decisions, is relatively rare." The study goes on to report that "a lack of economic and marketing data are mentioned more often than any other factors as key obstacles to the successful development of overseas research." Some 70 percent of the executives responded that their respective firms were doing less overseas research than they should. For example, nearly half of the consumer marketing firms had never done any consumer behavior or attitudes studies. Only 28 percent of the 490 had ever done any political analysis.[30]

Though a firm may thus have established a priority of target markets geographically defined, it must proceed to an internal examination of these markets to determine the degree to which it should attempt penetration; that is, the percentage of the total market it should seek.

1.3 MARKET PENETRATION

To what depth a firm can or should try to penetrate a target market is related to the time horizon of management (see below), product quality and design, degree to which a product use is specialized, price, access to channels, availability of funds for investment in promotion, and the relationship between promotional intensity and added sales. Some of the significant questions to be asked are:

1. Are the assumptions made about necessary durability and performance standards really justified in respect to the target market?

2. Is the design of the product such as to generate maximum demand? (Included are such considerations as packaging, marketing, color, size, measure.)

3. Is the degree to which the product is specialized in use or function necessary?

4. Is the product so designed as not to rely unnecessarily on the presence of other products or materials in the target market?

5. Can the price be shifted significantly by reason of those considerations listed in one, two, three, and four above, or by alternative sourcing?

6. Would access to channels of distribution be made less costly if the firm were to go into partnership with local interests of some variety?

7. Is the present promotion budget for the target market really adequate if national bias toward further penetration of the firm's domestic market were eliminated?

8. Are the indicators of potential penetration used by management reliable in the foreign environment (for example, income-demand elasticities)?[31]

---

[30]International Research Associates, Inc., "International Research Practices," pp. 16, 17.
[31]See Glossary.

9. Does the buyer in the target market respond to various promotional strategies any differently from buyers in other markets? (That is, is the per capita cost of generating an additional sale higher or lower than elsewhere?)

If one can achieve within the target market minimum product price at the appropriate quality, and minimum market access cost, then the problem becomes one of achieving equal marginal sales cost (the cost of generating the last sale) across national markets, within a given time horizon.

TIME HORIZON   1.4

Prior to an on-the-spot market survey, management should normally have made explicit the time horizon it will use in determining the return from company resources committed to the exploration of that market. (See Figure 1.5.) If the time horizon is very short, only a minimum commitment is justified, possibly no more than a reading of the aggregate statistics and talking with one or two persons familiar with the area. In such case, management will be concerned only with existing conditions in the market, not its dynamics. A short time horizon also normally implies no consideration of supply sources other than those already existing, certainly not new direct investment in productive facilities either in the home country or abroad from which to supply the target market. Although risk is thereby reduced because market conditions of the near future can be predicted with greater probability of accuracy than those of the more distant future, market opportunities inherent in aggregate growth and structural change in the target market are likely to be hidden from view.

Relevant variables in setting an appropriate time horizon include the firm's available resources, its present geographical spread, nature of the product, and growth conditions within markets in which the firm is presently operating (particularly in the domestic market). If one or more of these factors do not rule out a time horizon longer than the current fiscal period, then management should not impose such a time restraint on its foreign market strategies. Figure 1.5 suggests some of the relationships that may exist between selection of time horizon and acceptable strategies, but is not meant to be definitive in any sense. The point is that it is wasteful of time and effort and, hence, of money, to permit analysis to consider strategies that management cannot accept. Bear in mind that there is a significant difference between what management *can* and *is willing to* accept. This difference should be made explicit after careful study of the company's resources and its commitment to present markets.

Having thus established a priority of target markets, the depth of penetration desirable in each, and the appropriate time horizon, the firm moves on to consider its choice of channels to reach each market.

	Now	1 yr.	2 yr.	3 yr.	4 yr.	5 yr.	10 yr.	20 yr.
	Sell Present Product		Consider By-products (Services, Rights, Finance)			Full Consideration of By-products →		
	Market Research = Statistical Study		Market Research = Detailed Study of Selected Target Markets			On-the-spot Market Analysis	Continuing Market Analysis →	
	Limited Penetration (Skimming)		Moderate Penetration			Full Penetration →		
	Limited Promotion (Largely Spillover)		Some Specially Designed Promotion			Full Promotion →		
	No Servicing		Provision for Servicing			Full Servicing →		
	No Investment Related to Foreign Sales		U.S. Investment Related to Foreign Sales			Foreign Investment →		
	No Product Modification		Minor Product Modification			Product Redesign	Special Products →	
	Use Present Supply Sources		Overseas Assembly in Leased Facilities or Contract Manufacturing			Overseas Manufacturing	Global Integration Among Manufacturing Facilities	
Acceptable Strategies	Direct Mail Order and/or Independent Exporters		← Either →			Overseas Agents or Representatives	Foreign Sales Branch or Subsidiary →	
	No Specialized Personnel		Specialized Expert Personnel			Specialized Staff Personnel	Internationally Oriented Staff	Internationally Oriented Operation
	No Organizational Changes		Slight Organizational Changes			Major Organizational Changes	Internationally Oriented Organization	Multinational or Transnational Organization
	Tight Control from U.S.		Tight Control			Looser Control	Decentralized Control	Near Autonomy for Foreign Operations (but See Chapter 8)
	Correspondent Relationships Only		Contractual Relations or Branch			100 Percent-owned Foreign Subsidiary	Joint Ventures	Multinational or Transnational Ventures

Figure 1.5
TIME HORIZON OF MANAGEMENT AND ITS IMPLICATIONS

CHOICE OF CHANNELS TO REACH A FOREIGN MARKET 1.5

The first decision to be made in this category is whether the firm itself should undertake the responsibility and risk of moving its product to the target market itself or should employ an external agency. In making this decision, management should consider market size and profit potential, the availability of specialized export skills presently within its organization, the desirability of direct relation with its foreign markets (the feedback effect), the likelihood of eventual assembly or manufacture within the target market, the possibility of supplying that market from a third source, and the cost of developing internal exporting expertise. All of these considerations are related to management's time horizon and to the potential importance of the target market in relation to the firm's total sales, not to mention the firm's overall size.

It should be clearly understood that export requires a set of highly specialized skills having to do with packaging; marking; documentation; selection of carriers; insurance; foreign import regulations; foreign exchange regulations; export finance; and the selection of overseas commission houses, representatives, and/or agencies; as well as the sensitivity to know when direct entry into the market through a foreign sales branch or subsidiary is advantageous.

The firm should be prepared to quote c.i.f. (cost, insurance, freight) at the nearest port to the buyer and not f.o.b. (freight on board) or f.a.s. (free alongside ship) for some point in the home country (see Figure 1.6). The firm should also give competitive credit terms (not insist on irrevocable letters of credit), provide adequate information about its products in a language and in measures useful to the potential customer, reply promptly and fully to overseas inquiries, provide adequate instructions in a useful language for a product's user, assure overseas customers of supply as regular as that promised domestic customers, and prepare and move overseas shipments so as to encounter the least delay and damage. To do these things requires specialists. Independent export packagers, freight forwarders, translation services, and so on may be employed on a fee basis. But even so, someone has to put it all together, as a prime contractor integrates subcontractors.

In the event management opts for an export channel external to the firm, it has the alternatives of using an export house, foreign buyers resident in the foreign country (for both government and private principals), a combination export manager (or independent export management company), an export commission house, a cooperative export association (a Webb-Pomerene Association[32] or Joint Export Association in the U.S. case), or an export broker. The risk and, hence, financial liability is generally least for the firm when it sells outright within the confines of its domestic market to unrelated parties for export on the latter's account. The risk is generally moderate in the case of combination export managers who operate on a commission basis, and

---

[32]Named for its congressional sponsors in 1918.

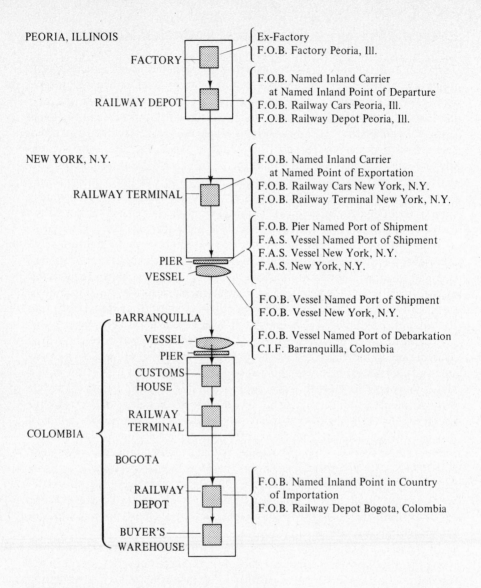

Figure 1.6
THE APPLICATION OF EXPORT TERMS

Source: Gerald R. Richter, "Basic Principles of Foreign Trade," in Leslie L. Lewis (ed.), *International Trade Handbook* (Chicago: Dartnell Corporation, prepared in cooperation with The American Institute for Foreign Trade, 1965), p. 32.

somewhat greater for export brokers, who simply negotiate sales contracts but assume none of the risk, and for the combination export manager who operates on a flat fee basis. In the case of some government purchasing, the firm may not have the option; the only buyer may be a government office located either locally or abroad. In many centrally controlled economies, the firm has only one alternative, sale to the appropriate import entity abroad, a foreign trading organization (FTO). It appears that a number of the Eastern bloc countries, including the U.S.S.R., have recently liberalized their rules to the extent of permitting the establishment by foreign firms of local representative offices, which may be staffed by either foreign or local personnel.

Least familiar are the combination export managers (CEM) or export management companies (EMC), Webb-Pomerene Associations, and Joint Export Associations, the latter two being creations of U.S. law. The CEM or EMC may provide virtually all of the services of an export department. The relationship rests on an agreement defining territories, products, functions, reimbursable expenses, promotional responsibility, and fees and commissions. A combination export-management firm generally works for several noncompetitive manufacturers. It conducts business in its own offices, handles all correspondence pertaining to its clients' exports, appoints overseas agents and representatives, and assists in preparing advertising copy and selecting media. A variation is the combination consulting-and-export service, which is of special value to the novice exporter who is unaware of the organizational and technical problems inherent in export sales (packaging, invoicing, design, degree of preassembly, instructions). This type of service tailors a program to a particular company and follows through by sending men into the firm to explain why and how the domestically oriented system must be changed.

The Webb-Pomerene Association is a device by which a group of U.S. firms may join their export activities without becoming vulnerable to antitrust prosecution. Such an association, which is a U.S. domestic corporation, must engage solely in export trade; foreign manufacturing facilities may not be included. Nor may it engage in any domestic business except that incidental to export. The law authorizes, for export purposes only, joint facilities, price fixing, allocation of orders among members, and a requirement that members export only through the association. A Webb-Pomerene Association may not, however, restrain nonmember exports in any way and may not enter into agreements with foreign companies that are illegal for independent U.S. firms, nor may they affect domestic business in ways contrary to provisions of the antitrust laws.

Japan has something similar to the Webb-Pomerene Export Association in that Japanese manufacturers and traders are specifically allowed to form export cartels to prevent excessive competition in foreign markets and to promote "orderly marketing" of exports.

The Joint Export Associations are groups of firms willing to cooperate in a joint export effort and that, thus, qualify for financial assistance from the federal government. In practice, CEM firms seem to be the principal recipients of such support. The chief advantage to participating producing firms, of course, is the marketing economy of scale which may be realized.

Management should note that it is contrary to the interest of these external exporting devices to recommend the development of another source of supply vis-à-vis a target market, for example, some variety of overseas assembly or manufacturing, even though there be strong arguments in its favor. Hence, even though employing such external agencies, management should undertake periodically an internal or independent check on its foreign markets. Furthermore, promotion, servicing, and/or product design feedback may be substantially less than optimum. Management should be forewarned not to finance the *development* of market expertness external to the firm.

A specialized agency of recent origin is the broker in international license, technical assistance, and management contract. Other relative newcomers are the mutual funds companies concentrating on overseas portfolio investment and specialists in the overseas marketing of used capital equipment.

A firm may in a sense also export its distribution services by buying goods and services of overseas origin—that is, imports—for distribution in the domestic or third markets. Inasmuch as importing, as well as exporting, requires a set of highly specialized skills, not the least of which is moving goods through home country customs, the firm is faced with a similar set of alternatives as in the exporting situation, and a similar set of variables is relevant. (See Section 2.2.)

One of the dangers in comparing the cost to the firm of these various channels is that at least a portion of those activities performed by the firm itself may be charged to general overhead and not be allocated to the export or import function. Therefore, the marginal costs of the various alternatives are not strictly comparable.

This comment leads into a discussion of the firm that opts for performing these functions itself. What this really means is that the firm is shouldering the risk for the movement of the goods or services involved to or from the foreign market. It may merely go to the frontier if what is involved is only a mail order or long-distance purchase business. Other alternative strategies involve penetration into the foreign market to a greater or lesser degree. The establishment of a foreign sales subsidiary possibly represents the greatest degree of penetration, for in that case the firm comes face-to-face with the internal distribution system or supply channels of the foreign market. Again, the size of the market, the nature of the product, the importance of the market feedback, and the resources available to the firm (including the necessary associated skills) are controlling. And again, management should be cautioned not to make domestically conditioned assumptions about any one of these factors.

In everyday usage many of the terms in Figure 1.7 are used interchangeably, which is a legally dangerous practice. Indeed, problems not infrequently arise because the precise nature of the relationship is not spelled out and is left ambiguous. In the first place, it should be made clear whether the relationship is that of a principal and agent or principal and distributor. In the latter case, title passes and the principal is absolved of certain risks and liabilities from that

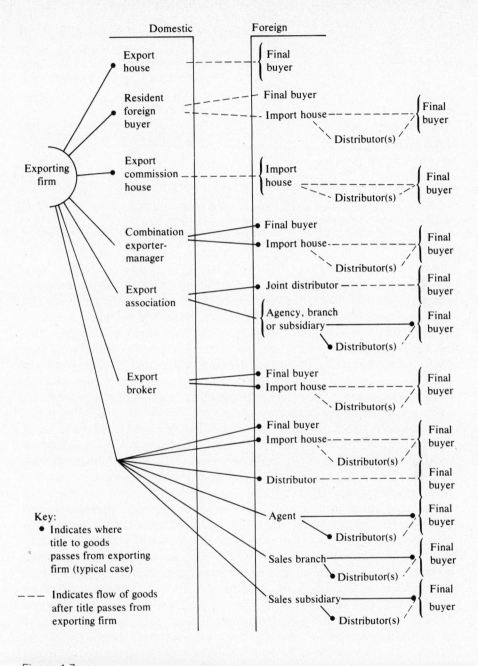

Figure 1.7
ALTERNATIVE EXPORT ROUTES

Definitions: Export (or import) house or merchant—an integrated distributor who buys, stocks, and distributes on his own account. Includes trading companies and foreign trade organizations (whether export or import depends on where the purchasing is done).

Figure 1.7 (Footnotes continued)

Resident foreign buyer (governmental or private)—the subsidiary, branch, or agent of an overseas buyer charged with the responsibility of buying on behalf of its overseas principal or owner.

Export commission house—an indent merchant who acts as the representative of specific foreign buyers and who negotiates purchases on behalf of his foreign clients.

Combination export-manager (may be combined with a consulting service)—one who acts as the firm's export manager on a fee basis.

Export association—a cooperative activity undertaken by several firms, sometimes under a separate incorporated entity. (In the United States could be a Webb-Pomerene Association and/or a Joint Export Association.)

Export broker—a negotiator of export sales contracts for a fee.

Distributor—one who contracts to buy a firm's goods or services for sale to third parties.

Agent—one who buys nothing from the firm, its principal, but acts on its behalf as defined by agreement (in a sense, acts as a branch of the firm), for which the agent receives a fee and/or commission. (A "manufacturer's agent" sells in the name of the principal; an ordinary "commission agent" sells in its own name.)

Branch—an unincorporated entity, legally and financially indistinguishable from the parent firm (that is, an act of a branch is an act of the parent, for which the parent is fully liable.)

Subsidiary—an incorporated legal entity, in which the parent owns a controlling interest, possessing legal liability distinct from the parent and, hence, a separate financial structure.

point forward. This means, of course, that sales through distributors are more expensive if these risks and liabilities are perceived to be significant by the exporting firm. Antitrust laws in the United States and elsewhere generally permit a firm to make a much more restrictive agreement with an agent, for in a very real sense an agent is merely an extension of one's self. In such a case the firm employs another firm, or an individual who is not a full-time employee of the firm, to act for it. As in a parent-branch (or parent-controlled subsidiary) relationship, generally there can be no question of conspiracy to restrain trade, to fix prices, to define territories, and so on. The situation is different for distributors, for then the firm is entering into agreement with other legal entities who will traffic in the firm's products on its own account and on its own liability. For much the same reason, it may be costly not to specify who controls whom when two associated firms are involved in agreement, such as two firms linked by equity.

For a variety of reasons it may be important to transfer title to exported goods outside the country of origin. For example, in the U.S. case, for a sale to be deemed legally an export, title must be transferred outside the United States. This is important in qualifying revenues as *export* revenues for the purpose of gaining special tax treatment (as formerly in the case of the Western Hemisphere Trading Company, now for the Domestic International Sales Corporation, see Chapter 7), or to shield the transaction against attachment by parties with unsatisfied claims against the purchaser, such as a foreign government in default on U.S. obligations. For example, it is wise practice to transfer title of goods sold to the People's Republic of China outside the United States. Chinese-owned goods within the United States may be vulnerable to court-ordered attachment in that China has never paid compensation for certain private U.S. properties seized by the previous regime in the 1940s. (Such default, whether on private or public obligations, also blocks any direct borrowing in the U.S. by the offending government. Only in 1976, for instance, was Hungary declared exempt from the Johnson Debt Default Act, thus paving the way for direct borrowing in the United States.) It should be borne in mind that title passage other than in the seller's country may preclude the domestic financing of the export sale by the seller, although the foreign branch or correspondent of a local banking institution might be utilized. This restraint may mean that the seller will be unable to extend as liberal payment terms as might otherwise be the case.

An agency or distributor agreement should include a number of other provisions. Chief among these are (1) duration and termination, (2) territory (exclusive, nonexclusive), (3) special reservations by seller to sell directly or at reduced commission to certain categories of buyers (such as to associated firms headquartered in the seller's domestic market or in respect to orders originating in other territories, governments, and so on), (4) products and/or services covered, (5) tax liabilities, (6) payment and discount terms, (7) right to fix and/or change prices and other terms, (8) sales support to be given by both parties, (9) responsibility for customs clearances, (10) limitation on right of assignment of rights, (11) information to be supplied by an agent or distributor to the seller (for example, that relating to customers, competitors, government regulations, prices, other lines carried), (12) inventory maintenance, (13) services and information to be supplied by seller and on what terms, (14) clarification of warrantees, (15) right to audit, and (16) the arbitration system to be used.

A related subject is the definition of the precise parties to an agreement. The principal may wish for tax, administrative, and/or liability control purposes to insert a subsidiary firm in its stead, possibly, in the U.S. case, a U.S. Possessions Corporation, a Domestic International Sales Corporation, or a less developed country corporation (see Section 7.3 on taxation). Other countries have somewhat similar provisions, often in the form of foreign trading corporations that enjoy certain tax advantages. Meanwhile, to the extent possible, the principal will wish to assure itself that it is contracting with a legal entity that has some real assets, not a paper firm. Perhaps a parent company guarantee should be required.

It is obvious from the foregoing that expert legal counsel should be employed to draft and/or review such agreements before finalization.

It has been suggested[33] that a firm tends to pursue an entry strategy involving greater control over overseas activities (that is, it selects routes lower down in Figure 1.7) as the country's environment becomes more attractive to the firm in terms of (1) political stability, (2) market opportunity, (3) level of

---

[33]See Litvak and Banting, "Conceptual Framework."

economic performance, (4) cultural unity, (5) legal barriers, (6) physiographic barriers (internal communications and market density), and (7) geocultural distance (language, physical distance, degree of coastal orientation). Empirical research tends to support this hypothesis,[34] although the finding may simply indicate that firms tend to enter the most attractive market first, gain experience and confidence over time, and consequently develop a willingness to assume a higher level of risk in respect to goods and services flowing into second-choice markets into which they enter subsequently. Also, many of the less attractive markets are relatively small, thus not justifying very much overhead commitment on the part of the firm.

One generalization can be made: As the market for a firm's products or services develops and matures in a particular national environment, the firm may be well advised to move closer to the ultimate consumer up to the point of direct selling through its own employees based on a local branch or subsidiary. To facilitate a move downward on Figure 1.7, a firm should attempt to maintain a flow of information relating to export packaging, documentation, freight, insurance, handling, and tariffs; the identity of the final consumer and the terms of final sale; the channels through which the product or service moves to the final consumer; the devices used to promote sales; and feedback from both the distribution channels and the final consumer in respect to product quality, design, terms of sale, delivery, and servicing. Even though a firm may be selling through export houses, resident foreign buyers, export commission houses, or a combination export-manager, it may (1) require that these intermediaries supply the firm with the above information and (2) employ one or more people simply to monitor the system and to internalize the experience thus gained. It should be kept well in mind that it is normally against the interest of such export intermediaries to facilitate a move by the client firm, such as a more direct relationship with the final consumer, that would eliminate their role.

Special comment about the trading company, particularly the Japanese, is warranted because of its importance and almost unique character. As one writer notes,

Trading companies handle more than 80 percent of Japan's foreign trade; they form a firm understructure for its entire domestic business establishment; have had an important part in the recasting of the Japanese product-image around the world, and have probably done more than any other Japanese agency or enterprise to open Japan's windows on the world.[35]

---

[34]J. D. Goodnow and J. E. Hansz, "Environmental Determinants of Overseas Market Entry Strategies: An Empirical Analysis Concerning U.S. Corporate Behavior," paper delivered to the Association for Education in International Business, New Orleans, December 1971, mimeo.

[35]John A. Marino, "Japan's Trading Companies: The Two-way Bridges of International Trade," *Business Review*, Boston University, vol. 11, no. 3, Spring 1965, p. 3.

The largest trading companies in the world are Mitsubishi Shoji Kaisha and Mitsui & Co. All told there are some 6,500 trading companies in Japan, but only 300 or so are engaged in foreign trade, and of these only about 50 are large *general* trading companies that handle highly diversified lines and are organized on a worldwide basis. These have major offices in all of the major trading centers, thereby providing the structure for a vast information system.

The general trading company defies our previous classification of international trading routes because it can assume the role of virtually any type of intermediary. The only functions that the general trading companies do not perform are production and retailing, but they may become involved even in these activities through joint ventures. Their export-import services are complete and expert, providing possibly the best Japanese agency the foreign seller can find. The trading company conducts thorough detailed market studies and advises the seller. It will then supervise the overseas shipment in all stages from packaging, scheduling, insurance coverage, inland shipment, stowage, overseas shipment, warehousing, distribution, to the choice of wholesale outlets. For potential buyers, the trading company provides the reverse set of services and on occasion will actually trade on its own account. It also provides financing, from short- and medium-term commercial credit to long-term production financing. The latter has led the trading company to be active in establishing overseas joint ventures on behalf of third parties, but frequently involving the trading company as well. (It would appear that many, if not most, of the joint ventures established overseas by Japanese firms include at least one trading-company partner.) Of recent years, these companies have become increasingly active in the international transfer of technology. Many now research available technology for sale or license in one country for possible buyers in another. Indeed, the larger trading companies have in-house engineering and technical capacity to advise on the construction of factories and public works.

But who owns and manages a Japanese trading company? Although formally associated with industrial-banking cartels (that is, the Zaibatsu), since World War II these groups have tended to fall apart and to be replaced by a number of less formal relationships. Still, the larger trading companies are linked with groups of Japanese banks and manufacturing firms as much through debt financing with banks as through equity. And, many of the trading companies have plowed their profits into equity holdings of Japanese growth industries so that the trading company itself may approach the status of holding company. In short, the trading company is a corporate entity whose stock is held in large part by related banking, commercial, and manufacturing enterprises.

In dealing with the trading company, one should realize that the top management level is involved with coordination of policy and financial agreements with affiliated producing and service companies. Operational control is usually at the managing-director level, of which there may be 20 or more but only a few involved with import-export. So the foreign seller's real point of contact is the department head or section chief. Initial contact is often through one of the branches located in the exporter's home country.

A new form of collaboration between Japanese trading companies and non-Japanese commercial groups is appearing. An example is a small U.S. corporation that entered into a joint venture with one of the Japanese trading companies for the purpose of stimulating U.S. firms to export through the trading company's worldwide network. For a relatively small fee, the U.S. company's products are plugged into the Japanese firm. If and when products are sold, a commission is paid to the joint venture. The Japanese trading company is motivated to sell U.S. products in Japan or in third markets because of the pressure on them from both the Japanese and U.S. governments to help improve the U.S. balance of payments, the imbalance of which is due in large measure to the imbalance in U.S.-Japanese trade.

The only non-Japanese firms similar to the general trading companies of Japan would be the former Dutch and British East India companies. Of existing enterprises, the United Africa Company in the African trade, Denmark's East Asiatic Company (which operates principally in Africa's English-speaking countries), Cie Française de l'Afrique Occidentale and Societé Commerciale de l'Ouest Africain (which sells and distributes chiefly in former French Africa), and the W. R. Grace & Co. (in Latin America) approximate the Japanese pattern, although the Japanese trading company does not typically confine itself regionally. Very recently, a few U.S. and European-held manufacturing firms have begun moving into the general trading area, but as yet have only a fraction of the turnover handled by the largest Japanese trading companies. Two of these are the Kaiser Trading Company (organized in 1969 as a wholly-owned subsidiary of Kaiser Aluminum and Chemical Corporation), which specializes in bulk commodities, and Volume Export and Trading Corporation, a U.S.-based subsidiary of Volkswagen of Germany. The latter has expanded from automotive products into chemicals and textiles.

Some have speculated that one or more of the larger international oil companies may develop into trading companies by expanding from oil to petrochemicals, synthetic fibers, textiles, thus gradually diversifying their product lines.

The United Africa Company (UAC) is the largest trading organization in Africa. It owns department stores, is involved in industrial partnerships, has a shipping subsidiary, and markets products on the continent for about 200 firms. Generally UAC avoids client firms that have a history of setting up their own sales organization once a market has been established, and it insists that clients agree to a 50 percent UAC interest in any sales organization set up in an area in which UAC has developed the market. UAC also protects itself by rarely selling one firm's line throughout its entire network. Increasingly, UAC is offering technical services. The firm and most of these trading companies may trade on their own account as distributors or operate as agencies.

Having thus selected the channels to reach each market, the firm is faced with a choice of strategy for reaching *within* each market toward the ultimate consumer.

CHOICE OF CHANNELS WITHIN THE TARGET MARKET 1.6

A firm may go still further, of course, by pushing on toward the ultimate consumer. Various alternative paths of distribution and the possible functions and characteristics of each layer, which are imposed traditionally, are diagramed in Figure 1.8. In each case, management should analyze the cost of changing the system to conform to its policies elsewhere. For example, for a given product in country X, wholesalers may traditionally carry large inventories, finance the retailers, and assume responsibility for promotion vis-à-vis the consumer. Can the firm, or the retailers, perform these functions as effectively at comparable cost? That they do so in the home country may not be important. Relevant variables are: The ability of one layer (including the manufacturer or foreign sales branch or subsidiary) to perform functions of the next, the degree of control of each layer by competitors, the adequacy of coverage by each layer, the degree to which flow is confined to fixed channels (extent to which retailers purchase direct from manufacturers or from primary wholesalers), the nature of the customer (mass market, industrial market, limited number of consumers), the nature of product (durability, need for special handling facilities, the ease of adulteration, the amount of customer service needed, unit cost), and the existence of a turnover or transactions tax (which may have a pyramiding effect).

The Sino-Soviet bloc countries pose special problems for the international marketeer. In these countries the respective ministry of foreign trade administers the national import/export business through a series of state-owned enterprises—the Foreign Trade Organizations (FTOs)—each of which specializes in a specific area of international commerce. Thus, the first task in selling is to determine the appropriate FTO. Contact with the end user is frequently difficult, possibly even prohibited, although even within the U.S.S.R. recent reports have indicated that not infrequently one can communicate directly with potential industrial customers. On occasion an overseas mission or office of an FTO, or a government trade mission on which the representatives of several FTOs may be represented, takes the initiative in contacting specific Western firms producing products in which they are interested.

Normally, each FTO has full authority to purchase and/or sell all goods and services covered by its charter. Nonetheless, one should exercise special care to be certain that one is dealing with an organization properly authorized to handle the product or service in question. If the product or service is new in international trade and does not fall into well-established categories, a real problem may arise. Soviet law specifies that negotiations outside of an FTO's charter are not binding. In any event, it becomes critical to locate the decision-making authority within the relevant FTO; there are frequently internal politi-

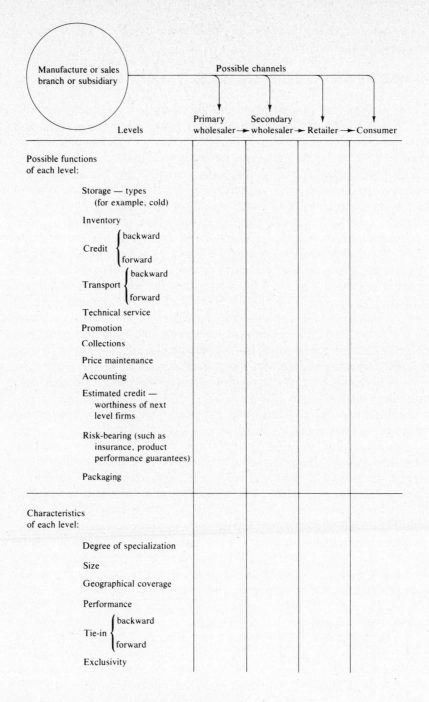

Figure 1.8
ANALYSIS OF A DISTRIBUTION SYSTEM

cal frictions of which the foreign seller may not be aware. Old hands in East-West trade urge the employment of a knowledgeable person to lead the way. If that much time and patience are required in negotiating East-West trade deals, the establishment of a permanent sales office may be helpful. As of mid-1972, some 55 Western firms were maintaining offices in Moscow. Of these, two were U.S. and 22 were Japanese. Among the latter were several of the larger Japanese trading companies. Also represented: eight French firms, five West German, ten Italian.[36] As of late 1976, it was possible for U.S. firms to establish such offices in all of the socialist countries other than Albania and the People's Republic of China.

It is important to note that the socialist countries vary significantly in respect to their relations with individual nonsocialist countries. For example, in the U.S. case, differences may be noted in respect to diplomatic recognition, most-favored-nation treatment, availability of Export-Import Bank facilities, availability of assistance from the Overseas Private Investment Corporation, the existence of a double taxation treaty, the presence of a relevant science and technology agreement, the existence of a trade agreement or long term economic cooperation agreement, freedom to borrow in the U.S. money market, and the possibility of joint equity investment. One should note also that these countries differ in respect to membership in various international economic and commercial institutions, such as the General Agreement on Trade and Tariffs, the International Monetary Fund, the World Bank, the Berne Convention on Copyright Protection, the Paris Union on the Protection of Industrial Property (patents, trademarks), membership in the Liaison Committee of the International Chamber of Commerce[37] and willingness to accept external arbitration.

In general, as one moves away from the U.S.S.R., the People's Republic of China, and Albania, the system tends to be somewhat less rigid. Also, for highly technical imports requiring close liaison with the end user the exporter may have some opportunity to develop direct linkages. This is particularly true in the smaller countries of Eastern Europe where individual factory managers have acquired more influence in respect to their own imports. One anticipates a slow change in this respect even within the U.S.S.R. Yugoslavia has gone further than any, for it would appear that the typical Yugoslav industrial enterprise has almost complete freedom to select its own imports within the limits of the foreign exchange available to it. Likewise in Poland, Hungary, and the German Democratic Republic, certain manufacturing enterprises are authorized to deal with foreign markets directly in that they receive allocations

---

[36]See James Ramsey, "An Office in Moscow? Not So Fantastic As You Might Think," *Worldwide Projects and Installations*, July–August 1972, p. 16 ff.

[37]See *East-West Trade Update: A Commercial Fact Sheet for U.S. Business*, Overseas Business Report, OBR 76–46 (Washington: U.S. Department of Commerce, Bureau of East-West Trade, November 1976). For details in respect to China, see *Doing Business with China*, Overseas Business Report, OBR 76-43 (Washington: U.S. Department of Commerce, Bureau of East-West Trade, November 1976).

of foreign exchange and are given the freedom to conduct their own commercial transactions. And, in all four of these countries it is possible to approach end-users through joint economic commissions (usually set up within the framework of bilateral trade agreements for the purpose of implementing agreed patterns of trade), advertising (through official advertising agencies), fairs and exhibitions, establishment of permanent business representation, and contacts through the national Chambers of Commerce.[38]

It seems increasingly true that selling on any scale into the socialist countries may require involvement in other than straightforward commercial transactions. A typology of East-West business arrangements has been suggested by St. Charles (Table 1.4).

Increasingly, as a prelude to sales, a Western firm may enter into a technological cooperation agreement with the U.S.S.R. As of early 1975, some 160 such agreements had been reported, most having been signed with the Soviet Committee for Science and Technology. Under such agreements, companies participate in technological discussions with interested industrial ministries and, in some cases, joint research work in the company's own laboratories. A major reason to enter into an agreement is to promote the image and presence of the firm. The point is that the agreement signifies the committee's general endorsement of the firm's technology, which fact greatly facilitates introductions to possibly interested ministries. And, in event that Soviet enterprises ever become authorized to enter into coproduction or joint production ventures, Western firms with technology cooperation agreements may have a competitive edge. It may also be possible to negotiate an agreement, one provision of which would give access to Soviet raw materials at a somewhat reduced price. On the debit side is the substantial cost involved in negotiating these agreements. Characteristically, if products result from an agreement, the firm markets them in its area, the Soviet within the COMECON countries, and in other areas sales responsibility is negotiated and royalties split.

At best, the options a firm may have in selecting channels in the more centrally controlled economies are limited, and include some vehicles not generally known within the market-oriented economies. It is equally obvious that great patience and a high level of skill are required in selling successfully under these circumstances, which suggests that smaller firms with limited resources are at a disadvantage unless they develop their Eastern European business wholly through intermediaries, including the Japanese trading companies.

1.7 CUSTOMER SERVICE

For many consumer goods no customer service is required, although the matter of guarantees of quality and performance may remain. Are such guaran-

---

[38] *The Decision-Making Process in Respect to Imports of Selected Socialist Countries in Eastern Europe* (New York: United Nations, 1971).

Table 1.4
A TYPOLOGY OF EAST-WEST BUSINESS ARRANGEMENTS AT THE ENTERPRISE LEVEL

LEVEL I: Straightforward commercial transactions Category types	LEVEL II: Business and industrial cooperation — functional or operational arrangements Category types	LEVEL III: Business and industrial cooperation — institutional arrangements Category types
1. *Merchandise trade:* International transactions are basically similar to domestic exchanges, but the act of crossing a frontier can make a major difference in how the sale is handled because of such special factors as import duties, quotas, currency payments, language, and customs. 2. *Trade in services and management contracts:* The former involves the buying and selling of insurance, transportation, financial, and a number of other services. The latter is a variant of exporting services, under which management skills will be provided for a specific period. Such arrangements often include the training of local citizens to	1. *Payment in resulting production for the delivery of plant or equipment and/or technology:* An enterprise (usually a Western firm) supplies (or arranges) the necessary plant or equipment and technology (possibly involving a licensing agreement) and receives partial or complete payment through products made with this equipment. 2. *Contract manufacturing and subcontracting:* Contract manufacturing requires an enterprise (usually Eastern) to deliver a contractually agreed upon quantity of final products (built to specifications) to a principal. In a subcontracting agreement, an enterprise (usually Eastern) supplies a Western principal with certain parts or components (built to specifications) that are incorporated into a final product. 3. *Co-production and specialization:* Through reciprocal deliveries, the co-production partners supply one another with the necessary components or parts so that each is capable of assembling the	1. *Joint marketing and servicing ventures:* The contracting parties pool their resources to establish a joint marketing and/or servicing organization (usually in the West) jointly to provide distribution and after-sale servicing. This is in contrast to the comarketing and servicing of Level II-4, which entail a prearranged contractual division of markets. 2. *Joint ventures for the provision of other services:* The joint marketing and servicing concept has led to the emergence of joint ventures in the provision of other services, especially in the area of banking and financial services, usually in the West.

assume management functions.

3. *Turnkey projects:* This is in essence a variant of exporting, but here enterprises are involved in exporting a complex package of goods and services to create a fully operational production system.

4. *Licensing arrangements:* An enterprise (licensor) may license its patents, copyrights, and know-how to enterprises (licensees) in other countries.

final product. Specialization necessarily entails that certain final products within a product line are produced by the Eastern and others by the Western enterprise. The exchange of the end products among enterprises usually results in the full range of a particular product line being offered by each participating firm.

4. *Co-marketing and/or after-sale servicing:* This is almost invariably a part of many co-production and specialization arrangements providing for a contractual division of marketing and/or servicing responsibilities. The resultant output may be marketed and serviced by each enterprise in its respective markets with the possibility of joint deliveries to third markets.

5. *Project cooperation:* The enterprises involved (usually through previous cooperation arrangements) jointly supply the necessary mix of plant, equipment, and technology for projects in third markets.

6. *Joint research and development:* This usually involves enterprises with a certain technological parity or complementary specialization who agree to coordinate their research and development activities. Such agreements may also embody co-production and/or comarketing arrangements.

3. *Joint production ventures:* The joint venture in production (of which there are examples in both the East and West) is characterized by two or more partners contracting to pool their assets in a mutual endeavor in which production operations are jointly managed and profits and risks jointly shared.

Source: David St. Charles, ''East-West Business Arrangements: A Typology,'' in C.H. Macmillan (ed.), *Changing Perspectives in East-West Commerce* (Lexington, Mass.: D.C. Heath, 1974), p. 106—7.

tees really necessary and, if not, what is the effect on cost? Where foreign exchange controls operate and time-consuming transport is involved, guarantees of this variety may be inoperable unless local inventories are maintained. In event the complexity, unreliability, and/or use of a product is such as to require servicing, the firm has the choice of putting its own servicing agents into the field or leasing or contracting for these services. Prior to the development of a significant market, both courses may be unduly costly and thereby may generate pressure in the direction of some sort of regional arrangement. This latter is feasible if freedom and cost of movement within the area are within reason. In some instances a joint arrangement with competitors may be possible, thereby making service costs lower for all concerned. For products exported from the U.S., a Webb-Pomerene Association or a Joint Export Association may provide a way out by permitting a sharing of service costs and activities. (See Figure 1.6 above.)

PROMOTION VEHICLES   1.8

Whether the firm itself undertakes promotion in the target market or farms out this task to an external advertising or promotional agency depends in large measure upon the availability of the necessary expertise within the firm and the potential size of the target market, plus management's time horizon. Also, if the firm is likely to move into production within the overseas market within the foreseeable future, the rationale for employing an external agency may be somewhat weakened. It may be less costly to internalize this expertise in preparation for the more complex problems that local production entails.

Relevant variables in the decision between a U.S. and foreign agency would include: (1) national identification (with the U.S. or a third market) with desired attributes of the given products or services within the target market, (2) similarity between the domestic and target markets, (3) "spill-over effect," and (4) linkages. "Spill-over effect" relates to the creation of demand in one country by reason of promotion in another. "Linkages," on the other hand, have to do with demand created in other than the initial market by reason of the movement either of the product or of the customer, or both. An example of linkage would be an international hotel system, which can be used for channeling customers from one hotel to the next, or to improved cargo handling equipment aboard a ship, which creates demand wherever it is seen in operation. A special type of spill-over effect is that created by the "pre-sell." For example, one entry into a foreign market is through demand stimulated on the part of local nationals who have spent time in the company's home market or third markets, such as tourists, students, participants in professional meetings, and the like.

There is a further strategy alternative in the selection of an advertising agency: should it be the agency used by the firm in its home country or a different one? If the latter, should it be foreign; that is, indigenous to the target market or identified with a third market? In making this choice, of course, the entire international program of the firm should be considered. Directly relevant are the firm's ownership and control strategies and the likelihood of developing foreign profit centers. Major pitfalls are (1) centralizing *control* of foreign promotional campaigns in corporate headquarters, whether firm or agency conducted, with the attendant danger of overlooking environmental variables, (2) utilizing a home-based agency for overseas promotion which does not have adequate experience or staff in the target market to be effective, (3) having *no* department, subsidiary, or agency directly responsible for promotion in the target market, (4) permitting the overseas promotion effort to be overshadowed by, and become subsidiary to, the domestic effort.

Sensitivity to local taste and legal restraints relating to advertising is obviously demanded. In reference to taste, some publics, such as the French, seem to reject the hard-sell, boastful type of advertising and react more favorably to informative presentations. In the area of legal restraints, certain European countries are vastly more restrictive than is the U.S. For example, on French television, which is government operated, advertising is very limited in time. A very large consumer goods company might *at most* secure five minutes of exposure per day. Automobile advertising is not permitted at all. In general, advertising in France must be truthful in all respects, and may not mention, much less malign, a competitor. Advertising can also influence the channels through which a product may be sold. An example: if a room deodorizer is advertised as a bacteriological disinfectant, it must be sold in a pharmacy, not in a supermarket.[39]

A related problem has to do with labeling. Compulsory labeling, a legal requirement that articles bear specified information, has been adopted in many countries for a variety of reasons: to protect the consumer's health and safety, to provide more accurate information so as to facilitate a more rational choice by consumers. There are, however, wide variations among countries. Additionally, there are two forms of noncompulsory labeling widely used: systematic labeling and labeling devised and provided by producers and sellers. The first refers to systems of informative labeling devised by special bodies, many of which are partly supported with public funds, designed to convey information on the composition and performance of products. These have been of particular importance in Denmark, Finland, Germany, the Netherlands, Norway, Sweden, and, most recently, France. The pioneer is the Swedish Institute for Product Labeling. The main difficulty with the systematic labeling schemes, other than their non-use by some manufacturers and sellers, is that the only sanctions are contractual or civil. The problem with producer or seller-devised

---

[39]As reported in Daniel A. Picard, "Strategic Planning of the American Multinational Firm in France," unpublished S.M. thesis, Massachusetts Institute of Technology, Alfred P. Sloan School of Management, 1972, chap. 3, p. 10.

International Care Labelling Code for Textiles			Grade	3	2	1	0
International Symbols			Treatment	Symbol	No special caution required	Some caution prescribed	Special care necessary	Treatment prohibited
(This set of symbols has been established by the International Symposium for Care Labelling of Textiles, which represents national groupings of manufacturers of textiles and clothing, detergents, coloring agents and other groups interested in having a common international system of visual symbols. It has been adopted on a voluntary basis in Austria, Belgium, France, Germany, Israel, Italy, Luxembourg, the Netherlands, and Switzerland. With modifications it will be used in a number of other countries as well.)			WASHING	Wash-tub	95°	60°	⊔*	⊠
			CHLORINE BLEACHING	Triangle	△cl		*	⊠
			IRONING	Iron	⬒•••	⬒••	⬒•	⬒✕
A = All solvents can be used in cleaning process P = Can be cleaned in perchlorethylene or mineral oil. F = To be cleaned only with mineral oil (white spirit etc.) *54° or 72°F. according to the articles. *Reproduced courtesy of the International Symposium for Care Labelling of Textiles, Paris, France.*			DRY-CLEANING	Dry-cleaning cylinder	Ⓐ	Ⓟ	Ⓕ	⊗
				Color	Green	Green/Orange	Orange	Red

Figure 1.9
**INTERNATIONAL CARE LABELLING CODE FOR TEXTILES:
INTERNATIONAL SYMBOLS**

labels is that very frequently they are misleading and lead purchasers to buy products not appropriate to their needs.

An example of well advised compulsory labeling is in the textile field. A number of the OECD countries are developing new, more precise standards of flammability. Compulsory declaration on the label of fiber content of most clothing and textile goods is required in member countries of the European Communities, in Canada, Spain, and the U.S. An interesting example of an international labeling code for textiles has been developed by CARE (Figure 1.9). This effort may represent a prototype of more general international requirements to come, possibly first out of the European Community and the OECD.

In October 1976, the EC Commission was proposing to introduce stiff new rules on product liability and to encourage the harmonization of national laws in this regard by the member states. Meanwhile, in virtually every place, pressures were mounting from activist consumer groups. In response, various private industry groups were creating self-regulating bodies to set advertising standards, to anticipate controversy, and to provide the mechanism for objective arbitration. Of the major countries, only Japan and Brazil lacked such bodies by 1975.[40] The soaring cost of product liability insurance in the U.S. was a source of business complaint by 1977, premiums having gained five-fold

[40]*Effective Advertising Self-Regulation: A Survey of Current World Practices and Analysis of Interest and Patterns* (New York: International Advertising Agency, 1975).

in some cases over the 1974–76 period. The U.S. was probably the bell-ringer for similar developments elsewhere.

In the international case special problems also arise in the selection of brand names. Some firms go to great effort to compile lists of meaningless four, five, or six letter nonwords. Such companies as Esso and Pfizer undertake arduous computer research before naming a product for use internationally. The problem is that a good name in one language may have unfortunate meanings or connotations in one or more other languages, and dictionaries may not reveal possible slang expressions in common use. Compounding the problem are those countries that have many dialects, such as India. There is also the problem of finding a name that can be pronounced easily in any language. In some cases, in which the difficulties are great, the firm may emphasize a trademark instead of a name. In many countries mere registration, not prior use, as in the U.S., bestows ownership of trade name or trademark. Hence, a firm must protect a name or mark selected for use in international trade and must monitor infractions. An increasing number of firms seem to be moving to the strategy of establishing global trademarks and trade names, thereby facilitating the international flow of the firm's goods and permitting the firm to exploit the spill-over effect of promotion within one national market to another through internationally circulated media, travelers, and so forth. One may anticipate this spill-over effect to become greater as time passes.

General practice in respect to brand name policy is to maintain the closest possible relationship between new brands and packages and established ones. However, when extending a name from one national market into another it should be examined with care from the point of view of (1) semantics (that is, different meanings and connotations), (2) pronounceability (Spanish and several other languages lack a "w"; Japanese and Koreans find little difference between "r" and "l"; Turks generally insert vowels between consonants, for example, "proof" would transliterate to "pūf" or "pōrūf"), (3) similarity to foreign brand names, (4) foreignness (may be either an advantage or disadvantage), (5) illegality (for example, ownership by others or registration deemed invalid because the word is generic). Even if the brand name must be altered, a corporate symbol may be standardized, although even here certain symbols may have unpleasant connotations in some parts of the world.

In the case of most of the Sino-Soviet bloc countries, it is of critical importance that the firm keep the appropriate Foreign Trade Organization fully informed as to pricing and product availability. It is also of special importance that Western experts attend East European trade shows, for here one has an opportunity to tell his own story directly to those responsible for preparing the details of the next planning cycle and also to find out what goods are available for possible purchase. The latter is important, for the willingness to buy an amount equivalent to or exceeding in value that which one is trying to sell is an important competitive factor in these markets.

The technical institutes are important in all of the East European countries, for they have an influence in the decisions as to what is to be bought from whom. These institutes are normally attached to specific industries and are supposed to provide technical counsel both to the industry and also to the FTOs in their area of expertise. In the past, it was difficult for a Western businessman to get past an FTO and to confront the ministry or technical institute directly, let alone the final user. This is still generally the case in the U.S.S.R., but in the other countries of Eastern Europe the demands of the technical organizations have become so urgent that the FTOs no longer block direct exchanges between the Eastern and Western engineers and technicians, and increasingly advertising is becoming more important in Eastern Europe.

Increasingly important in the promotion of certain goods and services in overseas markets are trade fairs, trade centers, and trade missions. The first tend to be annual affairs in all of the major trading centers of the world. Trade centers often house permanent exhibits and/or market information channels. Trade missions (in the U.S. organized and sponsored by the Department of Commerce and/or one of the regional world trade centers—New Orleans, Boston, New York, San Francisco) may be important links. The varying degree of continuity each institutional device offers, plus the different exposure of each (the public in the case of trade fairs, commercial buyers for trade centers, and specific interested parties for trade missions) determine their relative value to the firm.

A frequent criticism of U.S. government representatives overseas is their unwillingness to speak to local customers, perhaps the government, on behalf of specific U.S. firms interested in selling to them. It must be recognized that such representation is illegal under U.S. law, even though officials of other governments may feel free to support their national firms in this way. It goes without saying that state trading organizations active in foreign trade receive such official support in foreign markets.

NATIONAL SOURCE OF PRODUCT   1.9

Management should be aware of the fact that price alone may not determine optimum strategy in respect to national source of supply from the point of view of the buyer. The reasons are:

1. Given balance-of-payments pressure, foreign exchange controls, relatively high interest rates, and distance, the customer may be most concerned about the currency in which payment is to be made, and, in descending order, in credit terms, delivery time, durability, and, lastly, price.[41]

2. Production within the foreign market may be justified even though the resulting product price be higher than for a comparable import, in that official exchange rates on lesser developed countries undervalue the local currency (in respect to

---

[41]Expert financing options are detailed in Appendix 2, Chapter 6.

comparative purchasing power) in terms of convertible currencies,[42] which is equivalent to a subsidy for imports, a tax on exports. If this were not the case, there would be no need for a controlled exchange rate. Certain foreign exchange (that is, currency) is "hard" because it is scarce, and it is scarce because it is underpriced at the official exchange rate. The result is the importer is permitted to buy fewer hard currency units per local currency unit than may be economically justified; the exporter receives more local currency units of value sold. Therefore, an import-substituting industry should be measured not only by the recorded values of the imports thereby rendered unnecessary, but by something more, typically 20 to 30 percent more for many underdeveloped countries. Up to that inflated unit price, the local economy gains even though it could import the same item more cheaply. The point is that, using the official exchange rate, the convertible exchange saved is worth more than the local resources used, in the calculus of national economic growth. As government economists become more sophisticated, these things are recognized, and official pressures favoring the locally-sourced product can be expected.

3. In some instances, regulations enforced by customers limit the nationality of source, such as the tied-aid regulations of the U.S. Agency for International Development (AID), NATO, and other national and regional entities. Management should be aware that what constitutes the definition of source may vary from ownership of productive facilities to place of sale, or to where a certain percentage of value is added.[43] (See discussion of nontariff barriers in Section 2.2.) Of relevance has been the reluctance of the People's Republic of China to buy from the United States or from U.S.-owned firms producing overseas. In 1972, for the first time in many years, a few U.S. firms were invited to participate in the Kwangcho (Canton) Trade Fair, through which virtually all Chinese buying from overseas is accomplished. Also, it became Chinese policy in 1972 to permit the display of Canadian goods (including those produced by U.S. subsidiaries in Canada) if produced substantially from Canadian materials and shipped via Canadian ports. More recently, of course, this Chinese reluctance has disappeared.

4. In a given target market, certain countries tend to be associated with the more desirable attributes of the product in question; for example, German optics, Turkish tobacco, English woolen goods, and French wine; in some instances, a foreign-made product is assumed to be "better" than a local manufacture.

5. As already indicated, in the Sino-Soviet bloc a sale is frequently linked with a compensating purchase. And where one is trading under a bilateral trade agreement (for example, Soviet-Turkish or Canadian-Chinese), the product source is defined for a Western firm (Turkey and Canada in the above example). It is

---

[42]See Glossary.

[43]Of relevance is the U.S. "Buy American" Act, which permits the Department of Defense to award a contract to a U.S. producer whose price is 50 percent higher than that of a foreign bidder, and other governmental agencies (for example, the General Services Administration), which will award contracts when the supplier's prices are 6 percent higher, or 12 percent higher if the supplier is located in a distressed area. In 1976 the U.S. General Accounting Office was urging the Department of Defense to bring its more stringent application of the "Buy American" Act (the 50 percent differential) into conformity with the practice of other government agencies (a 6 to 12 percent differential).

possible, however, for a firm to unlink sale and purchase (in respect to source) through either switch trading or parallel trading. These vehicles may be defined as follows:

Switch trading. Switch trading involves selling products or services to a Sino-Soviet bloc country, or to any country under a bilateral trade agreement, in return for the credit of that country. This credit may be stated in clearing dollars in that the temporary imbalances in trade between two trade partners in a bilateral trading system are so denominated. Inasmuch as a ceiling to the imbalances is often specified, there is pressure on both trading countries to reduce the balance of clearing dollars in favor of one or the other, thereby enabling trade between them to continue. However, a so-called clearing dollar can only be sold to those who will use these credits to purchase goods and services from the countries that created the deficit in the first place, or who will ultimately sell them to a third party who will do so. Obviously, if one sells these credits for a convertible currency, he must expect to sell at a substantial discount. These transactions can be very complicated and are usually handled through switch trading specialists headquartered in Vienna or Zurich.

Parallel trading. Parallel trading involves taking a country's goods as partial or full payment for products or services sold there. Usually, the goods are unrelated and one disposes of the goods received through a special barter house, which sells them to a third party. The exporter's price should, of course, be adequate to cover the added cost.

These relationships may be diagramed as in Figure 1.10, bearing in mind that many more intermediaries may be involved than those shown here. Countries X and Y in this example are bilateral traders with a clearing account arrangement. The reason for bilateral trading is that by so restraining trade, the parties can maintain a balance of trade within a given plus or minus margin (represented by the credit limit) and thus to a degree can insulate domestic pricing, employment, and monetary and fiscal policies against balance-of-payment pressures. Particularly for socialist countries, bilateral trading is an important mechanism in that domestic prices may have little relevance to international market prices.

Generally, in determining the best supply source *from the point of view of the buyer*, management should consider (1) trade patterns (often frozen by bilateral commercial agreements, reparations, or foreign assistance or biased by free or preferential trade relationships), (2) the extent and sophistication of government trade controls, and (3) comparative costs. The last includes the possibility of using a third nation's export credit and insurance facilities (see Section 5.4) if the firm can satisfy the value-added requirements normally imposed by a government. The use of a third country's export financial facilities may result in lower cost and/or risk. A firm may likewise benefit if the third country's tax system is such that export earnings are taxed at a lower rate than by the firm's parent country, and the parent country taxes can be de-

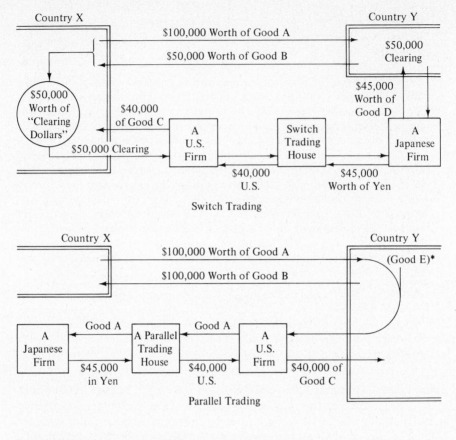

Figure 1.10
DIAGRAM OF SWITCH AND PARALLEL TRADING

---

*Or good E may be delivered in payment, good E being in excess supply in country Y.

Note: In each case, the trading house has made a profit of $5,000 in yen, which it can use in reverse transactions or sell to someone else. The U.S. firm must price good C so that the discount on the clearing dollars or on the goods delivered to the trading house will be covered. It will be seen that parallel trading does not necessarily affect the balance between countries X and Y unless Y uses the goods received from X as part of the deal with the U.S. firm.

ferred. (See Section 7.3 for further details.) For all of the reasons outlined in Section 1.1 above, in which relative costs are discussed, the optimum supply source cannot be determined by a simple cost comparison built on a firm's domestic factor mix, the domestically designed product, the domestic definition of a plant (the particular bundle of processes housed on one site), domestic scales of economy, its parent government export credit or insurance programs, or its parent government tax rates.

INTRACOMPANY COMPETITION 1.10

A firm may limit the sales efforts of its various subsidiaries and associated firms by means of exclusive territory or price fixing arrangements so as to avoid competition among the associated overseas enterprises. Factors to be considered are legality, degree of product differentiation, enforceability of agreement, relative levels of involuntary expenses of the various enterprises (including those implicit in collective labor contracts, governmental agreements, and community responsibility), likelihood of intracompany competition's forcing revenue below involuntary costs for some environments, and price-demand elasticities[44] in the various markets. For example, assuming no legal barrier or product differentiation, a firm might impose an exclusive territorial arrangement on its subsidiaries and associated firms if involuntary expenses varied substantially among the related enterprises and if price-demand elasticities were less than one (that is, if total revenue would fall with a decrease in price) in the markets concerned. Otherwise, the enterprise with the lowest involuntary expenses would simply establish a monopoly by undercutting all of the other enterprises. But by doing so, total revenue would fall; that is, with a very low price-demand elasticity, the increase in sales revenue generated by a decrease in price would not compensate the firm for the price decrease. But in erecting barriers, management should be aware that both U.S. and foreign antimonopoly law may apply (see Section 7.3) and that every marketing agreement should be reviewed by legal counsel.

INTERCOMPANY COMPETITION 1.11

Restrictions imposed on foreign entities neither controlled through ownership by the U.S. firm nor acting as agencies of the U.S. firm involve a very real danger of running afoul of U.S. antitrust law or that of foreign states, particularly if the associated foreign firm is a manufacturer. (See Section 7.3.)

Increasingly, foreign governments seem to be looking skeptically at restrictions imposed by foreign firms on the sale of goods and services. For example, under the Andean Pact, contracts for the importation of patents, trademarks, technology, and know-how into the member countries must be registered with designated local authorities. Apart from a general cost/benefit analysis, approval presumably will not be given if the contract includes provisions (1) limiting the recipient's choice of sources for capital or intermediate goods, raw materials, or other technology; (2) setting prices for the goods manufactured under the agreement; (3) restricting production; (4) purchasing options in favor of the supplier; (5) requiring the feedback of inventions or improvements; (6) paying royalties on unexploited technology or unused trademarks;

---

[44]See Glossary.

(7) placing territorial restriction on the sale or export of products bearing a licensed trademark; (8) permitting the choice of law for resolving conflict; or (9) specifying the payment of royalties between related foreign and domestic companies or for readily available technology.

1.12 PRICING

As Cateora and Hess observed, "Two basic choices are available to a company in setting its price policy. It may view pricing as an active instrument for the accomplishment of marketing objectives, or it may consider prices to be a static element in business decisions."[45] What distinguishes the international case is that the firm can follow several pricing strategies at one and the same time. (It should be noted that credit terms could properly be considered as part of pricing strategy. However, export financing is treated more in Chapter 6, especially in Appendix 2.)

Essentially there are three alternative policies in the pricing area: (1) a standard worldwide base price, (2) a domestic price and a standard export price, and (3) a market differentiated price. But, in each case the pricing policy may be cost-oriented or market-oriented, thereby generating six possible policies. Additionally, the firm may opt to control final prices (resale price maintenance) or to control the net price received by the firm. If the firm carries the product all the way to the final consumer, the two strategies become one. In some instances, the former may be illegal. In fact, the desire to control final price may control the firm's choice of channels. Hence, one can generate a 12-box matrix of pricing strategies (see Figure 1.11).

Cost-oriented pricing is typically associated with either intracorporate transfers or with dumping. Any policy may, of course, include a discount system. But because of the different priorities given by some foreign buyers, discounts for waiving performance warranties, claims for services, payment in certain foreign currencies (for example, dollars), or delivery within a specified time may be more important than the typical domestic discounts based on quantity, terms of payment, or purchase of associated goods or services.

The standard worldwide base price is most likely to be looked upon by management as full-cost pricing, including an allowance for manufacturing overhead, general overhead, and selling expenses. Often ignored are (1) the necessarily arbitrary nature of these cost allocations, (2) differences in costs from market to market (in labor, capital, materials, and management in the case of overseas manufacture; in shipping, crating, insurance, tariffs, taxes, internal transport, distribution, and promotion in the case of exporting), (3) possible lower marginal cost of goods moving into foreign markets (particular-

---

[45]R. P. Cateora and J. M. Hess, "Pricing in International Markets," in H. B. Thorelli (ed.), *International Marketing Strategy* (Middlesex, England: Penguin Books, 1973), p. 209.

	Cost- Oriented	Market- Oriented	
Standard worldwide price:			
with net price control			
with final price control			
Dual pricing (domestic/export):			
with net price control			
with final price control			
Market differentiated prices:			
with net price control			
with final price control			

Figure 1.11
MATRIX OF INTERNATIONAL PRICING STRATEGIES

ly in reference to domestically oriented research and development), (4) differences in competitive position within the foreign markets, (5) differing degrees of optimum penetration for different foreign markets, (6) price controls enforced by a government or by a dominant supplier, (7) the cost of unforeseen and uncontrollable delay (for example, this factor induced one firm to price unassembled plants in Eastern Europe at the same price as assembled plants elsewhere), and (8) the equally unforeseeable cost associated with anticipating performance ratings under certain types of contracts, such as training.

The use of a special export price, which is generally lower than the domestic, is justified to the extent the marketing cost is external to the firm. Also, if the firm is exporting out of a country, whose basic tax is the value-added tax, into a country in which the value-added tax is not employed, the tax burden on the exported product may be lower to the extent that the value-added tax is rebated by the exporting country. This rebate is not restored by the importing country unless it too has a value-added tax. Of course, a firm may use a foreign market in which to dump products. Insofar as something over and above the variable cost of production is captured by the firm, a special price may be justified in the short run so long as such sales do not affect full-cost price sales, either domestically or in other markets. Such a strategy is sometimes called marginal cost pricing.

In that it may be easier to insulate national markets than sub-national markets, marginal cost pricing is very common in international marketing. Dumping charges frequently result. Where fixed costs are abnormally high, as in the Japanese case, there may be an unusual tendency to "dump." For products otherwise unsalable, sale at a price that contributes something to fixed costs has a strong appeal, particularly where those fixed costs are very high and where the domestic market is well protected. A somewhat similar situation exists where products are manufactured according to a central plan and not in response to market pressures. Surplus products thus generated, because of planning errors or a mismatching, in physical terms, of supply and demand, can be substantial and continuing. Eventually, the surplus will be seen as representing "sunk cost," which is the equivalent of a fixed cost in that it cannot be avoided. Sale at any price thus represents gain. Also, in socialist countries "costs" are likely to be less than complete because of a possible systematic undervaluation of the capital used in production, including R&D, so that even full-cost socialist prices may appear to be at a dumping level by nonsocialist traders. Finally, if at least a portion of a country's trade is essentially on a barter basis, it is the internal tradeoff (perceived relative marginal utilities) of the exported and imported goods that sets the export price. In a centrally controlled economy, the imported goods may be so valued in terms of the goods traded against them (exported) that, translated into international market prices, the exporting country appears to be guilty of dumping. Of course, it should be recognized that virtually every major trading country, except the socialist, has antidumping laws and, by dumping, the firm may run the risk of losing trading rights within that market or at least of paying a compensating import duty.[46]

On the other hand, some firms fail to recognize that special costs are associated with exports, which perhaps justify an export premium rather than a discount. Some of these costs are special labelling, packaging, and documentation; lower volume; added insurance and freight; heightened credit risk; a longer wait for payment; and higher cost intermediaries.

A market-differentiated pricing policy, on the other hand, assumes that the head office knows enough about the target market to set the correct price for that market. The best policy in some circumstances is for headquarters to set a price floor and permit local management full pricing discretion beyond that point. A variation is a headquarters-determined price guideline, with local discretion to price below and above, within certain percentage limits. The commonality of ownership between the corporate headquarters and the associated foreign firm is obviously an important consideration. If ownership is the same, that is, if the foreign firm is a branch or 100 percent owned by the American firm, the degree of price discretion given may be substantial. Profit is 100 percent owned wherever generated.

---

[46]See also Section 2.1, n. 23.

Also, decisions in all of the other marketing strategy areas (particularly in regard to degree of penetration, time horizon, choice of channels, source of product, and degree of intracompany and intercompany competition) are directly relevant to setting pricing policy. It should be noted that the price used by a firm may or may not be the price recognized by local customs officials for the purpose of determining *ad valorem* duties. (In international tariff negotiations, a recurrent criticism of the United States is its use of American selling price regardless of the foreign price.) Also, inasmuch as transfer prices determine in part the jurisdiction within which profits are generated, local tax officials are concerned. (See Section 7.2 for further discussion of this point.) It should be borne in mind that many countries impose some variety of *retail* price control system, as in France and the United States.

Recent research[47] would seem to indicate that U.S. firms are generally more cost-oriented in their international intracorporate (transfer) pricing policies than their foreign-based counterparts. Also, although as a group the U.S. subsidiaries of non-U.S. firms were found to be singularly independent operationally, their parents nonetheless retained absolute control over intracorporate pricing. All firms (U.S. and non-U.S.) were found to consider essentially the same external variables in setting transfer price policy: levels of competition, taxes, tariffs, probability of changes in foreign exchange rates, foreign exchange controls, export subsidies, expropriation risk, the need to make a floundering subsidiary look better, or the need to bolster the financial performance of the parent. Some of the internal parameters found to be relevant were the management evaluation.system, the degree of control over subsidiaries' operations, corporate goals (such as income tax minimization, maximizing return on investment), and ignorance of alternatives. The research concluded:

> There presently does not exist a universally optimal system of international intracorporate pricing. Corporate goals are too diverse and the international environment too complex. No single system has proven optimal for all firms at all times, or even for one firm over time. Theoretical treatments have been essentially indeterminant, and no consensus exists among business practitioners. Minimizing conflicts with host governments is becoming a major criterion for optimality.[48]

On this last subject, it should be noted that market-oriented pricing produces the least conflict with host governments, although cost-oriented pricing provides for the greatest flexibility. The research referred to here makes it quite clear that subsidiaries rarely enjoy any autonomy in setting prices; the deci-

---

[47]Jeffrey S. Arpan, *International Intracorporate Pricing: Non-American Systems and Views* (Bloomington: unpublished Ph.D. dissertation, Indiana University), subsequently published by Praeger (New York, 1972), summarized in Arpan, "International Intracorporate Pricing: Non-American Systems and Views," *Journal of International Business Studies*, vol. 3, no. 1, Spring 1972, p. 1 ff.

[48]Quoted from an abstract of the Arpan thesis, distributed at the 1971 Annual Meeting, Association for Education in International Business, New Orleans, December 1971, mimeo.

sions are almost always made by the highest financial executives in the parent corporation.

Special comment relative to the pricing of technology is merited, for here the duration of the contract is obviously an important element. Also the supplying firm may face special difficulties in costing a technology transfer to a specific customer because the fixed cost is so high relative to total cost. It would appear that in practice, license and technical assistance agreements covering the transfer of fairly rudimentary technology to developing countries very commonly ran for 20 years or more during the 1950s. In more recent years, ten years seems to have become general practice. Royalty or fee rates, most often linked to ex-factory value of sales or to production volume, were commonly in the 10 to 15 percent range two decades ago, but now range from 5 to 7 percent. In the Indian case (1961–64), only 12 percent of the agreements stipulated rates of over 5 percent; in the Japanese case (1963–66) 11 percent indicated rates over 6 percent and a further 10 percent between 5 and 6 percent.[49] A number of countries are now setting maximum limits for royalties and fees. A case in point is Brazil. For patent licenses, royalty limits of between 1 and 5 percent of net sales (net of direct taxes and cost of imported components) are set by a government office. For technical services, engineering services, and consulting services, fixed payments are accepted, but the maximum payment admitted (that is, accepted as an expense for Brazilian tax purposes) for technical personnel entering Brazil to render services is fixed at $6,000 per month. If 50 percent or more of the Brazilian firm is owned by the licensor, no royalty payments are tax deductible and, hence, are taxable as a distribution of profit. Fee and royalty limits of 2 to 4 percent of sales are becoming quite common among LDCs, although it can be argued that such a generalized ceiling makes no economic sense. Even the Soviet Union has no such ceiling, although it bargains hard for what it wants. But in the end it pays what it has to. In some cases, as in Mexico, patent protection has been eliminated in certain priority sectors. What may not be adequately appreciated is that such moves have the effect of enhancing risk in the eyes of business decision-makers and, hence, push the price of technology even higher. Also not adequately appreciated are the rising cost of corporate R&D and the relative unproductiveness of government R&D. Although it would thus appear that during the period 1950–66 the cost of technology transfer was somewhat reduced, in fact the imposition of restrictive features renders such a comparison invalid. These restrictions may appear in the form of tie-in clauses

---

[49]Based on a report of the Indian and Japanese experience with licensing and technical assistance agreements as reported by Savak S. Tarapore, "Transmission of Technology to Developing Countries," *Finance and Development*, vol. 9, no. 2, June 1972, pp. 16–21. The Indian study covered 1,057 agreements in force as of April 1, 1961, up to March 31, 1964. Also, *Foreign Collaboration in Indian Industry—Survey Report* (Bombay: Reserve Bank of India, 1968); the Japanese agreements approved between 1949 and 1966 (R. H. Patil, "Foreign Collaboration in Japanese Industry," *Reserve Bank of India Bulletin*, February 1970).

(a requirement that the licensee purchase raw materials and equipment from a source approved by the foreign licensor), quality and design control and export and sales restraints. In an Indian study it was found that "a higher proportion of tie-in clauses applied to companies without any foreign ownership of capital than to foreign subsidiaries." Some 43 percent of the Indian agreements restricted exports and 3 percent banned them completely. Over half of the Japanese agreements approved (1950–61) included export restrictions. In the Philippines, about one-third of the 254 agreements studied by UNCTAD included export restrictions, 60 percent being in the form of a global ban. A study of 109 Mexican agreements revealed that about half included global bans on exports.[50]

Another hidden cost is the secrecy clause in many of those agreements, which leads to repetitive import of technology by more than one firm in a country. "Even Japan has been faced with [this problem]; . . . some 57 percent of its technology introductions in 1965/66 was repetitive imports."[51]

In the face of these facts, one is not surprised to find rising pressure to liberalize the conditions under which technology is sold internationally, which is another way of saying to reduce market imperfections. Even the more developed industrial countries of Western Europe are moving toward rendering a number of restrictive provisions illegal. For example, under European Community law in respect to technical assistance agreements, it appears that export prohibitions or restrictions are illegal. In most of Europe, any restriction on a contractee's R&D effort is probably illegal, so likewise is tied-purchasing, the setting of a contractee's prices, or limitations on his choice of customers.[52]

The principal effort to improve the international market for technology is, of course, being spearheaded by the less developed countries, which are becoming increasingly aware of the size of the payment burden for access to modern technology being imposed on them. Some of the specific proposals sponsored by the World Intellectual Property Agency, a specialized agency of the United Nations, are discussed below in Section 6.8.

In the final analysis, sales strategy must be adjusted and readjusted by reason of the feedback from strategy selections in other areas; that is, no final choices should be made before possible problems in other areas of decision have been thought through. In a sense, everything could be subsumed under sales strategy, as some marketing "specialists" are wont to do.

Discussion questions

1. Outline the arguments for considering the export of skills and services rather than of physical goods.

---

[50]Tarapore, "Transmission of Technology," p. 19.
[51]Tarapore, "Transmission of Technology," p. 19.
[52]See *Business International*, April 12, 1974, p. 116, for a tabulation of relevant European laws.

2. Why is the use of historical export sales data to predict future trends of exports likely to be misleading?

3. Specify some products in which the degree of literacy would be directly relevant to the size of the potential market.

4. Relate the four methods for in-place market surveys to the several variables listed subsequently in the test.

5. Criticize the causal model for forecasting camera sales (Figure 1.3).

6. Describe the function of a Japanese trading company.

7. Typically, through what channels does one sell to Soviet-bloc countries? How might one influence sales?

8. Should control over international advertising and promotion be centralized?

9. How does a bilateral trade agreement operate? What is its purpose?

10. Under what circumstances is a firm likely to limit competition among its associated overseas enterprises?

11. How does the fact that the United States does not have a value-added tax affect its international trade?

12. Why is dumping likely to be more of a problem internationally then domestically?

13. Explain the Japanese tendency to dump. The socialist tendency.

14. Why is market-oriented pricing likely to produce the least conflict with the host government?

15. Why is pressure mounting to improve the market for technology?

16. Of what value in international marketing research are statistics relating to Gross National Product?

Assignment

Analyze the market for Agchem's products in an assigned market (see Case L).

Recommended references

Alexandrides, C. G., and George P. Moshis. *Export Marketing Management.* New York: Praeger Publishers, 1977.

Boddewyn, Jean, ed. *Comparative Management and Marketing.* Glenview: Scott, Foresman, 1969.

Carson, David. *International Marketing: A Comparative Systems Approach.* New York: John Wiley & Sons, 1967.

Fayerweather, John. *International Marketing.* Englewood Cliffs: Prentice-Hall, 1965.

Guttmann, H. Peter. *The International Consultant.* New York: McGraw-Hill, 1976.

Heck, Harold J. *International Trade: A Management Guide.* New York: American Management Association, 1972.

Managing Global Marketing: A Headquarters Perspective. New York: Business International, 1976.

Miracle, Gordon E. *International Marketing Management.* Homewood: Richard D. Irwin, 1970.

Pizer, Samuel. *Coexistence and Commerce, Guidelines for Transactions between East and West.* New York: McGraw-Hill, 1970.

Root, Franklin R. *Strategic Planning for Export Marketing.* Copenhagen: Einar Harcks Forlag, 1964.

Sethi, S. P., and J. N. Sheth, *Multinational Business Operations, Marketing Management.* Pacific Palisades: Goodyear, 1973.

Terpstra, Vern. *International Marketing.* New York: Holt, Rinehart and Winston, 1972.

Thorelli, H. B., ed. *International Marketing Strategy.* Middlesex, England: Penguin Books, 1973.

Thomas, Michael J., ed. *International Marketing Management.* Boston: Houghton Mifflin Company, 1969.

Appendix to Chapter 1
NATIONAL INCOME-PRODUCT ACCOUNTING AND INTERNATIONAL COMPARABILITY

Definitions. The definition of Gross National Product (GNP) used generally by nonsocialist countries is the market value of all domestically produced products and services (that are legal) of the private and public sector exchanged in all markets (foreign or domestic, money or barter). Excluded are most products of the family economy, except self-consumption by commercial producers or farmers and utilization of residential real estate. Imputed values are used in estimating the market value of these three items. Also included is the imputed value of the services provided to the ultimate consumer by publicly owned facilities, such as roads.

Self- or household-serving personal services are not included (for example, housekeeping by a housewife, child care by parents, do-it-yourself home repairs, home cooking services, a self-administered shave). However, the income paid a servant, a nurse, a carpenter, a cook, or a barber would be included in gross national product. In short, if one adds up all the net value added by firms (the difference between gross income and payments for goods and services produced externally to the firm) and the total income received by self-employed individuals, one derives the total (or gross) national product. Another way of saying the same thing is that gross national product is the sum of payments made to the factors of production (in the form of wages, interest, rent, taxes, corporate profits, income of self-employed persons). Gross national product, so defined, must equal personal consumption expenditures plus government purchases plus investment both public and private. Net national product is derived by deducting depreciation or capital consumption allowance; that is, that production necessary to maintain a nation's capital stock.

Included in these totals are payments made to and from foreign countries, either for consumption (exports and imports) or investment. If one subtracts (or adds if positive) net foreign investment from the totals (that is, receipts derived from exports and outgoing investment less all payments for imports and in-flowing foreign investment), the balance constitutes gross domestic product. If a further deduction for depreciation of capital assets is made, one has the net domestic product. The relationships are shown schematically in Figure 1.12.

A more dynamic view of these various concepts is diagramed in Figure 1.13. The easiest way to follow the flow is to start with the components of national income at the far left (wages, noncorporate profit, personal interest, personal rents, corporate earnings), which are made equal to personal income if one takes out undistributed corporate profits, corporate profit taxes, and social security payments, and adds back in transfer and interest payments from the government sector. Personal income equates with disposable personal income if one extracts personal taxes paid. Disposable personal income flows into consumption, and savings. The former, plus government expenditures for goods and services and private investment, equates with Gross National Product. Deduct capital consumption, that is, expenditures to maintain the existing stock of capital goods, and one derives Net National Product. Take away indirect taxes and government subsidies, and one derives National Income, which in turn is paid out as indicated. To link these flows one needs the government revenue and expenditure box and the private savings and investment box. These are really reservoirs linked by borrowing in either direction. Not shown separately are the flow of external (foreign) savings into the system and the flow of domestic savings out of the system. The inflow of foreign savings is represented by foreign investment and foreign goods and services (imports) flowing into the system; the outflow of domestic savings, by domestic investment and goods and services (exports) flowing out of the system. One can then derive gross and net *domestic* product.

All of these national measures, if comparable trends are to be demonstrated, should be deflated or inflated according to the relevant price level index in order to make them "real." Dividing by the population generates per capita figures, which are often used to make international comparisons.

International Comparability. These definitions beg a lot of questions, which may be answered differently by different societies, hence casting considerable doubt on the validity of their international comparability in terms of level, growth, and structure. Some of the questions that generate the ambiguities are:

1. Definition of legality. Growing the opium poppy is legal in Turkey, not in the United States. Production for private profit may be illegal in a socialist country, not elsewhere. Gambling is legal in some places, not in others.

2. The volume of imputed prices and errors implicit in such imputation. In a less developed country, the barter or noncash economy may be very large, and the errors correspondingly great. In a socialist or centrally controlled economy, the

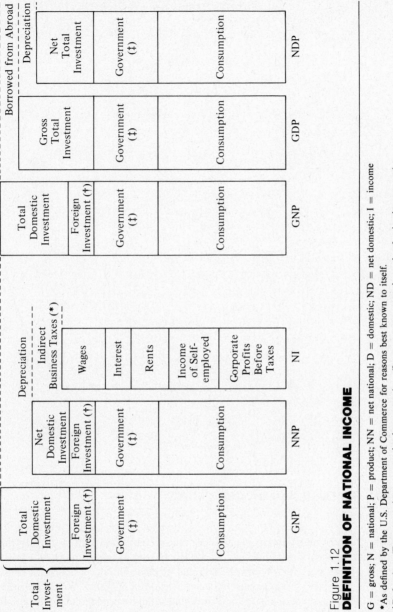

Figure 1.12
DEFINITION OF NATIONAL INCOME

G = gross; N = national; P = product; NN = net national; D = domestic; ND = net domestic; I = income

*As defined by the U.S. Department of Commerce for reasons best known to itself.

†Defined as: (Export earnings + outgoing investment) — (Import payments + incoming foreign investment). If positive, constitutes an addition to total domestic investments; if negative, a deduction. A negative total implies net borrowing from abroad.

‡Government itself, of course, either invests or consumes.

"prices" at which goods and services are exchanged are probably centrally controlled and the amount rationed. Hence, their prices do not represent full market prices comparable to those in a relatively free market situation.

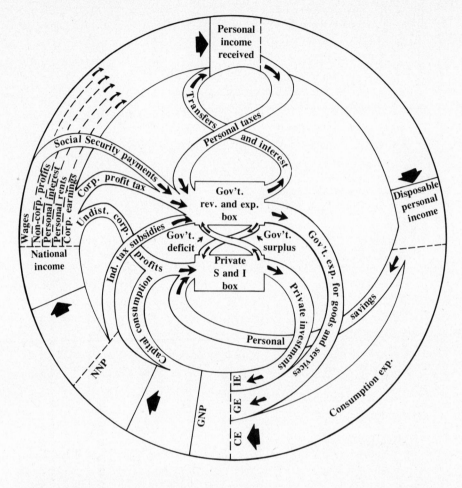

Figure 1.13
NATIONAL PRODUCT AND INCOME FLOWS

3. The inclusion of many goods and services that are culturally determined. In the United States, most households buy bread. Hence, the payments received by and made to bakeries are included in the national product. In poorer countries, most bread may be baked within a household and is thus not included. Where a significant part of the population resides within extended family households, many goods and services may be performed within the household that would move through the market in a society more oriented to the nuclear family. Since both self-service and the extended family are characteristic of poorer societies, their national product calculations tend to be biased downward.

4. Costs arising out of social structure. A highly urbanized society generates many costs not incurred in a more rural society, such as distribution, housing, and

communication costs. Hence, a somewhat lower national income in rural per capita terms within the more rural society could be equated with a higher national income for the more urban society.

5. Costs arising out of climate. Canadians must produce and buy more energy for heating purposes than Cubans. Yet, if this item were the only difference in the real per capita product of the two economies, could one say that the difference was real?

6. Different firms and national legal systems that use and encourage different systems of depreciation, thereby rendering net national products not strictly comparable.

7. Treatment of external diseconomies. If a paper mill causes water pollution to the extent that another plant has to be built to purify the water, should the costs associated with the second plant be an additive to net national products? Differing degrees of environmental disturbance are found in the more and less developed countries.

8. Imputed value of public sector services—military, police, education, public health. If output is simply equal to the cost of the inputs no net value is added. Hence, countries investing relatively heavily in these areas are penalized. Is $1,000 spent on education equal to $1,000 spent on the wages of a soft-drink salesman?

    For example:

	Country A (in millions of dollars)	Country B (in millions of dollars)
Education, health, research expenditures	1	2
Wages	2	1
Profits	1	½
GNP	4	3½

One might remove the penalty on education, health, and research expenditures by imputing a value-added equal to at least the marginal return on capital.

9. Differences arising out of political ideology. The U.S.S.R. includes income only of those engaged in the production of material goods. Excluded is "exploitative income," for example, the salaries of enterprise managers, all sales from farms with an income over that normally paid to hired labor, all nonfarm income of unincorporated businesses such as doctors and small tradesmen, interest, land rent and royalties, and enterprise profits before tax. The United States includes all goods and services passing through a legal market regardless of perceptions of social utility.

10. Noncomparability of sectors—consumption, investment, government. The more welfare-oriented is a country, the more consumption expenditures will be made in the government sector, such as in public health, public education, radio broadcasting, and public transport. The investment sector may be substantially reduced in countries relying heavily upon government investments. The level of the government sector will vary dramatically with the perception of external threat, such as

defense expenditures, which, in terms of growth of production, are more in the nature of consumption than investment.

11. The exchange-rate problem. If one is comparing levels of national products or income, a common denominator is needed. Use of the official rate causes a serious distortion for several reasons. First, only a relatively small percentage of the nation's goods and services are traded internationally. An exchange rate is designed to bring about a balance between outflows (imports, investment out) and inflows (export earnings, investment in), not to establish an equilibrium exchange value for all goods and services. The following example illustrates the problem:

	Country X			**Country Y**		
	Price/Unit	Production	Total Product Value	Price/Unit	Production	Total Product Value
Good A	$20	300	$6,000	£ 2	1,000	£2,000
Good B	$10	200	2,000	£50	100	5,000
GNP			$8,000			£7,000

Assume that only good B is traded internationally. Perhaps good A is perishable, or that tastes vary so that good A is not wanted in country X, or that country X has a tariff against good A. The exchange rate in terms of goods traded (that is, in good B) is $1 = £5. Thus, the GNP of country X equals $8,000; that of country Y, $1,400 (that is, 7,000 divided by 5). But the exchange rate in terms of good A is $10 = £1. The economy of country Y may be substantially better off relative to country X than the exchange rate indicates.

For purposes of comparison of GNPs, one really needs an exchange rate that measures the *internal* purchasing power of the two currencies. Therefore, the prices used should be weighted by local purchasing patterns. If one uses country X prices, it will be seen that the GNPs would be $8,000 and $21,000, respectively. If country Y prices were used, the GNPs would be £10,600 and £7,000, respectively. In fact, to use either Y's prices in X or X's prices in Y is not supportable. It is suggested by research that prices on those goods enjoying relatively high demand are relatively low. In our case, it would appear that the demand for good A in country Y is relatively greater than in country X in respect to the demand for good B. For instance, a 1954 study found that in 1950 a dollar's worth of European currency would buy substantially more in Europe than a dollar would in the United States at official rates.[53] It was concluded that one reason was that those products with relatively high consumption in Europe carried relatively low prices. Figure 1.14 illustrates this.

This curve indicates that as the units measured per capita increased in the United Kingdom as a percentage of U.S. consumption, the £ price (at the

[53]See Milton Gilbert and Irving B. Kraus, *An International Comparison of National Products and the Purchasing Power of Currencies* (Paris: Organization for European Economic Cooperation, 1954).

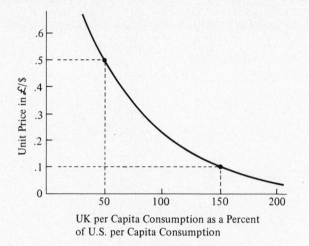

UK per Capita Consumption as a Percent
of U.S. per Capita Consumption

Figure 1.14
**RELATIONSHIP BETWEEN TOTAL UNITS CONSUMED
NATIONALLY AND PRICE**

official exchange rate of £.36/$) became lower. At 150 percent of U.S. per
capita consumption, the United Kingdom price was £.5/$.[54] In general, it was
concluded that:

*The domestic purchasing power of the European currencies, when utilized to purchase
the European pattern of products, is about 60 to 90 percent greater than the exchange
rate suggests, but only about 8 to 25 percent higher than on the basis of the United States
pattern of expenditures.*[55]

Clearly, anyone using national product and income figures in a direct comparison among different countries should have many reservations. When one says
that the per capita GNP in country X is $150, it should be clear that that is
a virtually meaningless statement. No one could survive on less than 50 cents
a day in the United States. Obviously $150 buys more goods and services in
country X than in the United States. How much more? All one can say is that
as the level drops the multiple necessary to produce a comparable consumption
level probably increases. Some have suggested that for a country with a per
capita GNP of $200, a multiple of three should be used; that is, the goods and
services the $200 will buy in country X probably approximates a $600 level

[54]Gilbert and Kraus, *International Comparison.*
[55]Gilbert and Kraus, *International Comparison,* p. 24.

Table 1.5
GNP PER CAPITA AS A PERCENTAGE OF THE UNITED STATES

Country	Old	New
Kenya	3.2%	5.7%
India	2.3	7.1
Colombia	7.1	15.9
Hungary	33.6	40.3
Italy	37.0	45.8
Britain	47.7	60.3
Japan	40.3	61.5
West Germany	61.6	74.7
France	65.1	75.0

in the United States (roughly $2 a day); at a $400 level, the appropriate multiple may be about 2½; at a $600 level, about 2; and so on.

An effort to establish a basis for making better international comparisons of income and purchasing powers—free of the distorting effects of either fixed or floating exchange rates—was undertaken by the United Nations and World Bank in 1975.[56] The results, based on careful comparative pricing of several hundred items in each of ten countries, were strikingly different from past measures (see Table 1.5).

As a by-product, this same study pointed out the enormous differences in relative prices. For example, construction costs were found to be 24 percent lower in West Germany than in the United States. Indeed, U.S. construction costs were found generally to be higher than elsewhere except for Japan. Likewise, medical care was found to be far cheaper in other countries than in the United States: 51 percent less in West Germany, 54 percent less in France, 57 percent less in Britain, and 73 percent less in Japan. But food, clothing, energy, transportation, and communications were much cheaper in the United States. Energy, in part due to heavier government taxes, was about 70 percent more expensive in France and Japan. Educational costs varied. In France, the cost was 47 percent above that in the United States; 7 percent more in West Germany; 29 percent less in Britain; and 40 percent less in Japan.

The difficulty of coming up with firm estimates on income distributions is reflected in a 1975 World Bank compilation.[57] Estimates for the same year for the same country are frequently widely disparate, so much so that the establishment of an unambiguous trend toward greater or lesser income inequality is difficult to track for many countries.

---

[56]Irving B. Kravis et al., *A System of International Comparisons of Gross Product and Purchasing Power* (Baltimore: Johns Hopkins University Press for the World Bank, 1975).

[57]Shail Jain, *Size Distribution of Income* (Washington: International Bank for Reconstruction and Development, 1975).

Obviously, countries with similar GNPs per capita could have very different income distributions. The gross average imbedded in the per capita notion may be very misleading.

A 1976 Organization for Economic Cooperation and Development study of income distribution reported that regardless of the measure of income inequality one looked at, three countries (Australia, Japan, and Sweden) seemed to record the lowest degree of inequality of post-tax income distribution. At the other end, France was ranked consistently as having the most unequal distribution. (See Table 1.8.) If one uses *pre*-tax inequality, Australia and Japan, in that order, ranked as the least unequal countries on most measures, and France was joined by the United States at the opposite end of the scale.[58] The study warned, however, that "in a strict sense, a comparative study [of income distribution] is impossible in the present state of knowledge."[59] The reason for this proviso is apparent when one lists the methodological problems encountered in making international comparisons of income distribution. Some of the major ones:

1. Underreporting of income of higher income groups because of omission of capital gains, fringe benefits and understatement of investment and entrepreneurial income.

2. The use of annual income, rather than lifetime income.

3. Variations in age distribution from one population to another in that the income of the young and the elderly tends to be less than that of the middle aged. (Hence, income distribution might differ from country to country for purely demographic reasons, but note four below.)

4. Differences in the age distinctions of household heads in that the income of a household is influenced by the age of its head, with the income of the young and the old tending to be less than the income of others.

5. Difference in the definition of the income receiving unit, specifically the household[60] and variations in average household size. (With the same national product and population, per household income could vary substantially as between a society characterized by nuclear families and one characterized by the extended family.[61] Use of per capita income corrects for this aberration, but runs into the problem suggested in three above. Further, it can be argued that there are economies of scale in the size of household and that children do not need as much income as adults to achieve a given level of welfare.)

6. Some national data exclude nonprivate households such as inmates of prisons, orphanages, military personnel not living on bases, servants living with their employers.

---

[58] Malcolm Sawyer, *Income Distribution in OECD Countries* (Paris: Organization for Economic Cooperation and Development, Occasional Studies, July 1976), p. 16.

[59] Sawyer, *Income Distribution*, p. 3.

[60] In Turkey, for example, the household has been defined as those individuals normally eating together.

[61] In Spain, 30.7 percent of the households contain five or more persons, 6.6 percent, only one person. In Sweden the figures are almost reversed, 6.2 and 37.6 percent, respectively. (Sawyer, *Income Distribution*, p. 18.)

Table 1.6
AFTER-TAX INCOME DISTRIBUTION BY COUNTRY

The poorest 10 percent of the households in:	Receive the following percentage of the national income:
France	1.4
Spain	1.5
Australia	1.6
Canada	1.6
United States	1.7
Britain	2.4
Norway	2.4
Sweden	2.6
Japan	2.7
Germany	2.8
Netherlands	3.2
The richest 10 percent of the households in:	
Sweden	18.6
Netherlands	21.8
Norway	21.9
Britain	23.9
Canada	24.7
Australia	25.2
United States	26.1
Japan	27.8
Spain	28.5
France	30.5
Germany	30.6

7. Some national data exclude the self-employed (such as farmers) and nontaxpayers.

8. The Lorenz curves of two national distributions may cross, so that comparison of some measures of inequality are ambiguous; it depends upon whether one stresses the shares accruing to the poorest or to the richest.

9. The nature and progressivity of the tax system if one is comparing pretax income distribution. (One can reasonably assume that pretax income distribution will be more equal than posttax in a country in which the tax system is not very egalitarian than in one in which it is, and vice versa.)

10. Point measures of income distribution inequality are static. (They do not tell one whether income distribution in Country A is becoming more or less equal than in Country B. A historic series would correct in part, but note eleven below.)

11. If countries are at different points in the economic cycle, or undergoing widely disparate growth rates, income distribution will be affected. (One may be left only with a measure of unequal economic activity or unequal growth.)

Nonetheless, a 1976 study of income distribution claims to provide "strong support for the proposition that relative inequality increases substantially in the early stages of development, with a reversal of this tendency in the later stages." It was also found that there were a number of processes occurring with development that correlate with greater income equality and which plausibly could be causally related. These are: (1) intersectoral shifts in the structure of production, (2) expansion of educational attainment and skill level of the labor force, and (3) a reduction in the rate of population growth. It is observed that "these processes appear to explain some of the improvement in income distribution in the later stages of development, but they do not serve to explain the marked deterioration observed in earlier stages. Nor does the analysis support the hypothesis that "the deterioration in relative inequality reflects prolonged absolute impoverishment of large sections of the population in the course of development. The cross country pattern shows average absolute incomes of the lower percentile groups rising as per capita GNP rises, although slower than for upper income groups." Finally, this study did not support the notion that "a faster rate of growth is systematically associated with higher inequality."[62] But questions about basic data leave one unconvinced.

In the case of the United States, the figures show a small but distinct shift toward a more equal distribution of income. In 1935–36 the bottom fifth of the families received only 4.1 percent of the country's income, while the top fifth pocketed 51.7 percent. Some change occurred during World War II when the United States got its first taste of full employment. Between 1950 and 1968 the share of the lowest fifth inched up steadily from 4.5 percent to 5.6 percent. This trend seems to have been halted for the past six years, which suggests that the great inflation has hit the low incomes somewhat harder than the top brackets.[63]

Gunnar Myrdal, the Swedish economist and sociologist, was asked a few years back about the adequacy of the GNP measure of the development process in the less developed countries. Here is his response:

The concept is flimsy in developed countries and still more so in underdeveloped countries. It does not take into consideration how the product is distributed, and, generally the "noneconomic factors" or even what is growing—whether it is real growth from a national point of view or merely costs caused by various developments some of which are negative, etc. Second, anyone who looks into how the basic statistical data are assembled and analysed in underdeveloped countries must find them grossly unreliable.[64]

---

[62]Montek S. Ahlinwalia, "Inequality, Poverty and Development," *Journal of Development Economics*, vol. 3, 1976, p. 32. Ahlinwalia suggests a curvilinear relationship between income per capita and income inequality of the form $Y = X + X^2$, where Y equals income and X, a measure of inequality of income.

[63]John Cobbs, "Egalitarianism: Mechanics for Redistributing Income," *Business Week*, December 8, 1975, p. 86.

[64]Gunnar Myrdal, "I Have No Respect for Diplomacy in Research," *Ceres*, vol. 4, no. 2, March–April 1971, p. 31.

The Lorenz curve (see Figure 1.14) is frequently used to depict the inequality of income distribution. In this application, the Lorenz curve shows the relation between the cumulative percentage of population shares (on the horizontal axis) and the cumulative percentage of income shares (on the vertical axis), very frequently shown in deciles. A specific measure of inequality is the Gini coefficient, which is defined as the ratio of the area on a graph which lies between the Lorenz curve and the line representing perfect equality (A), which forms a 45 degree angle with both the vertical and horizontal axes, to the area of the entire triangle formed by the egalitarian line and the two axes (A + B). The Gini coefficient thus ranges from 0 to 1; the larger the coefficient, the greater the inequality. An alternative measure is the Kuznets index, which is computed for 20 intervals, that is, for each 5 percent of the population (or active population, or working population, or households). The absolute mean deviation of the income share of each 5 percentile group from 5 percent (which would be equivalent to perfect equality of distribution) is calculated. The arithmetic averages of the 20 absolute deviations range from zero in the case of perfect equality to 9.5 in the case of maximum inequality. Division by 9.5 is necessary to standardize the measure to a range from zero to 1.

The pattern of income use, quite apart from disparities in level and distribution, likewise differs significantly from country to country and, not infrequently, over time for a single country. Table 1.7, compiled by the Organization for Economic Cooperation and Development (OECD), is revealing on this score. "Pure private consumption" is defined here as private consumption less "publicly supported consumption." The latter phrase refers to "decisions about how money will be spent . . . made directly or indirectly by governments." Examples are medical, education, and living expense reimbursements made to private individuals by governments.[65]

As may be noted, despite the rise of what has been dubbed "consumer societies," in fact, the share of GNP devoted to private consumption declined in every OECD country over the 15-year period ending in 1969. This decline was particularly sharp (over 10 percentage points) for Japan, Belgium, Denmark, Ireland, Netherlands, Sweden, Switzerland, and Greece. According to OECD projections, the decline will probably continue into the 1970s for all OECD countries other than the United States. Also, the proportion saved has increased in all OECD countries except in the United States, Denmark, Luxembourg, and Sweden.

These changes probably imply a shift in spendable income to the aged, the unemployed, the underprivileged, all who benefit from increases in social welfare payments. In general the analysis leads to the conclusion that in many major national markets the amount of money over which those who earn it

---

[65] *The OECD Observer*, no. 59, August 1972.

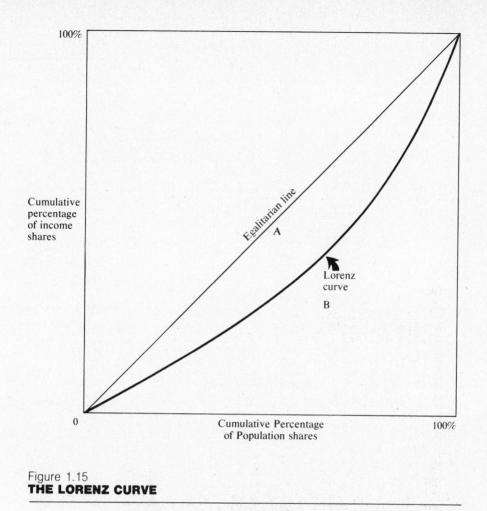

Figure 1.15
THE LORENZ CURVE

have control has been falling, and the public-sector control over income utilization is increasing commensurably.

One of the questions suggested by these comparisons is how fast and how great a shift can be made in the 1970s, from "pure private consumption" to social expenditure (financed by private investment, government expenditures, and transfers) without seriously aggravating inflation.

It should be noted that government expenditures in the United States as a percentage of GNP have risen only slightly, from perhaps 26 percent in 1948–50 (16 percent federal and 10 percent state and local) to 33 percent in 1973–75 (18 percent federal and 14 percent state and local). Over that period, it can be seen that much of the increase in the ratio was due to state and local governments. Employment reflected the same phenomenon, with 12 percent

Table 1.7

FROM "PRIMARY" INCOME TO "PURE" PRIVATE CONSUMPTION

(as percentage of GNP, 1955 and 1969)

	"Primary" Income		Net Current Transfers from Government		Direct Taxes		Net Current Transfers from Abroad		Disposable Income		Saving as a Percentage of GNP		Private Consumption		"Pure" Private Consumption	
	1955	1969	1955	1969	1955	1969	1955	1969	1955	1969	1955	1969	1955	1969	1955	1969
Major Countries																
Canada	72.9	72.9	6.4	10.0	5.8	11.0	−0.2	−0.1	73.3	71.8	8.6	10.7	64.6	61.1	58.3	51.1
United States	79.3	78.8	4.2	6.1	11.5	16.2	−0.1	−0.1	71.9	68.6	7.9	7.3	63.9	61.3	59.7	55.2
Japan	78.0	72.0	2.7	3.2	5.4	7.6	−0.1	0.0	75.2	67.6	13.4	16.1	62.1	51.5	59.4	48.3
France	74.5	73.4	12.3	17.0	13.4	19.5	0.1	−0.3	73.5	70.6	9.3	10.8	64.3	58.8	52.0	42.8
Germany	71.3	71.9	12.2	13.3	14.4	19.2	0.0	−0.7	69.1	65.3	9.2	10.4	59.8	54.9	47.6	41.6
Italy	77.3	77.1	8.5	13.7	10.3	16.5	0.7	0.8	76.2	75.1	9.8	12.3	66.4	62.8	57.9	49.1
United Kingdom	74.9	76.8	4.9	8.3	9.4	15.8	−0.4	−0.5	70.0	68.8	3.2	6.0	66.8	62.7	61.9	54.4
Other Northern European Countries																
Austria	77.6	75.8	9.3	13.6	13.6	18.8	0.1	0.6	73.4	71.2	11.1	12.6	62.3	58.6	53.0	45.0
Belgium	78.6	77.3	9.1	13.6	11.4	17.6	0.0	0.4	76.3	73.7	6.4	11.1	69.9	62.4	60.8	48.8

Table 1.7 (continued)

	"Primary" Income		Net Current Transfers from Government		Direct Taxes		Net Current Transfers from Abroad		Disposable Income		Saving as a Percentage of GNP		Private Consumption		"Pure" Private Consumption	
	1955	1969	1955	1969	1955	1969	1955	1969	1955	1969	1955	1969	1955	1969	1955	1969
Denmark	80.6	75.0	6.0	9.6	10.4	16.2	0.0	0.0	76.2	68.4	7.3	6.8	68.9	61.6	62.9	52.0
Finland	73.8	74.6	4.5	7.3	9.1	14.9	0.0	0.0	69.2	67.0	8.1	11.2	61.2	55.8	56.7	48.5
Ireland	78.7	75.4	5.7	7.5	3.3	7.4	2.2	1.3	83.3	76.8	5.4	8.7	77.9	68.1	72.2	60.6
Luxembourg	71.9	74.0	10.0	15.4	14.7	19.5	0.0	0.0	67.2	69.9	9.3	8.9	57.8	61.0	47.8	45.6
Netherlands	73.1	75.9	6.6	16.2	13.2	24.7	0.2	−0.1	66.7	67.3	7.5	10.4	59.2	56.8	52.6	40.6
Sweden	77.5	76.5	5.4	10.0	13.5	26.1	0.0	0.0	69.4	60.4	7.5	6.0	61.7	54.2	56.3	44.2
Switzerland	77.3	75.3	3.1	6.9	10.0	13.4	−0.6	−1.8	69.8	67.0	4.3	10.1	65.6	56.9	62.5	50.0
Other Southern European Countries																
Greece	84.7	77.2	4.0	8.3	6.2	8.6	2.3	3.7	84.8	80.6	7.1	11.6	77.7	68.9	73.7	60.6
Spain	79.0	78.1	1.1	4.2	3.6	7.7	0.3	1.5	76.8	76.1	6.1	7.6	70.6	68.5	69.5	64.3
OECD Total	77.4	76.6	5.7	8.2	10.8	15.9	0.0	−0.1	72.3	68.8	8.3	9.0	63.9	59.8	58.2	51.6
OECD excluding U.S.	75.4	74.2	7.3	10.5	10.0	15.6	0.1	−0.1	72.7	69.0	8.7	10.8	63.9	58.2	56.6	47.7

Source: National Accounts of OECD Countries, *1953-1969 and Secretarial estimates.*
The OECD Observer, no. 59. August 1972, p. 5.

of total employment in the government sector in 1950 (4 percent federal; 8 percent state and local) and growing to 18 percent in 1975 (4 percent federal; 14 percent state and local).[66]

Such considerations must be borne in mind by those plotting marketing strategy.

Recommended references

Beckerman, Wilfred. *International Comparisons of Real Incomes.* Paris: Development Center of the Organization for Economic Cooperation and Development, 1966.

Gilbert, Milton and Irving B. Kravis. *An International Comparison of National Products and the Purchasing Power of Currencies.* Paris: Organization for European Economic Cooperation, 1954.

Kravis, Irving B. et al. *A System of International Comparisons of Gross Product and Purchasing Power.* Baltimore: Johns Hopkins University Press for the World Bank, 1975.

Sawyer, Malcolm. *Income Distribution in OECD Countries.* Paris: Organization for Economic Cooperation and Development, Occasional Studies, July 1976.

---

[66] *Commerce America,* October 25, 1976, p. 2.

Case B
SYSTEMICS LOOKS AT BRAZIL

The management of Systemics was under increasing pressure from the company's Latin American distributor, who was headquartered in Rio de Janeiro, Brazil. He felt that in view of Brazil's balance of payments situation Systemics would lose Brazilian sales unless it produced within the country. (Subsequently, an importer was required to make a cruzeiro deposit in his local bank equivalent to 100 percent of the value of the import as soon as an import license was issued to him.) Furthermore, he argued, export sales from Brazil to the rest of Latin America would reduce the cost to other Latin American consumers and, hence, enhance the firm's competitive position in these other markets. The president of Systemics, Mr. Lee Roberts, and the director of marketing, Mr. Sean Nelson, were not entirely convinced. No one in the company had had very much experience in Brazil in that all business had been conducted through the distributor. He was characterized by Messrs. Roberts and Nelson as energetic, emotional, and secretive.

Systemics, headquartered in Lee, New Jersey, manufactured phototypesetting equipment for use by the printing industry. The product line consisted of 20 different models, of which eight were considered basic. There were some components common to all. The machines consisted of electronic circuit boards, an optical system, a motor system, a lighting system, and a chassis. It used specially prepared film strips on which a variety of types had been developed. The price of the various models ranged from $3,500 to $35,000, the mode being about $6,000. Sales had grown rapidly and presently stood at $80 million per year, roughly $15 million of which was in exports (excluding Canada). If Canada were included, total foreign sales would come to about $20 million.

In the United States, the company enjoyed a market share of about 60 percent in terms of unit sales, about 45 percent in terms of value. Management did not know its market share in Brazil, but guessed that it was somewhat lower than in the United States because of its relatively recent entry. Total Latin American sales ranged between 100 and 125 units annually ($600,000 to $750,000), about half of which constituted sales within Brazil. Some post-sales servicing was required, but this was performed by the distributor. No comparable machines were being manufactured in Brazil. Systemics' only competitors, of which there were four or five, were located in the United States. Competition was almost wholly on the basis of price. No important patents or production secrets were involved. In the United States, Systemics manufactured only about 30 percent of the equipment itself. The manufacture of the balance was through subcontract with unrelated U.S. firms. Its only U.S. plant was in Lee.

The weight-volume-value relationships were such as to permit air shipment for long distance delivery.

With but two exceptions, Systemics sold overseas through national distributors. The two exceptions were the East Asia Company for Southeast Asia and the Brazilian distributor for Latin America.

Discussion questions

1. Should Systemics produce any or all of its product line in Brazil?
2. If it should, what strategic options should it consider?
3. How should it proceed to analyze these options?
4. In your opinion, what seems to be the most likely strategy?

Chapter 2
SUPPLY STRATEGY

Having determined, as far as possible, optimum strategy in respect to sales, management is faced with a set of production and procurement decisions. Given the nature of the product, a sales target, product specifications, promotional agency, source of product (in terms of nationality *from the point of view of the consumer*) and competitive restraints, management needs to address itself to these queries in the production area: (1) to what extent should the firm itself undertake production (degree of integration), (2) where and what should it buy, (3) should it produce in one plant or many, (4) with what sort of production equipment, (5) on what sites, (6) in new plant or acquired, (7) fed by research and development located where? Obviously, optimum answers to these questions set up a feedback into the sales strategy area, particularly in respect to product specifications and national source of supply. In each case, trade-offs must be considered. The market may suggest modifications in the product, but modifications often mean extra costs. Likewise the market may indicate preference for a particular source, be it local or third country, but cost considerations (and risk) may give an advantage to another source.

DEGREE OF INTEGRATION   2.1

Degree of integration regarding a particular product may be viewed as a continuum from 100 percent purchase on one end to 100 percent manufacture on the other, with all degrees of external supply and assembly in between. Of course, any degree of external input implies make-or-buy decisions in respect to both the individual plant and the company at large, thus introducing a second dimension (see Figure 2.1); that is, the single plant or subsidiary may buy from the parent (or other associated firms) or from entirely independent sources. In reaching a decision, the relevance of product nationality, discussed in Chapter 1, should be weighed.

Various political factors may militate against company integration—whether vertical or horizontal—within a given national market, particularly if

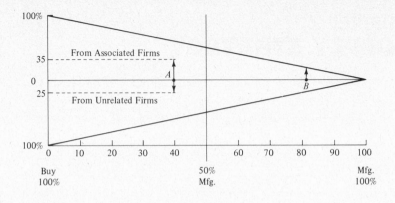

Figure 2.1
THE SUPPLY PROFILE FOR A SINGLE PLANT

Example: Point *A* indicates about 60 percent bought—approximately 25 percent being procured externally to the company, 35 percent internally. At point *B*, the plant manufactures about 80 percent, buying all of the balance from associated firms.

the contemplated enterprise would constitute a large and obvious part of an important sector of the host economy, either nationally or regionally. An extreme case of the latter is the stimulation of large communities virtually dependent upon the enterprise; that is, the company town. Avoiding such a situation may well be worth higher cost of external sources of supply.

Some firms have attempted to build themselves into the local economy by a process of *local integration* by subcontracting all processes and services for which local skills are adequate, even to the extent of providing training, financing, and technical assistance to indigenous entrepreneurs. Sears, Roebuck in Mexico and the Arabian-American Oil Company in Saudi Arabia are two cases in point. In a 1970 Conference Board study, well over half of the cooperating executives believed that international firms are well advised to use local suppliers whenever possible, in some cases even when the local subsidiary would have preferred to use materials from the parent company. And a large number used locally available professional services, legal, accounting, auditing, medical, advertising, public relations, and architectural.[1] The extreme case is *contract manufacture* and/or assembly by otherwise independent local firms. In this case, the initiating firm simply contracts with a local firm for the production of certain goods or services according to the former's specifications for delivery to it. The contractor often provides some technical service and reserves the right to monitor quality. Some debt financing may be involved as

[1] James R. Basche, Jr., *Integrating Foreign Subsidiaries into Host Countries* (New York: The Conference Board, 1970), pp. 25–28.

well. A further alternative is *licensing* a local manufacturer who produces on his own account for sale to parties of his own choice, although possibly restricted in respect to territory.

Some observers feel that the frequent over-building of industrial plants, and the subsequent idle capacity, in the less developed countries has created many opportunities for profitable contract manufacturing. Indeed, the UN Industrial Development Organization (UNIDO) proposes the establishment of a "sub-contract exchange" for bringing the owners of excess manufacturing capacity together with those who need additional and more diversified sources of supply. The "marketing" of excess industrial capacity would be the primary function of the exchange.[2]

Optimum strategy may call for changing one's supply or production profile in planned steps from one alternative to another. If so, care should be taken not to lose something valuable in the process without adequate remuneration, such as secret processes, personnel in whose training the firm has invested heavily, or market position. Not infrequently this shift is compelled. An example of such *forced manufacture* is a Spanish government decree that 95 percent of all autos assembled there must be produced locally. (Ford was able to negotiate the 95 percent down to 66 percent.) In other instances, a firm may be compelled, as part of its entry permit, to commit itself to the development of a certain percentage of local manufacture in a series of steps spread over time, a process known as *phased manufacture.*

A few further examples of recent pressure toward local manufacture or purchase are: (1) in Canada the Canadian Guidelines of Good Corporate Behavior urge local purchase when feasible; (2) in India international joint ventures must be independent of raw materials, components, and small parts within three years (not an official ruling, but derived from decisions taken on foreign collaboration applications); (3) in Bolivia, special incentives are offered to enterprises using a certain percentage of national raw material; (4) in Chile enterprises using 80 percent or more domestic raw materials are exempt from import duties; (5) in Columbia certain tax exemptions are given to enterprises launched before 1965 that use at least 60 percent domestic raw materials; (6) in Indonesian entry agreements and elsewhere, firms must frequently commit themselves to increasing local content over time by specified percentages.

Please note that these pressures are distinct from the nationality preferences from the *point of view of the customer,* as discussed in Chapter 1 (an example of the latter is the "Buy American" regulations imposed by the U.S. federal and several state governments). Further details of these latter restrictions, which constitute important nontariff barriers, are given in Section 2.2.

The problem of control, of course, is greatly compounded by the shifting

---

[2]See E. Edwards, "The Subcontract Exchange" (Paris: U.N. Industrial Development Organization, mimeo, ID/WG.41/9, May 1969).

of supply sources. If a firm is involved in phased manufacture, it may start with the assembly of knocked-down kits from its parent or another subsidiary. As local manufacture develops, parts must be deleted from these kits, which initially can add to cost at the source rather than reducing it. If offshore sources, that is, unrelated foreign suppliers, are used initially, purchase contracts must be written so that their termination coincides with the development of local sources, but the latter may not be known with precision.

Assuming that the firm opts for some degree of manufacturing in its own facilities in order to supply the target market, whether that market be local, home, third country, regional, or global, management is then faced with determining the best *national* location for those facilities. Logically, the relevant factors would be costs (if a factor is not available, its cost is simply infinitely high), political risk (the probability of politically-imposed costs up to and including expropriation of assets and stream of earnings), and trade relationships between the supply country and the market country or countries (which likewise translate into costs). Theoretically, the size of the national market local to the manufacturing facility becomes relevant only through these same intervening variables; that is, the target market has already been identified in our schema and should be supplied from the least cost source, which may or may not be within that market.

In measuring comparative costs, the same concerns as listed in Section 1.2 should be kept in mind, likewise the difficulty of translating these costs from one currency to another.

A 1976 Conference Board survey indicated that a large majority of corporate respondents agreed on one point: production costs had been rising all over the world in the past three years. In most cases, the rise in production costs had been more rapid at their overseas facilities than at home.[3] Although most of the survey respondents reported that rising production costs had had no major effect on their overseas business plans and operations, a number reported otherwise. In some cases exports from the United States had been expanded, expansion abroad restricted, subcontracting expanded, and supply sources shifted. With the advent of more flexible exchange rates and freer trade, effective price relationships had changed quite rapidly. And among the more industrialized countries one suspected that a fairly rapid convergence of labor, energy, and materials costs was taking place. Of course, nontariff barriers and transportation costs might remain significant, depending upon the nature of the product. It was also revealing that a number of executives, although a minority, reported to the Conference Board that for various reasons their companies did not monitor comparative production cost data, which suggested that relative costs were not important in investment decisions. The danger is that executives might use short-term cost changes, such as those

---

[3]James R. Basche, Jr., *Foreign Production Costs* (New York: The Conference Board, 1976).

induced by adjustments in foreign exchange rates, as justification for longtime investment commitments. One wondered whether Volkswagen, in its 1976 decision to invest in a U.S. manufacturing plant, was not unduly influenced by what might prove to be short-term changes in the Deutschmark-dollar rate.

A 1974 study by Schollhammer, based on responses to a questionnaire returned by 140 corporations (in the U.S., Europe, and Japan) with foreign production facilities, indicated that locational decisions at the country level evolved in a haphazard fashion;[4] that is, they were "frequently made after only an incomplete and preconceived investigation of the consequences of a particular locational choice rather than on the basis of a comprehensive and systematic evaluation of locational alternatives on a global scale."[5] Factor analysis of his data led Schollhammer to conclude that the decisions were most strongly affected by perceived risks and uncertainties and only to a lesser extent by production factor availability, market potential, cost conditions, local competitive pressures, a country's infrastructure, and by what he called "nuisance factors" (labor problems, government intervention, trade restrictions). It was his judgment that firms should consider a much wider range of factors, undertake more comprehensive and systematic investigations, and examine more alternative national locations than in fact they appeared to do.

At odds with Schollhammer's factor analysis is Kobrin's analysis of direct foreign investment (FDI) flows of U.S. origin. He concluded:

The research findings appear unambiguous. Market related variables would seem to be the overriding factor in the allocation of manufacturing FDI. Furthermore, even when one holds market size constant—when one asks, in effect, on what factors the FDI decision would be based if an investor was faced with a number of comparable markets— no relationship can be established between FDI and any of the other environmental variables.[6]

Kobrin specifically attempted to relate various measures of political risk to the flows of FDI, but was unable to do so, even while holding market size constant. There thus seems to be some conflict between the micro data reported by Schollhammer and the macro data with which Kobrin worked. The latter suggested that this apparent contradiction lay in the definition of political instability or political risk. Kobrin defined political risk in the structure and functioning of basic political institutions.[7] But, "political activities which do

[4]Hans Schollhammer, *Locational Strategies of Multinational Firms* (Los Angeles: Center for International Business, Pepperdine University, 1974).

[5]Schollhammer, *Strategies*, p. 32.

[6]Stephen J. Kobrin, "The Environmental Determinants of Foreign Direct Investment: An Ex Post Empirical Analysis," (*Journal of International Business Studies*, Fall 1976, p. 37).

[7]Regime type (civilian, military civilian, military), changes in effective executive (number of changes per year to an independent successor), major cabinet changes (change of premier and/or 50 percent of the cabinet), general strikes (involving over 1,000 workers and aimed against the national authority), riots (involving more than 100 persons), government crises (any rapidly developing situation, other than revolution, that threatens

not significantly alter the business environment do not represent political risk." That is, political discontinuities in themselves do not necessarily create unexpected costs for the investor. "Risk may result from political disruption, but only to the extent it constrains operations."[8] Kobrin notes that political variables may well intervene between FDI and market size. (His measure of market size consisted of gross domestic product and population.) It may be that present market size, which is a function of past growth, implies minimal politically-induced costs imposed on production. Otherwise, one might argue, the growth would not have taken place. It may also be true that the most populous countries represent relatively high orders of political stability, a necessary condition for holding together large population masses. Thus, a populous country with a large GNP is identified with low political costs in the past, and investors simply project that record into the near future.

But why investors should necessarily invest within a market to supply that market is not at all clear. Yet there seems to be a strong bias in that direction. Possibly it can best be explained in terms of trade barriers and the cost of international shipping.

Trade barriers can be defined in terms of special institutionalized commercial relationships among nations (from negotiating groups through producers' cartels and common markets to federations), plus the more general institutions of tariffs and nontariff barriers. The first of these—the institutionalized relationships—is the subject of the appendix attached to this chapter.

Almost all countries have some sort of tariff barrier, an import tax or duty,[9] although these tariffs may be waived in respect to imports from certain countries (partners within a free trading area) or lowered (generalized LDC preference system). If "most-favored-nation" (MFN) treatment is given by Country A to Country B, it means that any reduction in tariff negotiated by Country A with Country C is extended automatically to Country B. The U.S. has denied MFN status to all of the Sino-Soviet bloc countries other than

---

the immediate fall of government), purges (systematic elimination by the political elite of opposition leaders by imprisonment or execution), assassinations (any politically motivated murder or attempted murder of government or political officials), armed attacks (acts of violent political conflict by one organized group against another), coups d'état (extra-constitutional changes in the governing elite), guerrilla warfare (armed attacks by irregular forces or bands of citizens aimed to overthrow the existing government), revolutions (an armed attempt by a part of the citizenry to form an independent government or force a change in the governing elite), irregular executive transfers (any change in the national executive accomplished outside of legal or customary procedures and accompanied by actual or threatened violence). The data was sourced either in Arthur S. Banks, *Cross-Polity Timeseries Data* (Cambridge, Massachusetts: M.I.T. Press, 1971) or Charles L. Taylor and Michael C. Hudson, *World Handbook of Political and Social Indicators* (New Haven: Yale University Press, 2d ed., 1972).

[8]Kobrin, "Environmental Determinants," p. 37.

[9]A *tariff* is a schedule of rates at which imported goods are taxed upon entry. A *duty* is the money amount of the tax collected by reason of a tariff. *Customs* refers to the act of imposing, or the administration of, a tariff. In common parlance, the three words are often used interchangeably. In the case of bilateral trading a tariff is virtually meaningless. In the case of centrally controlled economies where international trading is the monopoly of the state and trading companies and prices in the usual sense are meaningless, tariffs may be irrelevant.

Poland, which has meant significantly higher tariffs on U.S. imports from these countries, hence higher prices and lower imports.

The range of duties charged varies enormously from country to country, from many hundreds of percentage points on imported luxury goods by LDCs to zero. The basis may be either on physical quantity (specific) or value (*ad valorem*). The average duty levied on imports in the United States peaked at 59.1 percent in 1932 and subsequently has declined to something between 10 and 11 percent, which reflects a worldwide reduction in tariffs. The U.S. is the only major trading nation in which the tariff schedules are part of national legislation and, hence, changes require congressional authorization.

There is also some evidence, at least in the U.S., that the impact of the tariff is "at least slightly regressive in its incidence on consumption"; that is, a low-income family pays a higher percentage of its overall consumption than does a higher-income family. One reason for this phenomenon is that goods moving in international trade "represented a progressively smaller share of consumption as consumption rises."[10] For example, the higher a family's income, the greater the tendency for the percentage of total family consumption going into housing and services to increase, items that essentially do not move in international trade or at least are not subject to duties (such as travel and entertainment).

Another significant feature of tariffs is the apparent global tendency for rates to be higher on labor-intensive imports than on capital-intensive imports regardless of whether a country is relatively well endowed with capital in relationship to labor or poorly endowed with capital in relationship to labor; that is, both industrialized countries and less developed countries tend to tax labor-intensive imports more heavily than capital-intensive ones. This tendency makes some sense for the less developed (poorer, labor-rich) countries; not for the industrialized (richer, labor-poor) countries. The result is that the poorer countries are denied access to the more developed markets in which their labor-intensive products would otherwise have a competitive advantage. The upshot is that these countries cannot earn the wherewithal to purchase the more capital-intensive products of the more industrialized countries. And both categories of countries suffer a negative income effect, the industrialized countries because they continue to produce labor-intensive products behind tariff walls, the cost of which is higher than need be the case if imports from the less developed countries were admitted duty free. The inflationary impact of this higher cost indirectly results in higher production costs for the capital-intensive goods, thereby having an adverse income effect on the less developed countries as these goods are sold to them. This argument has led to the generalized preferential treatment of LDC exports discussed above and to a general lowering of tariffs among the industrialized countries.

---

[10]Norman S. Fielke, "The Incidents of the U.S. Tariff Structure on Consumption," *Public Policy*, vol. 19, no. 4, Fall 1971, pp. 648–49.

The reasons for the tendency to tax the import of the more labor-intensive goods more highly are several:

1. Political vulnerability and pressure for protection tend to increase with labor intensity, for increased imports reduce employment (temporarily) more seriously than do capital-intensive imports.

2. Large-scale, extensive agriculture is relatively capital intensive, but basic agricultural crops are frequently subsidized in the more industrialized nations, thereby increasing price beyond the capacity of many poorer countries to pay and causing relatively high-priced agricultural production to be maintained in those countries.

3. The protection of domestic agriculture and mining (through import quotas), which are characteristically capital intensive, by some of the more developed countries, most notably the U.S., under the pressure of well organized lobbies which wish to maintain high commodity prices. (A quota is equivalent to an infinitely high import duty.)

4. Most countries have a tendency to levy a higher import duty on a completely assembled machine than on its component parts. (The former obviously is more labor-intensive than the latter.)

Most countries publish their respective tariff schedules following the Brussels Tariff Nomenclature (BTN), sometimes known as the Customs Cooperation Council Nomenclature (CCCN); some use the UN Standard International Trade Classification (SITC) or a variation thereof (such as the Tariff Schedule of U.S., or TSUS); and a few use their own system of classification (such as Canada).

Complete English-language translations of national tariff schedules are printed in the *International Customs Journal* (*Bulletin International de Douanes*) published by the International Customs Tariff Bureau in Brussels. This organization translates and publishes the tariff schedules of most of the world's countries into five languages.

The EEC uses the BTN classification system, and its common external tariff (CXT) rates are not excessive. Most raw materials enter duty-free or at very low rates, and rates on manufactured goods range generally from 5 to 20 percent. Some food products enter at higher rates. Free trade areas (such as EFTA) permit the duty-free movement of goods among themselves, but maintain their own external duties on imports from nonmember countries. In the case of free trade areas, there is normally either a value-added or a change-of-BTN-classification test for goods imported into one member and re-exported to a second member; that is, certain value must be added, or certain transformation of a product undertaken, in the original importing country if the good is to qualify for duty-free shipment into other member countries belonging to the free trade area.

In the case of the United States, as for most nations, a variety of import quotas and prohibitions are enforced, specifically:

Absolute quotas—excess imports being placed in bonded warehouses until the quota period is ended,[11]

Tariff rate quotas—tariff rate increases with quantity imported,

Quotas by source—such as sugar, for which quotas are assigned to certain supplying countries (characteristic of commodities subject to international commodity agreement or to long-term arrangements),

Absolute prohibitions—any imports from Cuba, North Korea, Vietnam, and, until 1971, the People's Republic of China; import of any product manufactured by forced labor, import of agricultural commodities deemed by the President to interfere with the domestic price-support program,

Special tariffs—following a finding of dumping, a duty designed to equalize the price with a fair market price may be imposed; in the event of foreign export subsidies, a countervailing duty may be imposed by the importing country,

Voluntary import quotas—in the U.S. case, oil until 1959, at which time the quota became mandatory,

Voluntary export quotas (or voluntary restraint arrangements)—such as that imposed by the Japanese government on certain exports to the U.S.

In the last case, voluntary export quotas, these quotas are enforced unilaterally by a supplying country (Japan vis-à-vis the U.S.) as a result of diplomatic pressure and/or the fear of the imposition of special protective tariff legislation by the importing country. As one commentator wrote of the Japanese export quotas:

It is not enough to say that most of these restrictions are made by Japan and can be altered by Japan. As a matter of law, this is true; but it does not accurately describe the relationship between the United States and Japan. The Japanese have shown great sensitivity to U.S. views; and leading U.S. officials have frequently praised and endorsed Japan's "self-restraint." In some cases, the unilateral abrogation by Japan of self-imposed export regulations would be regarded here (in the U.S.) as a breach of moral obligation by Japan. Such restrictions by Japan are truly voluntary only when the United States government ceases to endorse them and makes clear that they are inconsistent with fundamental U.S. trade policies.[12]

If a voluntary export quota is a multilateral arrangement, it may be known as a voluntary restraint arrangement (VRA) or long-term agreement (LTA). An example is the LTA on steel imports into the U.S. under which steel producers

---

[11]In the U.S. case, an important example was for many years the import of oil and certain agricultural products. The U.S. also has a long-term cotton textile agreement under which the U.S. controls the imports of cotton textiles under separate bilateral agreements with 24 countries, which account for 80 percent of U.S. cotton textile imports.

[12]Noel Hemmindinger, "Non-Tariff Trade Barriers of the United States" (Washington, D.C.: paper delivered to The United States–Japan Trade Council, 1964, abridged, mimeo).

of the United Kingdom, Japan, and European Community member-countries (who collectively accounted for 85 percent of total steel mill products imported into the U.S. in 1971) limit steel shipments to the U.S. to an increase of 2.5 percent per year.

A recurring problem is the selection of value of the imported good on which an *ad valorem* duty is to be assessed. Possible options (see Table 2.1) are (1) domestic price of competing products within the market into which it is being imported, such as American Selling Price (ASP), (2) invoiced price, (3) fair market price within the local market of the exporter, and (4) the price at which the seller exports a certain percentage of his product (if he can show that he exports, say, more than 50 percent of the product at a given price). Insistence by the U.S. in using an ASP basis has been the source of much friction between the U.S. and several of its major trading partners, notably those of the EEC and EFTA. The valuation basis can be an f.o.b. or c.i.f. price.

Products that do not fall neatly within BTN categories also cause problems. Very frequently a complete machine and its parts will carry different rates, rates for the parts generally being lower. If the parts can be used in machines listed in different BTN categories, the problem of classification arises. Tariff schedules of the U.S. (TSUS) vary from the BTN somewhat in that the TSUS frequently classifies items so that parts are not listed with the product to which they belong. In any event, an importer generally must pay the assessed duty and then appeal.

The general rule in the United States is that only the federal government may constitutionally levy taxes on imports. But at some point, of course, an import loses its "import" status and becomes vulnerable to taxation by individual states and municipalities. For the past century, the "original package" doctrine has held. Basically this provided that an import lost its distinctive character as an import, and became subject to state and local taxation, only when it was removed from the original package in which it had been brought into the country and mixed with other property in the state or locality. But a 1977 case narrowed that protection by a court ruling to the effect that a good loses its import status when it is "no longer in import transit," and at that point a nondiscriminatory personal property tax may be assessed by state or local government. Presumably the courts will follow the rules developed for goods in interstate commerce, likewise only taxable by the federal government.

One method of retaining foreign commerce status of goods is to place them in a foreign-trade zone. Even purely domestic goods are shielded from state and local taxation if the goods are moved into a zone for eventual export. There were free trade zones in 22 U.S. port communities as of early 1977, and more were contemplated.

Although imported goods in a bonded warehouse are considered outside U.S. Customs territory, as a free trade zone, such goods are treated somewhat differently. Those which can be withdrawn for export only, as ship's stores, are exempt from state and local taxation. But other goods that can be withdrawn

Table 2.1
METHOD OF DUTY ASSESSMENT

Country	Valuation basis	Duty assessment on specific rates
Australia	Transaction value, f.o.b. or current domestic value in the exporting country	Generally net weight
Austria	Brussels definition of value*	Gross weight if duty not over S 50/500 kgs., net weight if subject to higher rates, additional taxes for liquids, gases, and certain other products
Canada	Fair market value of like goods sold under similar conditions at place from which goods are exported or equivalent	Net weight or volume unless other specified
European Economic Community	Brussels definition of value	Net or gross weight as specified in customs tariff
Finland	Brussels definition of value	Generally net weight
Japan	Brussels definition of value	Net weight
New Zealand	Current domestic value in the principal markets of the country whence exported	Net weight
Norway	Brussels definition of value	Generally net weight
Sweden	Brussels definition of value	Generally net weight
Switzerland	Value at frontier	Generally gross weight
United States	Generally export value f.o.b. ASP for certain chemical products, alternative methods used in certain other cases	Generally net weight

Data: Tariffs and Trade Profiles by Industrial Product Categories, GATT, Geneva, May 1974.

*"Brussels definition of value" refers to normal price, plus freight, insurance, commissions, and all other charges and expenses incidental to the sale and delivery of the goods to the point of entry.

and placed in domestic commerce after payment of duty are generally not exempt from local or state property taxes. A few states have what are called "free port laws," which in general provide that goods in the process of being transported out of the state or out of the country are exempt from property or inventory taxes. Sometimes, as in California, the transit of such goods may be interrupted for repackaging and relabeling without becoming vulnerable to local taxation.

U.S. companies that import dutiable goods to be incorporated into export merchandise can get a refund of 99 percent of the duties paid when the goods are actually exported, the so-called "draw-back" provision. Similar provisions are found in the laws of many countries.

Nontariff barriers (NTB) to international trade are legion. We have cited but two examples here, the basis for assessment and classification. All of these NTBs must be taken into consideration in the decision to purchase offshore (to import) rather than to buy or produce locally. Added cost may be in the form of delay or additional paper work and documentation.

An important nontariff barrier in the U.S. case flows from the Buy American Act of 1933, which requires the federal government to buy only domestic materials unless (1) they are not available, (2) their purchase would not be in the public interest, or (3) the cost would be unreasonable. Unreasonable is defined by a 1954 Presidential order (still in effect) as more than 6 percent higher than the foreign bid. Another 6 percent differential is added if the material would be produced in a "depressed area" or by "small business." Materials are considered to be foreign if the cost of the foreign component constitutes 50 percent or more of the total cost. The Defense Department normally applies a 50 percent differential, whether for use domestically or overseas.[13] In fact, all U.S. government agencies, except A.I.D., purchase domestically for use overseas unless the domestic product is more than 50 percent above the delivered cost of comparable foreign goods. In addition, at least 17 of the 50 states discriminate in their purchases against foreign goods, sometimes without apparent statutory basis.[14] Other examples of U.S. nontariff barriers are legislation preventing the import of more than 1,500 copies of any English-language book authored by a U.S. citizen, a law requiring that all subsidized ship construction be done in U.S. shipyards and that related purchased equipment be of U.S. origin. Another example was the 1971 provision that the 10 percent investment tax credit (which was to become 5 percent after August 15, 1972) could be taken only if the investment were in capital goods of U.S. origin.

The U.S. government is not alone in pursuing buy-national policies, although most seem to base their discriminatory purchasing on internal administrative directives with a minimum of publicity, not as a matter of formal law as in the U.S.

---

[13]An exception is embedded in the United States-Canadian Defense Production Sharing Program, which places Canadian defense industry in the same position as U.S. industry.

[14]See Norman S. Fieleke, "The Buy-American Policy of the United States Government," *New England Economic Review*, Federal Reserve Bank of Boston, July–August 1969, p.7. In mid-1976 the New York State Court of Appeals nullified that state's "Buy American" policy, thus bringing to three the number of states whose protectionist purchasing policies had been struck down as unconstitutional. The others were Texas and California, whose rules were voided in 1963 and 1969, respectively.

Thus in France, the customary practice is to invite bids only from those contractors known by the administration, i.e., from only French contractors; in the Netherlands, government contracts are as a rule awarded only to persons domiciled in the Netherlands; in Japan a cabinet order authorizes the heads of ministries and agencies to limit competition in order to suppress the procurement of certain goods from foreign sources.[15]

Even though not made explicit in law or regulation, most European governments, in fact, automatically buy in the home market regardless of price and often do not even accept bids from foreign firms. And, of course, the public sector in some countries is relatively large, including all railroads, power generation, gas distribution, airlines, and sometimes oil refining and distribution. It is reported, for example, that only about 50 percent of the U.K. market is open to foreign manufacturers on a competitive basis, and that

U.S.-made transformers, generators and circuit-breakers are virtually excluded from Europe. The electrical industries of West Germany, France and Italy buy exclusively from large domestic manufacturers, and those that do buy abroad (usually because the equipment is not made locally) go to traditional European suppliers.[16]

An interesting example of national bias in government buying is embedded in the purchasing regulations of the Republic of South Africa. Government procurement in the republic is highly centralized, with responsibility vested in the State Tender Board, the deputy chairman of which is designated as the state buyer. He is responsible for calls for tenders and arranges the terms of contracts for the government. Briefly, the relevant rules are:

1. Tender notices are published only locally unless the product cannot be obtained domestically, in which case the board will approve the publication of tender offers abroad.

2. Only firms with agents in South Africa are eligible to render bids.

3. All bids must be c.i.f. and normally must include rail charges inside the republic.

4. Based on the local content of the goods, a specified percentage of the bid is deducted from the price up to 10 percent of the total bid. The board is then free to grant an additional 15 percent deduction for locally produced goods, another 2.5 percent deduction for goods bearing the mark of the South African bureau of standards, and an additional deduction if the Board of Trade and Industries recommends one.

5. In considering a foreign bid, the board will add on to the bid the applicable customs duty even though it will not have to be paid since the government is the recipient of the product.[17]

Other common, nontariff import barriers include withholding customs apprais-

---

[15]Fieleke, "Buy American Policy," p. 15.

[16]*Dun's*, October 1971, p. 48.

[17]A useful compendium of official regulations relating to buying by governments is *Government Purchasing* (Paris: Organization for Economic Cooperation and Development, 1976).

al in respect to imported goods, safety standards, labeling requirements, health standards, special documentation. Also important is national legislation requiring that certain services, often including common labor, as well as technical and professional personnel, be secured only from national sources. This may mean, for example, that foreign construction, engineering, and architectural firms are required to secure special permits to work locally. For a number of countries, such service firms can enter the local market only through joint venture with a local firm. In some countries the requirement for a security clearance for personnel employed by firms in defense-related industries may impose difficulty for the alien firm. Normally the U.S. requires that voting control be in the hands of U.S. nationals and that the management be almost wholly of U.S. citizens before issuing such clearances for a firm's personnel. Maintaining foreign ownership is thus exceedingly difficult. "Tied-buying" is another important type of NTB. This very commonly occurs in the case of economic assistance flowing between countries, such assistance being available only for the purchase of goods and services from the donor country. For example, certain U.S.-origin products were given a competitive edge in the Israeli market as a result of the U.S. commodity import assistance accorded to Israel in 1977. The consequence was that Israel received some $585 million in grants and loans, which could be used only to purchase designated U.S. products at market rates. Also, shipment on U.S. flag vessels of at least half of those goods purchased with U.S. economic assistance funds has been a long-standing rule.

The following classification of NTBs has been established by the UN Committee for Trade and Development (UNCTAD):

Type I *Commercial-policy measures designed primarily to protect import-competing suppliers from foreign competition*
Group A *Measures working through quantitative restraint*

1. Import quotas, globally administered
2. Import quotas, selectively or arbitrarily administered
3. Licensing, discretionary or restrictive
4. Licensing for statistical purposes and *"toute license accordee"*
5. Voluntary export restrictions, bilateral and multilateral
6. Import prohibitions—embargoes
7. Import prohibitions that are selective with respect to origin
8. State trading designed to protect import-competing suppliers
9. Domestic procurement policies and discriminatory government purchasing
10. Mixing, milling, and domestic-content regulations
11. Export restrictions

Group B *Measures working through increased costs and prices*

1. Variable levies, supplementary import charges, tariff quotas

2. Advance or preshipment import deposit regulations[18]

3. Anti-dumping duties and countervailing charges

4. Credit restraints on imports

5. Fiscal benefits for import-competing industries

6. Direct or indirect subsidization of import-competing industries

7. Discriminatory international transport charges by carriers under government influence

Type II *Measures designed to deal with problems not directly related to commercial-policy questions but which are from time to time employed for trade-restrictive ends*[19]

Research has shown that voluntary export restraints are the groups of NTBs most frequently applied to manufactured exports from less developed countries. Out of a total incidence of 2,950 Type I and Type II NTBs applied by 20 industrial countries to these exports, there were:

444 cases of voluntary export restraints

379 barriers due to safety and industrial standards

313 global quotas

273 selective quotas

246 barriers arising from customs–classification procedures

219 cases of discriminatory or restrictive import licensing

187 barriers due to customs–valuation procedures[20]

At a general level of aggregation, it does appear that manufactured exports from the developing countries have been more often subject to NTBs than have world exports of similar goods. It has been estimated that in 1967, 10.4 percent of the industrial countries' imports of manufactured goods from the less developed countries, excluding textiles and clothing, were subject to Type I NTBs, while only 4.3 percent of these advanced nations' total imports of the same goods were similarly restricted. The addition of textiles and clothing, which were most severely restricted of all the developing countries' manufactured exports, would greatly increase this 6 percent difference.[21]

If this finding be true, NTBs—as well as tariffs—tend to discriminate against the sale of products from the less developed countries in the more developed

---

[18]Refers to a requirement that a certain percentage of the value of an import be deposited in local currency with the government at the time the good is ordered, a deposit on which no interest is paid. An example: in 1972 Ecuador was imposing a 50 percent prior import deposit for essential goods, 100 percent for luxury goods.

[19]"Liberalization of Tariff and Non-Tariff Barriers" (Geneva: U.N. Committee on Trade and Development, TD/B/C.2/R.1, Annex 1, mimeo, 1969).

[20]"Liberalization of Tariff and Non-Tariff Barriers."

[21]Caroline Pestieau and Jacques Henry, *Non-Tariff Barriers as a Problem in International Development* (Montreal: Private Planning Association of Canada, 1972), summarizing the UNCTAD study.

countries. Little wonder that the LDCs exhibit a chronic balance-of-payments deficit.

But NTBs are by no means limited to trade between LDCs and the more developed countries. There is some evidence that NTBs have increased generally in relative importance as tariff barriers have been reduced. The Commission of the European Communities has for years been trying to break down NTBs within the community. A graphic illustration of the complexity of the EEC problem is provided by Table 2.2.

So onerous have the NTBs become that the 1977–78 round of GATT trade negotiations, known as the "Tokyo Round," focused on them for the first time. NTBs relevant to a firm's product must be considered in plotting supply strategy.

Technically speaking, the General Agreement on Tariffs and Trade (GATT) forbids member countries, which include all major trading nations outside the Sino-Soviet group, to discriminate in the application of import and export duties among member countries in that all contracting parties are bound by an MFN clause. Secondly, the GATT provides that protections shall be afforded domestic industries exclusively through the customs tariff and not through other measures such as quantitative quotas and other nontariff devices. However, import quotas may be used to redress a country's balance of payments, but only under specific circumstances and after consultation. In practice, many LDC members have maintained a quota-import licensing system without interruption. Also, most countries have restrictive legislation concerning the import of services, such as engineering, construction, architectural, and medical. (Curiously, international trade negotiators continue to think almost exclusively in terms of commodity trade, not at all in terms of the sale and purchase of services.) GATT also provides a framework for multinational negotiation for the purposes of reducing international trade barriers and avoiding damage to the trading interests of the contracting parties. There is one noteworthy exception to the nondiscriminatory provisions: adjacent countries (for example, the U.S. and Canada) and regional blocs (such as the EEC) may introduce preferential or zero tariffs vis-à-vis each other, but only with prior consultation. Within the GATT, free trade areas, customs unions, and common markets normally negotiate as units in respect to external tariff reductions.

In 1969 the GATT inventoried the nontariff barriers in place within member nations (the result: a 276-page catalogue of 844 categories of NTBs) and instituted a search for a basis for multinational negotiation toward their reduction. Specialists have learned that NTBs are extremely difficult to deal with in such negotiations, principally because many of the national negotiators do not have the authority to offer concessions in that the NTBs are embedded in statutes unrelated to foreign trade, and legislative action is required for liberalization.

Prior to 1962, the U.S. executive was authorized to negotiate reciprocal,

Technical standards:

1. German law prohibits importing of fuel with a high lead content (blocks the imports of French and Italian cars).

2. Technical equipment entering France must go through massive red tape and examination by the Ministry of Science and Industrial Development.

3. Strict German standards for packaging will inhibit imports of packaged foods and beverages after January 1, 1974.

4. The U.K. requires a costly "Air Worthiness" certificate for all aircraft.

5. Belgian law labels "pure wool" as 97 percent wool; this restricts French wool, which is 85 percent wool.

6. Italian standards on milk production require a health certificate of inspection at the time of milking and pasteurization, necessitating Italian customs inspection at plants in other countries (costly to Bavarian milk dealers).

7. French cheese standards do not permit importing of cheese produced from milk powder (protects market against some Dutch exports). The French also require health certification for honey and tinned fish.

Licenses:

1. Ireland requires licenses for imports of egg albumen and tobacco.

2. Italy requires licenses for imports of vinegar, cork, silk, umbrellas.

3. Germany requires licenses for worsted yarn and vinegar.

4. Belgium/Luxembourg require licenses for petroleum and chemical imports.

5. France requires licenses for petroleum and electronic components.

Restrictive sales practices and administrative obstacles:

1. French insurance rates place a special burden on the vehicles from other countries.

2. French auto manufacturers limit the amount of their cars that dealers in EEC countries may sell, which artificially keeps prices higher.

3. French repair shops, often directly controlled by the manufacturers, will sometimes delay their obtaining of spare parts for foreign makes to create an obstacle to their use.

Charges on imports:

1. Italy and France levy huge taxes on grain-based spirits.

2. Imports of wine into France must pay a special "wine-transport fee."

State aids which divert trade:

1. Germany gives assistance to the industry that regenerates waste oil by an equalization levy on regenerated oil imports.

2. France subsidizes the clock and leather industries through a quasi-fiscal charge levied on imports.

3. Italy taxes chemical pulp and paper imports to subsidize its own newspaper industry.

State-trading:

1. France has a state monopoly on phosphates that has sole selling rights.

2. Germany has an import monopoly on ethyl alcohol.

3. Italy and France have state monopolies on matches and alcoholic beverages.

Government (national) procurement policies:

1. All European governments have commitments to purchase domestically.

2. Germany limits use of architects on its projects to German nationals, even if the contract is with another country.

3. The Netherlands allows state industries a first call on resources, even if they have been reserved by another government.

4. Italy gives out its construction bids secretively and selectively without Community-wide announcement.

5. The French Electrical Company deals solely with French producers, allowing them to recoup research and development overheads.

Table 2.2
NONTARIFF BARRIERS IN THE EEC

Source: *Business International,* Oct. 12, 1973. p. 335.

item-by-item reductions of duties under the Reciprocal Trade Act of 1934, renewed eleven times by Congress. These laws were amendments to the high-tariff Smoot-Hawley Tariff Act of 1930, parts of which are still in effect, particularly the tariffs on imports from countries not granted "most favored nation" treatment. But in anticipation of a multinational negotiation within GATT toward the end of greater trading freedom ("the Kennedy Round"), the U.S. enacted the Trade Expansion Act of 1962, which gave the president latitude to negotiate. The most recent trade act, that of 1974, empowered the president to:

1. Reduce rates higher than 5 percent by 60 percent (if the reduction is greater than 10 percent, it takes effect over a 10-year period at an annual rate of no more than one tenth of the total reduction);

2. Eliminate duties in certain cases (such as in trade agreements with the EEC, where the United States and EEC accounted for 80 percent or more of free world export value; generally on products carrying rates of 5 percent or less; and on articles of tropical agriculture or forestry if not produced in the United States and provided the EEC has assured access to European markets comparable to that which the article would have in the United States);

3. Increase import duties up to 15 percent, to take such action as necessary to control imports when faced with balance of payments problems, or to increase duties up to 50 percent if imports have either caused or threaten to cause serious injury to a domestic industry;

4. Modify existing import restrictions other than duties (quotas, quarantine, inspection, licensing, documentation, and so forth);

5. Extend MFN treatment, grant Export-Import Bank credits, provide guarantees for credit and investment, and conclude commercial agreements with a socialist country if that country does not restrict immigration. (The Soviet Union's objection to this proviso has blocked ratification of a Soviet-U.S. trade agreement, which would have given MFN treatment to Soviet goods entering the U.S.);

6. Extend duty-free treatment to eligible imports from LDCs for a maximum of ten years.

Legislation limits the president in reducing tariffs on goods to a three-year commitment. He is also limited in respect to which there are outstanding proclamations under the national security provision, under the escape clause provision, or if the Tariff Commission has made a finding of injury but the president has not acted. In the last case, the president may either accept the findings and execute them or, if in disagreement, notify Congress and explain his reasons. Congress may override such presidential resolution. Otherwise, the president is free to act as he deems best within the limits of international agreements limiting the amount of import into the United States, such as international commodity agreements. A finding of injury can lead to either tariff rate increases or adjustment aid (such as low interest import-injury loan and retraining). The traditional tests used are: (1) has there been an increase in imports? (2) was the increase due to tariff reduction? (3) has U.S. industry been injured or threatened? and (4) was the injury due to increased imports? Obviously, unambiguous answers to (2) and (4) are difficult, and there has been a tendency for the Tariff Commission to ease up and to rely principally on (1) and (3). The escape clause mechanism is set in motion when a domestic industry feels threatened or is experiencing serious injury and petitions the Tariff Commission. A petition for relief may be filed by a trade association, firm, labor union, or groups of workers representative of an industry. Something like 1,000 petitions for adjustment assistance for workers were being received per year by the end of 1976, with possibly half resulting in some form of help.

Politically motivated sanctions by one country in respect to goods originating in other countries, as the past U.S. embargo on imports from the People's Republic of China, and the Arab country sanctions on Israeli goods, likewise may be an important consideration in the purchase of goods for sale in the target market.[22] Officially, as of mid-1972, the People's Republic of China would not trade with manufacturers and enterprises in Japan that (1) traded with or invested in Taiwan or South Korea; (2) were active in South Vietnam, Laos, or Cambodia; or (3) were joint ventures with U.S. firms or were subsidiaries of U.S. firms. In addition, the Japanese firm had to reject the Japanese government's position that Sino-Japanese trade should be separate from any political considerations. Specifically, the Japanese trader had to agree (1) not to take hostile policies toward China, (2) not to join any conspiracy supporting a two-China policy, (3) not to prevent restoration of normal relations between China and Japan, and (4) to support an official trade agreement between the two governments.

As noted in Section 1.12, most major trading countries have antidumping laws, under which a finding of dumping can lead to the imposition of either a countervailing tariff or a quota. Dumping occurs, of course, because of the geographically and politically segmented nature of the international market. Any time an exporter has idle capacity, he can justify exporting at a price sufficient only to cover the variable cost of the incremental production, plus some contribution to fixed cost. Any contribution to fixed cost is a net gain. Where fixed costs are relatively high (as in Japan, because of the high debt-equity ratios and the lifetime employment commitment), the pressure to use idle capacity to sell at variable cost-plus pricing (which in the Japanese case is relatively low) is irresistible. But how does one on the receiving end differentiate between that sort of situation (which represents true dumping), price

---

[22]Of interest is the fact that the U.S. government refused, until 1977, to adhere to the economic sanctions invoked with U.S. support by the U.N. Security Council against the white-dominated government of Rhodesia. However, a U.S. firm must be sensitive to the possibility of a customer boycott in one country by reason of its production or sales in another, as the threatened boycott of certain U.S. firms by U.S. customers because of the firms' activities in the Republic of South Africa or because of their import into the U.S. of goods from communist countries.

cutting because of greater efficiency, and marginal pricing by a firm that enjoys a monopoly or oligopolistic position in its domestic market?

In general, dumping refers to sales below "fair market value," which is equated with a price at which the product is freely offered in the country where produced. But under monopolistic or oligopolistic conditions (such as cartelization of an industry), or in a segmented market (one in which the same product is offered at different prices), what is the fair market value? One is then forced to consider cost of production plus a fair return, but few firms will release cost data, particularly to a foreign government. Indeed, they may be restrained from doing so by domestic law.[23]

Another element in the differential costs of purchases from various national sources may be export subsidies. Though technically illegal under the GATT, what amount to export subsidies are paid by a number of governments. These can take the form of (1) permitting export proceeds to be exchanged for local currency at an advantageous rate, (2) allowing the exporter to retain for his own use a portion of the foreign currency earned, (3) exempting exports from certain taxes (corporate income tax, value-added tax, and so forth). Consider what happens if one country relies heavily on corporate income tax (with no special treatment for export earnings) and its trading partner, on a value-added tax (that is, each party handling a product pays a tax based only on the value added by that party, which tax is shifted forward cumulatively to the final customer). It is relatively easy for the latter government to remit to its exporter part or all of the value-added tax and to justify doing so in that the consumer is foreign and should not be taxed. On the other hand, it is difficult for the income-tax-based country to separate out that tax income associated with exports and remit it to the seller. It is for this reason, among others, that the U.S. introduced in 1971 the concept of a domestic international sales corporation (DISC), a subsidiary corporation through which export sales could be invoiced. Generally, half of its income is not taxed in the United States until remitted to the parent. (See Section 7.3.)

The cost of physically moving goods internationally is likewise relevant to

---

[23]The usual test used by the U.S. is whether net f.o.b. factory price to a U.S. importer is less than net f.o.b. factory price to purchasers for consumption in the country of export. If the amount sold there domestically is so small (under 25 percent of the total) as to be an inadequate basis for comparison, then the test is the f.o.b. factory price for exports to countries other than the United States. If neither of these tests is feasible, then a "constructed value" is used, which consists of the sum of the direct cost of materials and labor, general expenses and profits characteristic of such goods (but general expense must be at least 10 percent of the direct costs, and profits at least 8 percent of both direct costs and general expenses), plus packing and other costs incurred in readying the goods for shipment to the U.S. From 1955 through 1963, only six antidumping findings (out of 286 investigations) were made that led to the imposition of countervailing duties; from 1964 through 1969, 14 cases (out of 87 investigations). The U.S. antidumping law requires the imposition of a countervailing duty once the fact of dumping or possible dumping is established. No injury need be found. In contrast, GATT rules require that injury must be proven before imposing a countervailing duty. At the time of entry into GATT, the U.S. entered a reservation on this matter. Export grants, preferred tax treatment for exports, government price support systems leading to export subsidies or government assumption of export losses, preferred export financing rates, special export foreign exchange rates, even the rebate of the value-added tax on export can be used to establish dumping.

the choice of supply source. This cost consists of insurance, freight, and handling charges (stevedoring, storage, special packaging). Curiously, it is often exceedingly difficult for a firm to secure specific rates prior to shipping. For instance, a firm might want to know the difference in freight rates for moving a product to the U.K. from, say, Boston, New Orleans, and Buenos Aires. The differential could be relevant to the decision as to which source to use in supplying the U.K. But both shipping lines and freight conferences seem reluctant to quote specific rates prior to the actual commitment.

The setting of rates is in the hands of so-called steamship conferences, sometimes called freight associations, which are simply groups of steamship owners (including governments, as in the Soviet case) operating in a particular direction over established routes (for example, the North Atlantic Westbound Freight Conference). Over 100 conferences are involved in U.S. trade. Their function is to eliminate freight rate competition among member lines (by allocating sailing dates, ports and schedules, or by pooling revenues), to standardize shipping practices, and to provide regularly scheduled service between designated ports. U.S. law exempts conference agreements from antitrust vulnerability, if agreements are filed and approved by the U.S. Federal Maritime Commission. The point is that once a ship is scheduled, approximately 70 to 75 percent of the costs of the voyage are fixed. In an overcapacity situation, competition for cargo would drive rates down below full cost and even approach the variable cost level, thereby endangering the shipping industry and leading to instability. The conferences were formed in order to prevent this sort of competition and to offer scheduled sailings over specified routes. It is a curious anomaly that the rate for the same commodity over the same route, but in different directions, may vary. For example, westbound rates across the North Atlantic are often lower than eastbound.

Rates are classified as an ordinary tariff (which is that specified by a conference), an open rate (a rate which by agreement is not set by the conference but by individual carriers), deferred rebate (refers to refunds of a percentage of one's freight payments to a shipper who does not use nonconference carriers for a stipulated period, a practice illegal in U.S. trade), contract (or dual) rates (exclusive contracts, which may reduce rates up to 15 percent), or project rates (exclusive contracts relevant to particular projects, which may reduce rates by 50 percent).

Rates are generally quoted on a commodity basis, but items for which no specific rates are quoted pay a general cargo rate (n.o.s.—not otherwise specified). So long as a commodity rate yields revenue somewhat in excess of direct costs of lifting and discharging that commodity, it makes a net revenue contribution. It is not essential that each commodity over each route make the same net revenue contribution per ton. Hence, there is some latitude in conference rate-making for promotional and other special-purpose rates. Therefore, shippers with some leverage may find it advantageous to negotiate with a conference for a special rate. In general, rates are a function, not of sea distance, which represents only a very small part of total cost, but rather of (1) commodity value per unit of weight; (2) relative cost of transport to total product cost; (3) potential volume of movement; (4) competition on the route; (5) urgency of the shipment; (6) special direct costs or risks, such as susceptibility to damage and pilferage, need for special storage and heavy lifts, extra length, turnaround time in ports, port costs, canal tolls; (7) relationship of weight to volume; (8) possibility of securing return cargoes; (9) pick-up and delivery at nonscheduled ports; (10) relationship between carrier and shipper (contract or dual rates); and (11) political and public relations considerations.

Air freight rates are set by the International Air Transport Association (IATA), the members of which include virtually all of the international air carriers other than charter companies. IATA's rate-making function is performed through three regional traffic conferences (Conference One—Western Hemisphere; Conference Two—Europe, Africa, Middle East; Conference Three—Asia, Australia, South Pacific). The rationale for rate setting, scheduling, and so forth, is roughly the same as in the case of the marine carriers. Air cargo rates have been decreasing steadily over the past decade. The saving to the shipper and/or user in going to the air comes, of course, from faster delivery, less likelihood of stoppages, lower inventories, lower working-capital requirements, and hence, lower interest charges. It can also close the time between financial commitment by the firm and collection, which in an explosive inflationary situation could be critical.

2.2 PURCHASING

In the event the firm opts to purchase rather than to manufacture, the question arises as to whether the firm should limit purchases to its local market or scan the international horizon for the best deals. This decision is very largely a function of:

1. Local shortages (persistent, seasonal, cyclical);

2. Foreign exchange controls;

3. Differential costs (tariffs, nontariff barriers, export subsidies, insurance, freight);

4. Internationalization of the firm in terms of sales or production;

5. The availability to the company at reasonable cost of the skills needed for successful importing;

6. Effectiveness of antiforeign bias on the part of the ultimate customer (for example, how apparent is the foreign component or the foreignness of the product?);

7. The sensitivity of organized labor (which possibly mounts with the labor intensity of the component or product concerned);

8. The appeal of foreign goods (particularly to market segments; for instance, the appeal of Israeli goods to the Jewish community in the United States).

Also relevant, of course, are the restraints imposed by intercompany or intracompany agreements (see Sections 1.7 and 1.8). A parent firm with surplus inventory may force it upon an associated foreign enterprise. Whether legal or not, license or technical assistance contract may provide for *tied buying*, a requirement that the recipient of the license or of assistance buy certain products from the contractor in order to retain the contractual rights (see Section 1.12). It should be noted that what constitutes the "best deal" for the foreign enterprise may be defined more in terms of delivery time, ability to effect change orders (such as deletions from assembly kits as local manufacture increases), the currency required, terms of payments, and quality, rather than in terms of mere price.

Local shortages translate themselves, of course, into high or unstable prices. Where a country is deliberately trying to maintain relatively high price levels to protect local industry, legal barriers in the form of import prohibitions or quotas may exist. In the U.S. case, this reasoning has applied to certain price-supported agricultural products and to oil, zinc, lead, textiles, and steel. To hedge against seasonal or cyclical shortages, that is, price changes, a firm may deliberately develop offshore sources, even at higher short-run cost. In some cases, of course, the materials wanted are simply not available locally, nor can local sources be developed economically, given economies of scale and production and the availability of the relevant technology.

Overseas purchase involves both foreign export controls (see Section 1.2) and local import restrictions, the latter being linked frequently in less developed countries to a foreign exchange control system. Both an import license (often based on a quota system) and a foreign exchange permit (a permit to use local currency for the purchase of foreign currency) may be required, in which case a smooth flow of imported components may be impossible to maintain. Huge inventories of some components, shortages of others, and interrupted production may be the results. Much longer lead time is often required than in the case of local purchase and, hence, the importance of planning is magnified. Inventory control then becomes critical. An additional cost element may enter the picture in that the importer may be required to make an interest-free, local currency deposit in the Central Bank of a specified percentage of the price of the imported good at the time of applying for, or receiving, an import license and foreign exchange permit. This obligation can easily add another 10 to 20 percent to the cost of the imported good.

Relevant to the selection of supply source for a given market is the variety of special international trade relationships described in the appendix to this chapter. These may both hinder (increase cost) or facilitate (reduce cost) international movement.

Not widely appreciated are the highly specialized skills required for efficient importing. Briefly, they may be summarized as follows:

1. Finding a reliable supplier;

2. Predicting shortages or stoppages (at the source or in transit, such as a dock strike);

3. Advising sellers as to appropriate markings, documentation, packaging, means of transport;

4. Selecting the least-cost method of moving the goods if the firm has opted for an f.o.b. or f.a.s. purchase rather than c.i.f.;

5. Passing the tariff barrier (that is, determining the value of the goods, placing them in the appropriate lowest duty category, anticipating the final assessment of duties —which may occur many months after an actual import, arguing various official rulings before relevant bodies);

6. Identifying all relevant nontariff barriers and devising ways of dealing with them at least cost;

7. Maintaining an import equilibrium in respect to locally manufactured competitive products (so as to avoid retaliation by domestic producers through price wars or politically pressured dumping charges and/or increase in duties);

8. Assuring the availability of associated services to customers which, of course, may be oneself if the importing firm is the user (such as effective guarantees of quality and measure);

9. Following changes in legally imposed local import restrictions and foreign export controls.

The degree of skill required is related to the degree the firm penetrates toward the foreign source in its buying. Relatively low-level skill is perhaps adequate if the importing is done external to the firm; that is, through independent importers, resident foreign sellers, combination importer-managers, cooperative import associations, import brokers, or locally situated distributors. A much higher level of skill is needed if the firm buys abroad direct from overseas export commission houses or merchants, or through its own buyers, agencies, branches, or subsidiaries located overseas. As in the case of exporting, the choice of channel rests largely on volume, legal restraints, degree to which competitors control existing channels, the international structure of the firm, and existence within the firm of the relevant skills.

2.3   INTERPLANT RELATIONSHIP

When management determines the productive processes that the firm itself should undertake within the supply area chosen for the target market, a secondary question emerges: Is a single plant or a multiplant setup optimum? This problem comes up quite frequently in an emerging common market or free trade area. There may be immediate advantages to unity in manufacturing, but, on the other hand, a concentration of productive facilities in one national market creates a certain uneasiness about the possibilities that the trade area or common market may eventually pull apart. As soon as one moves into a multiplant operation—a decision that is in part a function of perceived risk, lumpiness in economies of scale, the nature and diversity of the product line, and the domestic pattern of production—the choice ranges from plant specialization (by product or process) to the absence of such specialization. For long-established plants in Western Europe, for instance, this process of *rationalization* may be costly, both financially and psychologically, as plants are split apart and new bundles of processes or products brought together. But delay may be even more costly. A third alternative is *manufacturing interchange* whereby each plant manufactures a specified set of parts, all exchange with one another, and all assemble the same products. For a highly complex product, the problem of flow control is almost insoluble. Also, a work stoppage at any one plant shuts down all. Hence, there is a pressure for large inventories to build up in the system. Different governments may impose varying standards as to size, content, durability, load, quality, and so forth. Organized labor may offer effective opposition to the introduction of certain labor-saving innovations in one country, and not in another. Nonetheless, some companies have moved in the direction of manufacturing interchange. In 1976, the president of Ford Motor Company reported:

> *In 1967, we established Ford of Europe to coordinate the activities of our national companies throughout Europe so that our car and truck business could be conducted on a more integrated basis. Until then, our operations in Britain and the other Western European nations had been separate and distinct and virtually autonomous. (The cars we built in Germany and Britain were so different that most of the components were not interchangeable.)*
>
> *Today, Ford engineers in Germany may work on bodies and British engineers on engines of basically the same automobile for assembly in both countries or in a third country.*
>
> *Through this multinational sourcing, we avoid duplication of tooling costs, maximize product quality by limiting the number of industrial processes for which each affiliate is responsible, and achieve lower unit costs through higher volume production. The consumer benefits, we benefit. And the economies of the host nations benefit most of all.*[24]

Closely associated with the notion of manufacturing interchange is the production-sharing concept, which is a form of international barter. A company exports an entire industrial plant and receives products from that plant in payment. A large European textile group spins, weaves, and dyes fabric, all high technology, capital intensive processes, and then airlifts the cloth to Morocco, Malaysia, or Indonesia for conversion into garments, bedding, rugs, towels, upholstery fabrics, or curtains. The finished product is airlifted back for sale in Europe. The participating firms are not related through ownership. Peter Drucker wrote:

---

[24] Lee A. Iacocca, address to the National Foreign Trade Convention, November 16, 1976.

Production sharing may, in the last quarter of this century, become as dominant in the world economy as the traditional multinational corporation became in the world economy of the last 20 years. Paradoxically, the multinational that organizes production sharing will be more controversial than ever.[25]

The reasons for the controversy: increased LDC dependency upon external relationships with the "wicked capitalists," and intensified trade union opposition in the home country as the number of displaced workers grows (even though production sharing is likely to create more jobs than it displaces, but different jobs, for better educated workers). Some have suggested that a U.S. management may find itself under some obligation to discuss with labor any action that eliminates jobs, including a shift to foreign sourcing. In 1969, the International Union of Electrical Workers proposed to General Electric a contract clause that would have prevented the company from transferring any operation abroad without union approval. GE refused and was upheld in this refusal by the National Labor Relations Board. In 1970, the United Auto Workers Union challenged Ford's decision to produce Pinto engines in Europe for cars to be assembled in the United States. Ford successfully resisted.[26] But the situation could change.

An obstacle to production sharing is the diversity of industrial standards, although there is considerable pressure to develop either regional or worldwide standards, whether related to truck loads, navigational aids, railroad gauges, electrical connections, dress and shoe sizes, voltage and frequency, building codes, fire insurance underwriter codes, automobile safety and pollution, food preservatives, color televisions, tire sizes, pharmaceutical standards, screw threads, pipe and pipe fittings, building modules, shaft and flange sizes, or environmental pollution. The absence of international standards may be a significant obstacle (added cost) in the international transfer of technology.

A study of inducements to foreign investment in the U.S. revealed that safety and health restrictions were mentioned by pharmaceutical manufacturers as a principal reason to invest.

The Pure Food and Drug Administration will not accept the results of testing done outside the United States. Manufacturers, therefore, have to maintain duplicate laboratories inside and outside of the United States in order to carry out testing and to assure that there is not too great a time lag between the time that a new drug is developed and the time the companies are given permission to sell in the United States. Once they are ready to produce the goods, they find it practically impossible to import. They can import ingredients if the final mixing and assembly is done in the United States. A manufacturer of films in which foods are wrapped likewise found it impossible to import into the United States due to health regulations.[27]

---

[25]"The Rise of Production Sharing," *Wall Street Journal*, March 15, 1977, p. 22.

[26]Duane Kujawa, "Foreign Sourcing Decisions under the Duty to Bargain under the NLRB," *Law and Policy in International Business*, 1972, pp. 497 ff.

[27]John D. Daniels, *Recent Foreign Direct Manufacturing Investment in the U.S.* (New York: Praeger, 1971), p. 54.

Curiously, the greater intensity with which the U.S. examines new drugs and pharmaceuticals, and the delay thereby induced before a new product can be sold to the public (often three to five years), generates the movement of research and development in the opposite direction as well. Inasmuch as the licensing of new drug and pharmaceutical products tends to take less time in most European countries, there is a temptation for U.S. firms to introduce them there first, and indeed, much to the dismay of some of the U.S. public, many new products are available in Europe years before introduction in the U.S. Producing companies are inclined to locate their manufacturing facilities in Europe for this reason, in which case the location of research and development facilities in Europe as well becomes attractive. National differentials in regulation of this sort can set up flows of both investment and technology.

Recognition of the need for harmonization of national standards has led to the creation of international standards bodies of a nontreaty nature, notably the International Organization for Standardization (ISO) and its 100-odd technical committees, the International Electrotechnical Commission (IEC), and the Pan-American Standards Commission (COPANT). Many of the national members of these organizations are supported and funded by their respective governments. By way of contrast, the U.S. member, the American National Standards Institute, has been supported entirely by the private sector. Federal participation has been limited to the supply of certain technical information and some experts. In a few cases, a purely private organization may enforce standards so that nonstandard products are blocked effectively from the market, either by law or by the nonavailability of insurance. An example is the Underwriters Laboratory in the United States, whose approval must be obtained, according to the laws of some of the 50 states, if an electrical appliance is to be sold within those states. Otherwise insurance is vitiated. Are foreign products judged by the same criteria as competing domestic products? On occasion, foreign producers have seemed skeptical.[28] Other countries have similar organizations, such as the Swedish Institute for Testing and Approval of Electrical Equipment.

Members of the national standards bodies of the EEC and of EFTA have formed the European Standards Coordinating Committee (CENEL). Because of the nonparticipation of non-European countries in CENEL's product testing and certification procedures, these may be used as the basis for nongovernmental, nontariff barriers.

A major problem in the international standards area has been the nonuse of the metric system by the United States, along with Brunei, Burma, Liberia, and Yemen. The U.S. finally committed itself to metrification in late 1975 with

---

[28]Recently, the U.S. government actually brought an antitrust case against a U.S. trade association and the testing organization used in the trade on the grounds that the two were conspiring to restrict U.S. imports by means of refusing to certify that the imported goods fulfilled U.S. technical specifications even when they did.

the passage of legislation on the subject, although open-ended and without any compulsory features. The United Kingdom, long a holdout, had decided on such a course a decade before.

A measure of the difficulty in the standards area is the fact that something like 20,000 engineering standards are needed to maintain an industrialized society and that in the U.S., national standards are issued by some 400 organizations. Obviously, many LDCs are unable to generate their own national standards, even if they so desired and, hence, have adopted those of the ISO and IEC, which have emerged as the strongest international standard bodies.

Whether a management opts for a single or multiplant solution—and if the latter, whether specialized or autonomous—depends upon a set of considerations, chief among them being the cost of moving products, economies of scale to be achieved through plant specialization, relative ease of introducing new products, the cost of reshuffling existing productive facilities (transfer of machines, workers, managers; customer reaction; response by organized labor; political reprisal; legal barriers), effect on inventory levels (and, hence, on working capital), adequacy of new local suppliers, the risk (and, hence, cost) inherent in specialized plants, probability of controls on product or service movement among the plants becoming unduly costly, nature of the product, nationality of management, and ownership of the various parts.

In respect to the last: if it is deemed necessary to have diverse ownership patterns, or, indeed, anything departing from equity-based control by a single parent, then the tie-in buying and selling inherent in the manufacturing interchange relationship may be deemed illegal under both U.S. and foreign antimonopoly law (see Section 7.3). In this case, the problem of mutually acceptable transfer pricing likewise comes up. Also, if the policy is for management of each plant to be in the hands of local nationals, the difficulty of instituting effective control over who makes what may be compounded if different products or components have varying prestige values in the minds of key executives (such as, degree of modernness, size, complexity), for then elements of national pride may become involved. And, in the event of varying degrees of strategic significance of the alternative products (military applications, basic pharmaceuticals), official intervention in the allocation may be expected.

2.4 PLANT DESIGN

A management may be so domestically oriented that a "plant" is assumed to be a *given* bundle of processes undertaken with a unique set of machines whatever the surrounding factor mix (for example, as reflected in a lower natural resource price, higher interest rate, lower unskilled labor/skilled labor wage ratio, higher profit expectations, lower tax rates). Only one part, at best a small part, of the production function is within the range of management vision.

But if management sees a "plant" as a variable, then the local environment becomes relevant, and a set of decisions is required, which in a general way has to do with determining the desired balance between machine and labor skill, given relative capital and labor costs. In other words, how much skill should be built into the machine? How much into labor? If skilled labor is scarce and costly, if publicly supported institutions are not producing the skilled persons, then it may be less costly to invest in the skilled machines. But skilled machines are often special-purpose machines that require long production runs to bring down per-unit depreciation cost to a feasible level. On the other hand, more general purpose machines often require a higher level of labor skill and closer quality control, which in many markets is difficult to come by at a feasible cost. An optimum solution in this case might be highly flexible (such as multipurpose) skilled machines. But given the range of present technical feasibility, it may be more practical to fragment jobs, thereby simplifying the training function, and to superimpose a few highly trained trouble-shooters. Capital costs may, of course, be brought down by the installation of second-hand machines if permission of the host government can be secured for their import and agreement reached as to their capital value.[29]

At least one firm (Gillette) introduced the notion of the mini-plant, a plant specifically designed to produce the *lowest* volume of product possible at a feasible cost. The General Motors Basic Transport Vehicle program was likewise designed to achieve economic efficiency at very low volume.

The actual purchase of the machines deemed most appropriate may well be influenced by considerations other than initial price, such as the currency in which purchase is made, durability (in a high capital-cost situation, investment locked in long-lived machines may be unduly costly), ease of repair, and safety features (requirements may vary nationally, as for electrical wiring).

In commenting on the appropriateness of automated techniques in less developed countries, Baranson observes that the solution rests upon several interrelated criteria and constraints, specifically, (1) the scale of production, (2) precision or quality requirements, (3) the stage of development of supplier industries, (4) the availability of management and technical skills, (5) wage rates relative to capital costs, (6) the supply of factory labor, and (7) national employment goals. He adds, "The necessity for using automated techniques is often implicit in the product."[30]

Baranson summarizes his study of the Kirloskar-Cummins venture in India to manufacture truck-type diesel engines in India:[31]

---

[29]An interesting example of the adaptation of production techniques is given by Jack Baranson, *Manufacturing Problems in India, the Cummins Diesel Experience* (Syracuse: Syracuse University Press, 1967), pp. 63–69.

[30]Jack Baranson, "Automated Manufacturing in Developing Economies," *Finance and Development*, vol. 8, no. 4, 1971, p. 12.

[31]Baranson, *Manufacturing Problems in India.*

At the U.S. plant in Colombus, Indiana, equipment was designed and selected for high-volume, capital-intensive production. Most of the machine tools were single purpose, multistation, and multispindled; this meant one machine might drill sixty holes in each of five cylinder blocks at one pass. Narrow tolerances on diesel engine parts required the highest precision in tooling. Automatic control devices generally replaced operators' skills, thereby building quality control into the machine and reducing the need for inspection of machined parts. But these more expensive, quality machine tools are warranted only in high-volume production. Some multipurpose, single-operation equipment was used for low-volume parts at the U.S. Cummins plant, but even there, machine tools were tape-controlled for economy and precision. In converting equipment and techniques to the Indian plant's low-volume requirements, machine precision and control had to be replaced by human skills and organizational capabilities. Virtually all of the extra tooling and fixtures required on the lower-volume equipment had to be custom made in the Indian plant's own tool-and-die shop. As a result, for a plant with one twentieth the output, the Indian plant required a tool shop with about twice the facilities and three times the skilled labor of the U.S. plant. The Cummins compromise in tooling—given the quality and volume constraints—is indicative of the dilemma faced by plants in developing countries, particularly in the replicating of sophisticated industrial components and little or no adjustment in product design.[32]

Baranson concludes his discussion as follows:

For developing countries, it is not an either/or choice between automation and handicraft technology. Technology should be viewed as a continuum of production techniques, with choices depending on the one hand on the scale and precision of production, and on the other on wage rates relative to capital costs—within the emerging framework of manpower skills and industrial capabilities. Developing countries should adapt appropriate technology, which will vary according to product lines, market opportunities, and the evolving capabilities of industry. In order to follow this path, however, long-term investments in research and engineering capabilities (manpower and institutions) will have to be made. The general tendency is for a widening of the technological gap between developing and advanced economies. This would seem to point to the need for the development of indigenous capabilities to adapt industrial product designs and production systems to help offset this gap.[33]

Writing in reference to Latin America, Stephen and Douglas Hellinger observed:

Although there exists no comprehensive data, the available information suggests that MNCs rarely adapt their production processes when they transfer them to Latin America.

---

[32]Baranson, "Automated Manufacturing," pp. 12–13.

[33]Baranson, "Automated Manufacturing," p. 17. An extreme example of the adaptation of technology is embodied in *Village Technology Handbook* (Schenectady: Volunteers for International Technical Assistance, Inc., 1970). VITA enlists the services of some 5,000 scientists and technicians from 64 countries to provide free technical assistance dealing largely with technology adaptation. Other useful volumes are *A Handbook on Appropriate Technology* (Ottawa, Canada: Canadian Hunger Foundation and Brace Research Institute, McGill University, 1976); the publications of the Intermediate Technology Development Group, International Development Centre of London, England; *Choice and Adaptation of Technology in Developing Countries* (Paris: Organization for Economic Cooperation and Development, 1974), and Kenneth Darrow and Rick Pam, *Appropriate Technology Sourcebook* (Stanford, Calif.: Volunteers in Asia, 1975).

Of the R & D they have done overseas, practically all has been performed so as to scale down production techniques for smaller markets, adapt them to local materials, or adjust them to conform to consumer tastes (especially in the case of food processing). Yet changes of this kind have been carried out infrequently.

Mason,[34] in his study of foreign enterprises operating in Mexico and the Philippines, found that the research efforts of the vast majority of them culminated in only minor adaptations in existing technology. Of greater concern, in light of Latin America's employment problems, is the extremely small amount of R & D that has been undertaken for the purpose of adapting to local factor problems.[35]

Another authority on international production problems wrote:

Scope for substitution of labor for capital by multinational companies is considerably greater than is typically put in practice. This is indicated by recent studies, which point out that closer attention could substantially alter current practice.[36] In cross-cultural transfers of technology, heated debates are not uncommon among qualified managers and engineers who work from different environmental assumptions and information with respect to machine output and tolerances, supervisor capability, operator performance, and—not least—discontinuities and bottlenecks. In addition, it has been noted that "the lack of 'disaggregated' analysis of equipment and process abroad appears to be due to the shortage of middle management experienced and competent in this sort of detailed analysis."[37] Steps to produce and disseminate evidence on the whole range of options relevant to least-cost performance are clearly important in the training and development of middle managers, supervisors, and skilled workers.[38]

In reference to this last point, it is quite clear from the deliberations on appropriate technology that took place at the OECD Development Center in 1972[39] that the range of possible technologies may be substantially greater than that suggested by the experience of U.S., European, and Japanese-based industry. One program, which originated in Mexico in 1964 and was based on ten years of experience accumulated by the development and engineering group of the du Pont Company of Mexico, resulted in the identification of some 1,100 chemical products of interest in the Mexican context and the development of a "basic modules language." This latter was simply an identification of separate transformations required for the production of these

[34]Hal Mason, *The Transfer of Technology and the Factor Proportion Problems: The Philippines and Mexico* (New York: United Nations Institute for Training and Research, 1970), p. 54.

[35]Stephen H. Hellinger and Douglas A. Hellinger, *Unemployment and the Multinationals* (Port Washington, N.Y.: Kennikat Press, 1976), pp. 84–85.

[36]Reference is to C. Wickham Skinner, *American Industry in Developing Economies: The Management of International Manufacturing* (New York: John Wiley & Sons, 1968) and to W. Yeoman, *Selection of Production Processes for the Manufacturing Subsidiaries of U.S.-Based Multinational Corporations* (Boston: Harvard Graduate School of Business Administration, unpublished Ph.D. dissertation, 1968).

[37]Quoted from Yeoman, *Production Processes.*

[38]Richard Morse, "Decision Factors in Comparative Manufacturing Advantage, An International Research Program" (Cambridge: Massachusetts Institute of Technology, Center for International Studies, mimeo, September 1971), p. 6.

[39]*Choice and Adaptation of Technology in Developing Countries* (Paris: Organization for Economic Cooperation and Development, 1974).

chemical products, but without specification as to process or hardware.[40] All reasonable processes to effect a given transformation were then listed, together with their cost characteristics. The engineer is thus in the position to select the optimum program. Obviously, the choice of one particular process for one module can impact on the choice of processes in other modules, so one comes up with a rather complex, iterative process that lends itself to computerization. Girai, the initiator of the Mexican study and a long-time du Pont employee, commented, "I was impressed by . . . [comments] . . . about the economies of scale being often exaggerated. Small and medium industries adapt more easily and contribute in countries such as Japan substantially to the national product and [to] exports . . . . We tend to be overwhelmed by the phantom of the scale problem."[41] It should also be pointed out that it seems very likely that private business will be asked increasingly to justify the technology that it uses in the developing countries. Governments can be expected to become ever more sensitive to the deepening unemployment confronting them. Grant writes, ". . . these countries will place a particularly high premium on foreign investments which promise to provide, directly or indirectly, significant added employment. If the developed countries encourage—or at least permit—the current trend toward the internationalizing of production that is by nature labor-intensive, the image of foreign investment should be enhanced."[42]

Obviously, there are some restrictions on capital substitution. Empirical studies by the United Nations on certain process-type industries (chemical, cement, and metal refining) demonstrate that certain restraints operate in the case of less developed countries. Among the reasons for relatively high capital/output ratios in the LDCs as compared with the more industrially advanced countries are (1) smaller scale of operations; (2) lower levels of efficiency in machine utilization by reason of poorer organization and control; (3) the need for each plant to maintain its own repair and maintenance facilities and, in some cases, its own power plant; and (4) long initial periods of overcapacity as market and production skills are developed.[43] And, if the firm must supply technical assistance or debt (possibly in the form of prepayment) to its subcontractors, its capital/output ratio may be increased still further. To these reasons can be added recurring periods of overcapacity—and possibly a build-up of inventories of incomplete products—as the flow of imported supplies is intermittently shut off due to the nonavailability of foreign exchange or the flow of supplies from local subcontractors is interrupted due to poor production and quality control and material shortages. If the firm's production machinery is of a specialized nature, it is not easy to shift

---

[40]OECD, *Choice and Adaptation*, pp. 79–85, 182–86.

[41]OECD, *Choice and Adaptation*, p. 128.

[42]James P. Grant, "Multinational Corporations and the Developing Countries: The Emerging Jobs Crisis and Its Implications" (Washington: Overseas Development Council, January 1972, mimeograph).

[43]United Nations, "Projection of Demand for Industrial Equipment," *Industrialization and Productivity*, Bulletin 7 (1964), pp. 11–12.

production temporarily to the manufacture of other products in the event of such interruption. One tractor producer in Turkey was able to do so only because it had inherited a building full of general-purpose machine tools. When the tractors could no longer be produced because the flow of essential imported components was shut off, the firm survived by turning to the manufacture of a simple agricultural pump which required no imported parts or materials.

One of the hypotheses raised in a series of UN studies on the transfer of technology and the factor-proportions problem is that the inability of less developed countries "to absorb labor at a more rapid pace is the result of inappropriate choice of technology rather than a matter of lack of technological alternatives."[44] It is argued that in the LDCs the interest rate or cost of capital is artificially depressed through subsidies while wage rates are raised unduly high by reason of social welfare programs modeled after those found in the more developed countries. Thus, the relative factor prices make attractive the utilization of too much capital and too little labor, and unemployment arises. It is suggested that "multinational firms could play a role in this process if they confront a different set of factor price relationships than do locally controlled firms."[45] Some of the possible reasons are as follows:

Capital is cheaper for the developed country's [DC] firm because it has access to a lower-cost capital market and enjoys various investment incentives (fast write-offs, tax forgiveness, subsidized land) which tend to cheapen capital.

Labor is more expensive for the DC firm because local firms are more knowledgeable of local customs and are more able to operate successfully in lower labor-cost areas, such as in villages and provincial towns; also the DC firm often opts to pay higher than the going wage.

The DC firm may require the use of more capital than is appropriate because it restrains the choice open to local subsidiary managers in respect to technology (that is, standardization on plant design developed elsewhere because it is "well known" or "most advanced" or because the interchangeability of parts and skills inherent in standardization generates perceived economies).

The availability of only capital-intensive production processes, many of which are proprietory to DC companies. (Thus, if such production is undertaken in an LDC, it is likely to be done by a DC firm.)[46]

In fact, in a study of Mexican and Philippine enterprises it was found that the local facilities of U.S. firms were indeed more capital intensive than their local counterparts in the capital-per-worker sense, largely because of heavier investment in buildings and inventory, not in machinery. But, at the same time, the U.S. subsidiaries reported a higher value-added per worker (productivity) and

[44]R. Hal Mason, *The Transfer of Technology and the Factor Proportions Problem: The Philippines and Mexico* (New York: U.N. Institute for Training and Research, Research Reports, no. 10, 1971), p. 1.

[45]Mason, *Transfer of Technology*, p. 3.

[46]Mason, *Transfer of Technology*, pp. 19–22.

higher wage rates than did the local firms. The result was that the ratio of wage bill to capital service flows for the U.S. firms was only slightly lower. Little evidence was uncovered suggesting that local firms systematically emulated their U.S. counterparts in terms of technology, wages, and skilled-unskilled labor mix. The UN Mexican-Philippine study concluded:

What is most interesting in comparing the two samples is that much different systems and technologies yield capital to labor flow ratios and total factor productivities which are not greatly different between the two groups. We conclude tentatively that a strong case cannot be made for multinational firms being a major source of the factor proportions problem. We should look instead ever more closely to the incentive systems provided by the developing countries themselves.[47]

Another UN-sponsored study concluded:

The material gathered by questionnaire and interviews with business firms by the present author as well as recently published literature supports the conclusion that in many if not most large-scale manufacturing operations, the opportunity for choosing from among the available technologies a more economically efficient and at the same time labour-intensive technique is extremely limited. Perhaps more important, there is a consensus that such successful modifications as have been made have resulted from disaggregating the production function and seeking out those operations that may be effectively modified, notably in the handling of materials in the plant. A significant number of replies to the UNITAR questionnaire indicate that foreign firms have looked into the possibilities with reasonable care and have made adaptations mainly in materials handling operations and in construction operations as well as in the simpler repetitive operations in technologically unsophisticated forms of food processing, pharmaceutical packaging and the like. There is also some evidence—of which certain paper and pulp mills in developing countries are an example—of reduced use of automation in control mechanisms.[48]

A UNITAR questionnaire directed to foreign direct investors contained the question, "In hindsight, would you change the original technical decisions in plant design, production techniques or product designs; if so, in what ways and for what reasons?" With very few exceptions, it is reported, the reply was negative. A number of managers did express awareness of the desirability of substituting labor for capital when possible. A "typical" response follows:

We have made no change in production techniques, excepting in some areas additional labour manhours are substituted for machine time and mechanical processes due to the lack of some machining capabilities in the Mexican plant. This substitution is possibly due to the lower existing wage rates.[49]

The modification of production techniques to use less sophisticated equipment

[47]Mason, *Transfer of Technology*, pp. 64–65.

[48]Walter A. Chudson, *The International Transfer of Commercial Technology to Developing Countries* (New York: Institute for Training and Research, Research Reports, no. 13, 1971), pp. 25–26.

[49]Chudson, *International Transfer*, p. 30.

and to scale down the size of the plant to serve the local market was emphasized by several executives responding to the UNITAR study.

Production techniques and equipment are usually adapted to the skills of the local
labour supply, and market requirements. This can mean the use of much smaller, less
sophisticated equipment than would be considered economical in the United States in
the case of fabricating facilities. Product designs have also been modified to suit local
conditions, particularly in the building (construction) field.[50]

The landmark Strassman study (1968) of technology and economic development, based on field work in Mexico and Puerto Rico among a sample of 70
firms, categorizes the four strategies in respect to technology choice: (1) *task
simplification*—more, but less skilled, workers; (2) *mechanization*—skill level
or employment or both fall; (3) *instrumentation*—the use of fewer, but more
skilled, workers; (4) *scale-related changes*—more skills, more workers, or
more of both (which implies higher total costs and, hence, is likely to be
selected only if unit costs fall; that is, when economies of scale can be
achieved).[51] Strassman found that the overwhelming part of his sample
reported no influence of interest rates (cost of capital) on the choice of
technology.[52] Yet, he reported an earlier study of the Latin American textile
industry in which plants were rated as using technology of the 1950, 1960, or
1965 levels, and that overall those plants using the earliest technology were
the most profitable.[53]

The Wells study of the choice of technology in Southeast Asia makes a
similar point:

In one instance, a foreign-owned company had automated the unloading of bottles from
the filler and capping operations. A local competitor had not. The foreign company had
invested approximately $3,600 per worker that it calculated it had saved by automating
the step. Assume, however, that at best the opportunity cost of capital was only 10%.
This represents a capital cost alone of $360 per year. When you add in operating costs
and a reasonable allowance for depreciation or maintenance, it is hard to believe that
the investment was economically justified in a country where the worker's wages and
benefits would amount to only some $100 to $200 per year.

In fact, I found many foreign companies making investments of more than $5,000 per
man; in one case, the investment exceeded $20,000. At no point in the foreseeble future
could the wages in a developing country have justified such an investment. A less
automated plant would have resulted in a substantial saving of capital and, thus, higher
profits.[54]

---

[50]Chudson, *International Transfer*, p. 31.

[51]W. Paul Strassman, *Technology Change and Economic Development* (Ithaca: Cornell University Press, 1968),
pp. 64–65.

[52]Strassman, *Technology Change*, pp. 146–47.

[53]"Choice of Technologies in the Latin American Textile Industry," Latin American Symposium of Industrial
Development, Santiago, Chile, March 14–15, 1966 (E/CN, 12/746), pp. 9, 31, 39, 44.

[54]Louis T. Wells, Jr., "Don't Overautomate Your Foreign Plant," *Harvard Business Review*, January–February
1974, p. 114.

Wells pointed up the dilemma facing many foreign investors in this way.

An American investor setting up a new plant in a less developed country found himself under great pressure from his local partner, a government-owned enterprise, to bring in ultramodern, automated equipment. At the same time, the country's minister of labor was strongly suggesting that the plant use a simple technology that would employ lots of workers. And the minister of industries was more than hinting that secondhand equipment, although perhaps using more labor and saving on capital, would not be allowed into the country—only the most modern technology should be brought in. [55]

The Wells study of Indonesian industry[56] reported that even where the effective cost of labor was low (25 to 35¢ per day), capital cost high (24 to 36 percent per annum), and a range of technology of varying capital intensity available, foreign firms tended to install the same capital intensive technology as used in their home markets with very different factor costs. He advanced a number of possible explanations, based on intensive interviewing of corporate managers: (1) the impact of engineering objectives (that is, technical efficiency, the prestige associated with technical sophistication and modernity, and the greater engineering interest in up-to-date technology); (2) the monopolistic advantage of trade names (which overshadowed any price advantage that might have been realized by using more appropriate technology); (3) greater flexibility of output in the face of uncertain market data (that is, rapid increase or decrease of labor was difficult, but adding shifts for a machine-intensive operation relatively easy; so, likewise, was its shutdown); (4) greater ease of managing machines than local labor, coupled with a shortage of managerial skills, especially at the foreman and supervisor levels; (5) response to government policies, which bestow greater rewards on more capital intensive enterprises (for example, the greater ease of getting loans for fixed assets than for working capital; also the impact of tax incentives such as accelerated depreciation); (6) greater consistency and higher quality of output; (7) the cost of developing a new, more labor intensive technology; (8) low productivity of labor, thereby making cost per unit of output relatively high; and (9) the desire to avoid "sweat shop" conditions where men and women do the work of machines. To this list should be added (10) the greater difficulty that a firm has in capturing the "rent" (the element of appropriability) from less sophisticated, more labor-intensive technology for which entry barriers are lower than in the case of sophisticated, more capital-intensive technology (for which patents, secrecy, and scarce high-level skills may be involved); and (11), the fact that a foreign control system undervalues local currency, thereby decreasing the cost of imports and

---

[55]Wells, "Don't Overautomate," p. 111.

[56]Louis T. Wells, Jr., "Economic Man and Engineering Man: Choice of Technology in a Low Wage Country," in *Public Policy*, Summer 1973.

increasing the cost of exports (the former tend to be more capital-intensive than the latter).

World Bank–sponsored research as to the optimum mix of capital and labor in earth-moving projects (such as road building) has revealed a number of relevant variables, specifically soil types, moisture, incentives, nutritional levels, and the quality of management (that is, the capacity to arrange work efficiently so as to avoid bottlenecks in the flow of work, particularly at the interface between men and machines). In this case, the quality of the product was not directly related to capital or labor intensity.

Possible management guidelines coming out of these findings were listed by Wells:

1. Control the engineering bias, possibly by requiring a comparison of the proposed plant design with technological alternatives from the point of view of anticipated profit.

2. Use local wages rates in the profitability studies.

3. Look at local technologies, and analyze the rationale for their use.

4. Consider the use of secondhand machinery.

5. Consider the use of machinery built in LDCs; it may be less expensive, less automated, and, thus, easier to operate and repair than that made in North America, Europe, or Japan. (India, Mexico, Argentina, Brazil, Iran, and Turkey may be sources worth exploring.)

6. Require justification for all expenditures on materials-handling equipment (and earth-moving machinery).

7. Eliminate the biases in reporting systems, such as using the number of workers per unit of output as a measure of efficiency.

8. Check whether the company's "standard" plant designs are appropriate for low-wage countries.[57]

It is of interest to note that a number of LDC governments have apparently begun to heed the impact of their investment incentive packages. By mid-1974, the Philippines Investment Board was using two measures of labor intensity in its investment screening process. Indonesia had indicated that its attitude toward continuing foreign ownership of industry would be somewhat more liberal in the case of labor-intensive enterprises. Malaysia had, by 1974, started giving "labor utilization relief" in the form of a two- to five-year tax holiday for projects employing specified numbers of workers.

What is rarely mentioned in the literature regarding appropriate technology is the underlying question, appropriate for what? There is no generalizable objective function determining appropriateness, just as there is no generalizable objective function determining how a nation should allocate its resources.

---

[57]Summarized from Wells, "Don't Overautomate," pp. 115–19.

Appropriateness depends upon the priority of objectives, whether they be maximum employment, technical efficiency, income equality, export development, national autarky, or whatever. The phrase "appropriate technology" standing outside of a politically determined priority of objectives is meaningless. Management should be sensitive to this truth.

2.5 SITE SELECTION

Once decisions have been rendered in respect to sales, supply sources, and plant design, one can move to site selection. Curiously, there is some evidence that firms expend more effort in selecting a site within a country than in selecting the country.[58]

Although both decisions [selection of national site and local site] are made formally at the top of the company . . . , they have rather different characteristics. While the decision to invest in a country is often unstructured, the selection . . . of a specific location is more formalized since it is embedded in the formal procedure for approval of funds. Funds do not seem to be granted merely for an investment opportunity, but only to a specific project at a specific location. There, it is possible that the final and formal decision to invest at all is coupled with the location decision. This does not seem logical, and one of the executives explained, "In our company, the overall analysis for an investment opportunity in a foreign country is not done as carefully as the comparative analysis of potential locations, which is largely formalized."[59]

A further finding in this same study was that companies did not select the location promising the highest net present value but, rather, the site which was likely to create the fewest problems. The actual evaluation of competing sites was found to be highly subjective and unstructured. Only a small number of the companies surveyed professed to use any formalized procedure, such as the weighted criteria method[60] described below. There are publications that provide checklists of site selection factors[61] and reports on which factors companies have actually used in their decisions.[62]

Among those factors sometimes overlooked are free trade zones. A growing number of countries have designated one or more zones into which goods may be imported and exported without tariff or control. Traditionally located near important ports, many are now placed near major international airports. Their significance lies in the fact that a firm may mix foreign inputs with local (including labor) and re-export to the target market, and pay little or no tax.

---

[58]Hans W. Hagenbuck, "The Selection of Plant Locations Abroad" (Cambridge: Alfred P. Sloan School of Management, M. I. T., unpublished S.M. thesis, 1973).

[59]Hagenbuck, "Plant Locations," p. 71.

[60]Hagenbuck, "Plant Locations," p. 92.

[61]"Checklist of Site Selection Factors," published annually by *Industrial Development*.

[62]An example is *Characteristics of Modern Industrial Plants* (Washington: U.S. Department of Commerce).

One of the oldest and most famous is the Colon Free Zone in Panama. Profits recorded by companies operating in the Zone enjoy a 90 percent exemption on the regular Panamanian rate of 34 percent, or an effective rate of about 3 percent. Of course, any product from a zone plant sold into the host country market is subject to all the usual entry controls, including tariffs, on the value added to any local inputs.

In many countries, the selection and acquisition of a site may be much more time consuming than the firm is accustomed to domestically. It is reported, for example, that as long as a year may be needed to acquire a site in Indonesia, quite apart from the search time. The only other generalization significantly different from those applying to a purely domestic enterprise is that the relative cost of factor and product mobility may vary widely from market to market. It may or may not be less costly to locate relative to the center of market gravity on the one hand or, on the other, near an existing power source, an important raw material input, a stable labor supply, in a locale in which management will reside contentedly (availability of intellectual companionship, familiar entertainment, schooling facilities for children), in a well-policed area, or—of growing importance everywhere—where the cost of maintaining a tolerable impact on the environment will be the least in the long run. The weights applied to each factor, and the degree to which geographic areas thus defined overlap, will determine the solution.

The Weighted Criteria Method. A great deal of time and effort can be saved by first narrowing down the choice of potential sites to the most promising few. Once the requirements of a new facility are firmly decided, in terms of size, land, manpower, utilities, and services, they can be superimposed on a number of possible locations and compared against the same set of criteria. By assigning numerical values to each criterion to show its relative importance for the particular project, the potential sites can be weighed and compared to find the preferable ones.

In the hypothetical example (Table 2.3), sites B, C, and D would be eliminated from the contest for scoring too low. Sites A, E, and F would be worth investigating in detail from the point of view of legal, engineering, and economic feasibility. The final selection of a site would be made by comparing the feasibility studies. But the number of such expensive and time-consuming feasibility investigations would be limited to the top contenders—all acceptable sites—as measured by the weighted criteria method.[63]

Domestic U.S. weights may not be appropriate. A point to bear in mind: a characteristic of many less developed countries is that they are developing at a quickening pace; their internal markets are expanding and perhaps shifting quite rapidly. Power, resource, and community development at a very fast rate

---

[63]E. S. Groo, "Choosing Foreign Locations: One Company's Experience," *Columbia Journal of World Business,* September–October 1971, p. 77.

Table 2.3

Criteria	Maximum Value Assigned	Sites					
		A	B	C	D	E	F
Living conditions*	100	70	40	45	50	60	60
Accessibility†	75	55	35	20	60	70	70
Industrialization‡	60	40	50	55	35	35	30
Labor availability§	35	30	10	10	30	35	35
Economics††	35	15	15	15	15	25	25
Community capability and attitude#	30	25	20	10	15	25	15
Prestige: Effect on company reputation**	35	25	20	10	15	25	15
Total:	370	260	180	165	225	280	265

* General appearance of community; availability of housing; community services and education facilities; attractiveness of climate and environment; freedom from disruptive problems; living costs for transferred employees.

† Accessibility to markets, suppliers, services and other company facilities; quality of local transportation and of facilities for visitors; availability of communications networks.

‡ Level of industrialization; desirability of industrial and nonindustrial neighbors; potential for area's industrial growth.

§ Wage rates; population within commuting radius; size of local labor force and level of employment; availability of skills and of training programs; history of local labor problems.

†† Relative cost of construction and site development; local costs of doing business; e.g., corporate and personal tax structure, utility rates.

Quality and type of schools; adequacy of public services; local issues; attitudes toward industry and possible effect of introducing new facility into community; evidence of community planning for future growth.

**General reputation of area; specifically, reputation that may relate to the type of facility planned; freedom from special problems that could create unfavorable reputation; desire of community to welcome type of activity planned.

Source: E.S. Groo, "Choosing Foreign Locations: One Company's Experience," *Columbia Journal of World Business,* September-October 1971, p. 77.

may be expected in some instances. Also, some of these countries have not yet discovered the environmental problem, but they will—sooner rather than later, one expects. Static analysis may thus be dangerous, as it was for a company that located a plant near its largest market, only to find that the market center shifted several hundred miles away in a matter of five years. Similar shifts in the domestic U.S. market, given its size and more leisurely expansion rate, often move much more slowly, but even so, the environmental problem has exploded into general view very rapidly.

It was noted in a 1967 study that the comparative weights given to site selection motivation for U.S. companies in Europe had shifted since 1958. They had become increasingly sensitive to market access and community development; less sensitive to service and materials input, labor availability, and taxes. (See Table 2.4.)

Table 2.4
COMPARATIVE WEIGHT OF SITE SELECTION MOTIVATION FOR U.S. COMPANIES IN EUROPE

Characteristics cost or availability of:	1958	1966
Physical property	5%	6%
Utilities and services	10	4
Materials input	10	5
Access to markets	5	20
Labor and staff	40	30
Community environment	10	25
Taxes and incentives	20	10

Source: Severo Mosca, "Changing Approaches to Plan Location in Europe," *Worldwide P&I Planning,* September–October 1967, p. 23.

In a specific discussion of the European (EEC) manufacturing site problem, it has been suggested that a firm has three possible solutions:[64]

Solution One. **A plant or plants that are suboptimal in that capacity and site are selected to serve the "final" market.**

Solution Two. **A plant or plants suboptimal by default, aimed only at serving the partial markets immediately accessible.**

Solution Three. **A mixed strategy derived from a comparison of costs and benefits relating to serving each successively accessible market segment or area (that is, a historical development).**

Solution one would call for "a large-acreage, highly-integrated, single-story manufacturing complex, located at the weighted center of the Common Market, which is the Strasbourg area of Eastern France," or was before the entry of the U.K. Solution two would be represented by "an assembly-limited-fabricating type of plant, placed in any of a half dozen areas of high market concentration and aimed at serving the cream of the market in such area." Examples would be the greater Frankfurt area or the Antwerp-Rotterdam port zones. Solution three is typical of the old-time multinational firms that operate a heterogeneous collection of plants, none of which were planned with the EEC in mind.[65]

Not to be overlooked are the many thousand industrial estates located around the world, including both private and public sponsors. The term "industrial estate" designates a planned clustering of industrial enterprises on an already developed site and occasionally in prebuilt factory accommodations. In a number of LDCs, the industrial estate is a major instrument for encourag-

---

[64]Adapted from Severo Mosca, "Changing Approaches to Plant Location in Europe," *Worldwide P&I Planning,* September–October 1967, pp. 18–19.

[65]Summarized from Mosca, "Changing Approaches," pp. 18–19.

ing and supporting small-scale industry or a device for stimulating industrial development in less congested, less developed parts of a country. Firms locating facilities within such estates may enjoy publicly subsidized facilities.

2.6 PLANT ACQUISITION OR CONSTRUCTION

If the firm opts to supply a market from its own facilities, the question arises as to whether the construction of new facilities or the acquisition of an existing plant is desirable. Obviously, the choice rests on the extent to which the facilities or companies up for acquisition satisfy decisions (and the weight given those decisions) made in respect to interplant relationships, plant design, and plant site. But there are other factors that should be brought to bear on the problem. For example, how important in a cost/benefit sense is it to acquire a management, a labor force, or access to otherwise closed channels of distribution? to save time in market entry? to eliminate competition? to preempt purchase of the facilities by another? to build in technological innovation (new plant versus old)? to anticipate political reprisal? It is quite clear that the acquisition of locally owned firms and their physical facilities can generate more political heat than the construction of new. Such countries as Canada, Japan, Australia, France, and the U.K. have demonstrated tangible opposition to American takeovers. And the ANCOM countries specifically forbid foreign takeovers of local enterprises except in cases of bankruptcy.

Japan, of course, is peculiarly vulnerable to takeovers by reason of the high debt-equity ratios characteristic of Japanese corporations (although in July 1971, regulations prohibiting a takeover bid on the Tokyo Stock Exchange were dropped).[66]

Under certain circumstances, the acquisition of, or merger with, a foreign enterprise may run afoul of U.S. antitrust laws. For example, if the acquired company is a member of a cartel that restrains the foreign commerce of the U.S., the U.S. firm may be vulnerable. Other risky situations:

1. A merger with, or the acquisition of, a foreign firm if the latter has U.S. subsidiaries that compete with the U.S. firm and its subsidiaries within the U.S.

2. If a merger or acquisition linking a U.S. with a foreign enterprise eliminates actual or potential competition within the U.S. market.

A variety of questions remain without clear answer, such as which products compete (for example, do razors compete with electric shavers; coal with oil; copper with aluminum) and at what point in terms of market concentration is competition significantly restrained?

---

[66]"Internationalization of the Japanese Stock Market" (New York: Nomura Research Institute of Technology and Economics, June 26, 1972).

There is the reverse situation of an acquisition by a foreign firm of a U.S. enterprise. Apparently, the same rules apply; witness the U.S. Justice Department's concern when British Petroleum acquired Sohio in 1969; that is, if the acquisition or merger has an adverse effect on competition in any section of the country, the courts may force a dissolution or prevent the acquisition or merger. Of relevance here is the so-called "toe-hold doctrine" which refers to the notion that a common entry strategy for a foreign firm is to acquire an existing company, often relatively small, and then expand from that base. By so doing, the firm starts with a locally-experienced management, a going enterprise, a developed distribution system. Also, the cash flow may begin much sooner than would otherwise be the case. The antitrust question has to do with the maximum size of firm that may be acquired by a new foreign entrant into the U.S. market without reducing actual or potential competition to such a point as to run afoul of antitrust law. By way of contrast, EEC anticartel law would prevent a merger or acquisition only if it were deemed to have an adverse effect on internation trade within the EEC and if the benefits accruing to the larger enterprise were not passed on in significant degree to the public through lower prices, better service, accelerated research and development, and so forth. The one exception to that statement would now—since the Intercontinental Can Company case of 1975—arise in event of the acquisition of an EEC firm by another EEC firm held to be dominant, whether defined by sector or by geography; that is, such an acquisition might be held to be a *per se* misuse of dominant position; hence, in violation of the Rome Treaty. Since 1975, the EEC Commission has taken the position that mergers and acquisitions should be notified to the commission. A foreign-owned firm (that is, non-European) and a European-owned firm are treated without distinction in this regard.

In the absence of effective EEC law relating to alien takeovers within individual member states, such countries as Germany, Belgium, and France have set up screening mechanisms that tend to render alien takeovers more difficult. For example, the French Finance Ministry has repeatedly warned that the government will not approve takeovers in which the foreign investor merely wants to use the French company as an entry into the domestic market. Japanese restrictions in this area are, of course, notorious, although substantially liberalized in the last few years. The U.K. has transformed its Monopolies Commission into a stronger body with the power to approve mergers and acquisitions and to enforce the legal requirement that the holding by a single entity of 10 percent or more of the voting equity in a corporation be published. The thrust clearly seems to be to make foreign takeovers more difficult. Canada has created a government corporation to help ailing Canadian firms, thereby lessening the danger of foreign acquisition, and in 1972 created a committee to screen pending acquisitions of Canadian firms by foreign corporations, currently known as the Foreign Investment Review Agency

(FIRA). A capital gains tax was also enacted so as to reduce the financial benefit derived by Canadians selling out to foreign firms.

It is generally recognized that there is often an asymmetry between a multinational firm and a local enterprise in that the owners of the latter have a higher liquidity preference (future earnings are more highly discounted). The reason is that the local firm is generally much smaller and represents a bigger proportion of the total wealth of the owners than it would of a multinational corporate owner. Therefore, the multinational firm can "afford" to offer a compellingly attractive price. The nontaxation of capital gains in some countries further increases the attraction of a sell-out.

2.7   RESEARCH AND DEVELOPMENT (R&D)

Much that has been said in the preceding paragraphs emphasizes the need for a situationally oriented research and development effort, whether one speaks of product, process, machines, or site. A research and development division embedded in a domestic operation, that is, one in which foreign markets are only in the peripheral vision of management, is unlikely to develop the interest and skills necessary for devising optimum solutions to the set of problems posed above. Also, the cost of R&D may be significantly lower abroad than within the United States. A half-and-half solution devised by some companies is the employment of technical liaison personnel to provide the linkage between the foreign market environment and domestically based R&D sections. This linkage, of course, may prove to be the transmission belt for a valuable two-way technical flow as a firm's competitors abroad or local foreign researchers come up with new ideas and products. This externally induced stimulation may be important in devising the optimum entry into a given market. There is, of course, an important feedback into sales strategy area; constant adjustment is needed. Organizational structure should be such as to facilitate this need.

A 1970 Conference Board study observed:

The research and development function is not one that can be easily decentralized. In spite of their desire to make maximum use of the capabilities of their foreign units, most companies cooperating in the survey make limited use of them for R&D. In spite of pressures to decentralize research activity, most companies carry out the bulk of it in the United States.

When R&D work is done overseas, it most often takes the form of product modification or adaptation to meet the particular needs of local markets.[67]

Generally, it seems that there is an overwhelming concentration of R&D in

---

[67]Michael G. Duerr, *R&D in the Multinational Company* (New York: The Conference Board, 1970), p. 1.

the home country, 94 percent in the case of internationally active U.S. corporations in 1964, the latest data available.[68]

There is reason to believe that this situation is changing. Although no statistics seem to be available, it is possible that the R&D done by U.S. manufacturing firms overseas, as a percentage of their total R&D budget, may be increasing. Six general trends lead one to this conclusion: (1) growing aggregate R&D expenditures by Europe and Japan, (2) increasing cost advantage of doing R&D outside of the U.S., (3) increasing awareness of the tax advantage of doing R&D in a low tax country so that the subsequent patents may be owned by a subsidiary in that country, (4) improvement of the protection of patents and commercial secrets in many countries, (5) increasingly onerous U.S. government regulation of the introduction of new products (as in the pharmaceutical sector), (6) increasing host government pressure to undertake local R&D, and (7) an unwillingness by many LDC governments to permit subsidiaries to pay related foreign companies for technology either through royalties, fees, or assumption of a general overhead burden. Table 2.5 provides a measure of the alleged cost advantage. As an expansion of point three above, let it be noted that since the introduction of the 1962 tax reform in the U.S., there has been a tax incentive for locating of R&D in a country that either does not tax foreign source income, or does so at a very low rate. So long as the U.S. subsidiary *owns* the relevant patents or trade secrets, or has substantially developed them, then income derived by that subsidiary through license (and technical assistance agreements in some cases as well) is not taxable in the United States until remitted to the United States. If the subsidiary does not own the patents or secrets, income derived from the license of those patents and secrets (and from technical assistance agreements in some cases as well) will be fully taxed to the U.S. parent as earned, even if not remitted to the U.S. Moreover, the transfer of a patent or valuable secret by a U.S. company to its foreign subsidiary is a taxable transaction, and the gain is taxed to the parent as ordinary income. Hence, it can be very worthwhile for a U.S. firm to develop substantial R&D facilities abroad.

Jerome Wiesner observed in mid-1976 that the rate of development of new technology in the United States appeared to be slowing. Several factors were cited: increasing government regulation in some areas, the retreat of some important government agencies (notably the Department of Defense) from sponsorship of basic research, the short national attention span for technical issues, lack of capital for important industries, and inflation-induced money problems of major research-oriented universities. He identified certain U.S. industries that had not fully exploited available technology, specifically, steelmaking, shipbuilding, and the railroads.[69] Some would add the automotive and

[68]Karl P. Sauvant and Farid G. Lavipoor, eds., *Controlling Multinational Enterprise* (Boulder, Colorado: Westview Press, 1976).

[69]Reported in *New York Times*, April 20, 1976.

Table 2.5
OFFICIAL VERSUS RESEARCH EXCHANGE RATES FOR SELECTED COUNTRIES IN 1962

	U.S.	France		Netherlands	U.K.
Official exchange rate in $U.S.	1.00	4.90	4.00	3.61	.35
Research exchange rate in $U.S. (including labor, capital, materials, and overhead)*	1.00	3.27	2.35	1.94	.25
Research exchange rate as percentage of official exchange rate	100	67	59	54	71
Official exchange rate	100.00	67.90	69.00	65.61	71.35

* The research exchange rates are calculated on the comparative normal inputs for research activity.
Source: Christopher Freeman and A. Young, *The Research and Development Effort in Western Europe, North America and the Soviet Union* (Paris: Organization for Economic Cooperation and Development, 1965), p. 94.

pharmaceutical industries. An important related question was whether the United States was developing new technology at a somewhat slower pace than such countries as Japan and Germany. Some observers by 1977 thought so. If the number of patents being issued were any barometer, Japan was clearly catching up. In 1976, Japan issued nearly three times as many patents as did the United States Patent Office. Of course, it could be that Japanese investors relied more on patent protection, less on secrecy, than their U.S. counterparts. Also, Japan issues utility patents; the United States does not. Finally, the patent applicant need not be Japanese.

One highly competent observer of U.S. technological development pointed out in 1976 that in the United States "the *socialization* of R&D had been instituted as national policy."[70] He estimated that more than half of all scientists and engineers in the United States depended upon government funding for their employment. He expressed growing concern with the extent to which this *fourth sector* (the defense/aerospace industry, government laboratories, and quasi-government, nonprofit institutions whose activities depend almost exclusively on federal funds for survival) is now employed by the government to plan and manage commercially oriented development programs, i.e., programs that involve the ultimate operation of processes or the development and sale of products by the private industrial sector. The point is that this "socialized R&D," although recording many technical

---

[70]Richard S. Morse, "Socialized R&D," *Sloan Management Review*, vol. 18, no. 1, Fall 1976, pp. 81–85.

achievements, has seldom successfully applied its management talents or technology in the competitive commercial world. It is alleged that the bureaucracy of socialized R&D has greatly reduced the effectiveness, and probably doubled the cost, of many research programs. Also, in that a disproportionately large number of innovative ideas come from smaller technically-based companies, and because of the cost of dealing with the federal government and the absence of any real champion for the small business community at the federal level, these small enterprises have a particularly difficult time. Furthermore, "the spirit of technological innovation and risk taking is declining within many large corporations." The conclusion: this overall slowdown in U.S. technical innovation, plus the increased flow of U.S. technology overseas, is rapidly eroding the technological lead enjoyed by the United States.

In recent years, as profit margins have been reduced by inflationary pressures and a slowdown in economic growth, many companies have had to review costs, particularly those of a discretionary nature. Often at the top of the list is R&D. With R&D expenditures most frequently ranging between 5 and 10 percent of gross sales, it is natural for companies to reduce such commitments to long-range profit growth when the immediate concern is for survival in the short run. Also, it is argued, with some justification, that a centralized R&D facility serving the entire corporation is the least costly way to accomplish the research objectives of the company. So, even if some decentralization of the R&D function had been planned, pressures seem to be pushing in the opposite direction. There can be no denying the fact that duplicate laboratory facilities are costly, that staffing foreign laboratories can lead to increased hiring and training costs, and that total cost control is made more difficult by the decentralization of research activity. The real issue, however, is cost effectiveness, not simply cost control. One must consider benefits as well as costs in determining the optimal solution to the problem of research location.[71]

Closely tied to cost effectiveness is control. Perhaps the most important element in a research program is the effective integration of all components of the effort. Obviously, integration is most readily accomplished when all aspects of the R&D program are under one roof, let alone scattered around the globe. A frequent criticism of decentralized research is the likelihood of redundant activities appearing in various laboratories. Researchers naturally wish to become involved in the most promising projects. This tendency can lead to the deliberate disguise of projects in order to counter charges of redundancy, or to flagrant duplication of effort. Should such situations exist there is certain to be loss of cost effectiveness.

---

[71]This paragraph and the following general discussion of arguments pro and con decentralized R&D have been extracted from comments made by J. Kermit Campbell, Director, European R&D, Dow Corning International Ltd., November 1976.

Many, if not most, of the firms involved significantly in international business take pride in their R&D efforts. It can be expected that top management in such firms feels a need to be in close touch with this activity, either to make inputs into the programs or merely to remain informed of progress. But whatever the reason, this personal interest can be a decisive influence in locating R&D.

Some have argued that research work can be conducted at lower costs in certain foreign locations, for example, in Great Britain. The relatively low salaries paid to highly trained British technical employees is one factor. A second is the declining value of the British pound vis-à-vis the U.S. dollar. But one must be alert to cost-effectiveness as well as absolute cost.

Another central issue is the *relevance* of a research effort. International managers find that the best opportunities for the growth of their respective firms are outside their home countries. A very strong case can be made for locating R&D activity within a firm's principal markets in order to improve the responsiveness of the company's technical programs to local needs. This responsiveness can be measured in both time and relevance. Too often the U.S.-based company attempts to promote its U.S.-developed products overseas without considering its appropriateness. Without an effective technical staff on the scene it is very difficult to ascertain the peculiar product characteristics desired, and certainly is most difficult to determine the needs in a timely manner. This can prevent the firm from either acquiring, or maintaining, a competitive edge.

Closely related to the above issue is the desirability of developing and maintaining a global product. Often it is possible to design in characteristics of a product that will satisfy multiple market areas. But for this to be done during the development stage it is imperative that market needs from around the world be known and appreciated. Acquiring such knowledge is difficult without experienced technical personnel on hand to ascertain market needs and to funnel these through design requirements into the central laboratories. Such organization can result in cost saving in the R&D program since the need to redesign products is minimized.

Another strong argument for locating technically trained staff in foreign locations is related to industry leadership. For example, the electrical power transmission industry is more highly developed in Western Europe than in the United States. Failure to participate in this leadership by not employing European R&D personnel can lead to competitive disadvantages. Selectivity may be designed into foreign research programs and personnel strengths in order to position the effort in relation to such industry leadership.

Most R&D-oriented firms utilize their technical personnel to support sales and marketing efforts. Beyond the obvious use of technical service personnel, the deployment of research and product development personnel within a market area can lend credibility to a firm's sales program. In countries with indigenous competitive firms that maintain full R&D facilities the foreign-based company relying totally on home country R&D may find itself at a considerable sales disadvantage. Regionally based research activities may also be useful in keeping technical service personnel up-to-date on the latest corporate technology. The technical service engineer who does not have the opportunity to work with his research and product development colleagues on a continuing basis may well become technically obsolete within two or three years. This obsolescence could reduce his effective product knowledge to that of a mere salesman, thereby wasting the money spent to maintain him in the area and reducing the competitive edge of the firm.

High technology companies often develop management personnel from the ranks of the R&D departments. If the firm operating internationally wishes to follow a similar pattern overseas, a research department will be essential to any foreign subsidiary enterprises. Continued reliance on more marketing-oriented management candidates can seriously alter the profile and competitive characteristics of a firm engaged in the application of high technology.

An important activity for a high technology company is that of maintaining liaison with the academic community in the principal areas of operations. Obviously, this is not possible without the benefit of technically trained and active company personnel on the spot. The firm that fails to keep in touch with the main institutions around the world involved in basic research relevant to the industry is very likely to miss opportunities for growth and innovation. This same principle applies to active participation in professional societies and similar industry associations. The existence of a solid R&D function in the major areas of involvement is central to establishing these kinds of relationships.

A final argument often advanced for maintaining a research activity in selected countries where the firm does business concerns corporate citizenship. There is a definite trend developing for host countries to demand total participation by the foreign firm wishing to operate in that country. The existence of a company-sponsored R&D facility that can employ the technical expertise of the country's universities, as well as adding to the technical base of that country, may become an issue as criticism of foreign-owned enterprises mounts in many countries.

An optional strategy is for the firm to enter into a continuing supportive relationship with one or more of the relevant research institutes within the host country, either through R&D contracts, the loan of personnel, or by general financial support. These research institutes, often industry-specific and often at least in part supported by government funds, are a common feature of the contemporary LDC landscape. Unfortunately, there seem to be relatively few that devote their energies to the development of technologies appropriate to local conditions and are responsive to commercial needs. But there are a few.

It should be noted that among the explanations advanced for Japan's dramatic economic growth is that the productivity of Japan's R&D is significantly higher than in the U.S. case for several reasons:[72] (1) relatively little R&D is done in the public sector (for example, relating to defense) and, hence, the payoff period (in terms of goods and services demanded by consumers in the market place) is substantially shorter; (2) the permanent employment system of Japanese firms leads to a stability and continuity in R&D teams and projects (whereas U.S. and European firms tend to cut back on R&D personnel and discontinue projects when business is bad. In fact, Japanese firms probably intensify their R&D effort during such periods); (3) the cost of competent R&D personnel in Japan is relatively low; (4) government encouragement of R&D allocation among companies makes for less wasted effort; (5) the permanent employment commitment on the part of many Japanese firms eliminates labor's fear of unemployment arising out of technological change and, hence, such changes can be introduced more rapidly.

That this last factor is of possible importance is suggested by the fact that the most rapid improvement in technology seems to be associated in the U.S. with the fastest growing industries, that is, in those sectors where firms can most readily absorb labor that would otherwise be made redundant. Hence, labor resistance is minimal. Various approaches to the problem of labor resistance to technical change other than a permanent employment system are:

1. Public adjustment assistance to those threatened with loss of job and income in the form of free retraining, free employment services, subsidized loans, subsidized moves. Perhaps among the best examples is that of the U.K., which taxes an industry on the basis of labor turnover and uses the proceeds to retrain workers made redundant by reason of technological changes;

2. Providing labor with a vested right vis-à-vis the employing firm in respect to training, either to add skills or to upgrade them (as embodied in French legislation).

Both of these approaches tend to reduce labor resistance and reduce institutional rigidities blocking the rapid introduction of technological change and attendant improvement in efficiency (such as labor-initiated building codes and protectionist international trade policies). Hence, investment in R&D becomes more productive, and, as a consequence, it is seen as less costly.

---

[72]Supporting evidence: Japan's technical development level (a composite of four indicators: number of patent applications, value of technology trade, value of the export of technology intensive products and total value-added) stood in the first half of the 1960s at 19.2 as against 100 for the U.S. In the second half, Japan's index was 29.1, compared with 43.7 for West Germany, 23.0 for France, and 27.7 for Britain. In other words, Japan's position relative to the U.S. improved by over 50 percent. As for the capability of technical and scientific development calculated on the basis of research resources, the number of technical innovations, and other factors, Japan's relative position is 16.1 as opposed to 100 for the U.S., 22.3 for West Germany, and 18.5 for Britain. (Summarized from a Japanese government "white paper" on science and technology [*New Needs and Response to Them*, Tokyo, 1972] in the *Japan Economic Journal*, May 2, 1972, p. 10). Applications for patents in Japan reached an all-time high in 1975 or 343,000, roughly three times the number of applications received by the U.S. patent office. Two explanations are advanced: Japan accepts utility patents (see Section 6.8), and Japanese investors are more prone to seek patents for inventions (*The Japan Economic Journal*, February 1, 1977, p. 12).

The many hundreds of transnational research cooperation agreements being reported out of Europe suggest a certain economy to be achieved from increasing scale. Because of the difficulty of assigning to the member firms commercially valuable discoveries and developments emerging out of these collaborations, there may be a tendency for jointly-owned subsidiaries to exploit the R&D. Over time, with repeated joint venturing of this kind, the parent firms will have merged in effect.

A *Business International* report observes,

Companies are directing special efforts to develop research within Latin America. Johnson & Johnson reported that the research departments of its larger Latin American affiliates are among the most active of such organizations engaged in pharmaceutical development. Ralston Purina's Latin American research programs, staffed 100% by nationals, have yielded such a high level of expertise that two or three staff members are candidates to head the company's world-wide R&D program. The Argentine subsidiary of General Tire has even gone further in promoting R&D by teaming up with a local group to explore advanced rubber technology.[73]

But generally speaking it seems quite clear that most firms operating internationally are exceedingly reluctant to put any significant R&D effort into their LDC operations. Among those factors discouraging the location of R&D in the LDCs can be cited: (1) import restrictions, in that they reduce competitive pressures; (2) relatively small size of many LDC markets; (3) shortage of trained personnel; (4) the ineffectiveness of local law regarding patents and protection of commercial secrets. However, "as research costs soar at home and standards of university education rise abroad . . . research work could well begin to move to less expensive areas close to the production site."[74] It remains to be seen how rapidly this movement will, in fact, occur.

A Soviet analyst, projecting present trends into the future, estimates that by the end of the century the LCDs' bill for imported technology will be 20 to 35 times the present annual expenditure of between $3 and $5 billion. The degree of present technological dependence is illustrated in Figure 2.2. Noting that U.S. "transnational" corporations spend only about 4 percent of their total R&D funds abroad, he doubts that such corporations will do other than increase technological dependence. He advocates that technology transfer contracts be made to cover the setting up of laboratories, pilot and training facilities, "so that the imported technology can serve as a threshold for further progress on the spot," and goes on to point out, "We in the U.S.S.R. generally insist that R&D facilities be supplied with the production lines."[75] But what

---

[73]*Business Latin America*, February 25, 1971, p. 58.

[74]Hellinger and Hellinger, *Unemployment*, p. 86.

[75]Ivan Ivanov, "Transfer of Technology: Your Own R&D Is the Key," *Development Forum*, vol. 5, no. 3, April 1977, p. 3. Ivanov is Chief, Economics Division, Institute of U.S. and Canadian Studies, Moscow, and an UNCTAD consultant.

Technological dependence: selected indicators
(averages expressed as medians for 1970 or latest year available)

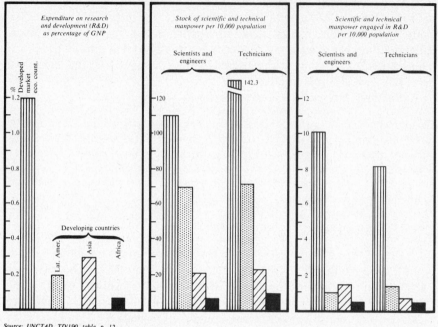

Source: *UNCTAD, TD/190, table, p. 12*
UN Statistical Yearbook 1974, Table 208
UNESCO Statistical Yearbook 1973, Table 8.3

Figure 2.2
TECHNOLOGICAL DEPENDENCE: SELECTED INDICATORS

Taken from Ivan Ivanov, "Transfer of Technology: Your Own R&D Is the Key," *Development Forum*, vol. 5, no. 3, April 1977, p. 3

he does not say is that the Soviet market and consequent scale of production is far different from the typical LDC, and he himself warns against any country shutting itself off from external technological development.

Another aspect of R&D should be noted: some countries offer subsidies, from outright grants to tax write-offs, if the activity satisfies certain criteria. For example, in the Canadian case:

To qualify for a grant, expenditures must be for scientific research and development carried on by a corporation for the purpose of strengthening or extending its business in Canada. Corporations must therefore undertake to exploit the results of their research and development work in Canada unless, according to sound business judgment, it would be uneconomic to do so. Furthermore, corporations must normally be free to market products resulting from their research and development to all countries of the world.[76]

In France, DATAR (the government's regional and national development agency) offered as of 1975 direct grants up to 20 percent of an investment in R&D (depending upon size and location) for fixed assets and relocation and training of personnel. And R&D centers in certain regions enjoyed a number of tax relief measures. Additionally, various government agencies were authorized to enter into R&D contracts and to provide loans and credits for their execution.

Another country offering official inducement for R&D is Japan. The vehicle for assistance is the Research Development Corporation, the purpose of which is to stimulate the development of commercially valuable technology out of research produced by universities, private research institutes, and private companies unable financially to carry out development. The corporation selects that research deemed to be of greatest developmental value and advertises for bids by private firms for development. A successful bidder then borrows the necessary funds from the corporation, which are to be repaid (within five years at no interest) if the development turns out successfully. No repayment is required in case of failure. If a company thus commissioned exploits the technology commercially, it must offer a certain rate of royalty to the corporation, which in turn divides it with the original owner of technology.

In 1972 the EEC moved to strengthen intra–European Community technological cooperation through a new device, the *Community Industrial Development Contract* (CIDC). A CIDC is drawn up to fund a Community-based joint effort of two or more companies established in two or more member states, through low interest loans administered by the European Investment Bank. A CIDC is granted for a project of sufficient financial and/or technological risk that it could not be realized without community or national assistance. Some additional criteria used in evaluating proposals include: (1) contribution to the technological development of a specific industrial sector; (2) degree to which imports from non–European Community countries could be reduced; (3) creation of new export opportunities; (4) satisfying major economic or social needs.

The original provisions of the CIDC gave high priority to certain advanced technology industrial sectors, including pharmaceuticals. Subsequently, however, these sectors were removed from priority status in order to provide equal access to a CIDC for a range of sectors. Presumably, subsidiaries of non–European Community firms are not discriminated against. Industrial property rights arising out of a CIDC belong to the companies involved, subject to the general provision of the European Community patent. Some expect an addi-

---

[76]Government of Canada, Department of Industry, *Annual Review*, 1967 (Ottawa, 1968).

tional clause which would require exploitation within a reasonable amount of time.

It has been suggested that there are two types of R&D operations:

1. The international interdependent laboratory, which concentrates on research (not development) and is closely connected to an international research program that emanates from corporate headquarters. Such a facility may or may not interact with local manufacturing facilities, depending in part upon the extent to which production is rationalized internationally;

2. The support laboratory, the main activities of which are (a) to act as a technical service center (that is, to assist in the adaptation of products to the local market) and (b) to adapt foreign manufacturing technology to local conditions by implementing the process of technology transfer, to adjust production technology to shorter runs.[77]

It would appear that as far as U.S. firms are concerned, there is no single method of charging a subsidiary for technology. Some corporations distinguish between work specifically requested by the subsidiary and that done in general support of the corporation's activities. There may be a specific charge for the former, not for the latter. Other corporations follow the policy that the payment of a royalty or a fee entitles a subsidiary to technical services, as well as a bundle of other benefits.

The foregoing discussion is adequate to demonstrate the difficulty of decisions in the supply area, whether one refers to the make or buy decision, the local or foreign-sourcing decision, the single or multiple plant decision, choice of technology and of site, the build or acquisition decision, or the location of the relevant R&D. Part of the problem, of course, lies in the highly dynamic nature of many of the relevant variables, such as relative cost, intermarket relations, political vulnerability, and law and government regulation. The accuracy of forecasting in these areas becomes critically important, just as much so as in forecasting the size and location of the market.

Discussion questions

1. Cite examples of customer preference regarding national source of product and of producer's preference.

2. Discuss the pros and cons of a tariff preference on the part of the more developed countries vis-à-vis the less developed.

3. List possible nontariff barriers (NTBs) not mentioned in the text.

4. Why might firms in certain countries be more prone to dump in foreign markets than those in other countries?

5. Do you feel that buy-national law or regulation is ever justified? Why?

---

[77]Arthur Cordell, *The Multinational Firm, Foreign Direct Investment, and Canadian Science Policy* (Ottawa: The Science Council of Canada, 1971), pp. 42–43.

6. Do you feel that setting international sea and air cargo rates should be done by agreement among the carriers? Why?

7. Under what circumstances, if any, should a firm rely on a single supply source within the EEC?

8. In selecting the technology to be used in an overseas plant, to what extent should a firm be sensitive to factor proportions within that country?

9. If you were locating a small pleasure craft manufacturing plant in Western Europe, what criteria would you use in site selection? Using these criteria, where would you locate it?

10. Under what circumstances should a U.S. firm purchase an existing manufacturing plant overseas as opposed to constructing a new one?

11. On the basis of Tables 2.6 and 2.7, which commodities seem the most likely subjects for effective producers' cartels?

12. Taking one of the commodity associations, producers' cartels, commodity agreements, regional cooperation agreements, free trade areas, or common markets, evaluate their current stability and the probability of achieving higher levels of integration.

Recommended references

Baranson, Jack. *Automotive Industries in Developing Countries.* Washington: International Bank for Reconstruction and Development, 1969.

_____, *International Transfer of Automotive Technology to Developing Countries.* New York: U.N. Institute for Training and Research, 1971.

_____, *Manufacturing Problems in India, the Cummins Diesel Experience.* Syracuse: Syracuse University Press, 1967.

Basche, James R., Jr., and Michael G. Duerr. *International Transfer of Technology.* New York: The Conference Board, 1975.

Chang, Y. S. *The Transfer of Technology: Economics of Offshore Assembly, the Case of Semiconductor Industry.* New York: U.N. Institute for Training and Research, 1971.

Chudson, Walter A. *The International Transfer of Commercial Technology to Developing Countries.* New York: U.N. Institute for Training and Research, 1971.

Mason, R. Hal. *The Transfer of Technology and the Factor Proportions Problem: The Philippines and Mexico.* New York: U.N. Institute for Training and Research, 1971.

Organization for Economic Cooperation and Development. *Choice and Adaptation of Technology in Developing Countries.* Paris: 1974.

R&D in the Multinational Company. New York: The National Industrial Conference Board, 1970, pp. 65–74.

Savage, Charles H. "Village and Factory Ways." Cambridge, Mass.: working paper, Alfred P. Sloan School of Management, M.I.T., 1965.

Site Selection Handbook. Atlanta: Conway Research, Inc., 1971.

Skinner, Wickham. *American Industry in Developing Economies.* New York: John Wiley & Sons, 1968.

Stobaugh, Robert B. *The International Transfer of Technology in the Establishment of the Petrochemical Industry in Developing Countries.* New York: U.N. Institute for Training and Research, 1971.

Wortzel, Lawrence H. *Technology Transfer in the Pharmaceutical Industry.* New York: U.N. Institute for Training and Research, 1971.

Appendix to Chapter 2
INSTITUTIONALIZED TRADING AMONG COUNTRIES

The special institutionalized trading relationships among various groups of countries constitute a trade barrier for those countries not belonging, trade incentives for those on the inside. It seems useful to classify these trading relationships into 17 groups, from the least integrated to the most integrated, in theory if not in practice.

1. *Negotiating groups*, organized for the purpose of joint commercial negotiation with other countries. An example is the Special Coordinating Committee for Latin America (ECLA) for coordination in negotiating trade preferences with the European Community and the United States. The European Community (see below) often acts as a negotiating group. It may be important for a firm to try to influence such negotiations. Special mechanisms may be in place to facilitate the expression of industry views, such as the new Industry Center for Trade Negotiations in the United States.

2. *Exporters' clubs*, organized for the purpose of consolidating the commercial debts of a specified country and to extend further credit, such as the Hague Club (for Brazil) and the Turkish Consortium. The credit-worthiness of local buyers is thus affected.

3. *Commodity associations*, groups of countries concerned with specific commodities (see Table 2.6), either as producers or consumers (see Table 2.7). Their function is limited to the gathering of statistics, to research, and to providing forums for international consultations between producers and consumers. The principal examples are the International Cotton Advisory Committee, dating from 1939, the African Groundnut Council (1964), the International Lead and Zinc Study Group (1960), and the International Wool Study Group (1947). The U.S. belongs to the latter two. Such associations are obviously important for firms dealing in these commodities, so likewise the existence of commodity cartels or agreements.

4. *Producers' cartels*, organized by commodity-producing countries to stabilize and/or increase prices, and, hopefully, thereby to maximize revenues in the long run. The most successful has obviously been the Organization of Petroleum Exporting Countries (OPEC), founded in 1960 and with a membership currently consisting of Iran, Iraq, Kuwait, Saudi Arabia, Venezuela, Qatar, Libya, United Arab Emirates, Indonesia, Ecuador, Gabon, Algeria, and Nigeria. It produces nearly 55 percent of the world's oil. OPEC shocked the world's economy in 1973 by collectively increasing the price of a barrel of

Table 2.6

COMMODITIES (EXCLUDING OIL) OF EXPORT IMPORTANCE TO LESS DEVELOPED COUNTRIES, 1972

Commodity	LDC exports (millions of U.S. dollars)	LDC share of world exports	Rank	Concentration (number of countries supplying 75%)	Principal exporters (with share of world exports in percent)
Coffee	3,049	100	1	10	Brazil (31); Colombia (15); Ivory Coast. Uganda. Angola (5 each).
Cocoa	723	100	9	4	Ghana (32); Nigeria (22); Ivory Coast (13); Brazil (9)
Tea	609	82	12	4	India (33); Sri Lanka(31); China (8); Kenya (7)
Sugar	2,235	67	3	12	Cuba (26); Brazil (11); Philippines, Australia (8 each); France (7)
Bananas	533	86	13	10 account for 55%	Honduras (17); Costa Rica (12); Panama (11)
Wheat	160	4	20	4	U.S. (35); Canada (23); Australia (14); France (11)
Rice	440	39	15	6	Thailand (28); U.S. (26); China (10); Burma (6); Egypt (6)
Corn (maize)	331	14	16	4	U.S. (54); France (16); South Africa (8)
Vegetable oils*	2,000	substantial	4	minimal	(Dispersed)
Meat	1,400	28	6	4	Netherlands (15); Australia (12); Belgium, France (5 each)
Cotton	1,757	62	5	17	U.S. (21); Egypt (14); U.S.S.R. (10); Turkey (8)
Natural rubber	904	100	8	2	Malaysia (53); Indonesia (23); Thailand (10)
Jute, incl. manufactures	670	88	10	2	Bangladesh (44); India (42)
Wool	161	12	19	3	Australia (50); New Zealand (20); South Africa (7)
Hard fibres, incl. manufactures†	84	96	22	5	Brazil (22); Mexico (21); Tanzania (18); Philippines (12); Angola (7)
Phosphates	300 (approx.)	55	17	4	Morocco (31); U.S. (29); U.S.S.R. (15); Zaire (13)
Copper	2,395	58	2	8	Zambia (22); Chile (20); Canada (16); Zaire (13)
Iron ore	992	38	7	7	Canada. Australia. U.S.S.R.. Brazil. Liberia. Sweden. India
Tin	632	87	11	4	Malaysia (43); Bolivia (16); Thailand (12); Indonesia (11)
Bauxite, incl. alumina	516	56	14	10	Jamaica. Surinam. Guyana. Australia. Yugoslavia
Zinc	194	23	18	11	Canada. Peru. Mexico. Spain
Lead	116	28	21	10	Peru. Canada. Ireland. Australia. Sweden

*Soybean, cottonseed, peanut, olive, sunflower, rape, linseed, palm, coconut, palm kernel, castor and tung oil. Oilseeds, oil cake and animal fats are included.
†Sisal, henequen, abaca, and coir (coconut husk).

Source: Jon McClin, *Governments and Commodities* (Hanover; American Universities Field Staff, January 1976). pp. 4-5.

Table 2.7

UNITED STATES, WESTERN EUROPEAN, AND JAPANESE IMPORT DEPENDENCE OF SELECTED RAW MATERIALS, 1972

	United States		OECD Europe		Japan	
	Import Volume (Thousands of tons)	Imports as a Percentage of Consumption	Import Volume (Thousands of tons)	Imports as a Percentage of Consumption	Import Volume (Thousands of tons)	Imports as a Percentage of Consumption
Aluminum	721	14	285	10	333	23
Bauxite and Alumina	13,389	88	3,726	51	4,996	100
Chromium ore	408	100	970	100	875	100
Copper ore and conc.	49	} 17	562	} 93	2,179	} 90
Copper	334		1,877		332	
Iron ore and conc.	36,334	32	75,307	37	111,519	94
Lead ore and conc.	92	} 19	356	} 75	199	} 76
Lead	222		433		5	
Manganese ore	733	95	3,696	98	2,921	90
Nickel ore and conc.	21	} 90	176	} 89	3,165	} 100
Nickel	119		64		14	
Phosphate rock	52	*	20,514	100	3,040	100
Tin ore and conc.	4	} 100	76	} 96	†	} 97
Tin	52		40		32	
Tungsten ore and conc.	2.7	42	21.5	100	2.4	100
Zinc ore and conc.	231	} 55	1,561	} 61	1,115	} 80
Zinc	484		302		8	

* Net exporter.

† Negligible.

Source: U.S. Council on International Economic Policy, *Special Report: Critical Imported Materials,* December 1974.

crude from roughly $3 to $9. In that oil is a price-inelastic good (within a broad range, a change in price does not change consumption significantly), total revenues to the producing countries rose by approximately the same order. Other factors explaining OPEC's success: member countries controlled most of the oil moving internationally and consumed relatively little; all were LDCs with pressing developmental needs; the cost of developing adequate supplies of an alternative energy source was somewhat higher than the $9-per-barrel price. A cartel can work only if most of the major producing countries are willing to restrict output and to desist from cheating. Other cartel-like organizations, in part inspired by the OPEC success, are the following:

The Council of Copper Exporting Countries (CIPEC), organized in 1974 to restrain exports, increase prices, install a pricing system in which raw copper prices were to be tied either to refined and processed copper or to a general index of industrial prices, and establish a buffer stock to be financed either by the International Monetary Fund (IMF) or OPEC. Members: Zaire, Chile, Peru, and Zambia, with Indonesia, Papua New Guinea, Mauritania, and Australia possibly soon to join. The first four account for about 30 percent of global output.

Association of Iron Ore Exporting Countries (AIEC), which became operative in 1975. Membership: Algeria, Australia, Chile, India, Mauritania, Peru, Sierra Leone, Sweden, Tunisia, and Venezuela. Together, they produce about 75 percent of the noncommunist world's iron ore. AIEC's intent is to provide a structure for consultation and a clearinghouse for information with emphasis on independent government decision-making. The ultimate intent would seem to be formation of a cartel, although thus far Australia and Sweden have pressured against any price-fixing or output restriction provisions.

The International Bauxite Association (IBA) is a ten-nation group dating from 1974. Its purpose is to develop a common pricing policy. Members: Australia, Dominican Republic, Ghana, Guinea, Guyana, Haiti, Jamaica, Sierra Leone, Surinam, and Yugoslavia. Collectively they account for about 70 percent of world production.

The Association of Natural Rubber Producing Countries (ANRPC) was organized in 1970 to stabilize price but not to create a producer-dominated cartel. Its program called for limitation of natural rubber exports from member countries, establishment of an international buffer stock, and a supply rationalization scheme. Membership: Indonesia, Malaysia, Singapore, Sri Lanka, Thailand, and Vietnam.

Union of Banana Exporting Countries (UBEC), consisting of six Latin American states, appeared in 1974. Explicitly inspired by OPEC, it was designed to control production and increase prices. As of 1977, it had yet to prove effective although it had organized a marketing corporation to open up new markets for member countries and to increase their direct participation in the banana trade in competition with the three firms currently dominating such trade. The corporation was also designed to offer technical assistance to producers' associations. Membership: Panama, Costa Rica, Honduras, Guatemala, Columbia, Dominican Republic.

The tungsten-producing nations met in 1975 and agreed to form a producers' association in order to create price stability. The major problem in the path of effective organization lies in the fact that world production is nearly evenly divided among ten market economy countries, the People's Republic of China, the Soviet Union, and North Korea. As of 1977, no permanent organization had appeared.

5. *Commodity agreements*, multilateral agreements among producing and consuming countries for the purpose of stabilizing prices and earnings. Frequently, they include specifications for buffer stocks, allowable price ranges, export quotas, import quotas, quality controls, and joint promotion. A proposal was introduced in the United Nations in 1975 to establish buffer stocks for 18

major commodities, at a cost of $10.7 billion, to stabilize prices and assure supplies. Present agreements relate to wheat, coffee, cocoa, sugar, tin, olive oil, and whales.[78] The International Wheat Agreement obligates exporting and importing countries to buy and sell certain guaranteed quantities at stipulated prices, although importers limit their obligation to buy only a specified percentage of their commercial imports from exporting member countries. The International Coffee Agreement, with 48 members but now largely ineffective, is based on an adjustable quota restriction on exports and the reduction of surplus production through agricultural diversification, financed by a fund to which all member countries contribute. The International Cocoa Agreement, to which 42 countries adhere, attempts to set maximum prices and export quotas and maintain buffer stocks. The International Sugar Agreement, with 49 participants, sets up a target price range and uses quota restrictions on exports. The International Tin Agreement, supported by 35 countries, uses buffer stocks (largely depleted as of 1976–77) to keep prices within target ranges, the seven major producing countries (all members) bearing the entire cost. The agreement was reported near collapse in early 1977. The International Agreement on Olive Oil, with 21 participants, attempts to regulate the volume of trade by compensatory exchanges on a voluntary basis between deficit and surplus producing countries and by stockpiling the unsold surplus. The International Whaling Agreement, supported by 14 countries, attempts to establish limits to the annual whale catch and to assign national quotas. Its purpose is conservation, not the establishment of a producers' cartel for the purpose of maximizing revenues. The U.S. adheres to the wheat, coffee, tin, and whaling agreements, but has recently withdrawn from the sugar agreement.

A recently-introduced innovation through the Lomé Convention, 1975, to which the European Community and 46 African, Caribbean, and Pacific LDCs have committed themselves, is a commodity earnings stabilization plan. The plan calls for the community's commitment of some 375 units of account[79] to protect member countries heavily dependent upon the export of certain raw materials and agricultural items against price and production fluctuations. When receipts drop by a certain percentage, countries can request compensation. The mechanism triggering the fund operates sooner for the poorest countries, which will not have to reimburse the fund. Other recipients must repay when the price rises. Products affected include: peanuts, cocoa, coffee, cotton, coconuts, palm nuts and kernel, hides and skins, timber products, bananas, tea, raw sisal, and iron ore. This comes very close to some of the presently proposed global schemes for commodity revenue stabilization,

[78]In each case, there is an organization, specifically the International Wheat Council, the International Coffee Organization, the International Cocoa Council, the International Sugar Organization, the International Tin Council, the International Olive Oil Council, and the International Whaling Commission.

[79]A multiple currency unit, valued at $1.2063 in mid-1975.

which in essence call for a pooling of revenues by commodity-producing countries and a division according to some predefined formula. The theory is that aggregate revenues derived from a variety of commodities would be more stable than revenues from one or two.[80]

6. *Long-term arrangements* (LTA), bilateral or multilateral agreements calling for the restriction of exports of a specific commodity by one or more countries to one or more other countries whose markets are being disrupted. The objective is to lessen the export-induced disruption of the market in the importing country without the imposition of quotas or tariffs, since these devices tend to be difficult to remove. Properly used, a long-term agreement provides the importing country with time to shift resources so that the import restrictions may be lifted with minimum injury. The U.S. government has negotiated LTAs (under the GATT) in order to limit imports of textiles and steel. Although the principal concern initially was the increase of Japanese textile and steel imports, the LTAs are multilateral. Under these agreements the U.S. could unilaterally restrict imports from countries that disrupted or threatened to disrupt the U.S. market. Subsequently, injured U.S. importers brought legal action against the government on the grounds that such agreements restrained U.S. trade and, hence, were illegal under U.S. antitrust law. The government successfully defended itself on the grounds that they were voluntary, not legally binding. Indeed, LTAs are sometimes called voluntary marketing agreements (VMA), or, if multinational, orderly marketing agreements (OMA).

7. *Friendship, commerce, and navigation (FCN) treaties,* bilateral agreements designed generally to facilitate trade and commerce between the signatory countries. Typical provisions include the principles of reciprocity, right of entry, right of establishment, right to national treatment (such as access to courts), freedom of travel and communication, most favored nation (MFN) treatment,[81] guarantees against confiscation of property, establishment of certain tax exemptions (for nonprofit institutions, nonresident aliens not engaged in trade or business, foreign-source income received by aliens), freedom of currency exchange except as necessary to maintain or restore adequate monetary reserves as authorized or requested by the International Monetary Fund, enforceability of private arbitration awards, establishment of the private legal nature of state enterprise (so that state sovereignty cannot be used as a shield against legal action), plus certain limitations (such as on the employment of aliens and on alien entry into certain types of enterprise).

---

[80]This idea first appeared in print in 1958. See *Private Foreign Investment,* Hearings before the Subcommittee on Foreign Trade Policy of the Committee on Ways and Means, House of Representatives, 85th Congress, Second Session, December 1–5, 1958, testimony of Richard D. Robinson, p. 579.

[81]The U.S. has refused to extend MFN treatment to the U.S.S.R., and most members of the Sino-Soviet bloc. The sole exception as of mid-1977 was Poland. The lack of MFN treatment means that in the absence of a special agreement no tariff reductions negotiated with other countries apply and that duties will therefore be higher on goods traded with that country.

8. *Bilateral trade agreements*, a two-nation agreement calling for the exchange of specified commodities at specified trade-offs up to stipulated amounts. Provision for a clearing account is generally included, which is a device for permitting temporary imbalances up to agreed-upon limits. Much of the trade between the Sino-Soviet bloc countries and the rest of the world moves under such agreements. Other countries under severe balance-of-payments pressure may attempt to maintain a balance in their trade accounts by entering into a series of such agreements. The problems attendant on marketing successfully within a bilateral trading agreement are discussed in Section 1.1.

9. *General Agreement on Trade and Tariffs (GATT)*, a multilateral agreement (85 full members plus 14 others which *de facto* apply GATT rules)[82] providing the mechanism for facilitating reciprocal reduction of tariffs and other trade barriers, the standardization of trade formalities, and the resolution of trade disputes. MFN treatment is guaranteed all members except that granted within common markets, free trade areas, and other international agreements specifically excepted by GATT members (for example, the Canadian-United States vehicle accord).

10. *Regional cooperation agreements*, a group of nations with a special relationship in regard to economic planning and investment in joint projects and very frequently linked by a regional development bank (for example, the African Development Bank, Asian Development Bank, Arab Development Bank, Caribbean Development Bank, Inter-American Development Bank). Another common linking device is a trade preference or liberalization program. Important among these are:

Organisation Commune Africaine Malgache et Mauricienne (OCAM), essentially French West African states (Benin, Central African Republic, Ivory Coast, Mauritius, Niger, Ruanda, Senegal, Togo, Upper Volta).

Association of Southeast Asian Nations (ASEAN), consisting of Malaysia, Indonesia, Singapore, Thailand, and the Philippines. Late in 1976 ASEAN was reported as having taken two steps toward implementing plans for five major industrial ventures to serve the regional market. In February 1977, the ASEAN Foreign Ministers signed an agreement to establish a preferential trading arrangement.

Regional Cooperation for Development (RCD), membership which consists of Turkey, Iran, and Afghanistan. Its avowed purpose is to coordinate trade and infrastructure development, to map out joint industrial projects, and to evolve a system of preferential trade agreements. By the end of 1976, 17 projects had gone into operation and 21 others were being negotiated.

The Eastern European Council for Mutual Economic Assistance (COMECON), whose membership consists of all of the Eastern European socialist countries except Albania

---

[82]GATT includes seven communist countries: Hungary, Czechoslovakia, Poland, Rumania, Yugoslavia, Cuba, and Bulgaria (as an observer).

and Yugoslavia. As of 1976, progress in COMECON toward market integration had slowed. The 1976–80 plans of the member countries were to have been coordinated to achieve a rational division of labor and avoid duplication of production facilities. Among the barriers to integration were the absence of joint administrative responsibility for cooperative projects (the management for all of them has rested in Soviet hands) and reluctance by member countries to rely on each other's commitments for product quality and delivery dates. Nonetheless, COMECON countries do rely heavily upon one another, and it was estimated that intra-COMECON trade would increase 50 percent between 1976 and 1980 to an annual level of $400 billion.[83]

Organization for Economic Cooperation and Development (OECD), a 23-country organization consisting of the North Atlantic Treaty Organization (NATO) members, plus Japan and Australia, with Yugoslavia and the Commission of the European Communities enjoying limited participation. It provides a forum for the discussion and harmonization of a wide range of economic issues. Additionally, it compiles a wealth of statistical data and undertakes research into issues of common interest. Many observers anticipate that the OECD will eventually emerge as the organizational vehicle for the creation of a common international law in respect to trade and investment.

Council of the Entente, consisting of Benin, Ivory Coast, Niger, Togo, Upper Volta, which has institutionalized a number of joint development projects in communications and industry.

East African Community (EAC), whose specific purpose has been to expand cooperative regional projects. Members: Kenya, Tanzania, Burundi, Ethiopia, Somalia.

Latin American Economic System (SELA), created in 1975 by 23 Latin American states, is designed to provide a permanent regional organization operating in the fields of joint economic and social consultation, cooperation, and promotion. Its specific purpose is to promote regional cooperation in order to achieve self-sustained and independent development and to support regional integration.

The League of Arab States[84] is a loose association whose most effective activity has been the anti-Israeli boycott. From its start in the early 1950s, the boycott forbad all direct trade between the Arab countries and Israel (although there has been much leakage through Israeli-occupied west bank of the Jordan where goods are relabelled). Subsequently, this "primary boycott" escalated into a "secondary boycott" of all foreign companies doing business with Israel that might contribute to the Israeli economy or its war potential or were controlled by "Zionists." This move led to the creation of the "Arab blacklist," on which was listed the names of those firms operating contrary to the Arab boycott rules. More recently, the Arabs have tried to prevent any foreign firms that do business with blacklisted firms from doing business in the Arab countries, the so-called "tertiary boycott." The U.S. government reacted in 1969 with a requirement that U.S. firms report boycott requests. In 1976, the lists of reporting U.S. firms were made public. It was already illegal for any U.S. firm to

---

[83] *Business International,* February 27, 1976, p. 69.

[84] Members: Algeria, Bahrain, Egypt, Iraq, Jordan, Kuwait, Lebanon, Libya, Mauritania, Morocco, Oman, Qatar, Saudi Arabia, Somalia, Syria, Tunisia, Sudan, United Arab Emirates, Yemen Arab Republic, Yemen's People's Democratic Republic.

engage in a "discriminatory boycott," which in this context referred to a boycott by one U.S. firm of another by reason of the fact that its owners or officers were Jewish. In 1975, the U.S. Justice Department brought an anti-trust suit against the Bechtel Corporation on the grounds that its refusal to subcontract with blacklisted firms was a conspiracy to restrict competition. (The case was subsequently settled out of court through a "consent decree.") The 1976 Tax Reform Act denied certain foreign tax benefits to U.S. firms participating in an international boycott, which it is deemed to have done if, as a condition of doing business in a particular country, it agrees not to conduct business with another (the secondary boycott), or if it refuses to do business with another U.S. firm that does business in that country (tertiary boycott), or because of the nationality, race, or religion of the owners or officers of the other firm (discriminatory boycott). If found to be participating in a boycott, the firm could lose (1) the credit it might otherwise claim against its U.S. tax liability for foreign income and wealth taxes, (2) any right to defer the payment of U.S. taxes on income not remitted to the United States, and (3) the capacity to defer U.S. tax on half of the income of a domestic international sale subsidiary (see Appendix 1, Chapter 7). In addition, a number of states legislated penalties against firms participating in the Arab Boycott,[85] which laws, however, were preempted by a federal law in 1977 which made it a criminal offense for U.S. firms (including overseas affiliates "controlled in fact") to comply with the Arab boycott provisions other than the primary boycott.

11. *Currency area (franc, sterling, dollar),* a group of countries whose currencies are relatively freely convertible, which enforce similar foreign exchange control systems, if any, and hold reserves of scarce or "hard" currencies in a common pool. Two variations: monetary area (a group of countries having a special relationship with a currency not their own; for example, Bahama's use of the U.S. dollar and, until recently, the Persian Gulf principalities' use of the Indian rupee), and a currency union or area (two or more countries that share the same currency, as Liberia's use of the U.S. dollar and the Communauté Financière Africaine use of the CFA franc in West and Equatorial Africa[86] and the East African shilling). It is suggested that this is a highly unstable relationship short of a federation.

12. *Customs preference area,* a group of nations that either reciprocally maintain lower tariffs with each other than with other countries (historically, the British Commonwealth, the United States and the Philippines; currently, EFTA and its associate members, Finland and the Soviet Union)[87] or do so unilaterally (that is, without "reverse preference") as does the EEC in respect to some 53 LDCs. Virtually all of the industrialized countries now extend a generalized preference to various categories of imports from LDCs, a system pioneered by Japan and Australia, subsequently by the Soviet Union and the

---

[85]Jack G. Kaikati, "The Challenge of the Arab Boycott," *Sloan Management Review,* Winter 1977, pp. 83 ff.

[86]Benin, Niger, Senegal, Togo, Upper Volta, Ivory Coast.

[87]Finland extends to the Soviet Union the same preferences, on a reciprocal basis, as it gives the European Free Trade Association, with which it has "associate" status. It is apparently true that in this case there is no nationality or sourcing test; that is, the Finnish subsidiary of a U.S. firm could re-export U.S.-made goods through Finland into the U.S.S.R. under the Finnish-Soviet trade agreement.

EEC. In the U.S. case, the president is authorized by the Trade Act of 1974 to provide duty-free treatment of eligible imports from "beneficiary developing countries," which are so designated by executive order issued by the president after notifying Congress of his intent. Excluded are all communist countries except those participating in the International Monetary Fund and the GATT, members of OPEC, and those that have expropriated U.S. property (that either owned directly by U.S. citizens or by a firm at least 50 percent owned by U.S. citizens) without compensation. A variation of the customs preference is the favorable treatment given by the Mexican government in respect to imports of materials and components from the U.S. as an incentive to the industrialization of the high unemployment zone along its northern border and by the U.S. to the import of the final product.

13. *Free Trade area*, a regional group with no internal tariffs. Since national external tariffs may vary, rules of origin must be enforced.[88] It is permitted by the GATT if 85 percent of the trade is free. Major operating free trade areas are the European (EFTA),[89] the Latin American (LAFTA),[90] the Anzac (Australia and New Zealand), and the Anglo-Irish. In the EFTA and LAFTA cases, there are two subgroups somewhat more highly integrated than their fellow members, the Nordic customs union (Finland, Norway, and Sweden, plus Denmark, an EC member) and the Andean Group Common Market (ANCOM) countries (see below). Characteristic of LAFTA are the so-called complementarity agreements, which are bilateral national agreements for the mutual exchange of related products, without MFN extension to other member states. In gaining more liberal treatment of its own industry, it is important for an interested firm to influence negotiations at the LAFTA sectoral meetings by persuading the national industrial delegates of possible

[88]The most precisely stated rules of origin are those worked out by EFTA and introduced in 1973 in their present form. Obviously, those commodities wholly produced within the member states from materials indigenous to the group qualify for free trade. By definition, materials included on the "basic materials list" were considered as of EFTA origin even though imported. For those commodities produced within EFTA but from imported goods or a mixture of indigenous and imported goods, the rule is that to qualify for free trade a product had to be sufficiently transformed by processing that it was classified under a different tariff heading of the Brussels Tariff Nomenclature (BTN) or Customs Cooperation Council Nomenclature (CCCN), which are one and the same, than that of each of the products worked or processed. To adjust for those cases in which a change in classification results from relatively unimportant processing or those in which extensive processing fails to change the classification, two lists (A and B) were constructed. List A lists those cases in which even though processing induces a change in tariff classification, further processing must take place to confer on the goods the status of "originating products." List B enumerates those manufacturing processes that, although not resulting in a change of tariff heading, nonetheless confer the status of originating products. It should be noted that the origin of the energy, the equipment, machinery, and tools used in production has no bearing on the origin of the product. The origin rules both in EFTA and under the Free Trade Agreements (FTAs) negotiated with nonmember states (for example, with the European Community, Switzerland, Portugal, Finland) are identical except that FTAs with these associate members do not define "basic materials" as indigenous. If a product has "originating status" when imported into a country from which it is subsequently exported to another country linked by FTAs, and not more than 5 percent "nonoriginating" materials are used in the further processing, then the idea of "multilateral cumulation of origin" is recognized.

[89]With the admission of the U.K. and Denmark into the European Community as of January 1, 1974, EFTA membership now consists of Austria, Iceland, Norway, Portugal, Sweden, and Switzerland.

[90]LAFTA membership: Argentina, Bolivia, Brazil, Chile, Colombia, Ecuador, Mexico, Peru, Paraguay, Uruguay, Venezuela.

gains. The U.S. counterparts of these sectoral agreements are the Canadian-U.S. accord on vehicles[91] and the United States-Canadian Defense Production Sharing Program, both of which establish a virtual free trade regime within the two sectors. Another example of a sectoral arrangement is Intermetal, the East European organization to promote specialization and close cooperation of national steel industries.

14. *Customs union*, a regional group with a common external tariff and no internal tariffs, examples of which are the Benelux countries (Belgium, Netherlands, Luxembourg) and the Southern African Customs Union. It should be noted that the application of a common external tariff does not mean that the same duty will be collected by all member states, in that the determinants of the value of the imported goods, on which basis the common *ad valorem* rates are applied, may include import cost, insurance, and port handling charges, all of which may vary from one port of entry to another.

15. *Common market*, a regional group with no internal tariffs, a common external tariff, and harmonization of domestic law in order to facilitate unrestricted factor movement, the major attempts in this direction being the European Economic Community (EEC),[92] the Central American Common Market (CACM), the Andean Common Market (ANCOM), and the Caribbean Common Market (CCM). A common market may be of a general character (as the EEC), or based on the integration of certain sectors of the members' economies. This last approach is used in the CACM[93] in its "industries of integration" scheme, which is designed to encourage the establishment of new or expanded industries by giving plants certified as regional access, on a

---

[91]The U.S.-Canada Automotive Agreement (1965) gives duty-free treatment in both directions to motor vehicles (with some special exceptions) and parts used as original equipment in manufacturing motor vehicles (but not replacement parts). To gain duty-free access to the U.S., Canadian products may contain no more than 50 percent third-country content. To gain duty-free access into Canada, U.S. products must be imported by a Canadian vehicle manufacturing firm approved by the Canadian government and, in 1964 and each following model year, has produced vehicles of the type being imported. In any event, the ratio of net sales value of vehicles produced in Canada to the net sales value of vehicles of the same type sold by the same company in Canada must be at least 75 and at least equal to the ratio in the 1964 model year. Also, the Canadian value added in the Canadian-produced vehicles must be at least equal to that of the 1964 model year. Finally, the Canadian government required Canadian motor vehicle manufacturers to sign "letters of undertaking" in which they commit themselves to (1) increase in each model year the Canadian value added in its Canadian production by 50 to 60 percent of the growth in the market over the 1964 model year, and (2) increase the dollar value of Canadian value added over the 1964 model year by a stipulated amount during the 1968 model year and by no less an amount in each subsequent year.

[92]With the union of the European Coal and Steel Community (ECSC) and the European Atomic Energy Community (Euratom) with the EEC, the resulting structure is now known as the European Communities (EC). In this text the more common acronym EEC is used. Present membership: France, Germany, Italy, Belgium, Netherlands, Luxembourg, United Kingdom, Denmark, Ireland. Early in 1977, it was reported that all contending factions in Spain aspired to EEC membership, possibly through a five- to ten-year transitional period. Greece expected to join the community within a year or two. Portugal felt that it would be ready to do so shortly thereafter. Turkey, on the other hand, did not expect to be economically ready for EEC membership until possibly 1995.

[93]Membership: Guatemala, Honduras, San Salvador, Nicaragua, and Costa Rica. As of 1977 efforts were underway to negotiate a new "framework treaty" that would establish the Economic and Social Community of Central America (CESCA) in order to reactivate Central American economic integration. Honduras, a *de jure* member, had withdrawn from active participation. It was expected that Panama would be included in the new CESCA.

preferential basis, to all of CACM. ANCOM[94] is pursuing a similar strategy through a series of sectoral programs for industrial development, which locate specified industries within certain of the member states. The member designated to receive preferential treatment in respect to a particular industry is to enjoy special tariff advantages within the ANCOM for the products of that industry for a specified number of years. There is a general agreement that member countries would not encourage new investment in sectors assigned to others, and authorization for foreign investment in these reserved industries is forbidden. The first sectoral program approved was in the metal-mechanics area, which assigned the manufacture of 180 products to individual ANCOM countries. Other sectoral programs involve the steel, automotive, electronics, and fertilizer industries. Approval was expected in mid-1978. Other than the extinguishing of all internal tariffs and the mounting of a common external tariff, the EEC has dropped internal barriers to capital and labor movement, developed a Community-wide antitrust law, and has stimulated various levels of harmonization in the tax, corporate law, accounting, industrial standards, export financing, and industrial relations areas. The EEC has also entered into a free trade agreement with EFTA and one-directional preferential trade agreements with Spain, Israel, Greece, Turkey, the Maghreb countries (Algeria, Tunisia, Morocco, Libya), and 46 developing countries of Africa, the Caribbean, and the Pacific (ACP). The 46 ACPs were parties to the Lomé Convention convened in Togo in 1975 (see Figure 2.3), thereby replacing the Arusha (1969) and Younde (1973) conventions, which had previously associated a number of African countries with the Community. With the admission of the United Kingdom to the EEC, some 23 members of the British Commonwealth had automatically become eligible for association with the Community. The Convention covers the duty-free access of ACP products to the EEC, an export revenue stabilization scheme (see above), a sugar agreement, and financial and technical cooperation.

The Caribbean Common Market (CCM), formed out of the Caribbean Free Trade Association (CARIFTA) and the Eastern Caribbean Common Market[95] in 1973, consists of the Barbados, British Honduras, Guyana, Jamaica, Trinidad and Tobago, Windward and Leeward Islands.[96] Members are signatory to the Lomé Convention. Other common market efforts not yet realized: East African Economic Community (Kenya, Uganda, Tanzania), the Maghreb Common Market (Algeria, Tunisia, Morocco, Libya), the Economic Community of West African States (Communauté Économique des États de l'Afrique et l'Ouest, or CEDEAO),[97] and the Central African Customs and

---

[94]Membership: Bolivia, Colombia, Ecuador, Peru, Venezuela. Chile withdrew in late 1976.

[95]Just prior to joining CARIFTA, the seven territories of the Leeward and Windward Islands had joined to form this subregional group.

[96]Antigua, Dominica, Grenada, Montserrat, St. Kitts-Nevis, St. Lucia, St. Vincent.

[97]Members: Mauritania, Senegal, Gambia, Guinea-Bissau, Guinea, Sierra Leone, Liberia, Ivory Coast, Mali, Upper Volta, Ghana, Togo, Benin, Niger, Nigeria.

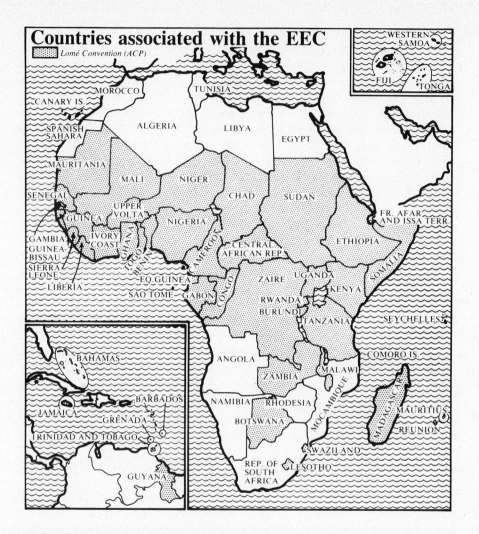

Figure 2.3
COUNTRIES ASSOCIATED WITH THE EEC

Economic Union (Union Douaniere Économique de l'Afrique Centrale, or UDEAC).[98] A mature common market, such as the European, is under great pressure either to move toward higher levels of integration so as to harmonize national laws affecting capital, labor, and management, *or* to pull apart as unequal national laws compete in the pursuit of such national interests as full

[98]Members: Congo People's Republic, Gabon, Cameroon, Central African Republic.

employment, monetary stability, and so forth. In the former situation, a federation is likely to evolve; in the latter, a customs union or free trade area. A variation of the common market is the sectoral common market, examples of which are the Canadian-U.S. Automotive Agreement and the Canadian-U.S. Defense Production Sharing Agreement.

16. *Economic union*, a combination of a common market and a currency union. The European Community moved in the direction of union a few years ago, but subsequently drew back. It would seem virtually impossible to maintain an effective economic union short of federation, for political decision-making organs at the regional level are necessary. Once the EEC holds direct elections to the European Parliament, scheduled for 1978, further movement in the direction of union, and ultimately federation, may develop. Efforts to create a Nordic Economic Union (Nordek) in 1970 failed. Examples of effective economic unions: the Belgium-Luxembourg Economic Community (BLEU); Monaco and France.

17. *Federation*, a grouping of former nations under a single law-making body, which implies special trade relationships, the most likely being an economic union (the West Indies Federation, which broke down in 1962; the United Arab Republic, which has become defunct; United Arab Emirates,[99] and Malaysia, which subsequently lost Singapore and only in 1972 began effecting a real common market among its constituent parts).

---

[99]Formerly the Trucial States, the UAE consists of seven sheikdoms: Abu Dhabi, Dubai, Sharjah, Ajman, Fujaireh, Ras-al-Khaimah, and Umm al-Qaiwain.

Case C
SINDEL DO BRASIL

Sindel do Brasil was a joint venture between a United States manufacturer of diesel engines, Sindry Incorporated, and a Brazilian firm, Deller S.A. of Sao Paulo. In 1973, Sindel had purchased the Sao Paulo plant of one of its European competitors. In that some 5,000 to 6,000 Sindel engines were already in Brazil, management felt that some degree of local manufacture was feasible and desirable. Given official pressures to develop a local source of diesel engines, it was felt that Sindel should move in before a competitor preempted the market by developing local manufacture first.

Shortly after purchasing the plant, Sindel approached Deller to join the enterprise, the upshot being a joint venture 55 percent owned by Deller and 45 percent by Sindel. Despite its minority shareholding, Sindel had the right to name the general manager. In fact, the general manager, financial vice-president, and technical director were all Sindry appointees, U.S. citizens, and had been employed by Sindry in the United States. Of the total capital, equity and debt together ($12 million), Sindel had contributed some 65 percent. Reasons given by the Sindel management for the joint venture were (1) the need for capital (Sindel-U.S. being under severe financial pressure in respect to liquidity and debt/equity ratio), and (2) the favorable experience with Deller in a Venezuelan joint venture for some eight years. The latter experience had convinced management of the usefulness of a local partner in a Latin American venture.

Sindel do Brasil was manufacturing diesel engines (230 to 400 horsepower) for sale to firms producing construction machinery, generator sets, and trucks. It was not yet selling to agricultural tractor fabricators, nor was it doing any direct exporting, although management was in the process of negotiating soft currency exports to other Latin American countries. Thus far, the company had not enjoyed any of the export-based incentives offered by the Brazilian Government. Sindel did export a few parts to Sindry-owned enterprises in Europe and elsewhere. In addition, some 20 percent of Sindel's Brazilian output was exported indirectly through a local customer who was in the business of building construction machinery. The Sindel plant was currently producing about 70 engines a month, but a major expansion was under construction which would treble production.

The Brazilian-made diesels were reported to be of comparable quality to those made in the United States, but the cost was somewhat higher. Labor input in hours-per-unit-of-output was roughly twice that in the U.S., likewise overhead as a percent of direct labor. But Sindel was producing only three engines a day, not 300, which was the rate in Sindry's U.S. plant. Sindel employed 486 persons, of which 45 were classified as managers and technicians and 200 as administrative personnel.

The Brazilian authorities had permitted all of the start-up costs to be capitalized. Virtually all of the technology and know-how to build and operate the plant was supplied by Sindry-U.S. Sindel engines carried the Sindry trade name, which was well-known worldwide. Sindel had reimbursed Sindry for technical assistance provided subsequent to plant start-up, but only on a direct cost basis. The Sindel management pointed out that there was no point in Sindry's charging more for the technology and technical assistance transferred to Brazil until Sindel started making money, which was unlikely to happen for two or three more years. Sindry did have technical assistance contracts and patent-trademark licenses with its enterprises in Turkey, Iran, Japan, and Venezuela, all of which were owned 60 to 80 percent by Sindry. It also had wholly-owned operations in the United Kingdom, Germany, Canada, and Australia.

Sindel was buying about 40 percent of the 90 percent Brazilian content in its diesel engines from local subcontractors unrelated to either of the parent firms. Among these were three foundries to which Sindel was supplying technology and some equipment. Technical personnel from Sindel visited them at least twice a month. The 10 percent not of Brazilian origin were purchased from Sindry-U.S. at standard cost plus a fixed percentage.

It was reported that inventory control continued to be a problem. When a shortage of an imported part developed, it had to be air-shipped from the U.S., but bureaucratic obstacles at the Sao Paulo airport caused long delays, the average time in getting a shipment out of the airport being some 18 days. Rio de Janeiro was said to be less difficult and hence management was planning to ship to Rio and truck to Sao Paulo.

On average, Sindel undertook some 600 to 700 man-years of training per year. For each of the past two or three years, something like 15 persons had been brought to Brazil and five Brazilians sent abroad, almost entirely to the United States and Canada. In addition it maintained a training center at its Sao Paulo plant for customers and employees on the use and maintenance of Sindry engines. About 20 persons were accommodated at a time in a week-long course.

Discussion questions:

1. Do you feel that Sindel was wise in trebling its capacity at this time?
2. What is your reaction to Sindry's policy in respect to providing technology and technical assistance?

Case D
MINNEAPOLIS-MOLINE

In February, a four-man mission from the Minneapolis-Moline (MM) Company, a manufacturer of farm machinery, arrived in Ankara, Turkey, to negotiate some sort of arrangement whereby MM could get its equipment into the Turkish market. MM management realized that participation in a local manufacturing enterprise would probably be necessary, and discussions toward this end were commenced with representatives of the Turkish government, largely from the Machine and Chemical Industries Association, a government-owned industrial combine.

The first obstacle encountered had to do with management control. The initial negotiation was with Mithat Dulge, an official of the MCIA. The MM board chairman had laid down the principle that either MM must have a management contract or a majority on the board, despite the fact that it was not proposing to subscribe a majority of the capital. The Turks rejected the latter of these alternatives, the board majority, at once, and no agreement was achieved on the idea of a management contract. On this point the initial meeting broke up, and it seemed likely that the project would collapse. Mr. William Foss, head of the MM group in Turkey, later recalled, "We were all set to go home and were even discussing the European cities we would visit on the way back to the States." At this point, Vecdi Diker, MM's Turkish representative, tried to talk the MM group into giving way on its insistence on management control. But the group maintained that it could not do so. Vecdi Diker then talked with Mithat Dulge and found that the Machine and Chemical Industries Association might be induced to give ground on the issue. It was then arranged that Mr. Foss and Mr. Fikret Bey, a technical advisor to the Machine and Chemical Industries Association and former works manager of the Turkish Air League's aircraft factory, would write a management contract. But agreement on details was obviously going to be difficult.

Three months later, the Turkish government and the MM group signed a protocol (see Appendix to Case D) which called for a management contract, but the discussion over the terms of such a contract continued. The reason for signing the protocol at this time was a desire by the government that an agreement be announced prior to the next general election. The administration seemed to feel that publicity about the impending opening of a tractor factory in Turkey would be a point in its favor.

Discussion between William Foss and Fikret Bey in respect to management control continued. In the final analysis, Fikret Bey insisted that all details, specifications, and drawings of equipment that might be built by the Turkish company in the next ten years be sent to Turkey immediately. This demand included copies of every drawing for every piece of equipment manufactured by MM in the United States. Not only would this have involved a considerable expense on the part of MM, it would have been a useless effort inasmuch as the designs for much of the equipment would undoubtedly change during this period of time, equipment the Turkish company would not initially undertake to produce. Mr. Foss pointed all this out to Mithat Dulge, Fikret Bey's superior, who agreed that Fikret Bey's request was an unwarranted one and signed the management contract as it stood. Later Mr. Foss observed that during those months of negotiation the Turks apparently had become convinced that MM was serious about its manufacturing project in Turkey and could be trusted. He observed that though one of Mithat Dulge's friends was the Turkish distributor for Klockner-Humboldt Deutz, A.G., a German competitor, which had also been discussing a tractor manufacturing venture in Turkey, Mithat Dulge had become convinced that the Germans were not really interested in manufacturing, and, in spite of what representatives of the German firm said, he refused to sign a contract with them.

The next issue facing the MM group related to financing. Although the Turkish company had been incorporated and the Turks had signed a management contract, Mr. MacFarlane, the MM board chairman, did not want to make a final commitment until financing could be found, as the project would involve several million dollars. Mr. Foss had been authorized to sign the protocol and the articles of incorporation, but not in such a way as would bind the company in any way in respect to financing. By this time everything had been settled other than the dollar financing. Mr. MacFarlane communicated with the Chase Manhattan Bank, and it was agreed that the bank would establish a revolving credit of $2.5 million to be repaid at six month intervals over two years. The terms having been agreed to in principle, one of Chase Manhattan's vice presidents and the bank's Middle East representative (who was headquartered in Beruit) came to Turkey and entered into the discussion. In a meeting in Mithat Dulge's office, agreement was reached that if the Machine and Chemical Industrial Association could secure a guarantee from the Turkish government for this credit, Chase Manhattan would make the funds available. Two weeks later a guarantee was in fact received from the Turkish government, signed by the Counsel of Ministers, to cover the $2.5 million. Mr. Foss believed that this guarantee was the only one of its kind given to a private company by the Turkish government up to that time. In a meeting with the United States Ambassador in Ankara and the chief of the AID mission to Turkey, all agreed that this arrangement was reasonable. But the Chase Manhattan Bank found the agreement unsatisfactory. It then developed that what the bank was really insisting on was a *gold-backed* guarantee by the Turkish government. Chase Manhattan was holding some $32 million worth of Turkish government gold, $13 million of which had been committed, and $19 million of which was free. Chase Manhattan was asking that an additional $2.5 million of the free gold be committed as security for this credit. As soon as Mithat Dulge heard that Chase Manhattan wanted a gold-backed guarantee he went to the Deputy Prime Minister and made known this condition. The request was transferred to the Counsel of Ministers, at which level it was turned down. This was five months after the signing of the protocol.

As soon as he learned of this failure, Mr. Foss rushed a program to the Deputy Prime Minister for a foreign exchange allocation covering the first year of the company's program in Turkey. This called for $3.6 million in dollar exchange for component parts for tractors. The request was approved in late October. Even with this guarantee by the Turkish government for foreign exchange availability, MM management felt that it had to get some dollars out immediately in order to be certain of the good faith of the Turkish government. Thereupon, the Deputy Prime Minister was induced to set up the first letter of credit. According to Mr. Foss, "We then felt we were in business." The company was known as Minneapolis-Moline Turk Traktor ve Ziraat Makineleri A.Ş.[1] Mr. Foss was its first general manager and Mr. Huff, another member of the MM negotiating team, the general sales manager. The firm was physiclly located in the aircraft plant formerly owned by the Turkish Air League, just outside of Ankara. Recently, the plant had been turned over to the Machine and Chemical Industries Association.

The production machinery in the Turkish plant was of a general purpose nature; there were no special purpose machine tools. Management felt that direct labor costs were so much lower in Turkey and the dollar allocations so uncertain that the company could not justify the purchase of labor-saving machines.

As part of the agreement, it was stipulated that the United States company would bill parts to the Turkish firm at a standard price charged all distributors. The management of the Turkish company could buy from any source that it so desired; it was not obligated to buy from MM-U.S. It was obligated, however, to produce an MM tractor, for which certain parts were manufactured only by MM. MM was to receive a 3 percent royalty. Eventually, of course, it would secure income from the repatriation of profits or dividends on whatever shares were issued to it for its services and equipment.

The production program of the Turkish company for the first five years rested upon the availability of $8 to $10 million a year in foreign exchange, half to be used for component parts and half for the purchase of machinery and equipment. The Turkish government insisted that MM agree to this five-year program for developing local manufacturing rather than simple assembly. For the first 35 months, the Turkish company would require each month $275,000 worth of parts and $25,000 worth of equipment. By the 36th month, the monthly expenditure would be about $150,000 for parts and $150,000 for equipment.

---

[1] Minneapolis-Moline Turkish Tractor and Agricultural Machinery Anonymous Society (Anonim Şirketi).

Appendix
PROTOCOL

T. C. Ziraat Bankasï, Makina ve Kimya Endustrisi Kurumu, Ziraî Donatïm Kurumu, and Minneapolis-Moline Company have agreed as follows:

ARTICLE I. A company (Société Anonyme) shall be organized in Turkey with its principal office in Ankara under the name of Minneapolis-Moline Türk Traktor ve Ziraat Makineleri A.Ş. The company will be entitled to use this name as long as the Agreement referred to in Article 9 hereunder continues to be in force. Provision will be made in the statutes of the Company to the effect that in case the Agreement referred to above is terminated, the words "Minneapolis-Moline" or letters "MM" shall be eliminated from the name.

ARTICLE 2. The duration of the Company shall be 25 years and its capital, initially, shall be subscribed for and paid by the following in percentages facing their names:[2]

T. C. Ziraat Bankasï	60%
Makina ve Kimya Endustrisi Kurumu	8%
Türkiye Ziraî Donatïm Kurumu	10%
Tariş (Izmir Incir, Uzum ve Zeytinyağï Kooperatifleri Birligi)	12%
Cuko Birliş (Çukurova Pamuk Satiş Kooperatifleri Birliği)	10%
	100%

Provided, however, that in case the members of the first board of directors are included among the founders, in the statutes, the amount of shares they are legally required to own shall be deducted from the participation of T. C. Ziraat Bankasï.

Ziraat Bankasï, as one of the participants in the formation of the company, expresses his willingness to assist the company in borrowing money for the purpose of acquiring necessary working capital.

ARTICLE 3. The object of the company shall be:

1. To manufacture in Turkey and to distribute in Turkey and to export elsewhere Tractors, Combines, Agricultural Machinery, and Equipment all as manufactured or to be manufactured by Minneapolis-Moline, U.S.;

2. To manufacture in Turkey and to distribute in Turkey and to export elsewhere Agricultural Machinery and Equipment designed especially for the needs of Turkey or the company's export market, it being understood, however, that no such manufacturing program shall be entered into without the prior written approval of Minneapolis-Moline Company, U.S.

---

[2]Translation of names: Agricultural Bank of the Republic of Turkey; Machine and Chemical Industry Association; Turkish Agricultural Equipment Society; Izmir Union of Fig, Grape, and Olive Oil Cooperatives; Çukurova Union of Cotton Sales Cooperatives. The first three were government owned; the latter two were of a semipublic character.

The Company shall import such Machinery, Component Parts, and Raw Materials as may be required to implement the production program attached hereto as Exhibit I, and as Exhibit I may be amended from time to time.

ARTICLE 4.   Minneapolis-Moline represents that it has no present intention to establish and, therefore, undertakes not to establish, factories in countries (Europe and the Middle East) to which exports can be made from Turkey. Provided, however, that in case due to reasons beyond the control of Minneapolis-Moline, exports cannot be made from Turkey to the countries above mentioned and after consultation with the Company or in case the Agreement referred to in Article 9 comes to an end, Minneapolis-Moline shall have full freedom in this respect.

ARTICLE 5.   The Company shall be organized instantaneously and all the capital shall be paid in cash by the founders, as shown in Article 2. Immediately upon the organization of the Company, the patent rights and trademarks of Minneapolis-Moline Company required for the manufacturing in Turkey shall be purchased for 30 percent of the capital of the Company. Simultaneously, the Motor Factory of Makina ve Kimya Endustrisi Kurumu described in Exhibit II[3] attached hereto, shall be transferred to the Company upon completion of the legal formalities and at values determined under provisions of the law, and under procedures agreeable to the parties. Provided, however, that both Minneapolis-Moline Company and Makina ve Kimya Endustrisi Kurumu undertake to use the amounts thus obtained, less any amounts previously invested by them in cash, for the purchase of shares of the Company and that T. C. Ziraat Bankasi undertakes to sell such shares to them.

ARTICLE 6.   The land, building, and machinery described in Exhibit II attached hereto,[4] together with all the furniture, fixtures, tools, materials, and supplies now located therein (referred to herein as the "Factory") shall be turned over to the Company after agreement is reached under the provisions of Article 5, and the Company shall be entitled to receive full title and sole and complete occupancy of the factory. Provided, however, raw material, semi-finished, finished parts, special tooling for water meters and Gipsey Major Engine Production, and special machinery for water meter production shall be removed from the factory by Makina ve Kimya Endustrisi Kurumu before the factory is turned over to the Company. The Company plans to erect or otherwise acquire additional building and to purchase and install additional machinery to enable it to carry out its estimated production programs.

ARTICLE 7.   The share certificates of the Company shall be nominative and more than one half of the capital shall be in the hands of private persons. In the duration of the Company, Minneapolis-Moline shall reserve the right to increase its participation in the capital up to 40 percent and if and when it

---

[3]Not included here.
[4]Not included here.

decides to use this privilege, the Ziraat Bankasĭ shall be obliged to sell such shares to it at market prices. In case of the increase of the capital of the Company, its shareholders shall have priority in proportion to their participation in the Company.

ARTICLE 8. The Board of Directors of the Company shall consist of five members, two of whom shall be selected from among the names given by Minneapolis-Moline. One of the directors recommended by Minneapolis-Moline shall be appointed managing director. The managing director shall have the powers and responsibility of a general manager and the Board of Directors of the Company shall, by appropriate resolution, delegate to the managing director, effective during the life of the Management Agreement referred to in Article 9, full authority and control over and responsibility for all manufacturing and sales operations of the Company with the exception of maximum prices for sales in Turkey, including the following powers:

1. The acquisition or construction, repair, or remodeling of the Company's factories, offices, warehouses, or other buildings and the machinery, equipment, parts, tools, and supplies contained therein;

2. The purchase or manufacture locally or importation of materials or parts needed in manufacturing operations;

3. The manufacture or assembly of machinery or accessories or repair and replacement parts and the sale, distribution, and servicing thereof;

4. The selection, training, and discharge of employees and the determination of their salaries and the nature of their work, including the salaries and work of employees lent by Minneapolis-Moline as provided in Article 9.

The managing director will at all times be responsible to the Board of Directors for the operation of the Company for the best interest of the shareholders.

ARTICLE 9. Immediately upon the organization of the Company, a Management Agreement on the basis laid by this Protocol shall be entered into between Minneapolis-Moline Company and the Company.

Minneapolis-Moline Company agrees to provide to the Company the necessary managerial, administrative, and technical personnel who will have the authority and responsibility for the management of the Company. Such personnel will undertake to train Turkish personnel, including production and design engineers, and within a period of not more than five years the percentage of the Turkish personnel in these positions shall be at least 90 percent.

ARTICLE 10. In compensation for the responsibility of the management assumed by Minneapolis-Moline and for its undertaking to make available to the Company the results of its researches, Minneapolis-Moline shall be paid a fee of 3 percent (three percent) of the sales prices of machinery and spare parts manufactured in Turkey in conformity with Minneapolis-Moline specifications.

Provided, however, Minneapolis-Moline within the first five years undertakes not to take out of the country the amounts accruing from the 3 percent above mentioned, net after taxes paid thereon, and to allocate these sums to the purchase of new shares in the Company.

T. C. Ziraat Bankasĭ
Makina ve Kimya Endustrisi Kurumu
Türkiye Ziraî Donatĭm Kurumu
Minneapolis-Moline Company, U.S.A.

EXHIBIT I

It is estimated that with present facilities plus the erection of additional buildings, the following approximate percentage of local manufacturing can be obtained in four successive steps.

First Year

1. Develop patterns, jigs, and fixtures for manufacture of replacement parts for Minneapolis-Moline equipment.

2. Assemble the component parts received from abroad that in our judgment cannot be obtained locally, on the following items:

    1000 Model U Tractors (800 standard, 200 row crop)

    900 Disc Plow

    100 One-way wheatland plows

    1000 Disc harrows

    225 Attachers

    225 Cotton planters and listers

    225 Cultivators

Tractors will be equipped with diesel and kerosene engines in proportions to be determined after further study.

Second Year

1. 2000 Model U Tractors of which approximately 30 to 40 percent of parts will be manufactured locally, providing foundry facilities are available.

2. Further develop manufacturing requirements for additional parts for both repairs and production.

3. Increase the implement line proportionately of which approximately 30 to 40 percent of parts would be manufactured locally providing adequate foundry facilities are available.

Third Year

1. 3500 Model U Tractors of which approximately 75 to 100 percent of those parts now in manufacture by our U.S. plants will be manufactured locally.

2. Increase the implement line proportionately of which approximately 75 percent will be manufactured locally.

3. Start production and assembly of another size tractor in accordance with market requirements at that time.

4. Start assembly of combines, the size to be determined in accordance with market requirements at that time.

Fourth Year

1. Manufacture 5,000 Model U Tractors with implements.
2. Increase balance of line proportionately to the production capacities then available.
3. Introduce additional implements in accordance with requirements of the market.

Discussion Questions

1. What production problems should Mr. Foss anticipate?
2. What should he do about them? When?
3. Could MM enter into a phased manufacturing contract in good faith?

Simulation: This case has proven useful as the basis for the negotiation of a management contract within the general terms of the Protocol. (The Protocol is really a mutual statement of intent.)

Chapter 3
LABOR STRATEGY

Once a firm has made preliminary strategy choices in regard to the market and related supply, management must consider the resources required to implement these choices—labor, management, and finance. Of these, perhaps of greatest difficulty and political import is the labor area, for it is here that possibly both the greatest cost and the greatest risk are entailed.

In the labor area, six basic questions face the firm with an overseas management responsibility:

1. What range of responsibility toward its employees should management feel, in depth and over time?
2. What degree of labor participation in management should be encouraged?
3. What should the policy toward local unions be?
4. What factors should influence recruitment and job assignment in an overseas enterprise?
5. On what basis should training, development, and promotion be undertaken?
6. Should pay scales and other benefits be the same or more liberal than those in the surrounding business community?

RESPONSIBILITY TOWARD EMPLOYEES   3.1

The range of possible attitudes runs from a highly paternalistic one to a highly formalized, impersonal one closely regulated by law and collective contract. Such responsibility runs from a short-term commitment, for example, the life of a contract, to a lifetime commitment, as in many of the larger Japanese corporations. Some observers have concluded that in an increasing number of countries labor is a semifixed cost, reducible only via natural attrition or bankruptcy. In such circumstances it follows that public assistance will be forthcoming if the survival of the enterprise is jeopardized, such as in the Lockheed case (U.S.) and Chrysler case (U.K.).

In many less developed countries, where the values of traditional society still persist, the foreign employer may be forced into a paternalistic relationship whether he desires it or not. An employee expects the relevant elite, whether official or civilian, to assume certain personal obligations toward him. This paternalistic relationship is a functional one, given a traditional society in which status is determined ascriptively, that is, by means other than demonstrated ability, typically by birth into a certain group or class and, to a lesser extent, by age. An elite in such a society remains an elite only so long as a system of reciprocal obligations operates between elite and nonelite. Responsibility on the part of members of the elite cannot be delegated, for that would challenge the validity of claims to eliteness. Upward mobility based on achievement likewise constitutes a challenge to claims to elite status based on ascriptive qualities. Therefore, achievement per se carries little weight in determining status as between elite and nonelite; only the fulfillment of traditional obligations does so. The system becomes even more functional if one stipulates (1) subsistence level of living for the mass and (2) an ineffective central government that fails to assure minimum services to all individuals, including ability to protect life and property. Then the employer, patron, landowner, officer, governor, chief, or sheikh becomes a protector as well as a master. Subsistence living requires periodic support by others of greater wealth, hence personal loyalties tend to be strong, far stronger than loyalty to abstract values. The system also implies social immobility and a low level of innovation and, hence, of technical skill.

As one experienced observer commented, the introduction of technical managers "with neither the inclination nor the economic resources to play the paternal role" may create a "malaise" among the workers who have previously known "no other source of vertical job relationship." Unfortunately, the pressure from workers to cast such managers in the "paternal context" may only sharpen "their maneuvers to resist the stereotypes."[1]

To retain new employees, in whom a substantial training investment may have been made because of the low initial level of skill relevant to a modern economic enterprise, the employer may be forced to assume the paternalistic obligations expected of a patron in traditional society. Paternalism may be equated with decision-making authority on the part of one's boss that encompasses much that would be considered reserved for personal decision and institutionalized implementation in a less traditional society, such as loans, personal assistance in time of disaster, housing, medical care, marital relations, children's education. Furthermore, nothing less than the *personal* assistance of the patron himself is demanded, for these responsibilities cannot be readily delegated for reasons already suggested. The patron's authority, his ability to command loyalty, might well be undermined by such delegation.

The psychological difficulties thrust upon an alien management in this

---

[1]Charles H. Savage, *Social Reorganization in a Factory in the Andes* (Ithaca, N.Y.: The Society for Applied Anthropology, monograph no. 7, 1964), pp. 3–4.

situation are readily apparent and may constitute a compelling reason for employing local nationals to manage the enterprise. In any event, the transition from a new, relatively small undertaking to a large industrial establishment requires a change in management-labor relations. The door of the boss's office cannot remain open to anyone with a personal problem. Possible steps in this transition are:

1. Delegation of responsibility for handling personal problems to someone other than the boss but closely identified with the boss socially, for example, a member of his family;

2. Institutionalization of certain functions, such as a housing corporation, a cooperative loan office, a company health clinic;

3. Externalization of all nonbusiness functions as rapidly as possible, by interesting the local government, employing subcontractors, and so forth;

4. Encouragement of the employees themselves to assume added responsibility through various clubs, associations, a company union;

5. Restraint in discouraging the organization of an independent labor union and, if representative, insistence on bargaining with it collectively.

A trap a number of foreign managements have fallen into is to make irreversible decisions in this area; a perfect case in point is the construction of a company town. Initially, the employer's responsibility to supply decent housing and related services may be entirely acceptable, indeed, expected, by the employee. The government may well be unable to provide what is needed. A differential between company town and traditional community in terms of living standards is thereby created. If, as is so frequently the case, the extended family system prevails, the company town grows far more rapidly than expected. Cash income may be sent home, but income in the form of houses and services can only be shared by moving into the town those to whom the employee feels obligation. Services become strained. As the town grows and the population becomes less traditional, friction with the company frequently develops. There is a tendency to blame the company for anything that goes wrong in the community. Once the situation has progressed to this point, how does the firm backtrack so as to limit relations with its employees to matters relating directly to the job? Unless outside interests, possibly the local government, are willing to take over responsibility, the firm may eventually be forced to withdraw entirely.

The alternative route is to externalize as rapidly as possible all functions not directly related to the principal business of the firm. The firm may subsidize housing, education, health facilities, transportation services, and so forth, but actual responsibility remains in the hands of local government or entrepreneurs. For example, providing daily transportation from traditional communities to the place of work may, in the long run, be far less costly than becoming involved in a company town. Ideally, either the government or local entrepreneurs would be paid to provide such services. Subsidies of this sort may be fully justified in that the firm is creating external costs that should be borne by the enterprise. The subsidies may take the form of grants, training, or technical assistance. The rapid externalization of such social services is particularly important for a foreign-owned firm that might otherwise generate the hostility of local political leaders by appearing to weaken the nationalistic loyalty of its employees. The social services provided by the firm may be seen as a challenge to the government, an exposure of its weakness, and hence, as a force against the creation of a politically cohesive state.

A further step in the creation of a modern labor force—modern in the sense of being more particularistic in its relations with management (that is, more limited to matters directly related to the job), more achievement-oriented, more individualistic in problem solving—is the appearance of employees' associations within the plant and eventual affiliation with an independent labor union.

A still further step in the modernization of manager-subordinate may be the "speak-up" and "open-door" policies introduced by some firms. "Speak-up" refers to encouraging anyone to register complaints to supervisors; "open-door" to the access that everyone has to higher management in order to complain about the behavior of one's supervisor. This system can operate effectively only if the investigating process is done objectively and well. Sometimes complementing these processes is an employee opinion survey run periodically in which individuals are asked to express opinions about working conditions, compensation, impact of job requirements on family, and the like.

Some have said that the paternalistic nature of management-labor relations in Japan, plus the astonishing rate of Japanese economic growth, challenges the notion that there is a unique relationship between "modern," as defined above, and high levels of productivity and creativity. Possibly the notion is faulty, but the Japanese case does not prove the point, for it is not paternalistic in the usual sense. True, the range of company-bestowed benefits is wide, and the company seems to be all pervasive in the lives of its employees, but, unlike the true paternalistic model, the employees appear to have a great deal to say about company policy in this regard. They participate in important decisions by means of the company union and other devices. What appears to be paternalism (that is, intimacy of decision-making *external* to the individual), plus some degree of participative management, is not paternalism; it is expression of a collective responsibility to the individual as determined by the *collectivity*, including the individual. Furthermore it is institutionalized.

A more obvious case is the Yugoslav enterprise, obvious because its structure is prescribed by law. To the uninitiated, such an enterprise would appear highly paternalistic vis-à-vis the individual worker in terms of the range of benefits received and the pervasiveness of the enterprise on his life. Yet, one does not think of the Yugoslav enterprise in these terms because of the system of self-management through which the workers, through their elected workers' council, select the managing board and general director and consider important policy alternatives, including the funds to be expended on various employee benefit plans.

Perhaps the sort of identity between manager and worker that the Japanese and Yugoslav systems may in some cases generate within the context of modern industry is the next evolutionary step, something beyond what North Americans are inclined to call "modern" (in which management and labor are seen as independent adversaries negotiating contracts). One does not know, but it is well to maintain an open mind on the subject, particularly given the rapidly evolving notions of job-enrichment and industrial democracy. More will be said of these subjects later on.

There is a further dimension in management's responsibility to employees: the time dimension. The laws of many countries inhibit management's freedom to discharge employees; in others, collective agreements have a similar effect but generally over a shorter run. In any case, a discharge may be a very costly business if there is a terminal pay requirement and the individual has been with the company for many years. Although not embedded in law, most of the larger Japanese firms pursue a lifetime employment system (*shushin koyo seido*), which means a lifetime job commitment on the part of the firm. Indeed, there is relatively little interfirm movement of labor within Japan, particularly among the larger firms. Such a system has definite advantages: (1) employees work in stable work groups over long periods of time, which probably contributes to better communication and a higher level of company loyalty; (2) the employees (and their unions) need not fear technical innovation; (3) these stable work groups may generate unusually high levels of both effort and innovation; (4) the time horizon of the worker is likely to be longer and, hence, his objectives more likely to coincide with those of the firm. The disadvantages include, of course, the difficulty of shaking loose less productive employees, or redundant employees, thus incurring a high fixed labor cost, and the elimination of the incentive implicit in the employee's latent fear of his inability to meet physical and culturally induced needs. But, given the total Japanese context, the lifetime employment system obviously has not interfered seriously with Japan's economic growth.

As one observer wrote,

Japanese management practices such as consensus decision-making, the reliance on middle management ability to resolve conflicts, the employment-for-life and promotion-by-seniority patterns, all have their merits. In fact, research into these practices (so far surprisingly lacking) might well show that some of their strengths could be "exported" for inclusion as new elements of western management practices.[2]

To what extent could, or should, a *non*-Japanese firm operating in Japan adopt

---

[2]Achim A. Stoehr (principal of McKinsey & Company), "Through Foreign Eyes," *The Japan Economic Journal,* November 23, 1971, p. 20.

the lifetime employment system? Clearly, a typical Japanese worker must look upon a job with a foreign firm as more risky. The firm is unlikely to have a long record in Japan. It is only a relatively small subsidiary operation. The Japanese government through the central bank is unlikely to support the firm if it runs into difficulties. The results are that (1) the foreign firm will have to pay the worker more to compensate for the perceived higher risk and (2) a natural screening process is likely to operate whereby the firm attracts individuals to its employ who are less motivated by security, more individualistically oriented, than are their average compatriots. The very fact that at least one internal study by a large international firm showed an astonishing similarity of employee expectations in Japan and elsewhere tends to confirm the suspicion that an important screening process indeed operates in Japan in respect to at least some foreign firms. If that be the case, the foreign firm would be ill advised to attempt to follow traditional Japanese practice in regard to lifetime employment without prior examination of the sort of local employees it is attracting.

Japanese question whether foreign businessmen, for example, could be expected to develop enough understanding of the complicated giri *and* ninjo *psychological concepts in the short time most of them stay in Japan to operate harmoniously. Giri, which plays a compelling role in Japanese society, may be defined as "sense of duty," or "recognition of a debt of gratitude." One of the meanings is akin to keeping "face." In business, much manoeuvering is in response to* giri *influences. Ninjo is humaneness, sympathy and kindness. The occasional mass layoffs in Western factories, and the coldness with which Occidentals are believed to dismiss employees, seem to the Japanese to demonstrate a lack of* ninjo.[3]

A 1976 survey of the opinion of 305 Japanese company presidents in respect to lifetime employment elicited this response: 31.1 percent reported no need to change but an expectation that change would nonetheless occur; 14.1 percent reported neither a need to change nor the expectation that it would occur; 29 percent wished to change but foresaw considerable difficulty in doing so; 24.6 percent wished to change the system and were sure that it would. The split was almost 50–50 between those who felt the need for change and those who did not.[4]

Lifetime employment may be edging into the United States. Among the demands of the U.S. Steelworkers Union in 1977 was lifetime income security, thereby adding to the suspicion that indeed labor was becoming a fixed cost.

---

[3]Howard F. Van Zandt, "Japanese Culture and the Business Boom," *Foreign Affairs*, January 1970, pp. 354–55.
[4]*Nikkei Business* (Tokyo), September 27, 1976. p. 71.

DEGREE OF LABOR PARTICIPATION IN MANAGEMENT 3.2

Obviously, one cannot speak of responsibility toward employees without reaching the subject of the latters' right to participate in important decisions affecting their welfare, present and future. The real question is, to what extent should workers influence the decision-making process in the firm? Increasingly, the answer is legally determined as the notion of voluntary cooperation—even in Scandinavia—fades.[5]

Speaking in front of Belgian TV in 1971 about European moves toward greater labor participation in management, pundit J. K. Galbraith raised a few European hackles by proclaiming, "It (participation) is a pipe dream. I advise you to give up the idea of this kind of reform. . . . The very nature of organized and bureaucratic management of a large concern concentrates the power in the hands of men who share the information of specialists in technology and management. Neither the capitalist nor the worker has a part in it."[6]

Notwithstanding such views, a change in the traditional relationship between employee and employer is obviously worldwide as dissatisfaction with the traditional forms of hierarchical corporate control mounts. Labor is demanding a larger role in decision-making, at both the job and the enterprise level. Perhaps this pressure arises out of an evolutionary process that, despite apparent short-term evidence to the contrary, is reflected in the increasing awareness of individuals everywhere of their humanity. The need for autonomy and self-fulfillment is now part of the world industrial culture. Whether it leads to maximum economic efficiency may be irrelevant. Responses take many forms, from flexible work hours (flexitime), group-assigned tasks, group assembly operations, workers' councils, codetermination (labor participation at the board level), self-management (labor selection and control of management), role change (managers working periodically as ordinary labor), to employee ownership. The response may be ideologically justified, introduced for purely pragmatic reasons, or appear as the result of labor dissatisfaction and pressure. In any event, in the process the prerogatives and roles of both managers and workers are redefined, and the social-economic disparity between managers and workers narrowed. In the ultimate model, they become one or are so heavily overlapped as to be virtually indistinguishable. (In some places, such as the United States, the notion that consumers as well should have a voice in the direction of enterprises is gaining support.)

In that the traditional function of organized labor is challenged by many of these reforms or, at least, seriously altered, the vested interest of big labor often perceives a threat. Its power could be damped by workers' management and

---

[5]As of January 1977, a Swedish law became effective, which provided for trade unions to conclude agreements with companies on codetermination, and for wage earners, through their unions, to have a voice on managerial and supervisory questions. Management became legally obliged to consult unions on various contemplated moves and to give progress reports on production, personnel policy, and related matters.

[6]Reported in *Worldwide P & I*, November/December 1972, p. 18.

ownership, for then distinctions between employee and employer tend to melt. Internal accommodation in decision-making replaces direct confrontation supported by resources and pressures external to the firm. Therefore, one can anticipate that big labor will tend frequently to resist these changes. Theoretically, the labor union could still serve critically important functions in the articulation of grievances, protecting the minority from the tyranny of the majority, reporting irregularities to competent authorities, in satisfying a variety of social and educational needs of employees, and in bringing attention to important income disparities among similar enterprises. Or, the unions may become an integral part of the decision-making system, in part as a compromise solution.

There are many systems and degrees of labor participation in decision making.[7] The following categories would seem to include most of these, although this section should perhaps be read in association with the section on participative management in the following chapter, Section 4.5.

Labor or self-management, where the authority of labor is theoretically preeminent to that of management. Examples are the Yugoslav case, already described, and theoretically the Israeli case, where 12 to 15 percent of manufacturing and perhaps 40 percent of construction work is provided by Histadrut-owned[8] and managed companies. In addition there are producers' cooperatives in manufacturing in most of Israel's 200-odd *kibbutzim* and in more than 125 separate industrial enterprises.

A key variable in such systems is the extent to which the workers recognize management as a profession requiring certain skills and judgment. It would appear that in Yugoslavia, the workers' councils have bid up managerial salaries as enterprises compete for competent managers. And, the average tenure of managers has lengthened, possibly meaning that they are being given greater authority.

Histadrut-owned industries, which employ about one quarter of the Israeli labor force, were established on the premise that the collective ownership of industry by labor would provide the best guarantee of labor-management harmony. But, over time, the pattern and nature of labor-management relations within Histadrut industries became essentially undifferentiated from those found elsewhere in Israeli industry. A renewed effort by the Histadrut to bring reality closer to ideological assumption has resulted in the introduction of employee participation schemes, the joint management program. Officially endorsed by the Histadrut, it builds on the earlier workers' (blue collar) and employees' (white collar) committees, which communicate with management through the secretary of the respective unions of the local labor council.

---

[7]See *Workers' Participation* (Paris: Organization for Economic Cooperation and Development, 1976), final report on an international management seminar convened by the OECD in 1975, and a second volume of documents prepared for the seminar under the same title.

[8]General Federation of Jewish Labor in Israel.

In the joint management scheme, workers' representatives are present within the central management of the Histadrut (the rough equivalent to the U.S. corporate board level) and on the plant management level. On the latter level, the management group consists of an equal number of labor and management representatives, plus the director (who is a member of management). The labor representatives are elected by the work force; the management, by the central managing group (which consists of one-third workers' representatives and two-thirds management representatives, both groups being selected by the Havrat Houvdim, the General Cooperative Association of Jewish Workers in Israel). At the plant level, the joint management body and the workers' committee (trade union) are recognized as two separate bodies. Thus, theoretically workers' self-interest is reflected on the workers' committee; the common interest of workers and managers, in the joint management group. An evaluation of the scheme is not yet possible.

The Israeli concept differs in theory from the Yugoslav, where virtually all industry is owned by "society" (not the government) and held in social trust by the workers' community, consisting of all employees of an enterprise, the terms of which are defined in charter or statute. The community (the rough equivalent of stockholders) periodically elects a workers' council (somewhat similar to a board of directors), which in turn names the managing director (president) and the management board (supervisory board). The latter, consisting of both council members and noncouncil community representatives, selects all other members of management, performs an auditing function, and initiates action at the council level. Given the recent growth record registered by Yugoslav industry, Yugoslav self-management must be operating with some degree of effectiveness.

The effectiveness of workers' self-management in Yugoslavia has been researched in respect to the relationship between (1) degree of participation in the workers' councils as defined by the social-psychological relations among all members of the organization and (2) the distribution of control and organizational effectiveness.[9] The study was based on two pairs of organizations comparable in plant size and technology. In each pair, one enterprise was judged to have a relatively participative council as measured by the proportion of members taking part in the council discussions and by the quality of debate. In each case the sample consisted of all council members and approximately 120 noncouncil members, the latter being randomly selected. The criteria for organizational effectiveness were productivity, economic success, wages, quality of management, degree of self-management, quality of social-psychological relations. The four organizations were ranked by

[9]Bogdan Kavcic, Veljko Rus, Arnold S. Tanenbaum, "Control, Participation, and Effectiveness in Four Yugoslav Industrial Organizations," *Administrative Science Quarterly*, vol. 16, no. 1, March 1971, pp. 74–86. See also Josip Zupanov and Arnold S. Tanenbaum, "The Distribution of Control in Some Yugoslav Industrial Organizations as Perceived by Members," *International Bulletin of Applied Psychology*, vol. 16, no. 2, 1967, pp. 93–110.

knowledgeable people, with a high degree of agreement among them, and with such objective measures of effectiveness as were possible to construct. Some of the more interesting findings follow:

1. Council members were more likely than noncouncil members to be male, older, more educated, members of the Communist Party, to hold supervisory or managerial positions, and to be more highly involved and motivated in their work.

2. Differences between council and noncouncil members were less in the more effective enterprises, in reference to identification with the enterprise and to favorable attitudes toward their work situation.

3. The amount of influence (control) exercised by six levels (workers' council, managing board, managers, unit heads, supervisors, and workers) was perceived by these groups as being consistently greater in those enterprises ranked more effective.

4. In all cases the managers were perceived as having the most control; workers, the least. But in the two more effective organizations, the workers' councils were seen as having significantly more control than the councils of the less effective enterprises.

5. The more equal distribution of control was associated with the less effective organizations.

6. The "ideal" distribution of control in all four enterprises was seen as significantly higher than was actually the case, and the difference among the six levels substantially reduced, with the councils being the highest, but the slope was still slightly negative (from workers' council, managing board, managers, unit heads, supervisors, to workers).

7. The "ideal" distribution of control did not correlate with the effectiveness ratings; the profiles for the four enterprises were a very close match.

8. The less effective organizations reflected lower levels of motivation, involvement, and identification.

In general, the workers' councils, though exercising substantial influence, "were not as influential as the members wished them to be, nor as influential as the ideology required."[10] The effectiveness of the councils was rated fair to good in all four enterprises by council and noncouncil members, the former rating the councils slightly more effective on average. Within the councils, manager-members were consistently rated as most influential and workers the least influential, with staff and supervisory members in an intermediate position. The general conclusion was that the "council by itself may not have the far-reaching effects that many advocates believe."

In a more recent study, ten pairs of Yugoslav industrial organizations were used, each pair containing one high-performing and one low-performing organization. Using the four managerial systems as developed by Rensis Likert and summarized in Table 3.1, the study concluded that the profile of the more

---

[10]Kavcic, Rus, and Tannenbaum, "Control," p. 83.

successful Yugoslav enterprises was consistently higher than the less successful in that all of the former group were within system 3 for virtually all
characteristics and the latter, in system 2.[11]

Generally agreement is reported among Yugoslav academics that the reforms of the 1960s, "in which the state had retreated in an effort to force
factories to take care of their own business in a self-management manner, had
not fully worked. Although workers' strength in the decision-making process
had increased on paper, in reality managers and leading personnel often dominated the decision-making process." The upshot was that the 1974 Constitution was drafted which "called for an organizational restructuring based on a
downward movement of the decision-making power." Since then, the fundamental unit of authority has shifted from the firm level workers' council to a
smaller unit, the Basic Organization of Associated Labor (BOAL), defined as
"a section of an enterprise or part of the production process whose production
can be measured as a value," either in the market or internally. Each BOAL
within a firm is an autonomous organization with its own books and authority
to disperse income earned by the labor of the BOAL, and to make decisions
on internal structure. A BOAL is organized into an assembly of all the workers
and an elected council of workers, members of which serve a two-year term
and who are not permitted to serve more than two consecutive terms. Members of the worker's council at the firm level are chosen by each BOAL, but
these councils are being replaced gradually by assemblies of delegates who are
chosen by the BOAL councils. Major decisions at the firm level must be
unanimous since a majority vote cannot bind a dissenting BOAL.[12]

Balzer enters a word of caution concerning the Yugoslav system:

> *Yugoslavia's self-management system is probably not exportable to Western Europe
> for, as the Yugoslavs themselves are fond of pointing out, it cannot exist unless there
> is social property. However, it is possible that Yugoslav experience in the sixties may
> point out some dangers of the type of participatory system, which is becoming increas-
> ingly popular in Western Europe. Yugoslav experience suggests that worker representa-
> tives, even when directly elected on the shop floor, cannot help but become alienated from
> the work force when they serve on a rather distant works' council or, as increasingly
> popular in Western Europe, on a board of directors. The problems of bigness cannot,
> the Yugoslav experience seems to indicate, be solved by structuring a hierarchical
> representative system. To be involved, workers must be more directly involved in the
> lowest levels of decision-making. This does not imply, as some might wish to infer, that
> the only place for involvement is at the lowest level.*[13]

But regardless of many criticisms, it is obvious that labor self-management

---

[11] Arnold S. Tannenbaum et al., "Testing a Management Style," *European Business*, no. 27, Autumn 1970, pp.
60–68. See also Howard M. Wachtel, *Workers' Management and Workers' Wages in Yugoslavia* (Ithaca and
London: Cornell University Press, 1973).

[12] Summarized from Richard Balzer, "Socialism with a Human Face" (New York: Institute of Current World
Affairs, Newsletter RJB-51, January 11, 1977).

[13] Balzer, "Socialism," p. 10.

Table 3.1

THE FOUR STYLES OF LEADERSHIP—THEIR CHARACTERISTICS

	System 1	System 2	System 3	System 4
Leadership				
1. How much confidence is shown in subordinates?	None	Condescending	Substantial	Complete
2. How free do they feel to talk to superiors about job?	Not at all	Not very	Rather freely	Fully free
3. Are subordinates' ideas sought and used, if worthy?	Seldom	Sometimes	Usually	Always
Motivation				
4. Is predominant use made of (1) fear, (2) threats, (3) punishment, (4) rewards, (5) involvement?	1, 2, 3, occasionally 4	4, some 3	4, some 3 and 5	5, 4, based on group set goals
5. Where is responsibility felt for achieving organization goals?	Mostly at top	Top and middle	Fairly general	At all levels
Communication				
6. What is the direction of information flow?	Downward	Mostly downward	Down and up	Down, up, and sideways
7. How is downward communication accepted?	With suspicion	Possible, with suspicion	With caution	With open mind
8. How accurate is upward communication?	Often wrong	Censored for boss	Limited accuracy	Accurate
9. How well do superiors know problems faced by subordinates?	Know little	Some knowledge	Quite well	Very well
Interaction				
10. What is the character of interaction?	Little, always with fear and distrust	Little, usually with some condescension	Moderate, often fair amount of confidence and trust	Extensive, high degree of confidence and trust

11. How much cooperative teamwork is present?	None	Relatively little	Moderate amount	Very substantial throughout organization

Decisions

12. At what level are decisions formally made?	Mostly at top	Policy at top, some delegation	Broad policy at top, more delegation	Throughout but well integrated
13. What is the origin of technical and professional knowledge used in decision-making?	Top management	Upper and middle	To a certain extent throughout	To a great extent
14. Are subordinates involved in decisions related to their work?	Not at all	Occasionally consulted	Generally consulted	Fully involved
15. What does the decision-making process contribute to motivation?	Nothing, often weakens it	Relatively little	Some contribution	Substantial

Goals

16. How are organizational goals established?	Orders issued	Orders issued with some chance to comment	Orders issued after discussion	Group action (except in crisis)
17. How much covert resistance to goals is present?	Strong resistance	Moderate resistance	Some resistance at times	Little or none

Control

18. How concentrated are review and control functions?	Highly at top	Relatively high at top	Moderate delegation to lower levels	Quite widely shared
19. Is there an informal organization resisting the formal one?	Yes	Usually	Sometimes	No—same goals as formal
20. What are cost, productivity, and other control data used for?	Policing, punishment	Reward and punishment	Reward, some self-guidance	Self-guidance, problem solving

Source: Arnold S. Tannenbaum, Stane Mozina, Janez Jerovsek, and Rensis Likert, ''Testing a Mangerial Style,'' *European Business,* no. 27, Autumn 1970, p. 64.

in Yugoslavia cannot be written off as a failure. It is equally obvious that Western firms will face unusual problems in joining forces with such enterprises.

To what extent the Yugoslav model will be seized up by other societies is not yet clear, although innovations introduced in 1971 and in Peru in 1974 seem to have been influenced. For example, the Zambian 1971 Industrial Relations Act introduced the concept of workers' committees, a move reportedly explicitly modeled on the Yugoslav example. In the Peruvian case, the "social property enterprise" embodied the Yugoslav notion of social ownership.[14]

Corporate managers operating internationally cannot ignore the challenge thrown up to the more traditional ways of organizing production by the Chinese and Cuban "models." Unfortunately, very little really hard data seems to have been reported out of China as to the actual allocation of managerial authority within either rural or urban commune or factory. To what extent does self-management actually operate? Unlike Cuba, Yugoslavia, or Peru, it should be noted that in China the commune is at once both the basic unit of government and of production and is subdivided into brigade and team. The administrative unit above the commune is the county, the managing body at that level being a revolutionary committee. At each level are the "cadres," or leaders who operate within the ideological context that demands an intimate contact with ordinary people. The appeal of the Chinese model for many lies in the apparent emergence of a uniquely egalitarian society, at least in terms of obvious consumption, and the solution of the basic problems of housing, food, clothing, education, and health services. Also appealing to many is the anti-elitist thrust of the society and its deemphasis on an ever increasing consumption.

In the Chinese case, commune brigade and production team level "cadres" are directly responsible for production decisions. The task of these cadres is to administer and direct. "They are individuals with a wide range of knowledge, who are skilled in transmitting information from one administrative level to another and in encouraging and utilizing particular social groupings."[15] This same observer reported:

But the extent of individual cadres' knowledge, although important and very significant for our work, was merely one of their characteristics that we found impressive. Another was the way they conducted themselves in their dealings with other cadres—at all levels—and with the people with whom we saw them interact. Whether walking through a village, a county town, a factory, or a kindergarten, they did not hold themselves aloof or behave in a manner that marked them off as a group of people who were privileged

---

[14]For an analysis of the Peruvian system, see Richard D. Robinson, "The Peruvian Experiment, the Theory and Reality of the Industrial Community" (Cambridge: Alfred P. Sloan School of Management, M.I.T., working paper, 1976).

[15]Elizabeth Johnson and Graham Johnson, *Walking on Two Legs; Rural Development in South China* (Ottawa: International Development Center, 1976), p. 31.

or unused to seeking the opinions of others. Relations with workers in a factory, peasants in a field, or passers-by on a street were relaxed and casual. There are rarely any signs of distinction in terms of dress between cadres and noncadres at the local level.[16]

What does not seem to be well understood in the Chinese case is exactly how the managers (the "cadres") are selected and trained. Are cadres in any sense rotated? In fact, to what extent do they simply carry out decisions made by the teams, brigades, and commune members, that is, self-management.

It would appear that there is somewhat less self-management in a factory context.[17] Johnson and Johnson describe the organization of two county-run factories. A revolutionary committee, consisting of leading cadres plus worker and militia representatives, were reported to have a role something like a managing board. This committee was divided into a number of functional departments, production, supply, maintenance, design, enterprise management, and political. "Questions of production" were determined by the industrial department at the county level. The county cadres entered into regular consultation with the leading cadres of the factory (top management). Production plans were discussed in the revolutionary committee, on which workers' representatives were present. After a preliminary discussion, monthly production plans were sent down to the squads for discussion in their monthly meetings. From this description it is not clear precisely what degree of control the workers have over the management, either in selecting cadres or in initiating or ratifying important decisions.[18]

Another observer of the China scene reports:

Factory workers and peasants are apparently being brought into the decision-making process. Instead of traditional management personnel (cadres) only, all institutions, scientific and otherwise, are now run by elected Revolutionary Committees constituted according to the "three in one" principle: cadres, ordinary workers or peasants, and army or militia. (The army does not seem to be included as a military presence, but rather because of its political loyalty to Mao.) The net effect is to increase participation of and answerability to ordinary people, and at the same time to control political direction. Although we had little chance to observe the interplay of central and local planning, I had the impression of some flexibility and independence at the local level within broad guidelines set by the government.[19]

Likewise, the Cuban system of collective management has registered unexpected successes of recent years in upping productivity and the standard of living for the ordinary Cuban worker. Cuba's system of management, as it has evolved since 1970, has been described by Zimbalist in 1975 on the basis of extensive field interviews and observations as follows:

---

[16]Johnson and Johnson, *Two Legs*, pp. 31–32.

[17]Johnson and Johnson, *Two Legs*, p. 39.

[18]See Barry M. Richman, *A Firsthand Study of Industrial Management in Communist China* (Los Angeles: University of California, 1967).

[19]Ethan Signer, "New Direction in Chinese Science," *Technology Review*, December 1971, p. 9.

The superior administrative body of all work centers in the Consejo de Direccion *(Mangement Council) . . . composed of administrator, his/her top assistants, the worker-elected representatives, representatives from the local party nucleus and representatives from the local branch of the Communist Youth Organization. This Council usually meets once a week, but often . . . more frequently. From my interviews with administrators, party representatives, union representatives and workers, it seems that the workers' input at these meetings is quite significant. The Management Council, like the Worker Production Assemblies [all enterprise employees], discusses all matters concerning production and social relations in the work center. Effective worker input is facilitated by the posting of information on output goals and fulfillment on a weekly or monthly basis on factory bulletin boards.*

Worker Production Assemblies, in general meet monthly or bi-monthly. . . . According to my interviewees, attendance at these meetings is extremely high, ranging from 80 to 100 percent, and worker participation is extensive and vocal. Many reported that substantial production reorganization and consequent productivity gains resulted from these meetings. [20]

During July and August, 1974, the preliminary economic plan for 1975 (and in September, Cuba's first Five Year Plan) was circulated in all enterprises to be discussed and modified at the Production Assemblies. Above the enterprise level, elected union representatives participated in the consideration of municipal, regional and provincial plans. . . .

The foregoing participation scheme is young and is still largely confined to the enterprise level. Thus, worker involvement in the setting of national priorities, investment, and trade policy is as yet highly inadequate. However, a central point is that the Party leadership is openly calling for participation at higher levels, thereby fanning the desires and expectations for such participation. [21]

In the Cuban system, the differentiation between manager and worker is minimal. Managers generally, in 1974, were receiving wages of between 200 and 300 pesos per month, manual workers something over 85 pesos (the minimum wage). Several observers have reported that the ratio of highest to lowest wages was almost never over 3.5 and in some cases not over 2 to 1. Although managers did not usually participate in manual labor during the week, they belonged to the same union as workers and participated in voluntary labor on Sundays. Workers were observed to address managers as *companero* (comrade) or by first name and very frequently they themselves were former production or farm workers.

Zimbalist went on to observe:

As factory life has changed since 1970, the economy has improved. Absenteeism is well

---

[20]Although there has been a systematic elimination of material incentives, a function of the assemblies is to distribute among their members those durable goods (refrigerators, televisions, radios, etc.) allocated by the state to the enterprises. This is done on the basis of merit and need, via the vote of the assembly.

[21]Andrew Zimbalist, "The Development of Workers' Participation in Socialist Cuba," paper prepared for presentation at the Second Annual Conference on Workers' Self-Management, Cornell University, June 6–8, 1975, mimeo., pp. 19–20.

under control. Industrial production has been growing rapidly in the last four years, and in his staff report to the Committee on Foreign Relations of the U.S. Senate Pat Holt says that the per capita income in Cuba is currently $1,587. This is "by far the highest in Latin America with the possible exception of Venezuela where everything is distorted by oil."[22] Based on his visit during the summer of 1974, Holt concludes that "the Cubans are on the verge of constructing a socialist showcase in the Western Hemisphere."[23]

One suspects that Castro's Cuba does not need to resort to violence and intrigue to be a powerful influence on the rest of Latin America and elsewhere.

Codetermination, a 50–50 management-labor representation on the board of directors, the principal example being until 1976 in the iron, coal, and steel industries of the Federal Republic of Germany. Introduced in 1951, the law provided for equal representation on the supervisory boards, *aufsichstrat.* After many years of urging by the German Trade Union Federation (DGB), codetermination (*mitbestimmung*) was extended in 1976 to all German enterprises employing 2,000 or more (roughly 650 firms employing some 4 million)[24] but with several important differences:

1. Under the new law, high-level white collar personnel (employees with managerial responsibility below that of the senior management group) elect one of the employee representatives. (If this representative votes with the shareholders, there is no longer real parity.)

2. The chairman of the supervisory board may be chosen either from the shareholders or employee representatives. But a two-thirds vote of the entire board is required. If a candidate is unable to generate the required votes then the shareholders may appoint one of their own representatives. (This would seem to assure the shareholders of the chairmanship in most cases.)

3. The board Chairman has a double vote in that first he may vote as any other member, but if the board is deadlocked, he may vote again as chairman.

Possibly the most revealing remark reported about the law was made by a German industrialist who did not wish to be quoted: "The new law doesn't bother me. It doesn't matter if the majority is one or five votes; the important thing is that the new law leaves power with the stockholders."[25] Others, however, feared the union influence. Henry Ford II was moved to declare that the scheme "could lead to a denial of basic property rights."[26]

The point was that of the employee representatives on the supervisory board, the unions were to nominate either three (in the case of a 20-member

---

[22]Pat Holt, "Cuba," (Washington: U.S. Government Printing Office, Staff Report Prepared for the Committee on Foreign Relations of the U.S. Senate, 1974), p. 2.

[23]Zimbalist, "Workers Participation," p. 22.

[24]Multiple companies are aggregated.

[25]Richard Balzer, "What Determines Co-determination?" (New York: Institute of Current World Affairs, newsletter RJB-44, April 27, 1976), p. 5.

[26]*New York Times*, 17 October 1975, p. 10.

board) or two (in the case of a 12- or 16-member board); employees, the balance through an indirect system in firms with over 8,000 employees. In the latter case, the electoral body, it was widely supposed, would have a high degree of labor-union affiliation.

The real test would come when these new boards would select the managing boards (*vorstang*) in that a two-thirds majority was required. If such a majority were not forthcoming, the vote would be thrown to the shareholders' meeting. But this procedure, many felt, was so cumbersome as to encourage a widespread tendency toward log-rolling, with stockholder and employee representative saying in effect, "we will elect your candidate if you will elect ours."[27] In any event, one member of the managing board must be the Director of Labor, who is in charge of personnel and social matters. It was expected that it was unlikely that he would be appointed against union objections.[28]

In late 1973, executives in 24 U.S. firms (out of 80) responded to a survey regarding attitudes to codetermination in Germany. All had substantial German interests. The general conclusion (21 out of 24) was that while their firm could live with minority labor representation on the board, albeit reluctantly, parity representation was considered to be "harmful not just to . . . corporate interest but to the national economy."[29] The reason for this opposition did not seem to rise from a doctrinaire position, but rather "skepticism about the motive of the promoters—from a feeling that the push for this form of management comes from labor leaders whose ambition is not so much improvement of the position of the workers as it is power for themselves."[30] Additionally, responding executives felt that parity representation "would make for delay and partiality in decision-making and thus impair efficiency."[31] The idea that with time the worker members of a board would come to have views similar to stockholder representatives was rejected almost unanimously (23 out of 24).[32] A clear majority (16 of 24) believed that codetermination was not going to disappear, but only seven out of 24 felt that the idea would spread to the United States.[33] At the same time, 21 of 24 agreed that workers should have a voice in management, but through stock ownership, consultation, and the like, not by reason of board representation. Opinion was almost equally divided as to whether codetermination was an attack on private property.[34] Likewise evenly divided were responses to the assertion that pressure for

[27] *The Morgan Guaranty Survey*, November 1974, pp. 11–12.

[28] G. Vorbrugg, "Labor Participation in German and European Companies" (Munich: mimeo, August 1976), p. 8.

[29] Stewart Schackne, "Report to Respondents to Survey on Codetermination" (New York: typed manuscript, February 21, 1974), p. 2.

[30] Schackne, "Report to Respondents," p. 3.

[31] Schackne, "Report to Respondents," p. 3.

[32] Schackne, "Report to Respondents," p. 5.

[33] Schackne, "Report to Respondents," p. 7.

[34] Schackne, "Report to Respondents," p. 13.

extension of codetermination was evidence that top management did not pay enough attention to the human factors in business.[35] Fifteen of the 24 felt that parity codetermination would reduce productivity and most (21 of 24) answered that it would have a deterrent effect on investment in Germany.[36]

It should be noted that the ultimate phase in the evolution of an "industrial community" in Peru, a concept introduced by law in 1971, is 50 percent ownership and participation on the board of directors by employees.

Although supported by the British Trade Union Congress (TUC), the codetermination proposal put forward by a royal commission in England in early 1977 did not seem to have much chance for enactment into legislation. Basically what was proposed was equal management, labor representation on the corporate board with one-third of the seats being reserved for a neutral group selected by both parties. The idea was that in corporations over a certain size, a union representing 20 percent or more of an enterprise work force could call for a secret ballot on the subject. A simple majority would be adequate to force the change to a joint board, provided the majority represented a third of all full-time workers. The labor representatives were to be chosen by the joint committee of shop stewards. Already, it was customary to appoint union members to the boards of government-owned companies.

Minority board participation, such as the one-third representation given to employees in German firms—other than in the coal, iron, and steel industries —by the Shop Consititution Law of 1952. This provision still applies for firms with over 500 employees and not more than 2,000. The European Corporation Law drafted by the EEC Commission would require one-third labor representation on the supervisory board. As of 1977, at least six other European countries had introduced minority board participation: Sweden, the Netherlands, Norway, Luxembourg, Denmark, and France. How has it worked? *Business International* reported in mid-1976:

> *Most companies in Europe have found industrial democracy less alarming than they feared. In fact, in those countries where it is most advanced, e.g., Sweden, Germany, the Netherlands, labor strife is virtually unknown, in stark contrast to the situation in the U.K. and Italy.*[37]

Although insofar as is known there are no legislative proposals in the United States on the subject, there are a few straws in the wind. The United Auto Workers Union asked Chrysler in 1976 to consider granting seats on the company's board of directors to labor representatives. Chrysler had been singled out because its subsidiary in the U.K. had proposed to admit two union representatives to its board in a bid for industrial peace. The demand in the United States failed, but one could expect repetitions.

---

[35]Schackne, "Report to Respondents," p. 14.
[36]Schackne, "Report to Respondents," p. 15.
[37]May 28, 1976, p. 172.

In early 1977, an AFL-CIO spokesman pointed out that in Germany union members sit on boards and receive stipends, often more than they are paid by their unions. In that the deciding vote is on management's side, codetermination, he claimed, was a "fraud." In the United Kingdom, labor wants to go further, he added. "But once labor becomes two-headed, it may swallow itself. Codetermination could destroy the unions. Hence, U.S. labor will never tolerate having their representatives sit on boards and managing."

In late 1976, reports out of Japan indicated that events in Europe were sparking lively interest in labor participation at the board level. Japan's two leading labor organizations, Sohyo (General Council of Trade Unions of Japan) and Domei (Japanese Confederation of Labor), were taking quite different positions. Domei showed interest in participating in joint decision-making. In contrast, Sohyo had declared itself as favoring the expansion of the collective bargaining system.[38] However, according to a 1977 survey of 50 large and 50 medium-sized Japanese firms, only five top executives expressed willingness to introduce the West German type of labor participation in corporate management. Eighty-eight were opposed and seven abstained from comment.[39]

In 1975 the Shah of Iran decreed that 49 percent of many privately-owned factories and 99 percent of government-owned industries be sold to their workers, and if rejected by them, to the general public. Although designed as a wealth and income distributing scheme, ultimately there may be management implications as well. And, of course, until the industrial community concept reaches full maturity in Peru, one has minority board participation by labor rather than full codetermination.

Works councils, bodies through which management-labor relations have been institutionalized at the enterprise level. A council may consist only of workers' representatives or of both workers and management, as in a joint works council in the United Kingdom. These bodies may or may not have legal status, may or may not be mandatory under the law, may or may not be established by agreement between trade unions and employers' organizations at the national level.

An example is the German law that requires that the works council (*Uetriebsrat*) required in any private firm employing five or more people, be a party to company decisions as they relate to working conditions, training, all methods of payment, hiring and firing, promotion, transfers and regrouping, and work allocation. A council is composed entirely of work force members. Curiously, although there is no requirement that a council member belong to a union and although union membership nationwide is only about 30 percent of the workforce, something like 80 percent of the works council members are

---

[38] *The Japan Economic Journal*, 16 December 1976, p. 10.
[39] *The Japan Economic Journal*, 15 February 1977, p. 20.

in fact union members. In that nominations are made by list, which must be supported by a minimum number of workers, the union has a substantial edge. Also, the union members seem to wield greater influence on the councils than nonunion members. The explanation is that the union, even though in a minority position, is organized.[40] Works council chairmen have a lot of power, and 98 percent of them are union members.[41]

Norwegian legislation in 1973 established "company assemblies" with one-third worker representation. These bodies were given final jurisdiction over major investments, reorganizations, and other substantial decisions. It is clear that as the authority of such bodies is enlarged so as to include all-enterprise policy matters the distinction between works councils and board participation becomes blurred. Even in Italy, where the Communist party has traditionally rejected workers' direct control in favor of channeling labor demands through union and party and rejects the idea of codetermination in the strongest possible terms, unions have begun demanding that management consult with them on major decisions. As David Jenkins noted, the *effect* of current labor relations in Italy is similar to codetermination.[42] Indeed, Italian opinion surveys show that employers increasingly see improving working conditions, encouraging employee participation, and granting more decision-making responsibility are critical to attracting and keeping an efficient work force. And a 1976 interview with Agnelli, the managing director of Fiat, supported this view. He stated that Italian management must encourage full involvement and participation of all segments of society. Only a pattern of consultation and cooperative decision-making could enable a return to more productive management in Italy.[43]

Similarly, although the French labor movement, likewise heavily impacted by the Communist party, had rejected the codetermination model, the reality below the surface was somewhat different. After the events of May 1968, the unions were given official representation within enterprise representative bodies, and by 1972 unionists held over 50 percent of their membership. A 1969 national collective agreement required employers to consult with the works councils in advance of proposed layoffs. In 1971, legislation extended the councils' function to worker training; and, in 1972, legislation permitted four nonvoting workers to sit on management boards of directors. In 1975, a government commission recommended one-third worker representation on supervisory boards. And along with these changes came a rather surprising

---

[40]Richard Balzer, "German Works Councils: First Impressions" (New York: Institute of Current World Affairs, newsletter RJB-46, May 8, 1976), pp. 2–6.

[41]Balzer, "German Works Councils," p. 6.

[42]David Jenkins, "Italy: Metal Workers Ask Broader Consultation," *World of Work Report*, vol. 1, no. 1 (March 1976), p. 8.

[43]"Problems Faced by the Manager: An Interview with Agnelli," *La Stampa* (Turin), 16 June 1976, translated in *European Press Roundup*, National Quality of Work Center, Washington, D.C., undated, p. 5.

shift in management opinion in the direction of support for worker participation.[44]

It should be noted that the Dutch Works' Council Act of 1971 provides for councils in firms with over 100 employees and gives them a voice equal to that of management in such matters as pensions. The councils must be consulted in respect to personnel policies, annual reports, mergers, expansion plans, and closures.

Some firms have gone beyond the letter of the law. Shell Oil's central works council in recent months has discussed inflation, unfavorable developments in the Dutch economy, antipollution measures, commuting problems, and restructuring of the company. The directors of another firm, Hoogovens, felt they should not decide on the merger with Germany's Hoesch until it had been agreed upon (not only discussed, as the law provides) by Hoogovens' works council. Other subjects that have been included on council agendas are production problems, recruitment of foreign workers and satisfying their housing needs, technical training, influenza inoculations, and new investment plans.

Works councils have from seven to 25 elected delegates, depending upon company size. (A council is required for every plant or subsidiary of affected companies.) In firms such as Philips, Shell, Unilever, Hoogovens, and Dutch State Mines, the elections are run with all the organization, publicity, campaigning, excitement, and seriousness of Dutch political elections. Last January (1971), for example, about 40,000 Philips workers went to 53 polling stations to vote for delegates to 29 works councils. There were 948 candidates for 425 seats, making the election the largest outside the normal elections for parliament.

However, not all companies are enthusiastic about the works councils. Subsidiaries of U.S. companies in particular find it difficult to adjust to decision-making by committee. It runs counter to normal policy in such firms as IBM Nederland, in which key decisions are made at the top. IBM also laments the fact that delegates do not fully understand financial and management problems.[45]

Particularly worrisome to the MNCs was the fact that local input into decision-making of the sort we have been describing could well undermine the centralized control necessary to maintain an internationally-integrated production system. Even some U.S. unions were trying to secure a veto power over managerial decisions in respect to foreign sourcing if there were an adverse domestic impact on jobs. (See Section 2.0.)

Job enrichment, any scheme that provides greater autonomy, that is, decision-making capacity, to workers or groups of workers on the shop floor.[46] Flexible work hours, ("flexitime") is one of these. The idea apparently originated in certain German enterprises about 1970. Ideally, the individual worker determines his own daily and weekly work schedule. In some cases, employees may borrow time to be made up later or bank time by working more

---

[44]David Jenkins, "European Report," *World of Work Report*, vol. 1., no. 1, March 1976, pp. 3–4.

[45]*Business Europe*, March 17, 1972, p. 83.

[46]See David Jenkins, *Job Power* (Garden City, N.Y.: Doubleday, 1973).

than the contracted number of hours, which can then be drawn down as desired. Obviously, it is not easy to apply such a system where the public is served or on production lines. A number of pressures push in the direction of such a scheme, specifically, the rising levels of education (which engender a demand for individual self-determination), the expansion of adult education, the growth of special programs to keep older workers at work, the growth in the number of women with a demand for intermittent or part-time work, the expansion of the service sector, continuing urbanization (which creates a need to stagger working hours to avoid congestion of services), the growing importance of shift-work designed to utilize the capacity of increasingly capital-intensive industries, the rising level of real income and relative job security (which permits workers to react against rigidity), and a weakening of the work ethic.[47]

As of 1976, the proportion of workers covered by flexitime was by far the greatest in Switzerland, 65 percent in a number of Swiss cities and with a national average of some 40 percent. In other countries, flexible working hours were less common. In Germany, where the first experiments took place, only 5.7 percent of the workforce were affected by 1972 (latest available figures). In the United States, flexitime was just getting underway.[48]

Another dimension to job enrichment is group assembly as opposed to assembly line organization. The record seems very mixed. In 1973, in a new plant, the Swedish car company, Saab, completely scrapped the assembly line. In its stead, work was organized in teams of from three to ten people, who set their own rhythm and divided the work among themselves. Their only obligation was to finish a batch in the same measured time as the assembly line production. After a year, Saab tallied the costs and savings. The biggest saving came from a drop in absenteeism and turnover, which more than offset the increased training costs. Shortly thereafter Sweden's other car company, Volvo, designed an entire automobile manufacturing plant built to accommodate team (15 to 20 people) assembly work.[49] Olivetti, another alleged success story, had by 1976 switched about half of its 5,000 assembly workers in Italy from conventional assembly lines to "production islands. The result? Higher productivity and lower indirect labor costs."[50] Early in 1974, General Motors Truck and Coach Division experimented with the team approach to assembly, but it was dropped after a few months. The complexity of assembly proved too difficult for a team approach and was too slow to meet GM's production standards.[51]

[47]Gösta Rehn, "For Greater Flexibility of Working Life," *OECD Observer*, no. 62, February 1973, pp. 3 ff.

[48]"Lifelong Allocation of Time," *OECD Observer*, no. 81, May/June 1976, pp. 25–26.

[49]*European Business*, no. 36, Winter 1973, p. 13, and "Volvo Designs a New Factory," *EFTA Bulletin*, vol. 14, December 1973, pp. 17 ff.

[50]*Business International*, December 19, 1975, p. 406.

[51]Mitchell Fein, "Job Enrichment: A Re-evaluation," *Sloan Management Review*, Winter 1974, p. 76.

Job rotation is another vehicle for reducing boredom and alienation. United Biscuits of the U.K. launched such a program in 1972. Subsequently, employees asked if they could learn more about supervisors' jobs in order to understand the work process better. Management allowed them to take over their supervisors' jobs a day at a time, handling production scheduling, paperwork, and liaison with other departments. So successful was the experiment that the number of supervisors was cut in half over the next two or three years. The result has been lower supervisory costs, less absenteeism and turnover.[52]

But, despite these seemingly positive results in Europe, some authorities argue vigorously against any attempt to generalize or to transfer such experiments to other environments, particularly that of the United States. One such:

> *Studies from around the world, including the communist countries, demonstrate that the concepts . . . regarding workers' need to find fulfillment through work hold only for those workers who choose to find fulfillment through their work. Contrary to popular belief, the vast majority of workers seek fulfillment outside their work. After almost twenty years of active research in job enrichment, it is clear that only a minority of workers is attracted to it.[53]*

The *Wall Street Journal* reports Leonard Woodcock, President of the United Automobile Workers, as "outspoken in his denunciation of government officials, academic writers and intellectuals who contend that boredom and monotony are the big problems among assembly workers. He said 'a lot of academic writers . . . are writing a lot of nonsense.' "[54]

But whatever the negative views on the subject, there is clear evidence of a worldwide movement toward more participative management, whether on the work floor or in the board rooms. It may be useful to think of the various alternatives that have been discussed as a series of concentric rings of authority or self-determination around the individual employee. (Figure 3.1)

Negotiating committees, assembled periodically to bargain collectively with management, may be on a national level between one or more national unions and an employers' association (in which case, a question arises as to labor's capacity to enforce an agreement at the local level) or on a local level between national or local unions and management; may have a legal basis or may not (that is, the resulting agreement may have the legal status of a contract and be enforceable as such, as in the United States, or it may not); may or may not be legally required. In any case, there seems to be a worldwide tendency for labor negotiators to broaden discussions to cover matters formerly considered to be purely managerial, such as hiring and firing, training, production scheduling, bonuses, promotion, trade and investment policy, and now environmental considerations.

---

[52]*Business International*, December 19, 1975, p. 406.

[53]Mitchell Fein, "Job Enrichment," p. 77.

[54]February 20, 1973, p. 5.

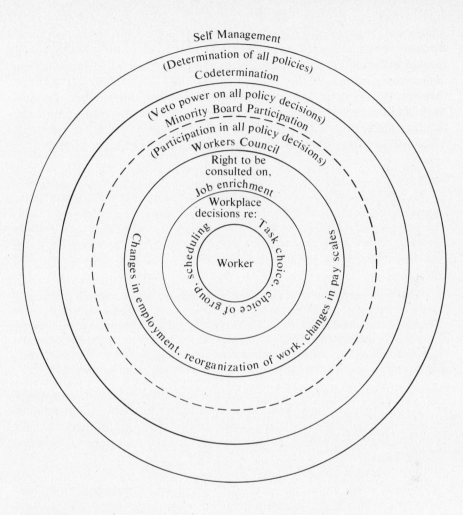

Figure 3.1
THE CONCENTRIC CIRCLES OF WORKER PARTICIPATION

Compulsory negotiation, a national or state network of conciliation and arbitration commissions and courts, as in Australia. Bargaining may take place at both industry and plant level, but it is largely informal and supplementary to the arbitration process. Even more than a collective bargaining system, the *compulsory* settlement of agreements would seem to place labor and management in adversary positions.

Role change, only known to exist on a compulsory basis in the People's Republic of China, although note the previously cited U.K. case (United Biscuit). Chinese factory administrators are apparently required to spend two days a week working on the factory floor as ordinary labor (likewise periodically required of bureaucrats and intellectuals). It is theorized that such a practice, though incurring a social cost because individuals are not fully exploiting their comparative advantage, that is, their differential skills, may in fact lead to a net gain by lessening social costs generated by increasing job specialization, inability to communicate, social fragmentation, and interpersonal conflict. The Chinese system attempts to achieve closer identification among all people by role change. One visitor describes the process thus:

The attempt to disestablish scientists as a privileged elite—while continuing to accept them as useful members of society—is being done partly through political education that stresses the virtues of workers and peasants. In the early days of the Cultural Revolution, extensive reorientation classes for intellectuals were apparently quite common. Many still spend several months at the May 7 Cadre Schools (named after the date they were proposed) where they learn to serve the people by accustoming themselves to manual labor, learning peasant skills such as farming and building huts, and studying Mao's ideology.

"Serving the people" is expected in ordinary jobs, too, where those in positions of authority still take turns doing the necessary menial work, and everyone is expected to spend time studying and discussing Mao's precepts—as at Chungsan University where the professors meet to do so for an hour a day. At Peking University, faculty duties are said to include research, teaching, and manual labor in agriculture or industry; faculty are expected to spend several months to a year alternately in each occupation. [55]

This practice is reaffirmed by more recent observations in South China, where it was reported that "as a general principle, cadres in county administration spend three months per year doing manual labor." And four times a year there is an investigation to check on how the cadres have approached their labor responsibilities. [56]

The Chinese system can hardly be called a failure.

Informal communication, particularly strong when management deliberately removes obstacles to direct communication, as in Imperial Chemical Industry (ICI) in Britain. It took ICI and nine unions several years to formalize the scheme. Without going into detail, two key sections of the agreement are revealing:

Relations in the workplace. **Management should accept the fact that employees have knowledge and skills which can contribute to the solution of work place problems. Employees should understand the management point of view, the needs of the business, and also have regard for the interest of other groups of employees. Where alterations to working or manning practices seem necessary to improve plant efficiency there should be joint discussion and agreement among those directly concerned.**

Organization of work. **Work should be organized so that each employee's time, skills,**

---

[55] Ethan Signer, "New Directions in Chinese Science," *Technology Review,* December 1971, p. 8.
[56] Johnson and Johnson, *Two Legs,* p. 37.

and capacity to accept responsibility can be fully and effectively employed. The joint cooperation of employees and management will be needed to achieve this. The outcome should be more interesting, more responsible, and, therefore, more highly rewarding jobs. All rearrangement of work will be consistent with the company's policy of safe working.

The pattern of labor management for which a firm opts is very much a function of law and local custom over which the firm may have little control. The real question is whether management wishes to move toward a higher level of worker participation than that compelled by law and/or custom, or to invent devices to circumscribe such participation. Management's choice rests very heavily on (1) its perception of man generally (theory X or theory Y?)[57] and (2) its perception of the capabilities and motivations characteristic of a particular labor force at a particular time and place. In this latter regard, management should be situationally oriented; that is, it should adapt its policy to a given place and time and be sufficiently sensitive and flexible so as to be able to shift that policy as relevant variables change. And, incidentally, direct labor participation in management may make the employment of nonnational managers very difficult. This difficulty is circumvented in the Yugoslav case by permitting the workers' council to delegate certain managerial authority for a joint business enterprise (Yugoslav-foreign) to a joint managing board or business committee, which board apparently may designate the managers of the joint enterprise for limited periods of time. Presumably, by prior agreement, non-Yugoslav nationals could be placed in this position, although none seem to have been appointed up to 1976.

It should be noted that legally imposed conditions vary substantially from country to country in regard to the *procedures* for determining wage and nonwage conditions of employment, the *substance* of such conditions (including employer contribution to employee welfare through the state or other external agency), and *structural relationship* (codetermination or labor representation on the board of directors or at other levels of management, disclosure of company financial records to labor representatives, employee participation in profit). What may be the subject of negotiation in one country may be dictated by law in another. On the other hand, some aspects of labor-management relations may have no legal basis at all, such as until recently the collective agreement or union-management contract in the United Kingdom. Until mid-1971, such contracts were held to be mere gentlemen's agreements, not legally enforceable contracts. The United Kingdom's Industrial Relations Act of 1971 (changed in 1974) made labor contracts legally enforceable, prohibited dismissal of an employee after two years' service without adequate cause, required a statutory notice of termination, recognized a worker's right to join a union (or not to do so), introduced the strike vote and a cooling off period,

---

[57]See Glossary.

and required employers to give employees and labor unions they recognized a variety of information on the company and its performance. Among all of the industrialized countries, the United States relies most heavily on collective bargaining.

3.3   POLICY TOWARD LABOR UNIONS

The role of the union varies from country to country for some of the reasons suggested in Figure 3.2. For example, if the level of union income is low due either to high labor mobility (difficulty of holding members), low employment, low per-capita labor income, and/or the lack of labor homogeneity, then a labor union has need for other sources of income and support. Also, limited income means that it has but little capacity to suspend work, support research, or undertake welfare on behalf of its members. Therefore, it is driven into alliance with other organizations—political party, church, or government— and bargaining becomes very emotional. Under these circumstances, it is very easy for political or religious issues and ideological commitments to become involved. The result is that economic and political issues tend to dominate collective bargaining. What is not shown is a relationship developed by Douglas A. Hibbs, who demonstrated that industrial conflict tends to drop in rough relationship to the success of welfare-state policies in making government the instrument for allocating shares in the GNP.[58] He concluded that the primary explanation for major changes, for example, in 12 leading market-oriented industrial countries lay in the effectiveness of social democratic and labor parties in moving the power center for distributing national income from the collective bargaining table to the political marketplace. His thesis is summarized in Figure 3.3. From Figure 3.4, the wide disparities among countries in respect to man-days lost due to strikes is apparent, from a high of 1,849 lost days per 1,000 employed for Canada to a low of 49 days for Sweden.

In the United States the union selected by the majority of workers in a plant has a legal monopoly over all bargaining with the employer, which means that there is no bargaining through other institutions. In Europe this right by a union to represent all employees is unknown. Further, a characteristic European institution, quite apart from the unions, is the works council consisting of elected employee representatives. The works council may act as a consultative agency vis-à-vis management and function as part of the grievance procedure and, as already described, participate in a variety of other decisions. Another major difference is that European collective bargaining, unlike that in the United States, is typically between representatives of an employers'

---

[58]Douglas A. Hibbs, Jr., "Long-Run Trends in Strike Activity in Comparative Perspective" (Cambridge, Mass.: mimeo, August 1976).

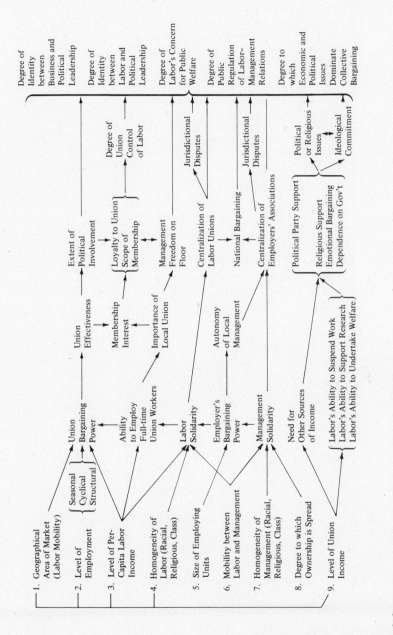

Figure 3.2
**ENVIRONMENTAL INFLUENCES ON STRUCTURE AND POSTURE OF ORGANIZED LABOR
(feedback loops not shown for sake of simplicity)**

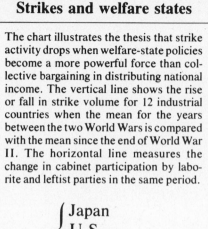

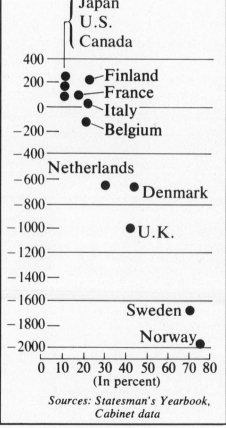

Strikes and welfare states

The chart illustrates the thesis that strike activity drops when welfare-state policies become a more powerful force than collective bargaining in distributing national income. The vertical line shows the rise or fall in strike volume for 12 industrial countries when the mean for the years between the two World Wars is compared with the mean since the end of World War II. The horizontal line measures the change in cabinet participation by laborite and leftist parties in the same period.

Sources: *Statesman's Yearbook,* Cabinet data

Figure 3.3
STRIKES AND WELFARE STATES

Note: Strike volume is equal to the man-days lost per 1,000 nonagricultural civilian employees for one year.

Source: The New York Times, Dec. 6, 1976.

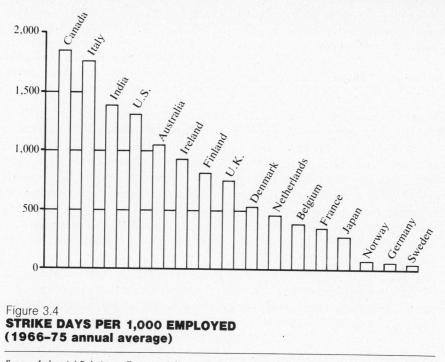

Figure 3.4
**STRIKE DAYS PER 1,000 EMPLOYED
(1966–75 annual average)**

Source: Industrial Relations—Europe, vol. iv, no. 50, January 1977, p. 2. Data from the International Labour Office, Italy.

association and representatives of a confederation of unions, sometimes on a national basis but usually on a regional basis. Agreements so negotiated often set the minimum conditions for an entire industry. In the United States, collective bargaining is more likely to be at the local or company level and any agreement is limited in its application to the union and firm involved in the negotiation. Also, in the United States the collective agreement negotiated between employer and a labor union supercedes any individual employment contracts. This is not necessarily true in Europe. In Japan, the national and regional confederations are relatively weak, and most negotiation is done by what are essentially company or plant unions.

Unions also differ markedly from one country to the next in respect to their degree of political involvement. One generalization that can be made is that characteristically the poorer the union, the more likely it is to turn to external sources of support, typically to a religious or political organization. There is also the historical input.

The more intimate relationship between unions and political movements or governments in newly independent countries is particularly the result of earlier identification of unions with movements for independence from Colonial powers, and partly the result of other pressures (economic development plans, Communist threats, etc.), which cause governments to control labor movements more than we have in the West. Unions have some freedom and influence even within the "one-party" democracies, such as Egypt, India, and perhaps even Ghana. In many developing countries, there is, as Maurice Neufeld has put it, "the inevitability of political unionism."[59] *Thus, our view of the trade union as virtually free of government influence or control will be a long time in developing in these countries at their present stage of political and economic growth.*[60]

If the firm has been able to limit its responsibilities essentially to those related directly to the job at hand, it will be in a better position to negotiate with trade unions on strictly economic issues. The broader the range of subjects included in negotiations, the more likely is the negotiation to take on a political coloration. Note that negotiation with a union in a company town situation is by definition of a political nature. That the union may become politically active on behalf of the company when its "golden egg layer" is under political attack is beside the point. The firm then becomes vulnerable at best to charges of undermining national solidarity, at worst to charges of subversion of national loyalty.

It is a safe assumption that sooner or later, regardless of its environment, the firm will be faced with the problem of dealing with a local labor organization. The degree to which union organization is centralized, politically committed, able to capture members, and responsible for its commitments is a function of a number of variables, the most important of which are plotted on Figure 3.2. Under most circumstances, it would appear in management's best interest to deal with unions that are strong locally, essentially nonpolitical, representative of the workers, and responsible to their members' best interests. The problem lies in how to encourage whatever unions there are to develop in those directions.

Some international businessmen suggest the following policies:

1. Resist vigorously bargaining with unions dominated by, or committed to, a political party or religious establishment, or to particular political or religious ideologies.

2. Resist, but give ground to, labor leadership that seems primarily concerned with bettering working conditions (rather than enlarging support for a political or religious cause). Some resistance, but not overwhelming, tends to strengthen such leadership. Outright company encouragement may torpedo its appeal.

3. Bargain with local unions rather than with a national organization if at all feasible. (Possible restraints: legal requirements, a demand for national negotiations through an employers' association because of the industry-wide repercussions, unwillingness on the part of the national labor union to permit local negotiation because of the weakness of local labor leadership and financial resources.)

---

[59]Maurice F. Neufeld, "The Inevitability of Political Unionism in Underdeveloped Countries: Italy, The Exemplar," *Industrial and Labor Relations.*

[60]Charles A. Myers, "The American System of Industrial Relations: Is It Exportable?" Reprinted from the *Proceedings of the Fifteenth Annual Meeting,* Industrial Relations Research Association, 1962, p. 8.

4. Encourage the development of responsible labor leadership by contributing to seminars and training courses sponsored by the host government, the International Labor Organization, the World Federation of Free Labor Organizations, the AFL-CIO or other responsible noncommunist agencies.

5. Avoid conditions permitting the creation of an independent "third force" between local and national unions, such as interunion, plant-wide shop stewards' communities in the United Kingdom.

Two points need expansion. The first is that bargaining with local unions rather than on a national level may so strengthen local labor as to make it virtually independent of national union control. If labor is organized on a craft basis and is represented locally by means of a shop steward system, as in the United Kingdom (which probably means one shop steward per shop regardless of the mix of unions represented in that shop), then one is facing a nonunion power center. In fact, a plant-wide shop stewards' committee may deliberately neutralize union authority on the local level. Given this situation, if the firm opts to negotiate only on the national level, it is in trouble, for the union negotiators are in no position to implement agreements at the plant level. The only leverage they can develop vis-à-vis the local shop stewards would be public appeal or control of funds or valuable services. But it is likely that the shop stewards have developed a virtual communications monopoly through a regular plant newspaper, as well as independent sources of funds through football pools and similar activities. In that they perceive their authority as being challenged by management's refusal to negotiate with them, they are constantly in need of proving their authority. Hence, the probability of wildcat strikes over relatively trivial incidents is high. In an overly simplified form, we have described the pattern of Ford's management-labor relations in its Daggenham plant in Britain during the 1950s.

Exacerbating the situation in many countries is the fact that the national unions supply the locals with very few services. For example, in 1962, there were 60,000 full-time union officers in the United States, about one for each 300 members. In Britain, the ratio was approximately 1:2000, which was just about one seventh the U.S. ratio.[61]

The second point meriting emphasis is that international channels of communication of organized labor are rapidly improving. An agreement reached with labor in country X may become relevant to negotiations in country Y. In some internationally oriented firms, a representative of the parent firm either sits in on all important negotiations or approves all important labor-management agreements. The critical variable here is the degree of management responsibility held in the local enterprise by the associated international firm. This feedback through international labor channels may be a valid reason for not retaining overall management responsibility in a foreign enterprise, or in

---

[61]S. M. Lipset, "Trade Unionism and Social Structure: II," *Industrial Relations*, February 1962, p. 93.

centralizing control over labor-management relations regionally or worldwide.

It is important to realize that nationally-based unions face many disadvantages when it comes to dealing with the MNCs. Prof. David H. Blake described some of the disadvantages as follows: (1) "... union officials must deal with management personnel who ... are subject to pressures or control from a foreign source"; (2) "... job security [is] more or less dependent on the global operation and performance of the firm"; (3) "many of the usual union tactics are less effective than in the relations with domestic firms"; (4) "... different states and their labor forces may be competing with each other for the favors of the corporation."[62] Finally, it should be noted that while "an increasing number of corporations are effectively coordinating their resources and productive facilities ... the trade unions have not kept up with the increasingly internationalized and integrated world economic structure."[63] An interview-based study in 1976 concluded that U.S. labor union officials perceived the multinational corporations (broadly defined) as both a "threat to the well-being of the United States and to union power." Most union leaders were found to be dubious about multinational unions as a means of restoring labor power vis-à-vis the multinationals.[64]

The trade union's response to the growing internationalization of business has taken a variety of forms. Initially, a great deal of time and effort was spent on union-to-union activities. In general, this took the form of encouraging, subsidizing, and helping to organize trade unions in less advanced countries. The principal national unions with international support programs have been the British Trade Union Congress (TUC), the AFL-CIO, United Automobile Workers (UAW), the United Steelworkers of America (USW), the West German Trade Union Federation (DGB), Force Ouvrière (France) and the Histadrut (Israel). An outgrowth of this concern was the appearance in 1962 of the American Institute for Free Labor Development. A nonprofit organization, it was founded and financed by the AFL-CIO and supported by some members of the U.S. business community with Latin American interests (notably W. R. Grace and Pan American). Its objective was to "assist the democratic labor movement in Latin America and the Caribbean in building strong, viable trade unions capable of improving the socioeconomic condition of their memberships."[65] Active throughout Latin America except Cuba and Haiti, the Institute leadership and technical seminars had undertaken such action programs as housing, community, and agricultural development.

Subsequently, the more aggressive Western unions focused their attention

---

[62]David H. Blake, "Corporate Structure and International Unionism," *Columbia Journal of World Business*, March/April 1922, pp. 19–21.

[63]David H. Blake, "Corporate Structure," p. 20.

[64]Franklin R. Root and Bernard Mennis, "How U.S. Multinational Corporations, Unions, and Government View Each Other and the Direction of U.S. Policies," *Journal of International Business Studies*, Spring 1976, p. 19.

[65]Statement appears in many institute publications.

on the expansion of international business, and many started to play a more active role in those organizations that had been established over the years to provide labor with an international forum; i.e., the World Trade Union Federations, the International Trade Secretariats (ITS), and the International Labor Organization (ILO).

The most active multinational union organizations have been the International Confederation of Free Trade Unions (ICFTU) and the International Trade Secretariats (ITS) (see Table 3.2). In 1973, the ICFTU and the ITS agreed that the former should focus its efforts on trying to influence governmental and intergovernmental organizations, while the secretariats should concentrate on the development of relations between corporations and unions on the international level.

In fact, on the international level there are two main groups of trade unions: (1) the World Federation of Trade Unions (WFTU, headquartered in Prague) of the Sino-Soviet bloc, plus a few communist-dominated unions elsewhere, notably in France, Italy, and India, but also in 25 other countries (however, something like one half of the WFTU membership is from the Soviet All Union Central Council of Trade Unions, the AUCCTU); and (2) the International Confederation of Free Trade Unions (ICFTU) of the American-European-Japanese bloc (headquartered in Brussels). Prior to the withdrawal of the AFL-CIO in 1969, about a quarter of the ICFTU's 50–60 million membership was U.S.; about 40 percent, European; 13 percent, Latin American; 12 percent Asian and Australian; 5 percent, Canadian; and 3 percent, African. There is a third grouping, the World Confederation of Labor (WCL, formerly the International Federation of Christian Trade Unions), likewise headquartered in Brussels, whose influence is limited largely to the Christian trade unions of Europe, but with some strength in Canada (Quebec) and Zaire.

Possibly of more immediate significance to corporate managers are the 18 International Trade Secretariats, which are really international federations of national trade unions operating in the same or related trades or industries. They cooperate with the ICFTU and each has its own liaison offices. Some 40-odd U.S. unions belong.

The significance of the ITS from the point of view of management lies in the fact that behind local unions may lie the expertise and resources of an ITS, oftentimes of U.S. origin. The AFL-CIO, until its withdrawal in 1969, directed most of its international effort through the ICFTU, its regional organizations (such as the Inter-American Regional Organization of Workers, ORIT) and the ITS. Regional ICFTU organizations other than ORIT include the ICFTU African Information Service and the ICFTU Asian Regional Organization (ARO).

A recent development is the appearance of the European Confederation of Free Trade Unions in the Community. It consists of ICFTU-affiliated unions in EEC member countries. An important role is given to the committee of representatives of individual unions in the same branch of industry—transport,

Table 3.2
THE INTERNATIONAL TRADE SECRETARIATS

		Total Membership of Affiliates*
International Metalworkers' Federation	(IMF)	11,500,000 in 65 countries (July 1972)
International Transports Workers' Federation	(ITF)	5,600,000 in 80 countries (Dec. 1972)
International Federation of Commercial, Clerical and Technical Employees	(FIET)	6,000,000 in 46 countries (Mar. 1973)
International Textile, Garment and Leather Workers' Federation	(ITGLWF)	5,250,000 in 40 countries (May 1974)
International Federation of Plantation, Agricultural and Allied Workers	(IFPAAW)	3,999,359 in 45 countries (Jun. 1969)
Public Services International	(PSI)	3,932,319 in 61 countries (Oct. 1970)
Postal, Telegraph and Telephone International	(PTTI)	3,150,000 in 82 countries (July 1973)
International Federation of Chemical and General Workers' Unions	(ICF)	3,100,000 in 32 countries (Oct. 1970)
International Federation of Building and Woodworkers	(IFBWW)	3,000,000 in 44 countries (Jan. 1972)
International Union of Food and Allied Workers' Associations	(IUF)	2,150,000 in 54 countries (Jan. 1974)
Miners' International Federation	(MIF)	1,500,000 in 33 countries (Mar. 1971)
International Federation of Free Teachers' Unions	(IFFTU)	1,500,000 in 37 countries (July 1972)
International Federation of Petroleum and Chemical Workers	(IFPCW)	1,176,089 in 58 countries (Jun. 1970)
International Graphical Federation	(IGF)	840,000 in 31 countries (Nov. 1973)
International Secretariat of Entertainment Trade Unions	(ISETU)	470,000 in 29 countries (May 1971)
International Federation of Journalists	(IFJ)	60,300 in 23 countries (May 1968)
Universal Alliance of Diamond Workers	(UADW)	10,350 in 6 countries (Dec. 1967)

*Latest statistics available.

Source: David C. Hershfield, *The Multinational Union Challenges the Multinational Corporation* (New York; The Conference Board, 1975).

agriculture, metalworking, food, and catering. Their ulimate objective is to engage in collective bargaining on a European level.

A factor slowing down the integration of European unions for negotiating purposes is that in many EEC countries the unions have always relied more heavily on legislation to provide improvements in working conditions for their members than have their counterparts in Britain or the United States. This modus operandi is for the time being impossible within the EEC in that there is no EEC political body with the necessary powers. In general, organized labor on the Continent has been slow to become involved on an EEC level, and the trade unions have official representation only on the Economic and

Social Committee, which has a purely consultative status. Nonetheless, both the Socialist unions (through a special secretariat) and Christian unions (through the IFCTU's European organization) have established EEC liaison offices in Brussels.

There are several independent regional labor organizations of some significance: the International Conference of Arab Trade Unions (ICATU) headquartered in Cairo, the African Trade Union Confederation (ATUC) in Dakar, and the All African Trade Union Federation (AATUF) in Tanzania.

In devising a position vis-à-vis a local labor union, the firm is well advised to be conscious of these developing transnational linkages.

The International Labor Organization (ILO), another international chamber of labor communication and support, is a specialized agency of the United Nations. Essentially, it is involved in the collection and analysis of statistics concerning labor around the world and in the creation of international labor standards. It deals with such subjects as employment, international labor mobility, skill development, wages and hours, child welfare, social security, and safety standards. There are now about 130 conventions embodying internationally endorsed standards concerning various aspects of working conditions. Such a convention is not legally binding unless formally ratified by a government, but it may become relevant to local labor-management negotiations. Additionally, the ILO has issued some 125 recommendations. These conventions and recommendations, collectively, are known as the International Labor Code. At various times and places it may be quoted to management.

Research based on 65 interviews with U.S. and European union leaders[66] produced the following responses: only two rejected the multinational corporation outright (the impact was all bad and the MNC should be done away with); all non-U.S. union leaders suggested that the most disturbing factor was the inability to find where decisions were made in the industrial relations area (unionists felt that they were given a "runaround," that local negotiation was a facade); several mentioned the reduced ability to influence management in the multinational case because of the multiple profit centers, the MNC's vast staying power (based on the MNC's capacity to shift production), and the threat of its withholding or diverting investment. Also mentioned was the tendency of the MNC to introduce too many foreign practices. Trade union wants were enumerated: (1) consolidation of national unions, (2) political pressure to regulate the MNCs in respect to union rights (particularly on a regional basis), (3) political pressure to introduce national laws to establish union rights, and (4) political pressure to restrict the MNCs. During the study, 181 instances of international union cooperation were listed, 50 percent involving information interchange and consultation (80 percent of which were of a continuing nature). Virtually all cases involving active

---

[66]David H. Blake, "The Internationalization of Industrial Relations," presentation to the Association for Education in International Business, Annual Meeting, New Orleans, 1971, unpublished.

interunion cooperation were of an *ad hoc* nature. ITCs were involved in 95 percent of all instances of interunion cooperation. The conclusion was that there was growing concern on the part of unionists over the inadequacy of international union linkages. The pressure to create such linkages mounts because of the growing percentages of foreign employees (for example, 36 percent for IBM, 26 percent for Kodak, 76 percent for Philips); the growth of overseas employees in absolute numbers (4 million employees for U.S. and European electrical and electronic firms outside the parent country and 2½ million for the automotive industry); and the increasing number of Europeans employed by alien firms (in 1967, 35 percent of all employment in the Belgian metal-working industry was provided by subsidiaries of foreign-based firms). The researcher concluded, "Industrial relations are going to be internationalized."[67]

Some have observed that the ITSs in fact provide a basic framework for labor's response to corporate multinationalism. Eric Jacobs feels that ". . . [by] working through the international trade union secretariats in Geneva, the unions are beginning to build up the foundations of countervailing power on the international scale equivalent to the power that unions created in their own countries years ago."[68]

Of the 18 international trade secretariats, the largest are the International Metalworkers' Federation (IMF)—not to be confused with the International Monetary Fund—with 11.5 million members and the International Transport Workers' Federation (ITF) with 6.5 million members. Among the more active are the IMF, the International Federation of Chemical and General Workers' Union (ICF), and the International Federation of Petroleum and Chemical Workers (IFPCW).

Charles Levinson, the General Secretary of the ICF, who has probably done more than anyone to advance the cause of multinational unionism, predicted that the relations between unions and MNCs will evolve through at least three phases. According to Levinson, the first phase was the growing awareness of the MNCs by the unions; the second phase produced the development of information centers by the ITSs; the next stage will be to establish organizational structures that will provide a basis for international bargaining.[69]

Blake, on the other hand, has argued that the more active of the secretariats have adopted one or more of four general strategies in trying to deal with the MNCs. The first strategy has been to collect and disseminate information between and among the affiliated unions. According to Blake, "this activity is now highly developed and widely utilized." Blake also points out that "some types of information collection and exchange seem to be capable of supporting

---

[67]Blake, oral comment, December 1971.

[68]Eric Jacobs, *European Trade Unionists* (New York: Holmes & Meier, 1973), p. 117.

[69]Charles Levinson, *Capital, Inflation, and the Multinationals* (London: George Allen & Unwia, 1971).

more dramatic efforts at coordination."[70] The IMF, ICF, IFPCW, and the International Federation of Commercial, Clerical, and Technical Employees (FIET) have all engaged in this type of activity.

The second strategy has been to facilitate international consultation between its affiliates. For example, the ITS has sponsored worldwide meetings focused on specific corporations and encouraged smaller meetings on a bilateral basis between two or more specific unions where the interests of both could be served by mutual consultation. The IMF, as a case in point, has established a system of "world councils," which represent four different industries within the federation: (1) an automotive group, (2) a steel group, (3) a shipbuilding group and (4) an electrical and machinist group. The World Auto Council, established in 1966, is the oldest and most completely developed of these world councils. Within it, three separate divisional councils have been created for dealing with the following companies: (1) General Motors, Ford, and Chrysler-Fiat-Simca-Rootes; (2) Volkswagen and Daimler-Benz; (3) Toyota-Nissan Motors.

To date the World Auto Council has made some notable contributions to the multinational labor movement. In 1966, delegates from the World Council met with Ford and GM officials in Detroit to discuss a number of issues. Although these meetings were not collective bargaining sessions, they represented one of the few times that management has even agreed to meet with representatives of a multinational union of any sort.

In 1967, a historic breakthrough took place when the major automobile companies agreed to establish parity in wages between U.S. and Canadian workers. This action removed the incentive for companies to shift work between the two countries in order to take advantage of lower wage rates. Some unionists also feel that this action could turn out to be a useful precedent for eliminating wage differentials that exist in other areas of the world.

In 1973, Ford became the first U.S.-based company to hold any sort of meeting with IMF officials. While Ford refused to commit itself to a substantive discussion of its multinational labor policies, it may be significant that Ford consented to a meeting even to discuss "procedural" matters.

The IMF-initiated World Electrical Council has focused its attention on the worldwide operations of General Electric and N. V. Philips. Led by the IMF, several unions have tried to initiate some actions against both companies. In 1960, for example, the Council met in Bogota, Colombia, to exchange information and lay the groundwork for future activities. In 1970, during the U.S. General Electric strike, an IMF official from Geneva participated in the initial negotiations. The Federation also made a token contribution to the union's strike fund. In addition, the Japanese electrical workers' council contributed $5,000 to the strike fund.

---

[70]David Blake, "Corporate Structure and International Unionism," *Columbia Journal of World Business,* March/April 1972, p. 21.

Hershfield reports "the IMF affiliates in the electrical industry in Europe have gone beyond their auto industry counterparts in getting substantive discussions of multinational labor policies with management representatives."[71] Under prodding from IMF affiliates, N. V. Philips has held informal meetings with unions representing Philips' employees in the original European Community countries. In 1973, when the unions asked to discuss proposals for specific EC-wide wage guarantees and redundancy rules, the company broke off the talks. Philips also refused to expand attendance to allow IMF observers to attend the next meeting.

Finally, it should be noted that the IMF supported the UAW's efforts to amalgamate seven Japanese single-company unions into one national auto workers' union. The Japanese union was then very instrumental in forming a world auto council for IMF affiliates representing workers at Toyota and Nissan Motors. Although these two actions had had, by 1977, no visible impact on the industry, they do represent another international union bridge.

The third strategy suggested by Blake has been to support a move toward international regional, or national controls on the multinational corporations.[72] He feels that the U.S. unions are particularly attracted to this strategy, because they see it as a way of stemming the export of jobs.[73] In 1971, for example, the AFL-CIO Executive Council endorsed a nine point program, the purpose of which was to provide national controls on the MNCs. In October 1973, ICFTU and the ITS proposed that the United Nations negotiate charters for the MNCs that would oblige them to recognize unions, observe fair labor standards, publish global accounts, reinvest profits in the developing countries, conform to economic and overall objectives of home and host countries, establish regional and worldwide company work councils, and use labor-intensive technology in the developing countries. Within the European Community, the unions have argued in favor of EC charters for the MNCs that would force them to establish workers' councils with veto and consultation powers over a wide range of labor-management policies.

The fact that none of these particular proposals had been adopted as of 1977 does not diminish the significance of what was proposed by the ICFTU and the ITS.

The final strategy suggested by Blake was to coordinate objectives, policies, and tactics for dealing with MNCs. Implementation of this strategy was, of course, the ultimate objective of the more ambitious internationally-oriented trade unionists. It is also the most difficult strategy to pursue for a variety of reasons. The ICF under Levinson had been the most active ITS in this regard. The most frequently cited examples of such ICF sponsored activity have been:

---

[71]Hershfield, *Multinational Union*, p. 25.
[72]Blake, "Corporate Structure," p. 22–23.
[73]Hershfield, *Multinational Union*, p. 1.

Saint-Gobian (1969), American Cynamid (1969), Hechst (1969), Dunlop-Pirelli (1971), Michelin (1971 and 1972), and Akzo (1972). There seems to be some controversy, however, over whether the ICF really achieved anything because of its involvement in these relatively minor incidents.

In the Saint-Gobian case (1969), the Italian unions requested the U.S. union postpone a proposed strike against Saint Gobian (U.S.) so that the action might coincide with that in Italy. The U.S. unions agreed. According to the unions, the threat of simultaneous strikes in the two countries led to more favorable terms for labor in both Italy and the United States. Charles Levinson, General Secretary of the International Chemical and General Workers' Union, "made this limited success into an international propaganda triumph ... which could be used as a convincing argument to overcome the skepticism and inertia of national trade union bodies."[74] Subsequently, he was able to persuade the unions in the chemical and rubber industries to establish international councils in a number of enterprises, among them Dunlop-Pirelli, Michelin, St. Gobian, Rhone-Poulenc, W. R. Grace, Ciba-Geigy.[75]

Other examples of active cross-border union cooperation since 1965 include:

1. a world meeting in Bogota of unions that negotiate with General Electric for the aim of creating a united front,

2. a Ford negotiation in Peru with a local union coached by the United Auto Workers,

3. creation of a Bauxite Federation of the Caribbean in Surinam to bargain with the big United States aluminum companies operating in the region,

4. advice by the United Steel Workers to their Jamaican counterparts when negotiations in Jamaica broke down,

5. successful United Auto Worker pressure on Ford headquarters in Dearborn to rehire discharged Venezuelan union leaders,

6. agreement by union leaders representing automotive workers from 14 European countries to cooperate in narrowing wage differentials,

7. organization of an international meeting of unionists representing 300,000 agricultural implement workers,

8. support by British unions of a U.S. strike against National Airlines,

9. resolution of a labor dispute in a German subsidiary in Turkey by pressure brought on the German parent by the International Chemical Workers Union in Geneva,

10. demands by the Industrial Section of the Dutch Federation of Trade Unions on Philips, the Dutch electrical corporation, in connection with a strike of 1,000 workers over wage increases in Philips' Colombian subsidiary,

---

[74]B. C. Roberts, "Multinational Collective Bargaining: A European Prospect?" *British Journal of Industrial Relations*, vol. 11, no. 1, March 1973, p. 9.

[75]See Herbert R. Northrup and Richard L. Rowan "Multinational Collective Bargaining Activity: The Factual Record in Chemicals, Glass, and Rubber Tires," *Columbia Journal of World Business*, Spring 1974. pp. 112 ff.

11. pressure by the Dutch Federation of Labor to make Philips reinstate suspended workers in Philips Barcelona subsidiary.

On the other hand, European unions failed in 1970 to bring off solidarity in a strike action when Flemish workers struck Ford's Genk plant and the British shop stewards refused their appeal for support. Nor did German labor support a United States–Canadian UAW strike against General Motors, although the former did agree not to do any work transferred from the strike-bound North American plants—an offer that had no substance since production could not be shifted in any case.

By 1973, Blake had tabulated some 256 instances of cross-national cooperation among trade unions, either in the form of cooperation in collecting information about specific corporations, consultation among unions confronting the same corporate employer, or joint action.[76] An interesting and little publicized example of international union activity is the annual meeting which takes place between Japanese and U.S. labor leaders (AFL-CIO) to discuss matters of mutual interest, very frequently trade-related problems.

A 1975 Conference Board survey revealed that more than one-quarter of the largest U.S. and foreign-based corporations that responded (134 out of the 555 U.S. companies queried, 34 out of 173 foreign companies) had been the targets of multinational union activity. For example, of the 134 U.S. corporations, approximately 10 percent had been contacted across national borders. Another 15 percent reported that their unionized employees had engaged in some form of multinational coordination.[77]

Of foreign-based MNCs surveyed, approximately 20 percent had been contacted by multinational unions and about 25 percent knew of intraunion activities at the international level.

The 21 U.S. and foreign companies that had been contacted by multinational unions cited the following 35 instances of union tactics (ranked in increasing order of force):

(1) Higher management is asked to change company policy toward employees in another country (eleven instances).

(2) Company's labor dispute in another country is publicized with the objective of reducing company's sales (four instances).

(3) Union officials from another country join local company employees at serious negotiating sessions with company (eight instances).

(4) Union officials from another country join local company employees in arbitration or court proceedings against the company (four instances).

(5) Company employees refuse to work overtime to compensate for production lost by foreign strike (one instance).

---

[76]David H. Blake, "Labor's Multinational Opportunities," *Foreign Policy*, no. 12, Fall, 1973, pp. 137–138.
[77]Hershfield, *Multinational Union*, p. 9.

*(6) Company employees refuse to make shipments to company's struck foreign oper-
ations (three instances).*[78]

The Conference Board's survey also revealed that target firms tended "to be
larger, more internationally involved, more centralized in their labor relations
policies, and more often members of employee bargaining associations.[79]

Those who advocate more active international labor collaboration face a set
of problems militating against the establishment of effective multinational
union bargaining positions, such as: union rivalries; political orientation of
unions; structural variations; ideological considerations; personality clashes
among leaders; desire to maintain independence; lack of funds and staff support at the international level; union discipline; lack of common contract
termination dates; the simple inertia not to change one's tactics. In addition,
proponents confront problems that emanate from the much broader context
of society as a whole: differences in the social, economic, and political environment within which the national unions must operate; the ideology and foreign
policy orientation of host governments; national customs and laws; the need
for full employment; and rising exports everywhere.

BASIS FOR RECRUITMENT AND JOB ASSIGNMENT   **3.4**

Labor may be recruited on the basis of social status and/or competence. In
many societies, quite apart from demonstrated ability, social status is very
largely a complex function of family background and ties, wealth (however
defined), sex, number of children, education, race, nationality, regional origin,
politics, religion, and former military rank—to mention a few factors. Because
of the vast complexity of this subject in view of the variety of social structures
in which the firm may be operating, all one can do is to suggest some guidelines
that emerge from accumulated experience.

In situations where patterns of dominance-subordination are socially determined, and not a function of demonstrated ability, management should be
cautioned about promoting those of inferior social status to positions in which
they are expected to supervise those of higher social status (for example, an
ex-corporal over an ex-sergeant in societies where this factor is important). A
complete breakdown in communication and morale may be the result.

Similarly, nepotism—in the sense of permitting supervisors and foremen to
hire kinfolk, fellow tribesmen, or villagers—may result in maximum efficiency
even though the individual worker may not measure up to other candidates for
the job in terms of *individual* ability. In his group, however, the "insider" may
be more effective than the "outsider" with superior ability.

Discrimination in employment by sex may also have to conform to tradi-

---

[78]Hershfield, *Multinational Union*, p. 9.
[79]Hershfield, *Multinational Union*, p. 10.

tional practice to gain maximum efficiency. Innovation on this score by a foreign management in a highly traditional society may lead to a variety of difficulties.

In a multiracial society where social status is related to race by both law and prevailing national values, the firm must either conform or withdraw from management responsibility. In determining its policy, the firm should be sensitive to the effect of its behavior in such a society on attitudes toward the firm in other societies in which it is operating. A relevant query is whether or not by restructuring itself legally and administratively the firm can avoid hostility in these other societies. That is, can it insulate itself from being identified with the enterprise in the country that assigns status on the basis of race? Mining companies operating both in the Republic of South Africa and in areas north of "the line," say, in Zambia, have had to face up to this problem. Another relevant query is how long the status quo is likely to last. The conforming firm may find itself trapped by a racial revolution. Total loss of assets may be expected unless the firm is supplying something in terms of skills, external sales channels, and so forth not available from other, more acceptable sources. It should be noted that a firm's home government policy may be applied subtly to the firm's overseas operations, encouraging it to be less officially repugnant in the host country.[80] Or, the reverse might be true. An example would be the pressures against apartheid (racial separation) by U.S. firms operating in the Republic of South Africa.

The problem of the multiracial society manifests itself particularly in reference to promotion and pay. An "equal-pay-for-equal-work" policy may not be acceptable to the politically dominant but racial minority group (perhaps white), even though the policy's strict application would mean job fragmentation and thus lower pay per worker for the "racially inferior" (black). In societies in which the dominant value system permits advancement of members of the numerically superior racial group, who are opposed socially by a higher status minority racial group, management may choose to phase out the latter group. This situation formerly prevailed in the copper mines of Northern Rhodesia (now Zambia) where the white minority dominated, but where advancement of Africans was permitted by the white elite and opposed by the middle-class whites. This breakthrough can be accelerated in some cases by an attractive pension system, by offering scholarships to children of the group who seek education abroad (thereby encouraging their emigration), and by similar measures which reduce the resistance of the recalcitrant group, which in the Zambian case was the skilled white worker. Meanwhile, an intensified training effort to upgrade members of the racial majority may be instituted.

---

[80]And sometimes not so subtly. By 1976 the U.K. government was explicitly encouraging U.K.-based firms operating in South Africa to change their pay schedules so as to upgrade blacks in relation to whites. In addition, it required companies to publish annual statements describing how they were developing black employees and encouraging trade unionism in South Africa.

Optimum strategy rests on a careful assessment of relative costs during the relevant time period, including the risk of loss of assets as the racial majority gains political control, as it eventually will.

A related, but different problem, is the employment by a foreign firm of members of a racial minority group that is considered to be more or less an outcast group by the larger society. Often, these racial enclaves are likewise differentiated by religion, for example, at various times in history, the Armenians and Greeks in Turkey, Indians in East Africa, Jews in Europe, Chinese in Southeast Asia, and English in French Canada. Because these groups are not fully accepted by the surrounding traditional society of the majority, they may turn to nontraditional ways of securing power (and, hence, status), the most frequent being commercial enterprise. In virtually all traditional societies, commercial enterprise other than the sale of one's own handicraft and farm products has been looked down upon as something not really respectable. Trafficking in the products of others for financial profit was not considered a prestigious occupation, and was certainly ranked far below military, administrative, religious, professional, or agricultural careers in many of the more traditional societies. Hence, the way was cleared for outcast national and religious minorities to dominate commercial enterprise. Indeed, financial power has been one of the few devices available to them to prove their importance to the majority community. The danger to the foreign firm is that it may find itself employing a disproportionate number of members of racial or religious minorities in key positions and thus become identified with these outcast groups. There is considerable pressure on a firm to employ members of these minorities, for they frequently carry a higher level of commercial-industrial skills, are more cosmopolitan in outlook because they are less nationalistic, more knowledgeable of the outside world, more likely to speak useful foreign languages, and more aggressive in behavior (a response to the frustrations of their outcast social position). Thus, there is often a definite short-run cost advantage to the firm in employing such individuals, not to mention the greater ease of communication with them on the part of a foreign company. But the insulation of management from the host society by a wall of racial and religious outcasts can, in the longer run, be disastrous. Relevant variables are the importance to the firm of government relations, the importance of internal markets (such as those outside the cosmopolitan centers), the size of the labor force recruited from the majority community, and the degree of area expertise within the foreign management itself.

The laws of virtually all countries require the employment of local nationals if adequate numbers and skills are available. Specific exceptions are granted for contrary cases, examples of which have been Mexican farm workers in the United States and the recent influx of Italian, Spanish, Greek, and Turkish workers into Germany and the Benelux countries. Puerto Rican émigrés into New York City, Jewish émigrés of different national origins in Israel, and the movement into the United Kingdom from the Commonwealth countries (particularly of West Indians, Indians, and Pakistanis) are special cases. In addition to these streams, substantial numbers of North Africans, Black Africans, Asiatics, and even Latin Americans have begun showing up in the European labor market.

United States immigration laws require that all permanent alien residents enter with immigration visas, a prerequisite for which is a work certificate. Persons with professional training and other needed skills are given priority, as are persons with relatives living in the United States. Work certification, which is granted by the Department of Labor, is given only if there are no qualified U.S. nationals available and willing to work or if the foreigner's entrance will not hurt the U.S. labor market. As an example of the latter, the United States has terminated the import of foreign farm workers from Mexico since (1) this alien labor was seen to serve as a wage-depressing device and (2) the jobs these seasonal workers occupied represented thousands of additional jobs otherwise available to American workers. Certain professions in which there is deemed a shortage of U.S. personnel are given blanket work certifications. The point is that an immigration visa is not granted unless work certification has been given; however, the issuance of the visa itself does not follow automatically.

Temporary personnel may be imported into the United States under a nonimmigrant visa at the request of a U.S. employer, such a visa being valid for six months and renewable twice. This visa takes about a month to obtain in comparison with several months for an immigration visa. Persons who hold a visitor's visa or student's visa are not allowed to work during their residence in the United States.

Many other developed countries seem to enforce fewer restrictions than the United States on the employment of foreign nationals. In general, they require work permits of all foreign employees but these permits are given fairly freely with few or no quota limitations. The high cost of living, of course, in some developed countries may be more restrictive than legal restraints towards the employment of non-nationals. An exception to the generally liberal policy of the more developed countries is Switzerland where, in 1970, foreign residents totaled 1.1 million out of a total population of 6.3 million. Switzerland enforced company quotas until mid-1970 and then adopted an overall quota system. A few countries have imposed special restrictions, such as those of Australia against Orientals (ended in 1973) and the Philippines against the Chinese.

The EEC countries are required by the Rome Treaty to permit free movement of labor among themselves, although they may, and do, require work permits of nationals of other countries. Residence permits may be necessary in some countries, but these too are granted with few restrictions. The United Kingom, one of the more restrictive, offers work permits freely in labor-short occupations but in certain fields may consider the availability of qualified UK personnel before issuing a permit at the technical worker level. The nonacceptability of professional diplomas and certificates across the borders in Europe constitutes an important barrier to easy mobility.

The less developed countries generally have stricter entrance procedures; in most cases businesses must employ a certain percentage of nationals, and work permits are granted only to technical and managerial personnel when qualified nationals are not available. The legal requirement for the employment of local nationals ranges up to 100 percent after a stipulated time, but in some countries employment is further limited by ambiguous definitions as to what constitutes a "qualified" national. It is not entirely clear how one defines a *prigumi* (indigenous Indonesian) or a *bumiputra* (indigenous Malay) in contrast to Chinese. What of those of mixed blood to some degree?

Occasionally, there appears to be an extraterritorial application of national law. An example is the alleged policy of most U.S.-owned companies in Canada who refused employment to U.S. draft evaders.[81]

Over the past decade, foreign workers have been making a vital contribution to all of the EEC countries except Italy, which is a major emigration country itself, and the Netherlands, where foreigners make up only slightly more than 2 percent of the labor force. But in West Germany there were close to three million foreign workers in 1974;[82] in France, just short of two million, the largest number coming from North Africa, mainly Algeria; in Belgium and Austria, about 230,000 each. The total for nine European countries: 4.6 million from ten countries, plus 2.9 million from elsewhere. Principal suppliers were Italy (1 million), Yugoslavia (.8 million), Turkey (.7 million), Portugal and Spain (.6 million each).

Non-European countries short of labor have likewise stimulated international mobility. Australia has been trying to attract labor from as far away as Turkey. In most cases, these workers are recruited through official placement offices and are hired on a two-year contractual basis. The United States, of course, has been host to large numbers of Mexican workers. Saudi Arabia has been employing Egyptians.

Japan, it should be noted, has been very reluctant to recruit foreign labor despite the extreme tightness of the domestic labor market (less than 1 percent unemployment in 1971; roughly 2 percent in 1976). There is reported to be a real fear of the tensions and social problems that might arise if many foreign workers joined the Japanese labor force. It is pointed out by the Japanese authorities themselves that Japan has had little experience with foreign workers and that generally the Japanese lack experience in living with foreigners. The Ministry of Labor was, nonetheless, by the end of 1971 actively promoting exchange of engineers and technical experts with Southeast Asian countries,

---

[81]Reported by the *New York Times*, April 10, 1968.

[82]Germany has had labor recruitment agreements with Spain, Greece, Turkey, Portugal, Yugoslavia, Tunisia, and South Korea.

although some of the non-Japanese participants were complaining that the Japanese did not seem to be very keen on revealing their technology to visitors. In any event, the presence in Japan of these foreign technicians was part of a technology export effort, not an import of labor.

Employment of nonnationals may involve lower direct labor cost, but the indirect costs may be substantial, depending upon the responsibility assumed by public authorities for language training, vocational training, health services, community services, recruitment, and transportation to and from their native countries. In any event, the firm incurs the costs of interpreters, translations of relevant documents, increased annual leave, transportation home in case of incompetency or ill health, and double holidays (local and foreign). Companies employing nonnational workers report that the following policies contribute to lowering indirect costs:

1. accurate information on working conditions prior to the worker's departure from home (hours, pay, nature of work, living conditions, social welfare, and pension benefits);

2. an understanding with the local unions as to the position of foreign workers;

3. reception of foreign workers by someome who speaks their language and is familiar with their culture;

4. provision of adequate housing and community services at reasonable cost to the workers, national groups being housed together;

5. employment of staff of interpreters of the same nationalities as the workers;

6. an initial guided tour of the plant with constant deemphasis of the complexities involved;

7. on-the-job training under foremen and skilled workers who do not look down on the foreign worker;

8. initial assignment to work teams of mixed nationality, then to a team of single nationality;

9. avoiding the use of piece-time rates as the standard for deciding norms for workers on hourly rates. (To achieve high levels of pay while abroad, foreign workers may produce at levels significantly higher than local nationals. They can do so because of their relative short time horizon, often two years or less; the local nationals cannot produce at a comparable rate for an unlimited time without risk of damage to health.)

10. encouragement of foreign workers to participate in a local language course;

11. maintenance of a balance between policies that appear to result in exploitation of the foreign worker and those seen by local nationals as giving preferential treatment to the foreign worker;

12. establishment of a direct channel of communication between representatives of foreign labor groups and management.

It should be noted that a major pressure stimulating the internationalization of business lies in the common need among the more developed countries to match their technological development with an adequate supply of relatively unskilled labor. In the less developed countries, the reverse is true; the greater need is to match a large pool of unskilled labor with technological development. Either the labor must move, or the technology.

For a time, some of the more developed countries could meet their unskilled labor demands from the flow of people off the land. The U.S.S.R. is apparently still able to do so. Japan, on the other hand, is beginning to require foreign labor, and has reluctantly admitted some Koreans, thereby releasing Japanese workers for more skilled, more pleasant, and more highly paid jobs. In the United States, it is the Mexicans and Puerto Ricans who move in at the bottom of the labor ladder. As has been noted, European Common Market members rely heavily on foreign workers for more unpleasant jobs. But, as one observer put it, "A type of second-class citizen is developing a place in all industrial countries and for reasons of economic logic rather than social prejudice."[83] The socio-political consequences of large-scale labor movement may be very great.

TRAINING AND DEVELOPMENT   3.5
(SEE ALSO SECTIONS 1.2 AND 2.5)

Inherently part of the recruitment problem is the employment of adequately skilled persons to do the job demanded. The alternative is training internal to the firm, whether it be on-the-job or in-school type. Employment of those trained outside the firm is undoubtedly easier, particularly for the nonnational management, but not necessarily the least in cost. In-the-plant training may be focused on a specific task rather than on the more generalized array of skills one trained externally is generally required to master, and for which demand and cost will be greater. A job may be broken down into relatively simple operations, with a skilled trouble-shooter taking over whenever a problem develops. The worker with the specialized skill has fewer opportunities for alternative employment. Also, literacy may not be required, but in hiring an externally trained worker, the firm pays for literacy. In fact, there is a growing body of evidence that would challenge the assumption of a significant positive correlation between formal education and earnings for at least certain types of workers in certain socioeconomic contexts.

The general experience of firms operating in various parts of the world is that relatively primitive people (in a technological sense) can learn the necessary industrial skills with surprising ease. For example, a Chrysler Corporation vice-president was quoted as saying:

> *[In the Philippines, young men] straight from the rice paddies have responded so well*

---

[83]C. L. Sulzberger in *The New York Times*, June 9, 1972, p. 33.

to Chrysler technical training that many of them are already first-class welders, uphol-sterers, painters and even inspectors.[84]

In South Africa, Chrysler's on-the-job courses for schoolboys were producing trained engineers in four years.

Difficulties may arise when the skill is associated with an innovation identified with a deeply embedded traditional practice or device, such as putting the boards on a native sailing craft or introducing an improved camel saddle.[85] The difficulty is much less when a completely new device is employed. Local military training of a technical nature may offer clues as to the most effective training methods and motivation given the local culture.

In mid-1970, an advanced program of vocational training was introduced in France by a collective agreement between the French Employers' Association and several French labor confederations. This agreement recognized the *right* of employees to receive training (with at least partial pay) and provided for leave *with full pay* of up to a year for certain categories of workers who wish to upgrade their skills or be retrained. The categories are two: (1) workers under termination notice because of lay-offs and (2) ten percent of the workers of an enterprise who have a minimum two-year seniority and at least five years remaining before retirement. If the training is provided by the employer, the trainee receives full pay regardless of length of the training period; in all other cases the employer pays up to one month's salary; for additional periods, the full salary is paid out of a special fund financed by a special tax for adult training. It remains to be seen how well the system will operate.

Motivation is of obvious importance in the training and development context, as well as remuneration (see Section 3.6). Motivation may run the gamut from fear of inability to satisfy biological or psychological and culturally determined needs (such as self-actualization), through habit (internalized values), to the lure of social gain (essentially nonfinancial). Social gain may be sought either for some definable group or identity such as family, community, region, nation, mankind, or for oneself vis-à-vis others, or for the promise of tangible financial or status gain for oneself or a group. Promising a worker a "clean" job may provide for greater motivation than a promise of higher pay, if clean versus dirty jobs are important to one's social status, which is of course always a relative measure. Promise of promotion to a position in which one may engage in some family or tribal nepotism may be of signal importance to the individual, if collectivist values have high priority. Some people are highly motivated by the opportunity to achieve seniority or position in which one enjoys greater freedom or opportunity for "self-actualization," such as longer vacation, financially secure retirement after a relatively short time, flexible work hours, and less authoritarian supervision.

---

[84]Paul E. McDonald, as quoted in *Business Abroad*, December 12, 1966, p. 31.

[85]Reported in Max Thornburg, *People and Policy in the Middle East* (New York: W. W. Norton & Company, 1964), p. 77.

To elevate the status of the worker and to enhance his self-image, IBM in Germany has obliterated virtually all distinctions between white-collar and blue-collar workers. This has been accomplished by the following policies: all employees receive a monthly salary (a practice now legally required in France); everyone up to and including the general manager submits himself to the same punch-clock control; there are no separate executive lunchrooms; and any employee with a complaint can circumvent his immediate superior and even take it directly to the general manager. In addition, the policy is to recruit executives from within the organization. Each employee is evaluated annually by his immediate superior, and such evaluations are shown to the employee for criticism or agreement and to add his own comment if he cares to do so. The complete report then goes on to the next higher superior.[86]

Still common among larger Japanese companies is the seniority pay system (*nenko seido*). As one Japanese writer explains its functional relationship:

> ... *wage is determined in accordance with educational background, age, experience and length of service ... [the system] was devised to guarantee the minimum needs of livelihood of employees throughout their life rather than to pay for the individual job, occupation, or ability.... The company expected in return a high employee morale.*[87]

The wide variety of fringe benefits in Japan is part of this same system of guaranteeing minimum lifetime needs, rather than linking pay and benefit directly with productivity, innovation, and responsibility. In Japan, the wage increases of those in the same seniority group tend to move together with but slight variation. Yet Japanese zeal is startling to the uninitiated. It may be that one's most direct reward for industry and creativity lies in the building-up of esteem—and influence—within the relatively stable group within which one works. It may be that lifetime employment and pay by seniority work in the Japanese context because of their interaction and because of the existence of at least a third characteristic, consensus decision-making, to which reference has already been made in differentiating the Japanese system from a truly paternalistic one. The alien management should realize that the whole system is highly integrated, and one tinkers with pieces of it only with great care.

It is perhaps significant that a recent survey of Japanese executive opinion indicated that 45.9 percent of those polled (305) indicated a need to change the seniority wage system and certainty that it would indeed change; 26.9 percent felt a need to change it, but agreed that change would be very difficult; 1.3 percent felt neither the need to change the system nor did they expect it to change; and 24.9 percent felt no need to change policies but nonetheless expected change.[88] All in all, 26.2 percent felt no need to change, 72.8 percent did; 28.2 percent expected no change, 70.8 did.

---

[86]Reported in *Business Europe*, February 28, 1969, p. 65.

[87]Toyonabu Domen, "Employee and Customer Policies in the International Company" (paper presented to CIOS, 13th Session, 1963, Concurrent Plenary 5, Paper No. CP5c), p. 2.

[88]*Nikkei Business* (Tokyo), September 27, 1976, p. 71.

A great deal has been written about what motivates people to work produc-
tively and to improve and expand their capabilities. There is substantial reason
to believe that there is no single management strategy generating the highest
levels of motivation under all circumstances. It is quite clear that in a highly
traditional, relatively poor, socially stratified society people are likely to respond to somewhat different strategies than those in a more modern, affluent,
open society. In short, one cannot generalize the validity (in terms of either
human satisfaction or maximum production and/or creativity) of the more
authoritarian "theory X" of management or that of the more modern "theory
Y."[89] For example, a study of workers' attitudes in Peru concluded that "in a
highly distrustful society marked by authoritarianism, certain participation
forms which involve man-to-group relationships will probably not be
successful when they are initiated."[90]

This research, based on a study of blue- and white-collar workers in two
large electrical utility companies, one in the United States and one in Peru,
revealed significant differences in that in Peru there was labor preference for
a boss who supervised one closely, greater acceptance of pressure for production, less identification with a work group, and a somewhat lower level of
interpersonal trust. Even when level of interpersonal trust was matched between Peruvian and U.S. workers, the former seemed to relate positively to
closeness of supervision and satisfaction; U.S. workers, negatively. However,
as level of trust rose, both Peruvian and U.S. workers tended to show increasing appreciation of the human relations dimension of management. The authors of the study generalized to the effect that U.S. culture tends to stimulate
the individual to take initiative toward change in his organizational situation:
"the worker tends to think and act as a member of a group and to channel his
initiative through the group."[91] In contrast:

> The individualism of the Peruvian seems to be a different sort of phenomenon. His
> organizational relation tends to be polarized in relation to a more authoritarian man-
> agement, which seems to result in isolation of the individual worker from his fellows.
> The worker does not see the work group in terms of psychological identification or of
> practical support to nearly the same extent as does the U.S. worker. A high faith-in-
> people orientation seems to go with the integration of the individual into the group and
> confidence in being able to solve problems through the group.[92]

On the other hand, a study of the 13,000 employees of the IBM World Trade
Corporation concluded that there was remarkable similarity in employee goals
around the world. "This finding has an extremely important policy implica-

---

[89]See Glossary.

[90]Lawrence K. Williams, William F. Whyte, and Charles S. Green, "Do Cultural Differences Affect Workers'
Attitudes?" *Industrial Relations*, vol. 5, no. 3, May 1966, p. 116.

[91]Williams, Whyte, and Green, "Cultural Differences," p. 117.

[92]Williams, Whyte, and Green, "Cultural Differences," p. 117.

tion: since the goals of employees are similar internationally, corporate policy decisions, *to the extent that they are based on assumptions about employee goals*, can also be international in scope." The authors then say, "It would be interesting to determine how much of the difficulty experienced in managing employees in other countries is due not to cultural differences at all, but, rather, to the automatic and psychological self-serving assumption of differences that, in reality, may be minimal or even nonexistent."[93] One might suggest that the differences may well be present, but that this particular study failed to find them because the employees surveyed (all were in the employ of a large U.S.-based multinational firm identified with computer technology) were self-selected to start with. Many had undoubtedly opted to work for IBM precisely because they felt more at ease in its employ than with a local firm operating with traditional relationships. (This process may work to a somewhat lesser degree for a small, decentralized firm headquartered in Europe, not at all for a joint venture in which day-to-day control is in the hands of the local partner.) Thus, the Sirota-Greenwood study would not appear either to disprove or prove the existence of significant culturally derived variations in employee goals and values.

PAY SCALES AND OTHER BENEFITS 3.6

Closely related to the problems of training and development and of identifying motivational priorities are those associated with selecting the appropriate strategy in regard to pay and benefit standards for local labor. A number of options are open to the firm if law does not foreclose on them. It may pay in cash or in noncash benefits. It may pay currently or defer payment of part of the remuneration. It may pay a fixed wage or incentive payments. Incentives can be of a personal nature (individual piece work), based on group performance, or linked to enterprise results (profit-sharing). National law and custom impact heavily, of course, on one's choice.

Quite apart from these strategy options is the question, should management apply an international policy of "equal pay for equal work"? Or should it pay the going local rates, something less than the local rates, or something above those rates? The last seems to be the most common practice. In this calculation, of course, total labor cost should not be equated with direct labor cost, for the rate of direct to total labor cost varies widely from one country to another, even from one region to another and from one national group to another (see Section 1.2). The problem of appropriate wage level is somewhat aggravated for the multinational corporation in that it is in a position to perceive international differences.

---

[93]David Sirota and J. Michael Greenwood, "Understand Your Overseas Work Force," *Harvard Business Review*, January–February 1971, p. 60.

While the productivity of foreign workers in U.S. affiliates [overseas] can rise rapidly with new capital and technology, their wages are still only a fraction of those in the United States. For example, the ratio of U.S. hourly earnings including fringe benefits to those in foreign affiliates in 1969 for the assembly of office machines was as follows:

Mexico	*6.2:1*
Taiwan	*9.8:1*
Korea	*10.1:1*
U.K.	*2.3:1*

Yet the productivity differentials are far less. The benefits are reaped principally by the international corporations.[94]

This last point is recognized frequently by labor both in the home country and in the host country. In the former, the firm is charged with exporting jobs; in the latter, with exploiting local labor in that the principle of equal pay for equal work is not being recognized.

Optimum strategy should probably be a function of (1) local law and government policy, (2) pay level required to recruit and *hold* competent workers, (3) union pressures, (4) vulnerability of the firm to charges of "exploitation," (5) levels established by the firm in adjacent or similar countries, (6) political and economic significance of local business hostility directed toward a foreign firm not conforming to local pay scales, and (7) need for encouraging greater productivity and initiative than found in traditional local enterprises.

For example, in Mexico there are legislative guarantees for an adequate minimum wage, adjusted for regional disparities and cost-of-living increases; a legal right to 20 percent of company profits, after taxes and deduction of certain allowances for return on capital; job security against dismissal without just cause after three months of employment, giving workers a choice between reinstatement or costly indemnification; an all-encompassing social security system, paid for mostly by employees; arbitration and conciliation in event of failure to resolve grievances on the enterprise level.[95]

As it turns out, a number of companies offer fringe benefits over and above those legally required. But voluntary benefits may soon be taken for granted and become irremovable.

In order to minimize local criticism if the foreign firm opts to pay at a somewhat higher level than prevailing local standards, a larger share of the total labor bill may be dispensed through indirect compensation. For example, special training courses for upgrading, scholarships, more liberal health insurance or retirement benefits than those required, interest-free loans to employees, educational benefits for children, various free or low-cost services

---

[94]Robert d'A. Shaw, "Foreign Investment and Global Labor," *Columbia Journal of World Business*, July–August 1971, p. 58.

[95]Taken from *Solving Latin American Business Problems* (New York: Business International, 1969), p. 107.

such as meals and work clothing, and special bonuses may be offered. This device may be particularly effective if the local labor union can claim at least some of the credit for winning these benefits. Such immobilized earnings may, however, encourage nepotism, theft, and compacted living if the extended family system is operating. Cash can be divided up and distributed over space; many benefits cannot. The ratio of fringe benefits (statutory and voluntary) to total remuneration varies widely even within Europe. Although difficult to calculate, the percentages seem to approximate 20 percent in the United Kingdom, 26 percent in Sweden, 30 percent in Switzerland, 45 percent in the Federal Republic of Germany, 60 percent in Belgium and the Netherlands, 66 percent in France, and over 100 percent in Italy. Comparable averages for Japan and the United States would appear to be 15 to 20 percent and 10 to 15 percent respectively. But how does one evaluate a lifetime employment commitment, as in Japan? Perhaps most extreme of all are the total benefit packages in certain communist countries, such as that reported from North Korea where it is explicitly stated that cash wages and salaries are unimportant compared to heavily subsidized food, housing, work clothes, education, entertainment, medical care, sanitariums, and vacation retreats. For instance, housing in North Korea allegedly costs no more than 3 percent of cash wage or salary. It should be noted that the relationship between legally required and voluntary benefits varies widely among countries. In Japan, statutory benefits are relatively low. For example, although the Japanese government pays unemployment insurance to the jobless, the lifetime employment system makes this type of public assistance less important than in many other countries.

As labor negotiations take on an international color, company negotiators may be faced with demands for a uniform package consisting of the relatively high cash wages of one country and the relatively high fringe benefits of another. Within the EEC, one can anticipate that over time the social welfare legislation of the member states will be harmonized effectively, and wage differentials narrowed. According to EEC rules, a national of one member working in another member state must be accorded full national treatment by the host country in respect to legally based fringe benefits. There is evidence that EEC wage indices are beginning to converge. There is also evidence that total labor cost in U.S. and Japanese manufacturing is now converging with the European. Although difficult to quantify exactly because of national differences in payroll taxes to employee and employer, social welfare systems and lifetime earnings patterns, plus the vagaries of floating exchange rates, it would now appear that unit labor costs in Germany and Sweden may have possibly moved ahead of those in the United States. Hence, a certain divergence in the opposite direction may be occurring. It should be noted that as rates of inflation heighten and persist, labor can be expected to assert pressure for the indexing of wages such as in Brazil and, since 1975, in Australia.

The piece-rate is used widely, particularly for unskilled or semiskilled labor.

There are several dangers inherent in the system. One of these is that the norms should not be set on the basis of temporary foreign labor performance; they may be unduly high. Quite apart from recent experience in Western Europe, Max Weber made a similar observation some years ago:

> the simple fact [that] a change of residence is among the most effective means of intensifying labor is thoroughly established. The same Polish girl who at home was not to be shaken loose from her traditional laziness by any chance of earning money, however tempted, seems to change her entire nature and become capable of unlimited accomplishments when she is a migratory worker in a foreign country. The same is true of migratory Italian laborers. That this is by no means entirely explicable in terms of educative influence of the entrance into a higher cultural environment . . . is shown by the fact that the same thing happens where the type of occupation, as in agricultural labor, is exactly the same as home. Furthermore, accommodations in labor barracks, etc. may involve a degradation to a standard of living which would never be tolerated at home.[96]

The real danger, of course, lies in angering domestic labor if the norms for setting piece-rates are set high because of the short-term, unduly intense effort on the part of foreign labor. In some situations, one may wish to introduce job rates, that is, assigning a task, upon the completion of which the worker is free to leave. The competition is then in terms of time, not in remuneration. But, in line with the drive for increased dignity of the individual on the shop floor, some firms have discontinued both piece-rates and hourly rates by placing all employees on a monthly salary, subject periodically to merit bonuses. IBM pioneered this innovation in 1958 and currently claims to have few hourly employees any place in the world.

In Italy, Japan, and certain other countries it is customary to add semiannual or annual lump sum payments equal to one or two month's pay. Such payments should not be considered as profit sharing but as an integral part of the basic pay package. These bonuses are preferred apparently by employees as a sort of forced savings plan. In Japan, these payments may contribute substantially to maintaining the relatively high level of personal savings so that the gap between income and consumption is sustained even though both increase rapidly. Some have observed that this is an essential part in the engine of Japanese economic growth. If so perceived by Japanese authorities, a foreign firm not paying the annual "bonus" might incur official displeasure.

Some companies have attempted some variety of profit sharing among their local employees overseas in order to create a greater area of common interest between management and labor. This scheme is appealing only if the enterprise is, in fact, a profit center and if the labor force is relatively stable. In any event, the time lapse between labor-input and payments under most profit sharing

---

[96]Max Weber, *The Protestant Ethic and the Spirit of Capitalism* (New York: Charles Scribner's Sons, 1958), p. 191.

schemes is such as to reduce their effectiveness. Also, given the frequent lack of financial and accounting sophistication on the part of local labor, any payment is likely to be taken as due the beneficiaries regardless of the year's profit record. Any reduction may cause serious friction.

Nonetheless, it has become quite clear that there is a worldwide push in the direction of some form of profit sharing, ownership sharing, and participative management. Initially, both labor and management almost invariably oppose such schemes; it is the political sector that forces the issue in the interest of industrial harmony and increased productivity and, therefore, overall economic growth. Constant wrangling between labor and management over how a very slowly growing pie of economic goods is going to be served up becomes politically intolerable sooner or later. In Catholic countries, the notion of sharing has, of course, been encouraged by Papal Encyclicals to the effect that workers must share in the profits of the enterprises in which they are employed and become part owners. In practice, socialist-communist countries such as Yugoslavia, Poland, and Hungary have been trying to institute both profit sharing and management participation (with greater or lesser success, depending upon the basis used for judgment). Profit sharing is legally required for all of certain categories of industry in Mexico, Peru, Pakistan, India, Egypt, and Iran among the LDCs; Yugoslavia among the socialist-communist group (and to some extent apparently in the People's Republic of China); France among the more developed countries. It may be legally encouraged in others (as in the United States, where delayed distribution of profits to employees is considered a cost for tax purposes, not a dividend) and is characteristic of still another group of the more developed countries, such as the cooperative movement in Scandinavia. A recent innovation in the United States is the appearance of the Employee Stock Ownership Plan, which permits a firm to loan pretax funds to employees with which to buy the firm's stock.

In the French case, a 1968 law requires all companies employing over 100 persons to establish a profit-sharing plan of one of three types: (1) distribution of shares of stock, (2) payment into special employee savings accounts (blocked for five years), or (3) creation of an employee-owned trust fund, which acquires securities and is managed by an independent financial institution. In any case, ownership rights are vested only after five years, and only employees with three months' seniority participate. In each case the employees' share of profits (not subject to corporate tax) consists of half of the "superprofits" (French-source profits exceeding five percent of net worth; includes export profits but not income derived from foreign subsidiaries or branches) multiplied by a variable coefficient. The latter is determined by the company's payroll divided by raw materials and equipment, which in all cases is necessarily less than one. IBM-France chose option three, the trust fund approach. The portfolio is managed by the labor-controlled financial institution, Inter-Expansion.

Several European countries have considered profit-sharing proposals. A

United Kingdom proposal would require firms to pay one percent of their capital plus 5 percent of their labor cost into a central fund each year.

More ambitious programs have been proposed in Germany, Denmark, Sweden, and the Netherlands. In all four, the essence of the proposals has been a compulsory company contribution to a central fund that the national unions would help manage, thereby gradually giving the unions substantial power over industry. The Swedish proposal would require that all companies with 50 or more employees set aside 20 percent of annual taxes before taxes in the form of a special stock issue to be transferred into a collective employee fund. These shares of stock would not be allocated to the company's own employees but would be held collectively in the fund system. In that the plan would continue in effect indefinitely, it implied that after some years virtually the whole of Swedish industry would pass into the control of the workers.

The Dutch scheme of "excess profit sharing" may have the best chance of passing into law within the foreseeable future. (See Figure 5.4.) The proposal called for entities subject to corporate profits tax to allocate a given percentage of excess profits to a national fund administered by the Dutch trade unions, not in cash but in special nonvoting shares (so-called VAD shares). If a firm's excess profits were less than 250,000 guilders, it was to be exempt. Excess profit was defined as the excess of domestic profit (profits less foreign profits) over the corporate profits tax and a "deemed return on fiscal equity." This latter was defined as the return on long term government bonds plus 2 percent to cover the risk factor. In 1974 the percentage of excess profits to be paid would have been 18 percent; in 1975, 10 percent; and in 1976, 12 percent. This percentage was to vary over time according to changes in the ratio of labor productivity to labor cost to a maximum of 20 percent; that is, gains in labor productivity showing up in increased labor cost would push up the percentage of "excess profits" paid out in the form of shares. The greater part of these shares were to go into a central fund, which would not sell them without approval of the company. The smaller part of the shares was to go into a fund destined for the employees of the company concerned. Each employee was entitled to an equal share of the fund. These amounts were to be blocked for a fixed period and thereafter distributed as shares, at which time they would become negotiable. Many problems are inherent in such a scheme, particularly for the foreign firms. For example,

1. What happens in the case of thinly capitalized foreign-owned subsidiaries or foreign-owned branches? Would the foreign parent company be obliged to issue stock?

2. What of VAD rights of non-residents?

3. How was this stock allocation to be treated by foreign parent companies for tax purposes? Would it be treated by home taxing authorities as a credit against domestic tax liability or merely as a deduction from taxable income?

4. What would happen in companies with already existing voluntary profit-sharing plans?

The most advanced LDC profit-sharing scheme was associated with the industrial community concept introduced in Peru in 1970. Through their industrial community, a firm's employees have a claim to 15 percent of the pre-tax, net annual profit of the company. With their share of the profit, employees are obliged to purchase an interest in the firm up to, but not exceeding 50 percent, through a fund owned collectively by the community. Once the 50 percent limit is reached, the industrial community issues its own shares to members (all permanent employees) according to seniority. The shares thus acquired by individual members cannot be sold and are redeemable by the employee or his heirs only through his industrial community and only in event of his severance from the firm. An additional 10 percent of the firm's net pre-tax profit is distributed directly to the employees, half in proportion to basic wage and half in proportion to number of months worked during the previous year. (See Figure 5.3.)

In socialist enterprises of the Yugoslav type, of course, all enterprise earnings (that is, gross income less cost of materials and services bought, sales expenses, capital charges, and other legal and contractual obligations) are divided into four funds by decision of the workers' council (but satisfying certain legal minimums): the investment fund (depreciation of fixed assets, expansion), the social fund (for community and social welfare), the wage fund, and the business fund (the residual, equivalent to the nonsocialist notion of profit). The objective of the workers' council is to maximize the wage fund over some time horizon. It is reported that as the system matures workers' representatives have expanded their time horizons and see more clearly the relationship between foregone income now, investment, and larger income in the future.

The point of giving this much detail is to emphasize the enormous difficulty firms operating internationally will face once national profit-sharing schemes become compulsory, which seems very likely. Tax, accounting, and control problems will be compounded.

It has been observed that labor-management relations can be of four basic types: (1) competition (collective bargaining from power positions), (2) arbitration, (3) sharing (rests on a preproduction agreement in respect to a formula for dividing profits generated by increases in productivity, however profits may be defined), and (4) cooperation (presupposes a convergence of rules and goals in that workers become owners, and managers are merely specially trained workers). The first two relationships rest on a power relationship; in the short run, neither party need be fundamentally interested in increasing productivity. The latter two relationships, theoretically, are based on mutual interest in increasing productivity and a sharing of the product in such a way as to generate increased productivity. Therefore, collective bargaining makes no sense, nor do labor unions as economic forces. Such is the theory.

In fact, significant problems remain in respect to determining the basis for dividing profit. (1) Who is going to participate? All employees or only those with certain seniority and/or rank and/or function? (2) What is the formula for sharing between employees (labor and management) and capital? The ratio of the coefficients in the production function? (But they change and, in any event, may not be known with any precision.) A 50–50 split on the grounds that both factors are essential? (But it is hard to support equal sharing in very labor-intensive or very capital-intensive plants.) Simply giving enough to employees so as to generate sufficient convergence of goals to minimize work stoppages, slow-downs, absenteeism, and idleness? (3) Finally, who makes the sharing decision? The board of directors? Management? A joint labor-management committee? Parliament? The executive branch of government?

If one assumes a significantly different level of income, education, and general sophistication between managers and labor, the marginal utility of additional income will differ between the two groups, and so likewise will time horizons. One would anticipate a tendency on the part of labor to demand that virtually all profit be paid out in current wage, and that reinvestment be kept to a bare minimum. In a situation where there is no obvious objective function to maximize, these differences are very likely to be resolved through competition or bargaining based on relative power positions or on arbitration, probably by a political entity, which means that we have merely shifted the locale of the competition to the political sector. The political sector may specify a formula in law or authorize the executive branch to do so. Whoever has the greater political muscle will win the larger share. It follows that unions and employers' associations will tend to be highly politicized in such situations.[97]

Despite these conceptual difficulties, the international manager must relate effectively with a growing number and variety of national systems. These systems include simple profit-sharing (either of a cash or deferred wage type),[98] profit-sharing with or without ownership sharing, and either profit or ownership sharing with or without some form of participative management on the part of labor. In judging how well a system is working, there may be several significant signals to monitor. Among these: *trend* in the percentage of retained earnings, *trend* in the tenure of managers, *trend* in managerial wages as a ratio to various categories of labor, *trend* in the work-years lost due to stoppages arising out of labor-management conflict and due to absenteeism, and *changes* in the role of unions. Curiously, there seems to have been very little hard research on the effectiveness in these terms of the various profit-sharing and ownership-sharing schemes around the world. It should be noted that the promise of mere economic award may not be very effective in certain economic and sociopsychological environments, a subject already treated in Section 3.3.

---

[97]In the Yugoslav case, it would appear that the minimum level of reinvestment is specified by regulation, which is generally defined as that amount necessary to maintain the fixed assets and working capital of the enterprise. Some observers of the Yugoslav system, which has been operating almost 25 years, seem to agree that in many enterprises the workers tend to be passive participants in the profit-sharing decision, the decision being dominated by management.

[98]Or possibly a shared savings plan in the case of a nonprofit organization or governmental department.

It would seem quite clear from the foregoing discussion that it is unlikely that the best policy is the worldwide application of the same strategies in respect to management responsibility vis-à-vis labor's participation in management, local unions, recruitment and job assignment, training and promotion, and pay scales and other benefits. Implicit in this generalization is sensitivity on the part of headquarters' management of the special conditions prevailing in various parts of the world and an information system adequate to monitor significant changes. For the international firm, local autonomy in respect to choice of labor strategy is not wholly adequate because of the growing linkages among national trade unions and the increasing international flow of information relating to working conditions to which employees have access. In general, "international companies seem destined to move more and more into total remuneration planning as a result of legislated pay and benefit requirements now in force or pending throughout Europe [and elsewhere]. . . . The 'participation movement' suggests significant implications in terms of both management prerogatives and labor costs. . . ."[99]

Discussion questions

1. Why might the characteristic pattern of management-labor relations in Japan be said not to be paternalistic in the sense that the term is often used?
2. Consider the advantages and disadvantages of codetermination in management and of a lifetime employment commitment.
3. What factors tend to determine the content of a labor-management negotiation?
4. To what extent should the labor negotiating authority be centralized within a multinational corporation?
5. What are some of the advantages and disadvantages of employing nonnational labor?
6. Is there a best style of labor management in a universally valid sense? In an evolutionary sense?
7. How might a multinational firm, faced with a highly politicized union in a particular country, move to depoliticize labor-management negotiations?
8. Multinational firms are accused both of exporting jobs and of exploiting foreign labor. In what senses are such charges true or false? How should spokesmen for the firm answer the charges publicly?
9. What aspects of U.S. unionism are exportable?
10. How can a multinational corporation cope with national codetermination and profit-sharing schemes?

---

[99] *Business Abroad*, January 1971, p. 2.

Recommended references

Chruden, Herbert J., and Arthur W. Sherman, Jr. *Personnel Practice of American Companies in Europe.* New York: American Management Society, 1972.

Crispo, John. *International Unionism, a Study in Canadian-American Relations.* Toronto: McGraw-Hill, 1967.

Descloitres, R. *The Foreign Worker, Adaptation to Industrial Work and Urban Life.* Paris: Organization for Economic Cooperation and Development, undated but probably 1966.

Galenson, Walter, ed. *Labor and Economic Development.* New York: John Wiley & Sons, 1959.

Jenkins, David. *Job Power.* Garden City, New York: Doubleday, 1973.

Joint International Seminar on Adaptation of Rural and Foreign Workers to Industry, Supplement to the Final Report. Paris: Organization for Economic Cooperation and Development, 1965.

Kahn-Freund, Otto, ed. *Labour Relations and the Law, a Comparative Study.* Boston: Little, Brown & Co., 1965.

Kamin, Alfred, ed. *Western European Labor.* Washington, D.C.: The Bureau of National Affairs, 1970.

Kujawa, Duane. *International Labor Relations Management in the Automotive Industry, a Comparative Study of Chrysler, Ford, and General Motors.* New York: Praeger Publishers, 1971.

Workers' Participation. Paris: Organization for Economic Cooperation and Development, 1976.

Case E
SIEMENS' FOREIGN WORKERS*

As was the case with most West German firms with the positive upturn in the nation's economy during the 1950/1970 period, Siemens had found it necessary to recruit foreign workers. In 1970 the managers of the firm were saying that regardless of the problems involved, an ever increasing number of foreign workers would be employed.

In 1972, nevertheless, Siemens went through a period of cost consciousness, and the previous policy of recruiting a high number of foreign workers, mainly Turkish and Yugoslavs, was submitted to review. Several top managers were not sure of the analytical rigor of their previous decisions, and decided to review corporate policy concerning foreign workers. In particular, the following questions seemed important to answer:

1. Did Siemens have any choice as between employing and not employing foreign workers?

2. What were the costs and the benefits of employing foreign workers?

3. What should be Siemens' policy regarding the percentage of foreign workers employed, the homogeneity or heterogeneity of foreign workers' nationalities at Siemens, the criteria to be used in selecting one or several given nationalities?

4. How should the firm treat its foreign workers in respect to wages, fringe benefits, housing, promotion, etc.?

The Company. Siemens, a German-based international firm, was founded in 1947 and had in 1971, 1.2 billion DMs capital, 16 billion DMs standing orders, and 14.7 billion DMs in annual sales.[1]

It occupied the sixth position in the list of world's ten largest firms in electrical equipment production. Of its current production, 4 percent was construction material, 14 percent computers, 31 percent energy production (i.e., measurement and process techniques, energy producing machinery, industrial energy, transportation, and research), 14 percent installation materials and know-how (auto electric, cables, time-equipment, telephone, etc.), 8 percent electrical house equipment, and 4 percent various other products. The firm had 47 branches in different parts of West Germany and numerous other branches in more than 100 countries.

---

*The basic material for this case was collected within the federal Republic of Germany by Ayse Sertel and Yilmaz Özkan during the summer of 1972 and reworked subsequently by Henri de Bodinat under the supervision of Richard D. Robinson, Alfred P. Sloan School of Management, Massachusetts Institute of Technology, 1973. All rights reserved.

[1]The parity exchange rate in mid-1972 was 3.10 Deutsche marks to U.S. $1.00. By March 1973, the rate had changed to DM 2.9 = U.S. $1.00. The rate prior to May 1971 had been DM 3.66 = U.S. $1.00.

Table E.1
DEVELOPMENT OF KEY GROWTH VARIABLES DURING POST-WAR CYCLES (ANNUAL AVERAGE RATES OF CHANGE IN PERCENT)

Growth cycles	1951 to 1954	1955 to 1958	1959 to 1963	1964 to 1967	1968 to 1972
Real GDP	8.8%	7.1%	5.9%	3.7%	5.1%
Change in capital stock	3.8	5.8	6.4	6.2	5.4
Capital-output ratio	3.8	3.4	3.4	3.6	3.8
Employment	2.4	2.3	1.0	−0.5	0.5
Labor productivity	6.0	5.7	5.6	5.1	5.0
Change in capital intensity	1.4	3.5	5.2	6.8	4.8

Source: OECD Economic Surveys, Germany, 1972, p. 32.

The investments of the firm in 1970–71 amounted to 916 million DMs. As far as sales were concerned, of its 5.9 billion DMs worth of exports, 26 percent was going to EFTA members, 24 percent to member countries of EEC, 13 percent to those European countries outside both EFTA and EEC, 17 percent to the U.S., 12 percent to Asia, and 8 percent to Africa and Australia.

In September 1971, Siemens had 234,000 employees in West Germany, and 72,000 working in different branches of the firm outside the country. Of the employees in the country, 36 percent were women; of those outside Germany, 58 percent.

The German economy and foreign labor. West Germany, one of the major labor-importing European countries, had a population of 61,279,000 in 1971. In the same year, its labor force was 27,414,000 and employment in industry was 12,207,000. The per capita gross national product of this highly industrialized country was $3,370 in 1971, with over 50 percent of the GNP originating in industry. Development of West German key growth variables during post-war cycles is shown in Table E.1. Some key measures of differences in the employment of foreign and local labor are given in Table E.2.

Table E.2
WAGE STRUCTURE IN GERMANY

Average hourly wage (general average)

DM	1963	1966	1972
	4.00	4.92	9.00

1. *By level of skill*

(1966)	Level of qualification	Percent of labor force	Wages (general average = 100)
	Skilled	43%	114
	Semi-skilled	32	96
	Non-skilled	18	84
	Others (beginners)	7	74
		100%	

Table E.2 (continued)

2. *By number of years in an enterprise* (general average = 100)

(1966) $\frac{2}{93}$ $\frac{2-4}{97}$ $\frac{5-9}{103}$ $\frac{10-19}{108}$ $\frac{70}{108}$

3. *By age* (general average = 100)

(1966) $\frac{18}{57}$ $\frac{18-20}{84}$ $\frac{20-24}{98}$ $\frac{25-44}{103-5}$ $\frac{45-49}{101}$ $\frac{50-54}{99}$ $\frac{55-59}{97}$ $\frac{60}{94}$

4. *By size of firm* (number of workers in the firm, general average = 100)

(1966) $\frac{10-1,000}{98}$ $\frac{1,000-2,000}{100}$ $\frac{2,000-5,000}{105}$ $\frac{5,000}{112}$

5. *Job variances and unemployment index (1963 = 100)*

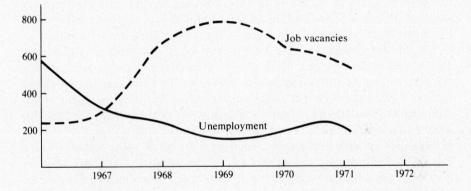

Siemens' Foreign Workers. As of September 1971, Siemens employed a total of 25,401 foreign workers within its various operations within the Federal Republic of Germany. This number constituted 20.8 percent of all Siemens' laborers in the country. The breakdown of the foreign workers by nationality was as follows:

Turkish	7,371
Yugoslavian	6,648
Greek	3,498
Spanish	1,507
Italian	1,578
Australian	1,146
Tunisian	451
Other	3,202

A large majority of these workers were between 20–39 years of age, while the German workers tended to be somewhat older. The precise age distribution and other social background characteristics of these workers were not known by the Siemens management. It was known, however, that not more than 30 percent of these workers came directly from rural areas. The migration to West Germany was usually a multistep process. This was especially true of the Turkish workers who tended to have some prior industrial work experience within Turkey, even though sometimes brief. Of all the foreign workers coming to West Germany, some 30 percent were classified in their respective countries of origin as skilled workers (though not all worked in this capacity when they arrived in Germany).

The structure of West German population and its projected trend would increasingly necessitate the import of foreign workers. In 1971, the age group over 65 constituted a rather large portion of the overall population. The age group below 14, on the other hand, had been growing very slowly. The size of the working German population relative to total population had been shrinking for the last several decades. The gap between projected demand for manpower and the capacity to fulfill this demand was estimated to be much larger in 1980 than it had been in 1970. In fact, this gap, currently being filled by import of labor, was expected to double within this ten year period.

For the last 11 years the unemployment level in West Germany had been consistently under 1 percent. Such a low level of unemployment, coupled with the current high rate of industrial growth (given the demographic structure) created a labor shortage that could only be fulfilled with labor importation. Although the country did not have a large number of vacancies prior to 1960, with the sudden change in the rate of unemployment in that year, the number of vacancies increased noticeably, reaching 750,000 in 1966. Vacancies still existed in 1972 despite the import of foreign workers. German industrial growth (6.2 percent between 1958 and 1964) called for increasing manpower. Yet the German labor force was expected to remain more or less constant for ten more years.

A recent OECD study had revealed that, taking 1972 as the base year, West Germany's population increased from an index of 100 in 1957 to an index of 112.1 in 1968. However, not all of this increase was natural. Excluding net immigration of foreign labor to the country, the 1968 index was about 107. During the same period, on the other hand, the population of one of the labor exporting countries to West Germany, namely Turkey, increased from an index of 100 to 132.8. This increase was less dramatic in the case of Italy and Spain.

The net flow of foreign labor into West Germany had shown a secular increase over the 1956–72 period. Starting from less than 20,000 in 1956, the migrant labor stock reached a level of 350,000 in 1969 (Tables E.3 and E.4). Though the yearly increases had not been uniform, yearly increments of labor before 1960 had been substantially less than those after this period. Although only rough estimates were available, the nature of the inflow reflected a very high labor turnover rate and an increasing mobility of workers between the importing and exporting countries.

The West German economy, being highly industrialized and developing at a fast rate, was dependent on competitive industrial production costs to sustain its exports and to compete with possible imports. In view of the demographic structure and the pressure to hold down costs and sustain a high level of exports, Germany found it imperative to employ foreign workers. Alternatives to the import of foreign workers would be either automation, increasing working hours, or inducing intersectoral labor displacement. As to the first alternative, one must note that Germany is the second most automated country in the world. Secondly, sharp increases in part-time employment as well as in working hours had been evidenced for some time. Nevertheless, the manpower shortage continued. Although intersectoral displacement of labor, or more exactly the transfer of agricultural population to industry, remained a serious alternative to labor importation from abroad, this alternative could be realized only in the long-run.

The social situation of foreign labor in Germany. A recent study undertaken by the *Spiegel Magazine* had provided some insight into the foreign labor phenomena. According to the study, five countries had sent approximately 80 percent of the total. Of the incoming workers one-half had been accompanied by their families, and 77 percent were between 20 and 39 years of age. The percentage of West German workers in this age group was, by way on contrast, only 27 percent of the total. The rate of illiteracy among the migrant group was very low, but they had, nevertheless, a lower education level on average than did indigenous workers in that 64 percent of the foreign workers had had less than eight years of education, which was the minimum required for West Germans. Not surprisingly, foreign workers earned, on the average, less money than indigenous labor. In 1971 the average monthly earnings of the migrant workers was 870 DMs. This amount was, for the same year, 98 DMs less than the average for local workers. Sex-based wage differences were also more visible for the migrant groups. While two-thirds of the female laborers received less than 800 DMs a month, this ratio was only one-fourth for the males. Some 38 percent of the foreign workers lived in public housing, another 38 percent in private houses, and the remaining shared a room or a flat with other workers, again, in private houses. Some 40 percent of the migrants expressed discontent with their living quarters. Of these, only 18 percent indicated high rents as the primary reason for their discontent. They said, in interviews, that it was not the rent but the landlords and the treatment by their West German neighbors that disturbed them most. These workers seemed more pleased with the facilities in West Germany than with its people. They were upset for having been treated badly by the indigenous population. In 1971

Table E.3
GERMANY: STOCK OF EMPLOYED FOREIGN WORKERS BY NATIONALITY, 1954-69[*][†]

	Total All Nationalities	Italians		Greeks		Portuguese		Spanish		Turks		Yugoslavs	
		Total	% Male	Total	% Male	Total	% Male	Total	% Male	Total	% Male	Total	% Male
1954	72,906	6,509	—	548				411				1,801	
1955	79,607	7,461	—	637				486				2,085	
1956	98,818	18,597	—	953				698				2,297	
1957	108,190	19,096	—	1,822				967				2,778	
1958	127,083	25,609	—	2,838				1,494				4,846	
1959	166,829	48,809	91.0	4,089	87.1			2,150	81.6			7,310	81.
1960	279,390	121,685	93.6	13,005	88.3	261	85.8	9,454	82.6	2,495	92.0	8,826	81.
1961	507,419	218,003		43,948				50,976					
1962	655,463	265,978	91.0	69,146	82.0	1,421	85.8	87,327	75.6	15,318	91.7	23,608	81.
1963	811,213	299,235	88.7	106,152	67.1	2,284	81.6	117,494	71.6	27,144	89.0	44,428	79.
1964	932,932	289,252	86.2	143,859	66.8	3,463	77.3	144,256	71.0	69,211	90.0	53,057	79.
1965	1,164,364	359,773	85.0	181,658	63.8	10,509	84.7	180,572	71.3	121,121	87.2	64,060	77.
1966	1,314,031	399,154	82.7	196,207	60.4	19,802	83.6	185,336	69.3	157,978	83.5	96,675	73.
1967	1,023,747	274,249	78.4	146,817	58.1	18,519	76.1	129,126	64.7	137,081	81.5	97,725	67.
1968	1,014,771	284,440	77.9	136,191	58.0	18,743	72.9	111,982	63.8	139,336	78.3	99,660	63.
1969	1,372,059	340,244	—	174,348	—	26,379	—	135,546	—	212,951	—	226,290	—
1970 (Jan.)	1,575,072	330,049	75.4	206,812	57.5	32,802	71.2	149,190	68.9	272,423	77.6	296,970	60.

[*]In the years 1954-60 all data refer to July, for years after 1960 to June.
[†]Data refer to wage and salary earners only; i.e., exclude self-employed.

Source: Bundesanstalt fur Arbeit.

Table E.4
GERMANY: INFLOW OF FOREIGN LABOR BY NATIONALITY, 1956-69 *†

	Greek	Italian	Portuguese	Spanish	Turk	Yugoslav	Other	Total	Net Inflow
1956	738	15,620		475		812	13,944	31,589	19,211
1957	1,550	14,894		736		1,997	26,106	45,283	9,372
1958	1,510	19,460		1,170		3,358	29,079	54,577	18,893
1959	2,479	42,455		1,935		4,189	34,253	85,311	39,746
1960	23,364	141,263		26,745		4,400	63,712	259,484	112,561
1961	36,606	165,793	913	51,183	7,116	9,962	88,918	360,491	228,029
1962	47,559	165,250	1,013	54,958	15,269	24,139	87,379	396,567	148,044
1963	58,009	134,912	1,545	51,715	27,910	19,440	83,969	377,500	155,748
1964	65,130	142,120	3,904	65,872	62,879	17,459	84,899	442,263	121,721
1965	61,822	204,288	11,140	65,146	59,816	30,983	91,705	524,900	231,432
1966	39,742	165,540	9,185	38,634	43,499	50,869	77,318	424,787	149,667
1967	7,605	58,510	1,782	7,785	14,834	15,379	45,999	151,894	−290,281
1968	37,348	130,236	6,709	31,995	62,376	76,782	45,533	390,879	− 8,973
1969	65,126	136,225	13,237	50,086	121,529	192,232	67,644	646,079	357,283

*Including frontier workers.
†Found as the annual increment in the stock of workers.
Source: Bundesantalt fur Arbeit.

more than half of the foreign workers earned enough money for a vacation and 20 percent possessed private cars. Job security, schooling, and health guarantees were among the most pleasing items, while family problems, housing, and climate were among the most disturbing aspects of life in West Germany.

Although they were responsible for about one-fourth of West German production, foreign workers did not have much job security. During the 1966–67 economic recession, some 600,000 foreign workers lost their jobs and were forced to return home. Although it might seem that there was not much difference between German and guest workers with respect to employer-employee relations, working conditions, and ability to change jobs freely, in practice there were important differences.

Foreign workers were brought to Germany on the basis of a one-year contract. No matter how unpleasant the working conditions might be, this contract could not be terminated short of a one-year period by the workers. Otherwise they would be sent back to their respective countries immediately. The salary specified in the contract was almost always the minimum set forth for the job in question. Although the same scale was used both for German and for foreign workers, German workers almost never started at the very bottom of the scale as did the foreigners. Thus, an automatic wage difference between the two groups was created from the beginning.

Moreover, the vocational training offered to the foreign workers in their own countries, and their definition of skilled workers, differed from those of the Germans. Therefore, even a qualified foreign laborer working in Germany in a skilled capacity often received a wage equivalent to that of a semi-skilled worker and was classified in such manner. Although this classification might change as the worker remained in his job for several years, the lower classification would hold true almost without exception for the duration of the first year's contract.

Current statutes regulating the behavior of foreigners required that every foreign worker obtain a residence permit from the German employment office. The newly arrived foreign workers obtained, by showing their contracts, a year's working permit, and consequently, a year's residence permit. These legalities made it impossible for workers to change jobs no matter how unpleasant the conditions might be. In case the worker wished, at the end of the first year, to renew his work and residence permit without renewing his contract, he was required to find a new job, obtain a favorable recommendation from his previous employer, and to leave the boarding house (*heim*) of his previous employer. Provided that he met these conditions, he could acquire a new work and residence permit. This new permit, too, was valid only for one year. The city police could refuse a permit, without which employment was not allowed. As was the case during the 1966–67 economic crises, the police would come up with rather abstract reasons for denying an application for residence. This same mechanism might force workers to remain in their former jobs under undesirable conditions. The threat to be sent back to his own country hung over the head of every foreign worker.

Every firm offering employment to foreign workers was under an obligation to provide housing. This obligation had been included in the bilateral agreements signed between Germany and the labor-exporting countries. Current statutes specified the minimum conditions of acceptability for workers' housing. Accordingly, no room could contain more than eight persons; women and men must live in separate quarters; every worker must be supplied with ten cubic meters air, wardrobe, a chair, and adequate table space. In addition, he must have facilities to dry his laundry and to cook. The bedrooms must at least be 2.30 meters high and the floors must be covered with some material to keep the workers' feet warm. At the most, five workers might share a wash basin and ten workers, a toilet. But even these minimum requirements were rarely satisfied. Only the largest firms, such as Siemens, had *heims* (boarding houses) with the above stated specifications. Control of the smaller firms was difficult to enforce. More importantly, rent control over the houses satisfying these specifications was almost impossible. Those firms with more or less acceptable housing facilities frequently were charging what seemed to be unduly high rents.

The German mass media frequently and critically reported these miserable housing conditions and the ineffectiveness of the attempts to better them. An example was *Brigitte* (September 1971, no. 18), which described the plight of an Italian family with six children. The family, it was claimed, was living in a house without running water, heat, or toilet and paid 235 DMs for a 25-square-meter apartment. The magazine claimed that miserable housing conditions and high rents characterized the living conditions of millions of foreign workers in West Germany. Caritas, an organization formed to help Catholic foreign workers, reported that although it was offering free legal assistance to the workers to improve their housing conditions, the workers, frightened by the threat of being forced to leave Germany or at least of being evicted from their apartments, were abstaining from legal action against the landlords. Despite the high frequency of these reports and research findings, West German officials did not seem to be reacting rapidly.

As noted, foreign workers were placed in *heims* upon their arrival to West Germany, but they soon started to search for private housing. Many workers found it difficult to live with six other persons in a room and that the rent was too high for such communal living. Even when the occupants were of the same country, they varied at least in respect to age, place of birth, custom, and socio-economic status. Such differences, needless to say, resulted in frictions. These frictions, when added to high rents and variations in work and sleeping hours, induced many to seek private housing regardless of conditions. Local landlords, fully cognizant of the workers' reasoning, felt quite confident in charging high rents. It was not considered unusual for landlords to ask for 2500

DMs as an *abstand* (guarantee deposit) from incoming tenants. The control of conditions in privately-owned residences, it should be added, was not an accustomed practice in West Germany.

Moreover, foreign workers were required to stay in West Germany for at least a year before they could have their wives join them. In order to get together with his family, a worker was required to leave the factory *heim*. The helplessness of the worker in this regard was also well known and exploited by the landlords.

The fact that workers, as long as they lived in *heims*, were not permitted to have visitors (of both sexes after a certain hour and of the opposite sex categorically) tended to force even the bachelors to look for private housing.

Still another factor inducing workers to search for private housing was their shift from one job to another upon completion of the first year of their contract. Once a worker started a new job he could no longer stay in the *heim* of his original firm. To gain flexibility in looking for better opportunities, some foreign workers found it advantageous to move into private apartments despite deplorable conditions and high cost.

Local prejudice directed toward the foreign workers caused further problems. There were frequently signs on bars and restaurants explicitly restricting entry of foreign workers. The aggression of local German youth against foreign workers in small towns was reported frequently in the newspapers, even some killings. As can be understood from various reference terms used for foreign workers (e.g., *Makkaronifresser, Kameltreiber, Messerstrecher*), many of the indigenous population considered the migrants second class citizens.

The children of foreign workers, of which there were an estimated 400,000, also constituted a problem. In accordance with the West German laws, these children had to remain in school until age 18. But, due to shortage of personnel and other educational facilities, this law was not being as strictly enforced for the children of migrants as it was for the indigenous population. After the death of two ten-year old children in the mines in 1970, West German authorities found 97,800 children working illegally. A control week in Berlin resulted in the fining of 98 firms for employing a total of 285 youths under 18 years of age. The West German Trade union had estimated the total number of illegally employed children to be around 1,000,000. The government found it difficult to enforce the obligatory schooling requirements in the absence of sufficient facilities, and many of the migrant parents, highly motivated to save, preferred to send their children to work. Moreover, due to a shortage of kindergartens, even for the indigenous population, migrant parents, if both were working, preferred to keep their older children at home to take care of the younger. This young migrant population, being separated both from their homeland and from the rest of the children in West Germany, constituted a totally alienated group.

Situation of foreign workers at Siemens. Siemens, as many other firms employing foreign workers in great numbers, was forced to incur a number of expenditures. First, there was the cost of recruiting and of transporting the workers from their homelands to West Germany. The transportation cost, of course, accrued only in the case of workers recruited directly from their respective countries and not if they were already employed elsewhere in Germany. Up until the first of 1972 a flat transportation payment of 165 DMs had been made to the foreign workers. Subsequently the payment was 300 DMs. This amount was paid directly to *Arbeitsamt*[2] and covered the recruitment costs incurred by this organization. In addition, every foreign worker was entitled to 200 DMs of vacation allowance upon the completion of his second year in the company. Those workers brought directly from their homeland who chose to return directly from the company also received 150 DMs as return travel allowance. There were, however, few foreign workers who did so. For example, it was estimated that only about five percent of the foreign workers in Siemens returned home directly from the company. Since the company was obliged to advertise any job opening in the German press should it decide to employ workers from within West Germany, the cost involved in such advertisement should be subtracted from the 300 DMs recruitment cost of the foreign workers brought directly from their homelands. The Munich branch of Siemens estimated that the initial training costs averaged 450 DMs for a West German worker and 500 DMs for the foreign. The respective figures reported by the management of the Berlin branch of the company were much higher: 593 and 820. The reason for these different estimates was unclear.

In addition to the above-mentioned costs involved in the employment of foreign workers, the company, under the provisions of German labor law, was forced to provide housing facilities. Several million DMs were spent in the building of boarding houses (*heims*). Siemens' *heims*, compared to those of many other firms, were well-kept and comfortable. The monthly rental of a four-person room was around 65 DMs per person (780 DMs per year).

It should be noted, however, that these *heims* were not really some sort of subsidy for the foreign workers. Given the stresses involved in sharing a room with four to six strangers with different habits and working hours, the rental was substantial. If the *heims* were to be filled most of the time, the firm could very well make a profit, but some beds were known to remain empty, sometimes for long periods of time. A study undertaken by the Munich branch of the firm estimated the average yearly cost of a bed to be around 888 DMs. (This figure was obtained by dividing the total cost of beds, empty and occupied, by the total number of foreign workers.) The management of the Berlin

---

[2]Refers to the branch offices of BAFA (see p. 273).

branch estimated 1380 DMs. It was believed by independent researchers that those figures were unduly high if used to calculate the extra cost of foreign workers in that a number of steps could be taken to fill empty beds, especially in West Berlin. The *heims* were not meant to house only foreign workers, and many West German laborers in fact lived in them. Thus, housing cost per worker could not be viewed as an extra cost of foreign workers. This point needed to be stressed, as many of the current studies viewed the construction of these *heims*, not as another prospective business for the firm, but as an extra cost of labor.

A genuinely important cost of the foreign workers to the company resulted from the organizational changes that had to be made to accommodate the newcomers and to provide a communication link between managers and workers. In the Berlin branch of the firm there was a department in charge of the numerous problems of foreign workers. Staffed by three administrators and several translators, this department handled housing and schooling problems of foreign workers and their families as well as any other problems that the migrant workers might have. There, through the intermediacy of an interpreter, the problems were recorded and hopefully solved. The administrators in charge of this office were deeply concerned with the problems of foreign workers and were trying to find equitable solutions for the problems brought to them. However, to the extent that many of the problems required a more systematic solution by the West German authorities, such as those relating to the schooling of workers' children and to housing, satisfactory answers were not always possible. Nevertheless the proximity and accessibility of the administrators to the workers was important.

Regardless of the extra costs cited above, employment of foreign workers was inevitable so long as Siemens maintained its current level of production. This was so because of several reasons. First, as explained above, the extra cost of foreign labor did not amount to a significant figure. Second, the indigenous labor stock had been exhausted and even during the 1966–67 recession Siemens had been forced to keep many of its foreign workers. There simply was no West German labor to replace the foreigners, especially in those categories of employment in which foreigners were working. One heard from all sources, including company managers, that German labor would under no circumstances do what the foreign workers were doing. Thirdly, it was a known fact that foreign labor was relatively cheap. Even if replacement of foreign workers with the West Germans were possible, equivalent wages would not have been offered to the latter. And as already noted, foreign and indigenous workers started from different points of the same pay scale, and a constant wage differential existed between equivalent quality of workers of these different stocks.

Foreign worker recruitment by Siemens. The control and administration of foreign labor recruitment in West Germany was handled by an autonomous public agency, Bundesanstalt fur Arbeit (BAFA).[3] It was headquartered in Nuremberg and had many branches throughout the country. BAFA was concerned not only with foreign labor but also with the administration of the social security system.

The major methods of foreign labor recruitment were three. Of these, the first was through BAFA, which accounted for about 70 percent of total recruitment. BAFA had established offices in those countries with which West Germany has signed labor agreements. BAFA was first informed of the need for labor by the German employer. It responded by making known to the employer the specifications of the available stock of registered potential workers. If the employer were satisfied with what was available, the necessary paper work would be completed, and BAFA contacted its representatives in the appropriate countries. The formalities following this last step varied, both in time and in procedure, in different countries. The second method of recruitment differed from the first in that the application might be made directly by the worker to the firm. BAFA still controlled permits for entry and final documentation as to employment. Although West German visas were in fact issued by the local German Consulate, this was done only after clearance with BAFA. The third method, only applicable in the case of Moroccan and Tunisian workers, consisted of recruitment by BAFA missions in the labor exporting countries. Companies might also obtain BAFA's permission to recruit directly on their own behalf in these two countries. Of these methods, the first two were most frequently used by Siemens.

Arrival procedures at Siemens. Foreign workers usually came to Siemens in large groups. Upon their arrival in Germany, they were met at the airport or railroad station by representatives of the West German employment office and by representatives and a translator from the firm. They were then taken immediately to the factory and shown around. A brief explanation of their job and pay was given and they were then taken to their living quarters, usually the firm's *heim.* Those who came with families and who had made other housing arrangements were also offered help in locating their quarters. The workers were then given a day to report to their jobs.

During their first day at work, a foreman or an engineer accompanied by an interpreter explained to them what was to be done. The training period varied considerably with the nature of the job, from two or three hours to two or three months.

There seemed to be a discrepancy between the length of the training period as perceived by managers and by workers. This was apparently due to the fact that the management identified a "training period" as the period during which laborers were not working at full productivity. Even for a low-skilled job,

---

[3]Federal Institute for Labor.

training might thus, in this sense, last one or two months. On the other hand, the training as perceived by labor often consisted of a foreman or an experienced worker's showing the foreigner what to do for one hour or so. In training for more complicated jobs, the nationality of the worker was quite irrelevant; no matter from where they had come, several weeks were often needed to acquire the skills if they were new on the job.

Labor turnover at Siemens. A recent study conducted in the Munich branch of the Siemens company had established a 54 percent turnover rate for foreign workers and 27 percent for the indigenous ones. Another study covering all departments of the Berlin branch had come up with a 113 percent fluctuation rate for foreigners and 37 percent for the West Germans.[4]

Foreign workers' jobs were being changed by the firm quite frequently. Those workers brought from their countries at minimum wages were generally first assigned to those jobs requiring nearly no training. After having worked in this job for several weeks, the workers adjusted to the work conditions of the firm. This adjustment was eased by their high motivation to earn and save and by the perceived threat of loss of employment in West Germany. Managerial complaints in regard to foreign workers' maladjustment to work were few. In fact company managers emphasized their satisfaction with these workers.

At the end of this adjustment period, the workers were likely to be assigned to a somewhat more complicated job. After having worked in several such tasks, the workers became eligible to work in a piece-rate job. The piece-rate was considerably higher than the hourly wage offered to the workers. If any particular worker were on a piece-rate he either produced the set minimum or norm and received a payment substantially above his hourly wage-level or he fell below this level and received his hourly wage. It had been typical for the foreign workers to exceed the minimum levels. For that reason these levels had been changed periodically in many industries with the result that a number of West German workers voiced their unhappiness with the presence of the foreign workers. Because the foreigners were so highly motivated to make as much money as possible in a short period of time, they concentrated very hard at least to achieve minimum production, if not to exceed it. As in other firms, the minimum levels were being set jointly by management and labor. Still, many German workers claimed that these levels were too high and the relevant pay levels were too low.

Workers received a substantial bonus for producing over the specified norm. For instance, by producing 850 when the norm was 800 the workers might receive 1–1.30 DM extra for every hour they worked for that particular day. Since labor costs increased considerably if workers were to exceed the minimum levels consistently, not only did these levels have to be set very carefully

---

[4]Calculated by dividing all interdepartmental shifts and all departures by the total number of workers and multiplying the result by 100.

but also the over-productive workers were shifted periodically from one task to another. For this reason many piece-rate workers were shifted within the firm among different piece-rate jobs. The discontent arising from such practices had been expressed by many workers. In general, task shifts were *intra* departmental to avoid union interferences (the union could intervene in cases of inter-departmental shifts).

The overall turnover rate for foreign workers in West Germany was 22.5 percent and 11 percent for indigenous labor. When these figures were compared with those of the Munich branch of Siemens (54 and 27 percent, respectively) it became apparent that the average for foreign workers in the firm was 2.5 times the national average. It had been suggested that the following were the principal causes for this differential:

(1) It had been the policy of the firm to maintain a certain level of labor turn-over. The workers brought directly from different countries were being employed at minimum wages for the first year. At the end of this period the contract could be renewed only by mutual consent and by a raise in salary in consideration of the worker's experience. The company, at this point, seemed to prefer to terminate the contract rather than raise salary.

(2) It took a year for foreign workers to acquire basic knowledge of the language and of the work conditions in other parts of West Germany. During their first year, foreign workers were extremely obedient and hard working. They even refrained from membership in trade unions, and in all labor activity. At the end of their first contract year, however, many bargained with the firm for a wage raise and became cognizant of their rights to demand such a raise. Needless to say, these were undesirable demands from the viewpoint of the firm. Less problem-prone labor, fresh from foreign lands, was preferred.

Opinions voiced by Siemens' workers. The interview of a limited sample of 20 workers who had already left the company and of another 20 currently employed may be summed up as follows. First and most important, was the view of the piece-rate workers. As explained by these workers, their jobs consisted of producing a given number of units within a work day. If they should fall below the specified number they received a cut in wage. If, on the other hand, they should prove to be more efficient, they were not allowed to continue that particular task for too long. Almost every one of the workers from Siemens and many other workers employed by other firms claimed that they found it very difficult to maintain the specified level of production on a daily basis. A young woman, for instance, said she could only finish about 1/3 of the specified number of units, and all the other women that worked within the same department as she did were in the same position. "A giant-like, strong Turkish woman" was the only exception. While the young girl received approximately 500 DMs a month for the amount she produced, the "strong" workers, regularly working above norm, received over 800 DMs. The young girl was forced to leave Siemens at the end of the third month of her arrival, in breach of her one-year contract. After two months of delay, the firm finally agreed to give her a clearance to seek other employment.

Many workers claimed that as they became more experienced in their jobs, the level of unit production specified by the firm was increased. In other words, if they were asked to produce only 100 units within the first 3–4 months of their experience in the firm, this number was raised to 110 for the next several months and perhaps higher later. A labor leader observed, "Of course, it would be to the advantage of the firm if every worker produced just 99 units when the specification is 100. This is why unit production is being kept at such an unrealistic level."

Workers also complained about the job conditions. Many said the work they performed was extremely heavy and dirty, and that they had to sweat for long hours in front of oily, steamy machinery. The words of a young woman perhaps best characterized these conditions:

When I first came to Germany I started in Siemens. We were many women in one large room. There was tremendous noise. Nobody smiled, nobody talked for we could not hear each other. I was in charge of a big machine which vomited oil and soapy water. Out of it came other machines which I was supposed to take out and put aside. As they came out I fed new materials into the machine. We were asked to cover our hair so that the machine would not catch it. We put gloves on our hands. All day we stood. We had an hour's lunch break, but nobody talked. When I went home, I did not have the power to say "hello" to my brother. I went directly to bed. Since my brother was living with me I could not live in the heim. It took me a full hour to travel from home to the factory. I had to get up at 3:30 in the morning and leave home at four to be at my work in time. This was in 1966 and I was getting approximately 400 DMs a month. Finally I found another job in a cleaning firm. That was more of a disaster.

Another worker expressed his complaint as follows:

I worked in Siemens for six years. Every day was more of a torture than the previous one. It was killing to get up so early in the morning, run out of the house to catch the train. Until the 9:30 coffee break I worked half asleep. I was then assigned to one of the heims as an heim director. That was a good job. But the conditions of the workers, the inhuman manner in which they lived in these crowded quarters was heart breaking. Then came the recession and the heim was closed. I was forced to go back to my old job. But this time I just could not take it any more. Bodily exhaustion was not so much the problem. It was sleeplessness that got to me. Finally I had an offer from this office to be a consultant to Turkish workers. This job has its own problems, but compared to the old one I feel I am in heaven.

The first made a rather clear cut point: when workers were forced, for one reason or another, to move out of the firm *heims*, which tended to be fairly near the factories, they sometimes ended up in neighborhoods very far from their work place.

Hours spent travelling from home to job became a clear addition to work hours. However, given recent legal changes, workers were no longer compensated for the hours spent travelling to their jobs. This consideration might apply to any one of the 4,700 foreign workers living outside the company *heims*. A shift in job occurred when a worker heard of a job opportunity nearer his home, provided that he was promised a wage at least equal to that in Siemens.

Many workers, after having moved out of the *heims*, were known to have returned, having found the conditions of private houses intolerable. This meant, on the other hand, deprivation of wives and children. Final departures on the grounds of family reunion were frequent, especially in the case of Turkish labor, a very large percentage of whom were married. Problems relating to the schooling of children, especially in cases where both wife and husband were working, were also mentioned frequently by workers as among the reasons for leaving the firm. It was uncertain, in such cases, however, whether the workers took employment in some other firm, or in some other part of West Germany, or simply returned home. Solution to baby-sitting and schooling problems varied from termination of the wife's employment to the bringing a close relative from the home country. There was a tendency for families to refrain from sending their older children to school and to either find them a job or have them baby-sit for the rest of their siblings. German law required that all children under 18 be in school, and workers were being constantly advised by the relevant authorities not to act in this manner.

Management-labor relations and the absence of opportunities for promotion did not appear to be important considerations for the foreign workers. They tended to be extremely obedient toward the foremen and managerial personnel and viewed their work environment less as a social milieu than as a place to earn a living. Workers were also very pessimistic about upward mobility in their jobs; they seemed to believe that as foreigners they were not entitled to such privileges. This was especially true for piece-rate workers. As one laborer expressed it:

There is no such thing as promotion for us. You might work for ten years on the same task. If you produce the specified number of units you get your money; otherwise you get less or lose your job. Of course, there are exceptional cases. But I know them too. They came here as skilled workers but were employed as unskilled. When finally their industriousness and skills were appreciated they were given a position which they deserved many years ago anyway. There is no such thing as a better or worse position; there are jobs with more salary and those with less. If you put up with more and heavier work you get more.

Yet another worker said:

After six years of work in Siemens I was the most qualified in the department to be the foreman. I was fluent in German and was even offering courses to Turkish workers. We had a mixed department. I don't remember it exactly, but there might have been more Germans than foreigners. Although I deserved it, I could not have been made the foreman. They explained to me at that time that if I were to be selected for such a position it would anger the Germans. This is still true. Only in those departments employing foreign workers exclusively does a foreigner have a chance to get promoted.

The following table (Table E.5) prepared by Siemens gives a list of reasons offered by workers and management for the departure of foreign workers from the Berlin branch of Siemens. As will be noted, 50.3 percent of the male and 50.1 percent of the female workers left the firm of their own choice. Some 34 percent of the former and 36 percent of the latter group, on the other hand, were asked to leave by the company administration.

Interview of the Turkish attaché in Berlin. "The German labor laws do not discriminate between German and foreign workers. However, in case of disputes the laws regulating the activities of foreign nationals play a largely restrictive role. Although it can be argued that the employers do not discriminate against the foreign workers, this does not change the fact that most of the foreign workers do what the German workers refuse to do. Today, not even the most uneducated, unqualified German would clean the bathrooms and sweep the floors.

"The contribution of the foreign workers to the German economy cannot

Table E.5
REASONS GIVEN BY WORKERS AND MANAGEMENT FOR DEPARTURE OF FOREIGN WORKERS FROM THE SIEMENS PLANT IN BERLIN

	Male		Female	
From the workers' viewpoint				
Dislike for the job	41	8.6%	73	6.6%
Job is too far	—	—	7	0.6
Low payment	84	17.7	102	9.2
Change in occupation	40	8.4	95	8.6
Sickness	4	0.8	37	3.4
Desire to attend a school	17	3.6	6	0.5
Desire to go to West Germany	11	2.3	51	4.6
Desire to return to West Germany	—	—	—	—
Desire to work in a different country	42	8.9	107	9.7
Need to care for young children	—	—	70	6.3
Marriage	—	—	4	0.4
Need to care for some other family member	—	—	19	1.7
Desire to quit working	—	—	6	0.5
From the viewpoint of the firm				
Inappropriate for the job	38	8.0	41	3.7
Sickness	4	0.8	14	1.3
Inattendance and inefficiency	44	9.3	100	9.1
Lack of appropriate work	10	2.1	16	1.4
Activities in breach of contract	—	1.3	44	4.0
End of contract period	35	7.4	122	11.0
Disgraceful dismissals	26	5.5	62	5.6
Other				
Termination of the contract by mutual consent	51	10.7	118	10.7
Retirement	2	0.4	—	—
Shifts to office work	—	—	1	0.1
Appointment to some other branch of the company	19	4.0	9	0.8
Death	1	0.2	2	0.2
Total	475	100 %	1,106	100 %

be overlooked. Today, a worker who earns 800 DMs per month spends about 200 for his housing, anywhere between 300 and 350 for his food and clothing. He can send only about 15 percent of his monthly savings to Turkey, or, in other words, he cannot save more than 150 DMs a month to take out of the German economy. His spending from his own earnings in Germany no doubt strengthens the German economy. Moreover, foreign workers, like the Germans, are now entitled to retirement compensation, and every month each worker pays, in proportion to his income, a certain amount of money as his contribution to retirement compensation. This monthly payment required of foreign workers augments the strength of the German social insurance organization. Many workers, as they go back to their country, withdraw these forced savings (without interest). Retirement savings accumulated in Germany can, if the worker so wishes, be counted towards his retirement benefits in his own country. Increasingly, a growing number of foreign workers grasp the advantage of not withdrawing their retirement funds from Germany on their return home.

"Many workers find it difficult to live in their country of origin after their return from European employment. Whether or not a worker applies for reemployment in Germany depends upon his socioeconomic status and his previous level of savings abroad. Also, not all of the workers return home voluntarily. For instance, during the 1967 recession thousands of workers were forced to leave Germany. Many of these then reapplied to come back to Germany, and both the government and the German representatives gave their demands a priority.

"The trade unions in Germany are open to every worker. Membership, however, is not obligatory. For many years only a few Turkish workers were willing to join the unions. Gradually, they considered the pros and cons of membership and now a majority pay their union fees regularly.

"The problems of foreign workers are many and much can be done to improve their conditions. The responsibility falls on both the receiving and the sending countries. What needs to be done changes from one country to another. Common to all foreign workers, however, is a problem of housing, schooling, and language and an immediate solution to these problems is a must."

Interview of head of the DGB[5] department in charge of foreign labor affairs. "The German economy needs foreign workers. Our own population does not expand as rapidly as our industry requires. We are unable to meet our manpower needs from within ourselves. Especially after 1961, with the construction of the wall, the manpower shortage in Berlin became acute. Before then every day around 60,000 workers were coming from the East to

---

[5]Deutsche Gewerkschafsbund, usually referred to as the German Trade Union Federation. It is the top-level organization consisting of 16 member unions organized along industrial lines.

work in the West. Until 1965 we tried to close at least part of this gap through attracting new labor from within West Germany. But even then the West was unable to meet its own labor requirements. After 1965 it became clear that unless foreign labor were brought to Berlin, continuation of our growth could not be attained. By 1972 the number of foreign workers in Berlin reached 78,000. The number of family members and tourist (illegal) workers together double this figure.

"DGB does not hesitate to give every possible assistance to the tourist (illegal) workers. However, only a very small percentage of such workers ever come to this organization for help. The estimates of the total number of such workers in Berlin fluctuates between 12,000 and 20,000.

"It would have been possible to satisfy the labor needs of West Berlin through the employment of more foreign workers. However, due to the special circumstances of Berlin we are unable to bring in as many foreign workers as we need. The most important of the many problems that face the foreign workers are the following:

"*Housing.* The employer is obliged to guarantee housing for those foreign workers brought in through the intermediacy of Arbeitsamt. Generally, the firms prepare *heims* for this purpose. In these *heims* at least four persons live in one room and despite this the price they pay for a single bed is rather high. The firms improve conditions of these *heims* only when there are complaints. This is why many of them deteriorate into unbearable living quarters. When the schedules of four or six workers sleeping in one room do not coordinate with each other, each gets to be extremely disturbed in a matter of just a few days. *Heims* also have strange rules regulating visitors, which adds to the laborers' discontent. To move out of these *heims* is also difficult for there is a rather acute housing shortage in Berlin. Thus, the housing shortage forces us to limit the import of foreign labor into Berlin.

"*The problem of language:* Because foreign workers do not speak German, systematic assistance needs to be given to them. Such assistance, however, is rather costly. The expenditures of the Berlin Senate in this regard are very high compared to similar expenditures in other areas of West Germany. There are many consulting agencies for employment-employee problems. The Senate's yearly housing expense averages four million marks. Land owners frequently refuse to rent apartments to foreign workers, and certain elements of the press stimulate this tendency. Differences in mentality and mutual prejudices cause relationships to deteriorate. DGB has been trying to establish an atmosphere of mutual understanding. We bring in foreign labor only because our industry needs it.

"The firms do offer to help the workers in respect to language training. Recently, the Berlin Senate appointed 80 Turkish teachers to instruct Turkish children. It is very costly to provide occupational training for children of foreign workers for they first must learn the language. Now we are planning a one-year language training program in cooperation with Landesarbeitsamt. This too is a matter of budgeting. There are certain occupational gaps in the German economy. If we had enough money we would establish intensive language and vocational training centers in different parts of the country for the children of these workers.

"Foreign workers arrive here without any prior knowledge about trade unions, social insurance, and other topics relating to working conditions. They show little interest in the information offered to them in their own countries before departure. When they first arrive here they maintain a passive orientation towards the unions. In time some become active and seek membership. Those who come to their respective country's consulting personnel here in DGB continue their contact with us. If they receive sufficient aid from us in their dealings with the courts, their attachment to the union strengthens.

"All foreign workers are informed, via pamphlets prepared in their own language, of their rights and of the services they may receive from the union. Once they become union members, foreign workers—especially the Turks—function extremely positively. Yugoslavs, on the other hand, perhaps due to their forced membership in unions in their own country, are rather disinterested in union activities altogether. The Spanish and Greek workers have the opposite problem. In their countries union membership is forbidden, and government representatives from these countries in Germany pressure their workers and discourage them from taking part in unions. This is why Spanish and Greek union members are very few. Italians, on the other hand, belong to the European Common Market. Unlike other foreign workers, they do not require a residence permit and are well integrated into the local society.

"Today DGB has 6.5 million members, of which some five or six hundred thousand are foreign workers. A more precise estimate is difficult to make. DGB does not differentiate between foreign and German workers. The rights and forms of membership are the same for both. I can say, however, that only about one-third of all Turkish workers, one-fifth of Yugoslav and Greek workers in Berlin are union members. In firms with well organized labor associations more foreign workers join the unions. However, because in some firms union membership is seen as undesirable, pressures are exerted on the workers. This tendency, too, decreases the number of union members.

"At the moment it seems impossible to solve the problem of tourist (illegal) workers in Berlin. This problem cannot be solved even if we give legal rights to all workers living and working illegally in Berlin, because the illegal workers will continue to come to Germany bringing with them a number of problems, the most acute of which is housing.

"In DGB we believe that a rather radical change in the laws regulating the life of foreigners in Germany must be brought about. When the law was modified in 1965 the phenomenon of guest workers was still being treated as a temporary pheonmenon. Now this law must be softened. Such a modification, needless to say, would have been easier if SPD[6] were in power. It is now impossible to allow a free movement of labor without solving the problems of education, schooling, housing, etc.

"The West Berlin Senate has established a commission to examine the projected needs of the region for guest workers. It is estimated that by 1978 the number of guest workers in Berlin alone will exceed 100,000.

"It is my personal opinion that the guest workers must participate in local elections. This is, of course, a legal matter. There is a small scale of participation now in West Berlin. In some locales guest workers, though not allowed to vote, participate in local administration in a consulting capacity. These representatives are elected by the trade unions. Although some of the Greek and Spanish organizations and the religiously oriented Turkish organizations have objected to the unions' interference in this matter the Berlin Senate recognizes DGB's right in the matter. DGB believes that under certain conditions (relating to the length of residence, etc.), guest workers must obtain the right to vote and be encouraged to vote. However, this is an issue which will receive little attention for the years to come and will be one of the last problems to be solved in relation to foreign workers."

Discussion questions

1. Consider the four questions at the start of the case.
2. How would you evaluate the foreign worker problem from the point of view of Siemens' management?
3. Would the situation of Siemens vis-à-vis foreign workers be any different if Siemens were the subsidiary of a U.S. firm?

---

[6]The German Socialist Party.

Case F

PALEY OF JAPAN*

The Paley Corporation had administered questionnaires to 7,500 of its employees in 19 countries outside of Europe. These questionnaires, within the restraints imposed by the difficulties of translation, included many of the same questions asked periodically of Paley's employees within the U.S.

The Paley management was shocked by the results from Japan in that they indicated a very high level of dissatisfaction among Paley employees there. Some suggested that the explanation was the introduction of U.S. management practices into a highly traditional and different pattern of social relations and values. A social scientist, one of Paley's researchers, was dispatched to Japan to look at the situation more closely. Normally such a level of dissatisfaction was associated with a high rate of attrition, but this was not so in Japan, which of all of Paley's affiliates had one of the lowest attrition rates.

Because of the similarity of Paley's operations worldwide, the people responding to the questionnaires in all countries were doing essentially the same things. The questionnaires were focused basically on two areas, (1) morale and (2) basic organizational behavior. The questionnaires were administered by organizational units, that is, departments, which normally consisted of about 20 people. In the domestic company, each plant was surveyed once every three years unless some special problem became evident, in which case it might be done once a year for a given length of time. Questionnaire answers were tabulated on a departmental basis. The response in all cases was virtually 100 percent since the questionnaires were administered during working hours on an anonymous basis. Only those persons absent from their place of work on the day on which the questionnaire was administered were missed. The results were made known to the departmental management about one month after the questionnaire was administered. No one other than the tabulators saw the data for any subordinate unit until the responsible manager had had an opportunity to study them. In each case, he was also given comparable enterprise-wide and company-wide data. He was expected to make this data known to his department's members and to discuss it with them. He was also required to write a report to his immediate superior on what he saw in the data and what he planned to do about it. It was company policy to discourage management at any level from using the data for punitive purposes. (Admittedly, this policy was not completely successful.) Rather, managers were encouraged to evaluate a subordinate manager on the basis of how he responded to the data.

---

*The name of the company is fictitious, but the data are accurate.

One set of questions had to do with what employees wanted from a job, for example, job security, security against transfer, opportunity for advancement, opportunity to develop personal skills, personal independence or autonomy, high earnings, challenging work, good working conditions, company security, working for a growth company, working for a technically advanced company. Each of these goals was rated on a five-point scale from "utmost importance" to "no importance." A European survey undertaken during the previous year of 6,500 salesmen and systems engineers (which constituted 85 percent of such employees in Europe) produced several interesting results when compared with comparable U.S. employees. For example:

1. Europeans were more interested in skill development than their U.S. counterparts.

2. Europeans were more interested in job security.

3. U.S. employees felt that personal time was more important (that is, regular working hours that did not impinge on family or personal life).

4. U.S. employees ranked residence in a desirable area more important (which implied that the Europeans were more mobile).

In regard to this fourth finding, the European survey revealed that 46 to 63 percent (depending upon the particular country) would accept foreign assignment and 25 to 35 percent "probably" would. Another relevant finding was that some 65 percent of the Europeans preferred to have the most competent individual assigned as his manager, even though of foreign nationality. Some 80 percent indicated that nationality made no difference if the choice were between equally qualified individuals speaking the local language. Unfortunately, comparable U.S. data on international mobility and management nationality were not available since these questions had not been included in the domestic survey.

It was found that in ranking job goals employees within certain countries tended to cluster with those of others. There was a Latin American cluster, a Chinese cluster (Taiwan, Hong Kong, Singapore), and an Anglo cluster (United Kingdom, Canada, U.S., Australia, New Zealand, Jamaica, Philippines—and Japan). The inclusion of Jamaica was rationalized on the basis of its association with the United Kingdom; the Philippines, because of its association with the U.S. In addition, there was a Scandinavian cluster, though this was somewhat rougher. Disparities were somewhat greater within the group. Other countries fell in between these clusters; for example, France came between the Latin American and Anglo clusters.

The hypothesis was advanced that differentials among these clusters were due to different levels of economic development, as measured by gross national product per capita. The highest correlations developed between job goals and GNP/capita involved (1) working for a financially secure company (which goal became of lesser importance as per capita GNP increased) and (2) the desire for challenging work (which goal increased in importance as per capita

GNP went up). The major exceptions were South Africa and Germany. In the former case, it was probably true that the relevant GNP/capita was that of the white population only, which would cause a shift in the relationships. In the latter case, Germany, a hypothesis was that the wartime experience of the Germans had something to do with their greater concern for company security and lesser concern with challenging work. It was known that South Africa had the highest attrition rate in the world insofar as Paley companies were concerned. It was thought that the higher the desire for a challenging job and the lower the desire for security the higher the attrition rate was likely to be.

As already mentioned, the Japanese response clustered with the Anglo countries in that employees rated high on the challenge and income goals, relatively low in respect to the security goal. But the overall employee response showed a very low level of satisfaction. Interviews elicited the following Japanese complaints: (1) work pressure, (2) large scale and arbitrary movement of people, (3) inability to get complaints handled. It was true that as a U.S. company in Japan, there was considerable pressure for efficiency and production from Paley's Asian area headquarters, which was located in Tokyo. It was also true that the all-Japanese management of Paley's Japanese manufacturing company had introduced certain U.S. practices, such as a performance promotion system and restricting the firm's involvement in providing employee housing. But certain traditional Japanese policies had been retained, for example, discouraging employees from taking a full vacation (the president of Paley-Japan had not taken a vacation in 40 years), paying salesmen a fixed salary rather than having a commission plan, paying employees the traditional low wages (about one-fourth that paid in the U.S.). Paley sold its technologically-complex products at the same price around the world. About 15 percent of the Paley's Japanese employees had been trained in the U.S. Japanese salesmen participated in the 100 percent club for salesmen filling quotas 100 percent, which resulted periodically in big international affairs at which the 100 percenters from all over the world met. Paley-Japan was relatively new, but had grown rapidly.

Discussion questions

1. What is the most likely explanation for the relatively high level of dissatisfaction among Paley's Japanese employees?

2. As a member of Paley's international headquarters, what steps might you recommend to correct the situation?

Chapter 4
MANAGEMENT STRATEGY

Given the communications and control problems involved, the selection, preparation, promotion, and remuneration of international managerial personnel become a matter of signal importance, so likewise the selection of managerial style. In many instances, circumstances compel overseas managers to operate more autonomously than their domestic counterparts; expert staff assistance is not always immediately available. Also, their principal function may be that of training rather than management per se. And, in any event, they are part of an intercultural communications system.

Despite so-called instantaneous communications, such communication is in fact often far from instantaneous, and frequently less than "communication" in the true sense of the word. In a single national setting, many relevant variables need not be made explicit; they are within the compass of the experience of both parties and are implicitly given similar values by both. Hence, their words are understood within a similar context. Not so for an international setting; much more need be made explicit, even the use of words. To communicate by writing is time-consuming and tedious. Yet oral communication is subject to gross misunderstandings. The mind wanders for a moment, the thread is broken. A word is not understood; too late, the conversation goes on. A nuance is lost; a tone of voice misinterpreted; puzzlement in a person's eyes not seen. The probability of such events is multiplied if the conversation is over radio or wire. It is not happenstance that speaking in a foreign language by telephone is more difficult than in face-to-face conversation.

It should be borne in mind that an overseas manager occupies several roles: (1) representative of the U.S. firm, (2) manager of the local firm, (3) resident of the local community, (4) citizen either of the host state or of another, (5) member of a profession, not to mention (6) head of family and all that implies. To the extent that these roles conflict, communication tends to be blocked. For example, if expectations created by the manager role cannot be realized due to the restraints imposed by the representative role, the individual is in a position of role conflict. The resident and citizen roles are likewise likely to conflict. Unless the parent management is sufficiently sensitive to these possible conflicts, the overseas manager's behavior may be inexplicable and communications become blocked or at least noisy.

An example would be an executive of a U.S. firm sent to India for an extended period of time as financial manager of an Indian subsidiary. Over time he finds himself identifying emotionally with India and grows impatient with the financial restraint placed on the subsidiary by the U.S. parent. More rapid growth, which requires greater parent company financial commitment, is required if the enterprise is to live up to Indian expectations, which objective the young man sees as increasingly important in the broad context of supporting the more liberal approach to rapid national development. He makes vigorous representation to the parent on behalf of the subsidiary, not necessarily on purely financial grounds, which becomes known in India and improves his status as one who "understands our problems." But because of his apparent inability to influence the parent company, he loses some authority within the Indian subsidiary itself. And, his colleagues back home, knowing far less about India and identifying very little with its problems, refer to our man as "unrealistic" and "soft." In addition, he himself may realize that he is getting out of touch with domestic developments in his profession, as well as losing contact with professional colleagues ordinarily maintained through attendance at periodic conferences and seminars. He begins to feel uncomfortable. So, likewise, does his family, some members of which are reaching high school age. Even though the Indian subsidiary may be in critical need of his services, the executive may now engage in a homeward-bound strategy. Again, he is making decisions and recommendations for reasons other than the immediate financial profit of the corporation. Perhaps he should; that is not the issue. The point is that unless the parent company management is aware of the pressures and needs to which his various roles can expose him, it may not be in a position to read his communications from India correctly. If one substitutes a qualified local national, one resolves some of these conflicts but intensifies others. For example, what if the financial manager were Indian, and the parent company had no process whereby nationals other than those of the parent country were considered for assignment to world corporate headquarters? Then, if the Indian were ambitious and wished to develop international status in the field of financial management, he would either seek to increase autonomy for the Indian firm or, failing that, leave the employ of the firm entirely. Whatever his action, it is likely that the headquarters management will misunderstand his motivations.

The critical importance of overseas managerial selection is heightened by the greater difficulty in assessing performance and in finding replacements than in a purely domestic situation. Performance measurement is rendered difficult by different factor inputs, differential inflation and foreign exchange rate moves, time delays in reporting, and the external restraints embedded in intercompany relationships (such as pricing, financial decision) over which local management has little control. An internal profit-and-loss accounting is unlikely to provide an adequate basis for judging managerial effectiveness in this situation. The replacement problem is aggravated by personal difficulties involved in international moves and by the severe shortage of management skills in many parts of the world.

How and where do firms find managers for assignment to international operations, whether in corporate headquarters or foreign affiliates? There seems to be little research into current practice. But one such, a 1974 survey of 62 U.S. firms, revealed substantial differences. About two-thirds took on U.S. nationals directly for work in international operations. The balance required previous experience in domestic operations. Just over half reportedly hired foreign nationals directly for management positions in the U.S.; another 20 percent only transferred them from affiliates abroad. The balance employed no foreign nationals in the U.S. Some firms would accept applications for foreign nationals in the U.S., such as foreign graduates of U.S. management programs, for jobs with associated overseas firms; others would not. It was clear that a more internationally-oriented set of hiring policies went together, that is, those firms hiring U.S. nationals directly into international operations also tended to employ foreign nationals in the U.S., and accept foreign applications in the U.S. for overseas positions. Hiring foreign national managers in the U.S. suggested relative absence of national bias at corporate headquarters. Accepting applications in the U.S. for foreign jobs suggested a high level of control by the U.S. parent over its overseas affiliates. One further point came out of this study: of those firms hiring foreign national managers in the U.S. (47 out of 62), 12 required a permanent U.S. visa; 23 did not. The latter firms were willing to support one's application for a permanent U.S. visa *after* a job offer.[1]

SELECTION OF OVERSEAS MANAGEMENT 4.1

Two decisions are involved in the selection of overseas management: choice of prerequisites (including nationality) and validation of those prerequisites.

Until recently there seemed to be a clear trend for U.S. firms to employ an increasing percentage of local nationals in management positions in associated foreign firms. For example, one report shows that some 70 percent of the managing directors of U.S. subsidiaries in Europe were local nationals by 1969, as were 55 percent of other key executives. Comparable figures for subsidiaries in Latin America were 30 percent and 50 percent.[2] And a 1970 study found

[1]Oscar DeShields and Richard D. Robinson, "An Inquiry into the Hiring Practices of U.S.-Based Multinational Companies" (Cambridge: Sloan School of Management, Massachusetts Institute of Technology, typed manuscript, 1974).

[2]"What It Costs to Hire Good Executive Talent for U.S. Subsidiaries Overseas," *Business Abroad*, vol. 92, no. 24, November 27, 1967.

a definite trend in the direction of sending fewer U.S. managers abroad.[3] In 1975, General Motors reported total overseas employment of 168,000, of which only 421 had been assigned to foreign subsidiaries by the Overseas Operations Division within corporate headquarters in the U.S. (presumably all U.S. citizens).

But the evidence is not all one way. A 1972 study by the Conference Board found that 268 major U.S. corporations then employed 3,455 U.S. citizens abroad. By 1975 the total for 213 of these *same* companies had *risen* to 5,300.[4] Also significant was the fact that the number of U.S. passports issued or renewed for business travel rose dramatically from 40,000 in 1970 to 268,000 in 1974. Obviously, these figures did not mean that the number of U.S. managers on long-term assignment abroad per million dollars of sales or of assets had increased. Possibly not. But at the same time, the number of expatriate U.S. managers seemed to be holding its own. Based on 1972 data relating to 250 U.S. and European firms, Franko[5] related the number of U.S. expatriate managers to the stage of internationalization of the firm (see Figure 4.1). If true, this pattern would conform to the evolutionary model of the control system of the internationalizing firm as outlined in Chapter 8. It may be that some of the mature multinational and transnational corporations actually plan on maintaining between 5 and 10 percent expatriates or third country nationals in local subsidiary managements. Unilever, the U.K.-Dutch transnational, reportedly does so on the assumption that there are benefits in mixed management, such as providing multinational experience and intensifying corporate socialization for all parties.[6] When General Motors set up its Australian operation in 1948, some 42 U.S. managers and technical specialists were required. Twenty years later, the number had apparently stabilized at about ten.

Franko found that European-based firms maintained their preference for home country nationals through the periods of initial manufacture and, unlike U.S. firms, foreign growth. Both ended up in stage six, however, employing fewer home country and third country nationals.

There is some evidence that there may be national differences in respect to a corporation's propensity to employ local national managers. A 1976 study of more than 60 U.S., European, and Japanese subsidiaries operating in Brazil produced the results tabulated in Table 4.1.

---

[3]James C. Baker and John M. Ivancevich, "Multinational Management with American Expatriates," *Economic and Business Bulletin*, vol. 23, no. 1, Fall 1970, p. 36. A similar finding was reported in respect to Latin America by Charles E. Watson, "Selection of Overseas Managers in U.S. Firms," unpublished M.B.A. thesis, University of Illinois, 1967.

[4]Burton W. Teague, *Selecting and Orienting Staff for Service Overseas* (New York: The Conference Board, 1976), p. 2.

[5]Lawrence G. Franko, "Who Manages Multinational Enterprises?" *Columbia Journal of World Business*, Summer 1973, pp. 30 ff.

[6]Reported by Doreen L. Wederburn, Public Affairs Manager, Unilever Ltd. (Conference Board seminar on "Coping with Host Country Tensions," New York City, January 19, 1977).

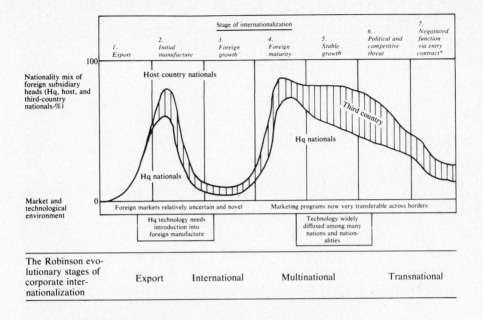

Figure 4.1
**STAGE OF INTERNATIONALIZATION AND NATIONALITY OF
FOREIGN SUBSIDIARY CHIEF EXECUTIVES: U.S. COMPANIES
WITH LOW FOREIGN PRODUCT DIVERSIFICATION**

*Which may be explicit or implicit.

Source: Adapted from Lawrence G. Franko, "Who Manages Multinational Enterprises?" *Columbia Journal of World Business,* Summer 1973, p. 33. Franko's version did not include stage seven nor use the Robinson classification system. For definitions of the latter, see Chapter 8.

It may well be true, however, that these apparent national differences arise more out of the fact that more European and Japanese firms are at lesser stages of internationalization than the U.S. than out of national differences. One would have to control for stage of corporate evolution.

Two reasons are generally given for the employment of local national managers: lower cost and more intimate environmental knowledge. A third reason is the difficulty a nonnational may face in assuming either the highly paternalistic role vis-à-vis employees that is expected of him in traditional society or the egalitarian or subordinate role required in some of the more collectivist societies (a subject developed more fully in Chapter 3). Two obvious disadvantages to the employment of local nationals as managers are nontransferability (hence, local management may become frustrated, inbred, and nationalistic) and poor communications (unless there is someone in the parent firm sufficiently familiar with the local environment to be able to interpret signals to the rest of management). An alternative is the use of a third-country national (multinational) or assignment without regard to nationality unless

Table 4.1
**PERCENTAGE OF LOCAL NATIONAL MANAGERS
IN FOREIGN-OWNED SUBSIDIARIES IN BRAZIL**

Nationality of Parent	Subsidiary Executives		
	Chief Executive	Marketing Manager	All Top Executives
United States	24%	52%	56%
European	8	68	38
Japanese	0	13	16
Total	13	53	40

Source: W.K. Brandt and James N. Hulbert, *A Empresa Multinacional No Brasil* (Rio de Janeiro: Zahan Editors, 1977), p. 45.

relating directly to managerial effectiveness. In some cases, of course, denial of entry visa or work permit may require the firm to nationalize management over a specified period of time. In other cases, the top management must be local, as in the case of a foreign investment in a Yugoslav enterprise in its entirety (as in contrast to an autonomous division). In the former case (foreign investment in the parent enterprise), the director must be a Yugoslav citizen; in the latter (a sub-entity), he could be a foreigner. In fact, virtually all directors of international joint ventures in Yugoslavia have been local nationals.[7] In still other cases it is exceedingly difficult to use expatriate managers effectively. A case in point is Japan. In a number of LDCs the development of local management may be legally required by the host government as a condition of entry. And, if some circulation of foreign national managers through assignments at corporate headquarters is anticipated, legal restraints imposed by the *parent* country can become important.

For example, although U.S. firms report relatively little delay in moving foreign nationals into management positions abroad, prior to 1970 months of advance planning were sometimes needed to move non-Americans into the U.S. In some cases this difficulty of entry into the U.S. for alien managers led to employment by a firm of more U.S. nationals in overseas positions than might otherwise have been the case. It has been possible all along for foreign managers to be admitted into the U.S. in training status for a period of two years, or on a temporary permit basis for six months, but the assumption of managerial responsibilities in the U.S. until 1970 required an immigration visa, which often meant a wait of anywhere from 10 to 18 months because the Department of Labor generally declined to certify executives as needed talent.

---

[7]Miodrag Sukijasovic, *Yugoslav Foreign Investment Legislation at Work: Experience So Far* (Belgrade: Oceana Publications, 1970), pp. 64, 146.

"If all countries had the same immigration set-up as America now [1970] uses, multinational corporations simply couldn't function."[8] The practice was for companies faced with long delays in gaining entry for much needed talent to fly in executives for short business trips at regular intervals, a procedure that was both expensive and personally difficult.

Fortunately, a 1970 amendment to U.S. immigration law permitted non-U.S. executives employed by a firm over one year to enter the U.S. on a temporary basis in a management or executive capacity in the employ of that firm or of an associated entity. Such visas are granted more swiftly than other types of visas and are valid for three to five years. Obviously, certain questions are begged: What is a manager or executive? What constitutes an associated entity?[9]

Rules controlling entry for managers are sometimes modified reciprocally on the basis of a bilateral commerce, friendship, or navigation treaty or convention of establishment. In the French-U.S. case, there is a 1961 Convention of Establishment, which specifies that those French or U.S. nationals qualifying as "treaty traders" or "treaty investors" will be given permission to reside, to work in a salaried position, and to carry on a business in the other country. Qualifications consist principally of establishing nationality, a history free of bankruptcy, and credit worthiness.

The key question is what are the relevant variables in determining optimum strategy: employment of parent country nationals, local nationals, or third-country nationals?

The use of parent country nationals in key managerial roles may be jusitifed in the following situations:

1. The foreign enterprise is just being established (start-up phase).

2. The parent firm wishes to develop an internationally oriented management for the headquarters (foreign assignments are seen essentially as management development).

3. No adequate management is available from other sources.[10]

---

[8]Reported in the *Wall Street Journal*, 14 January 1970, p. 1.

[9]See Esther M. Kaufman, "Visa Options from B to L: Bringing Foreign Staff to the U.S.," *Worldwide P&I Planning*, March–April 1972, p. 26.

[10]According to Baker and Ivancevich, inadequacies of local nationals reported by 254 international U.S. firms in 1969 are as follows:

Unfamiliarity with U.S. business practices*	36%
Lack of education or technical confidence	23
Lack of initiative or aggressiveness	9
Failure to communicate	9
Failure to delegate	8
Failure to plan	8
Nonprofit oriented	7
	100%

*Note: Unfamiliarity with U.S. business practices is essentially a communications problem.

4.   The parent firm has surplus managerial personnel toward which it feels responsible. (This reason, if relevant, should be examined with care if it implies pushing the least capable managers abroad.)

5.   The parent firm has no one sufficiently familiar with the foreign environment to interpret communications from a non-parent country management, and therefore needs to develop area expertise.

6.   Virtually no autonomy is possible for the foreign enterprise because it is integrated so closely with operations elsewhere.

7.   High-level technical knowledge and skill of a nature that cannot be protected legally is carried by top management (in a research oriented, service firm).

8.   The foreign enterprise is seen as short-lived.

9.* The host society is multiracial (or multireligious), and a local manager of either racial origin (or religion) would make the enterprise politically vulnerable or lead to an economic boycott.

10. There is a compelling need to maintain a foreign image.

11. The parent firm will be serving largely other firms of the same nationality operating abroad, most of which are directed by parent country nationals.

12.* It is felt desirable to avoid involving particular local nationals or families (former distributors or agents) in management, and the use of other local nationals would create dangerous animosities. (For example, U.S. executives are reported to be in demand in Europe to manage multicountry operations involving the supervision of managers of different European nationalities.)

13.* Local nationals are not mobile and resist assignment elsewhere.

14.* A parent-country national is simply the best man for the job, all things considered.

15.* Control is weak (see Section 8.6), particularly in cases where local nationals are highly nationalistic (patriotic) and more responsive to government appeals than would be an expatriate (but an expatriate may be less able to influence the government).

It will be noted that several of these conditions are not persuasive in the long run, such as condition 1. In regard to condition 2, there is no reason for parent-country nationals to occupy the *top* roles. In any event, U.S. firms are finding it increasingly difficult to induce their expatriates to return to the United States.[11] "Adequacy" is in part a function of a perception of one's superiors; that is, personal confidence. For an individual not known intimately on a person-to-person basis over a significant period of time, personal

---

*These items also show possible justification for employment of the third-country nationals.
[11]See *Business Abroad*, January 1971, p.21.

confidence is hard to come by. Hence, one way to build up adequate managerial skills in foreign nationals is through extended assignment to corporate headquarters. Condition three may be limited in time; local nationals may be trainable. Mere unfamiliarity with individual foreign nationals may be a valid reason to send in known nationals for a period of time, though not indefinitely. Condition four is also a limited phenomenon; management can be sloughed off. Condition five will change over time as the parent country nationals are rotated home. Condition six could be argued. Why should parent country nationals perform more adequately? In either case, the manager's role should be carefully defined so as to avoid conflict of roles. Condition seven begs a question: why should parent country nationals be more trustworthy in this regard? In fact, given their greater ease in securing jobs with domestic (parent country) competitors, the risk of loss of such knowledge and skill may be greater in the case of parent-country nationals. It might be argued, however, that the transfer of skills and know-how decreases a firm's external leverage against possible nationalization. Conditions eight through fourteen clearly seem to demand parent-country nationals under some circumstances. In the case of condition 15, the situation calls for a careful analysis as to the source of weakness and to the costs and benefits of enforcing greater control. What control is required and why is a parent-country national better able to control? Is this ability based simply on familiarity with both the local scene and the parent company? Very likely, in which case the key element here is an effective communicator in both directions, as indicated in Figure 4.2.

Perhaps the alternatives shown in Figure 4.2 should really be thought of as representing a continuum over time as individual communication abilities develop—from channel one, to channel two, to channel three, to channel four, to channel five. When the term "U.S.-trained Mexican manager" is used, what one means is a Mexican national who is able to communicate effectively with a U.S. management that includes no particular expertise in understanding Mexico or Mexicans. Channel five is characteristic of the multinational corporation, which has a cadre of international managers of different nationalities who can communicate effectively in all directions.

Because of the competition for such individuals, many firms may find it virtually impossible to move beyond channel three, which can be a perfectly adequate system of communications. The trouble is that the need for the person in headquarters who is knowledgeable of things Mexican is often overlooked. Words flow, and management is led to believe that it is communicating effectively with its Mexican management when in fact it is not.

For example, it is reported that:

About half the existing offices of foreign companies in Japan—mostly the smaller ones—are staffed exclusively by Japanese. One might think that this would solve the problem, but it doesn't. If executives at headquarters responsible for the operation are unfamiliar with Japan's customs and business practices, the indigenous staff is not likely

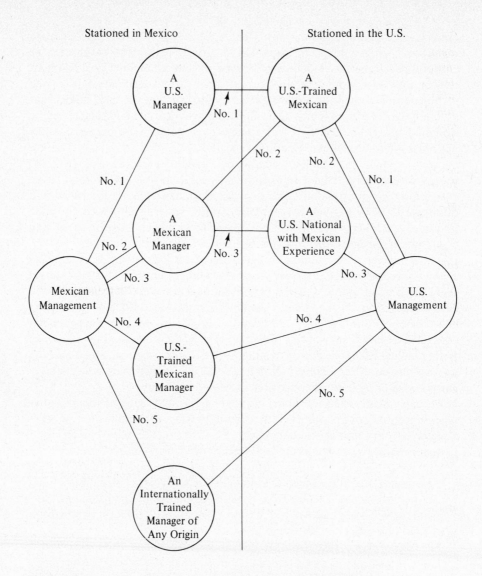

Figure 4.2
ALTERNATIVE CHANNELS OF COMMUNICATION BETWEEN A U.S. FIRM AND AN ASSOCIATED MEXICAN ENTERPRISE.

to receive the understanding or cooperation requisite for success and a smooth-running operation.[12]

A Scandinavian businessman speaks of another aspect of the same problem:

[12]Howard F. Van Zandt, "Japanese Culture and the Business Boom," *Foreign Affairs*, January 1970, p. 355.

Nowadays there seems to be a tendency towards "over-Japanization" of the foreign company in Japan; i.e., the top management is after the initial stages of starting up business staffed entirely with Japanese executives. It has been observed that this can create serious problems particularly in the communication with the head office overseas. In one actual case, the Japanese president of a joint venture company got so frustrated with this communication problem that he actually resigned and returned to the large Japanese corporation he originally came from. The occasional visitor from the head office cannot possibly understand all the complexities of carrying out business in Japan, and what the Japanese executive in the related case actually wanted was to have an able person from the head office permanently stationed in Japan and with whom he could discuss the various problems on the spot.

The language differences create difficulties not only for the foreigner but also for the Japanese executive in an international company. There are also many other difficulties for both. However, these can be overcome by having a team of two able executives, one Japanese and one foreign, working together to form a very effective and powerful combination. [13]

A dubious reason for employing a foreign national management is to insulate parent company personnel from direct involvement in making extra-legal payments to foreign government personnel.

On the other hand, Lord Cole of Unilever has written,

It may in some cases be expedient to keep an expatriate in a country to balance the pulls which can be made on a locally born manager and to be available to present cases to government, or to other agencies, which it is often difficult for a national to do without being suspected of lack of patriotism. [14]

A Swedish company (Volvo) reports that it prefers to use Swedish nationals to fill financial executive positions abroad, principally because they are more familiar with the financial and accounting procedures of the parent company. Particularly for firms preparing consolidated international financial statements, this consideration may be important. All in all, generalizations in this area are unwise.

The danger is that the firm will opt for a policy of using parent-country nationals in foreign management positions by default, that is, simply as an automatic extension of domestic policy, rather than deliberately seeking optimum utilization of management skills. For a parent firm inexperienced abroad, the selection of foreign nationals, whether of the host or third country, may be difficult. But a variety of approaches are open: (1) recruitment from among foreign students or foreign alumni of domestic schools of engineering, business, and management; (2) recruitment from among students and alumni of recognized management development schools abroad, the number of which

---

[13]Bengt Delaryd, vice president and representative for the Tokyo office of Skandinaviska Enskilda Banken, in *The Japan Economic Journal*, May 30, 1972, p. 20.

[14]*The Sunday Times* (London), 26 February 1967, p. 33.

is growing rapidly;[15] (3) application to the files of such organizations as the Institute of International Education in New York City; (4) development of a company-sponsored management training program for foreign nationals; (5) reference to the Home Country Employment Registry of foreign students in the U.S., located at Tulane University; (6) utilization of one or more management recruitment organizations operating in the countries of interest.[16] An increase in management mobility has been noted in Western Europe and Japan. In France and Germany, nonstate employment agencies are prohibited legally from soliciting or maintaining files of either job seekers or companies in the market for personnel. Management consulting firms, however, are apparently not prohibited from giving advice in this area.

Emerging from a number of studies in various parts of the world is the fact that the businessman is not rated highly in relation to those employed in government services, medicine, law, teaching, or the military. Therefore, an unduly large proportion of the more qualified and achievement-oriented individuals may seek careers in these more prestigious professions, thus depleting the flows into private management. Nonetheless, in that the cost advantage of a foreign over a parent-country national in a management position abroad is often substantial, a firm may justify considerable expense in finding and developing foreign nationals.[17] On the other hand, equally compelling is the need for channeling communications to the parent firm by someone sensitive to the implicit cultural and environmental variables under which the foreign management is operating and equally sensitive to the external and internal environment of the parent firm.

A firm can invest profitably in an individual's development only if he is likely to remain in the firm's employ for an extended period of time. This is an area, incidentally, in which the Japanese permanent employment system contains an advantage. But in societies in which there is high job mobility among managers, whether due to a shortage or other causes, the firm's interests dictate that it invest only in those managers committed to the company and likely to remain in its employment. Herein lies solid rationale for a hiring policy based on nepotism. Friends and relatives of owners and top executives

---

[15]To list a few: Institue pour l'Etude des Methodes de Direction d l'Enterprise (IMEDE, Lausanne), Institute Europeen d'Administration des Affaires (INSEAD, Fontainebleau), Escuela de Administración de Negocios para Graduados (ESAN, Peru), Instituto Centroamericano de Administracion de Empresas (INCAE, Nicaragua), Centre d'Etudes Industrielles (CEI, Geneva). For a complete listing see Nancy G. McNulty, *Training Managers, the International Guide* (New York: Harper & Row, 1969).

[16]As of 1977, there were six U.S. executive search firms operating about 70 branches abroad.

[17]One study estimated that the job of a U.S. executive in the United Kingdom costing $35,361 a year could be filled by a U.K. national at a cost of $6,600. (Roger M. Pritchard, "Incremental Cost Associated with the Use of United States or Foreign Personnel in Overseas Operations," unpublished S.M. thesis, Sloan School of Management, M.I.T., 1969, p. 97.) In 1977 the Arabian-American Oil Company investigated the costs of giving preference to U.S. personnel over other expatriates in Saudi Arabia. It found that it could hire 2.8 Britons in key executive and technical posts for the cost of one American, and 2.3 Britons for one American in jobs for young engineers just out of college. (Reported in the *Wall Street Journal*, 12 April 1977, p. 28.) It should be noted that the Tax Reform Act of 1976 significantly boosted the cost of employing Americans overseas (see appendix to Chapter 8).

are probably somewhat less likely to exploit the firm for training and development and then leave.[18]

Some have estimated that the turnover rate for U.S. expatriate managers may be as high as 30 percent. "Companies cannot long suffer such an astounding high percentage, given the cost of relocation and training and uncountables in good will and organization."[19]

A large international company, which draws most of the managers of its international operations from its international division, calculates its turnover as 5 percent to 10 percent; but also expects that this percentage will rise sharply when personnel from its domestic companies are sent overseas.

One of the main problems is the apprehension some executives feel when offered and placed in foreign locations. Is an overseas assignment a road to advancement or a road to nowhere? Are domestic colleagues the ones who carve up the pie? Where really does an international executive fit into the total corporate picture? Few companies face these questions on a systematic basis.[20]

Enough for the pros and cons of the expatriate-local national argument. What of other selection criteria for overseas managers?

There is very little hard data relating certain personal characteristics with overseas management success. One effort to do so was based on a study of 50 expatriate managers (49 were U.S. citizens) operating in U.S.-affiliated companies in the Mexico City area. These managers were asked to rank four abilities most important to success overseas. The results are given in Table 4.2.

The same study reports unusually high expatriate scores in respect to responsibility, moderately high scores in emotional stability, and low scores in sociability. Expatriates scored high in internationalism, but with fairly high variability. The study went on to say,

The executives interviewed were generally well-adjusted to the foreign environment but a rather wide range of acculturation existed, and many examples of acculturation failures were cited. This indicates a very spotty success in the selection and training of expatriates and again points up the need for improved knowledge.[21]

Qualities deemed most important for overseas success by managers of foreign operations in 127 large U.S. firms were (1) independence and ability to achieve results with limited resources, (2) sincerity and integrity, (3) technical knowledge, and (4) a positive attitude toward overseas work, in that descending order. Overseas managers in the same firms specified (1) a positive

---

[18]For an interesting discussion of this and other issues, see Joseph M. Waldman, "Management Practices in Pakistan—Another Vicious Circle," *MSU Business Topics*, Summer 1971, pp. 35–39.

[19]*Compensating International Executives* (New York: Business International, 1970), p. 1.

[20]*Compensating International Executives.*

[21]Hays, "Behavioral Aspects," p. 19.

Table 4.2

DETERMINANTS OF SUCCESS-FAILURE IN AN EXPATRIATE POSITION

Factors	First	Second	Third	Fourth
1. Job ability factors (technical skill, organization ability, belief in mission)	27%	8%	6%	7%
2. Relation abilities (ability to deal with local nationals, cultural empathy)	7	20	16	1
3. Family (an adaptive and supportive family)	12	15	12	3
4. Language ability	2	6	9	10
Percent of all responses in this rank accounted for by these four factors.	94%	96%	84%	41%

Source: Richard D. Hayes, "Behavioral Aspects of U.S. Expatriate Managers," Tulane University, Graduate School of Business Administration, working paper series, 1970, p.13.

attitude by the wife, (2) sincerity and integrity, (3) adaptability, and (4) a positive attitude on the part of the manager, in descending order.[22]

Another study, limited to canvassing the opinion of U.S. expatriate managers (1,161 in 40 countries), produced the results given in Table 4.3. Still another study of 70 U.S. based companies came up with the results shown in Table 4.4. All of these criteria can be grouped under: (1) experience in company, (2) technical competence (including managerial), (3) language, (4) area expertise, (5) age, (6) stability of marital relations (including spouse's attitude), (7) personal preference, (8) personality attributes, (9) career plans, (10) sex, and (11) social acceptability. Curiously, the last two are almost never articulated by U.S. managements. Not mentioned at all is physical stamina of both husband and wife.

It is clear that most U.S. managers overseas have been recruited from within their respective firms[23] and that there is a "trend away from using foreign-reared Americans as managerial talent in U.S.-based multinational firms."[24]

For an individual to be versed fully in company policies, procedures and products are often felt to be of prime importance. It is sometimes claimed that a foreign manager, operating at greater distance from the home office and under a severe communications handicap, must have internalized thoroughly the way the company operates and the nature of its products. In fact, however,

---

[22]See John M. Ivancevich, "The American Manager Overseas Representing Large U.S. Industrial Corporations," unpublished D.B.A. thesis, University of Maryland, 1969.

[23]Sixty percent of large U.S. international firms recruit over 80 percent of their expatriate managers from within the firm, according to James C. Baker and John M. Ivancevich, "Multinational Management," p. 35.

[24]Hays, "Behavioral Aspects," p. 18.

Table 4.3
IDEAL BACKGROUND FOR AN OVERSEAS CAREER

Wife and family adaptable	20%
Leadership ability	19
Knowledge of job	14
Knowledge of language of host country	13
Well educated	13
Respect for laws and people of host country	12
Previous overseas experience	4
Desire to serve overseas	4
Miscellaneous	1
Total	100%

Source: Richard F. Gonzalez and Anant R. Negandhi, *The United States Executive: His Orientation and Career Patterns* (East Lansing, Michigan: Michigan State University, Graduate School of Business Administration, 1967), p. 113.

Table 4.4
CRITERIA FOR SELECTING EXECUTIVES FOR OVERSEAS OPERATIONS: HOW 70 COMPANIES MAKE SELECTIONS

Criterion	Number of times mentioned	Percentage of companies citing
Experience	30	42.9
Adaptability, flexibility	28	40.0
Technical knowledge of business	24	34.3
Competence, ability, past performance	24	34.3
Managerial talent	16	22.9
Language skills/ability	8	11.4
Potential	7	10.0
Interest in overseas work, executive ambition	7	10.0
Appreciation of new management, sensitivity	5	7.1
Education	4	5.7
Initiative, creativity	4	5.7
Independence	3	4.3
Communication	3	4.3
Maturity, emotional stability	2	2.9
Same criteria as for other comparable jobs	2	2.9

Source: Compensating International Executives (New York: Business International Corporation), p. 2. Reprinted with permission of the publisher.

this may be the easiest prerequisite to satisfy by training and periodic conferences.

Technical competence is, of course, essential if by "technical" skills one refers to skills required to do the assigned job. Warning: the skill-mix for a successful manager abroad may differ somewhat from the parent country model. It is a truism that one of the elements most important in gaining acceptance for foreign management is demonstrated technical capacity. This quality is also important in providing the manager himself—be he or she of parent or of third-country origin—with that degree of confidence necessary to overcome "cultural shock." A person must be genuinely self-confident, although not arrogantly so.

A recent study of the international marketing function of the larger U.S. firms disclosed that 40 percent of the responding U.S. executives listed proven domestic marketing ability as the primary prerequisite for appointement to overseas marketing positions. One quarter cited foreign national status; 16 percent specified an expression of personal interest; only 10 percent, prior formal training; and a mere 2 percent, foreign language ability. Yet, 43 percent of the executives responding specified that adapting to different cultural concepts and overcoming the language barrier were the main difficulties faced by international marketing personnel, and 24 percent said that the chief characteristic favoring success was strong empathy with the cultural environment.[25]

Must a manager know the language of the host country? If we admit the validity of employing parent or third-country nationals under certain circumstances, then language may impose a severe restraint on recruitment. A second language may be most efficiently acquired either as a child or as a mature adult when a specific language need arises. With concentrated effort, a *casual* speaking knowledge of any language may be acquired within six to 12 months by an intelligent adult. With but exceedingly rare exceptions, an adult with no prior exposure to a given language cannot become bilingual in it. The rare exceptions are two: linguistic genius or complete isolation from the mother tongue for a long period of time (as confinement in a foreign prison). The major danger to management is that a person inadequate in the local language will nonetheless attempt to carry on as though he understood, or was being understood, at all times. The local community undoubtedly appreciates the foreigner's efforts to communicate directly, but these efforts should not be permitted to interfere with understanding. Pride should not stand in the way of employing a good interpreter.

For the novice in a language, there are at least three serious blocks to full understanding:

1. inadequate knowledge and understanding of the culture and, hence, of words. Many apparently equivalent words do not, in fact, carry the same meaning (for example, "education," "management," "fair play," "labor"—words which relate to institutions, values, or attitudes);

2. the use of words to carry other meanings because they are equivalent in a first meaning, the point being that the words may overlap only for a single meaning. Simply because the English word equivalent carries the other meanings is no guarantee that the foreign word expresses the same. Concept clusters vary;

---

[25]A. Kapoor and R. McKay, *Managing International Markets* (Princeton, N.J.: Darwin Press, 1971), pp. 9, 16, and 17.

3. the use of metaphors, similes, and analogies (for instance, "the sweater tickles her to death" is translatable as "the sweater scratched her until she died").[26]

Even the effective use of an interpreter requires an alertness to these difficulties.

Many nonlocal managers with no prior knowledge of the local language have been eminently successful. The skilled use of competent interpreters, plus coincidental study of the language to the point of being able to keep the interpreter on his toes, may be quite adequate. The pitfall here is the temptation to associate unduly with those speaking one's own language. In many non-Western countries, the U.S. businessman is surrounded by English-speaking "carpetbaggers," many of whom may not be ethnically or culturally part of the major community. He should be wary of becoming too closely involved.

Perhaps of greater importance than ability to use a given language is an awareness of the importance of language as a programmed thinking process. The capacity and structure of a language to a significant degree determine the nature of both thought and emotion and hence, of behavior. Granted, a language changes over time, but for a given experience it is fixed. Associated with this subject is that of the so-called "silent language," in the context of which only a spoken language can be understood. Essentially, the "silent language" consists of signals communicated by means other than words—spatial relationships, timing, movements, sequences. What may be insulting in one culture may be complimentary in another. The point is that *a characteristic of a good manager is a capacity to communicate effectively. How he does it is relatively unimportant.*

As Noer has pointed out,[27] an essential ingredient in effective communication has to do with knowing one's *own* cultural bias.

The dynamic nature of cultural values works at both ends of an international assignment. The German manager brought up in the aftermath of World War II has different cultural values from the young German worker. A 28-year-old U.S. technician selected by a 45-year-old middle manager in the United States and sent to work for a 50-year-old manager in Germany, where the peer group is 28-year-old German technicians, is caught in a crossfire of cultural values before he starts. If he and the individual who selected him are unaware of cultural differences and cultural bias, the chances for a cultural clash are greatly increased.[28]

A cultural clash simply signals a breakdown in effective communication. Individuals are speaking and acting from different premises.

Another prerequisite often specified for the foreign manager is area expertise, knowledge of the market or production area. Several points should be

[26]Taken from Thornburg, p. 33.

[27]David H. Noer, *Multinational People Management* (Washington: The Bureau of National Affairs, 1975).

[28]David H. Noer, *Multinational People*, pp. 47–48.

made. Firstly, prejudgment without personal experience can be very misleading. International communications are clogged with misinterpretation, bias, misinformation, propaganda, distortion, and outright lies. Secondly, experience has demonstrated that a man who has worked *successfully* in one national environment different from his own is very likely to operate with similar success wherever employed. Once he has breached an intercultural communications barrier, and once he has felt the essential unity of human society, the likelihood of failure is greatly reduced.

This last point needs expansion. By "essential unity of human society" is meant the fact that human life everywhere faces similar needs and drives. Given a historical input, certain institutions, relationships, personality types, and values emerge. All are functional, that is, rational, within a context. They are constantly changing as interactions slowly alter the historical input. The manager himself is one of these inputs. Once a person views human society in this manner, he always feels "at home" wherever he is. He realizes that bargaining in the bazaar, or elaborate rituals of politeness are not simply quaint old customs, but serve definite functions.[29] This realization does not mean that one is necessarily resigned to the *status quo*. On the contrary, he is then in a position to deal with his cultural environment more effectively. For example, he knows what is likely to reduce the pressure to bargain. In short, the successful international manager is one who sees and feels the similarity of structure of all societies. The same set of relevant variables are seen to operate, although the relative weights may be very different. This capacity is far more important than possession of specific area expertise, which may be gained quite rapidly if one has this capacity to see similarities and ask the right questions—those that will provide the appropriate values or weights for the relevant variables. Such an individual very quickly locates himself on the social-cultural map.

It could be argued that the manager's success in subsequent foreign environments after an initial success is not because he has learned anything but because he has demonstrated that he possesses a special set of qualities, perhaps most importantly a coherent identity and adequate ego strength. The counterargument is that identity and ego strength may be necessary conditions, but possibly not sufficient. It may be that the learning process in the initial experience shortens the time to relate effectively to a foreign culture in subsequent experiences.

Other than nationality, company experience, technical competence, and language and area expertise (communicative capacity), there are at least eight other prerequisites used in selecting overseas management either consciously

---

[29]Bazaar-type bargaining is functional when (1) customers differ greatly in wealth—from subsistence to affluence—the differences being known to the seller; (2) the selling unit is small so that profit and loss can be calculated almost continuously; (3) interest rates are high and turnover important and/or large margins are important; (4) the seller is the owner, or a close associate.

or unconsciously: health, marital relations (and attitude of wife), career plans and personal preference, age, social acceptability, sex, and personality attributes.

It has been noted by those experienced in this area that an individual's physical health is peculiarly relevant to success abroad. For example, the U.S. Foreign Service rejects candidates with not "*more* than average health." The health of one's family is also important. The point is that adjustment to the different working and living conditions encountered abroad generates psychological and physical strain. Undue worry about one's health, or that of one's family, can well subvert managerial effectiveness.

Virtually all analysts stress the importance of a strong and mutually reinforcing relationship between man and wife. In some circumstances sending an unmarried person overseas can be risky, particularly in socially sensitive (for example, where the sexes tend to be segregated) and racially conscious societies. In many, a single person simply will not have the access to families and homes that would a married couple, which may interfere with his or her effectiveness at work. Both husband and wife should have a positive attitude toward the proposed overseas assignment, but an attitude based on accurate knowledge of the working and living conditions they can anticipate.

Career plans and personal preference cannot really come into full play unless overseas job opportunities are posted within the company rather than communicated on an individual-to-individual basis either through formal or informal communication networks.

> *While there has been some movement toward intra-company job "advertising" in many corporations, the extension of such systems to the international arena is not common. A few companies have instituted programs—often using computerized inventories of employee skills—so that the corporate personnel department can quickly ascertain where qualified candidates are located, even on a worldwide basis. This type of system can be characterized as* company-initiated *rather than* employee-initiated, *since the prospective candidates usually do not know of the job opening until they are approached.*

> *The job posting scheme used by the U.S. Texas Instruments (TI) is a different system, in which the initial impetus to apply for a position within the company comes from interested employees themselves. Although oriented primarily to the domestic area, the program is being implemented for jobs outside the U.S. as well.* [30]

Management jobs abroad not limited by corporate policy to local nationals are posted worldwide by TI. Intracompany job opportunities in Europe are funnelled through the European regional office. A more recent innovation in the TI system is anonymous advertising by employees in search of new jobs, either domestic or foreign.

Influencing preferences for overseas assignment, of course, is the degree to

---

[30]*Business International*, August 9, 1974, p. 254.

which such assignments are seen as a necessary step on the ladder to the top.

Age may or may not be important to an overseas assignment. Should a Brazilian enterprise be run by a young or a more senior person? Obviously, managing an enterprise far removed from headquarters requires great responsibility and maturity of judgment. Within a broad range, no one has demonstrated that these latter qualities are closely related to biological age. In more traditional societies, of course, age may be an important status symbol, which fact may then become relevant to selection of management. Age may also be relevant if an individual's overall management career is considered to be a prerequisite for selection. Is a foreign assignment considered to be preparation for promotion or is it a dead end? If the latter, the parent firm may push its undesirables overseas. Very frequently, U.S. firms with policies of employing local nationals in overseas management do not consider these managers transferable, either to third countries or to the United States. Therefore, their career horizons are limited to the local enterprises. A few U.S. firms now require foreign experience for promotion to corporate level. If this be the case, career expectations may be an essential prerequisite for selection of a manager for a foreign enterprise. Indeed, a tendency seems to be evident among firms operating internationally—U.S., European, and Japanese—to make foreign experience a necessary step on the ladder to a top corporate position. The giant Japanese firm, Mitsui K.K., whose personnel policy is described in Case G, appears to be an example. A study based on a mailed questionnaire completed by executives in 81 U.S. firms having operations in one or more of six of the major South American countries came up with the results shown in Table 4.5.

In the list of prerequisites we have included social acceptability, by which is meant the reflection on the part of the manager of those social characteristics identified by his or her local colleagues and subordinates with a manager in that society. Particularly in a traditional society, where ascriptive factors, rather than demonstrated ability, predominate in establishing authority, care should be used to select one who possesses at least some of the characteristics, whether they be defined in terms of college degrees, knowledge of the fine arts, or manner of behavior. For a parent country or third-country national, family background may not be important, but if a local national is involved, social status may be a relevant variable, however social status may be defined in that particular society. Indeed, a more efficient organization may result than if one ignored such considerations and merely appointed the most *technically* qualified person.

Almost never mentioned in the literature is women's place in international business. In certain overseas managerial roles, particularly sales, a woman may have a distinct advantage. She is more likely to be treated with deference, may find it easier to gain access to distributors and customers, and may be more frequently invited into their homes. A case in point is the sale of pharmaceuticals in Western Europe and Latin America. Possible relevant variables are the area, the function, and the product. National differences in the degree to which

Table 4.5
HOW A SAMPLE CONCEIVED OF FOREIGN ASSIGNMENT IN TERMS OF MANAGERS' LIFETIME CAREER

Company's conception of foreign assignment	Firms accepting statements as description of company policy (choosing statement first with respect to other choices listed)	
	Number	Percentage
A training period for younger men who are expected eventually to fill top positions at home.	17	21.0%
A place where managers who are not needed at home can be sent.	0	0
A period of management rotation; that is to say, nearly all managers of our company are given a foreign assignment and then brought home.	7	8.6
Our company has a group of American managers who make foreign work a career. They rotate from one assignment to another as they are needed.	57	70.4
	81	100.0%

Source: Charles E. Watson, "Selection of Overseas Managers by U.S. Firms," unpublished M.B.A. thesis, University of Illinois, 1967, p. 82.

women are active in business are remarkable. For example, in Switzerland women constituted 47 percent of all those in business in 1966; in Japan, 4 percent. Other country ratios were: France, Germany, and Italy, 22 to 24 percent; Australia, 15 percent; Mexico, 12 percent; Canada 11 percent; Britain and South Africa, 9 percent; Sweden, 8 percent; and Spain, 6 percent.[31] More recent statistics might reveal a tendency to converge.

Even more seldom is race mentioned by researchers or practitioners as relevant to the selection of an overseas manager. For example, is a black American more likely to be more effective in black Africa than a white American or a Nisei (American-born Japanese) in Japan? There seems to be no research on the subject, although some experienced observers express doubt. It is possible that such individuals would be viewed with more suspicion—if not hostility—than one not racially identified with the host country population. It is known that some of the Japanese firms established in the United States have employed Nisei.

Even if we specified the prerequisites for overseas assignments, we still must validate certain of them vis-à-vis a given person. The problem arises particu-

---

[31] *Business Abroad,* December 26, 1966, p. 2.

larly in the language and area expertise areas, which we have redefined in terms of ability to communicate and capacity to grasp the interrelationship of societies. How does one increase the probability of selecting an individual who will perform effectively in a different culture, that is, one who will be least affected by culture shock?

Culture shock is induced by the removal of familiar cues. People are seen as behaving irrationally or stupidly; institutions, as not being functional. One is confronted by unexpected behavior and institutions and by different values and world perceptions. "When expectations are not fulfilled, stress and dysfunction are found to follow."[32] Such stress, or culture shock, may be manifested in a request for a transfer, the desire to leave a job before completion, dissatisfaction and indifference to work, quarreling, undue criticism, blaming failures on inherent qualities of the relevant nationality, adulation of the home country, withdrawal from social relations with local nationals (the compound or enclave syndrome), alcoholism, poor quality work. In Table 4.6 Shaw and Miccio summarize some of the more important American values and one possible set of "foreign values." (One might challenge the notion that the American values defined here are really held strongly by a significant majority of U.S. residents. Perhaps they reflect more a myth than a reality.)[33]

Methods for selecting individuals who are likely to be least upset by such a different value system and best able to work effectively include formal tests, training, personal preference, and none of these (that is, chance).

Formal tests are not widely used by companies to aid in the selection of personnel for overseas assignment, and there is some evidence indicating loss of confidence and decline in testing by former users. Even those firms employing tests do not seem to evaluate their predictability and, hence, are not in a position to relate scores with on-the-job performance overseas.[34] One writer claims, without offering any hard data, that "tests have proved to be valuable in at least some respects to psychologists in selecting American employees for assignments abroad." The tests so cited are the F scale (a measure of ethnic flexibility and adaptability), the Allport-Vernon Study of Values (a measure of personal convictions and values), the Guilford Zimmerman Temperament Survey (a comprehensive personality test), and the Individual Background Survey (a multiple-choice measure).[35]

The consensus of the U.S. international practitioners seems to be that testing has not proven very helpful. The most promising may be the "California Test" (The Indirect Scale for Ethnocentrism), in that from limited data it

---

[32]William B. Shaw and Joseph V. Miccio, "Executive Development and Cross Cultural Transition: A Proposal for the Multinational Corporations," *Trends*, vol. 4, no. 2, September 1971, p. 13.

[33]Another useful statement as to the cultural relativity of relevant values and practices can be found in Joseph M. Waldman, "Management Practices in Pakistan—Another Vicious Circle," *MSU Business Topics*, Summer 1971, pp. 85 ff.

[34]Baker and Ivancevich, "Multinational Management," pp. 38–39.

[35]Spencer Hayden, "Personnel Problems in Overseas Operations," *Personnel*, May–June 1968, pp. 22–23.

Table 4.6
COMPARISON OF AMERICAN AND "FOREIGN" VALUES

American	"Foreign"
Change: means improvement, and is an absolute necessity for survival. Corporations are expected to be dynamic and to be undergoing planned change constantly. Individuals within the corporation are expected to create change to increase efficiency.	*Change:* is to be accepted passively and not sought after. Life—and business—should proceed at a steady rhythmic pace in harmony with natural events. Failures when innovations are tried are accepted fatalistically, and the cause of failure may be defined in a culturally unique way.
Time: the familiar adage, "time is money," sums up the American view of time. To be idle is to be wasteful and non-productive. To make use of all the time available for productive endeavors results in admiration.	*Time:* is an unlimited resource to be used not to create efficient production but to be enjoyed while a task is being undertaken. Delays, cancellations and postponements are viewed with less concern than in the United States. Time is best spent by creating a pleasant interpersonal atmosphere.*
Teamwork: is an important ingredient of modern American corporations. Task forces and special commissions abound, and are believed to be the best avenue for mobilizing available resources to solve a problem. The individual serves the needs of the corporation by participating fully in a team endeavor.	*Teamwork:* may play second fiddle to a more authoritarian approach to problem solving. A highly stable social structure in which people are granted status by virtue of such factors as age, education, class, and parentage makes it difficult to approach tasks through teams. People are only made uncomfortable when told they have as loud a voice as a higher ranking teammate. Usually, individual assignments are made by people farther up the hierarchy.
Individual Initiative: is a major feature of the American self-image. At the same time as we are expected to work together as a team, each of us is expected to show initiative and creativity directed in the interest of the firm. Elaborate incentive and promotion systems are constructed to encourage individual initiative and creativity.	*Individual Initiative:* may be governed by role and status, and thus actively discouraged during a protracted development period. Only when one attains a senior role is he expected to exercise initiative as part of his job prescription. Credit for occurrences of initiative is channeled upward, and not infrequently the young, creative individual is ignored until he ripens into middle age. In the meanwhile he is rewarded for obedience and unobtrusiveness.
Pragmatic Approach: is a historic hallmark of U.S. business. A straightforward, no nonsense attitude is admired as being least wasteful of time and money. Activities not related to an organization's goals are viewed as trivial, and emphasis is placed upon a complete, factual analysis of a problem.	*Pragmatic Approach:* finds less favor than a problem solving approach that is based on a thorough review of past and present conditions. The human interactions occasioned by problem solving may receive more attention and energy than the future goal, and discussing of the ideal may overshadow discussions of actual conditions.
Judgment: Americans are culturally trained to evaluate events as being good-bad, practical-impractical, reasonable-unreasonable, efficient-inefficient, and so on. Such an "either-or" stance is severely limited be-	*Judgment:* is based not so much on evaluative categories as on historical and cultural precedents. Relevant situations from the past are sought out to shed light on what actions should be taken. Actions derived from judg-

Table 4.6 (continued)
COMPARISON OF AMERICAN AND "FOREIGN" VALUES

cause new situations are forced unnaturally to one pole or the other. Actions based on either-or judgments run a high risk of being ill-timed in human terms.	ments based on cultural and historical precedent have a low probability of being ill-timed.

*A further difference may be a tendency to view present conditions as a permanent given rather than a transient position from which one moves toward an explicit goal.

Source: William B. Shaw and Joseph V. Miccio, "Executive Development and Cross Cultural Transition: A Proposal for the Multinational Corporations," *Trends,* vol. 4, no. 2, September 1971, pp. 13–14.

would appear that high ethnocentrism is associated with overseas job failure. Various thematic apperception tests (TATs) may be useful in disclosing such characteristics as prejudice, a tendency to evaluate individuals in terms of stereotypes (or generalities), and compulsion to see things always in terms of absolute universal values. These characteristics would seem to be undesirable among international managers who must deal with multinational situations, for they are likely to make them unable to see the cultural relativity of either personal behavior or corporate strategy. Success in a special training course for a particular assignment, including language, may be an indirect measure of ability to adapt and to relate oneself to a different culture, and may provide as well an insight into motivation. But much, of course, depends on the quality of the training. The weight given to personal preference in the selection process depends on the reason for the preference; a keen interest in new and challenging social experience is very different from a mere desire for the glamour of the "international jet set." Possibly, one should be wary of those who speak of peoples and nations in broad generalities, who pass easy judgment as to the right or wrong of the acts of others, who "love to travel," who show little concern for their personal family responsibilities, or who are extremely extroverted. The personality of the wife and the quality of the husband-wife relationship are also of critical importance. There is evidence that many failures abroad are due to the inability of the wife to adjust satisfactorily or of the marriage relationship to sustain the compression of isolation from one's own culture. (Eventually, cases of a husband's inability to adjust to his wife's overseas assignment may be recorded.)

All in all, there seems to be no substitute for the in-depth interview of both husband and wife by one or more persons intimately familiar with the problems of intercultural movement, that is, one who has experienced them himself. "Mobil's four-hour environmental interview" is most revealing.[36] The Mobil interviewers first seek for above-average technical competence and solid marital relationship. The interviewing process includes the presentation of a

[36]See William Alexander, Jr., "Mobil's Four-Hour Environmental Interview," *Worldwide P&I Planning,* January–February, 1970, pp. 18 ff.

complete and accurate description of the overseas work environment (from housing, schools, medical facilities, and food, to the availability of girdles), and the requirements of the job (family separation, work schedules, vacation). Interaction between husband and wife is observed in the process. To hurry the process up would be to sterilize it; hence, the four hours. In addition, the applicant undergoes at least one functional interview confined to a job's technical aspects. The job offer is made after the lapse of a few days, and the applicant is permitted about two weeks to respond. The offer spells out the precise terms, such as base salary plus premium less U.S. tax and other relevant factors.[37]

The organizations, business and otherwise, with long success records in recruiting for difficult overseas assignments seem to depend very heavily upon similar in-depth interviewing, not by professional psychologists but by those with intimate familiarity with the sorts of problems the applicant will face overseas.

One experienced practitioner writes,

It is recommended that a system be designed to postpone an expatriate's acceptance of a position until he clearly understands the mechanics of his assignment—how he will be paid, how his taxes will be handled, and what will happen to him when currency relationships change.

Many multinationals are utilizing the "letter of understanding" concept to finalize the selection process. A letter of understanding is a summary of all the terms and conditions of an international assignment. It serves not only as a communications vehicle but also as a record of the details of an expatriation transaction.[38]

At the top of a series of recommendations made in a report sponsored by the South African Institute of Race Relations appears the following:

If United States companies are to engage in a serious attempt to effect social change in South Africa, they will have to exercise the greatest care in the selection of top management. The men at the top would not only have to be thoroughly versed in modern management and labour relations techniques, but also imbued with a sense of urgent necessity for evolutionary advance towards a more just society if sporadic violence and ultimate revolution are to be avoided. It is clear that they should have a thorough grounding in the problems of intergroup relations and that they should be well acquainted with the realities of the South African situation.[39]

Whatever the criteria used in selection, or the screening mechanism employed, expatriate U.S. managers are reported to be somewhat more educated than their stay-at-home counterparts, exhibit a somewhat higher career speed (dif-

---

[37]The same points are made by Teague.

[38]Noer, *Multinational People*, p. 57.

[39]Dudley Horner, "United States Corporate Investment and Social Change in South Africa," Johannesburg, mimeo., limited distribution by the African Institute of Race Relations, 1971, p. 14.

ference between the executive's age when first entering business and when achieving major executive status), are several years younger, and demonstrate lower interfirm mobility.[40] There is also some indication that the average U.S. top overseas manager is more satisfied with respect to Maslow's hierarchy of needs (security, social esteem, autonomy, and self-actualization)[41] than his or her domestic counterpart, with the one exception of social esteem. Overseas *middle* managers are more satisfied except in respect to security and social needs.[42] The lower satisfaction of social need probably rises from the more limited opportunity for social contact overseas, particularly given the inadequacy of preparation in the typical case. The lower level of satisfaction in respect to the need of security possibly arises because the individual perceives himself as out of the mainstream of company life, which understandably would be more acute for a middle manager than for a top manager.

A 1976 study based on data provided by executives in 33 major U.S. based international companies concluded:

The limitless variety of human personalities makes it virtually impossible to set out the ideal, or even the optimum, characteristics for foreign service. But most of the executives contacted indicated that what they find preferable is the person who is positive—even buoyant—about the assignment.

They also look for evidence of successful exposure to many different levels of society; an intellectual curiosity; and a talent for participating and sustaining group activities. The candidate who approaches the interviews in a wary, tense manner, whose manner is overly formal, painstaking and awkward, whose interests do not extend far beyond his profession, his home, family, and a small circle of friends, is less likely to succeed in foreign assignment, according to the executives interviewed.[43]

There are elements of this conclusion with which one might quarrel. The buoyant, back-slapping, extroverted, group-oriented type may not be the appropriate choice in a number of situations.

A 1971 inquiry into the practices and policies of 77 U.S. managers of foreign operations reported that 60 percent agreed with the statement that "the overseas American must have a broader and deeper professional training than he needs to perform the same kind of work in his familiar home environment." Only 26 percent disagreed.[44] The generalized need may be there, but precisely what sort of training or preparation is the best? And what is the practice? And, let it be noted that many international executives have observed that the cardinal quality for successful management in many countries lies in the

---

[40]Gonzales and Negandhi, "United States Executive."

[41]See Glossary.

[42]Ivancevich, "American Manager."

[43]Teague, *Selecting and Orienting*, p. 13.

[44]Alan F. White, "Preparation of Managers for Cross-Cultural Assignments" (unpublished S.M. thesis, Sloan School of Management, M.I.T., 1971), p. 22.

manager's ability to obtain the necessary permits, licenses, and approval from government. All else is secondary.

PREPARATION FOR OVERSEAS ASSIGNMENT 4.2

Very few U.S. firms appear to provide special training for managers slated for overseas assignment. A 1969 survey of 127 large U.S.-based international firms indicated that only 33 percent had any sort of predeparture training.[45] Of this 33 percent, only 41 percent (13.5 percent of the entire sample) offered language training for assignments in non-English speaking countries. Some 73 percent of the companies reported a time span of less than three months between selection for an overseas assignment and departure. Another survey of 50 U.S.-based companies revealed that 24 conducted regular in-house programs, largely in language training. This study concluded, "On the whole, less is done than might be expected in terms of providing environmental training prior to assignment."[46]

In an opinion survey of foreign operation managers and overseas managers as to the value of various types of preparation for working overseas, the subjects mentioned most frequently were language, living conditions, economic environment, and customs. Other areas given considerable value were business law, government and political structure, and geography. But of the 127 firms surveyed, only three exposed their prospective overseas managers to anything other than language and customs.[47] A 1976 survey of the practices of 33 large U.S.-based corporations revealed that only half had formal programs, and about one-third called upon outside consultants for assistance in their implementation. Of the 33 companies, 16 required at least some language training.[48]

Although virtually all commentators on the subject speak of the need to prepare a wife or husband for overseas experience, only 32 percent of the 127 firms surveyed in the 1969 Ivancevich study even asked the wives whether they wished to go abroad and an even smaller number allowed spouses to participate in predeparture training. This finding was supported by a completely separate study that concluded,

It seems to us that the greatest weakness of the selection process as now practiced by people in charge of selection at the twelve companies under review lies in the failure to realize that an assignment abroad is a family venture.[49]

---

[45]See John M. Ivancevich, "The American Manager Overseas Representing Large U.S. Industrial Corporations" (unpublished D.B.A. thesis, University of Maryland, 1969).

[46]*Business International*, August 14, 1970, p. 262.

[47]Ivancevich, "American Manager."

[48]Teague, *Selecting and Orienting*, p. 16.

[49]Louis Maertens de Noordhout, "Selection of Executives for Overseas Assignment—An Investigation into the Policies of Twelve United States Companies," unpublished S.M. thesis, Sloan School of Management, M.I.T., 1967, p. 55.

Yet, in another study, the U.S. managers of foreign operations overwhelmingly agreed that families should receive training or orientation prior to going abroad.[50]

There are many reasons for omitting formal training prior to overseas assignment; specifically, (1) the temporary nature of many such assignments, (2) lack of time because of the immediacy of the need for the employee overseas, (3) the trend toward employment of local nationals, (4) doubt about the need for special training, and (5) parallel doubt about the effectiveness of existing training programs. Nonetheless, a strong argument in favor of special cross cultural training is made by Shaw and Miccio. Van Zandt reports that "so different is the [Japanese] culture . . . that it generally takes about three years in residence, and faithful attendance at . . . training seminars before the average Westerner develops confidence in his ability to do business in Japan."[51] The seminars to which reference is made are conducted by the American Chamber of Commerce in Japan. Teague wrote in 1976, "It is becoming more and more apparent that American business in foreign lands will have to give more attention to adapting to local styles in product, method of operation, and approach."[52]

There are a few formal programs within the U.S. designed to improve the effectiveness of the international manager, whether posted to an overseas job or occupying a spot at headquarters within the international channels of communication. The best known of these are the American Graduate School of International Management in Glendale, Arizona; the Institute of the Business Council for International Understanding at the American University in Washington, D.C.; and the Monterey Institute of Foreign Studies in Monterey, California. In addition, such organizations as the Institute of International Education and Overseas Briefing Associates organize orientation programs that are on specific countries and are tailored to particular companies. Such organizations as the Asia Society, the Japan Society, and the Middle East Institute likewise periodically mount briefing sessions for businessmen. One of the more highly developed located elsewhere seems to be the Institute of International Training and Studies near Fuji, Japan. Created by the Ministry of International Trade and Industry, the student body consists of 120 young corporate executives (average age about 30) who are sent by their respective employees for an intensive year-long, full-time course of study. It consists of intensive English language training plus U.S. area study, general management training, international management study, a second language plus relevant area study, and, finally, a two-month study tour of some part of the world. Japanese industry is thus deliberately creating a trained cadre of international

[50]Alan F. White, "Preparation of Managers for Cross-Cultural Assignments," unpublished S.M. thesis, Sloan School of Management, M.I.T., 1971, p. 23.

[51]Van Zandt, "Japanese Culture," p. 355.

[52]Teague, *Selecting and Orienting*, p. 3.

managers. Communication skills and the demonstration of the cultural relativism of management policy and practice receive full treatment. There is nothing in the United States or Europe that can compare in quality and intensity. The major oversight is the isolation of Japanese wives from this sort of preparation, although, if traditional Japanese practice continues, few will live overseas with their husbands in any event. Another well-known institution is the Center for Education in International Management in Geneva, Switzerland. One should also note the course on directing foreign operations offered by the Administrative Staff College in Henley-on-Thames, England.

In a study of 403 Americans working in Asia,[53] it was found there was a high order of consistency in their ranking of training needs. The rankings of the first 15 are shown in Table 4.7.

With the hypothesis that Asians rank these training needs quite differently, the same question was put to 212 English-speaking Asian nationals with whom the Americans had worked. The rankings were remarkably similar for the first three, as can be noted in Table 4.8. The ranking of "orientation for service" reflected the greatest disparity. The author comments:

Apparently the motivation of Americans for working overseas appears somewhat more important to the Asian nationals than it does to Americans already overseas. The Asian nationals agree with findings of Cleveland, Mangone, and Adams that "belief in mission" is one of the five elements most relevant to success overseas.[54]

The low rating by both groups of language ability should be noted.

An open-ended question asked the Asian respondents to identify the most needed areas of training in an orientation program for Americans preparing to work overseas. Typical comments were:

Taiwan: **Attitude of humility. The greatest hindrance to working successfully overseas is the attitude of intellectual, cultural, and religious superiority. Although Americans are sent out to help, and possibly to change the lives of other peoples, they should also be ready to learn, to receive, and to be changed.**

Philippines: **Americans must not confuse a sense of service to the people with the imposition of their way of life; i.e., the development of other peoples does not necessarily mean their Americanization. I find most Americans I have worked with technically competent (in the area for which they were asked to serve) but terribly presumptuous, carrying around with them a tragic sense of "know-it-all" or self-superiority. A deep sense of partnership with local people and fellow workers is essential in their preparation.**

India: **Change in attitude. Most of them behave as if they are superior human beings,**

---

[53]Graduates of a five-month missionary orientation center program, one of the oldest orientation programs for Americans going overseas, and Peace Corps volunteers returning from service in Asia.

[54]Mary Johnson, "Training Needs of Overseas Americans as Seen by Their National Co-Workers in Asia," *IDR/Focus,* 1974, no. 4, p. 23. Reference is to H. Cleveland, G. J. Mangone, and J. C. Adams, *The Overseas Americans* (New York: McGraw-Hill, 1969). The five elements: technical skill, belief in mission, cultural empathy, a sense of politics, and organizational ability.

Table 4.7

TRAINING NEEDS FOR AMERICANS OVERSEAS
(N = 403)

1. *A sense for politics* (awareness of political conditions in assigned country; alertness to political consequences of everyday behavior)

2. *Skill as change agent* (the ability to work toward change)

3. *Ability to keep records* (skill in keeping simple records and accounts)

4. *Human relations skills* (ability to work with others, based on understanding oneself and the structure and dynamics of human society)

5. *Teaching skills* (an understanding of and ability to apply the principles of learning and teaching)

6. *Understanding of mission* (having a sense of the purpose of and enthusiasm about one's job and organization)

7. *Technical competence* (ability to do the job: knowing the subject matter and techniques in one's field)

8. *Health knowledge* (an understanding of the principles essential for maintaining physical and mental health)

9. *Orientation for service* (an understanding of the value of all human life and potential, such that one is motivated to serve fellow human beings)

10. *Organizational ability* (ability to combine personnel and resources into dynamic self-sustaining enterprises: ability to "work oneself out of" the job by developing self-sustaining institutions and by training local national personnel to manage them)

11. *Ability to adapt* (flexibility: ability to adapt learning to unlike situations; ability to adjust oneself to change)

12. *Understanding of other cultures* (cross-cultural understanding; the skill to understand the inner logic and coherence of other ways of life, plus the restraint not to judge them as "bad" because they are different from one's own ways; cultural empathy)

13. *Understanding of American culture* (insight into Western values, mores, attitudes, behavior patterns)

14. *Language ability* (a growing ability to express oneself in, and to understand, the language of the adopted country)

15. *Sensitivity training* (self-insight, self-understanding, sensitivity to feelings of others)

Source: M.B. Johnston and G.L. Carter, Jr., "Training Needs of Americans Working Abroad," *Social Change*, 1972, reprinted in Mary B. Johnston, "Training Needs of Overseas Americans as Seen by Their National Co-Workers in Asia," *IDR/Focus*, 1974, no. 4, p. 22.

although we do not believe they are. Some of them who are in the technical fields are not experts and they should be prepared to learn from their colleagues. . . . Americans who are undergoing orientation courses should be made to believe that Indians are intellectual.[55]

The reader may draw his own conclusion as to the relevancy of these findings to the expatriate business manager.

4.3 PROMOTION OF OVERSEAS MANAGEMENT

Three strategies are possible in the promotion of overseas management: national (limiting management careers to national operations), binational (possi-

---

[55]Johnston, "Training Needs," p. 24.

Table 4.8

RANKS OF IMPORTANCE OF TRAINING NEEDS FOR AMERICANS WORKING OVERSEAS AS DETERMINED BY RATINGS BY RESPONDENTS

Training need	Ranking by responses of Americans (N = 403)	Ranking by responses of nationals (N = 131)
Human relations skill	1	1
Understanding of other culture	2	2
Ability to adapt	3	3
Technical competence	4	6.5*
Sensitivity training	5	6.5
A sense of politics	6	12.5†
Language ability	7	9
Understanding of mission	8	5
Understanding of American culture	9	15
Orientation for service	10	4

*The two training needs that tied for sixth rank are both ranked 6.5.
†The two training needs that tied for 12th place are ranked as 12.5.
Source: Johnson, "Training Needs," p. 23.

ble promotion to parent corporate headquarters), multinational (no regard for nationality in promotion policy except where relevent to effectiveness). Valid considerations for the selection of an optimum promotion policy include:

1. legal restraints on emigration and employment of aliens (for example, on emigration and employment of aliens, such as are laid down by the United States law on communications and defense industry);

2. family participation in ownership and management of an associated foreign enterprise, which may result in conflicting loyalty if promoted to another associated firm;

3. inability to set up a consistent worldwide remuneration strategy (see Section 4.4);

4. degree of autonomy of associated firms in that the parent may not be in a position to dictate career paths;

5. preference on the part of key managerial personnel (they may not wish to move physically and, hence, one must weigh the risk and cost of losing them versus cost of replacement);

6. relative cost per comparable management-year for the various options;

7. ownership of the parent firm (if owned in significant measure by foreign nationals, a multinational management may become compelling);

8. relative size of foreign and domestic market (if the foreign is relatively large and has been developed by foreign nationals, the pressure to promote them to top corporate positions may be irresistible);

9. direction of major flows of technical development and skills (a similar phenomenon may take place here if the flows are obviously from foreign *to* domestic; then the appointment of foreign nationals to corporate headquarters would appear desirable);

10. availability of parent-country nationals able to interpret communications from abroad (if there are none, clearly foreign nationals must be used in headquarters);

11. involvement in foreign legal problems, thus requiring skills not available locally;

12. relative importance of foreign-source financing, thus possibly requiring special skills.

Insofar as U.S.-based international companies are concerned, there seem to be relatively few non-U.S. nationals in top corporate positions. But their number would appear to be growing, although admittedly the subject has not been well researched. A 1974 study of 62 U.S. corporations found that 47 hired foreign nationals for management positions within the United States.[56]

In a *Business International* study of 77 U.S.-based firms in 1970, only 14 were found to have rotated executives systematically through foreign and domestic posts, and only three indicated that it was stated corporate policy that to advance in the firm both domestic and foreign experience were necessary. These responses were softened somewhat by frequent observations that such practices were desirable.[57]

But another study seems to point to a growing trend in that it reports,

Personal experience of international operations is becoming increasingly important for the senior managers in the central office. Many presidents of multinational enterprises . . . were in charge of international divisions earlier in their careers.[58]

The authors of the study from which the above was extracted go on to opine, "The experience of senior executives in international business can help greatly to reduce the communications problem that exists between domestic and foreign units."

The multinational promotional strategy is particularly difficult for Japanese-based firms. The realization of this fact may be one reason that the Japanese generally seem to be internationalizing through the joint-venture and contractual route rather than through the creation of a family of centrally-controlled and integrated subsidiaries. Kobayashi writes,

---

[56]De Shields and Robinson, "An Inquiry."

[57]*Compensating International Executives* (New York: Business International, 1970), p. 1.

[58]John M. Stopford and Louis T. Wells, Jr., "Ironing Out the New Relationships," *Worldwide P&I Planning*, May–June 1972, p. 35. Reprinted fom Stopford and Wells, *Managing the Multinational Enterprise* (New York: Basic Books, Inc., 1972).

Despite the good will and intention to promote the locals in the overseas market, Japanese executives seem to experience a strong mental resistance when we discuss the stage of promoting the locals to managerial positions in their headquarters' organization. This is largely due to the closed culture of Japan and the resulting deficiencies of linguistic ability of many Japanese executives.[59]

Kobayashi feels that this situation may change in that a few Japanese corporations have bought out companies abroad, particularly in the more developed countries, and have retained the foreign managements. Consequently, there are examples, albeit very few, of large Japanese-owned companies presided over by non-Japanese executives. He feels that ultimately these executives must be appointed to "top board positions" in the parent Japanese companies.[60]

It is generally recognized that if the firm locks its foreign managers within their respective national firms eventually one of three things happens: (1) as the maturity and stature of the local management increases vis-à-vis that in headquarters, it becomes increasingly difficult for the headquarters to control, hence, local autonomy increases; (2) as competent, ambitious, foreign nationals hit the promotion ceiling, they leave the firm; (3) the company breaks its nationality policy and creates a multinational management. This last process is possibly accelerated—if not made compelling—if parent company equity is owned in significant amount by local nationals. It has been responsibly predicted that within a decade or so the headquarters of any firm operating internationally will "resemble a veritable U.N., peopled by dozens upon dozens of nationalities; the battle for the presidency will be a multinational one."[61] (See Chapter 8.)

There are some demonstrable differences in promotion policy from country to country. An example is the difference revealed by a 1968 survey of 138 business executives in Mexico selected from the largest business firms in Mexico (97 Mexican, 41 U.S. subsidiaries in Mexico).[62] It was found that the "Mexican firms prefer to bring a man from outside who has had some experience in management and make him president or vice-president." On the other hand, American firms in Mexico appeared "to emphasize hierarchical mobility and promotion from within more than the Mexican firms."[63]

---

[59]Noritake Kobayashi, "The International Manager Development by the Japanese Multinationals" (Tokyo: typed manuscript, February 1976), p. 12.

[60]Kobayashi, "International Manager," p. 12.

[61]*1985: Corporate Planning Today for Tomorrow's World Market* (New York: Business International, 1970), summarized in *Business Europe,* March 4, 1969.

[62]Guvenc G. Alpander, "A Comparative Study of Executives in Mexican Firms in Mexico," *Southern Journal of Business,* May 1971, p. 64.

[63]Alpander, "Comparative Study," p. 66.

4.4 REMUNERATION

Although an exceedingly complex subject, the choice of basic strategies relating to the remuneration of international management is limited to two: (1) multiple (that is, parent country personnel on a parent country salary scale, all others on the relevant local scales) or (2) an international base plus a variety of extras. Commonly included among such extras are a cost of living differential, an expatriate bonus to compensate for being away from home, and a number of personal adjustment payments (language training, moving allowance, children's education, home leave, entertainment, special health and accident insurance).

It should be noted that the salary differential between expatriates and local national managers is likely to vary according to job level, narrowing as one ascends the managerial pyramid. A large U.S.-based chemical firm found differentials at four levels, as shown in Table 4.9.

In some socialist countries the relationship between cash salaries paid to management may be a very low multiple of the wages paid to labor, not infrequently only three or two. However, there may be a much greater difference if all of the goods and services received by managers are taken into account, such perquisites as use of a car, large and well-located apartments, and access to special consumer goods denied the ordinary citizen.

A special problem arises in the international area due to the need (1) to provide inducement to leave the home country (or to return), (2) to maintain a home-country standard of living, (3) to facilitate reentry into the home country (through maintenance of a home and professional updating), (4) to meet the requirements of children's education, and (5) to maintain social obligations vis-à-vis friends and family. The obvious cost of these many payments to already highly paid U.S. or Northern European managers constitutes pressure toward the localization of management, or the employment of third-country nationals.

For example, a 1973 survey showed that the average American assigned to Paris received, in addition to his $18,000 base salary, an overseas premium of $2,411, a cost of living allowance of $4,693, a housing allowance of $5,503, an education allowance (for the schoolage children) of $4,600, airfare for a third child in a U.S. college of $879, and home leave transportation every second year for an annual average of $1,100. The total allowance worked out to be $19,186, for a gross annual cost of $37,186.[64] A frequently-used

---

[64]Calvin Reynolds, *1968–1973 Policy Changes Which Affect the Income of Americans Working Abroad— Preliminary Results* (New York: National Foreign Trade Council, 1973). (See also note 17.)

Table 4.9
U.S. AND EUROPEAN SALARIES AT
FOUR MANAGEMENT LEVELS

	Base Pay in U.S.			
	$10,000	$14,750	$21,300	$28,000
United States	100	100	100	100
Belgium	60	62	72	89
Germany	57	64	69	78
Luxembourg	52	58	63	71
United Kingdom	39	41	46	56
France	55	65	76	n.a.

Note: Thirteenth month pay is included in appropriate cases; comparisons were made between September 1969 and June 1970.

Source: Compensating International Executives, p. 10.

rule-of-thumb is to multiply a U.S. salary by 2½ to derive the total cost of the employee in an overseas assignment.

Almost inevitably, at some stage both parent-country nationals and foreign nationals are employed as managers within the same overseas enterprise. Additionally, there is a tendency to limit the use of parent-country managers more and more to start-up teams or for trouble shooting, which means transfer from one foreign assignment to another. Finally, as enterprises develop, and correspondingly their managerial personnel, nonparent-country nationals may well be shifted, including periods of assignment to the parent country. Therefore, a purely national wage policy becomes inoperative, for otherwise personnel cannot easily be transferred; they may refuse assignment to a post promising less total emoluments. Complicating the problem further are such factors as exchange controls and currency of payment (how much is to be paid in dollars, how much in local currency? what do the regulations permit?), national social security payments (benefits from which an alien national will never realize), exclusion from one's own social security system (by reason of prolonged absence), and diverse rates of taxation of personal income.

For illustrative purposes only, the compensation policy set up by one U.S.-based international firm is described. *For U.S. personnel overseas,* this firm paid a base salary equal to the U.S. salary, added to which was an expatriate or overseas bonus (varying between zero percent for Western Europe to 35 percent of base salary for more remote and unpleasant posts), a cost of living adjustment (zero to 70 percent of spendable income, which was estimated to be that amount of total income deemed actually spent on normal living expenses excluding housing, utilities, taxes, and insurance, the adjustment being based on the U.S. State Department's "Local Index of Living Costs Abroad"), and several personal adjustment payments (two-month home leave every two years, education expenses for children under college level, transportation and moving expenses between assignments, social and business club memberships, income tax differential).[65] American personnel were paid generally in local currency an amount equal to that paid to comparable local nationals, the balance being paid in dollars. In order to avoid income tax, local social security taxes (which would not benefit U.S. nationals), and foreign exchange control difficulties when the U.S. national wished to pay dollar obligations or create dollar savings, this dollar salary was generally not reported to the host government and was frequently paid into a Swiss account to the credit of the employee (a Swiss rather than a U.S. account so as to make certain that it had no appearance of having been earned within the United States and hence taxable within the United States).[66] *Local nationals* were paid the going local wage with no extra payment or dollar component. *Third-country personnel* were paid a base salary equal to that paid for a comparable position in the place where hired (not necessarily the country of national origin), plus a cost-of-living differential for which the place of hiring was used as the base. Income in excess of comparable local salary might be paid in the currency of country of origin.

The problems inherent in such a system are manifold and include the following:

1. It assumes that an individual's consumption function conforms to the average.

2. U.S. nationals receive more for the same job than either third-country or local nationals. (There is the possibility that a subordinate receives more than his superiors.)

3. Unreported "off-shore" (or split) income may be illegal vis-à-vis local tax authorities, and it cannot be shown as a cost against the local firm's taxable income. (Possibly not against parent company taxable income either. Yet, if the income were reported locally, it might be subject to foreign exchange control. Some attempt to justify the split income technique on the grounds that part of an expatriate's salary is directly attributable to the work he does for the parent company. At the very least, it is argued, a split income is justified to the extent that the manager travels outside of his base country.)

4. The value of off-shore income in the eyes of local nationals is very great and can set up tension.

5. A uniform, company-wide pension scheme is difficult to institute.

6. The transfer of local nationals often means higher cost.

7. Once having enjoyed higher income elsewhere, employees may resist reassignment to a lower income post, including their home country, even though costs may be lower (a money illusion may operate).

---

[65]If the foreign tax was less than the U.S. rate, the benefit was deducted from the cost of living differential.
[66]But the 1976 Tax Reform Act substantially reduced this rationale. See appendix to Chapter 8.

8. The necessarily arbitrary nature of expatriate bonuses and cost-of-living differentials sets up tensions.

9. Absence of local authority over salary structure may cause friction.

10. A company-wide profit-sharing system is virtually impossible.

11. Inclusion under the U.S. social security system must be considered.

12. Maintaining acceptable salary and benefit ratios among various levels of management and of labor may be desirable.

It is of interest to note that a few firms have a policy of reducing overseas allowances after a period of time. The assumption is that as time passes the transferee approaches the buying habits and customs of the local inhabitants, thus rendering the initial cost-of-living allowance untenable.

A general policy followed by a few firms is that of paying an international base salary without regard for nationality or place of hiring, plus whatever expenses are incurred by reason of employment with the company, including a cost-of-living differential (with the country in which the parent company is domiciled as the base). Each national enterprise may have its own pension plan in which local nationals continue to participate regardless of where they may be assigned. The entire base salary and cost-of-living differential is paid in the currency of one's citizenship directly by the employing enterprise. In case foreign exchange controls operate, the local firm must negotiate with the host government for currency exchange by its nonnational employees of a certain portion of their respective incomes. Special adjustment payments may be made directly in the relevant foreign currency by the parent company. Thus, an international management cadre consisting of career foreign service executives is created. Formerly commonplace in the large European firms, one suspects that as firms become truly multinational there is likely to be little or no distinction between foreign and domestic managers. Above a certain level, all will be placed on a global salary scale, subject only to cost-of-living and tax equalization allowances. Any pension and profit-sharing rights will be in respect to the consolidated corporate family. In poorer countries, of course, such a scheme has the effect of widening the disparities in income distribution.

As is well known in the United States, there are significant tax benefits for employees where deferred compensation is provided under a retirement plan qualified under the Internal Revenue Code of 1954 in that personal income tax is deferred until the income is actually received, at which time one's tax rate is likely to be substantially lower. Among the conditions a qualified plan must satisfy is the provision that its benefits extend to 70 percent or more of all eligible employees. Prior to the Employment Retirement Security Act of 1974 (ERISA), *all* employees of a corporate employer, regardless of citizenship or country of residence (or whether they had received income taxable in the United States), were considered "employees" for the purpose of applying the minimum participation standards. Hence, if a U.S. corporation operated through a branch overseas, all employees of that branch had to be included.

However, if it operated through a subsidiary, the employer was then a different corporation, and the subsidiary employees could be excluded. *But,* if one wanted to include U.S. citizens employed by such a subsidiary, they could be treated as employees of the U.S. parent but only if the minimum participation standards continued to be met including all of the subsidiary's employees. Also, U.S. expatriates would be so treated only if the U.S. parent had entered into an agreement to extend social security coverage to them. ERISA added a provision that for the purpose of applying the minimum participation standards, a corporation's employees would not include nonresident aliens who receive no income from the employer from sources within the United States. For these purposes a foreign subsidiary is defined as a foreign corporation, 20 percent or more of the voting stock of which is owned by a U.S. parent, and any 50 percent-owned foreign subsidiary of such a foreign corporation.

In practice, U.S. expatriate managers are almost invariably kept in the parent company pension scheme. It should be noted that a manager cannot be retained in a U.S. pension scheme unless he is covered by social security; that is, the payments made by the company will not be deductible from taxable income as a legitimate business expense. Coverage by U.S. social security is possible if (1) the U.S. firm owns at least 20 percent of the foreign firm employing the expatriate (and 50 percent of a second tier corporation if employed by such) and (2) if an agreement is executed with the Internal Revenue Service. Meanwhile, by local law, the manager and his employer may be required to contribute to a local social security system from which the employee is unlikely ever to benefit. Not infrequently, local national managers are excluded from headquarters' benefit plans, which fact causes another asymmetry in treatment of expatriate managers as contrasted to the local national managers. Nor are they generally eligible to participate in the qualified pension plan of the parent company. The firm really has three options: (1) set up local national pension plans, (2) pay local national managers from the U.S. payroll and thereby include them within the parent company program, or (3) set up a pension plan in a base company covering all non-U.S. executives. The first seems to be generally preferred. The third-country national may be included either under the pension plan where he is employed or under that within his home country. Unfortunately, many countries do not extend their social security systems to nationals employed abroad as does the United States.

4.5 SELECTION OF MANAGERIAL STYLE[67]

There would seem to be at least four significant dimensions to managerial style: (1) degree of subordinate participation in decision-making, (2) degree of cal-

---

[67]See Section 3.2 for a discussion of participative management, 5.1 for profit-sharing and ownership-sharing.

culation as contrasted with impressionism (intuition) in decision-making, (3) the degree of formality (for example, the presence of formal and informal channels of communication from one's subordinates to one's superiors and to those horizontally equal in power to the superior who may influence one), and (4) vertical consistency (the consistency in managerial style from one level to another). The relevant question for the international firm is whether the establishment of a universally applicable, single style along one or more of these dimensions is optimum.

A continuum of subordinate participation in decision-making would run thusly:

1. Superior makes own decision with no explanation and with little or no thought of subordinate (autocratic).

2. Superior makes own decision with no explanation but with considerable thought of subordinates (paternalistic).

3. Superior makes own decision, but with fairly complete explanation to subordinates so that they will be aware of why the decision was made (explanatory).

4. Superior makes own decision with no explanation because of prior knowledge of (or feel for) the attitudes, values, and opinions of subordinates, which he or she has taken into consideration (empathetic).

5. Superior makes own decision, but fairly complete explanation for the purpose of gaining the support of subordinates (supportive).

6. Superior makes own decision, but with fairly complete explanation to subordinates to indicate (1) that he or she has considered their known attitudes, values, and opinions, and (2) to gain their support (empathetic-supportive).

7. Superior makes own decision after consultation with subordinates (consultative).

8. Decision is made jointly by superior and subordinate, but is articulated by the superior to his boss (participative).

9. Decision is made jointly by leader and subordinates and is articulated to the superior's boss as a group decision (collective or joint).

10. Decision is delegated to subordinates, but is subject to superior's influence (partially delegated).

11. Decision is delegated entirely to subordinate (delegated).

Admittedly, styles 10 and 11 do not tell us how the subordinate makes the decision, who, in turn, may opt for any one of the styles listed.

The depth of management participation may be an important dimension. Participation may be limited to top-management levels (chief executives, principal staff directors, division managers), to upper-middle management (department heads and plant managers), to lower-middle management (section chiefs), to lower management (supervisors and foremen), or may be extended to include all employees (labor). This last form is discussed in Section 3.2. A closely associated subject is, of course, profit-sharing and ownership-sharing (discussed in Sections 3.6 and 5.1).

The point is that many studies of managerial style are too simplistic to produce valid findings. They assume either that the degree of participation is the only significant dimension to managerial style or that decision-making style is either participative or not. This latter assumption is like classifying all political systems simply into participative and nonparticipative without recognizing the essential difference between the single party regimes of Stalin and Ataturk or between the multiparty regimes of Sygman Rhee's Korea and Churchill's Britain. Even the four styles summarized in Table 3.1 (page 210) seem to be unduly restrictive.

When one considers the variables that must relate in some circumstances to choice of decision-making style as defined by degree of participation (see Figure 4.3), it is obvious that there can be no universally valid superior style. Even to dub one "modern" and the other "traditional," as some authors do, is surely misleading, given the state of present research.

In reviewing all of the major research of a comparative nature relating to managerial attitudes and behavior, Barrett and Bass concluded:

> *We interpret all the above studies on superior-subordinate relationships to indicate that there are differences among countries in preferred style of leadership. These differences in leadership styles appear to be largely culturally-based, and at this point of time it would appear naive to advocate one model of leadership style as being optimum for all cultural groups. The widely-advocated American model of participative management may not be optimum for all cultures, and in fact may be dysfunctional in some.*[68]

A 1973 survey of 75 expatriate U.S. managers apparently revealed a shift to a more authoritarian managerial style from that practiced in the United States prior to overseas assignment. First, the expatriates, on average, perceived their subordinates overseas as more resistant to change, but more loyal to the company, than their subordinates in the United States.[69] Furthermore, the executives tended to change their beliefs about subordinate employees after assuming overseas assignment. Very few of the respondents felt that U.S. subordinates were lazy, preferred to be led, did not want responsibility, or had to be closely controlled. The number of these same executives associating these qualities to their overseas subordinates tripled.[70] Several of the executives felt that the threat of firing was an effective motivational factor abroad, though not in the United States. And several felt that improving working conditions was an acceptable way of motivating subordinates to achieve higher productivity and was more effective in the overseas case. The

---

[68]Gerald V. Barrett and Bernard M. Bass, "Comparative Studies of Managerial Attitudes and Behavior," Chapter 8 in J. Boddewyn, ed., *Comparative Management—Teaching, Training and Research* (New York: Graduate School of Business Administration, New York University, 1970), p. 194.

[69]Gurenc G. Alpander, "Drift to Authoritarianism: The Changing Managerial Styles of U.S. Executives Overseas," *Journal of International Business Studies*, Fall 1973, p. 8.

[70]Alpander, "Drift," p. 9.

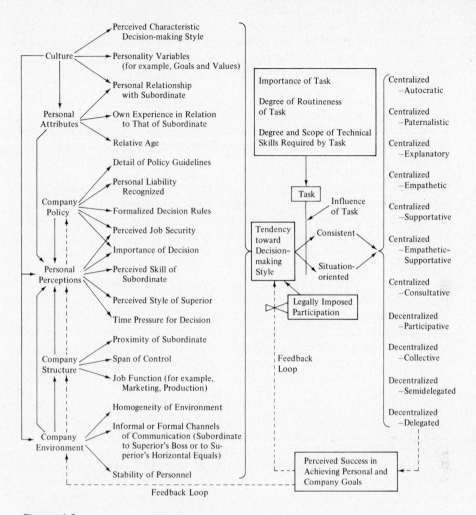

Figure 4.3
**DEVELOPMENT OF A DECISION-MAKING STYLE IN RELATION
TO DEGREE OF PARTICIPATION**

author pointed out, "This again concurs that what is good managerial style for the United States does not necessarily apply overseas."[71] "It is evident that the respondents in their present jobs overseas have become more authoritarian in decision-making."[72] "The findings conform to the situational theories of leadership behavior."[73]

[71]Alpander, "Drift," p. 9.
[72]Alpander, "Drift," p. 10.
[73]Alpander, "Drift," p. 13.

There has been little research and writing in reference to the second dimension of managerial style, the use of statistical information in making decisions versus own perception, intuitive assessment, or personal judgment, or in calculation versus impressionism. It has been observed that:

The American executive is number and fact oriented. This is often misleading in that facts and figures do not always contain all that is needed in making the "right" decision. The Latin American and European mind is much more well suited to the uniqueness of international business because they are humanistically oriented as opposed to the American factual orientation.[74]

One study of Mexican managers, previously referred to, reports a difference between managers of Mexican-controlled and U.S.-controlled firms in Mexico. In the former, about 70 percent said that they relied heavily on their perception and value judgment in making important decisions; in the latter, only 40 percent.[75] Giving some validity to the survey was the finding that regardless of types of business, 100 percent of the executives in the sample previously employed by the government indicated that they used perception and a "feel of the situation." It also came out that both the very small and the very large firms, whether Mexican or U.S.-controlled, had a large number of executives who could be classified as impressionists. It was the medium-sized organization (those with an employment capacity from 200 to 800 workers) that housed the majority of executives classified as calculatives. It was further found that the impressionists were promoted faster than the calculatives. Alpander observed:

In developing countries, such as Mexico, executives need self assurance, and they need to be quick in making their decisions in light of a rapidly changing environment. Therefore, expediency in decision-making by an intuitive approach is tolerated. This intuitive approach is not necessarily an asset in more developed countries like the United States, but it is definitely a characteristic that leads to success in environments like Mexico.[76]

The analysis goes on to conclude that "American firms in Mexico should take into consideration the decision-making characteristics of their executives in establishing recruitment and selection policies, since what is needed in Mexico is the ability to combine knowledge of scientific process with one's own judgment in making quick decisions." He also concludes, "Most of those executives who were classified as calculatives indicated that they could seldom

---

[74]Michael S. Werner, "Dealing with Governments in Developing Countries, Implications for the Multinational Enterprise," unpublished M.B.A. thesis, New York University Graduate School of Business Administration, 1971, p. 68.

[75]Alpander, "A Comparative Study of Executives in Mexican Firms in Mexico," p. 71.

[76]Alpander, "Comparative Study," p. 72.

derive a feeling of achievement, or a sense of personal growth, from their jobs."[77]

Very little can be said about the degree to which informal channels of communication from subordinate to superior or from subordinate to others on the same level as his superior are characteristic of enterprises in various societies. The subject seems not to have been researched. But it appears that there may be national differences on this score, in part a function of the status consciousness within a society and the degree to which voluntary, private associations are present. Who belongs to which clubs, associations (for example, Masonic lodges in some countries), churches, and political parties? What sort of off-the-job social intercourse takes place in such organizations may well influence the nature of the subordinate-superior relationship on the job and even the locale or forum in which decisions are made. If A knows that B, his subordinate, can talk freely and intimately with either C, A's boss, or D, who is on A's level, the relationship between A and B is likely to be affected and so likewise the decision-making style. It may be that really important decisions are not made in the office hierarchical context at all but within a more fluid group around the table at the club. In some cases, this circumvention of one's immediate superiors may be institutionalized, as reflected in the policy of some German companies previously commented upon (that is, if a subordinate wishes to speak with one above his superior, it is his right to do so and an interview will be scheduled within a certain period of time).

A fourth dimension of managerial style is vertical consistency, not only in respect to various forms of participation, but also to the degree of calculation and formality in decision making. To the extent that an elite upper management adopts a particular style that is inconsistent with managerial style at lower levels (whether a function of social, psychological, or educationally induced differences), lack of communication may become a problem on the interface, at whatever level that may be. An alien management from an industrially developed country operating in a less developed country may find itself precisely in this situation. If so, substantial inputs of patience, education, and training may be required to bridge the gap, or an adaption to the lower-level style by those functioning at the interface. Again, there seems to be very little research bearing directly on this problem.

No discussion of managerial style would be complete without some reference to the Japanese system, which is identified by the phrase *ringi-seido*, literally, "the system of submitting a proposal to one's superior and receiving his approval." The initiative for a decision may be at any level down to middle management, but the formal process starts with the preparation of a written proposal at the middle-management level. The proposal then works its way up

---

[77] Alpander, "Comparative Study," p. 73.

both laterally and horizontally. If anyone objects along the way, a meeting is called and the problem talked out until there is a consensus. The process then continues to the top level, at which point the decision is articulated by the chief executive. Four observations should be made. *First*, though certainly time consuming, this style of decision-making means that everyone is fully aware of the details of a decision, and of his respective role in implementing it at the moment of articulation by the chief executive. Hence, implementation is immediate. (Indeed, the point is made that the elapsed time from the moment a project is proposed to actual implementation is about the same for a Japanese and a U.S. firm. The former takes longer to reach a decision; the latter, to implement a project after a decision has been made. Consequently, each may be critical of the other for delay.) *Second*, this system may only work effectively in association with two other characteristics of the Japanese managerial system, life-time tenure and promotion by seniority. *Third*, a manager can through the *ringi* system be important without being president. Although many Japanese corporate chief executives are very important and much admired and respected men, one gets the impression that *as individuals* they are not as important in formulating decisions as, say, many of their U.S. counterparts. *Fourth*, in view of the sociopsychological evidence that decisions made in groups are more likely to be riskier than decisions made individually,[78] it may be that the Japanese system is less risk-averse than the U.S. or European. The individual does not bear the responsibility; the group does.

The idea of collective responsibility is related to a feeling called shu-jo-nu-on *(gratitude to nature and other human beings for one's success). To conform to this concept requires abandoning the idea of individual power domination in favor of cooperative group action where no man's success may be attributed to his brains and the strength of his two arms unaided and alone. The great emphasis on harmony sometimes surprises Occidental visitors; a manager may describe with pride the spirit of concord prevalent in his factory, rather than the profits it makes, even where the profits are high.*[79]

In Japanese, there seems to be no precise equivalent for the common phrase, "the self-made man."

In a 1976 survey of Japanese executive opinion (305 company presidents), the "*ringi*" system was felt by 42.0 percent to be a very effective way to encourage participation in decision-making and to maintain high morale. Another 21.0 percent felt that it helped to maintain better communication, both

---

[78]See James A. F. Stoner, "A Comparison of Individual and Group Decisions Involving Risk," unpublished S.M. thesis, Alfred P. Sloan School of Management, M.I.T., 1961; K. L. Dion, R. S. Baron, N. Miller, "Why Do Groups Make Riskier Decisions Than Individuals?" in L. Berkowitz, ed., *Advances in Experimental Sociology*, vol. 5 (New York: Academy Press, 1970), pp. 305–377; and Roger Brown, *Social Psychology* (New York: The Free Press, 1965), pp. 656–708.

[79]Van Zandt, "Japanese Culture," p. 348.

vertically and horizontally. Three percent felt that it encouraged the input of creative ideas by the junior echelon of management. Only 22.3 percent reacted negatively (for 10.8 percent it tended to blur responsibility and accountability in decision-making; for 9.5 percent it was time consuming; for 2 percent the process was likely to be stereotyped and bureaucratic).[80]

Finally, attention should be drawn to the Yugoslav system of workers' self-management and to the Chinese system of role exchange (and suppression of class or status consciousness). These three quite different systems—the Japanese, the Yugoslav, and the Chinese—all appear to be generating and sustaining a relatively high level of creativity and productivity. The problems inherent in a continuing relationship between a North American or West European firm with a Japanese, Yugoslav, or Chinese enterprise are legion. Experience is accumulating in reference to the Japanese. In the Yugoslav case, the age and number of international joint ventures are so restricted that generalizations are difficult. It has been observed that such ventures are normally managed by a joint operating board on which sit representatives of management of the two contracting firms. This board is required to submit certain matters to the workers' council for decision. These would include distribution of income belonging to the Yugoslav partner, salaries of personnel working for the joint venture, the joint venture's annual economic plan, the organizational structure of the joint venture, and the hiring and firing of workers.[81]

The thrust of this discussion is that the present practice of international firms in the selection, preparation, and promotion of international managerial personnel hardly seems to be the best. The remuneration problem is of a more tangible nature and, hence, has been given somewhat greater attention, but the interplay of conflicting laws and regulations and constantly shifting price levels and foreign exchange rates make the creation of an entirely equitable system exceedingly difficult without involving the firm in what would appear unnecessary cost. Finally, it is quite apparent that there is no universally best managerial style (in degree of participation, use of quantitative calculations, or in terms of formality and consistency). The latter observation relates to the selection and preparation of international managers in that individuals with very different personality attributes, managerial philosophies, and calculative skills may all perform well, but in different environments. The problem lies in matching people to situations, which implies an ability to measure both with something more than random success. Obviously, the measures are imperfect, but such imperfection does not preclude sensitivity to the problem and effort.

This view is challenged by the so-called universalists, those who insist that

[80]*Nikkei Business* (Tokyo), 27 September 1976, p. 72.

[81]For further details, see Miodrag Sukijasovic, *Foreign Investment in Yugoslavia* (New York: Oceana Publications, 1970), pp. 142–46.

there is a common pattern of behavior (based on similar values) among all managers regardless of the cultural milieu in which they operate. Induced by the discipline imposed by modern industry, this common pattern is seen as a world managerial culture. Differences among managers are thus perceived as reflecting personal, situational, or organizational differences. It should be pointed out that this definition begs a question, for if there is a *consistent* difference in personal behavior, situation, or organization, the impact of culture may thus be revealed.

A modification of the universalist view is that of the cultural cluster school, in which similarities of managerial values and behavior within multinational cultural areas are emphasized. Most frequent groupings are Nordic-European, Latin-European, Anglo-American, developing countries and Japan.[82]

A third point of view is that managerial behavior is strongly influenced by key environmental characteristics, particularly the economic (for example, the levels of industrialization and wealth). Other possibly important factors are size of relevant markets, occupational mix, density of population, level of popular education, prevailing politicoeconomic ideology, social structure, and ethnic-religious homogeneity.

These views may not be as inconsistent as would first appear. That is, the production function (as technologically defined) and the competitiveness of the international market (even if not the domestic) impose certain pressures on the managerial team of an enterprise wherever located. However, given the general cultural environment of a region (the degree of commonality being a function of common history, languages, depth of social-economic-political intercourse), managers within that area tend to react to these systemic pressures in a similar fashion in terms of values and behavior. But, in societies that are unique along some important dimension (such as size, wealth, politico-economic ideology, population density, social structure), managerial values and behavior are likely to be distinctive. Therefore, one may hypothesize that any study designed to demonstrate *globally* either the universality or cultural-relativity of managerial behavior will be inconclusive.

One difficulty in some studies directed to this subject is that they may not have homed in on the really key values and behavior patterns that differentiate managers operating within different cultures. Also, the samples have to be picked with great care. For example, should public sector managers be included in countries in which the public sector industry is a significant part of the total? If they are not, the results of a comparative study could well be vitiated in that among the essential dimensions of managerial values and behavior are those having to do with managerial motivation and organizational goals. These may vary substantially between public and private sector enterprise, and the fact that a society has opted for greater activity in the public

---

[82]For example, see M. Haire, E. E. Chiselli, and L. W. Porter, *Managerial Thinking: An International Study* (New York: John Wiley & Sons, 1966).

sector may be of signal importance. Another possibly relevant dimension is the occupational mix. Certain managerial values and behavior may tend to be associated with specific activities (such as banking, accounting, mass assembly-line industry, high technology industry, agro-business).

Barrett and Bass suggest seven variables in describing management behavior: (1) superior-subordinate relationship, (2) managerial needs or motivation, (3) interpersonal perceptions, (4) organizational goals, (5) perception of equity, (6) decision-making under uncertainty, and (7) managerial values. In respect to the first, the two authors, after surveying the literature of comparative organization, conclude that there are strong arguments against the view that the participative form of management has universal application throughout the world.[83] Without being inconsistent, one can go on to claim that participative management may represent the most highly evolved form of management. That it is not immediately effective in large areas of the world is not surprising. Effective participative management may require that labor and management have consistent goals and similar time horizons, conditions implying a fairly high level of sophistication and material well-being on the part of all concerned (a fairly rare condition).

Managerial needs and motivation, whether measured by a ranking of needs or of life goals, would appear to be remarkably similar around the world but with some significant differences. In order to be more certain of these findings, however, one would have to know (1) whether managers were more similar than nonmanagers, (2) whether public-sector managers differ significantly from private-sector managers, and (3) whether there were significant occupational differences.[84] Perhaps all that these studies tell us is that there is some hierarchy of human need that tends to be universal, at least among secularly educated people no longer directly concerned with daily survival. But these studies do not tell us how those needs are translated into personal or organizational behavior in a given environment.

In fact, what evidence exists would tend to demonstrate significant national differences among managers in respect to interpersonal perception (that is, accuracy of one's perception of others, degree to which one attributes his own traits to others, and the degree to which one assumes others to have a different priority of goals than oneself).[85] Also, in respect to ranking organizational objectives, significant differences among managers of various countries seem to have been demonstrated, with the key independent variables being economic. For example, more developed country managers seem to put more stress upon the objectives of growth and competition; less developed country managers, upon the maintenance of satisfactory organizational operations.

---

[83]Barrett and Bass, "Comparative Studies," p. 182.

[84]That occupational differences may be significant is suggested by David Sirota and J. Michael Greenwood, "Understanding Your Overseas Workforce," *Harvard Business Review*, January–February, 1971, pp. 55–56.

[85]Barrett and Bass, "Comparative Studies," p. 199.

Also, apparently significant differences have been demonstrated in reference to perceived equity in work rewards. In at least some less developed countries as opposed to some more developed countries, managers appear to be more inclined to give a smaller pay differential to above-average performers and to take into account in setting pay both extenuating personal circumstances and job conditions.

A recent study of the attitudes of Indian managers, using the same instrument as a comparable study of U.S. managers,[86] concluded,

Attitudes tended to differ between countries more than between senior and middle management levels....

There were significant differences between countries on 12 [of 19] scales. Compared to American managers, Indian managers tend to have a higher level of general cynicism, a high confidence in classical theory of management, a high faith in group decision making, and to see greater opportunities in larger companies. American managers tend to favor minimal intervention by labor and government, to see little conflict between personal morals and the managerial role, to have a high faith in workers, a high interpersonal orientation, a low cynicism about getting ahead and conformity pressures, and to favor specialization.

... an American manager in India might find a higher level of government and labor intervention in the processes of management. On the basis of this research, he could be expected to express attitudes against such intervention. However, he should not expect much agreement from Indian managers. On the other hand, an Indian manager in the United States might express general cynicism concerning the role of business in society and the possibility of conducting business on a high moral plane. He should not expect an American manager to be sympathetic to this view.

Furthermore, the American manager in India might confuse his Indian counterpart with his high expectations of Indian subordinates. He might find the Indian manager seeking a group decision in matters that seem best handled by allowing the individual to assume responsibility. He would find the Indian manager unconvinced by American beliefs regarding proper promotional practices in business. The Indian in the United States might observe that the American manager voluntarily structures his private life and personal behavior to fit the perceived norms of the organization. Therefore, the Indian could find the American to be relatively insensitive to external pressures to conform.[87]

Recent research also seems to have demonstrated national differences in decision-making under uncertainty, a finding based on the selection of given pay-offs at different risk levels. For example, Indian managers were found to be more likely to opt for an ideal outcome with high risk than for a moderately

---

[86]Schein's "Public Opinion Questionnaire II." See Edgar H. Schein, "Attitude Change During Management Education," *Administrative Science Quarterly*, vol. 4, March 1967.

[87]Bernard E. Smith and John M. Thomas, "Cross Cultural Attitudes Among Managers: A Case Study," *Sloan Management Review*, Spring 1972, pp. 46–47.

successful outcome with moderate risk (the choice of most U.S. managers).[88]

Some research would seem to support the idea that managerial values are perhaps similar cross-culturally, particularly in terms of degree of pragmatism.[89] But the public-private sector problem, the occupational base problem, as well as the linking of values to behavior and organizational characteristics, remain. Also, none of the research suggests that a certain set of values or behavior pattern is associated with the most *effective* management despite environmental conditions.

A 1970 study by Richard Wright based on matched pairs[90] of companies in Chile (U.S. subsidiaries versus Chilean-owned and managed firms) provides added support for the environmentalist view as against the universalist. In the Wright study, the critical environmental constraints consisted of rapid cost inflation, price control, labor law, and the small market size. Measures of managerial effectiveness used were net profit, a five-year trend in net profit, return on investment, a five-year trend in return on investment, and percentage change in sales and market share. The conclusion of the study was that the locally owned firms were doing better than their American counterparts. A study of the internal operations of the firm revealed that the U.S. firms were operated essentially according to guidelines set down by parent company headquarters whereas the management philosophy of the Chilean firms generally was "based on highly individualized patterns of policies and practices, usually characteristic of the personal value systems of the president and local boards of directors of those firms." These basic differences appeared to affect the relative ability "to adapt to the conditions of the Chilean environment in at least two different ways": (1) the U.S. firms had a more complex and costly management structure and (2) the U.S. firms responded more slowly to rapid changes in the environment.[91]

The evidence accumulates. A study in three very similar factories in France, England, and Scotland concluded,

Recent work in the field of cross-cultural research on business organizations by psychologists and economists has tended to lay stress upon the businessman as a cross-cultural phenomenon—motivated by the same needs and employing the same methods to achieve those needs. We believe, as the result of this research, backed up by twelve years experience of management in both countries, that such findings are extremely superficial.[92]

---

[88]Barrett and Bass, "Comparative Studies," p. 202.

[89]Barrett and Bass, "Comparative Studies," p. 203.

[90]Matched in terms of product, size, labor (hire from the same labor pool, preferably the same region), and market (preferably the domestic Chilean market).

[91]Summarized from Richard W. Wright, "Organizational Ambients: Management and Environment in Chile," *Academy of Management Journal*, March 1971, pp. 65 ff.

[92]Desmond Graves, "The Impact of Culture upon Managerial Attitudes, Beliefs and Behavior in England and France," *Journal of Management Studies*, vol. 9, no. 1, February 1972, p. 55.

A 1972 Norwegian study[93] came up with some fairly impressive evidence of significant cross-cultural differences in the attitudes of chief executives toward supervisory values and practices. Statistically significant differences among five regions (United States, Western Europe, Commonwealth nations, Latin America, Asia) were found in references to the following questions:

1. Are owners more interested in employee well-being than their managers? (highest agreement in Western Europe; lowest in Latin America and Asia)

2. Must successful leaders be exceptionally self-confident? (highest agreement in Western Europe; lowest in Asia)

3. Do successful leaders direct subordinates in exactly what they should do and how to do it? (highest agreement in Asia, lowest in the United States)

4. Do successful leaders involve as many people as possible in making important decisions? (highest agreement in Latin America and Asia, neutral in others)

5. Are major policy decisions made by a committee superior to those made by the chief executive alone? (a tendency to agree in Asia and Latin America, to disagree in the United States and the Commonwealth countries).

Significant differences were *not* found on some subjects. For example, executives in all areas were in strong agreement that successful leaders were interested in the ideas of their subordinates. Response from all areas was neutral in respect to whether subordinates wished to take on more responsibility than they are able to handle. All were in agreement that if subordinates see the likelihood of promotional opportunities, they will work harder. The overall conclusion: "the above findings suggest that culture does play an important role in determining the managerial philosophy, attitudes, and practices of chief executives."[94]

It should be pointed out that to say that the most *effective* style of management, however this may be defined, may vary with time and place is not to say that there may not be a global convergence of managerial style in terms of effectiveness over time. This evolutionary convergence is a legitimate problem for the organizational theorist, but the practicing manager must respond to the environmentally imposed requirements of a particular time and place. He should, however, be aware that the style that is effective at a particular time and place is not necessarily the most effective at a different time and place.[95]

Discussion questions

1. Describe some situations in which the manager of a local plant owned by a foreign firm would be caught in role conflict.

---

[93]Richard B. Peterson, "A Cross-Cultural Perspective of Supervisory Values," *Academy of Management Journal,* vol. 15, no. 1, March 1972, pp. 105 ff.

[94]Peterson, "Cross-Cultural," p. 114.

[95]Barry M. Richman and Richard N. Farmer suggested a checklist of relationships in monitoring the managerial environment in *Comparative Management and Economic Progress* (Homewood: Richard D. Irwin, 1965).

2. How would you go about selecting personnel for overseas assignment? Devise some questions you might put to them.

3. What sort of special training, if any, should managers slated for overseas assignment receive?

4. Under what circumstances might women be more effective in international management than men?

5. Do you feel that a U.S. citizen of Japanese ethnic origin would be more or less effective than others in a managerial position in the Japanese subsidiary of a U.S. corporation? How about a U.S. citizen of black African ethnic origin in a managerial position in the Nigerian subsidiary of a U.S. corporation?

6. Have you ever experienced culture shock? Under what circumstances? What were your symptoms?

7. Contrast and relate Table 3.1 and Figure 4.2. Are they inconsistent?

8. What assumptions are the universalists and relativists making? How valid are these assumptions?

9. Describe in your own words the differences between the Japanese managerial system and that of the U.S. Would any features of the former, in your opinion, be worth trying in the U.S. context?

10. Assignment: Prepare briefing material for an employee being considered for assignment to a specific country. Simulate a briefing session for the employee and his wife (other members of the class).

Recommended references

Chruden, Herbert J., and Arthur W. Sherman, Jr. *Personnel Practices of American Companies in Europe.* New York: American Management Association, 1972.

Davis, Stanley, ed. *Comparative Management.* Englewood Cliffs: Prentice-Hall, 1971.

Fayerweather, John. *Management of International Operations.* New York: McGraw-Hill, 1960.

Fforde, J. S. *An International Trade in Mangerial Skills.* Oxford: Basil Blackwell, 1957.

Floyd, Elizabeth R. *Compensating American Managers Abroad.* New York: American Management Society, 1958.

Gabriel, Peter P. *The International Transfer of Corporate Skills.* Boston: Harvard University Graduate School of Business Administration, 1967.

Gonzalez, Richard F., and Anant R. Negandhi. *The United States Overseas Executive: His Orientations and Career Patterns.* East Lansing: Graduate School of Business Administration, Michigan State University, 1966.

Haire, M., E. E. Chiselli, and L. W. Porter. *Managerial Thinking: An International Study.* New York: John Wiley & Sons, 1966.

Harbison, Frederick, and Charles A. Myers. *Management in the Industrial World.* New York: McGraw-Hill, 1959.

La Palombara, Joseph, and Stephen Blank. *Multinational Corporations in Comparative Perspective.* New York: The Conference Board, 1977.

Massie, J. L., J. Luytjes, and N. W. Hazen, eds. *Management in the International Context.* New York: Harper & Row, 1972.

Noer, David M. *Multinational People Management.* Washington: Bureau of National Affairs, 1975.

Rhinesmith, Stephen H. *Cultural-Organizational Analysis; the Interrelationship of Value Orientations and Managerial Behavior.* Cambridge, Mass.: McBer and Company, 1970.

Richman, Barry M. *Management Development and Education in the Soviet Union.* East Lansing: Graduate School of Business Administration, Michigan State University, 1967.

Shaw, William B., and Joseph V. Miccio. *Executive Development and Cross Cultural Transition: A Proposal for the Multinational Corporation.* Hilo: University of Hawaii. Published as vol. 4, no. 2, Sept. 1971 issue of *Trends.*

Teague, Burton W. *Selecting an Orienting Staff for Service Overseas.* New York: The Conference Board, 1976.

Torre, Mottram, ed. *The Selection of Personnel for International Service.* Geneva: World Federation for Mental Health, 1963.

Webber, Ross A. *Culture and Management.* Homewood: Richard D. Irwin, 1969.

Yoshino, Michael. *Japan's Managerial System.* Cambridge, Mass.: M.I.T. Press, 1969.

Case G
MITSUI K. K.*

The Mitsui method of identifying and grooming potential international managers starts before a candidate leaves school. Each September, Mitsui receives a thousand or so applications from seniors in Japan's top-ranking colleges who will graduate the following March. It runs these candidates through a culling procedure which weeds out about half of them: a careful analysis of school records; a battery of "yes or no" tests that check out factual knowledge; an essay-type test that reflects both common sense and business sense; and a multi-tier personal interview system that starts with in-company peer groups—junior executives who have been with the company two or three years—and works up the corporate ladder to a designated senior executive who puts his final "chop" on a candidate's eligibility.

Five to ten years of rotation. The process also produces the first indications of what direction the candidate's career path in the company should take. That direction, however, is not final. For five to ten years after these carefully screened candidates are hired, they are rotated within the company and systematically monitored to make sure they wind up in slots that best conform to their abilities.

The monitoring system includes an annual evaluation by the supervisor in direct daily contact with the executive, which is checked by the section chief and double-checked by the general manager of the department. In addition, an elaborate, written report provides detail under two headings: business ability and work attitude. The former contains such items as ability to administer staff, decisiveness, prejudices, perception, judgment, concentration, planning and negotiating ability, and business knowledge. Work attitudes are measured by such criteria as following proper reporting procedures, keeping apart personal and professional matters, accepting responsibility, maintaining required office hours, and obeying company regulations.

As a general rule, home-base executives are not moved into international jobs until they have been thoroughly pretested within the Mitsui system, i.e. at the middle management level. Three general criteria are applied: character —a combination of strength of character and adaptability; professional rating (Mitsui rates its executives on an A-through-D scale; candidates for service abroad must rank C or higher and for the major overseas posts B or higher); and language ability.

In addition, personal characteristics are put into the selection hopper. Ex-

---

*From *Business International*, July 18, 1975, pp. 228–29. Reprinted by permission.

ample: Is the executive's temperament right for the post? (Under Mitsui rules, a quick-tempered executive may be sent to North America but would not be assigned to a post where he might have to deal with *manana* attitudes.)

Finally, physical factors are weighed. Can the executive adapt to the food patterns of the country to which he is sent? Can he adapt to the lack of oxygen if the place of assignment is located at elevations of 5,000 feet or higher, such as Mexico City or Bogota?

Having met all criteria, the executive is put through a concentrated training and briefing process. He takes a three-month intensive language course at corporate expense and is briefed by in-house experts—staff and line—on political, economic, and business conditions in the country to which he has been assigned.

At the same time, the executive's wife is put through an appropriate language and culture course. A number of independent organizations offer such courses in Japan, with varying degrees of intensity and comprehensiveness. Mitsui picks the course and pays for it.

Once the executive is in his overseas post, Mitsui insists on intensive language training for another year. In some locations, the company finances university training, combining exposure to language with substance of valid interest to the firm. In the past, Mitsui has allowed its executives to choose these courses and take them on an audit basis. The new trend is to have executives take MBA degrees where the academic facilities are available.

Mitsui also takes care of the special schooling needs of executives' children. In Japan, high schools and universities are sharply competitive and inordinately decisive in shaping careers. Japanese executives are therefore particularly anxious to channel their children into the school system early and under the best auspices. Mitsui provides dormitory facilities for children of its executives, boys and girls, at both the high school and the university level. These facilities are situated in the company's residential quarters at various locations in Tokyo and Osaka, and are tightly supervised. Room and board are subsidized, but students pay their own transportation costs (daily travel can be two hours and more) and provide for tuition out of their own resources.

Two routes to overseas duty. At Mitsui, the assignment process for service abroad has two channels. Requests can initiate from the field, with specific requirements, or can be "self-initiated" with specific motivation. A typical example of the first would be Mitsui's North American manager, foreseeing substantial growth in the petrochemical industry in Houston, asking corporate headquarters for a candidate who knows the petrochemical industry, has a workable base of English, and is temperamentally suited to function in Texas. Such a request is fed into the Mitsui personnel computer, which currently has a pool of some 600 executives considered eligible for international service. Once the computer comes up with its choices, a negotiating-selecting process is set in motion between headquarters and the field. Depending on the urgency of filling the slot, this works by letter, telex, or telephone.

An example of self-initiated assignment is the executive who asked for—and quickly got—a post in Saudi Arabia. His main argument was that the country represented an important opportunity for the company.

Most Mitsui executives return to Japan—and the computer pool—after assignments of three years' duration. Hardship posts have shorter stints, and some of the plum assignments tend to last longer; but the general policy is to pull executives back to headquarters regularly to make sure they do not lose touch with how things are done at Mitsui and to make certain they continue to feel part of the mainstream. Occasionally, a particularly adaptable and well-regarded executive, especially at the higher echelons of middle management, is transferred directly from one overseas post to another international assignment, but that is rare.

The new concept at Mitsui—still very much in an embryonic state—is to "nationalize" expatriate executives, i.e., leave them in a post in which they are effective and which they find congenial for as long as they like.

At the senior management level, selected executives are sent each year to advanced management courses in the U.S. and Europe to such institutions as Harvard, the Sloan Management School at M.I.T. and IMEDE in Switzerland.

The "inbound" program. Mitsui also has a training system for "inbound" executives, i.e. non-Japanese executives with upward corporate mobility. That system has three channels. In one, candidates are selected from their home country's top universities and rotated in various departments of the local Mitsui subsidiary. London-based Mitsui & Co. Europe, for example, gets graduates from Oxford and Cambridge and, for about three years, trains them in-house, focusing at the same time on plotting long-term career paths. Career opportunities include staff and line positions, as well as the more specialized managerial activities in the commodity divisions of the Mitsui Trading Company.

A second channel sends promising foreign executives to the Mitsui office that commands a particular expertise. For example, a German executive with a career path in Mitsui's production division is sent to the New York office for a training stint of two to three years.

The third Mitsui channel for foreign managerial talent is reserved mainly for young executives from the developing countries, who are pulled into Tokyo for two to three years of training before a career path is plotted for them, preferably in their own countries or contiguous areas.

Mitsui pays particular attention to these young executives from the LDCs because it knows that LDC governments will increasingly insist on local managers as well as on local equity. As a Mitsui executive put it: "Sooner or later, we'll have to ask them to hold our company shares."

For its non-Japanese senior managers, Mitsui organizes a two-week in-house seminar once a year in Tokyo, at which key employees are immersed in company policies and techniques. Some 30 to 50 executives attend these seminars each year. English is the working language, with executives chosen from any and all of Mitsui's global operations, including its 230 joint ventures.

Mitsui policy in managing joint ventures is to recruit top local management wherever possible. In the U.S. and Canada, for example, the pattern is to have an American or Canadian serve as president of the venture, with a Japanese vice-president. In countries with fewer top managerial resources, the pattern is reversed. The newest trend at Mitsui is to look for top non-Japanese executives to serve on the boards of Mitsui companies in Japan.

Discussion questions

1. Analyze the strengths and weaknesses of the Mitsui system.
2. Would this system have to be modified in any way for a U.S.-based corporation? How?
3. What do you think of Mitsui's policy of nationalizing expatriate executives?
4. What personnel problems might Mitsui have that U.S.- or European-based firms possibly would not have?

Case H

TICE ELECTRICAL COMPANY*

The Tice Electrical Company was established in 1936 to manufacture electronic tubes and related items for sale to manufacturers and wholesalers. The company grew steadily, especially during World War II. Following the war an export department was set up which developed foreign markets, at first through distributors and then through sales branches in major markets. The export department was in New York City while the main company offices and plant were in Buffalo, New York. The export manager during this period was George Farley. Mr. Farley had been in the export business for 20 years prior to being hired by Tice to initiate the export operations and the success of the foreign business was generally credited to his aggressive management.

A few years ago, a Canadian factory was established. Previously, Canada had been treated as a sales territory under the domestic sales division. The director of sales for Canada was made head of the new manufacturing subsidiary, reporting directly to the president.

Two years later, the company decided to embark on further foreign manufacturing ventures, commencing with Pavalia, a major Latin American country. The export department was redesignated as the international division and under it a new department of foreign manufacturing operations was created. John Raines, who had been assistant to the director of foreign operations for a large electrical company, was engaged to manage this department. He was 58. In the next few months plans for the Pavalian operation were under constant discussion, and considerable friction developed between Mr. Farley and Mr. Raines. The approach of Mr. Raines to the manufacturing program received general support from the senior company officers and eventually Mr. Farley withdrew, accepting his privilege of retiring between 65 and 70. Mr. Raines became manager of the division. His former position was filled by Richard Birch from the domestic manufacturing organization. Some further adjustments were made, resulting in the organization shown in Figure H.1.

As work on the Pavalian project proceeded a number of administrative difficulties arose. The experience of John Martin indicates the general character of the problem.

The Pavalian experience. John Martin was transferred from the domestic treasurer's office to work in the newly-formed financial department in the

*From *Management of International Operations* by John Fayerweather. Copyright © 1970 by McGraw-Hill. Used with permission of McGraw-Hill Book Company. This case was prepared as a problem in international business as a basis for class discussion. It is not designed to illustrate either correct or incorrect handling of administrative problems.

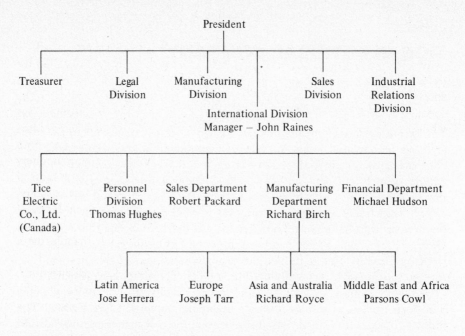

Figure H.1
TICE ELECTRIC COMPANY ORGANIZATION

international division where he was under Michael Hudson, former credit manager of the export department. The task of developing financial and legal plans for the Pavalian operation was assigned to Mr. Martin and he worked on them and other aspects of the Pavalian venture along with men in personnel, sales, and manufacturing during the following 12 months. That June, five years ago, plans for the new operation were completed and a staff of six men embarked for Pavalia to supervise construction of the plant and organization of the new subsidiary to replace the existing sales branch. Four of the men were production specialists who worked under the direction of Robert Loeb, an assistant to Mr. Birch, who was responsible for the construction program. Mr. Martin was the sixth member of the group. The manager of the division, Mr. Raines, and Mr. Hudson told him that he was to be responsible for establishing the financial and legal aspects of the new subsidiary and that he should serve a controller's function as watchdog for the general progress of the project. He was told to stay within the framework of the plans which had been agreed upon but beyond that he should use his best judgment in consultation with others in the group. He was to report back periodically to Mr. Hudson.

As work progressed a number of questions appeared and they were discussed by Mr. Martin, Mr. Loeb, and William Torrey, manager of the Pavalian branch. Mr. Martin found Mr. Torrey very knowledgeable about Pavalia and he gathered from his actions that he expected to be the manager of the new subsidiary.

The most troublesome questions arose because they found that the suppliers available could not provide materials of exactly the type or quality called for by company specifications. It was necessary to decide whether to require suppliers to change their methods and help them to do so or to alter the specifications. Mr. Loeb tended to favor enforcement of the specifications whereas Mr. Torrey was prepared to make some concessions to accommodate suppliers. Mr. Martin found himself usually agreeing with Mr. Torrey both because he trusted his knowledge of the country and because helping suppliers would have added to the financial burden of the venture. Mr. Loeb felt himself to be the senior officer of the group and adhered to his position quite strongly, but on several cases accepted the conclusions of the other two men. None of the specific problems which arose was of major importance so they were not referred back to the home office, the men feeling they could handle them adequately within their own authority.

Mr. Martin was also confronted by a number of strictly financial questions. He received several instructions from the treasurer, Mr. Hudson, which changed the original plan. While most of these were quite acceptable, a few of them seemed of doubtful value for the operation. For example, he was told that the working capital would have to be reduced and the deductions should be achieved by reducing the allotments for advances to suppliers, which seemed to weaken the operation at a crucial spot. Similarly, Mr. Loeb was receiving instructions from his superior periodically, most of them involving alterations in the manufacturing plan to incorporate innovations in domestic manufacturing processes. Mr. Loeb and Mr. Martin agreed on a general policy of accepting them. Mr. Martin did write to Mr. Hudson every four or five weeks, giving a summary of the progress to date and the work still to be done.

In March of the next year (four years ago), the plant was completed and the new subsidiary came into being with Mr. Torrey as president. The home office staff returned to the United States except for two of the production men who remained as advisors. On his return, Mr. Martin was disturbed to find his work in Pavalia subject to considerable criticism by Mr. Birch, head of the foreign manufacturing department, and Mr. Packard, the sales manager. They felt that he had injected himself unduly into decisions about the supply situation and that rather than take sides in the matter, his responsibility should have been to encourage Mr. Loeb and Mr. Torrey to refer their differences back to the home office. Mr. Hudson also expressed some displeasure at the extent to which the final financial structure varied from the initial conception, though he said he thought Mr. Martin had done a generally good job in handling the many problems of starting a new venture.

Mr. Martin's problems continued after his return. From time to time he received letters from Mr. Torrey asking his advice or approval of some action. For example, three weeks after his arrival in New York, Mr. Torrey asked if he would approve an advance to a supplier whose production was essential to the operation but whose quality had on several occasions fallen a little short of company standards. In view of the criticism he had received, Mr. Martin made a practice of routing all such inquiries to Mr. Hudson, Mr. Loeb, Mr. Birch, and Mr. Packard and of taking any differences of opinion through Mr. Hudson to Mr. Raines. He was distressed, however, at the time required for this process.

Reorganization. The recurrence of problems of this nature led to a major reorganization. Thomas Schilling, a consultant, was brought in as assistant to the director of the international division shortly after the Pavalian plant was completed. After consulting at length with members of the management, he established the structure shown in Figure H.2.

The regional directors shown on the left were given full line authority for their territories while the staff on the right were assigned advisory and support- ing responsibilities. The senior men in the organization were consulted as to what position they would like. Mr. Birch elected to become director for Latin America and Mr. Packard chose the marketing manager post. Men were then assigned to other posts according to the management's evaluation of their capacities.

In the months which followed, Mr. Schilling worked with the Tice execu- tives to make the organization function effectively as the operations grew with new plants in three other Latin American countries and one in Europe, in addition to expanding sales organizations in about 20 countries. Particular attention was given to keeping the staff from assuming improper authority or interfering with action without complicating the organization with excessive procedures. The success of these efforts was tested in many cases. One such was the handling of requests from the Latinian subsidiary for adjustments in salary scales.

The Latinian pay question. The Tice salary policies for overseas personnel had been established after an extensive review of the practices of other compa- nies. They were designed to assure adequate compensation to hold competent men in the organization. The company did not attempt to match the salaries of other companies exactly or to follow cost-of-living rises automatically, but rather it sought to maintain a pay level at which turnover was held to a reasonable rate. The main lines of the policies are given in Appendix 3 to Case H.

The Latinian subsidiary had initiated manufacturing operations two years ago. Previously the company had been organized solely for sales and service, with the manager, Timothy Finch, serving essentially as the sales manager, and the treasurer, Ramon Rivera, being the only other employee of significant management status. Mr. Finch had been in Latinia for several years and was made manager of the new operations with a salary increase to cover his enlarged responsibilities. Herman Kranz, a German who had been with the Pavalian operation for two years, was brought to Latinia as assistant manager.

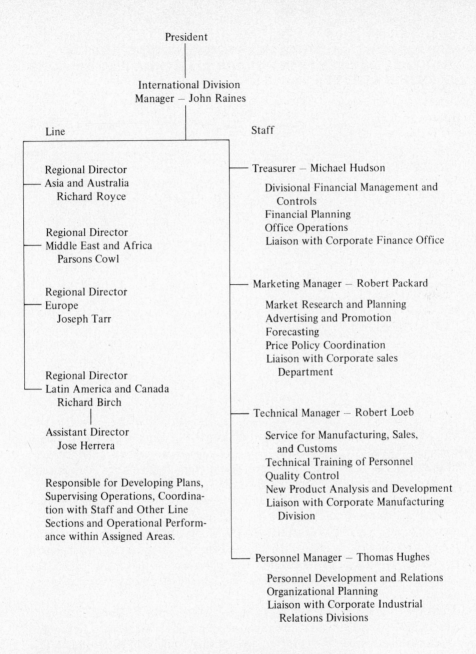

President

International Division
Manager — John Raines

Line

Staff

Regional Director
Asia and Australia
    Richard Royce

Treasurer — Michael Hudson

Divisional Financial Management and
    Controls
Financial Planning
Office Operations
Liaison with Corporate Finance Office

Regional Director
Middle East and Africa
    Parsons Cowl

Regional Director
Europe
    Joseph Tarr

Marketing Manager — Robert Packard

Market Research and Planning
Advertising and Promotion
Forecasting
Price Policy Coordination
Liaison with Corporate sales
    Department

Regional Director
Latin America and Canada
    Richard Birch

Assistant Director
    Jose Herrera

Technical Manager — Robert Loeb

Service for Manufacturing, Sales,
    and Customs
Technical Training of Personnel
Quality Control
New Product Analysis and Development
Liaison with Corporate Manufacturing
    Division

Responsible for Developing Plans,
Supervising Operations, Coordination with Staff and Other Line
Sections and Operational Performance within Assigned Areas.

Personnel Manager — Thomas Hughes

Personnel Development and Relations
Organizational Planning
Liaison with Corporate Industrial
    Relations Divisions

Figure H.2
TICE ELECTRIC COMPANY INTERNATIONAL DIVISION

Table H.1

MANAGEMENT SALARIES IN LATINIAN SUBSIDIARY*
(MONTHLY PAYMENTS IN POVARS IN LATINIA AND DOLLARS
IN UNITED STATES)

	June two years before	July two years before	April last year	September last year	February current year	April current year
Mr. Finch, manager	3400 P $300	3700 P $340	3700 P $340	3700 P $340	3700 P $340	4030 P $340
Mr. Kranz, assistant manager	($700†)	2900 P $265	2900 P $265	2900 P $265	2900 P $265	3160 P $265
Mr. Jesus, sales manager	1750 P	2150 P	2370 P	2370 P	2450 P	2540 P
Mr. Rivera, treasurer	1850 P	2150 P	2370 P	2370 P	2370 P	2370 P
Mr. Rojas, production manager		2400 P	2640 P			
Mr. Fales, production manager			($700†)	2640 P $340	2640 P $340	2640 P $426

*Company exchange rate: 5 Povars = U.S. $1

†Dollar equivalent of salary in home country

He received a new salary in accordance with the established policies (see Appendix 3), but no cost of living differential as Latinian costs were below those of Pavalia. Mr. Rivera also received a raise as his job was enlarged. One of the sales supervisors, Ricardo Jesus, was promoted to be sales manager and his pay was set by considering his former pay and that of comparable jobs in Latinia. Another Latinian, Alphonso Rojas, was hired from outside the company as production manager. He left in September of last year to set up a company with a group of friends, and Mr. Robert Fales was sent down from the parent company to handle the job until another competent Latinian could be located. His pay in pesos was set at the same level as that of Mr. Rojas, the balance due him being paid in dollars. The initial salaries of all these men are shown in Table H.1.

In April of last year, the union to which the Tice workers belonged demanded a 15 percent wage increase to compensate for cost-of-living rises. In the face of a threatened strike, the company agreed to a 10 percent increase and this advance was also extended to salaried local employees.

In the second week of July, Mr. Birch made one of his regular visits to Latinia. On separate occasions during his visit, Mr. Finch and Mr. Kranz talked to him about their pay situation. Both expressed the opinion that the cost-of-living had advanced to a point where they should receive an increase. (Cost-of-living data are shown in Table H.2.) Mr. Birch returned to the home office on July 20 and the next day talked with Mr. Hughes, the personnel manager, about the men's request. Mr. Hughes pointed out that the company did not pay cost-of-living allowances unless costs in the foreign post were determined to be higher than those in the United States, so that the situation would have to be studied. Because of the circumstances under which the men were assigned to their present jobs, there had never been any thorough check of their salaries in relation to comparative costs-of-living. Therefore, Mr. Hughes engaged a consulting firm that had done such work for the company before to survey the cost of living for the men in comparison with that in Pavalia and the United States. The survey in Latinia consisted of pricing a selected sample of products covering the following elements in the cost of living: food purchases, household services, household operations, housing, transportation, medical care, personal care, recreation, and tobacco and alcohol. The consultant made his survey accompanied by the two executives so that they would know the procedure for future checks. As a result of these studies, Mr. Hughes determined that the costs of living in Latinia and the United States were essentially equal. (See Table H.2.) He discussed the situation with Mr. Birch and they agreed that no increase should be given and Mr. Birch wrote the men to that effect on August 25.

On December 11 of last year, Mr. Finch wrote a letter to Mr. Herrera requesting approval for a general pay increase of 10 percent for all local employees. (Mr. Herrera had line responsibility for operational matters of this nature.) Mr. Finch included in his letter cost-of-living statistics since the time of the last general pay readjustment in the preceding April. He pointed out that the index had risen substantially and that the personnel were entitled to higher pay.

Mr. Herrera passed the letter on to Mr. Hughes and after discussing it, Mr. Hughes wrote the letter appearing in Appendix 1 to Case H, in which he proposed that a detailed survey of comparable jobs be made before any salary adjustments were made. He had several thoughts in mind in writing the letter. First, he regarded education of the field personnel as one of his major responsibilities and much of what he wrote was intended to convey specific information to Mr. Finch and to get him to thinking along lines of effective management, for example, in seeing the need to set salaries by competitive considerations, not just on cost-of-living indices. Second, he was relating the handling of the immediate problem to basic company policies. The observations on objectives of salary administration were derived directly from the company manual. Mr. Hughes had always found reference back to such policy statements both sound and safe. Third, he was using this situation as a vehicle for moving the Latinian operation toward a better personnel system. Specifically, he was pushing for better job descriptions. He had been encouraging

Table H.2
COST OF LIVING DATA

		Latinia	United States
Four years before		107	100
Three years before		109	100
Two years before	January	109	100
	February	110	100
	March	113	100
	April	114	100
	May	114	101
	June	115	102
	July	114	102
	August	113	102
	September	114	102
	October	114	103
	November	116	103
	December	116	103
One year before	January	117	103
	February	119	104
	March	122	104
	April	126	104
	May	128	105
	June	130	105
	July	133	106
	August	134	106
	September	137	106
	October	141	106
	November	142	106
	December	145	106
This year	January	145	107
	February	146	107
	March	147	108
	April	149	108
	May	152	108

them in this direction for some time but so far their approach had been rather haphazard. Now he hoped to get some real progress.

Ten days later Mr. Herrera received the letter from Mr. Finch (shown in Appendix 2 to Case H) suggesting that an interim raise be given immediately, with the full study to be made later. Mr. Hughes and Mr. Herrera discussed this letter and in the next ten days several telegrams were exchanged with Mr. Finch on the subject. Mr. Finch held firmly to his views and Mr. Hughes refused to recommend any increase without a survey. Finally, Mr. Hughes concluded that in view of the other pressures on the Latinia staff it was impractical to require a survey at this time so he undertook a survey in New York with the personnel managers of five companies with somewhat comparable operations in Latinia. He was not pleased with this as an approach to the problem because the records of some companies were inadequate and it was difficult to determine from their job descriptions what jobs were comparable with those in the Tice subsidiary. However, it did serve to give a rough measure

Table H.3
LATINIAN SALARY SURVEY

Average salesmen's salary

Company	Base	Commission or bonus	Total	Rate range
Tice	1,400	100	1,500	1,350–1,800
A	825	825	1,650	
B	1,300	100	1,400	1,075–1,750
C	1,654	—	1,654	1,125–2,100
D	650	850	1,500	600–1,300
E			1,500 (up to 2 years)	970
			(up to 4 years)	1,035
			(over 4 years)	1,130
				Commissions may vary radically from year to year

Job title	Factory and office employees Tice	B	E	A	F
Packers	175	150–200	156	150	
Watchmen	438		460	312	
Cleaning women	188			155	
Messengers	188		205	155	
Drivers	344		340	345	
Secretary, assistant manager	438	410	600	350	
Chief accountant	2,300		2,900	1,900	
Secretary to manager	875		1,000	935	1,270
Accounting clerk	375	300	300	414	
Secretary to chief accountant	400	250		391	
Stock clerk	225				300
Plant superintendent	2,300				2,500

of the competitive salary scales. The results of the survey completed on January 20 are shown in Table H.3. They indicated that the sales personnel were significantly underpaid and an increase of 7 percent seemed justified. For other jobs, however, the salaries seemed generally reasonable, though some individual jobs might be out of line. On this basis, Mr. Hughes and Mr. Herrera agreed to a 7 percent increase for sales personnel with no change for others except that individual adjustments might be made if inequities were determined to exist. Mr. Finch was then advised that no further increases would be considered until a full survey had been made.

In March of the current year, Mr. Birch visited Latinia and the two men again raised the salary question. They asserted that the cost of living had risen significantly and, if their pay had been correct in June, it certainly was not correct in the light of the rise in costs since then. Mr. Birch took the matter up with Mr. Hughes upon his return and they agreed that a new study was justified. Mr. Finch was directed to make a check of costs following the procedure the consultant had established. This study showed a 9 percent increase in costs since June of last year, and the men were given an increase in that amount on 70 percent of their total salaries. (See Appendix 3 to Case H.)

Discussion questions

1. How would you describe Tice's management style?
2. Evaluate Tice's personnel policy.
3. Define the Tice Company's compensation policy.
4. Evaluate the probable effects of that policy.
5. What alternative policies might be pursued?
6. How would you construct a relevant cost-of-living differential?

Appendix 1 to Case H
To: Mr. Finch
From: Mr. Hughes
Subject: Request for Cost-of-Living Increase

Mr. Herrera has passed to me your letter requesting cost-of-living increases for personnel in Latinia.

Your recommendations have been carefully considered in the light of the cost-of-living data you supplied.

We realize the urgency with which you make your request for a cost-of-living increase. Before being in the position to approve an increase of this nature there are certain relevant factors to be considered. It has not been a general policy of this company to give cost-of-living increases per se. We have considered cost of living, however, in conjunction with other conditions such as availability of labor and community rates in giving a "general increase."

Your recommendations were explicit and conformed to the cost-of-living changes as indicated by government statistics. Application of the pay ranges you have proposed, however, do not show that we are in step with community rates. It is possible that in some cases we may be lower than the community rates and in other cases perhaps higher and we feel that we should determine where we stand competitively before giving increases.

It is felt that this would be an excellent time to align ourselves with community rates. We do not wish to prolong this problem but we feel that you will find this approach to be more beneficial for you in the long run.

Objective. To determine whether or not our wages and salaries are adequate to attract and hold desired employees and also to assist in maintaining a high level of morale. It is our policy to pay wages and salaries that are fair to each job and each individual employee. We attempt to pay salaries that are fair and in line for comparable jobs with other companies in the community. To adjust these rates it is necessary to determine the prevailing rates for comparable jobs within the community surrounding our operations.

Step 1. Job description. Pay rates should be based upon a clear and accurate definition of the duties and responsibility of each job. To determine just what duties are performed by each individual, a brief but clear and accurate definition of the duties normally performed by each employee should be set down in the form of a job description. This job description should contain as concisely as possible the general and specific duties involved. This job description can then be used by you in making your survey to make sure that you are comparing like jobs with other companies. It is not necessary to compare every job but an adequate selection of key or benchmark jobs should be used. (Key or benchmark jobs would be those that have certain basic characteristics that are easily identified in any company such as a secretary, chauffeur, accountant, etc.)

Step 2. Selection of survey comparison. Pay rates should reflect market conditions and represent the amount required to attract and hold desired workers. To determine whether or not we are paying adequate rates, a selected group of companies within the community should be chosen. In selecting these companies we must first decide on the geographical area we plan to use as our "community" in which we will conduct our survey. This is usually the area surrounding our plant or office from which we normally expect to hire our people. For instance, we might draw a circle with a radius of 10 to 25 miles with our plant or office as center. The community would be represented by this circle and almost all the companies selected for the community survey would fall within this circle.

First choice of companies to be selected from within our community circle would be those in the same or closely allied businesses. Second would be those of comparable size, reputation, and working conditions. Third would be those we might not otherwise include but with whom we are in competition for labor. Within an area such as yours, your selection would include a broad category of industries of comparable size and reputation rather than just one industry.

Once such companies have been selected, they may then be contacted for salary and wage information. This may be made on a reciprocal basis.

Step 3. Comparison of jobs. Although other companies will seldom have identical jobs, it is possible to determine which jobs are close as to level of work (education and experience required, responsibilities and judgment involved, work hazards, pace of work, etc.).

In making a survey such as this it is best to make personal visits to the companies from whom you wish to obtain the information. If this is not possible, you should clear the path for the individual who will be assigned to the task so that the information will be given to him when he calls.

Whoever gathers the information should be qualified to discuss the positions, i.e., who knows the operations, has a good idea of the jobs being compared, and is a good analyst. He should be careful not to accept a job as comparable just because job titles might be the same. The job should be examined for content.

The foregoing information is general in nature but it is essential that some method such as this be used in determining what salaries are to be paid for various jobs.

In obtaining your information the following should be noted for each job: job title, date rate established, minimum of rate, maximum of rate, and actual rates being paid; also the approximate number of employees at each rate.

Upon completion of your survey, the information should be forwarded to this office for review and will be discussed with Mr. Herrera for salary adjustments. Your prompt cooperation would be appreciated so that we may conclude this matter as soon as possible.

Appendix 2 to Case H
To: Mr. Herrera
From: Mr. Finch
Subject: Request for Cost-of-Living Increase

The program outlined by Mr. Hughes in his memo represents the ideal approach to the problem. We are in agreement with various objectives set forth. In fact, we have attempted without much success to obtain this basic information from our local industry association. However, my personal opinion is that we will not obtain this information from them due to its confidential nature.

Also, we have requested to be included in a study by another United States company but have been refused because they have as many companies as they can handle. This survey for the most part includes big companies.

As you can appreciate, it requires considerable time to start and to complete our own survey. Frankly, with the number of problems we have relative to our new production plans, to our training program, and to the indoctrination of Mr. Fales, there just is not enough time to do everything.

However, we do know that industry, as reported by our association, has on the average increased salaries over 30 percent since last April. Thus, some leading companies must have increased salaries materially more than 30 percent to result in an industrial average of over 30 percent. Thus it is felt that the adjustment now proposed will not change our relative position in the industry; i.e., our new salary levels will not be out of line with other companies.

It is requested that you consider approving our request, and then in March when Mr. Hughes plans to come here to work with us in making a comprehensive wage survey, to help us make our personnel programs more effective and to review what has been done and future plans in connection with personnel training programs.

You have a certain degree of security if you do favorably consider our proposal and that is with the accentuated ascending cost of living index, another adjustment will probably be needed next year just to keep even.

Before this next adjustment is made, we can complete the comprehensive survey and adjust any unusual situations that might be found.

It will be appreciated if you explain in more detail to Mr. Hughes the problems we are facing with new production, etc., and request that he reconsider his request and postpone the formal salary survey. Honestly, I feel certain we will not find at this time that we are out of line with the industry.

Appendix 3 to Case H

All Tice overseas personnel were divided into three groups: (1) parent company personnel (hired in the United States and assigned to a foreign post other than their native country), (2) "third country" personnel (hired in one foreign country and assigned to another), (3) local personnel (employed in the same country in which they were hired).

A. *Parent company personnel.* 1. Salary. The basic salary was derived from the salary for a comparable position in the United States to which was added a geographic bonus ranging from zero to 35 percent depending on the nature of the foreign post. General increases in the United States pay scales were also applied to salaries of parent company personnel overseas.

2. Cost-of-living adjustment. When the cost of living in the overseas post was lower than in the United States no adjustment was made. When it was higher, a differential was given of 70 percent of the basic salary. This was the portion of the salary assumed to be spent by the average employee for living expenses at the overseas location. The differential allowed each individual was usually determined when initially assigned to a post by a study of all available data including comparative cost-of-living indices from the United States State Department, banks, and other sources. At the same time the company made a survey of costs for selected items and an analysis of the spending pattern of the particular individual. Subsequently adjustments in the cost-of-living differential were based entirely upon changes in the local cost of living without regard to the situation in the United States. The company felt that as an individual adjusted to life in the foreign post, it was the local costs only that were significant. An objective of reviewing cost-of-living changes every six months was set, but in practice the reviews were made at varying frequencies depending upon local conditions. Field personnel were asked to advise the home office when significant changes took place and they were never slow to do so.

3. Specific expenses paid by company. The company paid the cost of (1) travel required for company business, (2) two months' vacation every two

years in the United States, including transportation for employees and family, (3) costs of education for children where residence abroad forced the parent to pay more for education than he would have in the United States, (4) membership in social or business groups essential to company standing in the community, (5) income tax differential where taxes were higher than in the United States (when taxes were lower than in the United States this was considered as an offsetting factor in determining cost-of-living allowances), (6) transportation and moving expenses between assignments.

4. Pensions. Employees were treated like domestic personnel in pension benefits.

5. Method of payment. Basic salary and cost-of-living differential were computed in dollars but the company sought to pay the maximum portion in local currency (using the exchange rate determined by the treasurer's office for all intercompany transactions). As a general guideline employees were allowed to receive 30 percent of their pay in dollars in the United States, 70 percent being the portion assumed to be required for living costs. In some instances, employees were allowed to receive more in dollars and in others the company set a higher portion as desirable for employee relations. Tice, like other international companies, generally had to pay expatriates more than local personnel for comparable jobs. The management explained to the latter that this difference was justified by the fact that the expatriates had to be given an incentive to work away from their native land, but in view of the emotions involved, purely logical explanations were not always fully effective. Therefore, the company tried to restrict the amounts paid to parent company personnel in local currency to the same level as those received by local personnel in comparable jobs.

B. *Third country personnel.* 1. Salary. The salary was taken as the average between the salary for a comparable job in the place where the individual was hired and the salary for a parent company employee in the country of assignment.

2. Other provisions. Cost-of-living differentials and specific expense payments were made precisely as for parent company personnel except that the place of hire was used as the base rather than the United States. Third country employees were not eligible for the company pension plan unless they established the United States as their base. The portion of payment not received in local currency was generally paid in the currency of the country of hire but might be paid in dollars under special circumstances.

C. *Local personnel.* Salaries of local personnel were established according to local pay scales. General increases were based on overall local situation considering competitive rates, productivity, the cost of living, and other factors.

Chapter 5
OWNERSHIP STRATEGY

One of the most debated and critical areas in international business is the ownership of tangible and intangible assets by nonnationals. Discussion of the relative merits of 100 percent ownership versus joint venturing versus contracting goes on interminably. The 100 percenters speak of conflict of interest in joint ownership, and the need for control and integration; the joint venturers, of local national contribution and commensurate right of local nationals to share ownership; the contractors, of minimizing risk and taking full advantage of one's monopoly position in regard to either market access or technology, or both.

Over recent years, it would appear that U.S. firms have demonstrated a remarkably consistent ownership policy. A 1971 study reported that approximately 60 percent of the new enterprises established by U.S. firms overseas over the past ten years had been wholly owned (including branches which, by definition, must be wholly owned), 8 to 9 percent majority owned, 7 to 8 percent minority owned (the remaining 13 to 15 percent were unknown). There seems to have been little variation from year to year.[1]

By way of contrast, it was reported in 1971 that Japanese direct investment overseas was more inclined to be on a minority basis (37 percent), somewhat less on a majority basis (34 percent), and even less on a wholly owned basis (29 percent).[2] In a study of 50 major Japanese manufacturing enterprises, Yoshino found that of their 417 manufacturing subsidiaries in 37 countries in 1973, Japanese parent companies owned 50 percent or less in 304 (73 percent), less than 100 percent in 38 others (9 percent), and 100 percent in 75 (18 percent).[3] He also noted,

A recent study of international activities of Japanese enterprises undertaken by the Ministry of International Trade and Industry reported that of 661 major manufacturing

[1]A Booz, Allen, and Hamilton study, reported in *Business Abroad*, June 1971, p. 9.

[2]Gregory Clark, "Japanese Direct Investment Overseas," (unpublished manuscript, 1971), table 2.

[3]Michael Y. Yoshino, *Japan's Multinational Enterprises* (Cambridge: Harvard University Press, 1976), p. 143.

firms surveyed, in over half of them, the Japanese parent companies held only a minority position. The majority- or wholly-owned Japanese subsidiaries accounted for less than a quarter of the total number of subsidiaries. Although not directly comparable, nearly two-thirds of the subsidiaries of the 177 leading U.S. multinational enterprises were majority- or wholly-owned.[4]

The evidence of significant difference between U.S. and Japanese firms on this score seems to be overwhelming.

Yoshino went on to observe that this Japanese propensity to joint venture was in part a function of the relative lack of resources and international experience. "Though the data are still quite sketchy, the available evidence does suggest that as Japan's emerging multinational enterprises seek new strategies and gain greater competence and resources, they are also likely, as a result, to pursue different ownership policies."[5] Yoshino's own empirical research suggested that Japanese managerial evaluation of the contribution of local partners fell as the Japanese firm gained more international experience, which was measured by the number of overseas manufacturing operations.[6]

Also significant is the relatively low rate of income repatriated to Japanese parents. To the typical Japanese direct foreign investor the major profits are expected to be derived either from the import into Japan of raw materials or the sale out of Japan of components. In the United States and the United Kingdom cases, the data suggest that considerably less than 50 percent of the output of U.S.- or U.K.-owned enterprises overseas is imported by the parent companies. But for Japan, this proportion is substantially higher, possibly 80 to 90 percent.[7] Thus, U.S. and U.K. investors are somewhat more interested in securing a maximum dividend flow for their capital and skill; they are reluctant to share it. But the Japanese can afford to share the dividend flow because they perceive the major benefit to be derived from export or import. The heavy overseas investment is added evidence—their profits are derived largely from generating international flows of goods and services. Hence, the Japanese share in equity tends to be relatively low. There are possibly four other reinforcing reasons: (1) more Japanese investment is located in less developed countries (possibly 63 percent as of 1973),[8] where alien ownership tends to be restricted; (2) Japan's own restrictive policy in this regard;

---

[4]Yoshino, *Japan's Multinational Enterprises*, pp. 142–143.

[5]Yoshino, *Japan's Multinational Enterprises*, p. 156.

[6]Yoshino, *Japan's Multinational Enterprises*, p. 157.

[7]According to Japan Economic Deliberation Council, *Shihon Jiyuka to Kaigai Kigyo Shinshitsu* (Liberation of Capital Movements and Overseas Expansion of Business; Tokyo: 1969), p. 137, quoted in *Transfer of Technology from Japan to Developing Nations* (New York: UN Institute for Training and Research, 1971), p. 8.

[8]Terutomo Ozawa, "Peculiarities of Japan's Multinationalism: Facts and Theories," *Banca Nazionale del Lavero Quarterly Review*, vol. 28, no. 115, December 1975, p. 406.

(3) Japan's relatively heavy investment in resource investment[9] and more "mature" labor-intensive manufacturing (in which area pressures for local ownership are particularly strong); and (4) most Japanese firms operating overseas are possibly not true multinational corporations but are rather *international* corporations (see Section 8.1) which, even in the U.S. case, seem to have a relatively high propensity to joint venture abroad. (Unfortunately, most scholars have not differentiated the international from the multinational in their research.) A further point might be made. One suspects that at least some Japanese firms enter into joint ventures abroad as a means of blocking imports into the Japanese market in a preemptive sense.

It is suggested in Chapter 8 that the joint venture strategy tends to be associated with a firm's early moves overseas when it lacks expertise in respect to the markets it is entering and the capacity and resources to build an internationally integrated production/sales system. Such a strategy is more characteristic of "export-oriented" and "international corporations," the latter being characterized by an international division and a dual decision-making and control system. As management accumulates international expertise and the capability of integrating its far-flung operations into a global *system*, there is a natural tendency to centralize control and to build a structure to facilitate such. At this point, the true "multinational corporation" tends to emerge, which is characterized by the dissolution of the international division and a restructuring of the corporation into either a regionally-based, product-based, or functionally-based decision-making system, or a combination of two or more; in other words, a matrix organization. These developments are discussed in some detail in Chapter 8. Suffice to point out here that ownership strategy tends to be associated with the evolutionary stage through which the corporation is moving in respect to its global operations. Furthermore, in the early stages, the firm's foreign investment is very likely to be defensive in nature. As it becomes multinational, it begins to enjoy the synergistic effect of an integrated system. The peculiar competitive advantages accruing to the multinational corporation really arise by reason of international scale factors (that is, the full employment of certain scarce resources, such as high-level skills, technology, and access to global information and distribution systems); national differences in the cost of capital, labor, resources, government (taxes), and consumer satisfaction (product regulation, environmental protection); and the capacity of the multinational corporation to move goods, money, and people so as to exploit those differences. This last implies central control and very frequently 100 percent ownership of overseas operations. Increasingly, however, it would appear that multinationals are becoming aware of the advan-

---

[9]At the end of 1972, the ratio of extractive investment to the total was 36.8 percent for Japan, 35.7 percent for the U.S., 7.2 percent for Britain, and 5.3 percent for West Germany. Japanese Ministry of Trade and Industry statistics reported in Terutomo Ozawa, p. 408.

Table 5.1
IMPLICIT PARTNERS IN AN OVERSEAS ENTERPRISE AND THEIR AREAS OF CONCERN

	Project	Relationship	Operating policies
Domestic firm			
Associated foreign business interest			
Host government			
Parent government			

tage of doing the same thing through contract rather than ownership, and a few seem to be moving in the direction of transforming themselves into international service organizations.

It is apparent that ownership is a two-way proposition: both a domestic and foreign enterprise may own obligations or assets of the other. These obligations or assets may be defined in terms of the transfer by one firm to another of its assets, personnel, knowledge, or products through investment, lease, or sale. This transfer of obligations or assets may give rise either to rights based on contract (including debt) or equity. The first arises out of the possession by the contracting firm of valuable transferable assets, such as copyrights, trademarks, patents, trade secrets, managerial and technical skills, machinery, products, real estate, and access to information and markets. These may be transferred either by sale or, if recoverable, by a license or lease authorizing the use of specified assets for a given length of time under certain conditions. Or they may be capitalized and invested in the beneficiary enterprise.

In a very real sense, every overseas enterprise is a joint enterprise whether or not the participating interests are formally represented.[10] One might look at any enterprise as representing a choice of project (or choice of sector), a relationship (ownership of varying degrees and/or some contractual relationship), and a series of operating policies. These three must remain within the range tolerated by the parties involved; that is, the alien firm, the associated foreign business interest (partner, contractor, contractee, supplier, and/or consumer), the host country government, and the parent country government. Hence, we generate the matrix shown in Table 5.1; if each of the four parties perceive of their respective interests as being positively or neutrally affected by the nature of the project, by the relationship between the local and foreign parties, and by the operating policies pursued, then no conflict of interest is built into the situation.

Here, we concern ourselves with the "relationship" column, although it

---

[10]The term joint enterprise is used here to avoid confusion with the equity-sharing concept inherent in the phrase "joint venture" as commonly used. One can also enter into a *contractual* joint venture in which certain assets and liabilities are shared for a specific purpose and time as defined by contract.

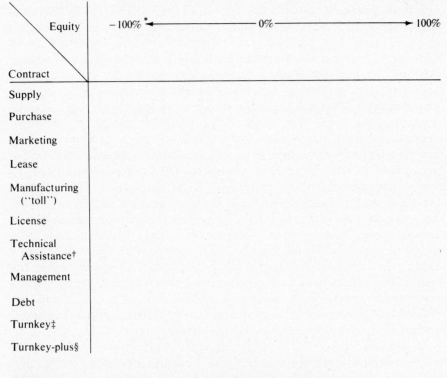

Figure 5.1
MATRIX OF ALTERNATIVE OWNERSHIP STRATEGIES

*Represents ownership of the equity of the domestic firm by the foreign firm.

†Includes contracts for engineering, architectural services, feasibility analysis, "know how," "show how," and consulting generally.

‡Commitment to design and build a working plant.

§Commitment to do "‡" and to train the operators, from skilled worker to top management.

should be kept in mind that what is perceived as a tolerable relationship depends in part on the nature of the project and the venture's operating policies. One hundred percent ownership may be tolerated by the host government for a consumer good manufacturing enterprise but not for power generation. Or, if the venture engages in serious technical training of its local employees, a higher level of foreign ownership may be tolerated for longer. It should also be noted that the full range of international business relationships runs the gamut from a 100-percent-owned subsidiary through zero percent ownership to a negative 100 percent (the ownership of the firm by the associated overseas business interest), and a range of possible contractual relationships, which can run likewise in either direction. (See Figure 5.1.)

Negative ownership may be represented by the exchange of stock of, say, a U.S. corporation for participation in a foreign firm or for some asset owned by the foreign firm. Two examples are a 1969 exchange by Minnesota Mining and Manufacturing Company of its convertible preference stock for the common shares of its U.K. subsidiary in the hands of 30 percent minority owners and a 1971 exchange by the Chrysler Corporation of Chrysler stock for an additional 20 percent of a Mexican firm in which it already had a 46 percent interest. (Japanese corporations find this strategy virtually closed to them because of a law preventing them from owning their own stock.) Or, the firm may simply list its stock in any of the 60-odd national stock exchanges operating around the world. Also, it should be noted that the sale in Europe of debentures that are convertible to shares in U.S. firms under certain conditions may transfer equity ownership. Of course, as ownership becomes multinational, we have the emergence of what may be called "transnational firms," a subject discussed more fully in Chapter 8. As time passes, national stock exchanges are facilitating the listing of foreign stock. (See Section 6.6.) Pushing in the direction of increased LDC investment in parent corporations is the accumulation of liquid balances in the hands of resource rich countries, notably the OPEC members thus far. Witness Iran's purchase of 25.1 percent of Krupp GmbH, the German steel firm, and Libya's purchase of 10 percent of Fiat, the Italian auto manufacturer. One also suspects that in time LDC policy makers, realizing the massive conflict in interest inherent in the joint venture strategy, will in some instances offer to swap access to local resources (labor, market, energy, land) for a negotiated amount of parent company stock.

Under some conceivable set of circumstances, any possible combination of contract and equity is possible, although as one approaches 100 percent ownership some of the contractual relationships become increasingly unlikely, indeed, may be forbidden by law. For instance, according to Brazilian law, if the foreign firm owns more than 50 percent of a local subsidiary, the subsidiary cannot enter into license agreements (for patents or trademarks) with the parent, and for know-how only for the first five-years after startup. The Brazilian authorities wish to have profits repatriated as such and not as fees and royalties, which are costed against the Brazilian subsidiary and thus paid out of pretax earnings.

The sale of services or lease of assets by the parent firm to a foreign subsidiary in which there is local equity investment is always a tricky business. Should the parent firm be compelled to provide services and assets at cost, which means that it will be dividing the profit derived therefrom with the local investors? Or, should the subsidiary pay the full price (cost plus profit)? The latter would seem to be the reasonable policy so long as the price is a reasonable one. Because governments realize that they do not have an adequate monitoring mechanism, it is easier simply to outlaw these nondividend payments from subsidiary to parent. Unmonitored, these flows can, of course, move profit from one subsidiary to another or from subsidiary to parent at the whim of management and at the expense of local stockholders and tax collectors. This movement is one form of "transfer-pricing."

Telesio has identified certain variables that appeared to be associated with the amount of licensing[11] a firm does as an alternative to foreign direct investment. The variables so identified:

1. the investment in research and development (R&D) as a percentage of sale (the higher the percentage, the greater the licensing propensity)

2. the relative size of a company in its industry (the smaller the firm, the greater its propensity to license)

3. the level of diversification (the greater the diversification of the firm, the greater its propensity to license)

4. degree of experience in foreign operations, as measured by the percentage of total sales manufactured abroad by controlled subsidiaries (the lower the percentage, the greater the firm's propensity to license)

Telesio speculates that licensing (i.e., technology contracting) becomes "an attractive way to obtain residual returns from technologies that are no longer unique."[12] This result was confirmed partially by a preliminary finding that *process* innovators license more readily than *product* innovators and receive lower royalties on their licensing agreements. The connection between this type of innovation (that is, process innovation) and the maturity of the technology had been suggested by another study in that product innovations were found to be dominant in the early stages of a product's life cycle and process innovations, in the later stages.[13] Therefore, Telesio reasoned, "the process innovators are more likely to have competitors for their technology, since process innovations occur as products age, and as products age, competition increases.[14]

Telesio's study generated those corporate responses listed in Table 5.2, which curiously include no direct observations that a firm licensed simply because it was more profitable to do so! Nor did Telesio appear to ask corporate executives what they would do if the return on corporate assets committed, appropriately discounted to the present, were clearly higher in the technology contracting case than for direct investment.

Telesio differentiated "licensing for reciprocity" from licensing as an alternative to direct foreign investment. By this phrase he referred to the policy of licensing to gain access to the technology of competitors through the reciprocal exchange of licenses. Variables associated with this policy were slightly

---

[11]Telesio included in "licensing" some technical assistance contracts involving nonproprietary technology and know-how, but excluding trade-mark licensing. He included licensing only to noncontrolled foreign subsidiaries and only for technology that the firm was itself using. Also excluded was "licensing for reciprocity," by which he referred to a policy of licensing to gain access to the technology of competitors through the reciprocal exchanges of licenses.

[12]Piero Telesio, *Foreign Licensing Policy in Multinational Enterprises* (Boston, Mass.: unpublished D.B.A. thesis, Harvard Graduate School of Business Administration, February 1977), pp. 8.4–6.

[13]William J. Abernathy and James M. Utterback, "Innovation and the Evolving Structure of the Firm," (Boston, Mass.: working paper, Harvard Graduate School of Business Administration, June 1975).

[14]Telesio, *Foreign Licensing Policy*, p. 8.7.

Table 5.2
AVERAGE OCCURRENCE OF REASONS FOR LICENSING ABROAD

Reasons for Licensing	Percentage of companies replying that a reason for licensing	
	has been of importance	total number of companies replying
1. Shortage of funds for investment	55%	46%
2. Did not have management for investment	36	39
3. Lacked knowledge of market	48	41
4. Market too small for profitable investment	73	45
5. Entry in market difficult because of strong competitors	58	45
6. Politically risky situation for investment	66	35
7. Government pressure for licensing	90	42

Source: Piero Telesio, *Foreign Licensing Policy in Multinational Enterprises* (Boston, Mass.: unpublished DBA thesis, Harvard Graduate School of Business Administration, February 1977), p. 4.10.

Note: Replies to the question: "Considering your recent licensing decisions, which of the factors below have been of importance in determining whether you license to an unaffiliated company or a minority-owned affiliate, instead of investing with a controlled manufacturing facility?" The possible replies were: (1) has been of importance, (2) occasionally of importance, and (3) never of importance. The first two possible replies are combined into one for this table.

different. Again, companies spending more on R&D as a percentage of sales and which were highly diversified tended to license for reciprocity, but, unlike the earlier case, so did the larger firms in an industry.

In fact, a prime reason for many technically oriented firms in the United States to enter into associations with the foreign enterprises is to share in technical developments (research and development) undertaken by the latter (notably European and Japanese firms), often at less cost than in the United States. Not infrequently, the domestic and foreign firms enter a cross-licensing deal, which in effect bestows the right of first refusal of any valuable industrial secret or patent developed by one firm upon the other. Technical assistance contracts running in both directions may be associated with these cross-licenses if personnel are to be transferred back and forth to assist in the installation of new productive equipment and/or to train employees. The two, the license giving the right to use a patented product or process or to use a trademark and the sale of associated technical assistance, may be found in a single contract or may be separate. Such agreements encompass such matters as definition of subject matter, warranty of title (for patents and trademarks), duration, payment of costs and fees (royalties), degree of exclusiveness, sales territory, quality control, confidentiality use of marks, reporting obligations, grant-back assignment, and arbitration of differences. These are difficult to write so as to protect adequately the interests of both parties and, hence, require expert legal counsel. Commonly, the fee or royalty is defined as a percentage of sales of those products incorporating patented parts or making use of the technology transferred. There are obvious problems of definition here. A lump sum, possibly paid in installments is an alternative. Another is a fixed royalty based on physical quantity produced or sold. Royalties may be either increased or reduced with the volume of production or of sales. Many governments limit the percentage of fees and royalties (often at a 2 or 3 percent level, almost never over 5 percent), also the duration of the contract (almost never over ten years). It is strongly suspected that the prices at which technology has been sold have been unduly low. Viewed initially as sort of a by-product, the firm applies a marginal pricing policy to technology; after all, its main output consists of tangible product, not technology or skills. Consequently, international business has gotten trapped in the 5 percent syndrome in that government approval is frequently required, and governments are strongly influenced by precedence. Indeed, research would indicate that virtually no manufacturing firms price technology either on the basis of full costing (including a reasonable return on investment) or on the marginal value of the technology to the recipient.

Sales and purchase agreements of a continuing nature likewise bestow valuable rights. If these are not linked to the licensing of a patent, trademark, or copyright and are exclusive in some sense (in respect to price, territory, credit terms, or delivery), serious problems relating to U.S. antitrust provisions may arise unless the associated foreign firm is the agent of the seller or at least 51 percent owned by the U.S. firm and, hence, unambiguously controlled. A special form of supply contract is contract (or "toll") manufacturing, which may or may not be associated with a technical assistance contract and/or debt. At the very least, on-the-spot quality control is often required by the contractor. In this case, the contractor is really leasing the manufacturing capacity of another firm.

There seems to be an increasing international traffic in management contracts. A 1975 study of 14 U.K.-based corporations operating internationally revealed a trend towards using management contracts. "Companies can reap substantial benefits from their use especially if they set out actively to sell their stock of managerial skills and resources."[15] The authors of this study went on to observe,

Although the research supports the advisability of short-term [management] contracts it would be a mistake to see this as limiting a company's long-term opportunities in a particular country. The successful completion of a particular contract (success often being based upon the speed of completion and withdrawal of the company) would in many cases lead to opportunities for undertaking further diversification phases of the local contract enterprise. Further, so competitive is the field becoming and so few are the companies which are experienced in operating such contracts, that successful oper-

---

[15]Richard Ellison, "Management Contracts," (Manchester, England: The International Business Unit, Institute of Science and Technology, mimeo., October 1975), p. 1.

ations in one country have often proved a decided advantage when opportunities arose in others. The 'world' of management contract operations is still sufficiently small to be considered almost a 'club.'[16]

This same research reported that if the contracting firm held equity in the local contract enterprise there was a tendency for severe conflicts to develop between the two parties, such that the management contract frequently broke down.[17]

Although ownership strategy should relate directly to sales, production, labor and management strategies, this principle is valid only if an effort has been made to select optimum strategies in these areas, given the particular set of circumstances. It is not valid if the firm has merely extended its domestic strategies into the foreign market without reexamination. In general, the firm should retain ownership of those rights and assets of greatest continuing value, as perceived by the associated foreign firm and by the host society and which cannot be supplied locally or by competitors. Maximum return with minimum risk is thereby assured. To retain ownership of assets and rights that have little or no continuing perceivable value, or which are available locally, is hazardous. By "continuing perceivable" value is meant a *continuing* inflow of assets and/or services perceived as necessary and, hence, valuable by both the local owners (if any) and the host government. Even such sophisticated governments as the Canadian, Australian, French, and British (not to mention the Japanese) have reacted negatively to foreign ownership under some circumstances. More recently many Alaskans and Hawaiians have become outspoken about the degree to which their control is being threatened by Japanese firms exploiting natural resources and tourism within their respective states. A bill was even introduced into the U.S. Congress that would limit foreign ownership of U.S.-owned firms to 5 percent.

The point has been made that "the foreign [direct] investor should look upon his investment as being continually 'on trial,' not only against alternatives open to the host country at the time the investment is made but even more so when it has matured.[18] The writer goes on to observe that once the stream of benefits slackens, whether in the form of new capital or skills, "the host government will become more susceptible to nationalistic claims that the foreign investor has outlived his usefulness."[19] And indeed he may have done just that. It was reported in 1970, relative to the impending socialization of the Chilean copper industry, that some foreigners were arguing that the Chileans would not be able to run the mines on their own. "But," the report continued, "copper men disagree. Says a U.S. executive, 'We've spent 15 years and

[16]Ellison, "Management Contracts," pp. 1–2.

[17]Ellison, "Management Contracts," p. 12.

[18]Peter Gabriel, "Foreign Investment in Less Developed Countries: Its Status, Risks, and Opportunities," typed ms., Harvard University, December 1963, p. 36.

[19]Gabriel, "Foreign Investment," p. 39.

millions of dollars training them to run copper mines. They can do it.' The number of American [U.S.] personnel is small, in any case. Kennecott, for example, has only seven Americans on its management. The mining supervisor of the great El Tiente mine is Chilean."[20] Another relevant fact: Chile was selling little of its copper to the United States, some 90 percent being shipped to Japan and Western Europe. The point is, in Chilean eyes, how could continued U.S. participation in ownership—and, hence, in earnings—be justified? As a patriotic Chilean decision-maker desperately worried about the economic plight of his people, one could become convinced quite easily that there was no justification unless there were some continuing inputs from the foreign copper companies that equaled or exceeded the cost of their ownership to Chile.

Many query the implicit assumption in the foregoing discussion that ownership across an international frontier is somehow different from the purely domestic, or uninational, situation. There are, one suggests, at least four reasons for making the assumption.

First. Political commitments differ among nations in that national priorities vary in respect to what is considered the appropriate allocation of a country's resources, of its land, its waterways, its minerals, its manpower, its energy, its skills, its R&D effort, its financial capital. Appropriateness is determined by national priorities in respect to allocating resources along several continua (see Introduction). The appearance of an alien business on the scene implies the use of some local resources. A national's allocational priorities will be influenced by its presence. The degree of penetration tolerated by an alien firm is possibly a function of

1. the relative size of the two national economies;

2. their historical relationship;

3. the size and importance of the enterprise relative to the host economy;

4. the nature of the enterprise (for instance, the degree of its public service, strategic and/or essential consumer content);

5. the nature of the international linkage, from complete alien control of decision-making to virtually no control (as in the case of a simple sale and purchase agreement);

6. the nature and effectiveness of the political elite of the host nation;

7. the "image" and political effectiveness of the alien's parent country and of the alien firm itself.

Second. One must consider international ownership differently from uninational because legal concepts generally differ more from country to country than within a single country, even those of a federal nature. Some nations do not even recognize the inherent right of private individuals, whether domestic

---

[20]*Time*, October 19, 1970, pp. 29–30.

or foreign, to own certain types of, or possibly any, real estate, mineral rights, buildings, productive machinery, or valuable intangible rights. For example, many nations of Spanish heritage deny the right of private persons to own underground mineral resources. Many countries (and some of the states of the United States) restrict alien ownership of real property. In socialist countries, the private ownership of certain types of real property is sharply restrained and, indeed, the derivation of private profit from real property may be a criminal offense. In the U.S.S.R. an inventor may be issued an inventor's certificate and receive recognition, monetary or otherwise, but he does not have the right to exploit the invention himself; that is a state prerogative. Even the development of personal skills and their employment may be subject to central control. Sometimes these rights vis-à-vis aliens are considered to be reciprocal ones. If the alien's country recognizes rights for nationals from another nation, the latter will recognize similar rights for aliens from that country. Even some of the U.S. state and federal laws in the areas of banking, property, and mineral rights ownership seem to be of this nature. In other cases, ownership may be considered in the nature of a lease or public trust—as in Yugoslavia—where the trustees are relatively autonomous working communities. Such a lease or trust may be subject to periodic revaluation and transfer if certain minimum conditions imposed by law are not met.

Third. A difference between international and uninational ownership may likewise appear because of differences in levels of national wealth. If the difference is great, the use of scarce resources (those that are capital- or foreign-exchange intensive, such as high-level skills, capital equipment, and already fully employed inputs of local origin) may be considered a matter of vital national interest. Given the vast disparity in time horizons between the decision-making political elite and the mass of consumers (who may be existing only slightly above subsistence level), market forces may not be perceived by the elite to be such as to achieve national development objectives. A responsible elite (responsible in terms of trying to act in such manner as to promote maximum, long-term national development) may well use measures for evaluating alien use of local resources other than internal, financial profit-and-loss. Some of these measures may be balance-of-payments effects, national income effect, public revenue effects, long-run growth effects, or allocational effects.[21] Thus, the reception an alien proposing to establish a local enterprise should anticipate may differ substantially from the purely domestic situation in which internal, profit-and-loss considerations are more likely to dominate. For example, within a much broader set of constraints, the allocation of resources induced by domestic market factors in the United States is assumed to approximate national interest.

---

[21]For a more complete discussion of this aspect, see R. D. Robinson, *International Business Policy* (New York: Holt, Rinehart and Winston, 1964), Chap. 3; also R. D. Robinson, *National Control of Foreign Business Entry* (New York: Praeger, 1976).

In a less developed country, because the consumer (that is, the ultimate buyer and user of goods) frequently has one time horizon and the governing elite one that is generally much longer, there can be no single set of equilibrium prices. In a more highly developed market economy, these two time horizons tend to converge. Prices have some relation to relative contribution to national development. For instance, the consumer in the more developed countries is willing to pay a great deal for education. A village farmer in a traditional society may not. In general, in the more developed countries, people approve of government expenditures designed to stimulate long-run growth (for example, education and R&D), although it means taking money out of their pockets to do so. In a developing country just moving off the subsistence level, this is not a popular thing for politicians to attempt. For these and other reasons, the price system may not allocate resources in an optimum way for maximizing long-run economic growth.

Furthermore, because of the rapid structural changes of many of these countries (for instance, the shift from capital-intensive agriculture to labor-intensive industry or the shift from a village society to an urban society) even if one could find an equilibrium price today, it would not be equilibrium tomorrow. One would have to assume the most sophisticated system of inter-related national markets and high elasticities in respect to demand and supply[22] if prices were to continue to reflect relative contribution to economic growth with any degree of accuracy.

If price cannot be assumed even to approximate the priorities desired by the elite in allocating resources, then the private property system as we know it cannot be permitted to operate. Why, one may ask, are we concerned only with an elite? Simply because it probably represents the greatest force for modernization and creativity; for investment in education, public health, and economic growth; and, eventually, for economic integration and, hopefully, one day, political integration as well. The mass of people living in their highly tradition-al communities at near subsistence level cannot in the near future be expected to demonstrate the sort of sophisticated and untraditional behavior that leads to modernization through a free market or liberal political system.

Fourth. Difference in monetary systems and wealth levels dictate a further disparity between the international and uninational cases relative to owner-ship. Assuming that the alien interest is of U.S. origin, profits must be repatriat-ed in dollars or something of value ultimately convertible to dollars. Because of the forced-draft development that a widening international disparity in per capita national wealth dictates, sooner or later a development-committed po-litical elite may be inclined to enforce its own consumption preference for that of the masses. One way of doing this is to husband scarce resources, including scarce foreign exchange such as dollars, and to allocate them through adminis-

---

[22]See Glossary.

trative procedures to high-priority imports. Hence, the exchange rate is not market determined, but is pegged, which means that scarce foreign exchange is undervalued; that is why it is scarce. The local currency buys more dollars, or the dollars buy fewer local currency units, than would be the case if the conversion rate were determined by a free movement of exports and imports. (Wherever there is a foreign exchange control system in place, this must be true. If not, there would be no need for the control system, for its purpose is to capture undervalued foreign exchange and ration it according to priority of use.) Therefore, an alien firm repatriating dividends at the pegged official rate may receive more dollars than its local currency earnings really justify, in that the marginal value of those dollars to long-term development is likely to be very much greater than that implied in the official exchange rate. The more local resources that one capitalizes through the reinvestment of local earnings, the more this is true. Even free exchange rates would be set by relatively few commodities being traded internationally within a limited range of time, which might or might not clear the market at a rate equal to the relative marginal value of the two currencies to long-run economic growth. At best, it would be a lucky coincidence if the two values (of a free exchange rate and of a marginal value to development) converged.

Taking an extreme case, suppose one invests $1,000, reinvests all earnings for ten years, and invests no new dollars, either directly or in dollar costs. If the project generates a 20 percent (after local tax) profit, one would have a total investment at the end of the tenth year of something over $6,000. Then assume that the alien owner starts repatriating all earnings at the rate of 20 percent. He would be taking home some $1,200 a year. This return is based on the initial $1,000 input plus $5,000 of earnings acquired through profits on local sales and invested in the acquisition of local assets. If the value of this flow of $1,200 a year starting ten years hence and discounted to the present[23] is felt by the local authorities to exceed $1,000 (plus the net external economies created thereby in the intervening years, discounted to the present), then they may perceive that the nation is losing more than it is gaining. If so, they will either shut the door on continued alien ownership or enforce reinvestment of all earnings over and above a certain percentage. *At some point in time*, as the tenth year draws closer, the perceived value of the $1,200 outflow is likely to exceed the value of the external input, *unless the inputs continue*. The existence of different monetary systems can thus make a difference.

Also, inflation rates tend to move ahead of the rates of change in an exchange rate. Say, 100 pesos buy a dollar at the official rate. Prices then move up, say, 50 percent, and the exchange rate (pesos per dollar) is increased by 25 percent. Now 125 pesos buy a dollar, but they are worth only 83 of the

---

[23]A very high discount rate is likely to be used, for the real marginal value of capital is high and the capital-output ratio is relatively low.

previous pesos. The dollar is now of less value than before in terms of local goods and services according to the official rate, but in fact it probably is not; rather it is worth more if one relates it to economic growth. The point is that the dollar can purchase the capital equipment and skills which, in combination with local resources, can maximize the productivity of the latter.

All of these national pressures generated by disparities in politically determined resource allocation, legal system, level of per capita wealth, and monetary system in turn generate a distinctive nationalism. This nationalism becomes relevant to the international manager when it leads to restraints on alien ownership of commercially valuable assets located within the national territory, on profits (through artificially high costs or controlled prices) or on the repatriation of earnings generated by such assets. Therefore, international ownership can be, and usually is, very different from uninational ownership in terms of how ownership is perceived and valued by the relevant authorities, which in turn may be equated with different sets of restraints imposed on alien ownership.

A 1969 survey of the opinions of 122 business leaders in 50 countries summarized the findings in these words,

Economic nationalism, narrowly defined and ineptly applied at the wrong time or in the wrong country, is bad. On some occasions and under certain conditions, a flexible and intelligently administered economic policy oriented to national end is good. But for most countries, and for the long run, the best and most feasible policy is one of progressive liberalism and interdependence in world trade and investment relationships. [24]

A Turkish business leader observed that there would be a clash of interest between rich and poor nations until there was a reorientation of thinking about materialistic values. He went on to observe, "Nationalistic behavior in reality exists in the rich, powerful, and imperialistic countries as an outcrop of individual egoism," and appears in backward and underdeveloped countries as a defensive reaction. [25]

This same study reported a strong undercurrent of feeling that foreign investors have an obligation to regard national susceptibilities and to conform to policies of countries in which they are located, particularly in respect to the abuse of a dominant or monopolistic position. [26] "To a substantial number of the survey participants, the most promising device for harmonizing the interests of the local economy with outside investment interests is the international joint business venture," although mandatory stipulations in this regard were widely criticized. [27] The question arises whether under the circumstances described on the preceding page a firm is well advised to invest

---

[24]Enid B. Lovell, *Nationalism or Interdependence: The Alternatives—International Survey of Business Opinion and Experience* (New York: The Conference Board, 1969), p. 1.

[25]Lovell, *Nationalism or Independence*, p. 64.

[26]Lovell, *Nationalism or Independence*, p. 37.

[27]Lovell, *Nationalism or Independence*, p. 58.

at all in the *ownership* of physical assets located in a less developed country. One suspects that there are, in fact, relatively few instances in which such investment is advisable on a long-run basis. For such investment to be advisable, the company must feel relatively certain that it can recapture its investment, plus an appropriate return, within a period of time during which it can demonstrate that its ownership is in the interest of the host society, both as presently perceived and in reality. (The corporate planner must assume that the two images of national interest will become similar over the planning horizon.)

Various measures of criteria may be (or will be) used, explicitly or implicitly, by host governments in evaluating what foreign business interests do locally. For the multinational corporation, long-run security of market position and business assets is anchored in the capacity of its management to think in similar terms and so structure overseas enterprises as to identify with the *perceived* interests of the host societies. Relevant economic measures are net-value-added, balance-of-payments, public revenue, and growth-generating effects—the last being a combination of allocational and innovational effects. It seems quite clear that the political vulnerability of a given enterprise is a function of all four of these measures, taken separately and in concert, plus certain essentially noneconomic measures of political impact that relate to (1) a firm's operational policies, (2) the structure of the enterprise, (3) the size of the enterprise, and (4) the nature of the product.

Curiously, research has uncovered very few multinational firms that have tried, in such objective terms, to *assess* the political vulnerability of its various foreign operations *and* to shift policies accordingly so as to reduce risk. One important policy variable here, of course, is ownership, for ownership creates an important outward flow of resources from a host society, a flow that may be unlimited in time. Foreign ownership also inhibits the freedom of the local society to allocate its own resources, which, for reasons already mentioned, may deviate from a market-determined allocation.

For example, a number of the less developed countries have reached a stage of development at which the perceived benefits of foreign business may be buried by the effect such investment has on inhibiting the growth of local enterprises. The result is a posture of hostility to foreign enterprise, the United States in particular because it is the home of so many of the large corporations. But again, research seems to reveal few U.S. firms willing to restructure their relationships with foreign affiliates when an affiliate's activities are, in fact, likely to block the growth of local enterprise.

Quite apart from political hostility, the foreign investor maximizes his return by limiting his investment and ownership to those rights and assets productive of the greatest return, which, in the long run, should be precisely those of greatest value to the associated firm and to the host society. On occasion, he may feel compelled to protect that profit stream by retaining ownership of other subsidiary rights and assets, for example, majority ownership, in order to assure continued purchase of intermediary goods from the parent firm or management contract to assure the purchase of technical assistance. Obviously, however, if a firm feels it necessary to "capture" its profit stream in this manner it must likewise feel that in the eyes of foreign associates or host governments, the value of what it is contributing may not measure up to what it is extracting. The firm is thereby admitting its vulnerability. The assumption that either contractual rights *or equity ownership* can be supported when its impact is contrary to the interest of either foreign associates and/or the host society has only short-run validity, if that. For example, if a firm has been securing an adequate product for the market through contract manufacturing undertaken by a locally-owned firm—or could do so—then the establishment of a foreign-owned manufacturing establishment may be considered unwarranted and therefore be opposed by both the host government and local business community unless there is some more attractive alternative employment for the local resources concerned.

The point is that, looked at from the side of the local society in which an alien-owned enterprise is embedded, the level of earnings and other costs imposed by its activity on the host economy should be of lesser value than the inputs or contributions made by the alien parent corporation. Some of these costs to local society are obviously very difficult to quantify, such as the amount of local enterprise growth being blocked. But the stream of earnings paid out by a society *is very visible.* To minimize risk, these returns should if possible be adjusted periodically as the perceived cost/benefit ratio for the local society shifts, as it almost certainly will over time. Typically, though admittedly not in all cases, as the foreign firm transfers resources and skills over time, its continuing contribution relative to its return will become less and less. In such event, one can expect mounting pressure in the direction of reducing the outflow of earnings to the foreign parent—perhaps to zero. In fact, however, some research would indicate that, although an international firm may be willing to limit its initial entry in respect to a new product to a license or joint venture, as the product matures (that is, as the relevant product and/or production processes become routinized and part of general industrial knowledge), the firm will try to protect its position through a 100 percent-owned enterprise. At this point, product differentiation, heavy promotional effort, and production specialization become critical, all of which push in the direction of centralized control and the elimination of any local partners.[28] But such a policy may very well lead to maximum political vulnerability. On the other hand, in the case of the conglomerate multinational firms, a countervailing pressure seems to be operating. According to the Harvard study of the multinational corporations, "those [firms] with broad product lines have

[28]See Lawrence Franko, "Strategy Choice and Multinational Corporate Tolerance for Joint Ventures with Foreign Partners," unpublished D.B.A. diss., Harvard University Graduate School of Business Administration, 1969.

a substantially higher proportion of joint venture among their overseas manufacturing subsidiaries than those with narrow product lines."[29]

It has been precisely this inflexibility on the part of Western business in readjusting benefits it derives from a foreign venture *so as to accord with the benefits received by the host country* that has induced many countries to introduce the "entry agreement." This phrase refers to an explicit agreement between host government and corporation upon the latter's entry through direct investment, a system first introduced in the early 1950s by India for certain ventures and more generally by Indonesia in 1956. The idea is now quite widespread among LDCs. The essential elements of such an agreement are: (1) a time limit on the right of the alien corporation to occupy and use industrial properties, most frequently 20 to 30 years but often extendable under certain conditions; (2) a host government guarantee that it will not expropriate the alien-owned enterprise limited to the same period; (3) a schedule for phasing out alien employees of various categories; (4) a schedule for increasing local value added over time. Most commonly there are provisions for the phased spin-off of foreign ownership, say 30 percent in 10 years, 60 percent in 20 years. Furthermore, approval may be given only to those projects meeting certain tests, such as employment, capital commitment, foreign exchange earnings, exports, production, and location.[30] Such an entry agreement, to all intents and purposes, means that rights arising from ownership are of a contractual nature. Only so long as the alien firm lives up to its agreement are those rights valid. In that a government, in entering into such an agreement, specifically states that the terms of such an agreement are in harmony with its national interests and development plans, the element of uncertainty from the corporate view may be reduced. And, of course, it forces the corporate negotiators either to justify or modify their relationships so as to conform to such interests and plans. A few countries (Indonesia and Malaysia) have given these agreements the coloration of international contracts by binding themselves to arbitrate disputes arising under such agreements before the International Center for the Settlement of Investment Disputes. Others may give the alien owner the right to sue the government locally in event of alleged breach of contract (Chile).

Curiously, on the basis of fairly intensive research, it seems apparent that exceedingly few corporations make a conscious, deliberate cost/benefit analysis of a proposed overseas operation for the purpose of determining the most profitable relationship; for example, 100 percent ownership, some degree of joint ownership, contract plus some degree of ownership, or entirely contractual. A study of United States–Italian joint ventures found no management that

---

[29]Raymond Vernon, *Sovereignty at Bay, the Multinational Spread of U.S. Enterprises* (New York: Basic Books, 1971), p. 142.

[30]See Robinson, *National Control of Foreign Business Entry* for a detailed study of entry agreements and other entry conditions.

had undertaken systematically to determine inputs and time horizons, without which a quantification of cost/benefit ratios was obviously impossible.[31] An earlier study of joint ventures entered into by English firms in Pakistan or India revealed the same omission.[32] So likewise did a more recent analysis of U.S. business operations in Canada.[33] A 15-country survey of international mixed ventures failed to turn up a situation in which the private firm appeared to have made a careful cost/benefit analysis of the possible relationships so as to determine which would be most profitable.[34] Rather, the arrangements that emerged were simply the result of a bargaining process, the outcome of which was based on the relative power position of the two parties at a particular point in time.

If one thing one can be certain, the relative power position of the corporation tends to shift downward once it is locked in the embrace of a government. In the case of a mixed venture, the embrace is more real than vicarious. However, were the firm to restrain its participation and earnings to that fraction of the total local enterprise representing continuing externally derived inputs (those not available locally), then its leverage should continue to be great. This strategy requires a continuing cost/benefit analysis. If, however, management's attitude is that joint venturing dilutes control, and somehow this is seen as apart from any comparative profit calculation, then it should be made explicit that management is maximizing power, not profit.

A study by Zenoff found that very few firms make a cost/benefit analysis in respect to international licensing.[35] His study concluded that, "Only a small number of companies are now adequately structured to evaluate fully foreign licensing opportunities." Zenoff points out that only by a comprehensive measurement of the value of projected marginal costs and benefits can one evaluate a licensing opportunity as compared with alternative methods of penetrating a foreign market. No company in his sample had made such an evaluation. Yet, the 43 companies in his sample had entered into 3,214 licensing arrangements.

---

[31]Dario Iacuelli, "Management Factors and Joint Ventures: Italy, a Case Study," unpublished Ph.D. diss., Sloan School of Management, M.I.T., 1970, p. 239.

[32]James W. C. Tomlinson, *The Joint Venture Process in International Business: India and Pakistan* (Cambridge: M.I.T. Press, 1970).

[33]A. I. Litvak, C. Maule, and R. D. Robinson, *Dual Loyalty, Canadian-U.S. Business Arrangements* (Toronto: McGraw-Hill, 1971).

[34]R. D. Robinson, *International Mixed Ventures*, unpublished country studies, 1971.

[35]David B. Zenoff, "Licensing as a Means of Penetrating Foreign Markets," *Idea*, vol. 14, no. 2, Summer 1970, pp. 292 ff. This statement is confirmed by a more recent study based on data reported by 40 U.S.-based and 26 foreign-based "multinational" corporations. In responding to a question as to why the company licensed abroad, *not one* indicated that it was more profitable to do so; that is, that it would generate a higher return on corporate assets than direct investment. "Licensing . . . appears to be a last resort alternative. . . . A common remark was: 'We are in the business of *manufacturing* and *selling* our products in many markets; we are basically *not* interested in selling our technology.' " Piero Telesio, *Foreign Licensing Policy in Multinational Enterprises* (Boston, Mass.: unpublished D.B.A. diss., Harvard Graduate School of Business Administration, February 1977), p. 4.8–9.

In the deliberate choice of ownership strategy, basically three questions are involved:

1. In what should the domestic (parent) firm hold ownership? Possible choices: equity (zero to 100 percent), debt, intangible assets (such as patents, copyrights, trademarks, trade secrets), managerial knowledge and skills, technical knowledge and skills, distribution networks, physical assets (machines, land, resources), other contractual rights (a lease, for example).

2. In what should the associated foreign business interest hold ownership?

3. What type of foreign associate(s) should the firm select? Possible choices: the general public, the host government, a limited number of identified private persons, a business entity, a nonprofit organization (for example, a labor union).

5.1 RIGHTS AND ASSETS OWNED BY THE INTERNATIONAL FIRM

Reasons advanced by parent managements for insisting upon 100 percent ownership of foreign ventures fall into these categories:

1. unpleasant past experience with joint ventures,

2. lack of confidence in the integrity and/or ability of foreign business groups,

3. uncertainty regarding the identity of those to whom the locally held equity may be transferred in the future,

4. difficulty in maintaining equity,

5. conflict of interest between the parent company and the foreign partners (for example, in such decisions as intercompany pricing, profit distribution, rate of growth, personnel policy, pricing, quality control),

6. desire to integrate the operation with the total corporate system in respect to export, production, marketing, and financial management.

It will be noted that reason one above is a matter of chance and reason two, possibly a function of reason one, reflects a generalized distrust. On the other hand, not a few experienced international businessmen have observed privately that the general level of integrity among businessmen is not significantly different across national frontiers. Dishonesty cannot be associated with nationality, only the form it takes. Levels of competence obviously vary, but training is always possible. The absence of any effort to develop a local management, given the frequently great cost advantage, throws one back to reasons one or two. In any event, a management contract need not be associated with participation in equity. The future transfer of locally held shares to "undesirables" may constitute a serious problem, although in some cases transferability can be limited. Equity can be maintained in a joint venture through special stockholders' agreement if possible under local law. Conflict of interest, on the other hand, is a very real issue, although many areas of conflict can be eliminated by working out operating policies ahead of time. One firm actually staged

Table 5.3
RELATIVE IMPORTANCE OF REASONS FOR DESIRING MAJORITY CONTROL OF FOREIGN MANUFACTURING AFFILIATES (19 JAPANESE FIRMS)

Reason	Mean score of answers*
To maintain quality standard	4.68
To protect company brand name	4.32
To protect company's technology	3.84
To coordinate export	3.00
To control dividend policy	2.95
To integrate production	2.58
To standardize marketing	2.52
To integrate financial management	1.58

*Scoring: from very important (5) to no importance (0).
Source: Yoshino, *Japan's Multinational Enterprises*, p. 155.

a "war game" with its prospective foreign partner, the result of which was 90 percent agreement. The 10 percent area of disagreement was worked out by compromise and committed to writing. Profit channels need not be the same for all participants; different classes of stock may be possible; special bonuses may be paid; and a minority interest represented on the board of directors may hold a veto power in certain decision areas. Many of these conflicts of interest arise because the foreign parent corporation views the local venture as one element in an integrated system, which came out quite clearly in Yoshino's study of 50 Japanese companies, of which 19 felt that majority ownership was important (see Table 5.3). Their reasons:

Forgetting for the moment personal preferences on the part of decision-makers and the extent of a firm's resources, five factors are in fact relevant to an optimum ownership decision: (1) competitive position, (2) availability of acceptable associates (or consumers), (3) legal constraints, (4) control requirements, and (5) benefit/cost relationships. (These are diagrammed in Figure 5.2.) We shall consider each in the order indicated.

Competitive position. Competitive position refers to the degree of uniqueness of what the firm has to sell. If the firm's good or service is, in fact, uniquely superior and has commercial value, it may well opt for 100 percent ownership if this relationship will better protect the uniqueness of its product than would lesser ownership and some contractual relationship. And the host government may be forced to accept it. If, however, another alien firm—or local firm—offers to do the same thing at a lesser cost in terms of scarce inputs (such as foreign exchange), the initial firm may find itself under pressure to reduce return, either by selling some part or all of its equity to a local firm and relying on a contractual relationship that generates an appropriately reduced income or, if already linked by contract, by reducing the percentage fee stipulated

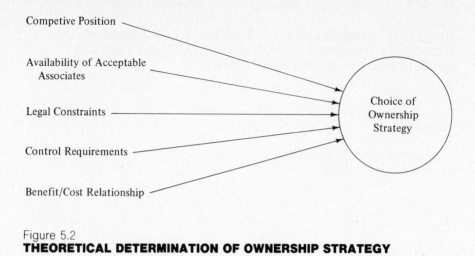

Figure 5.2
THEORETICAL DETERMINATION OF OWNERSHIP STRATEGY

therein. The latter is often easier to accomplish, particularly if forced on the firm suddenly. Reducing a royalty or fee is relatively easy; spinning off ownership is not. But for that very reason this strategy (choice of contractual relationship) may be suboptimal. The host government's attitude toward private property (for example, an ideologically based commitment to protect property rights) may tend to restrain it, for the time being, from forcing a readjustment in ownership and, hence, in income. In the short run, it may be much less restrained in forcing renegotiation of a contract, for the life of a contractual relationship is limited. In the longer run, however, ownership is in greater jeopardy because of the rigidity implicit in the idea that ownership runs forever so long as certain conditions are fulfilled (such as payment of taxes).

Of course, most firms fall in between a pure monopoly position (whether based on a unique product, unique process, unique access to market, relevant skills, or capital) and a perfectly competitive situation. In such case, willingness to meet competing offers in respect to ownership and contractual relationships is required. A flexible ownership policy is thereby indicated in the international case. Indeed, the entry agreement, even though it stipulates a spin-off of equity over time, may provide maximum stability.

Availability of acceptable associates. Whether a partner, contractee, contractor, licensor, licensee, supplier, or customer, the availability of acceptable associates obviously imposed a restraint. Even if one can find a suitable associate, how does one know that he will retain his interest and not transfer it to others who may be less than acceptable? In any event, everyone dies sooner or later. What of the next generation? Here, local laws of inheritance and the possibility of imposing legal restraint on stock or contract transference may be of critical importance. Barring this problem, and in the absence of an immedi-

Table 5.4
PARTNERS IN JAPANESE INTERNATIONAL JOINT VENTURES

Individuals (including closely held family corporations)		305
Entrepreneurs in manufacturing	102	
Entrepreneurs in commerce	119	
Individuals in other services	39	
Others	45	
Publicly held corporations		32
Government or quasigovernment organizations		24
		361

Source: Yoshino, *Japan's Multinational Enterprises*, p. 151.

ately available associate acceptable to the parent firm, the latter must consider the cost of finding and developing appropriate local nationals. Consequently, one perforce gets into a benefit/cost analysis, but this sort of analysis is anchored in one's expectations as to what the local associate will contribute to the enterprise. We postpone discussion of this dimension until later.

In a random sampling of 100 joint ventures owned by 50 major Japanese corporations, Yoshino found the distribution of joint venture partners seen in Table 5.4. "These data clearly demonstrate the dominance of individual entrepreneurs in particular as partners in Japanese manufacturing joint ventures abroad."[36] The majority of them had been engaged primarily in commercial activities, which tend to emphasize short term returns and possibly assume longer time conflict with the manufacturing-oriented parent company, albeit possibly less so in the Japanese case than for U.S. and European-based parents. As already pointed out, the Japanese seem less concerned with dividends, more with profits from external trade. Perhaps the conflict merely shifts to level of transfer prices.

Next, one might appropriately consider the *legal factors* bearing directly on the matter of selecting an optimum ownership, contracting policy. Certain legal restraints have already been touched upon, specifically, inheritance law, law on restricting transfer of ownership, entry controls, recognition of private property rights. Other legal variables directly relevant in some possible situations may be listed as follows:

1. Foreign tax credit; for example, for U.S. firms to credit foreign income and wealth taxes paid by associated foreign firms against U.S. tax liability, the U.S. firm must own at least 10 percent of the equity of a first-tier foreign subsidiary, which in turn

[36]Yoshino, *Japan's Multinational Enterprises*, p. 151.

must own at least 10 percent of the second,[37] and the second at least 10 percent of the third. (But in no case may the U.S. interest be less than 5 percent.)

2. Tax liability. If a U.S. firm owns more than 50 percent of the voting power of a foreign corporation, it is a controlled foreign corporation and some part or all of its income *may* be taxable currently in the United States even if not repatriated.

3. Reduction of withholding tax. The withholding tax imposed abroad on dividends paid to a domestic firm by an associated foreign firm may be reduced if the foreign firm is owned to a significant degree by the domestic. (For example, the French withholding tax is reduced from 15 percent to 5 percent if a U.S. firm owns at least 10 percent of the paying French firm.)

4. Withholding tax and local ownership. The withholding tax imposed abroad may be reduced if local ownership is permitted. (For example, the Canadian withholding tax on dividends is reduced from 15 to 10 percent on those paid by a Canadian subsidiary to a foreign parent if Canadians are permitted to participate in the equity and voting control of the Canadian subsidiary to the extent of at least 25 percent.)

5. Tax exemption and ownership. Some countries impose a low tax or no tax on dividends received from foreign subsidiaries if a minimum ownership test is met. (For instance, if a Canadian parent corporation owns 25 percent or more of a foreign subsidiary, dividends received from the latter are exempt from Canadian tax.)

6. Liquidation. For example, the redemption or sale of stock in, or liquidation of, a U.S.-controlled foreign corporation (a foreign corporation in which more than 50 percent of the voting power is owned by U.S. persons or entities) *may* result in ordinary income, not capital gain, and be taxable as such.

7. Investment guarantees.[38] For example, in order to qualify for a guarantee issued by Overseas Private Investment Corporation (OPIC), formerly a function of the Agency for International Development (AID), a U.S. corporation must be over 50 percent owned by U.S. citizens; in order for an investment made by an associated foreign firm to qualify, the latter must be at least 95 percent owned by such a U.S. corporation (or by U.S. citizens). Other capital exporting countries have different ownership tests in order to qualify for their respective schemes.

8. Antitrust vulnerability. International ventures involving a U.S. firm may make the U.S. firm vulnerable to prosecution. (Some unresolved questions are: How much of the foreign enterprise must the United States firm own to make itself invulnerable to charges of conspiracy with the foreign venture if the latter's trade with the United States is restrained, on the theory that one cannot conspire with one's self? Or, conversely, how little must it own in order to protect itself from prosecution if the foreign enterprise is a member of a cartel affecting U.S. trade?)

9. Export controls. For example, a foreign firm at least 35 percent owned by a U.S. firm is subject to U.S. export controls. (Even the sale under contract to a noncontrolled foreign firm of goods or services that are ultimately resold to a prohibited

---

[37]Changed from 50 percent in 1971.

[38]Issued for an annual fee against expropriation, noncurrenability of profits, and loss due to war and civil insurrection, plus commercial risk.

market may make the U.S. firm vulnerable, if it has reason to know the location of the ultimate buyer.)

10. Social security. In the U.S. case, for a firm to include U.S. citizens employed overseas under U.S. social security and in a qualified deferred compensation plan it must own at least 20 percent of the voting stock of the foreign corporation employing those citizens and, if they are employed by a second tier corporation, the 20 percent-owned foreign corporation must own at least 50 percent of the second tier.

11. Treaty rights. To take advantage of certain treaties among foreign countries (such as those relating to right of establishment, national and most-favored-nation treatment, access to local courts, double taxation, patent protection, and reciprocal dividend tax exemption), nationality tests in terms of ownership may be imposed.

12. Selling rights. To sell in certain restricted markets (government defense procurement, NATO, AID-financed projects, for example) the firm may be required to meet nationality tests, including ownership. For example Sulzer, the Swiss manufacturer of diesel engines and other products, was compelled to limit its equity in a French enterprise to 50 percent because, according to French law, the subsidiary had to be majority French-owned in order to qualify as a supplier of diesel engines and other products to the nationalized French industry, navy, and armed forces.

13. Consolidation of financial statements. In the U.S. case, such consolidation (which may be used to alter debt/equity ratios, rates of return, margins, and so forth) requires effective management control (generally interpreted to mean majority ownership) of the foreign firm by the U.S. parent.

14. Restrictions on ownership. The host government may restrict the percentage of foreign ownership. For example, for many years Japan banned majority foreign ownership of Japanese enterprises except in special cases. Mexico, Yugoslavia, and Turkey specifically limit alien ownership generally to 49 percent. Of the socialist countries, Poland, Rumania, Yugoslavia, and Hungary permit 49 percent foreign ownership in joint ventures with local enterprises. Many countries bar firms more than 49 percent foreign-owned from owning real estate or engaging in importing, exporting, local distribution, publishing, and trade-related services. Under the 1968 Philippine Investment Incentive Act, industries classified as "preferred," and hence a recipient of various incentives, must be at least 60 percent Filipino-owned. An interesting case in point was generated by the Philippine Retail Trade Nationalization Act of 1954, which went into effect in 1964, which decreed that only Philippine citizens could engage in retail trade. The sole exception was that the law did not apply to U.S. citizens or legal entities. This exception was based on the "parity clause" of the Philippine Constitution and the terms of Philippine-U.S. trade agreements,[39] the overall thrust of which was that until 1974, U.S. citizens were to have equal rights with Filipinos in all business activities. The Philippine view, however, was that to qualify U.S.-owned operations must be *wholly owned* by U.S. citizens, a requirement most large U.S.-based corporations could not satisfy. In mid-1972 the Supreme Court of the Philippines ruled that U.S. nationals,

---

[39]Particularly the Bell Act of 1947 and the Laurel-Langley Agreement of 1953. The latter expired in 1974 and both governments have stated that they do not intend to seek extension.

whether individuals or corporations, cannot own private residences, business enterprises, or real estate beyond July 3, 1974. (In general, most countries including the United States restrict foreign ownership in certain types of strategic industries. Typically, these include internal communication, domestic transport, coastal shipping, lease of government land, agriculture, insurance, banking, and sometimes mining.) The Andean countries (see item 18 below) prohibit direct investment in activities adequately covered by existing investments. Particularly vulnerable to entry restraints on foreign ownership are *acquisitions of existing enterprises*. The laws of many countries discriminate in this fashion. A recent example is Canada, which in 1972 moved to require official approval for the takeover by a foreign firm of any Canadian enterprise with assets in excess of Can $250,000 or gross revenue of more than Can $3 million.[40] As of 1975, a stake of more than 20 percent in a French company or in any operation which would give control to a foreign resident or corporation requires Foreign Ministry approval. A very recent innovation (1976) in Malaysia is the requirement that foreign-owned firms sell to Petronas, the state-owned oil company, special management shares (each equal in value to regular shares) totalling at least 1 percent of the company's paid-up capital. However, such shares carry voting rights equal to 500 ordinary shares whenever stockholders vote on the appointment or dismissal of directors and staff. In fact, such a formula gives Petronas something like a 5-to-1 voting majority.

15. Legally required ownership-sharing (with employees), such as under recent Peruvian law and various European schemes (France, Netherlands, Sweden), and others. The concept has been discussed generally in Section 2 in relationship to the whole notion of profit-sharing, a concept that seems to be gaining currency in many parts of the world. It should be noted that profit-sharing can lead to owner-ship-sharing; distribution of equity shares is one way in which a firm may respond to the legally required profit-sharing in France. In the Peruvian case, a certain percentage of pretax profit, which is otherwise considered a part of the workers' (and managers are considered workers) wages, is invested in a trust that purchases stock in the company up to at least 50 percent. Workers participate in the management of the trust (Figure 5.3). Some international firms have, of course, entered into voluntary ownership-sharing plans. Some years ago, prior to the independence of Zambia (then Northern Rhodesia), two U.S.-controlled copper companies announced plans whereby employees, both European and African, were allowed to buy stock in their companies under a system of payroll deductions, with the company contributing 50 cents for every dollar contributed by the workers. All those earnings over $11 a week were eligible for the plan. Somewhat less well known is the Iranian scheme for broadening company ownership launched in 1972 when the Shah encouraged the transformation of private companies into joint stock companies and the sale of shares to the public. Subsequently, a number of large industrial companies did sell some shares either to their own workers or to the public. By 1975, some 4,000 industrial workers had responded. In April 1975, the sale of shares in certain categories of companies became obligatory down to

---

[40]For further details regarding these restraints on foreign ownership, see R. D. Robinson, *National Control of Foreign Business Entry* (New York: Praeger, 1976).

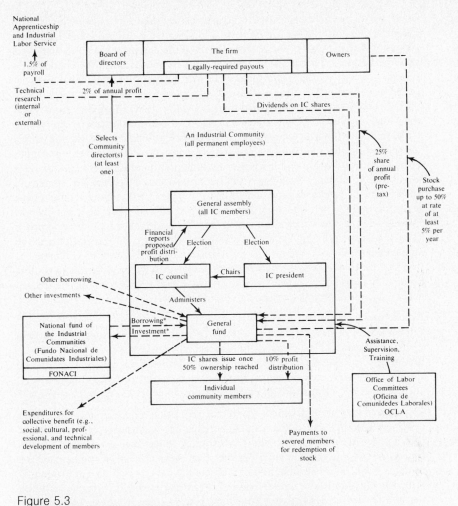

Figure 5.3
STRUCTURE AND OPERATION OF AN INDUSTRIAL COMMUNITY

*If 15% profit distribution to IC is more or less than that required to acquire 5% of the equity of the firm each year.

the 51 percent level for privately owned enterprises, down to 1 percent for government-owned industries other than those deemed to be "key." Qualifying for such divestment were firms with a registered capital of at least $1.5 million, with fixed assets of at least $3 million, or a turnover of at least $3.75 a year, and with a record of production of five years or more. It was reported that 320 firms would be affected, and that the divestment should be completed by October 1978. By January 26, 1976, a total of 64 firms had offered shares for sale, and 14,227 workers in 26 firms had received share certificates. The National Investment

Company of Iran had purchased 6 percent of the shares in 26 companies. The Financial Organization for the Expansion of Ownership of Production Units was created to buy the bulk of the shares offered by the companies coming under the share participation program for transfer to workers and farmers. The organization extends loans to workers and farmers to help finance purchase. The National Investment Company of Iran is charged with purchasing shares not taken up by the finance organization. Foreign partners in joint ventures affected by the scheme were also required to offer 49 percent of their shares. Management and voting rights written into the agreement could be retained as long as they did not violate the spirit of the law and had the consent of the partners to the joint venture. Upper ceilings for share-holdings for foreign investors in domestic joint ventures were established at not more than 25 percent for most sectors, 20 percent for some, and 15 percent for food industries and textiles. Foreign partners already holding a lesser percentage of ownership were unaffected by the share distribution law. Voting rights pass to workers and farmers as soon as formalities for share purchase from the financial organization are complete. However, during the period the shares are held by the organization, the organization may exercise no voting rights. The 1 percent share in state-owned enterprises retained by the government confers upon it full management and voting rights.[41] The most recent profit-sharing scheme is that of the Netherlands. (See Figure 5.4.)

16. Restricted access to local resources, such as the Andean countries' agreement that foreign firms (those not owned at least 80 percent within the Andean countries) be denied access to local credit or to Andean Common Market (ANCOM) trade preferences and the Brazilian requirement that foreign firms raising local capital through the public sale of equity (may be represented by nonvoting preferred shares) must reduce the foreign equity share to 49 percent within 20 years.

17. The right to increase investment. An Indian regulation requires that as an Indian company with majority foreign capital participation expands its activities it must seek a larger portion of Indian equity. According to the formula, companies with foreign ownership exceeding 75 percent must raise at least 40 percent of the estimated cost of expansion from Indian equity investors. The corresponding proportion for companies between 60 and 75 percent owned by foreigners is 33.33 percent; for companies between 50 and 60 percent foreign-owned, 25 percent.

18. Time limits on ownership. The host government may agree to recognize ownership for only a stipulated period, at the end of which time the relationship is to be renegotiated or terminated (always true for contracts). An example is the 1968 Philippine law: foreign investment in industries classified as preferred is limited to 40 percent. Foreign investment in "pioneer industries" may initially be 100 percent, but within 10 years, a foreign-owned pioneer firm must list its shares on the Philippine Stock Exchange. By the end of the 20th year it must have disposed of at least 60 percent of its shares to Filipinos unless an extension is granted.

The 1969 Foreign Investment Law of Indonesia stipulates that a foreign enterprise invests in Indonesia on the basis of a contract with the Indonesian government. The time over which foreign ownership rights will be recognized must be

---

[41]"Share Participation" (Teheran, Kayhan Research Associates, typed manuscript, March 1976).

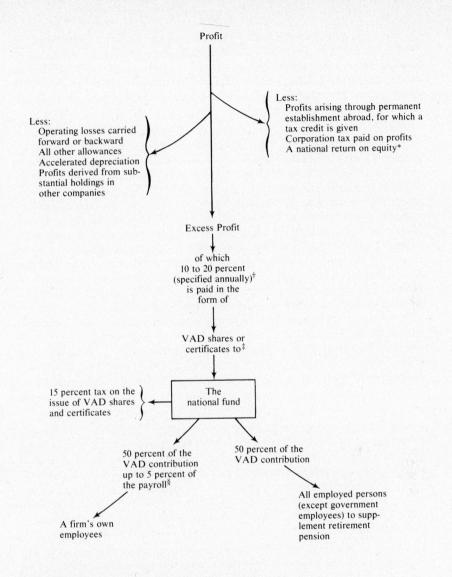

Figure 5.4
THE DUTCH PROFIT-SHARING SYSTEM

*The effective rate on long-term government bonds (about 8 percent) on net worth (less assets belonging to a permanent establishment outside Holland) and on the basis of a revaluation of certain fixed assets.

†Depends on the difference between the increase in labor productivity and the increase in labor costs (10 percent in 1975; 12 percent in 1976).

‡Certificates for a company not quoted on a stock exchange. Neither shares nor certificates have voting rights and are redeemable only in event of bankruptcy or liquidation. Each receive annual interest or dividend based on long-term government bond rate.

§If in excess of 5 percent of payroll, VAD contribution to a firm's own employees is reduced to 20 percent (from 50 percent). No individual can receive VAD of more than 2 percent of wages. The employees' shares remain frozen for several years at 7 percent.

specified, but 30 years is the limit. Extension may be negotiated toward the end of the period. To facilitate extensions, periodic reviews may be scheduled to measure performance against certain previously agreed-upon standards, such as production targets, employment, training, utilization of local materials, export development, cost reduction, and local capital participation. If these standards are met, extension may be guaranteed.

In general, the Andean countries (Bolivia, Colombia, Ecuador, and Peru), by virtue of a 1971 agreement, require that all new foreign investors must sell 51 percent of their equity to local investors within 15 years. For Colombia and Peru, local participation must reach 15 percent at start-up of production, 30 percent by the fifth year thereafter, 45 percent by the end of the tenth, 51 percent by the fifteenth. The schedule for the other ANCOM countries, and for established companies, varies slightly. Existing foreign enterprises have the option not to Andeanize provided they do not utilize the tariff preferences of the proposed Andean Common Market. (In fact, most of the ANCOM rules would seem to be vitiated by a provision in the agreement to the effect that any member state can declare an exemption. Acquiescence by the other members is not required.)[42] In general, there would appear to be a convergence on about 20 years as an appropriate limit on alien ownership. Note that this also corresponds to the most frequent length of the patent monopoly (in the United States, 17 years, an obvious compromise between 15 and 20 years) and of the modern oil concessions. Also relevant is the fact that the treaty under which the "New Territories" (Hong Kong) is leased to Britain by China expires 25 years hence (July 1, 1997), which must be considered a terminal point for foreign ownership of any commercial assets located there. Yet this knowledge does not seem to constitute a serious obstacle to foreign investment in Hong Kong.

19. Special requirements. Some countries impose certain requirements on foreign-owned firms. For example, New Zealand has special reporting requirements for firms more than 25 percent foreign owned. In Spain, for a foreign firm to have effective control it must own at least 77 percent; in France, 67 percent. (Otherwise, minority Spanish stockholders may prevent a company from undertaking an important step without first submitting it to a government "study," which could delay matters for months or even years.) In Germany, ownership of over 25 percent of a corporation's stock bestows a veto power over supervisory board action.

20. Protection of intangible property. Problems exist regarding the ownership and continued validation of patents, copyrights, and trademarks. For example, a firm might set up a foreign subsidiary to hold patents, copyrights, or trademarks so as to take advantage of international protective conventions or treaties to which the parent country is not a member. Will the host country recognize a 100 percent foreign-owned subsidiary as "national" and, hence, qualifying for convention or treaty coverage? If not, what measure will be used?

---

[42]For a discussion of the issues raised by the ANCOM rules, see Jack Behrman, "International Divestment: Panacea or Pitfall?" *Looking Ahead*, vol. 18, no. 9, November–December 1970; Paul Rosenstein-Rodan, "Multinational Investment in the Framework of Latin American Integration," a report presented to the Round Table of the Board of Governors' Meeting of the Inter-American Development Bank, Bogata, 1968; the *Colombia Journal of World Business*, vol. 6, no. 4, July–August 1971; and Robinson, *National Control of Foreign Business Entry*, pp. 252–89.

21. Special tax allowances. For example, depletion allowances and the right to include intangible development costs as current expenses (rather than capital investment) in respect to certain mineral explorations are available only for U.S. corporations, which means that any foreign ownership must be in the U.S. firm, not in the overseas venture (which must take the form of a branch to qualify for these allowances).

22. Special tax deductions. Certain deductions may be available only to *domestic* corporations, which rules out any non-U.S. participation in overseas enterprises in that foreign operations must be through branches.

23. Expropriation. For example, in the United States for the so-called Hickenlooper Amendment to the 1962 Foreign Assistance Act to take effect, which calls for the near automatic termination of all U.S. economic assistance to a government guilty of expropriating U.S.-owned property, the expropriated company must be at least 50 percent beneficially owned by U.S. citizens. In the U.S. case, expropriation losses incurred by a second-tier subsidiary (a subsidiary of a subsidiary), or a third or more, may not flow through to the parent corporations as either capital loss or an ordinary loss (deductible from taxable income), which would be the case if the loss were incurred by a first-tier subsidiary. Taking such loss as an ordinary loss is made easier if the foreign subsidiary is at least 80 percent owned by the U.S. parent, thereby qualifying it as an "affiliated corporation."

25. Government espousal. There is the general issue as to when a government will espouse a private claim in the International Court of Justice at the Hague; that is, what definition of nationality will be used in respect to a firm claiming an international wrong and requesting governmental assistance? The U.S. government, and apparently most governments, will not espouse a corporate claim vis-à-vis other governments or before the International Court of Justice at the Hague unless, in the case of a U.S.-domiciled corporation, at least 50 percent of the voting shares are owned by U.S. citizens or, if foreign-domiciled, at least 25 percent are so owned.

26. Securities regulation. For example, for a foreign financial subsidiary of a U.S. corporation to be exempt from SEC regulations in raising funds abroad, 90 percent of the subsidiary's assets must be invested in companies in which the parent concern has at least a 10 percent ownership interest.

27. Payment of royalties and fees. Brazil and the Andean Pact countries will not permit payments of royalties by local affiliates of foreign firms. The test in Brazil seems to be 50 percent foreign ownership.

28. Antiboycott laws. The 1977 antiboycott legislation enacted by the United States extends to the foreign branches and subsidiaries of U.S. firms and to foreign affiliates. The latter are defined as foreign corporations that are controlled "in fact" by a U.S. corporation. (It is suspected that in event of ownership of 30 percent or more by the U.S. corporation, the burden to prove no control will be on the side of the U.S. corporation.)

29. Restrictions on enforcement of contractual rights. The laws and regulations of many countries render invalid certain contractual conditions imposed on local firms by foreign corporations. Although particularly common in LDCs, Table 5.5 shows that such limitations are common elsewhere as well. In addition, a number of countries will not recognize patent rights in certain sectors, for example, in

Table 5.5

WESTERN EUROPEAN TREATMENT OF RESTRICTIVE CLAUSES IN TECHNICAL ASSISTANCE CONTRACTS

	EEC	UK*	Fr.*	Ger.*	It.*	Bel.*	Neth.*	Switz.	Spn.
1. Restrictions on territory where licensee can manufacture	No†	Yes‡	Yes	Yes	Yes	Yes	Yes	Yes	Yes
2. Exclusivity of license	No	Yes	Yes	Yes	Yes	Yes	Yes	Yes	Yes
3. Export prohibitions/restrictions	No	Maybe§	Maybe	Yes	Yes	Unclear‖	Unclear	Maybe	No
4. Restriction on licensee's manner, method, or field of use	Unclear	Maybe	Yes	Yes	Yes	Maybe	Unclear	Yes	No
5. Time restrictions on licensee's use of know-how									
a. contract with long duration	Yes	Yes	Yes	Yes	Yes	Yes	Yes	Yes	No
b. contract with short duration	Maybe	Yes	Yes	Yes	Yes	Yes	Yes	Yes	No
c. automatic extension/renewal	Unclear	Yes	Yes	Yes	Yes	Yes	Yes	Yes	No
d. termination provisions	Maybe	Yes	Yes	Yes	Yes	Yes	Yes	Yes	Maybe
6. Royalties/fees									
a. discriminatory between licensees of same know-how	No	Unclear	Unclear	Unclear	Unclear	Unclear	Unclear	Maybe	Unclear
b. based on production	Yes	Yes	Yes	Yes	Yes	Yes	Yes	Yes	Maybe
c. based on sales	Yes	Yes	Yes	Yes	Yes	Yes	Yes	Yes	Yes
d. minimums	Yes	Yes	Yes	Yes	Yes	Yes	Yes	Yes	No
e. charged on products not made from licensed know-how	No	No	No	No	Unclear	No	Unclear	No	No
f. excessive rates									
1. charged to independent licensee	Unclear	Maybe	Maybe	Maybe	Maybe	Maybe	Unclear	Maybe	No
2. charged to affiliates	Unclear	No	No	No	No	No	No	No	No
g. royalties/fees charged after licensed know-how has fallen into public domain	No	Unclear	Maybe	No	Unclear	Unclear	Unclear	Unclear	Unclear
7. Grant-back obligations for improvements, developments, refinements									
a. unilateral obligation for licensee	No	Maybe	Unclear	No	Yes	Yes	Unclear	Yes	No

8. b. comparable bilateral obligations	Yes	Yes	Yes	Yes	Yes	Yes	Yes	Yes	Unclear
Restrictions on licensee's R&D report	No	Unclear	Unclear	No	Unclear	Unclear	Unclear	Maybe	No
9. Noncontest of validity/secrecy of licensed know-how	No	Maybe	Unclear	Yes	Maybe	Maybe	Yes	Yes	Unclear
10. Control by licensor through licensing contract of licensee's management	Unclear	Unclear	Maybe	Yes	Maybe	Yes	Yes	Yes	Maybe
11. Licensor's obligation to grant licensee most favored terms	Yes	Yes	Yes	Yes	Yes	Yes	Yes	Yes	Yes
12. Quantity restrictions	Yes	Maybe	Yes	Yes	Yes	Yes	Yes	Yes	No
13. Nondisclosure of licensed know-how									
a. during term of contract	Yes	Yes	Yes	Maybe	Yes	Yes	Yes	Yes	Maybe
b. after contract ends	Yes	Yes	Yes	Maybe	Yes	Yes	Yes	Yes	Maybe
14. Non-use of licensed know-how									
a. during term of contract except as contract provides	Yes	Yes	Yes	Maybe	Yes	Yes	Yes	Yes	Yes
b. after contract ends									
1. where still secret	Yes	Yes	Yes	Yes	Yes	Yes	Yes	Yes	No
2. where no longer secret	No	Unclear	Unclear	No	Unclear	Unclear	Unclear	Maybe	No
15. Licensee's obligation to return documents, other objects after contract ends	Yes	Yes	Yes	Yes	Yes	Yes	Yes	Yes	Maybe
16. Licensee's obligation not to assign or sublicense	Yes	Yes	Yes	Yes	Yes	Yes	Yes	Yes	Maybe
17. Licensor's right to fix licensee's prices (not licensee's own customers)									
a. maximum prices	No	No	No	Yes	Unclear	Maybe	Unclear	Maybe	No
b. minimum prices	Unclear	Maybe	Maybe	Yes	Unclear	Yes	Unclear	Yes	No
c. suggested prices	No	No	No	Yes	Unclear	Maybe	Unclear	Maybe	No
18. Quality control obligations	Maybe	Yes	Yes	Yes	Yes	Yes	Yes	Yes	Maybe
19. Source of supply obligations (raw materials, parts, intermediates, etc.)	Maybe	Maybe	Maybe	Maybe	Maybe	Maybe	Maybe	Maybe	No
20. Tie-ins imposed on licensee	No	Unclear	Maybe	No	Maybe	No	No	Maybe	No
21. Licensee's obligation to use licensor's trademark on products	Unclear	Yes	Yes	Yes	Yes	Yes	Yes	Yes	No

Table 5.5 (continued)

	EEC	UK*	Fr.*	Ger.*	It.*	Bel.*	Neth.*	Switz.	Spn.
22. Licensee's obligation to affix reference to licensor on products	Maybe	Yes	Yes	Yes	Yes	Yes	Yes	Yes	Unclear
23. Restrictions on licensee's choice of customers	Unclear	Maybe	Unclear	Yes	Maybe	Unclear	Unclear	Yes	Unclear
24. Licensee's obligation to let licensor select or approve licensee's distributors	No	Unclear	Maybe	Unclear	Maybe	Unclear	Unclear	Maybe	No
25. Licensee's obligation to sell its production of licensed products to licensor or its designee	Unclear	Maybe	Unclear	Maybe	Yes	Unclear	Unclear	Maybe	No
26. Restrictions on licensee's right to manufacture and/or sell competing products									
a. during term of contract	No	Maybe	Maybe	No	Maybe	Maybe	Unclear	Maybe	No
b. after contract ends	No	Maybe	Maybe	No	Maybe	Maybe	Unclear	Maybe	No
27. Restrictions on licensee's right to acquire or use competing technology									
a. during term of contract	No	Maybe	Maybe	No	Maybe	Unclear	Unclear	Maybe	No
b. after contract ends	No	Maybe	Unclear	No	Maybe	Unclear	Unclear	Maybe	No
28. Contractual provisions re applicable law and courts	Yes	Yes	Yes	Yes	Yes	Yes	Yes	Yes	Maybe
29. Arbitration clauses	Yes	Yes	Yes	Yes	Yes	Yes	Yes	Yes	Maybe
30. Contractual provision that foreign language version of contract controls	Yes	Yes	Maybe	Yes	Yes	Yes	Yes	Yes	No

*Analysis based on "national law," excluding EEC antitrust rules.

†No = generally a serious legal problem is likely to exist by virtue of the restriction.

‡Yes = generally no legal problem generated by the provision.

§Maybe = no serious legal problem likely, yet considerable caution is nonetheless required.

‖Unclear = the law is unclear.

Note: it is assumed that no patents, trademarks or other forms of proprietary rights are involved. In that many definitional problems are involved, this table is indicative only.

Source: Abstracted and summarized by *Business International*, April 12, 1974, pp. 116–117, from Aaron N. Wise, *Trade Secrets and Know-how throughout the World* (London: Clark Boardman Company Ltd., 1974).

reference to pharmaceuticals (Italy, Brazil, Mexico). In 1975, Mexico likewise eliminated patents in chemicals, food processing and agriculture, fertilizers, pesticides and herbicides, pollution control, and nuclear energy. Owners of new technology in these areas may be issued an "inventor's certificate" (reminiscent of the Soviet notion), which would give rights to royalty payment for third-party use. However, the technology is considered to be in the public domain and within reach of anyone willing to pay for it. Likewise in 1975, the World Intellectual Property Agency (WIPO) developed at least a first pass at a "Model Law for Developing Countries on Inventions and Know-How." Proposed is a "Transfer of Technology" (T/T) patent, which would then proceed to take out a T/T patent locally on behalf of both firms. This "patent" would have the effect of prohibiting other companies from exporting comparable products to that LDC. Meanwhile, the LDC firm would be permitted to export anywhere. The proposal also suggests that all the relevant know-how be transferred to the LDC patentee at a relatively low fee (a maximum before-tax fee of 5 percent of sales is urged) and only for five years, though possibly renewable. Other proposals limiting the international rights of technology owners include shorter protection to developed-country technology than to LDC-owned technology, compulsory licensing of property rights or loss of such rights through nonworking, the granting of more favorable treatment to patent-holders in LDCs than developed country patent-holders (particularly in regard to fees). Even in the United States, the idea of compulsory licensing has been introduced in the areas of atomic energy and U.S. government-financed research. Also, there have been periodic legislative efforts directed to making patented inventions beneficial to consumers more widely available.

It is painfully clear that the legal restraints relevant to the choice of ownership strategy are legion, and they are by no means limited to LDCs.

In discussing *control requirements*, our fourth critical variable relative to choice of ownership strategy, it is important to make explicit the implicit assumptions held by those who simply equate equity ownership with control. These assumptions are:

1. Ownership rights resting on equity are, in the long run, less likely to be disturbed by a foreign government than purely contractual rights. (Empirically, this does not seem to have been the case.)

2. Total control by the international headquarters is necessary to accomplish corporate objectives whether they be defined in terms of maximization of corporate profit, return on investment, cash throw-off, growth, geographical spread, or market share. (May or may not hold true in a particular case.)

3. Adequate control without equity ownership is impossible. (This assumption implies that contractual rights cannot be enforced. Experience would not support this assumption.)

4. Total control by an international firm of a foreign enterprise is legally possible on the basis of majority or 100 percent ownership. (In fact, local law and regulation may seriously restrict freedom of decision in respect to personnel policies such as wage rates and hiring and firing, negotiation with unions, nationality of management and of labor, transfer pricing, product pricing, profit repatriation, local bor-

rowing, contracting with the associated U.S. firm or entering into tying agreements, market restraints, expansion of plant, reinvestment of earnings, purchase
of materials, degree of local manufacture, import of further capital, use of external
services, and plant location—to mention a few areas.) A parenthetical note: Curiously, one researcher has found an inverse relationship between the profitability
of joint ventures and the size of the foreign parent, *also with its predilection for
control.*[43] Another scholar observes,

*Foreign investors (notably in the oil industry) stress the fact that, in their experience,
cooperation between partners has not been any more difficult to achieve in contractual
joint ventures than in equity joint ventures. In the basic agreement, the partners have
every latitude to provide one or several executives with extensive powers and with the
means of using these powers. The senior executive in the contractual joint venture may
thus be granted powers as extensive as those of a managing director in an equity joint
venture. Moreover, the senior executive has to be provided with the financial means of
applying these powers. In principle, the management in a contractual joint venture
cannot exceed the precise budgetary limits that have been agreed to by the partners in
any given year. In practice, however, the budget may be planned so as to leave a sufficient
margin of financial freedom to the senior executive. Moreover, the rules of the agency
contract would, generally speaking, seem applicable in cases of emergency. It can therefore be concluded that the flexibility inherent in a contractual joint venture is far from
being necessarily an obstacle to the cooperation between the partners and to the efficiency of management.*[44]

Possibly it needs pointing out that equity-based control can be maintained with
substantially less than a majority interest, if the balance of the equity is held
by a large number of unorganized individuals or entities. And there are other
ways of diluting a majority ownership. One is to use a nominee or nominees
(literally "strawmen") which for one reason or another will do as the minority
owner decides. Some national laws prohibit this practice, for example, the
Mexican. Another way is the destruction of bearer shares, where bearer shares
are legal, so as to elevate the minority interest to a *de facto* majority. Still
another method is to put the majority ownership into a trust which the minority owner controls through his control of the trustees. Again, local law may or
may not recognize the trust as a separate legal entity for this purpose. Finally,
local law permitting, one might issue different types of stock—voting and
nonvoting, the majority of the voting stock being retained by the minority
owner.

The need for controls arises in anticipation of conflict of interest. Possible
conflict areas are:

1.   ownership—the sale or transfer of equity to third parties;[45]

---

[43]Tomlinson, *Joint Venture Process*, p. 161.

[44]Wolfgang G. Friedmann and Jean-Pierre Benguin, *Joint International Business Ventures in Developing
Countries* (New York: Columbia University Press, 1971), p. 418.

[45]A recent relevant case was the struggle between B. F. Goodrich and Goodyear of the United States over N.
V. Rubberfabriek Vredestein (RV) of the Netherlands. In 1946, Goodrich and RV formed a 21–29 percent joint

2. dividend policy—distribution versus reinvestment;

3. borrowing—acceptable debt/equity ratios;

4. plant expansion—what and where;

5. research and development—level, purpose, location;

6. production processes—degree of integration, degree of capital-labor intensity;

7. source of supply—external or internal, transfer prices;

8. quality standards—domestic or absolute, international standards;

9. product mix—diversification, competitive exports;

10. reinvestment—dilution of equity held by a minority;

11. terms of sales—credit, servicing, pricing;

12. market area—restricted or open;

13. market penetration—choice of channels, promotional effort;

14. labor-management relations—degree of paternalism, union recognition and negotiation, national versus international negotiation, levels of remuneration, profit-sharing;

15. management selection and remuneration—nationality, skills required, number, salaries, decision-making style (degree of participation, calculation and formalization);

16. political—honesty, company-government relations, degree of sensitivity to political decisions (for example, regarding desired allocation of national resources);

17. image projected.

The relevant query here is, given these possible conflict areas, what controls are needed to maintain a tolerable benefit/cost relationship for the firm? These controls may rest on the leverage the firm can mount by reason of:

1. ownership (control over the election of boards; hiring, development, and firing of managers; and/or determination of financial structure and profit distribution);

2. market access (control over channels, trademarks, brand names, and/or ownership of import licenses or business permits);

3. technology (control of patents, relevant R&D flow);

4. finance (ability to provide low cost debt and equity, and/or working capital such as commercial credit);

5. personnel (ability to provide scarce skills at relatively low cost—including management—and/or relatively cheap labor);

6. political assistance (greater ability to deal effectively with governments in preventing restraints or gaining largesse; and/or to gain customer or market acceptability);

---

venture in the Netherlands, 50 percent of the equity being sold to the public. Goodrich then transferred its radial tire technology to the joint venture. Subsequently, RV acquired all of the publically-held stock in the joint venture. In 1970 it became known that Goodyear had been buying RV stock on the open market, including controlling interest, of course, in the joint venture. Goodrich sought remedy in the Dutch court.

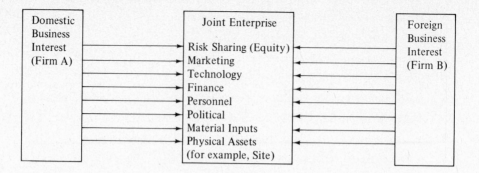

Figure 5.5
POSSIBLE CONTRIBUTIONS BY PARTICIPATING FIRMS TO A JOINT ENTERPRISE*

---

*The term "joint enterprise," it will be recalled, is used to avoid confusion with the equity-sharing concept inherent in the term "joint venture."

7. supply (limitation of source to the associated firm);

8. physical assets (control over sites, specialized transport, power sources).

In each case, the cost is that which would be incurred by the firm (firm A) if the relevant contribution of the associated firm (firm B) were to be interrupted. Hence, the ability of firm A to shut off any one of these flows is a control device and the ability of firm B to do likewise, a restraint.

In summary, a firm should determine what it proposes to do and where, define the essential elements of control relevant to accomplishing that purpose, and then decide upon the best means of assuring that control. The often-hidden cost of maintaining long distance control through equity should be included in this analysis. Otherwise, the benefit/cost analysis will be invalidated and corporate objectives not be achieved.

Finally, one moves into the general area of benefit/cost analysis of various ownership relationships. The costs, for example, of a domestic firm and its associated foreign business interests may be seen as two sets of flows converging on the foreign entity, which, in the terminology used here is always a joint enterprise, not necessarily in an equity sense but always in the sense of sharing common interests and responsibilities, whether recognized or not. These costs, or contributions (from the point of view of the joint enterprise), may be classified generally in terms of assistance in marketing, technology, finance, personnel, politics, supply and/or physical assets. (See Figure 5.5.) It is important to distinguish here between a one-time contribution (or transfer) and one that continues over time.

On the other hand, the benefits accruing to the domestic and foreign

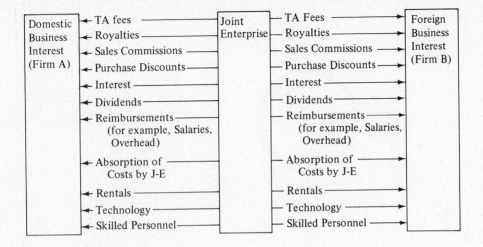

Figure 5.6
POSSIBLE BENEFITS FLOWING TO FIRMS ASSOCIATED IN A JOINT ENTERPRISE (JE)

business interests may flow through a number of channels, as illustrated in Figure 5.6. These benefits (costs from the point of the joint enterprise) should likewise be viewed over time. Some flows, however, may be of a one-time nature such as in a simple sale or a turnkey operation.

It is relevant to ask at this point, Is there agreement as to who contributes what, for how long, and receives how much, by what route, for how long? In other words, what are the expectations? As skills are transferred from the international firm, the flow of management contributions in terms of personnel and development of local nationals may dry up. Is this anticipated by both parties? How soon?

The appropriate ownership policy in a given case may be diagrammed as in Figure 5.7, using A to designate the domestic business interest and B, the foreign interest. The point here is not to quantify the relationships but to suggest an analytical structure.

The equations should be read in this fashion. The appropriate ownership policy for firm A at a particular time in reference to a given project overseas may be stated thus:

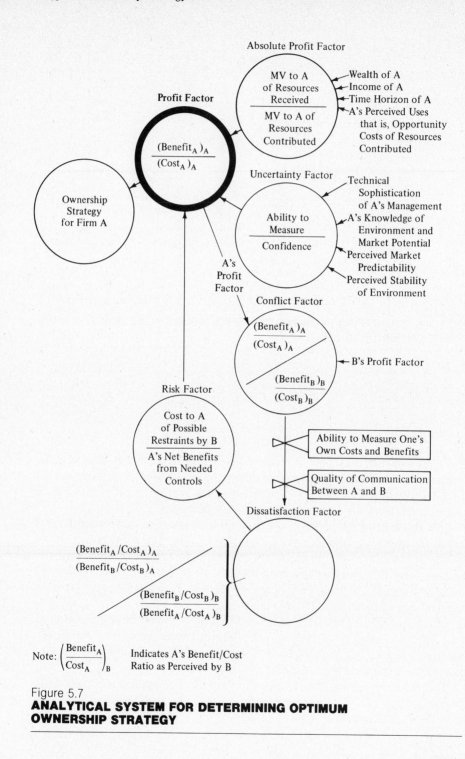

Figure 5.7
ANALYTICAL SYSTEM FOR DETERMINING OPTIMUM OWNERSHIP STRATEGY

[profit factor]   [risk factor]

$$\text{ownership} = f\left(\underbrace{\dfrac{\text{self-perceived}\atop{\text{benefit to A}}}{\text{self-perceived}\atop{\text{cost to A}}}}, \; \dfrac{\text{cost to A of possible}\atop{\text{restraints by B}}}{\text{A's net benefits from}\atop{\text{needed controls}}}\right). \qquad (5.1)$$

The first expression[46] in equation (5.1) is really the self-perceived profit factor, and the second, the generalized risk factor. Examining the first more closely, we may analyze it in this manner:

[absolute profit factor]   [uncertainty factor]

$$\frac{\text{benefit}_A\ A}{\text{cost}_A\ A} = f\left(\frac{\text{MV}_A\ \text{of resources received}}{\text{MV}_A\ \text{of resources contributed}}, \; \frac{\text{ability to measure}}{\text{confidence}}\right), \qquad (5.2)$$

where MV_A (marginal value to A), ability to measure, and confidence are functions of the variables shown in Figure 5.6.

In looking at the second expression in equation (5.1), cost to A of possible restraints by B as compared to A's net benefits from needed controls, we can see that the larger the term, the greater the risk. By definition, the ratio could not be less than one, for A's net benefits (benefits derived from control less the cost associated with that control) are limited to the costs incurred by A by reason of possible restraints imposed by B. They could not be more. In a one-to-one situation, there is no risk. We can break down this risk factor thus:

$$\frac{\text{cost to A of possible}\atop{\text{restraints by B}}}{\text{A's net benefit from}\atop{\text{needed controls}}} = f\left(\text{conflict factor, dis-}\atop{\text{satisfaction factor}}\right). \qquad (5.3)$$

These expressions can be defined in this way:

$$\text{conflict} = f\left(\frac{\text{benefit}_A\ \text{as perceived by A}}{\text{cost}_A\ \text{as perceived by A}}, \; \frac{\text{benefit}_B\ \text{as perceived by B}}{\text{cost}_B\ \text{as perceived by B}}\right); \qquad (5.4)$$

$$\text{dissatisfaction} = f\left(\frac{\text{benefit}_A/\text{cost}_A\ \text{as perceived by A}}{\text{benefit}_B/\text{cost}_B\ \text{as perceived by A}}, \right.$$
$$\left. \frac{\text{benefit}_B/\text{cost}_B\ \text{as perceived by B}}{\text{benefit}_A/\text{cost}_A\ \text{as perceived by B}}\right). \ast \qquad (5.5)$$

*May be written thusly:

$$\frac{(\text{benefit}_A/\text{cost}_A)\ A}{(\text{benefit}_B/\text{cost}_B)\ A}, \quad \frac{(\text{benefit}_B/\text{cost}_B)\ B}{(\text{benefit}_A/\text{cost}_A)\ B}.$$

---

[46]Bear in mind that a cost of A or of B is a contribution, or input, to the joint enterprise and a benefit to A or to B is a cost, or output, for the joint enterprise.

In equation (5.4), the degree of potential conflict is measured by the extent to which $\left(\dfrac{(\text{benefit}_A)\ A}{(\text{cost}_A)\ A} \right)$ differs from $\left(\dfrac{(\text{benefit}_B)\ B}{(\text{cost}_B)\ B} \right)$.

If the benefit/cost relationship for A differs substantially from that for B, as perceived by A and B, respectively, conflict of interest may emerge, *depending upon the quality of communication between A and B and on the ability of each to measure his own costs and benefits.* In equation (5.5), if either expression falls significantly below a value of one, dissatisfaction is likely to appear, for such a value would indicate that one or both parties expect less profit than they believe the other will realize. Bear in mind that in this latter case we are dealing with the relative value of benefits and costs for both firms as perceived by one of them. In each case, the other perceived ratios may be greater or lesser than the self-perceived.

All we have been saying is that the relevant ownership policy should be that designed to most nearly accomplish corporate objectives. We assume that these can be stated in terms of maximizing the self-perceived benefit/cost ratio, as discounted by a certain risk factor (that is, expressed as a cost-of-restraint/benefit-from-control ratio). These in turn are evaluated in terms of the marginal value of resources contributed and received as discounted (1) by one's ability to measure these resource flows as reduced by one's confidence in these measures, and (2) by degree of dissatisfaction as measured by the benefit/cost ratio of the firm and that ratio perceived for the associate. One may summarize this:

$$\text{ownership strategy} = f\left(\frac{MV_A \text{ of resources received}}{MV_A \text{ of resources contributed}},\ \frac{\text{ability to measure}}{\text{confidence}}, \right. \tag{5.6}$$

$$\left. \frac{(\text{benefit}_A/\text{cost}_A)\ A}{(\text{benefit}_B/\text{cost}_B)\ A},\ \frac{(\text{benefit}_B/\text{cost}_B)\ B}{(\text{benefit}_A/\text{cost}_A)\ B},\ \frac{(\text{benefit}_A)\ A}{(\text{cost}_A)\ A},\ \frac{(\text{benefit}_B)\ B}{(\text{benefit}_B)\ B} \right);$$

that is

$$\text{ownership strategy} = f(\text{absolute profit factor; uncertainty factor;}$$
$$\text{dissatisfaction factor; conflict factor}). \tag{5.7}$$

The restraints anticipated by firm A and the countervailing controls needed by it rest on the degree of dissatisfaction generated. Collectively, these are used to discount the profit factor, which is already discounted by the perceived market risk, that is, the uncertainty factor as defined here. The restraints and controls are interrelated; both generate costs and curtail benefits. The optimum ownership policy is one that maximizes this appropriately discounted ratio. If, by altering ownership policy, the reduction in conflict and dissatisfaction factors decreases costs more than benefits, or increases benefits more than costs, rationality would demand such a change of policy.

To simplify this discussion, let us assume two individuals. They would combine their resources in a joint undertaking only in the event that they both perceived their respective benefits flowing from a combined effort as surpassing those anticipated in an individual effort. A split in benefits is proposed, say, 50–50. In the first instance, Mr. A will look at the benefit/cost ratio as perceived by him, that is, the self-perceived value of what he will receive as related to the self-perceived value of what he will contribute. This will be discounted by his ability to measure these flows and his confidence in this measure. In order to assure this flow, he should anticipate the need for some degree of control over the joint operation, which effort will be encountered by some restraints by Mr. B (that is, by negative controls insofar as Mr. A is concerned), who is trying to do the same thing. If it is possible to reduce potential conflict of interest and dissatisfaction to a level that would leave the appropriately discounted flow of benefits still acceptably greater than the flow of contribution (that is, significantly greater than that anticipated in a one-man enterprise) for both parties, a joint enterprise should result. If not, it is because of the inability of Mr. A or Mr. B or both to adjust the expected flows of contributions and benefits, to design better measures for the flows, to develop a heightened confidence in them, or to shift the cost of control.

To avoid a critical level of dissatisfaction, Mr. A's self-perceived benefit/cost ratio must be approximately equal to, or exceed, the ratio he perceives for Mr. B. The reverse must likewise be true. Each must perceive his own ratio as approximately equal to or exceeding that of the other. Hence:

[self-perceived]   [other perceived]

$$\left(\frac{benefit_A}{cost_A} \right) A \geq \qquad \left(\frac{benefit_B}{cost_B} \right) A, \text{ and} \tag{5.8}$$

$$\left(\frac{benefit_B}{cost_B} \right) B \geq \qquad \left(\frac{benefit_A}{cost_A} \right) B. \tag{5.9}$$

Note that this condition implies nothing about the vertical or diagonal relationships. In fact, one should expect that over time Mr. A's perception of B's benefit/cost ratio will converge on B's self-perceived ratio, for both A and B should learn how to measure the flows better, and communications should be less subject to effective manipulation by either. Thus, a long-run equilibrium would require that:

$$\left(\frac{benefit_B}{cost_B} \right) A = \qquad \left(\frac{benefit_B}{cost_B} \right) B, \text{ and} \tag{5.10}$$

$$\left(\frac{benefit_A}{cost_A} \right) B = \qquad \left(\frac{benefit_A}{cost_A} \right) A. \tag{5.11}$$

These relationships imply further that

$$\left(\frac{benefit_A}{cost_A}\right) A = \left(\frac{benefit_B}{cost_B}\right) B; \tag{5.12}$$

that is, if the self-perceived benefit/cost ratios vary significantly, a potential conflict of interest is hidden in the situation. It is translated into overt dissatisfaction as one or both of the parties becomes aware of this disparity even though the initial conditions [equations (5.8) and (5.9)] were met. Note that there is no mention of the actual benefit/cost ratios, only the self-perceived and other-perceived ratios, for reality is only relevant as it is perceived.

At the present state of the art, no method suggests itself for quantifying these factors in any precise manner, least of all those relating to determining the tolerable limits of conflict and dissatisfaction. But many firms do not even consider the range of possible benefit/cost relationships, but rather rush into all overseas adventures in accord to some fixed ownership policy. Even for the conflict and dissatisfaction factors, it is useful to try inserting carefully considered subjective values and to consider at what point the inequalities in the conflict and dissatisfaction ratios are likely to bring about significant added restraints and to force a firm to incur added costs to maintain tolerable controls. A costing of various types of controls vis-à-vis possible losses (or gains) in terms of achieving corporate objectives may be useful.

The point is that this sort of exercise leads one to ask the relevant questions, such as, which of the contributions that firm A can make to the joint enterprise (costs to A) will firm B accept at the same, or higher, value than assigned by A. Presumably, this will result in the maximization of the benefit/cost ratio for A. This ratio should be adjusted until both the conflict of interest and dissatisfaction factors are approximately in balance, all else remaining equal. "All else" in this case refers to the cost of the added controls needed to balance any anticipated increase in restraints. Hence, the relevant questions for a firm are:

1. What value does the firm (firm A) place on what it proposes to contribute?

2. What value does firm B place on A's contribution?

3. What value does firm A place on the benefits to accrue to it?

4. What value does firm B place on the benefits to accrue to A?

5. What value does firm B place on the benefits to accrue to it?

6. What value does firm A place on the benefits to accrue to B?

7. How certain is A of its measure of resources received and resources contributed?

8. What restraints does A anticipate?

9. What are the likely costs to A of these restraints?

10. What controls does A perceive to be necessary to reduce the effect of these restraints to a tolerable level?

11. What is the cost of maintaining these controls?

12. How will the value of all of these factors shift over time?

The importance of the final query lies in the fact that, if any of the values shift significantly, mounting pressure toward a comparable shift in the flows of contribution and benefit should be anticipated. By anticipating such shifts, they may be made with minimum friction and cost, in both psychological and physical terms.

These questions suggest a possible technique for at least approximating the values required to make the evaluation system outlined in Figure 5.7 operative. Let each party to the proposed joint enterprise evaluate his own benefits and costs (self-perceived) arising by reason of the joint enterprise, both in its initial period and, say, ten years hence. Then let each party evaluate what he perceives the other party's benefits and costs likely to be, initially and ten years later. This "other-perceived" data should then be exchanged. Similarly, each party should determine an explicit discount rate for his own expected flows of benefits and suggest what the appropriate discount rate should be for his proposed partner. If the appropriately discounted cost/benefit ratio of A as perceived by A is seen to differ significantly from his benefit/cost ratio as perceived by B—which A now knows—A should expect an eventual conflicted relation. He may then wish to adjust his self-perceived flows of benefits and costs and/or the discount rate. B undertakes a similar exercise. Both parties are now in a position to compare self-perceived and other-perceived ratios. That is,

$$\text{if } \left(\frac{\text{benefit}_A}{\text{cost}_A} \right) \text{ A } \text{ approximates } \left(\frac{\text{benefit}_A}{\text{cost}_A} \right) \text{ B, and}$$

$$\text{if } \left(\frac{\text{benefit}_B}{\text{cost}_B} \right) \text{ B } \text{ approximates } \left(\frac{\text{benefit}_B}{\text{cost}_B} \right) \text{ A,}$$

then a tolerable relationship is possible. It is assumed that each firm has satisfied the conditions specified in equations (5.8) and (5.9). One should bear in mind, however, that if the two—the value of the self-perceived ratios $(\text{benefit}_A/\text{cost}_A)$ A and $(\text{benefit}_B/\text{cost}_B)$B—are in fact different, one can expect a shift in the other-perceived ratio over time and possibly an increasingly conflicted situation.

The central thesis here may be summarized thusly:

1. If there is a substantial disparity between each partner's concept of his own benefit/cost ratio, the potential for conflict exists.

2. Actual dissatisfaction arises from a disparity between the benefit/cost ratio a firm perceives for itself, and that perceived for its partner.

3. Since it is desirable to equalize the benefit/cost ratios to reduce potential conflict (while maximizing the value of each partner's self-perceived ratio), each partner should concentrate on making those contributions to the joint enterprise that it can make at lower cost than its partner.

4. Dissatisfaction stemming from differences in perceptions may be overcome by improving communications between partners and improving measures of control to reduce uncertainty arising out of each partner's ability to impose restraints.

One can then plot the profile of the optimum relationship in Figure 5.1.

But such a strategy is only valid for a point in time. Initially, we shall assume that the domestic firm, say, a U.S. company, supplies from sources outside of the host country, say, Peru, virtually all of the technology, managerial skills, financing, and marketing services for the 80 percent of the product that is exported. We shall assume that comparable services and assets are not available from alternative sources, either local or foreign. Given this set of relationships, 100 percent U.S. ownership of the Peruvian enterprise is perhaps justified. As time passes, several things happen: (1) the relevant technical and managerial skills are transferred to local nationals; (2) the market becomes essentially an internal Peruvian one rather than an export one; (3) local finance (debt plus reinvested earnings) sustains the operation; and (4) other firms are willing to supply the equivalent of the few remaining parent company inputs under contract. At this point, the parent firm is contributing little or nothing that would justify continued ownership.

Under these circumstances, although a 100 percent or majority ownership may be optimum for the first period over time, a subsequent reduction in foreign ownership to a minority position or only to a contractual relationship seems reasonable.[47] In other words, the marginal utility of the growth of the host country of the dollars being repatriated by the parent company becomes

---

[47]Popularized recently as the "fade-out" theory by Paul Rosenstein-Rodan. See his "Multinational Investment in the Framework of Latin American Integration," in *Multinational Investment in the Economic Development and Integration of Latin America* (Bogota: Inter-American Development Bank, 1968). The idea did not originate with him. It should be noted that the government of India in the 1950s was permitting entry of foreign firms into certain sectors only if they would agree to divest themselves of ownership within a stipulated period, often 20 years. Embedded in the Indonesian Foreign Investment Law of 1967 (indeed, in a 1948 law as well) was a similar provision. The first explicit discussion of the fade-out principle, although not under that label, appeared in R. D. Robinson, "Conflicting Interests in International Business Investment," *Boston University Business Review*, Spring 1960, pp. 3–13. For a recent analysis, see Guy B. Meeker, "Feasibility of Fade-out Joint Venture Principle as Form of U.S. Direct Private Investment in Latin America," unpublished M.B.A. thesis, George Washington University, School of Government and Business Administration, 1970, summarized in his "Fade-out Joint Venture: Can It Work for Latin America?" *Inter-American Economic Affairs*, Spring 1971, pp. 25 ff; also see his "How Will Multinational Firms React to the Andean Pact's Decision 24?" *Inter-American Economic Affairs*, Fall 1971, pp. 55 ff. The latter study was based on an interview of 20 large North American-based corporations. All expressed grave misgivings about the feasibility of the fade-out principle embedded in decision 24. Availability of local capital, finding a suitable partner, valuation of assets, and differences in business practices were the principal concerns. Nonetheless, one study revealed that the majority of some 90 U.S. companies with facilities in one or more of the Andean Pact countries might be candidates for the "fade-out joint venture," depending on conditions.

greater than the marginal utility of the current contribution of the parent company. One measure of this change is the willingness of others to do the same thing for less return. Such a consideration is particularly appropriate where the host country has been experiencing or anticipating a persistent balance-of-payments deficit because of asymmetric economic relationships between the host country and the domicile of the parent firm, an asymmetry inherent where wealth levels, growth rates, and political regimes are widely disparate.

It is precisely this logic that pushes countries in the direction of limiting alien ownership in time, as in the previously cited Indonesian, Philippine, and ANCOM cases. Such pressures have the effect of pushing the foreign firm to a greater utilization of local resources so as to be in a preferred position to sell by contract, or reduced equity, those external inputs still required, such as new technology and access to an international marketing network.

A further observation is suggested by the Franko and Wells studies of international joint ventures. The Franko study (1969), in respect to U.S. business practice relative to international joint ventures, reports that the tolerance of American firms of the influence of joint venture partners varied "with explicit elements of their strategies and the organizational implementation of those strategies."[48] It was found, for instance, that as U.S. firms *first* became involved in overseas production they tended to have a relatively high tolerance for joint ventures, many of which were highly autonomous. "Products tend to be new overseas in international product life-cycle terms. Demand and cost uncertainties and their concomitant, the need for close-to-the-market flexibility, are high."[49] The result is that the capital and the market knowledge of the joint venture partner "are seen as useful complements" to the international firm's monopolistic control over technology or natural resources.[50] But, as foreign markets become saturated, price competition threatens. Some firms respond by introducing new products; others by cutting prices and differentiating their products. In the first case, joint venture stability is relatively high; in the latter case, it is somewhat lower, particularly if the firm is operating overseas through a line area headquarters and not through an international division. The study concludes:

If this finding reflects the true state of the world, managers in firms following a strategy based on the pursuit of one end-use market may wish to consider avoiding some of the possible political and financial strains of disposing of partners by not entering into joint ventures in the first place. Alternatively, managers of such firms may consider the

---

[48]Lawrence Franko, "Strategy Choice and Multinational Corporate Tolerance for Joint Ventures with Foreign Partners" (Cambridge: Harvard University Graduate School of Business Administration, unpublished D.B.A. diss., 1969), p. 258. More recently (1976) Yoshino found the same phenomenon in respect to Japanese corporations (*Japan's Multinational Enterprises*, pp. 127 ff.).

[49]Franko, "Strategy Choice," p. 259.

[50]*Ibid.*

possibility that their joint ventures are distinctly transitional in nature. This possibility may merit special attention by managers of undiversified firms that have found joint ventures useful in the short run and have not yet reached area stages of multinational organizational development. They may consciously prepare for the shock that can come to corporate psyches when joint venture partners wish to go their own directions....

For managers of such firms, those pursuing a strategy of foreign product diversification, the results of this study suggest that the joint venture form of operation may not only be no hindrance to international growth but may be positively useful, both in the short and the long run.[51]

The Wells study measured the propensity of firms to enter joint ventures in terms of four strategies: (1) differentiation within a maturing product line, (2) the generation of new products to serve needs and customers similar to those of older products, (3) the generation of new products that are diversified as to function and customers, and (4) retention of control over raw material sources. It was found that firms following the third and fourth strategies had higher joint venture entry ratios. There also seems to be reason to believe smaller firms in an industry are more likely to enter joint ventures than larger firms.[52]

The point is, of course, that as multinational firms use the rationale of comparative input value to squeeze out foreign joint venture partners, then pursuit of a similar strategy by foreign investors and their governments cannot be too strongly contended when relative input value shifts to their side of the balance.

Some commentators have used the term "unbundling" to refer to the process of moving away from a general bundle of rewards as represented by a dividend stream to a matching of specific rewards with specific contributions. If a firm feels unable to follow such a strategy, it is possibly admitting its vulnerability. It is admitting that the self-perceived benefit/cost ratio apparently significantly exceeds that perceived for the other relevant interests, be they foreign business associates or political authorities within the host country. In short, the firm is admitting that

$$\left(\frac{\text{benefit}_A}{\text{cost}_A} \right) \ A > \left(\frac{\text{benefit}_B}{\text{cost}_b} \right) \ A.$$

5.2 RIGHTS AND ASSETS OWNED BY THE LOCAL FIRM

Here we have the reverse case with the same devices for transferring valuable rights being employed. In the transfer, however, the domestic firm should

---

[51]Franko, "Strategy Choice," pp. 261–63.

[52]See John M. Stopford and Louis Wells, *Managing the Multinational Enterprise: Organization of the Firm and Ownership* (New York: Basic Books, 1972).

exercise care not to lose unwittingly the assets from which such rights emanate by failing to secure valid local protection (see Section 7.2). For example, trade secrets, although recognized in U.S. law as a valid form of property giving rise to recognizable rights, are frequently not so protected abroad. But to assume that an American management is any more trustworthy than a management consisting of foreign nationals in this regard begs a large question.

The point can be made and defended that conflicts of interest in a joint venture between, say, a U.S. firm and foreign stockholders are probably unavoidable so long as there are significant differentials among nations in respect to tax level, commercial policy, monetary stability, remittance restriction, and resource allocation priorities. Maximization of profits at the joint-venture level may not be consistent with maximum profits for the integrated multinational enterprise. Therefore, as we have already seen, the international firm tends to develop profit centers quite apart from many of its individual overseas ventures through transfer pricing.

On the other hand, without local foreign participation in the profits generated by the employment of local resources, the conflict between the U.S. firm and the host government may be insurmountable, the latter probably desiring to maximize the balance of payments, income, public revenue, and growth effects of the local enterprise. And quite apart from the parent firm's desire to hold profits down in certain enterprises for legal and monetary reasons, the firm may find it difficult to establish mutually acceptable prices for goods and services moving among related enterprises. Also, the allocation of marketing areas as among subsidiaries, and between them and the parent, becomes awkward. If security of market position and assets is a function of the extent of perceived mutual interest as between an international firm, its foreign associates, and the host government, then the optimum long-run strategy may well be the transnational approach achieved through merger—that is, an exchange of ownership or the exchange of equity for that in a new, jointly-owned enterprise. With repeated international mergers, of course, a firm becomes truly *transnational* in that it loses virtually all national identity except that thrust upon it legally by its selection of a place of headquarter's incorporation.[53] And herein lies an odd dilemma, which may constitute the most important single problem facing international business.

It can be demonstrated that in order to quiet nationalist political pressures, to maximize the employment of local resources, and to minimize cost and expense, many international firms feel mounting pressure to withdraw all parent-country management personnel from foreign ventures and to share ownership in these enterprises with local interests. But if the ultimate form of much of international business is of the transnational variety, as seems possi-

---

[53]The prediction has been made that by 1985 ownership of the parent multinational firms will be spread worldwide through mergers with major companies elsewhere (*Business Europe*, March 14, 1969). See Section 8.1 for a more complete description of this process.

ble, how does one move from this highly localized (nationalized) structure to the transnational? Indeed, how does one recruit management personnel able to operate effectively in a transnational entity, if relatively few parent-country executives are getting any real management experience in foreign environments? It seems likely that without such experience few will achieve the ability to divorce themselves intellectually and emotionally from their native national identities long enough to make national bias-free decisions. The same could be said of European and Japanese firms.

The foregoing is not merely hypothetical. As noted, there have been a number of recent cases in which firms have traded their stock for an equity position in a foreign enterprise so as to push closer to full optimization of policy in regard to an integrated operation. A major obstacle is the psychological one on the part of the parent management. Is it psychologically capable of participating in a transnational enterprise? The Japanese, more than others, may encounter a real obstacle in making such a transition because of the unique managerial behavior and financial structure of many Japanese firms.

5.3 SELECTION OF FOREIGN ASSOCIATES

Quite apart from selecting an optimum strategy in regard to the ownership of assets and valuable rights, the choice of the foreign associate, whether he be a joint owner, contractor, contractee, or agent, can be of critical importance. The degree of criticalness depends upon the time duration of the association and the inability of the parent firm to mount adequate leverage against the foreign associates in event of behavior injurious to the interests of the parent. Of course, the foreign associate looks at the parent firm in precisely the same light.

Options in respect to selection of foreign associates are threefold: (1) sector (public or private), (2) dispersion (limited to named persons, named institutions or firms, the general public), and (3) nationality (local nationals, parent-country entities or nationals, multinationals).

Having gone through the exercise outlined in this chapter, a management must concern itself with its other two partners, whether explicitly or implicitly present; namely, the parent and host government. The important question here is the extent to which the values placed on the various flows by relevant official bodies vary significantly from those assigned by the business interests involved. It is probably a safe generalization that for a U.S., European, or Japanese firm the higher the capital intensity of its contribution the less likely are these assigned values to diverge significantly. Income from pure capital (debt) and from highly capital-intensive inputs (high-level skills and technology) and the sale of capital equipment are likely to be given priority in foreign exchange control systems over the repatriation of dividends representing, at least in part, return on less capital-intensive inputs, that is, those derived from the use of local land, labor, and materials.

Assuming the same overall risk in both capital-poor and capital-rich countries, capital-intensive inputs into capital-poor countries should enjoy relatively high returns. By diluting this input with more labor-intensive inputs, the rate of return can be expected to go down, all else being equal. Hence, maximization of rate of return, if this be the corporate goal, dictates limiting one's inputs and suggests a joint enterprise, whether through equity or some contractual relationship. The latter may, in some cases, minimize risk; there are relatively few cases of unilateral breaches (including forced renegotiation) of short term contracts (say, up to ten years). The initiating firm tends to maintain maximum leverage, for it has a minimum commitment in immovable assets abroad that may be sequestered or over which control may be lost. It is difficult for a government to sequester a flow of capital-intensive services or goods emanating from outside its borders.

Some firms have realized that the possible disparity between the values assigned to the flows in the system described here by the two associated firms and those assigned by the host government may be virtually eliminated by entering directly into an arrangement with an entity of that government; hence, the *international mixed venture*. In many cases, of course, the foreign firm is left no choice. But, even so, the risk inherent in any significant disparity between private and official valuations placed on the flows of benefits and costs (derived from the politico-social priorities suggested in the Introduction) may be reduced almost to zero. In such case, one need deal only with the first phase of this analysis, with some sensitivity, of course, to the restraints that may be imposed by the firm's *parent* government. Herein lies the rationale, other than sheer compulsion, for the international mixed venture.

In this age of the professional manager, development banks, economic plans and regulations, large-scale government buying, and monetary and fiscal control, it is often difficult to differentiate meaningfully between public and private economic institutions. For present purposes, it is suggested that state-dominated institutions may be of two varieties: (1) those in which decisions are dominated by internal profit considerations and (2) others. Clues as to the nature of a given institution are its legal basis (special statutes or ordinary commercial law), auditing authority, terms of office for directors, frequency of turnover of top management, political stature of both directors and top management, disclosure of financial statements, degree to which the product is subject to distribution and price control, and degree of official protection awarded (legal monopoly, tax and credit advantages, and so forth). The relevance of the distinction is that a *mixed venture*, in the sense of joint ownership of equity by public and private interests, assumes a certain area of mutual interest in generating an internal financial profit within the relevant time horizon. If the state-owned equity is concerned primarily with external economies or political power, then dividends should not be relied upon as the major profit route by the private partner. This does not mean that the foreign firm cannot find a profitable relationship through contracted sale (or purchase) of services and/or product, whether or not associated with debt or equity financing.

In some instances, the enterprise may be considered by the government to be a pioneer industry for purposes of training, development of supply (for example, agriculture-based industry), and market expansion. In such case, the private partner may wish to retain an option to secure equity when skills, supply, and market reach levels adequate to support an internal profit. Indeed, at that point, the government may wish to spin-off the entire enterprise into private hands. This move is possible if the state ownership is not seen as part of an ideological commitment but, rather, simply as a manifestation of a pragmatic policy. There is mounting evidence in many countries that the commitment to socialist ideology is weakening in favor of more pragmatic economic policies. Here then is a critically important variable.

But there are others. Consider the possible rationale for placing an economic activity in the public (government) sector and of the types of public sector enterprise possible.

1. Rationale for public (government) sector enterprise.

    a. Inability to internalize profit (social overhead and infrastructure type of enterprise, such as education).

    b. Tendency to monopoly, which is a function of the limited size of many national markets and which in turn transforms many industries into decreasing cost industries; that is, there is only room for one plant, if that.

    c. Need for pioneer industry, which implies an inability to internalize profit over a long initial development period (the school-factory and regional development concept).

    d. Inadequacy of private resources, in that by the very nature of a socio-political system a greater reservoir of capital, entrepreneurial capacity, and managerial and technical skills may appear in the public sector, thereby draining the private sector.[54]

    e. Need for public revenue with which to finance (a) above.

    f. Need for public control, as in defense-related industries, in industries whose output is inherently dangerous to public health or safety, and in activities involving an exhaustible resource (minerals).

    g. High risk due to uncertainty in respect to the timing and amount of the pay-out for a particular investment, such as space exploration. (It should be noted that in a small country individual private enterprises are likely to be small and, hence, the level of risk that can be tolerated is less. Therefore, there is greater pressure to spread risk by placing an investment in the public sector.)

---

[54]This may be due to the relatively high status of military-bureaucrats, the traditional low status of private business because of identity with racial or religious minority groups or a tendency to monopolize in a small market, or the appeal of the public sector (including the military) to those without the right family connections and to those more committed to long-run national welfare.

2. Types of public sector enterprise.

    a. By legal status (government department, autonomous government agency, specially chartered corporation, corporation established under general, that is, private, commercial law).

    b. By exclusiveness (close or public corporation).

    c. By scope of operation (multinational, national, regional, provincial, municipal, communal).

    d. By goal (internal financial profit, external economic-social benefit, general or regional economic development, personal prestige and power, employment).

    e. By economic status (monopoly or oligopoly, competitive with private).

    f. By philosophy (ideologically based, pragmatic).

Turning to choice of foreign associates in the private sector, one sees quite clearly that international firms most frequently limit their associations to either named persons or to specific legal entities. This is obviously required for contractual relationships. However, in the case of joint venturing through equity, the international firm has the option of a few or many local partners. If an important reason for moving into a joint venture is the purchase of a local management, which is available only if that management participates in ownership, or the need for a special relationship with suppliers, customers, competitors, distributors, government, and/or financiers, then the firm will usually opt for limiting the issue of shares to named persons or institutions, whether the shares be in the local or parent international firm. However, if the overriding reason for joint venturing is the need to effect maximum dispersion of foreign interests (hence, a need for local financing), to create a larger area of common interest with the host society (because of the utilization of local resources in generating profit), or simply to satisfy legal requirements, then the international firm may well decide to seek a public sale of equity. The ability to do so successfully rests on the reputation of the firm and the availability of a local securities market.

It should be noted that the assumption that there is no market for equity shares in most countries should be examined with some skepticism. Successful public issues in such countries as Turkey and Brazil may be straws in the wind. It is of interest to note that Brazilian subsidiaries of international firms have hesitated about going public locally to raise capital because they had been required under a 1968 law to sell over a 20-year period up to 49 percent of their equity. Although the Brazilian government favored such open corporations (*sociedades anonimas de capital aberto*) by granting them certain fiscal advantages, many firms hesitated to surrender 49 percent and the degree of control implied therein. Since mid-1971, however, after the required initial sale of 20 percent, firms may fulfill the 49 percent requirement by the sale of nonvoting preferential shares.

A serious problem in limiting local partners to named persons or institutions is that one can never be certain into whose hands the equity will fall in succeeding generations. Whether or not it is possible to limit the transferability of shares depends upon local law. In the United States, limitation is possible under certain circumstances. This problem need not arise for contractual relationships, which always can be limited in time and assignability. Therefore, the legal ability to limit the transferability of shares may determine the wisdom of joint venturing where public sale is not possible and/or desirable.

On some occasions, U.S. firms have seen fit to go into joint ventures abroad with other U.S. firms or financial interests (for example, an Edge Act Corporation). The same phenomenon is reported elsewhere. It is common, for example, for a Japanese manufacturing company to join a Japanese trading company in a joint venture abroad, which often includes a significant local equity interest as well. This domestic joint venture approach appears most commonly in response to pressure from an important domestic customer or supplier, the need for foreign area expertise (including access to the market) not available in the company, the desire to gain financing, or the desire to spread risk. Warning: a U.S. firm joining a domestic U.S. competitor in a joint venture abroad may be vulnerable to U.S. antitrust prosecution. Economic justification seems to be no bar. Multinational participation is becoming more common with the development of international financial consortiums, and the tied-sourcing of such international entities as NATO.

In summary, the only valid generalization is that a fixed policy in regard to ownership or choice of foreign associates, regardless of the circumstances, is very likely to lead to something less than optimum strategy. Firms insisting generally on 100-percent-owned enterprises abroad and favoring local national ownership of the parent, or insisting on limiting the association to contracts, are equally vulnerable to the charge that they are not really maximizing their return on investment. The same can be said of firms that refuse to associate with a government entity under any and all circumstances. It all depends on which entity, where. It seems likely that the best approach is a situational one, not conformance to a general ownership policy. Indeed, as national entry laws become more restrictive, the international firm may be required either to withdraw or to bend its policy. One has the feeling that the Indonesian, Philippine, and ANCOM rules on foreign investment may be prototypes for the LDCs generally. Also the appeal of the Japanese developmental model, restrictive entry for foreign firms coinciding with very rapid economic growth rate, should be noted.

The concluding paragraph of Friedmann and Benguin's work is appropriate.

It would be wrong to assume a general superiority of the contractual joint venture over the equity joint venture. The reverse would be an equally improper generalization. Nevertheless, developing countries have not forgotten the excesses of the colonial period and they are constantly on guard against a form of neocolonialism that would take the form of domineering foreign ownership in national enterprises. Therefore, it is likely that they will favor increasingly the development of cooperation with foreign investors based merely on contractual obligations.[55]

Discussion questions

1. It is said that maximization of profits at the joint-venture level may not be consistent with maximum profits for the integrated multinational enterprise. Develop some realistic, hypothetical situations in which this would be likely.

2. Under what circumstances might a firm opt for the international joint-venture strategy?

3. Should governments restrict the foreign ownership of domestic commercial assets? If so, what criteria should a government establish?

4. When might the mixed-venture strategy be appropriate for a foreign firm?

5. Do you feel that a government should ever force a foreign firm to reduce its ownership in a local firm? If so, under what circumstances?

6. Do you feel that a government is ever justified in expropriating a foreign-owned local firm? If so, under what circumstances?

7. Do you feel that a government is ever justified in confiscating a foreign-owned firm? If so, under what circumstances?

Recommended references

Basche, J. R. *Integrating Foreign Subsidiaries into Host Countries.* New York: The Conference Board, 1970.

Bivens, K. K. and E. B. Lovell. *Joint Ventures with Foreign Partners.* New York: National Industrial Conference Board, 1966.

Franko, Lawrence G. *Joint Venture Survival in Multinational Corporations.* New York: Praeger, 1971.

Friedmann, W. G. and J. P. Benguin. *Joint International Business Ventures in Developing Countries.* New York: Columbia University Press, 1971.

Garner, J. F. *Government Enterprise: A Comparative Study.* New York: Columbia University Press, 1970.

Kalmanoff, G., ed. *Joint International Business Ventures.* New York: Columbia University Press, 1961.

Lovell, Enid B. *Nationalism or Interdependence: The Alternatives—International Survey of Business Opinion and Experience.* New York: The Conference Board, 1969.

Robinson, Richard D. *National Control of Foreign Business Entry.* New York: Praeger, 1976.

Tomlinson, J. W. C. *The Joint Venture Process in International Business: India and Pakistan.* Cambridge: M.I.T. Press, 1970.

---

[55]Friedman and Benguin, *Joint International*, p. 418.

Appendix to Chapter 5
EXPROPRIATION

Although the terms expropriation, confiscation, nationalization, socialization, and intervention are used by some authors almost interchangeably, technically the terms are distinct. Expropriation refers to a formal taking of property with or without the payment of compensation; confiscation, to an expropriation without compensation. Nationalization, on the other hand, refers to limiting certain economic activity to local citizens, which may lead to forced sale, expropriation, or even confiscation if aliens are already present. Socialization refers to placing an economic activity in the public sector, which is even more restrictive than nationalization. Intervention describes a "taking of control" and may be of a temporary nature.

An expropriation may involve the seizure of contraband (the definition of which, incidentally, differs from country to country), the exercise of the right of eminent domain in order to accomplish a public purpose (as building a highway), an act of sovereignty in order to accomplish a general purpose perceived to be socially desirable (such as land reform or exclusion of alien owners), or the exercise of the police and judicial power to redress a wrong committed by the owner (such as nonpayment of taxes or gaining title by fraud). Obviously, in many of these situations, no compensation is paid, but problems arise even so because of varying practices and definitions, such as the amount of, and liability for, back taxes, the definition of contraband, and so forth. To this list, some would add simply unjust enrichment, that is, exploitation by reason of a firm's ability to charge monopoly prices for the services rendered to a national economy because of the absence of alternative sources of material, market access, technology, skills, or finance. For instance, "It has been estimated . . . that local participation in the form of wages, royalties, and taxes in the Bolivian tin industry amounted to only about 20 percent of the value of the minerals exported during the 1920s and perhaps 45 percent in recent years."[56]

Expropriation becomes confiscation when adequate, prompt, and effective compensation does not follow the taking. Confiscation may not be really questionable in a legal sense if the taking is based on illegal behavior by the dispossessed owner or is justified on the basis of a joint sharing by the owner in the social-economic benefits to be derived from the taking. But again, definitions of what is legal or illegal behavior, and belief wherein lies social-economic benefits, differ from nation to nation.

Even so, precisely what constitutes adequate, prompt, and effective compensation? The United States defines the terms in the so-called Hickenlooper Amendment to the Foreign Assistance Act of 1961, which automatically shuts

---

[56]Walter Heller, "Fiscal Policies for Under-Developed Countries," in Richard Bird and Oliver Oldman, eds., *Reading in Taxation in Developing Countries* (Baltimore: Johns Hopkins Press, 1964), pp. 19–20.

off U.S. economic assistance to a nation guilty of expropriating property and assets of U.S. citizens. For this purpose:

1. Expropriation consists of the seizure of "ownership or control of property," "repudiation or nullification of contracts or agreement," imposition of "discriminatory taxes or other exactions, or restrictive maintenance or operational conditions."

2. Nonpayment means failure by the responsible government to take appropriate steps, including arbitration, within six months to discharge its obligations under international law to the injured parties.

3. Adequate and effective payment means equitable and speedy compensation in convertible foreign exchange equivalent to the value of the property taken.

Such definitions really answer few questions. For example, how is the lost property or rights to be evaluated? Possible alternatives: tax assessed base, book value, or replacement value. One author has suggested that the "basic calculation is the determination of the time-adjusted difference between a cash inflow" from the foreign owners and a cash outflow to the foreign owners. One then assumes an appropriate cost of equity capital for the expropriated enterprise (after-tax return to the foreign owner). One can then calculate the net present compound value of the net cash flow for each year, the algebraic sum representing the "single transfer payment that should be made in order to reverse the entire history of the company and return the investor to its original status but with just compensation for the use of its funds over the period of operation."[57]

As of late 1971, a U.S. State Department analysis reported that the list of noncommunist countries that had nationalized, expropriated, or negotiated purchases of foreign assets since 1960, usually in connection with nationalization actions, included 34 countries (nine in Latin America, 15 in Africa, five in the Middle East, five in Asia). This report went on to state,

Studies of economic nationalism in developing countries suggest that, aside from fundamental changes in form of government, its causes are to be found in such factors as:

1. **increasing support for the widely held view in many of the LDCs that they are excessively dependent on foreign companies which export resources, take a disproportionate share of profits out of the country, and more generally exercise undue influence over governments and lives of people through their international economic power;**

2. **the increasing political responsiveness of developing country leaders to the popular sentiment outlined above, despite its debatable merits;**

3. **the increasingly positive and self-reliant attitudes taken by many developing coun-**

[57]David K. Eiteman, "A Model for Expropriation Settlement," *Business Horizons*, April 1970, pp. 85–91.

tries toward their development problems, partly as a result of increasing technical competence, partly as a result of frustrations over trade and aid issues, and partly because they have an increasing range of choices in a world of expanding capital centers and institutions; and

4. the appearance of infant industries that compete against foreign firms with easier access both to less expensive financing and more up-to-date technology.

In LDCs a primary aim of economic nationalism is to increase control over their economies and to reduce the role of foreign firms, even at the expense of economic growth and technological advantages gained from association with the developed countries. In the view of some LDC governments, the gains in self-confidence and national pride will outweigh this cost which they tend to minimize.[58]

Root, writing in 1968, reported six major expropriations of foreign business properties since World War I involving 187 U.S. companies in 240 separate acts of expropriation (171 being in communist countries, 137 in Cuba alone). The first was a result of the Bolshevik Revolution in Russia, with an estimated loss of $3.5 billion ($175 million U.S.).[59] The first significant noncommunist expropriation of foreign business property was the 1927 and 1938 Mexican seizure of foreign-owned real estate and in 1938, of international petroleum companies (though curiously, not all of them). Root calculated that the total estimated value of U.S. assets expropriated (1917–65) came to $2.3 billion, the biggest chunk from Cuba in 1959–60 ($1.4 billion). A more complete total (Root did not include the Mexican land nor the Ceylon oil seizures; also his Cuban figure may be low) would possibly be close to double this amount. Root observed that petroleum and public utilities have been most vulnerable to "selective expropriation" (selective in that the taking was limited to one economic sector, unlike the general expropriation as in the typical communist case).

A more thorough 1969 study of most of the expropriations suffered by U.S. and U.K. business interests overseas in the 1946–68 era (41 instances involving British firms, plus 110 seizures of insurance firms; 14 instances involving U.S. firms) found that 13 countries had been the sites for these takings. But, 33 of the 55 cases were in but four countries (Algeria, Burma, Ceylon, and Tanzania).[60] Since this study was completed, both Peru and Chile would have to be added to the list. Three countries (Ceylon, India, and the U.A.R.), it was found, were responsible for the nationalization (hence, expropriation, since

---

[58] *Nationalization, Expropriation, and Other Takings of the United States and Certain Foreign Property since 1960* (Washington: U.S. Department of State, Bureau of Intelligence and Research, Research Study RECS-14, November 30, 1971), pp. 1–2.

[59] See Franklin R. Root, "The Expropriation of American Companies," *Business Horizons*, April 1968, pp. 69 ff.

[60] John F. Truit, "Expropriation of Private Foreign Investment: A Framework to Consider the Post World War II Experience of British American Investors," unpublished Ph.D., diss., Graduate School of Business, Indiana University, 1969.

alien firms were already operating) of the 110 insurance companies. The most vulnerable industries other than insurance were petroleum, banking, and retail trade. Manufacturing accounted for ten cases out of the 53.

Considering the total amount of U.S. direct foreign investment, the risk of expropriation is low if the recent past is any measure of the foreseeable future. That risk would appear to be under 2 percent even in the riskiest areas (Table 5.6).

World events have, however, periodically caused much more extensive expropriation. For example, the high gross expropriation rate for 1914–19 reflects revolutions in Mexico and Russia. Between 1936 and 1950, the destruction and takeover of United States property in Austria, Germany, Eastern Europe, and China was reflected in high expropriation rates. During the 1955–60 period, Cuba confiscated United States property with a book value of about $1 billion. From 1970 to 1974, Chile nationalized property with a book value exceeding $2 billion, and Latin American and African countries expropriated oil investments with a book value exceeding $500 million.[61]

In 1974, a United Nations study compiled a listing of 875 cases of expropriations of foreign enterprises in 62 countries occurring between 1960 and mid-1974 (Table 5.7). It was found that 16 percent of the countries, each with more than 30 cases, accounted for over two-thirds of all expropriations, and a very high percentage of the cases had occurred in African states south of the Sahara. It will be noted from Table 5.8 that mining, petroleum, and agriculture accounted for 40 to 60 percent for each period. Public utilities and banking accounted for much of the balance. If one plots the number of expropriated enterprises by year from 1960, there would appear to be an upward trend line (Figure 5.8). Doubtlessly contributing to this trend has been the nationalization of the oil industry (Table 5.9).

Truit found in his study that country characteristics apparently associated most significantly with expropriation, although the author admitted that he could not establish any neat mathematical correlation, were as follows:

1. Internal political pressure by a vocal and powerful left wing of the ruling political party with a large constituency with a national election imminent.

2. Large and active presence of communist bloc trading, economic assistance offers and missions.

3. High ratio of public sector to private sector activity, with the public sector extended to the production of consumer goods.

4. Lack of domestic entrepreneurial class and activity, with that activity at present carried on by racial or religious minority groups, and tending to be speculative and commercial in nature (i.e., not industrial).

5. Typically Level II in respect to the "composite index of human resource develop-

---

[61]G. C. Hufbauer and P. H. Briggs, "Expropriation Losses and Tax Policy," *Harvard International Law Journal,* vol. 16, 1975, pp. 534–35.

Table 5.6
U.S. DIRECT INVESTMENT ABROAD AND ESTIMATED GROSS EXPROPRIATION 1914–74 (BOOK VALUE IN MILLIONS OF DOLLARS)*

Year	Latin America†			Africa, Asia, Oceania‡			Europe		
	Direct Investment	Gross Ex-propriation§	Annual Gross Expropriation Rate	Direct Investment	Gross Ex-propriation‖	Annual Gross Expropriation Rate	Direct Investment	Gross Ex-propriation#	Annual Gross Expropriation Rate
1914	1,300	80	1.2%	200	—	—	600	120	4.0%
1919	2,000	—	—	400	—	—	700	—	—
1929	3,500	100	0.4%	600	—	—	1,400	10	0.1%
1936	2,800	}180	}0.5%	600	}110	}1.3%	1,200	}620	}3.7%
1940	2,800			700			2,000		
1950	5,200	100	0.4%	1,300	—	—	1,700	—	—
1955	7,200	1,280	3.6%	2,600	—	—	3,000	—	—
1960	9,300	560	1.2%	5,600	40 #	0.1%	6,700	—	—
1965	10,900	810 #	1.5%	9,300	200 #	0.4%	14,000	—	—
1970	14,800	1,300 #	2.2%	16,100	2,700 #	4.2%	24,500	—	—

*The Department of Commerce has traditionally used book value figures in compiling direct investment statistics. The book value of U.S. ownership of a foreign corporation equals the sum of U.S. debt and equity claims. The book value of a branch equals the sum of branch net worth and U.S. debt claims against the branch. Book value figures were not always available to measure gross expropriation. In some cases, the amount of compensation was used as a proxy measure, though compensation may well understate book value. Note also that book value may be much less than the fair market value of seized property.

†Including Western European dependencies (principally in western hemisphere).

‡Including shipping and other ''international'' direct investment.

§Approximate five-year sums. For example, the figure in the 1914 row gives total expropriations from 1914–19, the figure in the 1970 row gives total expropriations from 1970–June 1974. Annual rates of gross expropriation (before compensation) were estimated by dividing annualized quinquennial gross expropriation amounts by the beginning year level of direct investment. Gross expropriation is defined to include cases of nationalization, intervention (assumption of managerial control), requisition (temporary assumption of managerial control), coerced sale, and concession renegotiation. An attempt was made to tabulate the book value of all assets acquired through compulsory measures, regardless of the amount of compensation.

‖Based on Treasury census rather than Department of Commerce survey.

#Excludes certain cases in Algeria, Iraq, and Venezuela from 1960–65; in CAR, Guatemala, Libya, Peru, Somalia, Sudan, and Yemen from 1965–70; and in Colombia, Ecuador, Ghana, Iran, Lebanon, Morocco, Pakistan, Togo, Venezuela, and Zaire from 1970–74.

Source: Department of Commerce, Bureau of Foreign and Domestic Commerce, American Direct Investments in Foreign Countries, Trade Information Bulletin No. 731, 1930; Department of Commerce, Bureau of Foreign and Domestic Commerce, American Direct Investments in Foreign Countries: 1936, Economic Series No. 1, 1938; Department of Commerce, Office of Business Economics, Survey of Current Business, August 1961, August 1962, August 1963, September 1965, September 1966, September 1967, October 1969, October 1970, October 1971, November 1972, September 1973; Department of State, internal documents; Department of Treasury, Foreign Assets Control, Census of American Owned Assets in Foreign Countries, 1947; Department of Treasury, internal memos and records; *Insurance Claims Experience to Date: OPIC and Its Predecessor Agency,* OPIC Press Release TX/261, February 1974; S. REP. No. 1535, 87th Cong., 2nd Sess., App. No. 8, at 91–95 (1962). Letter from Department of State to Sen. J. W. Fulbright, May 7, 1962, concerning expropriation of U.S. private investments, with attachment ''Major Instances of Expropriation of Property Belonging to U.S. Nationals Since World War II''; *Hearings on U.S.-Chilean Relations Before the Subcomm. on Inter-American Affairs of the House Foreign Affairs Comm.,* 93d Cong., 1st Sess. (1973); Chiona Lewis, *America's Stake in International Investments* (1938); *New York Times,* selected issues; *Oil and Gas Journal,* selected issues; *Wall Street Journal,* selected issues.

Source: G. C. Hufbauer and P. H. Brigg, ''Expropriation Losses and Tax Policy,'' *Harvard International Law Journal,* vol. 16, 1975, p. 562.

Table 5.7

EXPROPRIATIONS OF FOREIGN ENTERPRISES BY COUNTRY, 1960 TO MID-1974 (NUMBER AND PERCENTAGE)

Item	Total	Number of cases						
		1–5	6–10	11–15	16–20	21–25	26–30	31 or more
Countries								
Number	62	37	5	5	3	1	1	10
Percentage	100	60	8	8	5	2	2	16
Cases								
Number	875	85	33	62	54	23	27	591
Percentage	100	10	4	7	6	3	3	68
		Abu Dhabi (United Arab Emirates)	Malawi	Congo	Argentina	Burma	Libyan Arab Republic	Algeria
		Bangladesh	Malaysia	Ghana	Nigeria			Chile
		Bolivia	Mexico	Iraq	Peru			Egypt
		Brazil	Morocco	Somalia				India
		Central African Republic	Sierra Leone	Zaire				Indonesia
		Chad						Sri Lanka
		Colombia						Sudan
		Costa Rica						Uganda
		Dahomey						United Republic of Tanzania
		Democratic Yemen						Zambia
		Ecuador						
		El Salvador						
		Gabon						
		Gambia						
		Guatemala						
		Guinea						
		Guyana						
		Haiti						
		Iran						
		Kenya						

Khmer Republic
Kuwait
Lebanon
Liberia
Madagascar
Nepal
Pakistan
Panama
Philippines
Qatar
Saudi Arabia
Senegal
Swaziland
Syrian Arab
Republic
Togo
Trinidad and
Tobago
Venezuela

Source: Centre for Development Planning, Projections and Policies; Department of Economic and Social Affairs, United Nations Secretariat, based on the following sources: systematically examined were the *Africa Research Bulletin* (Exeter, United Kingdom, 1964–74), the *Asia Research Bulletin* (Singapore, 1970–74) and the *Arab Report and Record* (London, 1966–74). The *African Diary* (New Delhi), the *African Recorder* (New Delhi), the *Asian Recorder* (New Delhi), *Facts on File* (New York), and *Keesing's Contemporary Archives* (London), various issues, were used as supplementary sources.

Reproduced from *Permanent Sovereignty over Natural Resources*, "Report of the Economic and Social Council" (United Nations: General Assembly, A/9716, September 20, 1974), p. 20.

Table 5.8

EXPROPRIATIONS OF FOREIGN ENTERPRISES, SECTORAL DISTRIBUTION BY REGION AND COUNTRY GROUP, 1960 TO MID-1974 (PERCENTAGE)

Region and country group	All sectors	Mining	Petroleum*	Agriculture	Manufacturing	Trade	Public utilities	Banking and insurance	Others†	Mining, petroleum, and agriculture
Africa south of the Sahara										
All countries	39	50	25	52	37	57	45	30	63	40
Countries below the average . . .	48	66	36	89	30	50	46	75	—	50
Countries above the average . . .	37	31	18	49	38	58	44	27	69	36
West Asia and Africa north of the Sahara										
All countries	26	3	51	—	29	17	6	33	28	22
Countries below the average . . .	22	3	37	—	35	50	9	19	40	23
Countries above the average . . .	27	4	61	—	28	13	—	34	27	22
South and South-east Asia										
All countries	22	5	15	46	5	23	6	33	—	25
Countries below the average . . .	9	—	22	—	10	—	—	—	—	13
Countries above the average . . .	25	12	9	50	4	26	19	35	—	31
Western hemisphere										
All countries	13	41	9	2	30	3	43	3	8	12
Countries below the average . . .	21	31	5	11	25	—	46	6	60	14
Countries above the average . . .	11	54	13	1	30	3	38	3	4	11
All regions										
All countries	100	100	100	100	100	100	100	100	100	100
Countries below the average . . .	100	100	100	100	100	100	100	100	100	100
Countries above the average . . .	100	100	100	100	100	100	100	100	100	100

Source: Same as Table 5.7.

Note: Same number of cases as in annex table 1 above.

*Including refining and distribution.

†Including cases for which a sector could not be ascertained.

Number of cases

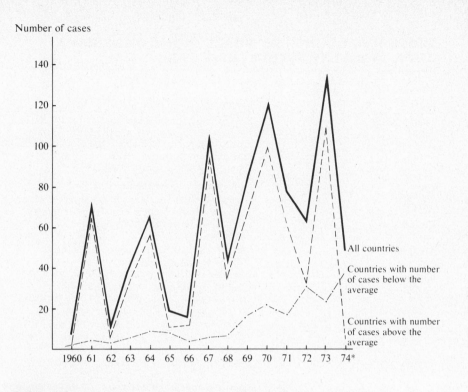

Figure 5.8
**EXPROPRIATION OF FOREIGN ENTERPRISES,
1960 TO MID–1974
(NUMBER)**

*The total for 1974 has been extrapolated.
Reproduced from *Permanent Sovereignty Over Natural Resources*, p. 25.

ment." But generally with a per capita income lower than the mean for all countries at that level.[62]

Truit also attempted to identify a firm's characteristics with vulnerability to expropriation. High on his list were

1.   Tactical vulnerability. Absence of any unique expatriate technical or managerial

[62]According to F. Harbison and C. A. Myers, *Education, Manpower and Economic Growth* (New York: McGraw-Hill, 1964), pp. 23 ff. The composite index is "the arithmetic total of (1) enrollment at second level of education as a percentage of the 15-to-19 age group, adjusted for length of schooling, and (2) enrollment at the third level of education as a percentage of the [20-to-24] age group, multiplied by weight of five" (p. 31). Of the 13 countries identified as expropriators in the Truit study, Harbison and Myers give a ranking for ten. Of these ten, five are given a Level II composite index, four of which had a per-capita GNP less than $182, the average for all Level II countries. One Level II country (Argentina) was higher. The other countries: two Level I countries, both with per capita GNPs lower than the group's mean of 84; two Level III countries, both well under the mean per capita GNP for the group; one Level IV for the per capita income well under the mean for that group.

Table 5.9

PRODUCING COUNTRIES' SHARE IN THE OWNERSHIP OF OIL INDUSTRY ASSETS (JUNE 1976)

Country	Government participation rate	Comments
Saudi Arabia	60	Sixty percent participation since 1974. Discussions for 100 percent takeover of ARAMCO's holdings nearing completion. Effective date of nationalization retroactive to January 1, 1976.
Iran	100	Nationalization in 1951.
Iraq	100	Almost total nationalization since 1973.
Kuwait	60;100	Gulf & BP holdings totally nationalized in March 1975; 60 percent participation for other foreign companies. However, their properties are to be nationalized soon.
Abu Dhabi	60	100 percent takeover under consideration.
Qatar	60	100 percent takeover is imminent.
Libya	51;100	BP, Bunker, Hunt, Amoseas, ARCO, and Shell's share of OASIS group totally nationalized; government owns a 51 percent share of Occidental's and remainder of OASIS group's holdings.
Algeria	100	Nationalization of all but Getty, CFP, and ERAP production since 1971, or approximately 80 percent of total.
Nigeria	55	Fifty-five percent participation in production of oil since 1974. Nigerian government has subsequently announced that it will assume complete ownership and control as soon as sufficient skilled local manpower is available.
Gabon	25	Although government participation is limited, Gabon has insisted on other stringent concessions from the oil companies.
Venezuela	100	Total nationalization in early 1976.
Ecuador	25	All petroleum is the property of the state. Twenty-five percent of Texaco/Gulf's operations taken over in 1974; government now plans to go to 51 percent.
Indonesia	100	Nationalization between 1963 and 1968.

See *Federal Energy Administration, The Relationship of Oil Companies and Foreign Governments* (1975); *Oil in the Middle East, Q. Econ. Rev.* (Ann. Supp. 1976).

Reproduced from William A. Johnson and Richard E. Messick, "Vertical Divestiture of U.S. Oil Firms: The Impact on the World Oil Market," *Law and Policy in International Business,* vol. 8, no. 4, 1976, pp. 966–67.

skills crucial to continued involvement by the owner, great visibility of foreign investment to the host population, high susceptibility to corruption in absence of incorruptible expatriate management.

2. Foreign exchange activity. The enterprise is a large net consumer of foreign exchange and consumes foreign exchange in a way that renders ineffective host government controls.

3. Nature of a firm's economic activity. Service or distribution investment, also one in which all commercial phases of the activity are located within the territorial jurisdiction of the host country.

4. Size of firm. For example, a relatively small firm in a relatively unimportant sector almost completely controlled by foreign firms.

5. Nationality of firms. Such as one related to a parent firm clearly identified with a country that was an unpopular foreign colonizer *and* with which the host government has severed relations.

6. Protective action by firm. One in which the original investment predates independence of the host nation and which does not participate in the development plans of the host government nor make a public relations effort to demonstrate its contribution to the host country.

7. Style of management. Such as one in which there is a minimum employment of local personnel other than those identified with minority religious or ethnic groups.[63]

What the Truit study seemed to indicate is that there has been a tendency for a country to expropriate when the gap between expectation and reality widens and political polarization sets in (that is, a commitment to radical reform by a significant number) and there is a perceived alternative source of capital and technology to the North American or European based firm, usually the Sino-Soviet bloc. Another alternative sometimes perceived in the manufacturing and mining sectors were those international firms geared to selling technology and skills on a contractual basis, very frequently but not invariably the subsidiaries of firms manufacturing capital goods (for example, oil drilling equipment, steel making machinery, paper mill machinery).

The other side of the coin, according to Truit, is that a firm enhances its vulnerability to expropriation by not cooperating with the host government (for example, in respect to foreign exchange conservation and development planning) and by losing the leverage that externally sourced inputs provide (external to the host country) for which there are no alternative sources. The dilemma for the international firm is that as it transfers technology and skill and develops the local market, it increases its vulnerability—but only if it adheres to a fixed ownership policy.

There are reasons to believe that all of these pressures will increase, thereby aggravating the risk of expropriation, whether by time-phased disinvestment as in the ANCOM case or in sudden taking as in the recent Peruvian and Chilean cases. The firm that insists on a fixed equity-ownership policy internationally simply compounds its risk, which means that it must discount its expected stream of earnings by a greater rate, thereby ruling out many opportunities that might otherwise seem attractive. One suspects that it is precisely because many international firms do not minimize risk by adequate environmental monitoring and flexible ownership policy that the international transfer of resources from the more affluent to the poorer countries remains at levels that are inadequate to close the gap in per-capita material well-being. Indeed,

---

[63]Adapted from Truit, "Expropriation," p. 235.

we know that by virtually every measure the gap continues to open, thereby further eroding confidence in the capacity of private international business to further world welfare and making expropriation even more attractive.

Recent take-overs (possibly temporary) of U.S. and European commercial assets overseas include the intervention of the Chilean subsidiary of the Pfizer Corporation (by reason of illegal gains from alleged smuggling of products to Bolivia and Peru); the occupation of Panamanian Light and Power, a subsidiary of Boise Cascade Corporation (because of alleged noncompliance with regulations); the official nationalization of the U.S., British, French, and Dutch-owned Iraq Petroleum Company (because of reduction in production and subsequent noncompliance with a request that the Iraqi government be given a 20 percent share in ownership); the unilateral termination of all existing exploratory oil concessions held by private companies in Argentina; and the expropriation of the Chilean subsidiary of the International Telegraph and Telephone Corporation (on charges of being a vehicle for CIA-directed political activity against the successful Marxist candidate for the Chilean presidency), and the seizure of Dow-Corning assets by the Venezuelan government (because of alleged noncompliance to government orders that the parent company not comply with certain demands issued by the kidnappers of a company executive).

It may come as a surprise to some that the United States has been considered by a few foreign firms a high-risk country from the point of view of expropriation. A 1969 study of 40 foreign direct investors in the United States revealed that only three of these firms had ever suffered expropriation in a foreign country, but two such experiences had been in the United States. "During World War II, enemy investments (namely German) valued at over $150 million were seized by the U.S. Alien Property Custodian. The two of these companies interviewed did not, however, consider the United States to be a high-risk country, although they did for some years following World War II and reported that many German firms had not invested in the United States because of fear of expropriation."[64]

An expropriation is really only disastrous if the firm has no warning, and hence no opportunity to adapt defensive strategies even if only to minimize losses (such as inventory reduction, cessation of new investment, cutback on receivables, payment of all debts owed to U.S. suppliers, reduction of parent-company guarantee on local borrowing, cutback in cash holdings, heavy local borrowing, an increase in remittance to the United States, shipment to the subsidiary on irrevocable letter-of-credit terms only, a cutback in production).[65] Other possible measures are maximizing shipments of goods to parent and other associated firms outside of the host country on credit, a

---

[64]John D. Daniels, *Recent Foreign Direct Manufacturing Investment in the United States* (New York: Praeger, 1971).

[65]Mentioned as most frequent defensive measures by Root (*Expropriation of Private*), p. 73.

stepped-up public relations policy, substituting a contractual relationship for that of equity, negotiating with the host government, and appealing to the parent government for diplomatic intervention or economic sanctions (in the case of the U.S. firm, invoking the Hickenlooper amendment, thereby stopping all U.S. aid).[66]

In any event, the financial effect of expropriation may be diminished by covering the risk with an investment guarantee issued by the parent government of the firm (see Section 6.8), through a write-off of the loss against the parent company's taxable income or tax liability, or by attachment of foreign assets within the United States.

Just how the tax write-off is handled depends upon the tax law of the country in which the parent firm is domiciled. In Japan, for example, a special reserve fund may be set up by the parent company to cover such risk, the input to such fund being a cost, thereby reducing taxable income in Japan. In countries where foreign-source income is not taxed, a tax write-off may be impossible.

In the U.S. case, loss due to expropriation is, first of all, a deductible business expense. If the expropriated foreign operation is conducted through a branch, expropriation loss can be offset directly against U.S. income. If it is conducted through a subsidiary, the parent company can claim a foreign expropriation loss either on its equity or debt (a capital loss) in the subsidiary or against taxable income from the subsidiary. This deduction is facilitated if the U.S. equity in the foreign corporation is at least 80 percent, thereby qualifying it as an "affiliated corporation." In any case, the loss must be recognized for U.S. tax purposes in the year of confiscation, even though there may be assurances of future compensation at the time. The deduction of an expropriation loss from taxable income is permitted only to the extent that it is not compensated for by insurance or otherwise. The loss may be carried back three years and forward five years, or longer under special circumstances (15 years in the case of the Cuban expropriation).

The seizure of a second-tier subsidiary (a subsidiary of a subsidiary) may produce a loss (and consequent reduction in tax liability) for the first-tier foreign corporation, depending upon local law. However, unless the expropriation renders the shares of the first-tier corporation worthless, the U.S. parent cannot recognize a loss prior to the actual sale of those first-tier shares. Thus, a firm might well invest in expropriation-prone areas and projects only directly. Or, if it anticipates expropriation, to sell the threatened second-tier subsidiary to the parent.

---

[66]The United States also uses its influence within the International Bank for Reconstruction and Development to exert pressure in such cases. In fact, it is long-standing bank policy not to lend to any country in dispute with another member country over expropriation where no reasonable and speedy attempt to negotiate a settlement is under way. The U.A.R. was barred from loans for a long period after seizure of the Suez Canal, for example. In that case, the United States froze all U.A.R. government assets in the United States, which, in that the blocking denied the U.A.R. the use of its assets, was a form of retaliatory expropriation of valuable rights.

It should be noted that by taking an expropriation loss as an "arbitrary" foreign loss (a deduction from taxable income), the maximum foreign tax credit that may be credited against the U.S. tax liability is reduced. The point is that the maximum credit is the product of the ratio of foreign taxable income to worldwide taxable income and its tentative U.S. tax, which is 48 percent of worldwide taxable income. Taking an expropriation loss as an arbitrary foreign loss reduces the numerator of that ratio and, hence, the maximum foreign tax credit. The result is a partial offset in the form of a higher U.S. tax bite.[67]

Another method of recouping losses occasioned by the uncompensated taking of assets by a foreign government is the attachment by injured parties of that government's assets located outside its jurisdiction. For example, attempts were made by foreign firms to recover such losses in Mexico (oil properties) and in Chile (copper properties) by seeking to attach shipments of Mexican oil and Chilean copper reaching foreign ports. In both cases the shield of sovereign immunity overturned the attachments. Likewise, there was the famous Sabbatino case in which U.S. interests whose assets had been seized by the Cuban government attempted to attach proceeds from the sale of Cuban sugar banked in the United States, but the shield of national sovereignty prevented recovery. The result was the Hickenlooper amendment to the Foreign Assistance Act of 1961, previously discussed, which in effect directs U.S. courts not to use the "act of state" doctrine to decline jurisdiction in event of a claim arising from a confiscation of U.S. property unless the executive branch specifically requests otherwise. Subsequently, the earlier Sabbatino decision was reversed.

Under the "act of state" doctrine, U.S. courts had previously refused to examine the validity of the *public* acts of foreign governments. "And under the related doctrine of sovereign immunity, U.S. courts have long recognized that certain public, as opposed to commercial, acts of foreign governments are presumptively nonjusticiable,"[68] that is, nonactionable. The United States, however, "assumes that the sovereignty of nations is seldom affronted when these nations are subject to suits arising from commercial law."[69] It would now appear that if a government acts in a purely commercial capacity and if the Department of State issues a letter to the effect that legal action would not be contrary to the national interest, then assets of a foreign government located within the U.S. may be subject to attachment and possible transfer to the injured parties. The case might be particularly strong if the foreign government is one the United States does not formally recognize.

For example, in December 1950, the People's Republic of China expropriat-

---

[67]See G. C. Hufbauer and P. H. Briggs, "Expropriation Losses and Tax Policy," *Harvard International Law Review*, vol. 16, 1975, pp. 533–64.

[68]Wayne Beyer, "Commercial Obligation Under the Act of State Doctrine." *Law and Policy in International Business*, vol. 8, no. 4, 1976, p. 1093.

[69]Beyer, "Commercial Obligation," p. 1093.

ed assets belonging to U.S. citizens subsequent to the freezing of assets belonging to the P.R.C. by the United States. As a result there is the possibility that Chinese assets within U.S. jurisdiction might be attached by American nationals to compensate for their unsatisfied claims against the P.R.C. government. "This threat has meant that no Chinese ships have entered U.S. ports, no direct banking relations have been established, no official trade agreement has been negotiated, no maritime or aviation accords have been reached, and no Chinese assets subject to attachment have knowingly entered the jurisdiction of United States courts."[70] Included, of course, would be any goods physically located within U.S. jurisdiction whose title has passed to any entity of the P.R.C. Hence, U.S. exporters to the P.R.C. exercise great caution in assuring that title to the exported goods not be transferred to the P.R.C. until they are outside of the U.S. jurisdiction.

This whole subject has been clarified somewhat for U.S. claimants by the Foreign Sovereign Immunities Act of 1976, which laid down guidelines under which a private citizen or company could bring suit against a foreign government or a commercial enterprise owned by a foreign government. These guidelines were in line with those applied in other countries in that they cover "private" (i.e., commercial) activities as opposed to public acts (i.e., governmental, those that could not be performed by a private person). The Act specifically states that:

A foreign state shall not be immune from the jurisdiction of the courts of the United States or of the States in any case . . . in which rights in property taken in violation of international law are in issue and that property or any property exchanged for such property is present in the United States in connection with a commercial activity carried on in the United States by the foreign state; or that property is owned or operated by an agency or instrumentality of the foreign state and that agency or instrumentality is engaged in commercial activity in the United States.[71]

The law specifically made property in the United States owned by a foreign state, used for a commercial activity within the United States, vulnerable to judicial attachment. The sole exceptions are property of a foreign central bank or monetary authority held for its own account or property of a military character and intended for a military activity or under the control of a military authority or defense agency. The glaring deficiency in the law is that "violations of international law" are not defined. And, inasmuch as there is substantial difference of opinion on "international law" in relation to a taking of private property by a sovereign government, the problem is not really resolved.

---

[70]Steven E. Carlson, "Expropriated Property, Frozen Assets, and Sovereign Immunity: Legal Obstacles to United States–China Trade Relations," *Columbia Journal of Transnational Law*, vol. 15, no. 2, 1976, pp. 245–55.

[71]Quoted from the text of the law published in *International Law Materials*, vol. 15, no. 6, November 1976, p. 1389.

Case I
COLONIAL SUGAR REFINING COMPANY LTD. IN FIJI

Early in 1969 it became apparent that the South Pacific Sugar Mills Limited (SPSM), the 98 percent-owned Fijian subsidiary of the Colonial Refining Company Limited (CSR), an Australian corporation based in Sydney, would be unable to renew its contracts with the growers due to disagreement as to terms. SPSM was the owner of all four of the sugar mills in Fiji. Neither SPSM nor the growers had resorted to industrial action, nor had they threatened to do so. They had agreed to go to arbitration, and the chairman of the Sugar Advisory Council, a public entity in Fiji, had certified that efforts to obtain agreement had failed and that "a dispute exists in respect of the question of a new contract of general application." Shortly thereafter, the Chief Justice of Fiji appointed an arbitrator (1) "to determine the issues in the dispute over terms of a new contract between the millers [i.e., the four SPSM mills] and the growers for the sale and purchase of sugar cane, and (2) to draft a standard contract that would be equitable to all parties."

The principal parties to appear before this arbitrator would be representatives of the Federation of Cane Growers, the Alliance Cane Contract Committee, and the South Pacific Sugar Mills Limited.

The new contract to be drafted by the arbitrator could not legally be forced on the parties without their consent. What an award would do, however, would be to prevent industrial action. Parties would be free to consider the terms of the new contract calmly, without undue pressure from anyone. Legally there could not be a threat of "no cutting" or "no crushing."

Background

In the 1880s a number of sugar companies had begun operations in Fiji, at one time there being more than 30 millers. Subsequently, one by one they had dropped out, and by the 1920s only the Colonial Sugar Refining Company Limited remained. It operated five mills, one of which, however, was closed in 1958. Sugar was Fiji's dominant industry, although tourism had increased recently. Sugar still accounted for something like two-thirds of Fiji's foreign exchange earnings and one-fifth of its GNP. Some 15,000 growers were involved plus 3,000 persons employed in the milling and transport of the cane. The average farm size was ten acres. Average yield was 21.0 tons of cane per acre actually under cultivation. Only about 75 percent of the sugar land was cultivated each year. (See Exhibit I.1 at end of this chapter.)

Initially, much of the cane had been grown by the milling companies—including CSR—which, over the years, had come to acquire substantial freehold and leasehold landholdings. As people of the Fiji race were not keen on farming, the British colonial authorities instituted a policy of bringing to Fiji indentured Indian cane farm workers. Such was the origin of the Indians on Fiji where, by 1973, they accounted for a little over 50 percent of the total population. The balance were people of the Fijian race, except for a small number of Europeans and Chinese.

The plantation system of cane production, under the ownership of sugar millers and with employed labor, was characteristic of the sugar industry in most parts of the world except Australia.

In the 1920s CSR took what was for those days a radical decision and decided that instead of operating plantations in Fiji it would establish the cane workers (almost wholly Indians) as independent farmers on company land leased to the farmers or sold to them where the farmers had a capacity to buy the land. In consequence, for many years CSR had not itself grown cane in Fiji (except for minor amounts on certain lands associated with the mills, basically for agricultural experimental purposes.) The cane supply for the CSR mills was thus produced by about 15,000 independent farmers of whom something over 12,500 were Indians.

Concurrently with this development, Fiji was evolving politically and, not surprisingly, the two major political parties grew out of the two main racial groups. From the Indian-dominated Federation of Cane Farmers evolved the Federation Party. The Alliance Party, was on the other hand, very much a party of the Fijian chiefs and their followers. Through the various stages of legislative evolution that preceded full independence in 1970, the Alliance Party was the major influence. In the 1961 and 1969 commission investigations the Federation and Alliance not infrequently presented contrary views on specific issues.

It was in this setting that CSR, the expatriate owner of all four Fiji sugar mills, conducted its sugar milling operation. In any sugar industry where there are independent farmers, there is a basic conflict of interest between millers and growers in respect to the price to be paid for cane. It is the sugar, not the cane, which is saleable, but sugar cannot be made without cane. And as the world price of sugar fluctuated violently, sugar proceeds were highly unpredictable and often very low, the reasons being that (1) over one-third of the average crop had to be exported to the so-called "world free market" at prices that were uncertain, and (2) unreliable weather gave rise to crops of variable size.

Customary practice

It is important to understand the organization of the industry. In Fiji it was customary for a number of growers to work together in a "gang" headed by a *sirdar*, essentially a cooperative arrangement. Each grower helped his fellow members with harvesting their crops, although sometimes a grower might pay a substitute to do his work for him. The miller, through field officers, arranged the harvesting program with the gangs, allotting portable rail lines to each gang along with hand, animal, or tractor pulled "cane trucks," which could be moved to a delivery point on the permanent rail system. The gang elected a committee to represent it for a year, appointed a *sirdar* to control its operations, and maintained a bank account. There was no book of rules; it was all done by custom and tradition.

Occasionally frictions arose within gangs and they split into separate groups. The miller then had to decide whether to supply the splinter group with portable lines and cane trucks.

The cane was delivered to the miller at a rail delivery point either by portable line or by tractor and trailer, or directly to the mill by truck. The cane was transported as much as 80 miles in some cases. In neither case was it weighed until it reached the "weighbridge" at the mill.

Obviously the allocation of portable lines and cane trucks constituted a logistical problem. At the start of each season the miller and the gang mapped out a harvesting program, in which daily quotas of cane required of each gang were allocated. As the harvesting season progressed, the miller allocated portable lines, rail trucks and/or highway trucks. The objective was to keep the mill supplied with sufficient cane to fill its crushing capacity, and no more. If cane were kept waiting, it blocked access to the mill and disorganized the rail system. Also, the cane lost weight and this caused loss to the growers. The upshot was that field officers were busy throughout the crushing season trying to maintain a steady supply to the mills. Even so, many problems came up. A mill might break down. There could be a derailment. A heavy rain could stop everything.

Delivery tickets recorded deliveries made by the growers to the miller. In the case of rail transport, the ticket showed the number of cane trucks loaded by the grower, the date of harvesting, the variety of cane, green or burnt, time of delivery to the main line. The original copy was given to the locomotive driver. When the cane got to the mill, each rail truck load was weighed, and a receipt returned to the grower through the *sirdar*, the process sometimes taking as long as 14 days. In the case a cane truck were derailed and the load spilled, the grower was credited with a weight equal to the average load of his trucks delivered to the mill intact.

Highway truck transport was paid for by the growers, many of whom owned their own vehicles or hired relatives who did so. In the case of rail delivery, the movement of the cane to a rail delivery point was at the growers' expense, but delivery to the mill over a main line at the miller's expense. The miller performed the maintenance on all the main rail lines, but not the 41 miles of horse lines that had developed out of portable lines made permanent. The miller had, however, supplied the growers in such cases with all materials free of charge, but the growers had done the actual maintenance.

For many years, the miller had made interest-free advances to the growers to enable them to meet their harvesting expenses. Also, the miller supplied growers with goods on credit, such as seed cane, rice and fertilizers. No interest was charged on the outstanding balance. If the grower were a tenant, the miller debited his account for the rent. The miller also, on a grower's request, issued orders to firms supplying agricultural implements to him and debited his account for the cost. Hence, the miller maintained a running account for each grower. A problem arose when a grower sought money from other quarters and gave liens or charges on his crops. As a result, the miller sought the consent of these other lenders—and of the grower—to give priority to the advance made for harvesting expenses and other agricultural services. In the absence of consent, the miller hesitated to grant these advances. Finally, each grower was given two bags of sugar at a special "concession rate" (about 60 percent of the current wholesale price) each year.

It was customary for teams of inspectors to roam fields looking for disease and removing and destroying diseased cane, a process dubbed as "roguing." The cost of roguing was borne by the growers, being apportioned among them. Many growers felt that the roguing should be done by themselves and only if they failed to follow the direction of their inspectors in this regard should the miller undertake the roguing (at the growers' expense.)

Both miller and growers were concerned with the closing of the crushing season. The miller desired an even flow of cane up to the end, and the growers wished to know the latest date so as to be able to deliver all the cane possible. The practice was that when there was about eight weeks to go, the growers were given preliminary warning and, when the time was down to one or two weeks, they were given an approximate date. Even so, rain or a mill breakdown might alter the day so that it was not possible to be certain more than a day or two before shutdown.

The Eve Commission

As in other cane producing countries, the price paid by CSR for cane had often created tensions, and during the 1950s the situation in Fiji reached quite serious proportions. The upshot was that the British government sent out the Eve Commission[1] in 1960 to establish an equitable formula for determining the price to be paid for cane in the circumstances of fluctuating market conditions for sugar. The Eve Commission devised a formula that was embodied in contracts between the miller and each grower and which operated throughout the 1960s, the so-called "Eve contract." CSR alleged that it had had the effect of reducing conflict between miller and growers to a minimum, although in the introduction of a subsequent arbitration (that of Lord Denning), it was held

---

[1] So-called because it was headed by Sir Malcolm Eve, subsequently known as Lord Silsoe.

that many of the growers still felt that they were being exploited for the benefit of the 6,000 shareholders in Australia. It was even alleged that at least some of the growers had been forced to sign the new contracts against their will. The "Eve contract" terms resulted in the following division of revenue from the sale of sugar.

Deductions from sales revenue to yield "profit"

1. All CSR costs incurred in the production of cane (e.g., salaries of field officers, research establishments, operation of the rail transport system which brought the cane to the mills).

"growers' services"   10%

2. All CSR costs in making sugar from the cane.
3. All CSR costs in bagging and storing sugar and in transporting it to the ships.
4. An allocation of head office expenses of 11½ percent of items 1, 2, 3.
5. A depreciation expense of 3 percent of the capital value of all the mills (on a present value basis).

"manufacturing costs"   20%

Basic sugar making cost   30%

Division of "profit"

To the growers (82½ percent of 70 percent)   (57¾%)
To CSR (miller)   (12¼%)

In an average year it was estimated, deductions would eat up about 30 percent of sales revenue, and that the price paid to the growers would equal 57¾ percent of the proceeds derived from the sale of refined sugar. In practice, it turned out that miller's costs were regularly less than 30 percent. Any improvement in costs—say a reduction to 26 percent—was divided between growers and miller according to whether the reduction occurred in "growers services" or "manufacturing services." If, of the 4 percent cost improvement, 1 percent were in the former and 3 percent in the latter, then the profit split would be changed as follows:

> To the growers' share of profit, add 2/3 of the 1 percent due to a reduction in growers' services, plus 1/3 of the 3 percent due to reduction in manufacturing costs, or a total of 1-2/3 percent.

> To the miller's share of profit, add 1/3 of 1 percent, plus 2/3 of 3 percent, or a total of 2-1/3 percent.

In this example, the final split would be:

> To the growers, 59-5/12 percent (57-¾ plus 1-2/3)

To the miller, 40-7/12 percent (26 percent for costs, plus profit of 14-7/12 percent; i.e., 12¼ plus 2-1/3.

If the actual costs exceeded the 10 percent and 20 percent standard, half of the excess in each case was deducted from the growers' and the miller's shares. In fact, between 1962 and 1968 CSR alleged that the growers' actual share was never less than 59.3 percent and in one season was 64.3 percent, the weighted annual average being 61.1 percent. From the miller's share, a steady dividend of 7½ percent on capital was paid by SPSM. Most recently, proceeds from sugar sales had been in the neighborhood of $30 million.

This complicated formula was founded on the assumption that there was a fundamental difference between "growers' services" and "manufacturing costs." The Eve Commission had stated that ". . . the costs of growers' services and cane transport can be influenced very considerably by growers. The costs of manufacture, transport and storing of sugar can similarly be influenced by millers." It was on that account that the commission provided in the formula that if there were any saving on "growers' services," two-thirds of it benefited the growers. But, if there were any saving on "manufacturing costs," only one-third benefited the growers. By so doing, the Eve Commission thought that it would provide an incentive to the growers to reduce costs on "growers services" and for the millers to reduce costs on "manufacturing costs."

International agreements

The existence of the Sugar Price Stabilization Fund should be noted.

Upon the outbreak of the war in 1939, the United Kingdom government had contracted to buy all the exportable sugar from Commonwealth sugar export-ers, including Fiji, under a series of bulk purchase contracts. The price paid by the United Kingdom under these contracts was negotiated annually. These contracts continued until the end of the 1952 crop, thus overlapping the Commonwealth Sugar Agreements (CSA), which was signed in 1951.

When the war ended in 1945, sugar producers of the Commonwealth were faced with an urgent need to rehabilitate plant and machinery, as proper replacement and maintenance had been hindered by shortages caused by the war. They were also faced with rising costs and thus, sought an increase in price. Hence, in 1946 the United Kingdom was paying to Commonwealth exporters £19.10.0 per ton.[2] The landed cost to the United Kingdom bulk purchasing authority was about £22.10.0 per ton for Fiji sugar. World prices at the time were substantially higher. The cost of Cuban sugar landed in the United Kingdom would have averaged about £26.18.0 per ton in 1946, and around £31.7.0 per ton in 1947. Moreover, available free market supplies came

---

[2] At this time the pound was worth $4.03.

mainly from "dollar" areas. With the United Kingdom and the whole sterling area desperately short of dollars, Fiji and other Commonwealth sugar (which was paid for in sterling) had special currency advantages for the United Kingdom, as well as the price advantage.

These were the circumstances in which the United Kingdom negotiated with the Commonwealth sugar exporters in 1946. It was eventually agreed that the price to apply from the beginning of 1947 should be increased from £19.10.0 to £24.5.0 per ton. But in the case of the colonies, including Fiji, the United Kingdom stipulated that part of the increase should be used to establish reserve funds for price stabilization, capital rehabilitation, and labor welfare. When the world sugar price went lower, the U.K. consumer was subsidizing the system; when it went higher, the supplying countries in effect subsidized the U.K. consumer.

The independent Commonwealth sugar exporters, Australia and South Africa, were not affected by the United Kingdom stipulation that the colonies should set aside some of the price increase. They received the same price but chose not to set up any funds. The full price was shared between their millers and growers.

Until the end of the 1961 season, a levy on proceeds from all exports from Fiji under the CSA was paid into the fund. These exports were not confined to sales made against Fiji's negotiated price quota to the United Kingdom, but also included exports at various prices to Canada and New Zealand (and in one instance to Hong Kong), which came within Fiji's Overall Agreement Quota under the CSA.

The CSA conferred benefits and imposed obligations both on the United Kingdom and on the exporting members. On the one hand, it gave the United Kingdom priority of supplies of export sugar available from the CSA exporters, even when (as had happened) sugar supplies were scarce and world prices high. On the other hand, it gave Fiji and other CSA exporters an assured outlet for a known quantity of sugar, at fair prices. These prices were defined in the CSA as being "reasonably remunerative to efficient producers." This principle for arriving at the price had prevailed since the inception of the CSA.

The commencement of the Sugar Price Stabilization Fund had been linked with the 1947 price increase under the bulk purchase contracts. However, the CSA, when it came into force, made no reference to the existence of funds in some colonies, or to any requirement that part of the CSA negotiated price should be paid into such funds. Moreover, it was significant that the negotiated price was the same for all territories, although there were no special funds in the dominions, and although the rate of deductions and number and style of the special funds varied from colony to colony.

In short, the Sugar Price Stabilization Fund in Fiji had accumulated from levies on proceeds that would otherwise have been paid to the miller and to the growers, as indeed happened in other countries. It represented proceeds withheld from the miller and growers, to be used to shield them both from a serious fall in sugar prices. Both the miller and the growers had an equity in the fund, and indeed the money in the stabilization fund was held in a "miller's general account" and a "growers' general account."

Up until 1960 Cuba had been the principal supplier of sugar to the U.S. But after the diplomatic break, the U.S. looked elsewhere, and Cuba began exporting its sugar to the U.S.S.R. and elsewhere in the communist bloc. Subsequently, the United States passed legislation giving quotas to specified countries, including—in 1962—Fiji. Fiji exports in recent years to the U.S. had been in the region of 37,000 tons. The price had been very favorable to the Fiji exporter, it being the same as the U.S. domestic raw-sugar price, less import duty, and was far higher than the world-sugar price.

Several attempts had been made to regulate the world-sugar market by international agreement, but they were largely unsuccessful till 1968, at which time a five-year agreement was made. A quota was given each exporting member, which was assessed by reference to estimated demand and supply. The object was to limit the amount of sugar coming on to the free market and thus support the price. But it did not provide a guaranteed price, and in fact the world price fluctuated. It was £16.10.0 a ton just before the negotiations in 1968; £39.5.0 in April, 1969; £29 in August, 1969; and £32 in November, 1969.[3] It was plain that to comply with the international obligations, the growers and millers in Fiji must likewise be subjected to a quota system, under which they were prepared to limit production.

SPSM contemplated that the total outlet for Fiji's sugar would be in the order of 341,000 tons a year, made up as follows:

	Tons
Local sales	19,000
Negotiated price quota (under CSA)	140,000
U.S. quota	37,000
International Sugar Agreement (ISA)	130,500
Stock to be built up under ISA	14,500
TOTAL	341,000

Other Eve Commission findings

Another finding of the Eve Commission had had to do with molasses, which was a by-product of the cane crushing process and had previously been sold and the proceeds added to those derived from sugar. The commission recommended that the value of the molasses should *not* be added to the proceeds from the sale of sugar, but credited against manufacturing costs at the rate of 50 shillings per ton,[4] thereby reducing manufacturing costs. The benefit of such a saving went two-thirds to the miller, one-third to the growers.

The Eve formula required that the proceeds of sugar and of the miller's costs

---

[3]The pound at this time was worth $2.40.

[4]As of 1969, molasses was being sold in Australia for 90 shillings a ton.

be certified jointly by independent auditors, but it was stressed that these auditors were required to keep much of the information given to them as confidential. Hence, the growers often had to accept decisions without disclosure of reasons. In that the miller had full information on all proceeds and costs, it was the growers who were kept in the dark.

The Eve formula also permitted the miller to deduct a 3 percent depreciation each year in capital assets. The capital value on fixed assets was based on a 1957 market value of such assets, except that any new assets acquired after 1957 should be taken at actual cost. A substantial upward adjustment of assets occurred in 1957; e.g., the railway system from £708,791 to £1,693,296; the telephone system from £20,311 to £96,000. Overall, assets were revalued by close to £6 million, from £5,548,364 to £11,269,526.

As indicated, 11½ percent could be deducted from revenues as "head office expense," to allow for costs of administration both in Australia and Fiji.

Organizationally, the Eve Commission recommended that either the CSR's Fiji activities as a whole, or at least the sugar-milling activities, be handed over from the present Fiji division based in Sydney to a subsidiary of CSR based either in Suva or Lautaka in Fiji. And indeed on December 19, 1961, CSR had formed a Fiji subsidiary, South Pacific Sugar Mills Limited (SPSM). For purposes of the transaction, the Fiji assets of CSR were set at £10 million, of which £7 million was paid in cash. This amount was then used to purchase the stock of SPSM. Subsequently an additional 2,250,000 shares were issued in lieu of a distribution to CSR of £2,250,000. In November 1964, SPSM had become a public company and CSR had made an offer to the Fiji public of five million of its SPSM shares, the original 9,250,000 £1 shares having been changed to 37 million five-shilling shares in the interim. Some 1,700 residents of Fiji had responded by buying 700,000 shares, or 1.9 percent of the total. Since then an annual dividend of 7½ percent had been paid regularly. The SPSM board included three local directors, all leading citizens of Fiji.

The Eve Commission also tackled the problem of burnt cane. Burning facilitated the harvesting of cane and was resorted to by growers who, for one reason or another, wanted to get their cane harvested at once—for instance, because they feared they might miss the crushing season or wanted the money for their crop quickly. Where labor was short and expensive, as in Queensland in Australia, burning made sense, although unless burnt cane was crushed within 48 hours, it deteriorated fast; it was more vulnerable to harmful bacteria than green cane. These bacteria could get into the sugar juices and make the compound more difficult to handle in the factory. The bacteria also appeared in the raw sugar and lowered its quality. Also, burnt cane reduced the milling rate and thus decreased crushing capacity.

The so-called "Eve contract" specified that payment for burnt cane should be 5 percent less than for green cane if delivered within two days of burning and an additional 4 percent less for each day thereafter up to seven days, after which it was to be rejected altogether. Further, if cane were burned without permission there were additional penalties—payment was to be withheld for three months and, although not written in the Eve contract, the miller did not advance harvesting expenses for cane burnt without permission. Permission was given only when the cane was badly fallen, heavily infested with weed, or swarming with hornets. Other conditions stipulated by the "Eve contracts" and subject to latter dispute:

1. That cane be said to be free of extraneous matter if such matter did not exceed 2 percent, and that the miller could refuse cane with a juice parity of less than 70 percent.

2. That the grower plant the variety of cane specified by the miller.

3. That the farm purchase allotment be expressed in so many *tons* of cane and not, as before 1962, in *acres* from which cane would be purchased.

4. That cane be weighed at the mill whether delivered by grower-operated truck directly to the mill or by rail operated by the miller. (In the latter case, substantial delay could occur and sometimes loss due to derailments.)

Differing views

It was considered very likely by the CSR-SPSM management that the Alliance (Fiji-dominated) and Federation (Indian-dominated) representatives would present somewhat different views to the arbitrator. Specifically, it was expected that:

1. The Alliance would support the present contractual provision relating to burnt cane, extraneous matter and "roguing"; the Federation would want more relaxed standards and greater grower autonomy.

2. The Federation would prefer to revert to the pre-Eve system of expressing farm quotas on acres from which cane would be purchased, not in tons per farm.

3. The Federation would propose a clause whereby the miller would be bound to recognize every gang, even a splinter gang, but the Alliance would urge that a gang not be permitted to split unless the new gang were of a specified size.

4. The Federation would propose that the miller should provide many weighbridges so that every grower would be within three miles of one; the Alliance would suggest that the miller be requested to pay compensation for any loss or delay after delivery.

5. The Alliance would seek an *obligation* on the part of the miller to make advances to the growers for harvesting expenses, rent, and fertilizing; the Federation would not seek such an obligation, but would suggest a prohibition against the miller's making any deductions from the proceeds of the cane without prior consent of the grower involved.

6. The Alliance would urge a division of the total proceeds from the sale of sugar and molasses in the proportion of 70 percent for growers and 30 percent to the miller, each to bear all of his own expenses out of his share; the Federation would urge the incorporation of a guaranteed minimum price to be paid to the grower.

7. The Alliance had already charged that the increase over the years of per unit costs

of sugar refining (6 percent per annum for wages and 3 to 4 percent for materials) was not due primarily to inflation and droughts—as management had alleged—but to bad management, obsolete machinery, and unwise capital investment. It was alleged that a prime reason was that there was no incentive for the miller to reduce its cost. It was also suggested that there might be duplication of costs, e.g., the cost of maintenance being paid out of revenue and as a result the capital base on which the 3 percent depreciation cost was calculated being increased. CSR management knew that such allegations were unfounded. The Federation would be silent on such issues.

On all other issues the two groups seemed to be in agreement.

During the summer of 1969, it was publicly announced that Lord Denning had been named as the arbitrator. He was Master of the Rolls in Britain, which was the third-ranking position in the entire British legal system. Personally, he was a lawyer of great repute. Assisting him as an advisor would be Mr. Robert McNeil, a leading British accountant and formerly President of the Institute of Chartered Accountants. Public hearings were scheduled to be held in Fiji during September.

Classroom exercise

A simulated arbitration of this situation, with class members assigned specific roles.

Discussion questions

1. Why, after so many years, should this situation have reached a crisis level?
2. What strategy should Colonial Sugar Refining Company Ltd. pursue?
3. Should the corporation expect a favorable or unfavorable award?
4. If the award proves to be unfavorable, what should the company do?

TABLE 26- SUGAR CANE

TABLEAU 26- CANNE A SUCRE

AREA = 1000 HECTARES
PRODUCTION = 1000 METRIC TONS
YIELD = 100 KG/HECTARE

SUPERFICIE = 1000 HECTARES
PRODUCTION = 1000 TONNES METRIQUES
RENDEMENT = 100 KG/HECTARE

NOTES	CONTINENT AND COUNTRY		1948/49-1952/53	1961/62-1965/66	1965/66	1966/67	1967/68	1968/69	1969/70	CONTINENT ET PAYS
2, 5	MADAGASCAR	AREA	15	25	24F	26F	21	22F	22F	MADAGASCAR SUP.
		PROD.	348	1068	1050	1210	1220	1300	1300F	PROD.
		YIELD	237	434	447F	465F	561	591F	591F	REND.
	MAURITIUS	AREA	64	82	82	83	81	80	80	MAURICE SUP.
		PROD.	3737	5135	5984	4843	5814	5152	5824	PROD.
		YIELD	585	630	727	586	719	645	733	REND.
14	MOZAMBIQUE	AREA	19	32	31F	32F	37F	39F	41F	MOZAMBIQUE SUP.
		PROD.	838	1598	1409	1500	1862	2000F	2150F	PROD.
		YIELD	441	498	462F	469F	503F	513F	524F	REND.
	NIGER	AREA	2F	2	2	1	1	1	1	NIGER SUP.
		PROD.	20F	36	41	12	21	25	25	PROD.
		YIELD	133F	178	199	179	211	204	183	REND.
	NIGERIA	AREA	...	1F	2	2	2F	3F	3F	NIGERIA SUP.
		PROD.	...	62F	110F	163F	180F	240F	240F	PROD.
		YIELD	...	437F	585F	750F	750F	750F	750F	REND.
	REUNION	AREA	22	36	36	36	35	42	43F	REUNION SUP.
		PROD.	1127	2009	2244	2002	2168	2273	2350F	PROD.
		YIELD	503	558	623	556	620	541	547F	REND.
10	RHODESIA	AREA	1	9	14	23	12F	11F	11F	RHODESIE SUP.
		PROD.	17	917	1525	2648	1200F	1050F	1140F	PROD.
		YIELD	412	981	1102	1169	1044F	1000F	1000F	REND.
10	SOMALIA	AREA	3	2	3	5	5F	6	7F	SOMALIE SUP.
		PROD.	59	146	246	350	277	393	420F	PROD.
7		YIELD	213	796	789	678	608F	624	627F	REND.
	SOUTH AFRICA	AREA	80	120	152	195	197	195F	195F	AFRIQUE SUP.
		PROD.	4789	9454	8406	14103	16913	13720	14788	PROD.
		YIELD	597	790	552	723	859	704F	758F	REND.
	SUDAN	AREA	...	3F	4F	12F	14	14	15F	SOUDAN SUP.
		PROD.	...	192F	270F	760F	969	939	965F	PROD.
4		YIELD	...	600F	675F	650F	673	674	666F	REND.
	SWAZILAND	AREA	...	10	14	11	12	12	12F	SWAZILAND SUP.
1		PROD.	...	755	1014	1301	1356	1328	1350F	PROD.
		YIELD	...	792	716	1191	1163	1130	1125F	REND.
	TANZANIA	AREA	2	26	32	32F	34F	34F	34F	TANZANIE SUP.
		PROD.	182	614	798	840F	930F	950F	900F	PROD.
1, 5		YIELD	735	240	251	263F	274F	279F	265F	REND.
	UGANDA	AREA	11	18	17	18	20	18F	17F	OUGANDA SUP.
		PROD.	496	1476F	1600F	1650F	1672	1650F	1530F	PROD.
		YIELD	450	837F	920F	906F	847	917F	900F	REND.
	U.A.R.	AREA	38	55	56	58	66	71	75	R.A.U. SUP.
		PROD.	2910	4959	5199	5261	6074	6667	6475	PROD.
		YIELD	771	909	930	908	927	962	930	REND.
	ZAMBIA	AREA	...	...	...	...	1	2	3F	ZAMBIE SUP.
		PROD.	...	...	...	...	183	180	270F	PROD.
		YIELD	...	...	...	...	1234	754	806F	REND.
	TOTAL	AREA	274	500	547	631	644	656	666	TOTAL SUP.
		PROD.	15329	30970	32706	40525	45136	42569	45001	PROD.
		YIELD	560	619	598	642	701	649	676	REND.
7	OCEANIA AUSTRALIA	AREA	112	176	204	225	224	230	213	OCEANIE AUSTRALIE SUP.
		PROD.	6686	12936	14382	16953	17026	18709	15782	PROD.
7		YIELD	598	733	706	752	761	813	742	REND.
	FIJI	AREA	18	38	43	43	45	46	47	FIDJI SUP.
		PROD.	908	1991	2206	2228	2197	2671	2377	PROD.
		YIELD	492	521	516	514	494	620	505	REND.
	TOTAL	AREA	130	215	247	268	269	276	260	TOTAL SUP.
		PROD.	7594	14927	16588	19181	19223	21580	18159	PROD.
		YIELD	584	694	672	716	715	782	698	REND.
	WORLD TOTAL	AREA	6571	9634	10505	10198	9788	10307	11343	TOT MONDIAL SUP.
		PROD.	277814	473284	520558	518945	515645	541452	581017	PROD.
		YIELD	423	491	496	509	527	525	512	REND.
	REG. TOTALS									TOT REGION
	EUROPE									EUROPE

Exhibit I.1

Production Yearbook, vol. 24, 1970, Food and Agriculture Organization of the United Nations, Rome, p. 92.

Exhibit I.2

Season	A Sales revenue	B Basic growers' share (57¾% of A)	C Growers' services	D Manufacturing costs	E Credit for molasses*	F Net mfg. costs (D-E)	G Extent growers' services fall below 10% of revenue	H Extent mfg. costs fall below 20% of rev.	I Growers' share of reduced growers' services (⅔ of G)
1962	$20,723,000	$11,968,000	$1,553,000	$2,530,000	$283,000	$2,247,000	$ 519,000	$1,898,000	$ 348,000
1963	35,713,000	20,623,000	2,003,000	3,556,000	332,000	3,224,000	1,568,000	3,919,000	1,051,000
1964	27,799,000	16,054,000	2,336,000	4,203,000	322,000	3,881,000	444,000	1,679,000	297,000
1965	24,523,000	14,162,000	2,162,000	4,033,000	304,000	3,729,000	290,000	1,176,000	195,000
1966	23,854,000	13,776,000	2,170,000	3,717,000	455,000	3,262,000	215,000	1,509,000	144,000
1967	23,435,000	13,534,000	2,348,000	4,004,000	414,000	3,590,000	−4,500	1,097,000	−3,000
1968	30,541,000	17,638,000	2,525,000	4,565,000	449,000	4,116,000	529,000	1,992,000	354,000
1969	26,635,000	15,382,000	2,495,000	4,819,000	521,000	4,298,000	169,000	1,029,000	113,000
Average	$26,653,000	$15,392,000	$2,198,000	$3,928,000	$385,000	$3,543,000	$ 466,000	$1,788,000	$ 312,000

Season	J Growers' share of reduced mfg. costs (⅓ of H)	K Total growers' share (B + I + J)	L Millers' share of revenue (A − K)	M Percent of revenue to growers	N Percent of revenue to miller	O Tons of cane crushed (2,240 lb/ton)	P Total payments to growers per ton of cane (K ÷ O)	Q Tons of sugar sold	R Price received per ton (A ÷ Q)	S After tax SPSM profit	T Percent on paid-up capital†
1962	$ 626,000	$12,942,000	$ 7,781,000	62.5%	37.5%	1,824,000	$7.10	246,500	$ 84.07	$1,322,000	9.4%
1963	1,293,000	22,967,000	12,746,000	64.3	35.7	2,337,000	9.83	315,800	113.09	3,128,000	16.9
1964	554,000	16,905,000	10,894,000	60.8	39.2	2,319,000	7.29	313,400	88.70	2,490,000	13.5
1965	388,000	14,745,000	9,778,000	60.1	39.9	2,171,000	6.79	293,400	83.58	1,935,000	10.5
1966	498,000	14,418,000	9,436,000	60.4	39.6	2,192,000	6.58	269,200	88.61	1,653,000	8.9
1967	362,000	13,893,000	9,542,000	59.3	40.7	2,163,000	6.42	292,300	80.17	1,414,000	7.6
1968	657,000	18,649,000	11,892,000	61.1	38.9	2,826,000	6.60	381,200	80.12	2,262,000	12.2
1969	340,000	15,835,000	10,800,000	59.5	40.5	2,339,000	6.77	316,100	84.26	1,472,000	8.0
Average	$ 590,000	$16,294,000	$10,359,000	61.1%	38.9%	2,271,000	$7.17	303,500	$ 87.83	$1,960,000	10.9%

*At a fixed price of $5.00 per ton.

†Paid-up capital works out to be $14 million in 1962 and $18.5 million thereafter.

Note: "Free" market price for sugar averaged 2.21 U.S. cents per pound, or $49.50 per English ton (2,240 lbs.) over the four years 1965–68. The price of molasses was fixed at 50 shillings per ton, or £2.50, which the company showed at $5.00 per ton.

Exhibit I.3
UNITED KINGDOM: U.S. DOLLARS PER POUND STERLING

Year	Par value	Annual average market exchange rate
	U.S. dollars	U.S. dollars
1929	4.8665	4.8568
1930	4.8665	4.8621
1931	4.8665 until Sept. 21	4.5349
1932		3.5060
1933		4.2368
1934		5.0393
1935		4.9018
1936		4.9709
1937		4.9440
1938		4.8894
1939		4.03
1940		4.03
1941		4.03
1942		4.03
1943		4.03
1944		4.03
1945		4.03
1946	4.03 from Dec. 18	4.03
1947	4.03	4.03
1948	4.03	4.03
1949	2.80 from Sept. 18	2.80
1950	2.80	2.8007
1951	2.80	2.7996
1952	2.80	2.7929
1953	2.80	2.8127
1954	2.80	2.8087
1955	2.80	2.7913
1956	2.80	2.7957
1957	2.80	2.7932
1958	2.80	2.8098
1959	2.80	2.8088
1960	2.80	2.8076
1961	2.80	2.8023
1962	2.80	2.8078
1963	2.80	2.8003
1964	2.80	2.7927
1965	2.80	2.7962
1966	2.80	2.7932
1967	2.40 from Nov. 18	2.4133
1968	2.40	2.3937
1969	2.40	2.3903
1970	2.40	2.3960

Year	Par value	Annual average market exchange rate
	U.S. dollars	U.S. dollars
1971	2.40	2.4168
		2.4866
	2.6057 from Dec. 19	2.5507
1972	2.6057	2.6031
		2.4076

World Currency Charts, 7th ed., American International Investment Corporation, San Francisco, California, December 1973.

Exhibit I.4
OVERSEAS SALES (IN THOUSANDS)*

	1962	1963	1964	1965	1966	1967	1968	1969
United Kingdom	$12,185	$16,693	$16,129	$14,308	$15,702	$14,506	$17,674	$14,196
Canada	4,345	8,962	2,540	3,843	2,031	2,912	2,655	4,438
U.S.	957	5,070	4,224	4,259	3,537	4,077	4,777	4,804
Japan					505	770	1,236	745
Malaysia			2,326	566	550		892	679
Singapore						267	340	690
New Zealand	2,813	4,297	2,022	912	755	334	2,350	260
	$20,300	$35,022	$27,241	$23,888	$23,080	$22,866	$29,924	$25,812
Other sales†	909	1,426	1,174	1,219	1,333	1,102	1,363	1,474
Deductions‡	−486	−735	−616	−584	−559	−533	−746	−651
Total proceeds	$20,723	$35,713	$27,799	$24,523	$23,854	$23,435	$30,541	$26,635

*Includes insurance claims and inter-season adjustments, after deducting freight and insurance on ship, expenses at destination, etc.

†Largely store sugar and special raws.

‡Port and customs service tax, expenses of marketing, expenses of the Sugar Board and Sugar Advisory Council and sundry expenses.

Chapter 6
FINANCIAL STRATEGY

Financial, legal, and administrative (control) structure should not be confused. Particularly in the international field, there may be wide divergences among the three. The flow of funds may not coincide with the legal or control relationships, and legal entities may have virtually no relevance to the channel of authority. For example, a firm may opt to organize its management on a regional basis, say, Europe, North America, Latin America, the Far East. Each regional headquarters may be virtually autonomous in a variety of ways. However, certain of the European subsidiaries, along with a number of Latin American subsidiaries, may be owned by a Panamanian holding company, thereby deriving a possible tax advantage. The funds accumulated in Panama on which very little tax has been paid may be used for investment in, say, India, where the subsidiary receiving the funds is owned directly by the U.S. firm although its management is a responsibility of the Far Eastern regional headquarters. Therefore, these strategy sets, financial, legal, and control, though related, are thus distinct.

In reading this chapter one should keep in mind three points. *First*, the international firm by reason of its presence in multiple markets is in a position to take advantage of any market distortions caused by governmental intervention. The greater the distortions, the greater the possible advantage accruing to the international firm. *Second*, in general what we are talking about is the management of financing options, the options being the choice of the transaction currency, the place where the transaction is legally registered, modification of risk by the firm's own behavior, and the degree to which risk is transferred. These options are present just as much for the exporting firm as for the investing firm. *Third*, one should be conscious of the sort of market with which one is dealing. Financial markets, as goods markets, are more or less efficient, depending upon information and the degree of intervention. For example, in a floating exchange rate world, the financial manager probably cannot do better by hedging his foreign exchange risk through the purchase of a futures contract than the interest rate differential between the two countries. But in a world of administered rates, he may do significantly better if his information is superior to the average, which is likely to be the case for the large corporation operating internationally. Concessionary export financing is another example of an imperfect market, which gives an advantage to the firm which is in a position to go shopping, which the purely national firm is in no position to do. The Euro-currency market, on the other hand, is a relatively efficient capital market; national markets may not be, depending upon their size and the degree of official intervention.

Essentially, there are eight questions facing management, the answers to which determine the firm's financial strategy.

1. Where are profits to be taken (location of profit centers)?
2. By what routes are profits to move to the profit centers?
3. Where are investment decisions to be made (location of investment centers)?
4. What type of financing is to be used?
5. What is to be the substance of investment?
6. What is to be the source of financing?
7. What legal instrumentality should be used?
8. How are claims to earnings streams to be made secure?

Although similar questions might be asked about a purely uninational operation, the nature of the relevant variables, their weighting, and the range of possible strategies differ when one is dealing with an international business. Indeed, there may be profound political consequences to the strategies a firm selects internationally. For example, in 1970 the liquid assets in the hands of private U.S. companies and banks probably amounted to between $30 and $35 billion, or three times the size of the U.S. government's foreign reserves.[1] Obviously, the larger firms operating internationally, if they acted more or less in concert, could bring great pressure to bear on the countries in which they do business by moving liquid assets in and out, thereby causing powerful inflationary or deflationary pressures. And, in many cases, there is little that the affected nations can do The international firm must be sensitive to the general economic-political implications of its financial strategies if it is to avoid political hostility and eventual exclusion from a national market.

6.1 CHOICE OF PROFIT CENTER

Within a family of interrelated enterprises, the profits recorded by any one are based on a number of arbitrary decisions regarding transfer pricing (the prices at which goods, services, and funds move among related companies), inventory policy and accounting, depreciation policy, cost allocation, assignment of

---

[1]As estimated by Prince Guido Colonna di Paliano, the former Commissioner in charge of industry in the EEC, *Wall Street Journal*, 17 February 1970.

production and sales, speed in effecting collection of receivables, dividend pay out, and debt repayment. In theory, the parent company may influence profit to the extent that it can affect the activities and costs of associated firms. In practice, the range of that influence is restrained by (1) the efforts of internal revenue authorities, abroad and at home, to collect taxes levied on corporate profits, transactions, and payrolls; (2) pressure exerted by local shareholders, if any, to maximize their return, and (3) the desire of local management to increase its autonomy, and, hence, its power.

Obviously, it is in the interest of the parent company to generate a maximum profit where tax rates are the lowest, where funds may be held with least restriction, and in currencies or securities freely convertible at predictable exchange rates to the currency of the parent country. Factors such as a legally enforced right by labor to see the firm's books (as in Italy) may be relevant because unduly high profits may generate agitation. If funds in a profit center are to be used to finance operations elsewhere, as is often the case, a further consideration is the relationship between the profit-center country and potential host countries in respect to double taxation, withholding taxes (on dividends, interest, fees), investment guarantees, and political boycotts (such as the Arab attitude toward Israeli-sourced financing, or the U.S. attitude toward Cuba). It should also be noted that if a subsidiary's profits are reduced through transfer-pricing, its capacity to borrow locally may be reduced.

The ultimate profit center may or may not be perceived to be the parent firm. The relevant variable here is the extent to which ownership is, or is likely to be, in foreign hands. Also relevant is the pressure or lack of pressure to repatriate foreign profits for distribution to domestic owners as opposed to reinvestment overseas.

A firm may opt to define a profit center by function (such as marketing or production), by product line, enterprise, or geographical area. A critical variable may be the administrative or control structure of the firm, for if that structure coincides with the system of financial reporting, a single accounting system may serve both a financial and a control purpose.

If profit centers are defined by enterprise, the profit centers will coincide with individual business entities (thereby leading to financial autonomy of these subsidiaries), or the parent firm may be defined as the profit center (which is the equivalent of full financial consolidation), or profit centers may be located wherever there is an advantage to be realized (which implies full financial integration). A word of caution: if profit centers are located by reason of a process of financial optimization, profit and loss statements of local firms cannot be used as a measure of managerial effectiveness, nor for purposes of internal control. For the latter purpose a second set of books must be kept showing "true costs," a practice that may be exceedingly dangerous from a legal (that is, a tax) point of view. In fact, where exchange controls operate and inflation is rapid, any measure of local profit may be very misleading. (See Section 8.5.)

6.2 PROFIT ROUTE

Quite apart from the dividend and capital gains routes, profits may be shifted from enterprise to enterprise by creating interenterprise costs, such as sales commissions, fees for contracted services (technical, managerial, entrepreneurial, distributive), salaries, interest, rent, purchase premiums or discounts (that is, special transfer prices) or royalties (on copyrights, patents, trademarks). Although tax and foreign exchange control systems invariably impose restraints, substantial latitude is often possible. In some instances, such payments are prohibited; for example, in Brazil, as noted elsewhere, it is illegal for a local firm to pay fees and royalties to a foreign company that owns 50 percent or more of its equity, such fees and royalties being held to constitute profit, and to be taxable as such. They are not defined as tax-deductible costs. However, if over 50 percent of the voting stock of the foreign firm is not *controlled* by a U.S. parent, any restrictive practices embedded in a contractual relationship, such as special discounts or tie-in arrangements, may run afoul of U.S. antitrust law, as well as EEC regulations on the subject. In addition, many LDCs limit the remittance of dividends to a specified percentage of registered capital (20 percent in the ANCOM group) and fees and royalties to a specified percentage of gross sales.

Although a firm may have some choice of profit routes, it must nonetheless be ready to defend its choice. The best defenses are consistency over time and geography, a business justification, or recording comparable profits/sales ratios for comparable enterprises unless special conditions can be demonstrated. It should be noted that the capital gains route may be used for the sale of intangible property, including commercial or industrial secrets of a patentable nature. In this case, equity may be taken in lieu of payment. Even direct payment, in lump sum or installment, may be considered a capital gain instead of income for U.S. tax purposes *if* the sale is to a foreign corporation not controlled by the U.S. firm.

In all fairness, more need be said on the subject of transfer pricing. Pricing is not of major value to most companies in moving profits from one incorporated entity to another so as to minimize taxes and/or customs duties. *First*, there is no significant tax differential as between the major industrialized countries among which the bulk of trade and investment takes place; hence, there is no advantage in artificially shifting profits from one country to another. *Second*, the use of a tax haven holding company located in such countries as Switzerland, Liechtenstein, Panama, Liberia, Bahamas, and the like, to siphon off profits from higher tax countries simply does not work for U.S. firms by reason of the 1962 tax law and subsequent amendments. More recently, other industrialized countries have likewise begun legislating so as to plug this loophole. In that these tax haven countries are well known to tax collectors worldwide, they are inclined to scrutinize very closely the prices of goods sold to, or purchased from, associated firms located within them. *Third*, artificially high prices often mean high customs duties, in that customs duties are most frequently levied on the value of a product. Conversely, artificially low prices mean low customs duties but increased profits and profit-based taxes. *Fourth*, even if a firm could accumulate profits in a low tax country through transfer pricing, this is an advantage only so long as those profits remain abroad. The real gain is limited to the interest free use of funds that would otherwise be paid out in taxes. *Fifth*, there is a real risk of double taxation arising from transfer pricing. Artificial pricing necessarily means that reported profits are too low in one country, too high in another. The tax collector in the latter is not likely to object, but in the former he is likely to, and at some later date to reallocate income, thereby increasing the taxable profits in his country. Bear in mind that these profits have already been taxed in the other country. If there is no tax treaty between the two countries, which is very frequently the case if one is an LDC, then there may be no relief at all. Even if there were a treaty, recovery may be slow and uncertain. *Sixth*, effective transfer pricing assumes a decree of centralized corporate control which simply may be inoperative. Significant transfer pricing means that subsidiary companies cannot operate as profit centers without substantial risk in that two sets of books would have to be maintained, one based on the artificially contrived prices and one reflecting the true state of affairs. Subsidiary managements are likely to be very jealous of their managerial prerogatives, and there is a natural tendency to try to make their profit performance look as good as possible unless local managers are being evaluated and rewarded explicitly on some basis other than profit.

On the other side of the argument, it should be noted that in 1970 only 298 U.S. firms accounted for 51 percent of all U.S. merchandise exports and 34 percent of U.S. merchandise imports. Data from this same survey indicated that over 40 percent of U.S. merchandise exports were identified as intra-firm in that they represented direct transfers from the U.S. reporting firm to a majority-owned affiliate overseas, while 45 percent of U.S. merchandise imports originated with these same subsidiaries.[2] Therefore, the opportunity for transfer price manipulation for U.S.-based companies is great. The same opportunity undoubtedly exists for European and Japanese-based corporations.

One only sees the tip of the iceberg. Why are the prices of certain goods manufactured by a given company so much higher in one market than another? Why, when ownership rights are forcibly spun off to local interest, does a firm then say that its transfer prices must be increased, say by 30 percent (which one U.S. management claimed would be the case if its equity in a Venezuelan subsidiary were lost)? Why do many U.S. firms impose no charge on their Canadian subsidiaries for R&D performed in the United States or for internal consulting services delivered to them by the parent U.S. firm? In many cases,

---

[2]U.S. Department of Commerce, Bureau of Economic Analysis, *Survey of Current Business*, December 1972, "U.S. Trade Associated with Multinational Companies," p. 20.

one suspects, such "unrealistic" transfer prices are not deliberate, possibly not even realized, on the part of management.

As already noted, the perceived gaps in per-capita economic well-being between the industrial and resource-rich lesser developed countries on the one hand and the poorer LDCs on the other seems to be widening. The evidence lies in the disparity of average rates of change in GNP per-capita for these groups of countries. It is only reasonable to expect that the poorer countries, the "Group of 77," will mount pressure for redistribution of income and wealth. And, in that private corporations are the most visible vehicles for the international transfer of capital, goods, knowledge, and services, one can anticipate that the attack on such corporations will become increasingly intense. To the extent that these corporations maintain centrally controlled integrated production and sales systems, they remain suspect to many people. Many of the prices attached to the funds, goods, knowledge, and service moving internationally are artificially determined. The relevant markets are too imperfect for them to be otherwise. Where markets are imperfect and entry barriers high, there is oligopoly pricing. The firm becomes vulnerable to charges of exploitation in the form of "unjustifiably" high rents on the inputs it controls. In an economic sense they are unjustifiably high so long as the beneficiary corporations contrive to restrain or eliminate competition through essentially nonmarket forces (for example, meaningless product differentiation through established brand names, deals with government whereby investment rights are traded for protection, illegal payments, massive lobbying for special legislative treatment, limiting access to knowledge by buying up inventions and patent rights that are subsequently not used).

6.3 DEFINITION OF INVESTMENT CENTERS

The investment center (that is, the locale of the investment decisions) may or may not coincide with the relevant profit center. The former may be located within the parent corporate headquarters; the latter in a foreign subsidiary or in a regional headquarters of some variety. The question arises as to why investment decisions should be centralized if decisions relevant to profit maximization are not. Possible reasons are (1) the need to know the cost of capital of different types and sources (internal and external, local and foreign) to select the least costly for any given enterprise; (2) the close relationship between investment and productive capacity, which may well have broader company-wide implications than a simple step-up in the utilization of present capacity; (3) the fact that investment decisions are likely to be longer-ranged (that is, induce more short-term rigidities) than operating decisions characteristic of the profit center.

From the point of view of a subsidiary operation, the *perceived* cost of capital may well be limited to its own or the parent's domestic cost of capital.

The subsidiary management may not perceive the third-country alternative, which implies a cost of capital equivalent to the corporate family's worldwide cost. Furthermore, a subsidiary management may not have the expertness to operate in this fashion, which requires moving through different currency barriers and the utilization of different hedging devices, both of which carry important costs.

TYPE OF FINANCING 6.4

Given the availability of both domestic and foreign financing, an international business has a wider range of types of financing from which to choose than does the purely domestic. In addition, a variety of specialized devices for financing exports have been developed by many countries. In general, the strategy lies among these choices: debt, participating debt, convertible securities, and shares in equity. But there are many variations.

First of all, debt includes short, medium, and long-term *export* financing through a variety of instruments, many of which are described in Appendix 2 to this chapter. Long-term *capital* debt is quite another matter in that it becomes part of the capital structure of the enterprise. Short or medium term borrowing for working capital needs is again distinct.

Several types of multinational debt-financing are of relatively recent origin: parallel financing, unit-of-account financing, and the Eurodollar. The first, which originated with the Deutsche Bank of West Germany, involves an arrangement by foreign borrowers (governments and businesses) with a consortium of banks in different countries to float largely identical bond issues in each country at the same time, each in the currency of the issuing country. Each bank takes a part (a "*tranche*") of the proposed loan and sells it locally. Interest rates and maturities are the same, but the issuing price and, therefore, the yield, may vary from country to country.

Unit-of-account financing involves securities denominated in several different currencies held in fixed relationship, sometimes in terms of SDRs (see Appendix 1 to this chapter). The investor pays in one of the currencies (may be stipulated by the borrower), receives interest in any one of the currencies, redeems in any currency desired.

A Eurocurrency loan is one designated in a currency other than that of the country in which debt contract is executed. The use of a Eurocurrency permits both lender and borrower to escape national controls. It should be pointed out that any difference in interest rates between a Eurocurrency loan and a domestic currency loan reveals market distortions. In that there is little or no intervention in the Eurocurrency markets, the divergence in rates reveals an intervention at the national level. The international firm is in position to exploit these market distortions much more easily than a purely national firm.

The preeminent Eurocurrency has been the Eurodollar, which simply refers to dollar accounts banked outside of the U.S. and which constitutes an important source of financing for both international trade and investment. The Eurodollar arose because of the inadequacy of gold production, the relatively large U.S. gold supply and the size, diversity, and productivity of the U.S. economy, the easy convertibility of the dollar, the U.S. balance-of-payments deficit (generation of dollar obligations abroad for which there was no immediate demand for use in purchasing U.S. goods, services, or long-term obligations), and the relaxation of exchange controls in Europe and Japan. Many international loans are denominated in Eurodollars, loans in which the creditor has no intention of utilizing the dollars directly. Any convertible currency can exist in a "Euro" form by simply being deposited in a bank in a country (not necessarily European) to which the currency is not "native." Of the Eurocurrencies, an estimated 80 percent is in dollars. Perhaps the easiest way of understanding the Eurocurrency phenomenon is by means of examples tracing the creation, employment, and extinction of a hypothetical Eurodollar deposit.[3] (See also Figure 6.1.)

1.   The Acme European Company, with a deposit in a bank in the United States, transfers $1 million to the branch of an American bank in London. This transaction turns the ordinary U.S. dollar deposit into a Eurodollar deposit. The initial effect on the bank in the United States is simply a change in the ownership of the deposit, from the original holder to the branch in London, not the loss of a deposit. When the transaction is completed, the Eurodollar deposit on the books of the American branch bank in London is reflected in an equivalent dollar liability in the United States.

2.   The London branch of the U.S. bank may subsequently redeposit the $1 million in the form of a time deposit with a bank in Belgium. The Belgium bank may then transfer ownership of the dollar deposit from the New York head office of the London branch to one of its regular U.S. correspondent banks, most likely another New York bank. The original deposit is still part of the U.S. banking system. But, note, there are now *two* European dollar liabilities—those of the London branch and those of the Belgium bank—based on *one* deposit in the U.S.

3.   The redeposit process may continue, with the Belgian bank lending the dollars to a Tokyo bank, which then lends the money to a Japanese importer to pay a Swiss exporter, who then purchases Eurobonds for his personal portfolio. This latter transaction would transfer ownership of the deposit to the multinational company floating the Eurobond issue, which then places the proceeds temporarily in the Eurodollar market until the capital expenditure outlay falls due, and so forth.

4.   Of course, just as Eurodollars are created, they may in the course of their redeposit chain also be extinguished. For instance, at some stage the deposit might be lent to a European importer who pays his New Orleans exporter by transferring the funds to the exporter's New Orleans bank account. In this way, the basic Eurodollar is extinguished. Or the multinational company exchanges the dollar proceeds

---

[3]Taken from *Euro-dollar Financing* (New York: The Chase Manhattan Bank N.A., 1968), pp. 13–14.

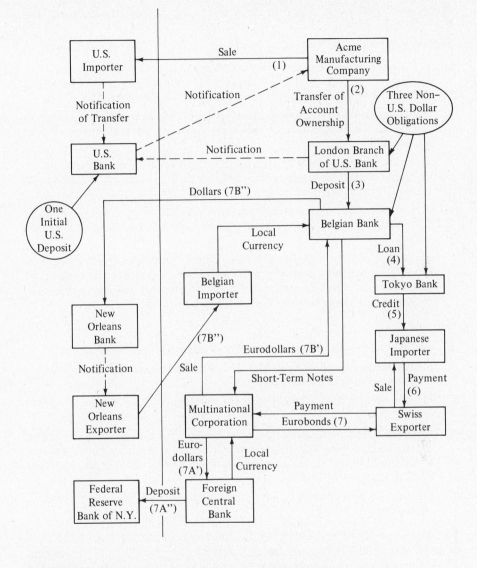

Figure 6.1
**TYPICAL TRANSACTIONS CREATING AND EXTINGUISHING
EURODOLLARS
(numbers refer to sequence of transactions)**

of its Eurobond flotation for local currency, thereby increasing the dollar holdings of a particular foreign central bank, which may hold such assets in a deposit with the Federal Reserve Bank of New York. In this way, the basic Eurodollar is also extinguished.

Business International reports ten ways of borrowing and lending Eurodollars.[4]

Short-term:

1. A straight bank loan in Eurodollars from a non-U.S. bank or a foreign branch or subsidiary of a U.S. bank for a fixed term at a fixed rate of interest. Rates are quoted daily in the London market for money from "overnight" to five years.

2. Bank loans on a revolving basis and at a floating rate of interest. The large majority of bank lending is now done on this basis, stipulating fixing of interest rates at six-month intervals.

3. Commercial paper (CP) for up to six months with renewal or refinancing anticipated. (Equivalent to negotiable corporate IOUs placed by an investment bank in its investors' portfolios.)

4. Private placement of promissory notes with maturity of up to five years. Most placements are completed through underwriters, but occasionally are done directly.

5. Certificates of deposit (CDs), the most suitable instrument for investors and depositors. They are available for terms of from three months to five years. The secondary market for CDs can be utilized by both investor and borrower if withdrawal or redemption becomes desirable before maturity.

Long-term:

6. Straight bond issues carrying a fixed rate of interest for the life of the issue.

7. Straight bonds with a floating coupon. The interest rate is established at six-month intervals and is valid for six-month periods.

8. Straight bonds with a detachable warrant, entitling purchase of stock at a fixed price.

9. Convertible bonds, convertible into parent company stock at a fixed purchase price over a period of years. The coupon rate is lower than on straight bonds, and can be fixed or floating. Convertibility into stock of a foreign subsidiary is rare, but is likely to grow.

10. Private placement of long-term notes with large investors, normally through an underwriter.

Morgan Guaranty has estimated that the total of the Eurocurrency market was approaching $500 billion as of the end of 1975. (See Figure 6.2.) In that this total included some double-counting of interbank obligations, the net volume was put at about $71 billion, of which about $54 billion was in U.S. dollars. Comparable 1970 totals were $57 and $46 billion. The problem for those in charge of national monetary policies is that the financial intermediaries that control the Eurocurrency flows escape rather easily from any national system of regulation. And it is difficult to envision international regulation that would stop those flows causing disturbances but at the same time would allow others

---

[4] *Business International*, June 26, 1970, p. 202.

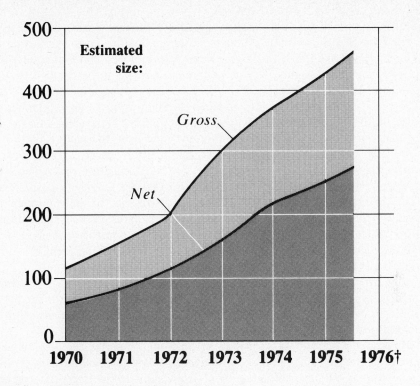

Figure 6.2
EUROCURRENCY MARKET*
(billion U.S. dollars, at end of year)

*Based on foreign currency liabilities of banks in major European countries, the Bahamas, Cayman Islands, Panama, Canada, Japan, and Singapore
†Data for June are preliminary
Data: Morgan Guaranty Trust Company of New York

to continue as before. International financial intermediaries have freedom in moving funds that is limited only by the practical requirements of communications.

A type of debt not common domestically is so-called participating debt, an example of which is the *partes beneficiaries* peculiar to some civil-law countries. This is a negotiable security, always callable and not considered part of a corporation's capital, but which bestows on the holder contingent credit rights in the form of profit participation up to a given percentage of annual net profits distributed. A sinking fund provision is generally required because the security becomes convertible to equity shares at the option of the holder when it is redeemed. The redemption price is determined at the time of the issue, although it may be represented as a multiple of average annual earnings over the last five years or so.

Closely associated with participating debt is the convertible debenture, a device that has grown more popular in international business as a device to counter inflation. A variation is the bond with attached stock warrants, the security being purchasable in one or more currencies to be decided by the purchaser at time of issue. Thereafter, the currency of the bond remains fixed. The purchaser of the bond also acquires the right to buy a given number of shares of the issuing company within a specified time. He exercises that right by converting his bond into shares without additional cash outlay.

Finally, the sale of equity shares is possible, such shares carrying one or more rights, voting, pre-emption, preference, cumulation, participation,[5] dividend payment in a specified currency. Regulations governing public issue vary, of course, from country to country in respect to such matters as disclosure, fees and taxes, minimum size, and legal status. In the United States, a quoted company (one whose shares are traded on a public exchange) with minority shareholders must be very circumspect in its management if it is to avoid legal trouble. A quoted company, on the other hand, can raise money through debt and rights issues. It can also use its paper to take over other concerns more easily than if it had to use cash. "And [speaking of foreign firms in the United States] finally and crucially, the [local] issue [of securities] is a demonstration that the company really has 'gone native.' "[6]

Inasmuch as corporate securities of some countries (for example, Japan) cannot be transferred physically to foreigners, a foreigner can hold them only by appointing a proxy and having them held locally. In the United States, the problem was solved by issuing American depository receipts (ADR), which have their origin in 1927. An expansion of the ADR, the International depository receipt (IDR), was announced in 1970 by one international bank. The IDR is a device designed to stimulate the international sale of corporate securities. In that the IDR is owned in bearer form and is not registered with the U.S. Securities Exchange, it may not be used within the U.S. market. An example of the IDR's utility: A Frenchman wishes to buy shares in a Japanese steel company. He goes to his local bank and advises those handling securities transactions that he wishes to buy, say, 1,000 shares in bearer form—that is, in IDRs issued by a bank doing business in IDRs. This latter bank (we will call it bank X) would place an order for 1,000 shares of the Japanese steel company to be deposited with bank X's custodian in Japan against authorization to bank X for the issue of the IDRs. Bank X would then deliver the IDRs to the French bank from which the order originated for delivery to the individual buyer.

A special problem arises when trading in registered shares (as required by U.S. law for U.S. corporations) on an exchange conducting business in bearer

---

[5]See Glossary.

[6]Nicholas Faith, *The Infiltrators, the European Business Invasion of America* (New York: E. P. Dutton & Co., 1972), pp. 49–50.

shares, as in Amsterdam. What happens is that the Dutch underwriters purchase the U.S. shares and transfer them for deposit to the depository company, which thus becomes the registered owner of the shares. It in turn issues bearer certificates to the underwriters against the original shares. These certificates constitute a personal claim on the depository company and require it to distribute dividends it receives in respect to the underlying shares to the holder of the certificate. The bearer certificate, known as the continental depository receipt (CDR), may be transferred without the service of the depository company simply by delivery of the CDR to the buyer. Attached to each CDR are dividend coupons upon which the depository company pays when surrendered to it.

In introducing its common shares on a European exchange, a U.S. or U.K. firm may use:

1. bearer depository receipts issued by a depository company, as described (Amsterdam).

2. bearer certificates guaranteed by, and introduced on the exchange by, a local bank (Brussels).

3. shares issued through a local firm acting as trustee on behalf of local shareholders. The shares are held for the stockholder's account with a nominee in the parent's country. The local buyer in fact acquires part ownership in a global share certificate that the local intermediary issues for clearing purposes on the basis of a London, or New York, deposit (Frankfurt).

4. a local intermediary who becomes the nominee for all shares traded on the exchange and who exercises all share rights for accounts of local shareholders (France).

Early in 1977 it was announced that the New York Stock Exchange had voted to admit foreign-owned brokerage houses to membership. It was anticipated that this would increase the flow of foreign funds into the exchange.

A recent major national stock exchange to permit the listing of foreign stocks was that in Tokyo (1973). Trading has been through transfer accounts handled by special Japanese settlement firms, with the original share certificates not physically transferred but held in custody in the parent-company country. There are certain conditions that must be satisfied, such as a minimum number of shareholders in Japan at the time of the listing (so as to assure a sufficiently broad market), a minimum size in terms of net assets and pretax profit, and prior listing on one of the 12 other major exchanges in the United Kingdom, Germany, France, Switzerland, the United States (American or New York), Netherlands, Belgium, Italy, Canada, and Australia.

As a further move to improve international securities market, the OECD Committee on Financial Markets issued in 1976 its recommendations as to minimum disclosure rules, which were prepared by government officials and experts of the securities industry.[7] Meanwhile, the U.S. Securities Exchange Commission, the public body regulating the U.S. stock exchange markets, the largest in the world, was reported to be moving toward a requirement that listed foreign firms (116 as of early 1977) provide as much detailed information as domestic listed firms. Since 1965, U.S. law has required that corporations with at least 300 American stockholders must meet Securities Exchange Commission requirements regarding financial disclosure, proxy solicitations, and the like, whether or not the foreign firm sought to sell its shares in the U.S. But apparently, the SEC has waived certain disclosure requirements from time to time when they would be at odds with foreign law or practice.

The Securities Exchange Law of 1934 introduced fairly rigorous control over the public sale of corporate securities in the United States. The extraterritorial reach of that law has been expanding in order to protect the U.S. purchaser of foreign corporate securities, although Congress did not provide the courts with any clear indication of the intended scope of application. There is no apparent problem with fraudulent action within the United States, which impacts on the value of corporate securities listed in the United States, even though the corporation be foreign-domiciled, such as the circulation of untrue information to potential American investors. And, if activity significantly related to losses arising from the fraudulent sale to U.S. citizens resident abroad occurs within the United States, the courts may find jurisdiction under the Securities Law. The application of U.S. law in this field has generated substantial conflict, for the degree of corporate disclosure required as a precondition for public sale differs substantially from country to country, despite some recent convergence. The problem is that some nations regulate the securities market by means other than disclosure. For example, disclosure requirements in the United Kingdom and Belgium are somewhat less exacting than in the United States. However, these two, similar to many other European countries, impose severe limitations directly upon the conduct of corporations listing their securities on national exchanges. The Belgian authorities have required the reorganization of a company's internal operations before permitting the marketing of its securities. And the London Stock Exchange has been known to demand the removal of particular officers from a firm before permitting it to sell its securities publicly. In other cases, the authorities may require detailed information not revealed to the public. The result is that the investor may be better protected against fraud in the United Kingdom and Belgium than in the United States. At times, some countries relax disclosure requirements so as to stimulate the market. In general, for an act to be vulnerable under the U.S. securities law, there must be some minimum connection with the United States, for example, the employment by a foreign corporation of a U.S. bank or accounting firm with headquarters in New York, even though

---

[7] *OECD Minimum Disclosure Rules Applicable to all Publicly Offered Securities* (Paris: Organization for Economic Cooperation and Development, 1976).

the security in question was not marketed in the United States but was purchased by a U.S. citizen abroad. The U.S. court may, on the other hand, refuse jurisdiction if it is satisfied that the U.S. citizen's rights are adequately protected by some foreign law.[8]

Even so, a trend toward greater disclosure is discernible for publicly-traded shares. Firms whose shares are traded on the London Exchange are subject to reasonably strict disclosure rules. Canada, France, and West Germany have amended their securities laws so that they are now closer to those of the United States.

A particularly onerous financial problem arises for firms selling services internationally through contract. In many cases, such firms are very thinly capitalized and need "front-end" financing in order to move into a major overseas project. Not infrequently, the foreign client will agree to a down payment of a portion of the fee shortly after the signing of the contract, but only on the condition that the contractor put up a bank guarantee or a surety bond for an equal amount. Even in the absence of advance payment, the client is very likely to request some sort of performance guarantee. Most frequently, these take the form of a bank guarantee. In the United States, a bank is prohibited by law from issuing open-ended commitments. Hence, a bank guarantee takes the form of a letter of credit, which has the effect of drawing down the contractor's line of credit. Against that letter of credit, the appropriate foreign bank issues a bank guarantee to the foreign client. Such a guarantee almost always gives the client a "first-call" right. If there is any dissatisfaction with the work being done under the contract, the client can simply demand to be paid the amount of the guarantee, and there is no recourse to arbitration. In the typical case, the beneficiary is paid promptly by a local bank, either a locally-owned bank or the branch of an international bank, which in turn will be reimbursed by the counterguarantor bank, which is the contractor's own bank. This bank will then collect from the contractor. Although the risk of an arbitrary (unjustified) call on a bank guarantee may be slight, calls have happened, sometimes by reason of bureaucratic mix-up, if the contractor's client is a government. Because an appreciable risk is there, this risk is covered by many European governments for their international service firms, also by the Japanese. Only in 1976 did the U.S. Overseas Private Investment Corporation (OPIC) initiate an insurance program for the United States exporter of services, which shifts the risk of an arbitrary call on a bank guarantee. Even so, the bank guarantee's effect on a firm's credit line is not thereby eliminated. But, in 1976, the Federal Reserve Board authorized banks to remove this credit burden if a surety bond were issued to the contractor, which is essentially a nonrecourse guarantee of performance. The system is so new that the cost of such a surety bond had not been well established by mid-1977, but it was

---

[8]Stevan Sandberg, "The Extraterritorial Reach of American Economic Regulation: The Case of Securities Law," *Harvard International Law Journal*, vol. 17, 1976, pp. 315 ff.

known that many insurance companies were not overly keen on issuing such bonds at what most would consider a reasonable price. As an alternative, the U.S. firm can cope with this restraint by turning to European banks to obtain bank guarantees and avoid straining domestic credit lines. But, if it does so, then the OPIC guarantee against the risk of an arbitrary call is not available to it.

In the United States, the Foreign Credit Insurance Association (FCIA), in cooperation with the Exim Bank, offers to U.S. international purveyors of services the opportunity to borrow against foreign service contracts to the extent that they call for payment in U.S. dollars for services performed by U.S. personnel. The FCIA in essence guarantees payment under these contracts, thereby making them bankable.

The strategy choice between types of financing, whether debt or equity, obviously rests on relative cost (availability), optimum leverage (given projected inflation and profit rates), legal restraints (including the maximum debt/equity ratio permitted by the parent government, also any foreign exchange controls, actual or potential), control considerations, degree to which risk may be spread, the relative utility of different currencies to the firm, and the ease of repatriation.

6.5   SUBSTANCE OF INVESTMENT

An investment may be in the form of cash, capital equipment, depreciated machinery, inventories, services, intangibles, or real estate. In that the last is immovable, it does not relate to international business except in the case where the investor transfers real estate from one local business entity to another. In most cases, real estate (including buildings) would represent a cash investment insofar as an alien is concerned. Note that in a world of perfect markets (no trade barriers, no tax differentials), the substance of an investment would become irrelevant.

The particular problem in this regard in international business lies in the valuation of assets for the purpose of capitalization in a foreign enterprise. *First*, there is sometimes a question of which exchange rate to use, a "free" rate or a controlled rate. The former creates more local currency value, but often obligates the investor to repatriate earnings likewise at the free rate in the future. *Second*, should capital equipment and inventories be valued at their U.S. or local values? *Third*, under what circumstances should depreciated machinery be used? Problems of local acceptance, maintenance, and operating cost may arise. In any event, the investor can expect a demand for independent expert appraisal and authentication by consular officials of the government involved. *Fourth*, how does one establish a reasonable basis for capitalizing services and intangibles? *Fifth*, should one shoot for a maximum capital base in view of the fact that (1) the repatriation of annual profits may be limited to a percentage of capital, (2) the local corporate tax based on percentage of capital may be progressive within a certain range, and (3) certain advantages may accrue if the foreign investment exceeds a specified minimum? An example of the last would be the Greek law that gives certain benefits to foreign investments over 60 million drachmae and the right to extend these benefits by special contract with the government if the investment exceeds 180 million drachmae. On the other hand, the large foreign-owned capital base may so dilute earnings as to make local participation unappealing, assuming that such participation is otherwise held desirable by the foreign owner. Bear in mind that in some cases local participation may be legally required, a subject already discussed in Chapter 5. Property taxes may also be relevant. In event of forced sale, understatement of value for tax purposes may constitute a trap.

SOURCE OF FINANCING 6.6

The basic strategy choices here have to do with (1) national origin—local (to the associated foreign operation), parent country, third country, or a mix of these (multinational), and (2) the choice between debt and equity in each case. Appropriate considerations include exchange controls, availability of investment guarantees at the source, tax treatment (withholding tax level, tax credits, tax deferral), ability to denominate debt and equity in source currency (whether local, foreign, Eurodollar, or unit-of-account), differential rates of inflation, possible changes in exchange rates, parent country balance-of-payments problems. All of these considerations could be appropriately aggregated in a single capital cost.

For example, one approach is to select the currency that appears to be weakest in the long run but which is presently convertible to the end-use currency. Let us assume an American firm contemplating a domestic United States venture. If sterling were available and the firm were willing to speculate that the pound would be devalued over the next 15 years while the dollar remained relatively stable, it might borrow in sterling then convert to dollars for its U.S. investment. Earnings would be in dollars. With a subsequently devalued pound, the firm could pay the loan back, converting from a relatively more valuable dollar (in terms of sterling) than was originally acquired. The profit would be roughly equivalent to the amount by which the pound had been devalued. This device assumes, of course, convertibility at maturity from dollars to sterling. On the other hand, should the pound remain stable and the dollar be devalued, the devaluation would result in a corresponding loss. The point is that capital-cost considerations must be modified to take these uncertainties into account.

Elimination of exchange risks by financing in local currencies seems to be a significant factor in pushing U.S. companies into borrowing overseas at interest rates substantially above those in the United States. If the proceeds of long-term borrowing are for use in, say, Brazil, and the firm's earnings are derived largely from Brazil, then from a hedging standpoint the cruzeiro would seem to be the currency in which to borrow, that is, the least costly. But such is not always the case.

Consider the choice between foreign and local debt financing—that is, the determination of relevant cost. We assume a two-country situation in which Country A is the domicile of the parent corporation and Country B that of the subsidiary corporation. Where is it cheaper for the subsidiary to borrow? The answer depends upon three factors: the interest rates in the two countries, the exchange rate, and taxes. For the moment we shall ignore taxes. As Shapiro correctly pointed out, "the relative rates of inflation are irrelevant when one currency is converted into another in the future, albeit unknown exchange rate. Comparative rates of inflation may help determine the future currency values but presumably this information is already incorporated in estimates of future exchange ratios."[9] That is, "imported debt is repaid in inflated local currency, just as loan debt."

First, if the exchange rate does not shift, which is the cheaper source to borrow, Brazil or the United States? Obviously, it is where the relevant interest rate (the cost of debt) is the lower. In either case, the Brazilian subsidiary has the same lack of earnings out of which it must repay the debt, plus interest.

Second, if the exchange rate does shift, then the lower cost of debt depends upon whether the change in the exchange rate more than compensates for the lower interest rate. Assuming that the loan is denominated in dollars and that the Brazilian cruzeiro is depreciated relative to the U.S. dollar, the Brazilian subsidiary will not have to expend more cruzeiros to repay both principal and interest. We can express this relationship mathematically.

Assume that the Brazilian subsidiary has the option of a loan from its U.S. parent repayable in full at the end of the year. Hence, the choice lies between:

$$L_\$ (X_o), \text{ or } L_{cr},$$

where

$L_\$ =$ a dollar denominated loan
$X_o =$ the cruzeiro/dollar exchange rate at the time of the loan
$L_{cr} =$ an equivalent loan in cruzeiros.

In the parent loan case, the subsidiary will have to repay at year end:

$$L_\$ X_1 + i_{us}L_\$X_1 = L_\$(1 + i_{us})X_1,$$

where

$X_1 =$ the cruzeiro/dollar exchange rate at the time of repayment of both principal and interest;

---

[9]Alan C. Shapiro, "Evaluating Financing Costs for Multinational Corporations," *Journal of International Business Studies*, vol. 6, no. 2, Fall, 1975, p. 26; see also, Clovis deFaro and James V. Jucker, "The Import of Inflation and Deflation on the Selection of an International Borrowing Source," *Journal of International Business Studies*, vol. 4, no. 2, Fall 1973, pp. 97–104.

then the cost of the loan to the Brazilian subsidiary is:

$$\frac{L_\$ (1 + i_{us}) X_i - L_\$ X_o}{L_\$ X_o} = (1 + i_{us}) \frac{X_1 - X_o}{X_o} = (1 + i_{us}) X_d,$$

where $\dfrac{X_1 - X_o}{X_u} = X_d$, the rate of devaluation (or evaluation) of the cruzeiro in reference to the dollar as between the beginning and end of the year.

If the Brazilian subsidiary were to borrow locally, it would receive L_{cr} at the beginning of the period and repay $L_{cr}(1 + i_B)$ at the end, for a cost of

$$\frac{L_{cr}(1 + i_B) - L_{cr}}{L_{cr}} = 1 + 1_B - 1 = i_B,$$

where i_B = interest on Brazilian source of debt.

Therefore: if $(1 + i_{us})X_d < i_B$, the subsidiary would be better off borrowing in the United States. If it were more, it would be better off borrowing locally. The point of indifference is where

$$(1 + i_{us})X_d = i_B, \text{ or where } X_d = \frac{i_b}{1 + i_{us}}.$$

Let us take an example: We assume that

$X_o = Cr50/\$1.00$

$X_1 = Cr60/\$1.00$

$X_d = .20$

$i_{us} = .08$

$i_B = .35$

$L_\$ = \$5$ million, repayable at the end of one year

$(1 + .08).2 = .216$, which is less than i_B, or .35;

therefore the subsidiary should borrow directly in Brazil.

One might then ask: How much would the exchange rate have to move to compensate for the difference in United States and Brazilian interest rates in this particular case?

$(1 + .08) X_d = .35$

$X_d = \dfrac{.35}{1.08} = .32407;$

that is, if the cruzeiro devalues relative to the dollar by .32407, it makes no difference where the loan originates. If the devaluation rate is higher, a local loan is cheaper than a U.S. loan.

We now plug taxes into these equations such that

t_{us} = rate of corporate profit tax in the United States
t_B = rate of corporate profit tax in Brazil

If the U.S. parent makes the loan to the Brazilian subsidiary, it will receive back at the end of the year the principal of the loan, plus interest. Any exchange loss is shown on the subsidiary's books for the loan was denominated in dollars. However, the subsidiary is part of an integrated system. Hence, it becomes important to talk about a net consolidated cost. As we have shown, the cost to the subsidiary of borrowing from its parent, without considering taxes, is:

$$(1 + i_{us})X_d,$$

where

i_{us} = the U.S. interest rate
X_d = the amount of devaluation between the beginning and end of the year.

Therefore, the total cost to the corporation of the loan to the Brazilian subsidiary is

$$\overbrace{\left[(1 + i_{us})\, X_d - t_B\, (i_{us}\, X_{1/X_o})\right]}^{\text{Net loss to subsidiary}} + \overbrace{\left[i_{us} - t_{us}\, i_{us}\right]}^{\text{Net gain by parent}}$$

Assume the same values as before, but with

t_B = .30
t_{us} = .50

The tax reduction rate in Brazil is thus $.3(.08 \times 1.2) - .0288$. The increased tax rate in the United States is $.5 \times .08 = .04$, so that net gain in the United States is $.08 - .04 = .04$. Hence, the net cost to the parent and subsidiary is .2272 (.216 − .0288 + .04) for the U.S. loan. The cost of the Brazilian loan is:

$$i_B - t_B i_B,$$

where $t_B i_B$ = Brazilian corporate profit tax reduction by reason of the local interest deduction from taxable income.

In our example, that cost would be .245 ($.35 - .3 \times .35$). Therefore, the cost of a U.S. loan is still cheaper, .2272 as against .245. Recall that without taxes, the comparable costs were .216 and .35. The difference has narrowed considerably.

The point of indifference is the point at which

Consolidated net cost of parent loan   Net cost of local loan

$$\left[(1 + i_{us})X_d - t_B(i_{us})\frac{X_1}{X_0}\right] - \left[i_{us} - t_{us}i_{us}\right] = \left[i_B - t_B i_B\right].$$

If the loan is non-Brazilian, say a Japanese yen loan, from an unrelated party, the tax reducing effect on the Japanese source is irrelevant. The foreign loan cost is simply

$$(1 + i_j)X_{jd},$$

where

i_j = Japanese interest rate

$X_{jd} = \dfrac{X_{ji} - X_{jo}}{X_{jo}}$ = rate of devaluation (or evaluation) over the period.

If that expression is less than $i_B - t_B i_B$, then the yen loan is less costly than borrowing in Brazil.

A major imperfection in this analysis is that it assumes perfect knowledge of future changes in exchange rates; also, it makes no provision for a possible inability to reconvert local currencies to dollars or another convertible currency at any price. For each of these variables, one should, of course, insert a probability of occurrence and expected dispersion of possible values, as Lietaer did in his hedging model (see Section 6.9). But, in fact, the inability to predict the path of these variables has led many companies to pursue the policy of borrowing locally for local use whenever possible, which is what Robbins and Stobaugh found.[10] And, according to Hoyt, the decision rule used by the Singer Company is, "if the exchange risk . . . [is] high and the amount of receivables large in any country, efforts . . . [are] made to borrow locally the total value of net receivables even though the interest rates incurred seemed exorbitant by American standards. If the exchange risk . . . [is] low, it might be decided to borrow less in local currency thus avoiding high interest rates, and to finance the receivables with dollar or other hard currency loans."[11]

One lesson learned by this exercise is that borrowing at the lowest interest rates does not always lead to the lowest cost debt. Table 6.1 shows the rates at which a good industrial borrower could have borrowed five major currencies for a five-year period as of June 30, 1971. The interest and redemption payments are translated back into U.S. dollars at the actual rate of exchange on the various payment dates (the intermediate rates are not shown). The true cost of borrowing is then calculated in U.S. dollar terms under two tax assumptions. In this instance, borrowing at the highest nominal interest rate, 10 percent in the United Kingdom, would have led to the lowest cost debt.

---

[10]Sidney M. Robbins and Robert B. Stobaugh, "Financing Foreign Affiliates," *Financial Management*, vol. 1, no. 3, Winter 1972, p. 7.

[11]Newton H. Hoyt, Jr., "The Management of Currency Exchange Risk by the Singer Company," *Financial Management*, vol. 1, no. 1, Spring 1972, pp. 17–18.

Table 6.1
IMPACT OF FOREIGN EXCHANGE RATE CHANGES ON COST OF DEBT

Currency	Exchange rate June 30 1971	1976	Nominal interest rate/yr.	Actual gross cost in U.S. dollar terms/yr. A*	B†
			%	%	%
U.S.$	1.00	1.00	9	9.00	9.00
D.M.	3.497	2.574	7¾	15.59	21.90
Swiss Fr.	4.097	2.473	6	17.55	28.16
French Fr.	5.515	4.743	7½	11.73	14.82
U.K.£‡	2.4197	1.7813	10	4.69	−1.28

*"Tax neutral." Profits (losses) on redemption are taxable (currently tax deductible) at the same tax rate as applies to interest deductions.

†Interest is deductible at a tax rate of 50 percent but the profit or loss on redemption has no tax consequences. (The figures are on a "gross equivalent" basis.)

‡$ U.S. per £. Other figures are units per $.

Source: J. F. Chown, "General Introduction to Investment in Europe," mimeo., 1976.

It will be noted that column A is calculated on the assumption that any exchange profit on repaid principal is taxable at normal corporate rates and that any exchange loss is deductible from taxable income. This is not always the case. For instance, in the United Kingdom, losses on long-term borrowing are not deductible. Empirical research has shown that in no less than 19 out of 20 three-month periods studied (1971–76) it would have been right for a corporate treasurer to have borrowed the most "expensive" (in terms of nominal interest rates quoted) of the major currencies available while it would have been correspondingly right for the investor in bonds to go for the currency offering lowest immediate yield.[12]

Chown points out that

Subject to these exchange risks and exchange control practice the basic rule of finance is simple: Money should be borrowed as an obligation of that company within the group that can obtain the most favorable deduction from taxable income. *The rule is, where possible, to take your profits in the company with the lowest effective tax rate but take your deductions in the one with the highest effective rate. Some countries (not so far as I know the United States) take a hard line on borrowing for purposes not designed to produce domestic profits and may as a result disallow the deduction for the interest on money borrowed for foreign acquisitions.*[13]

Chown also observes that there are two obvious alternatives in financing a new venture abroad.

First, *the parent company can provide substantially the whole of the capital required for foreign operations from U.S. sources, borrowing if necessary as a direct obligation*

---

[12]M. Marechal, "Is the Euromarket Rational?" *The Banker*, July 1975.

[13]J. F. Chown, "General Introduction to Investment in Europe," mimeo., 1976.

of the parent. The foreign subsidiary would then use local banks only for short term working capital requirements. Second, the parent might transfer a minimum capital (subject to any "thin capitalization" rules in the host country) raising the rest of the capital required outside the United States as an obligation of the subsidiary, probably with a parent company guarantee. These two extreme strategies are in practice often associated with different management styles, the first with centralized head office control (finance being regarded as a profit responsibility) and the second with decentralized profit responsibility. [14]

The choice, of course, may be limited by local law and regulation. In the United Kingdom, for example, foreign exchange rules do not usually permit a foreign-controlled company to borrow sterling, although it can borrow foreign currency as a direct obligation. The French have vacillated. Sometimes they have required that a portion of incoming foreign investment be financed in France; at other times, they have virtually prohibited the use of local finance for such purpose.

Bear in mind that there is no necessary relationship between the country in which one does business and the currency borrowed. A U.S. parent corporation may guarantee a Deutschemark bond issue as an obligation of its Swiss subsidiary to expand activities in Italy. The issue might be designed in London, with a substantial part of the money coming from Kuwaiti-owned balances in Zurich banks. It is not uncommon for the treasurer of a U.S. corporation to request a French franc line of credit from a London bank, whether controlled from Britain, Hong Kong, the United States, or Moscow. Currently, about 100 U.S. banks are represented in London, in part because many Americans find it easier to do business within a familiar environment.

The optimal financing decision becomes somewhat more complex, of course, when the options are expanded from local and foreign loans so as to include as well (1) retained earnings, (2) external equity (to the firm), and (3) intersubsidiary equity (ownership by one subsidiary of shares in another). Slavich developed a linear program for making the optimum financial choice, the objective being to maximize the value to the parent corporation's shareholders of a foreign investment decision. [15] To make the program operational, it is necessary to specify a number of constraints, specifically:

1. Equality of uses to sources of funds, both internal and external, for the subsidiary as well as the parent.

2. Total tax credit against parent country tax liability must not exceed the allowable limit.

3. Externally imposed limits on the amount of debt a company can incur.

4. Company-imposed limits regarding debt capacity and minimum dividend payout ratio (or a dividend at least as large as that paid in the previous year).

---

[14]Chown, "General Introduction."

[15]Reported in Dennis Slavich, "The International Financing Decision: A Programming Approach," unpublished Ph.D. diss., Sloan School of Management, M.I.T., 1971.

5.   Government-imposed limits on the magnitude of direct foreign investment (as
     formerly in the U.S. case) on dividend remittances and on repayments of loans and
     repatriation of capital (as in many LDCs).

The Slavich model takes into account such variables as the income tax rate of
the host country, the expected rate of devaluation of the local currency, the
financing sources available, and the cost of each. The output is a specification
of the optimum mix of financial sources for a project, optimum in the sense
of generating maximum value to the stockholders.

Although this approach is of interest, it does not provide a final answer
because of the many other factors involved in the real world, such as a discrete
change in the allowable dividend or interest remittance if the foreign investment exceeds a certain absolute amount, the fact that the impact of inflation
on a proposed project or on a subsidiary's operation cannot be foreseen with
accuracy, the fact that the cost of financing for various sources cannot be
known short of actual negotiation (note the discussion of various financing
institutions in the next section), and the fact that the tax relationships assumed
are grossly oversimplified. And, finally, it is by no means clear that a management need to—or, indeed, will—maximize in respect to shareholders' value.

Nonetheless Slavich does derive two important generalizations:

*First, the optimal financing decision in an international environment differs from the
purely domestic decision because of difference in taxation, currency, and government
regulations. Second, due to these parameters being unique for each entity of an international corporation, each such entity will have its own unique marginal cost of funds,
implying a different required return for investment purposes.* [16]

One of Slavich's constraints, the limits of debt a firm can incur, usually is
measured against equity in the form of maximum leverage or debt/equity ratio,
which in itself implies an inexplicable discontinuity. One can understand why
risk might increase as the debt/equity ratio increases and, hence, why both
debt and equity might become more costly. But why a financial institution
should impose a ceiling is not easily understood. Such a limit is reinforced if
the taxing authorities likewise recognize a ceiling. If the ceiling is exceeded,
interest may not be considered a cost to the payer nor repayment of principal
as tax free income to the payee if he is likewise an owner. What needs under-
scoring is the fact that permissible debt/equity ratios may vary substantially
from country to country, from perhaps 2:1 for the United States to possibly
10:1 in Japan. One observer wrote of the Japanese practice:

*It may first be said that debt-equity ratio in Japan when considered together with the
100 percent loans-deposits ratio of Japanese banks is without any doubt the most
efficient and flexible use of money to be found in the world. Whether Japan is or is not
short of capital—and it is now very unlikely indeed—this system certainly makes the*

---

[16]Slavich, "Note on Sources of Debt Financing," p. 307.

best of all available resources and, compared to it, the Western concepts can be described as a "waste of capital."

It is not infrequent for a Western firm to keep large cash balances in the bank and to have long term debts which even on Western criteria are insignificant. This results in a waste of capital, since these firms do not use the funds they have or could easily borrow.

The point can be made that this derives from the individualistic outlook in the West, where a firm, as a firm, as a person, is an individualized whole and must be prepared to take care of itself.

In Japan a person or a firm is not an individual but a link and, in a way, only exists through persons or organizations, or social groups or firms (and among them banks). Consequently, a Japanese firm cannot be described only through its balance sheet but also and sometimes mostly through the knowledge of its connections with other firms. [17]

The higher acceptable debt/equity ratio in Japan may suggest to a U.S. firm the wisdom of pursuing a joint-venture strategy in Japan (perhaps on a minority basis) so as to profit from the higher leverage but without running the risk that financial institutions in more conservative countries—as in the United States—might consolidate Japanese debt and equity with that held by the firm domestically and, hence, either impose a lower debt ceiling or increase cost.

If the firm opts for local (foreign) financing, then it has the choice of public institutions (a government-owned entity), private institutions (a private bank, a number of which now have New York offices), a local business firm, personal (limited to certain persons), public sale of securities, or internal (reinvested earnings). The criteria are, of course, availability (that is, relative cost), the degree to which financial disclosure is felt desirable, and preferred ownership and legal strategies (see Chapters 5 and 7).

Of special concern to the international businessman is the existence of blocked funds, that is, liquid assets that may not be immediately exchangeable into usable foreign currency but which may be remitted through the export of goods on deblockage lists[18] or invested locally under certain circumstances. Care must be exercised that such investment be considered foreign investment, the proceeds for which are subject to eventual repatriation. Blocked funds to be invested in productive enterprise (associated perhaps with newly imported capital) should be considered as "sunk cost."

Of growing interest is the development of organized security markets in an increasing number of countries, including several of the less developed countries. It is quite clear that more and more multinational firms have been listing their shares on foreign stock exchanges. A few companies have a policy of offering their stock in any country in which the firm has significant investment

---

[17]Xavier Remaux, Vice President of Nihon Gazocean KK (an affiliate of Gazocean S.A. of France), in *Japan Economic Journal,* March 14, 1972, p. 20.

[18]See Glossary.

in fixed assets. In some instances, the multinational firm has swapped its stock for a participation in its joint venture abroad, thereby creating a mutuality of interest and eliminating, at least in part, the suboptimization problem.[19]

A specialized institution now common around the world is the development bank or corporation. Quasipublic entities, these institutions channel both private and public capital into local projects deemed to have a high priority from the point of view of national or regional economic development. Foreign exchange resources have been made available to many of them by their respective governments and international financial institutions. Under some circumstances, debt and equity capital may be available to a foreign-owned enterprise through this channel. The circumstances not infrequently include a requirement that the enterprise be a joint venture with local capital, that local management and technical personnel be developed, and that there be complete financial disclosure, including transactions with the associated foreign firm.

Many countries, political subdivisions thereof (states, provinces, cities), and regional groupings (as the EEC) offer special financial incentives if the firm invests within their respective jurisdictions or within certain areas (such as economically depressed or less developed areas) or in certain types of activities (R&D, approved projects, activity generating foreign exchange). These inducements may run from tax holidays and low-interest loans to outright grants and permission for a larger share of foreign ownership than would otherwise be the case. A number of low interest loans have been granted to U.S. firms by the EEC regional development agencies, specifically the European Investment Bank (EIB, a major source of funds for firms setting up plants in Greece and Turkey and other associated countries or territories), the European Coal and Steel Community (ECSC, a source of loans to finance plants in regions where steel and coal facilities are being closed down or of loans to retrain workers displaced by coal and steel shutdowns), the European Social Fund (ESF, which finances up to 50 percent of the costs incurred in retraining and relocating workers), and the European Development Fund (a source of financing for the sale of goods and services to associated countries and territories). Other possible sources in the public sector are a variety of government agencies and public development corporations,[20] which provide equity and loan finance to joint enterprises and to local development banks in the LDCs. "Perhaps more important, however, is their role as catalyst and promoter of projects and expert intermediary between the foreign investors and bankers and the local public and private sectors in developing countries."[21]

---

[19]See Glossary.

[20]The more important public agencies and development corporations are British Commonwealth Development Corporation (CDC), Deutsche Entwicklungsgesellschaft (DEG), the Dutch Financierings Maatschappig Voor Ontwickelingslanden N.V. (FMO), the Danish Industrialization Fund for Developing Countries (IFU), the French Caisse Centrale de Coopération Economique (CCCE), the U.S. Overseas Development Corporation (ODC), and the Japanese Overseas Economic Fund (OCEF).

[21]Michael Emerson, "Foreign Investment in Developing Countries: Exporting Institutions and other Government Incentives from the Capital-Exporting Countries," *OECD Observer*, no. 50, February 1971, p. 32.

In the United States, foreign firms can qualify for Economic Development Administration (EDA) grants and loans if the project (1) comprises a new industrial or commercial facility (or an expansion) in a redevelopment area designated by EDA, (2) is consistent with the overall development program for the area, (3) is not in an industry experiencing overcapacity, (4) cannot be otherwise funded, and (5) includes at least 15 percent equity investment by the owner and 15 percent equity by a state, community, or an American Indian tribe. Also, the Small Business Administration (SBA) may be a source of loans and guarantee for bank loans either directly or through local development corporations. Several Canadian firms have secured such loans. There are numerous state and community development programs, such as the New York Job Development Authority, from which foreign firms may benefit.[22]

On the multinational level are several public institutional financial sources, most notably the International Bank for Reconstruction and Development, the International Development Association, the International Finance Corporation, the Inter-American Development Bank, and the Asian Development Bank (Table 6.2). General requirements are (1) evidence that normal commercial financing is not available, (2) acceptability by the host government, (3) demonstration that reasonable benefits will accrue to the host country from the contemplated investment. It should also be noted that *private* institutional arrangements of a multinational nature are multiplying; for example, the Iranian Oil Consortium, the Atlantic Community Development Group for Latin America (ADELA), and the Private Investment Corporation for Asia (PICA).

An example of how private and public investors might participate in a large project is detailed in Table 6.3. In this case the security for the lenders was an assignment of proceeds from exports, which were to be deposited in an external account (in London). The equity investors guaranteed completion of the project.

In addition, the UN Development Program (UNDP) constitutes an important source of preinvestment assistance to LDCs in the form of research projects, training surveys, and demonstration projects. In rendering such assistance, the UNDP may provide staff, experts, equipment, and supplies, or establish institutes, demonstration centers, or pilot projects. Proposals originate with member governments, but the implementation of the projects provides opportunities for private firms in member countries and may be related to longer-term interests.

Other significant sources of overseas financing are the local currency funds generated by the sale of U.S. surplus farm products under authority of Public Law 480, the Agricultural Trade Development and Assistance Act of 1954. A

---

[22]*See Investing, Licensing and Trading Conditions Abroad, United States—September 1970* (New York: Business International, 1970), pp. 987–88.

Table 6.2
MAJOR MULTINATIONAL FINANCIAL SOURCES

	World Bank Group			Inter-American Development Bank (IDB)		Asian Development Bank (ADB)	
	International Bank for Reconstruction and Development (IBRD)	International Development Association (IDA)	International Finance Corporation (IFC)	Ordinary capital resources	Fund for special operations	Ordinary capital resources	Special funds resources
Function	Promote the economic development of member countries primarily extending loans on conventional terms for specific high-priority projects.	Promote the economic development of less-developed member countries by making credits on concessionary terms, thereby lessening the burden on the recipient countries' respective balance of payments positions.	Encourage the growth of productive private enterprise in developing countries by extending loans and noncontrolling equity capital, providing underwriting and standby commitments, and attracting outside financing.	Contribute to the acceleration of the process of development of its member countries individually and collectively by providing loans on conventional and concessionary terms.	Contribute to the acceleration of the process of development of its member countries individually and collectively by providing loans on concessionary terms.	Finance loans on conventional terms and technical assistance for projects and programs to foster economic development in and among the developing countries of Asia and the Far East.	Provide loans on concessional terms for high priority development projects in developing member countries.
Criteria and limitations	Government guarantee required when borrower is a private entity; borrowing country must be credit-worthy; borrower must be unable to obtain funds from other sources on reasonable terms; loan decisions are made only on the basis of economic development considerations; loans must be for specific projects; funds may be spent only for purposes for which a loan was granted; project must have high economic priority; and recipient enterprise must have productive potential.	Government guarantee required when borrower is a private entity; borrowing country must be credit-worthy; borrower must be unable to obtain funds from other sources on reasonable terms; credit decisions are made only on the basis of economic considerations; credits must be only for specific projects; funds may be spent only for purposes for which loan was granted; project must have high economic priority; and recipient enterprise must have productive potential. Per capita income level of borrowing country should be below $250.	The corporation considers the degree of economic development of borrowing country; availability of sufficient capital from private sources on reasonable terms; prospects of profitability; evidence of sound planning; sponsorship from companies with proven industrial experience; extent of sponsor's share capital in enterprise; provision for local investor participation; and project's economic priority for the country. It will not lend where primary object is refunding, direct financing of trade, or land development.	The Bank must take into account the creditworthiness of the borrower, may finance only specific projects, must consider the ability of the borrower to get financing from private sources on reasonable terms, and may not finance a project on a member country's territory if the member objects.	The Bank must take into account the creditworthiness of the borrower, may finance only specific projects, must consider the ability of the borrower to get financing from private sources on reasonable terms, and may not finance a project on a member country's territory if the member objects.	Loans to be made in less-developed member countries of ADB.	Loans to be made in less-developed member countries of ADB.

Eligible borrowers	Member governments, their political subdivisions, and any public or private entities in their territories.	Member governments, their political subdivisions, any entities in their public or private territories, and public international or regional unit.	Private firms in developing member countries.	Member governments, private local firms or joint venture enterprises with local participation, and public or private re-lending agencies.	Member governments, private local firms or joint venture enterprises with local participation, and public or private re-lending agencies.	Any member government or any agency, instrumentality or political subdivision thereof, or any entity or enterprise operating in the territory of a member.	Governments of developing member countries.
Lending volume (FY 1975)	$4.3 billion.	$1.6 billion.	Total commitments of $212 million.	$1.1 billion.	$413 million.	$376 million.	$194 million.
Current interest rates and fees	8.85% interest, commitment charge of ¾% per annum accruing from a date 60 days after date of loan agreement.	No interest. Service charge of ¾% per annum to cover IDA administrative costs.	Interest rates are keyed to the IBRD rate.	8% annual interest, including 1% commission allotted to special reserve; 1¼% commitment fee on undisbursed balance.	1–4% interest per annum; service charge of ¾%.	8¾% interest per annum including 1% commission plus commitment charge of ¾ of 1% per annum on unused balances of loan. 9¼% interest for borrowers in countries with a per capita GNP of $850 or higher	Interest rates have ranged from 1½ to 3% per annum, including ¾ of 1% service charge.
Loan maturities	15 to 30 years, including grace periods, which run until projects are operational. Most are on 20 to 25 year terms.	50 years, including 10-year grace period, following which 1% per annum of principal is repayable over second 10 years and 3% per year over next 30 years.	Loans are usually 7 to 12 years. Amortization is generally on a semiannual basis after a grace period. Equity capital sold to private investors where appropriate.	15 to 20 years, including grace period.	20 to 40 years, including grace periods.	10 to 25 years with grace periods from 2 to 5 years. The average is 20.	From 16 to 50 years, including grace periods from 5 to 10 years; average maturity, 40 years.
Currency of repayment	Currency lent.	Currency lent or another convertible currency.	Generally currencies lent or invested, most commonly dollars.	Currency lent.	Mexico and Venezuela repay in currency lent; others may pay in their own currencies. Service charge payable in dollars.	Currency lent.	Currency lent.
Resources	$25.5 billion subscribed capital. Major sources of funds are sales of bonds on world capital markets.	About $3.2 billion in funds available for lending, of which about 70% is already committed.	Initial subscriptions and four replenishments plus transfers from IBRD.	$2.74 billion subscribed capital, of which $388 million paid-in. Major source of funds is sales of bond issues on world capital markets.	$2.33 billion in member contributions.	Subscribed capital, $3.2 billion; borrowings, equivalent to $451 million.	

Table 6.3
PROJECT FINANCING INVOLVING OPIC, EXIM, AND IBRD*

Capital cost		Financing plan		
Facilities	$677 million	Equity (35%)		$307 million
Pre-production costs	111	U.S.	$169 million	
Capitalized interest	77	Dutch	77	
Working capital	12	Local government	61	
Cash	8			
		Debt (65%)		578
		Eurodollar loan**	203	
		Suppliers†	300	
		IBRD‡	50	
		OPIC§	25	
Total	$885 million	Total		$885 million

*(Assume, for example, a mining project in an Asian country sponsored by two large U.S. companies)

**A floating rate loan (London interbank rate plus 2¾ percent), others at fixed rate (for facilities and preproduction)

†Financed by parent governments of suppliers. Eximbank involved to the extent of about $100 million (9 percent for 13 years)

‡At 8¾ percent for 20 years

§Guarantee for a private loan

portion of these PL 480 funds are subject to the approval of the host government and available for loans to the local enterprises of U.S. firms so long as they are not engaged in the production of commodities that would compete with U.S. sales at home or abroad. The loans are repayable in the currency borrowed.

Within the United States are a number of financial sources specializing in international operations, including such public institutional investors as the Export-Import Bank and the Overseas Private Investment Corporation (OPIC) and such private institutional investors as the "Agreement Corporation," "Edge Act Corporations,"[23] and investment houses and mutual funds concentrating on foreign securities (for example, the International Basic Economy Corporation and Private Enterprise Incorporated). The Edge Act authorizes equity financing in foreign enterprises by U.S. banks through special Edge Act subsidiaries, which are U.S. entities. Very frequently, these institutions require a convertible debenture or an option for stock interest from a borrower.

---

[23]Agreement corporations and Edge Act corporations are domestic subsidiaries of U.S. banks incorporated under the Federal Reserve Act to engage in international banking and to finance foreign projects through long-term debt and equity. Authorized in 1916 and 1919, respectively, such corporations were, unlike domestic banks, permitted to make equity investments and to have branches outside their own state. As a consequence, many non-New York state banks have Edge Act subsidiaries in New York City through which they do business overseas, including acting as a holding company for the bank's direct investments in foreign banking institutions.

Inasmuch as the Edge Act Corporation rarely desires control (other than in financial institutions), the borrower may frequently buy back these rights after a period of time. The Overseas Private Investment Corporation, although legally barred from making equity investments, is perceived as an important financial intermediary between U.S. investors and enterprises within developing countries in order to increase the flow of capital and technology. As a wholly owned government corporation, OPIC has no authority to increase its reserves by selling equity or borrowing in private capital markets or from the U.S. Treasury; any increase depends upon specific congressional appropriation. OPIC can, however, make direct loans through its direct investment fund and sell participations on the market. The typical OPIC loan is for 8 to 12 years, with a maximum of 20 years. Interest rates vary with OPIC's assessment of the financial risk. OPIC direct loans are limited largely to project loans in "friendly LDCs" for the purchase of U.S. goods and services.

In addition, of course, funds for overseas investment may be generated by a parent firm itself either through guaranteeing credit opened on behalf of its foreign associate or by loaning internally generated assets: that is, earnings, surplus machinery, services, intangibles. As already indicated, one device is to sell parent-company securities abroad and use the proceeds to loan to the local foreign enterprise or to exchange equity with a foreign joint venturer. A large and attractive foreign firm, including one in which a parent foreign firm has a direct interest, may, of course, tap the parent firm's home securities market directly.

Not to be overlooked is the possibility of using funds from third-country sources, particularly export credit facilities and commercial banking facilities (in such places as Switzerland and London). For reasons of tax considerations, it may be useful to utilize the funds of an associated firm in a third country. Also, joint ventures with either associated or nonassociated third-country firms may be an optimum financial strategy when those involved will provide a flow of valuable assets or services where uneconomic competition might otherwise develop. However, the relevance of antitrust law must be considered in such cases, also the availability of investment guarantees.

An important problem in the financing area as seen from the point of view of some less developed countries is set forth in the statement by the president of the Inter-American Development Bank.

There is a general consensus ... that the formulation of policies that stimulate exports, and the strengthening of Latin American enterprise are not sufficient to assure a more dynamic participation of our countries in international commerce, both in the exportation of raw materials and manufactured products. ... [E]xportation is an area where one must have enterprises which are specialized as much in marketing as in production techniques; indeed, perhaps even more so in marketing than in production. Finally, export projects, particularly when they involve the exploitation of natural resources, require huge amounts of capital investment. It is obvious that it would be very difficult for the developing countries to manage such projects depending only upon their own resources—technical, financial and marketing. It is largely as a consequence of this fact that the great international corporations have come to dominate the principal export lines of our countries.

It is evident, however, that this dominance cannot long continue. Conditions have changed in our countries and the international lending agencies must now reconsider traditional practices. These agencies, for example, have been reluctant to finance projects where it is believed that the international corporation by use of its credit worthiness can obtain the necessary resources from the private capital markets. Until now, it has been generally accepted that external public credit ought to be utilized to assist projects which could not be financed from other sources.

This practice has resulted in a situation in which the international corporations are left in control of the equity of the industry which is being developed; consequently, they are the principal, although not the only beneficiary of the industry in question. At the same time, there exists a false impression that, as a prerequisite to the transfer of the technical, administrative and commercial resources that are so essential for the success of this type of investment, the international corporation must be the equity owner of the project. It thus becomes very difficult, if not impossible, to reconcile the contribution of the international corporation with the principle of economic sovereignty that is so important to many developing—and developed—countries, with harmful consequences for both the developing country and the foreign investor.[24]

6.7   LEGAL INSTRUMENTALITY TO BE USED

A recent innovation by the larger American corporations operating internationally is to set up financing subsidiaries incorporated either abroad (typically Luxembourg, Liechtenstein, or the Bahamas) or domestically (New York or Delaware). These subsidiaries issue debentures in their own name either with or without parent-company guarantees and conversion features. The general purpose of a financing subsidiary, either foreign or domestic, is to avoid payment of the U.S. withholding tax imposed on interest and dividends flowing to foreigners that the U.S. parent would have to pay if it issued the securities itself. There may be a secondary purpose of interposing a corporate shield to protect parent-company assets from direct liability. Weighed in balance in each case are the following factors:

Advantages of a foreign corporation[25]

1.   Less vulnerability to future U.S. restrictions on foreign investment. For example, should the interest equalization tax be reestablished to cover direct investment by

---

[24]Antonio Ortiz Mena, address before the third meeting of the United Nations Conference on Trade and Development, Santiago, Chile, April 21, 1972 (Washington, D.C.: Inter-American Development Bank), mimeo., pp. 5–6.

[25]Adapted from W. S. Zeigler, "Financing Overseas Expansion," S.M. thesis, Sloan School of Management, M.I.T., 1966.

an American manufacturer, a finance subsidiary incorporated abroad prior to extension of the tax would probably be exempt, except for additional future direct investment by the parent.

2. Less danger that debentures issued by an overseas finance corporation and held by a nonresident alien would be subject to future United States estate taxes. Under present law, such debentures are included in the gross U.S. estate of a nonresident alien holder only if the securities were physically located in the United States at time of death.

3. Exemption from local income or withholding taxes on interest and dividends paid if incorporated in such countries as Luxembourg or the Bahamas. Nonetheless, net income of such a subsidiary generally falls under subpart F of the U.S. Internal Revenue Code and is considered taxable income to the parent whether or not such income is remitted to the parent. (See Section 7.1, Tax Deferral.) In any event, whatever foreign income and wealth taxes are paid by the overseas subsidiary may be credited against the U.S. income tax owed by the parent.

Advantages of a U.S. corporation

1. Offset of losses of the subsidiary against profits of the parent for tax purposes, provided a consolidated return is filed. Such consolidation would not be possible if the finance subsidiary were incorporated overseas.

2. Applicability of the many tax treaties to which the United States is a party. For example, the United States-Japanese treaty reduces the Japanese withholding rate on interest paid from Japanese sources from 20 percent to 10 percent effective January 1, 1966. A foreign country of incorporation might not have the same treaty or the extent of its agreements might be less than those to which the United States is a party.

    An important consideration here is the tax imposed by host governments on interest paid by foreign affiliates to the finance subsidiary. Some countries do not permit interest paid to a foreign affiliate to be considered a business deduction from corporate income for tax purposes. Britain is a case in point. If the United Kingdom manufacturing affiliate of, say, a Luxembourg financing subsidiary borrows funds from the latter, the British firm cannot deduct interest costs on the loan from its taxable corporate income in the United Kingdom. On January 5, 1966, the United States and the United Kingdom agreed on amendments to their treaty to the effect that interest paid by a British subsidiary to a U.S. parent or U.S. affiliate on or after April 6, 1966, may be deducted in the United Kingdom for corporate tax purposes. This treaty affects only U.S. corporations. Thus, until such time as a similar treaty is negotiated with Luxembourg, a Luxembourg financing subsidiary is at a distinct disadvantage compared with its American counterpart if the parent chooses to use it for financing in the United Kingdom.

    Other variations are possible. Mexico and Italy allow a deduction conditional on a tax being withheld from the interest. A Luxembourg company would not be able to recoup this tax since it is not subject to income tax in Luxembourg against which to credit it. A U.S. subsidiary would. (However, by arranging to pay dividends to its American parent, the Luxembourg subsidiary could claim a foreign tax credit for withholding taxes imposed on the Luxembourg company.)

3. Exemption from U.S. withholding tax on interest paid to nonresident aliens and foreign corporations if more than 80 percent of the finance subsidiary's income is derived from foreign sources.

4. In event the subsidiary's operations are curtailed or the corporation liquidated, the ability to carry out tax-free liquidation or sale of individual investments. By restricting its loans to foreign affiliates, the domestic financing subsidiary can qualify.

5. Exemption from U.S. tax of the transfer of stock in foreign affiliates to the American financing subsidiary, thereby permitting a build-up of equity without a commitment of cash.

If there is significant foreign ownership in the parent company, or such is desired, a useful device may be a local holding company owned entirely by local interests. Its capital might consist of shares of the parent company plus accumulated earnings. The holding company would issue shares to local nationals or business entities in exchange for real or intangible assets (cash, real estate, exploratory rights, mineral concessions, services). These assets could be assigned, for a nominal fee or no fee, to the parent company for use locally in a productive enterprise wholly-owned by the parent (either a branch or a subsidiary). Thus, in effect, the local assets are swapped for shares in the parent company. The parent company would, to the extent that local earnings from its operating branches or subsidiary were adequate, pay dividends on the parent-company shares owned by the holding company, and do so in local currency. This arrangement is represented in Figure 6.3. We here assume a U.S. parent and a Brazilian operation.

In real life, of course, the U.S. corporation would undoubtedly have to put some dollar assets into the Brazilian subsidiary. The advantages from the Brazilian point of view are:

1. Since Brazilian shareholders are assured the same dividend rate as U.S. shareholders, there should be no conflict of interest.

2. Changes in the dividend rate received by the Brazilian stockholders would be smoothed because of the broad investments of the U.S. corporation, of which the Brazilian subsidiary represents only one.

3. The U.S. parent is directly liable in that the Brazilian holding company holds shares in the U.S. parent.

4. The Brazilian holding company, by agreement of its shareholders, could sell the parent company stock at any time it wishes either on the Brazilian or U.S. market. (Because of the advantages to the U.S. company of having local stockholders, this threat provides the Brazilians with further leverage to assure fair play by the parent.)

5. This relationship provides Brazilians with an investment opportunity that might not otherwise be present.

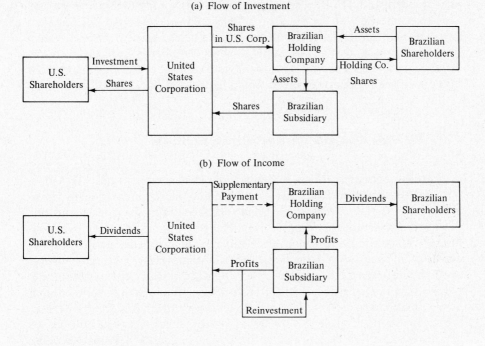

Figure 6.3
THE LOCAL HOLDING COMPANY

Note: The dividend per share paid to U.S. shareholders and that paid by the Brazilian subsidiary to the holding company on behalf of the parent must be equal, using some average rate of cruzeiro/dollar exchange for the calculation. If Brazilian earnings are inadequate, a supplementary payment will have to be made by the U.S. corporation. If Brazilian profits are excessive, the surplus may be either reinvested or remitted to the parent.

The advantages from the U.S. parent's point of view are:

1.   The need to commit a minimum of its own capital.

2.   The opportunity to share risks with Brazilians, but without dilution of control of its operating subsidiary in Brazil.

3.   The creation of some element of mutual interest between Brazilian investors and its other stockholders.

4.   The capacity to pay dividends on shares in the parent company stock in cruzeiros to the extent of cruzeiro earnings.

A problem arises if in the *long run* the Brazilian subsidiary is either significantly more or less profitable than the consolidated worldwide operations of the U.S. corporation. Also, agreement would have to be reached with the taxing authorities in both countries so that (1) the U.S. corporation would not be compelled to pay a withholding tax on the profits paid by the Brazilian subsidiary to the holding company (based on the assumption that these profits really were dividends paid by the U.S. corporation directly), (2) that the transfer of U.S. corporate stock to the Brazilian holding company was a tax-free transfer, (3) that the Brazilian holding company would not be taxed (that is, it would be treated as a conduit in that these earnings had already been taxed to the Brazilian subsidiary), and (4) that the taxes paid by U.S. and Brazilian shareholders on the dividends received would be roughly the same.

6.8 PROTECTING CLAIMS ON EARNINGS STREAM

A major issue in international business is the management of risk. As with a purely domestic corporation, the corporation operating internationally must attempt to maintain a reasonable balance between the risks it takes and the profits it expects to earn. Thus, in evaluating any business decision, whether it involves investing in new plant and equipment in a particular country or the choice of invoicing sales in the home or the customer's currency, risk must be traded off against expected return, either implicitly or explicitly. In structuring transactions, for example, the firm must decide which risks to take on and which risks to impose on the firm or individual with which it is doing business. Although the final result is often based on bargaining between the two, it nonetheless involves making risk-return tradeoffs. Once a decision has been made that exposes the firm to risks, it must then decide whether to "self-insure" these risks, thereby passing them through to its shareholders, or whether to transfer these risks to a third party in the form of insurance or other risk-bearing financial contracts.

Conceptually, there is no difference between this problem and that faced by the purely domestic firm. However, the firm operating internationally does face a larger variety of risk. Further, more risks may be of the type lying outside the influence and/or experience of the firm and are, therefore, better dealt with by someone else. Finally, and one suspects this is a major factor in the international firm's decisions, many "foreign" risks involve unknowns to management, thereby leading it to overreact. In this case, management may seek costly insurance even though within the home market it would readily self-insure risks of much greater magnitude.

Hence, a major problem in international business lies in reducing risk (loss of claims on a stream of earnings) to reasonable proportions as measured against expected return. A variety of devices are available, the choice of which depends upon the nature of the assets giving rise to the stream of earnings (physical, intangible, liquid), the nature of the risk (expropriation, dilution of control, destruction, dishonesty, inflation and devaluation), and the management's time horizon. In each case the firm may either avoid the risk (by not going into a project or transaction), self-insure, transfer the risk to another, or modify the risk by its own behavior. The risks themselves may be classified into commercial (see Appendix 2 to this chapter), casualty, political, and currency-related.

In order to protect earnings arising out of physical assets, the firm may self-insure through geographical dispersion or large size; take out commercial policies; utilize the investment guarantee schemes offered by certain governments; rely upon the specific guarantees of the host government; depend upon the leverage provided by a continuing flow from abroad of essential commodities and/or services (essential in the sense of not being available locally or from other international companies at comparable price); depend upon a high level of identity with the economic and political interests of the host country; employ company police; and offer special gratuities.

Commercial risk

A subject infrequently covered in most international texts is the conditions under which ordinary casualty insurance coverage (for fire, explosion, theft, liability) is available in various parts of the world.[26] The major problems are either the absence of any coverage at reasonable cost or coverage in an inconvertible currency even though the assets involved can only be replaced from a convertible-currency country. One may, of course, nonetheless take out so-called unadmitted insurance—that is, insurance issued by a foreign insurance company not legally authorized to do business in the country in which the insured assets are located. In such cases, the premiums paid out are frequently not recognized as legitimate business expenses and, hence, must be paid out of post-tax earnings, which in many cases considerably increases the cost. For example, in France unadmitted insurance is prohibited without government approval. Purchase of such insurance may be considered technically as tax evasion, and penalties could be imposed. In Chile, unadmitted insurance is permitted for exports and imports. Otherwise it is subject to a tax amounting to 60 percent of the premiums that would have been charged in the Chilean market. In Guiana, unadmitted insurance is not prohibited except for compulsory insurance, and premiums may be taken as a local tax deduction. So it goes; national laws vary and are constantly changing.

In protecting one's tangible overseas assets, the employment of company police (a device that modifies casualty risk), may be fraught with political danger in the less mature LDCs (hence, enhancing political risk), particularly if the enterprise is identified as being essentially foreign (with foreign nationals in top local management positions). A much better solution is, if necessary, to subsidize the local government to the extent of the cost of providing special

[26]Useful guides have been prepared by the American Foreign Insurance Association (New York City) for various regions of the world. See also Huntington Putnam, "Management's Stake in International Insurance," *World-Wide P & I Planning*, March–April 1967, pp. 21 ff.

police protection. Finally, the payment of special gratuities is exceedingly hazardous, particularly in a politically unstable situation, unless the time horizon of the firm is very short indeed. Many veteran international firms report a policy of desisting completely from politically motivated gratuities. Initial difficulties may be expected in some areas, but once a determined policy becomes known, companies report relative freedom from extralegal pressures. Bargaining, negotiating strategy, bureaucratic delay, hostility, and special payments for special services (so long as they are not secretive or illegal) should not be confused with bribery, nor should payments, presents, or trips given as rewards to private citizens who have been particularly helpful in accomplishing perfectly legal aims. One should bear in mind American practices in regard to Christmas gifts, commission men, lobbyists, expediters, and invitations to use company facilities (hunting lodges, yachts, stadium boxes).[27]

One rationale for a wholly owned international subsidiary incorporated domestically by the parent firm for purposes of entering into contracts with foreign clients, for executing foreign sales, and for holding equity in foreign enterprises is simply to shield the corporate assets of the parent against adverse —and possibly politically dictated—decisions of foreign arbitration and judicial bodies. In the United States, the parent company is generally permitted, and often required, by the Internal Revenue Service to consolidate the earnings of its domestic subsidiaries, and the intercorporate dividend tax is not a factor. The existence or nonexistence of a domestically incorporated international subsidiary has no direct relevance to the administrative control structure of the firm.

By far the best insurance against loss of one's assets overseas, whether tangible or otherwise, is the leverage the foreign firm can develop through the flow of services (managerial, distributive, technical, financial) it maintains that are not available locally. If the enterprise itself is also perceived by the host government as having a relatively high positive effect on net national product, balance of payments, public revenues, economic growth, and political development, the firm has little to fear. As the uniqueness (that is, the value) of what the firm contributes to the host society diminishes over time, the relationship between the firm and the associated foreign enterprise should likewise be altered.[28]

In the case of liquid assets, special precautions are necessary. Some alternative policies are personal bonding, external audits, the use of anonymous accounts, and the deposit of funds or securities where attachment is difficult. Given the time delay almost inevitable in controlling the flow of liquid assets overseas by an international parent firm, fiscal authority must be delegated. And given distance and isolation, the uncovering of irregularities may be

---

[27]For tax consequences of making illegal payments abroad by U.S. firms, see p. 7. See also Chapter 9.
[28]For a full discussion of this subject, see R. D. Robinson, *International Business Policy* (New York: Holt, Rinehart and Winston, 1974), Chapter 3.

delayed. Hence, it becomes doubly important to bond those with disbursing authority and to have periodic, though not necessarily regular, external audits by a reputable auditing firm. Several of the large U.S. and European auditing firms have worldwide coverage.

The only legitimate reason to use anonymous or confidential bank accounts (for example, the numbered account in a Swiss bank) is to prevent capricious attachment of the firm's liquid assets by act of a disgruntled foreign government, client, customer, partner, or stockholder. This risk is considered to be a real one, particularly by those in the contracting business where performance may always be questioned and damages claimed. Although the Swiss law makes disclosure of the ownership of a numbered account by a bank official a penal offense (and permits recovery of damages through civil suit), writs of attachment are relatively easy to obtain in Switzerland. The only problem lies in serving them on the right bank because of the difficulty of learning the location of deposits. However, serving writs on all of the leading banks is likely to include the right one, in which case the confidential nature of the account is no defense. The funds may remain attached until final judicial decision, which may be several years off. Writs of attachment are also relatively easy to come by in the United States. And a recent court decision has held that funds on deposit with the *foreign* branch of a U.S. bank may be reached by attachment served on the U.S. parent. The best protection against capricious attachment is gained by depositing funds in a bank in the United Kingdom where a reasonable cause for the attachment must be demonstrated prior to the blocking of an account.

Political risk

By most recent count, 16 capital-exporting countries offer foreign investment guarantees or political insurance. U.S. foreign investment guarantees (administered by the Overseas Private Investment Corporation, OPIC) are available for risk of expropriation, nonconvertibility of profits, and loss due to war, insurrection, and civil disorder in respect to new investment approved by the host government, but only in countries defined as less developed countries with which the United States has a guarantee agreement. These "specific risk" guarantees may be packaged with usual *commercial* risk insurance (covering defaults, bankruptcy, and so on) in the form of an "extended risk" guarantee. Guarantees may be issued to any U.S. entity, or to a foreign entity that is owned (10 percent or more) by a U.S. entity. Contractual arrangements, which embody some form of investment (such as withheld earnings or a performance bond) may likewise be covered. Three years is considered generally to differentiate investment from sale.

National schemes vary in respect to coverage (term, type and LDC limitation), cost (and, hence, level of subsidy), the requirement of prior host government approval, and nationality test of applicant. For example, because some national schemes are more extensive in their coverage than the United States, it may be important for a U.S.-based multinational corporation to qualify through a subsidiary for a guarantee under, say, the West German scheme. No one guarantees the rate of exchange applying in the case of blocked earnings other than the then current rate. Average premiums run about 1 percent ($\pm$ .5 percent), depending upon the type and amount of coverage. As in the case of export credit insurance (see Appendix 2), an investment guarantee insurance policy may make an otherwise unacceptable project into a bankable proposition.

Under congressional strictures to "privatize," the U.S. Overseas Private Investment Corporation attempts to involve private insurance and financial institutions to the extent possible. In the OPIC settlement with Kennecott for its loss due to expropriation of its assets in Chile, OPIC agreed to guarantee a debt issue to be offered private institutional investors. The issue consisted of participation certificates on the outstanding Chilean government debt due the Kennecott subsidiary whose property had been taken. The Bolivian settlement of payment for U.S.-owned lead and zinc property, expropriated in 1971, was covered by an OPIC guarantee. It involved an OPIC-guarantee loan by the Bank of America and nonguaranteed loans by the First National City Bank of New York and the Swiss Bank Corporation. The U.S. owners of the seized property were paid out of the proceeds of the loan.

A persistent question is whether national investment guarantee schemes may, in the long run, cause more difficulty than they avoid; that is, change the risk itself. The point is that offering investment guarantees to corporations may tend to consolidate the traditional manner of conducting international business —that is, direct equity investment on a majority or wholly owned basis with control centralized in the parent company headquarters. This traditional pattern stands in opposition to a movement out of ownership of the local firm into a set of contractual relationships that, by their very nature, possibly tend to render the firm more sensitive to the interests of the host society and also tend to reduce risk by associating specific inputs with specific benefits. This pattern is shown in Figure 6.4. It would appear plausible that the availability of investment guarantees for financial investment only tends to discourage the type of relationship envisioned here and thus sets companies (and the guaranteeing governments) on a collision course with foreign governments and business interests.

Despite the appearance of the national investment guarantee scheme, which gives the private investor some protection against political risk, international companies have been able to obtain this type of insurance protection only for a small portion of their total overseas investments due to the limitations of the various schemes in respect to the countries in which coverage is offered (only some LDCs) and the assets that can be covered (for instance, only new investment, not reinvested earnings). This gap has prompted the creation of a Lon-

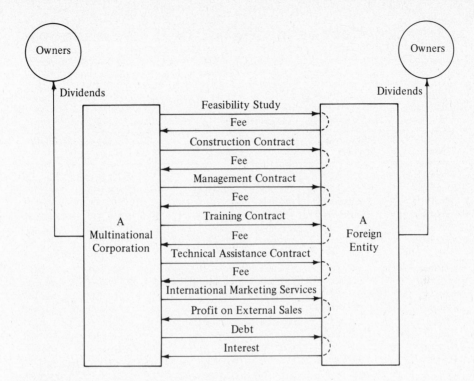

Figure 6.4
**RELATING SPECIFIC COSTS AND BENEFITS VIS-A-VIS A
FOREIGN ENTITY VIA CONTRACT**

don-based private market organized around Lloyd's for political risk insurance offering complementary coverage. Since the basic premise of this private market is the spread of risk, the insurer generally requires that a company insure its entire overseas assets against expropriation, including those located in low-risk countries. The Lloyd's scheme covers every country in the world (except Rhodesia), including those socialist countries where international joint ventures are possible. The amount of insurance available in each country, however, is limited and is sold on a "first come, first served" basis. Availability is determined by three factors, national origin of the investment, the country of investment, and industry. This allocation of available coverage is a device to spread risk in that the risk of expropriation is not the same for all nationalities, all countries, or all industries. Fees range from .2 percent to 10 percent per annum per country, depending upon the perceived risk in each case, which is based on the same three factors as determine the allocation of coverage. An example of the cost of such coverage is given in Table 6.4.

Table 6.4

EXAMPLE OF COST OF PRIVATE POLITICAL RISK INSURANCE

An unidentified U.S. company, whose worldwide overseas assets have a book value of $245 million, obtained a premium quote from AIGC* of $260,000 p.a., based on a $53 million indemnity. In this case the indemnity is 90 percent book value in each country except for those where the insurance company's capacity would have been exceeded if this rate were applied; e.g. Belgium and Italy. In the latter event, the insurance company proposed the specific, lower indemnity amounts. The average premium rate for the total $53 million insurance works out to 0.49 percent, which, interestingly, is lower than OPIC's fixed standard rate of 0.6 percent.

Country	Basis of value book ($)	Indemnity ($)	Country	Basis of value book ($)	Indemnity ($)
Argentina	2,752,000	2,476,800	Italy	38,225,000	2,500,000
Chile	885,000	796,000	Liechtenstein	2,853,000	2,567,700
Brazil	3,850,000	3,465,000	Netherlands	10,284,000	2,500,000
Venezuela	480,000	432,000	Spain	6,030,000	2,500,000
Mexico	2,285,000	2,056,500	Sweden	3,515,000	2,500,000
Jamaica	3,580,000	3,222,000	Switzerland	913,000	821,700
Aruba	12,000,000	3,500,000	South Africa	3,385,000	2,500,000
Dominican Rep.	700,000	630,000	Gabon	846,000	762,120
Austria	614,000	552,600	Australia	25,338,000	2,500,000
Belgium	26,473,000	2,500,000	Hong Kong	555,000	499,500
Denmark	1,012,000	910,800	Japan	3,890,000	2,500,000
Finland	291,000	261,900	Philippines	569,000	512,100
France	30,696,000	2,500,000	New Zealand	1,942,000	1,747,800
Germany	22,205,000	2,500,000	Canada	38,976,000	2,500,000
Greece	323,000	290,700	Total all countries	$245,467,800	$53,005,720

*AIGC refers to the American Investment Guarantee Corporation, the U.S. agent of the London-based Investment Insurance International, the only broker through which the insurance is available.

Source: Business International, April 19, 1974, p. 122.

Currency-related risk

Of special concern to the international businessman are the devices for the protection of earnings flows against devaluation and inflation effects: that is, *currency-related risks.* Which ones are appropriate in a specific case depends upon the legal restraints, relative costs, availability to local financing, price control, export potential (and legal capacity to retain export earnings), and the relation between relevant price increases and changes in the exchange rate. In addition to a variety of tax tools (see Table 6.5), the principal devices are listed below. It will be noted that the first eight of these devices are essentially risk-modifying; numbers nine and ten are forms of self-insuring; and the balance are devices for risk-shifting.

1. *Development of exports*, provided that the firm can retain any of the foreign exchange earnings.

2. *Price escalation.* Assumes the absence of price controls.

3. *Revaluation of assets.* Important only if profits are linked to capital base for purposes of taxation or repatriation, or if it is a joint venture. Otherwise asset

Table 6.5
TAX TOOLS TO OFFSET INFLATION IN EUROPE

Countries	Special depreciation provisions	Valuation of inventories	Special reserves provisions
Belgium	Accelerated depreciation is permitted for assets with lives from 6–19 years, using double-declining balance method. Maximum: 20% per year.	Valued at lower of cost or market by average cost or FIFO. (LIFO not permitted.)	Tax-free reserves to cover future losses and estimated expenses (5% of taxable profits for bad debts, but reserves for product warranty costs are limited only by type of business).
France	Machinery and equipment acquired may be depreciated at higher declining balance rates than usual.	Valued at cost or market, whichever is lower. Otherwise FIFO is used (LIFO not permitted).	Since mid-1959, base-stock allowances are permitted if prices rise more than 10% over a two-year period. If tax deduction is taken, it will have to be added back at end of sixth year. Otherwise, companies may set up a reserve for price variations of raw materials.
Germany	None.	Valuation at cost or market, whichever is lower; FIFO or LIFO, if justifiable; otherwise, average cost is used.	A tax-free reserve for price variations may be set up for certain inventories where costs have increased more than 10% above previous balance sheet date. (This reserve must be restored to taxable profits within next six years.) Also, 20% of cost of stockpiled imported raw materials may be written off.
Italy	Straight-line method based on historic cost plus accelerated depreciation of 45% (15% annually).	Valued at cost or market, whichever is lower; LIFO is used (but companies may use base-stock method if employed before end-1959).	None.
Netherlands	Special immediate write-off of 1975 investment in plant and equipment once contract is signed (and if jobs are created). Otherwise, 4% investment allowance for new equipment in each of next two tax years (108% depreciation) and 12% per year for buildings.	Valued at cost or market value, whichever is lower; FIFO, LIFO and base-stock systems are allowed.	Tax-free reserves for maintenance and uninsured losses. Also, replacement reserves for gains on disposal of fixed assets may be carried for four years.

	Depreciation	Inventory Valuation	Reserves
Spain	Accelerated depreciation may be negotiated for tangible assets: rates are 40% annually if useful life is more than five years, double straight-line rates if life is 1–5 years.	Valued at cost or market, whichever is lower; FIFO or other generally accepted system allowed, but not LIFO.	50% of undistributed profits (after legal reserve requirements) can be set aside in a special tax-free reserve. Another 30% (and sometimes 50%) can be set aside by exporting firms and must be reinvested in two years.
Sweden	Machinery and equipment may be written off either on a straight-line basis at 20% per year of purchase cost or 30% of book value on a declining balance basis. A third method allows "planned" depreciation. Depreciation may be deferred to a later year.	Inventories may be depreciated to 40% of the cost price or market value, whichever is lower. FIFO system is used; LIFO not permitted.	Investment reserves of 40% of pretax net business income may be set aside tax-free (46% in central banks, 54% kept in company). When used, reserve reduces depreciation.
United Kingdom	100% depreciation of machinery and equipment in first year; 40% initial allowance for industrial building and 4% annual depreciation thereafter.	Valued at cost or market. Since the 1973–74 financial year, a special tax deferral is allowed for "inflated" inventory once values have risen above 10% of trading profits.	No special reserves.

Source: International Accounting & Financial Report, September 20, 1976, p. 3.

revaluation is only of accounting significance. (An Italian firm assured itself that it would always have at least 50 percent ownership of a Brazilian joint venture by inserting in the charter a provision that the value of its initial investment would increase in accord with the effective exchange rate).

4. *Reducing import requirements:* eliminating products with a high foreign exchange content and reducing inventories of imported components (through use of air transport, better control), *if* management expects that the rate of increase of net cash flow to the local firm will exceed the rate by which the exchange rate used for the relative imports changes. In that case, imports cheapen in terms of local currency.

5. *Unit-of-account financing* or invoicing, see Section 6.4.

6. *Concentrating on the production of those goods with high margins that require relatively low hard-currency input*—but should not be done blindly; one should look at the risk-reward trade-off.

7. *Accumulating maximum credit in the United States on behalf of the foreign firm through fees, dividends, royalties, profits on intracompany sales or purchases.*

8. *Incurring local debt:* running up payables in relation to receivables. (A reduction of receivables may be accomplished by factoring. By altering their fiscal years, some firms have been able to borrow tax funds through a one-time deferment of taxes.) The point is that by borrowing locally the firm can reduce its net exposure.

9. *By manipulating leads and lags.* Involves the *prepayment* for imports or the early receipt of export proceeds (leads) or the postponement of import payments or a delay in the receipt of export proceeds (lag). In the first case the length of the transaction is shortened in anticipation that the currency being received will soon devalue or that the currency being paid will soon revalue. In the second case (lag), the length of the transaction is lengthened in anticipation that the currency received will soon revalue or that the currency being paid will soon devalue. Leads and lags may be limited by regulation. For example, France, as of early 1975, limited an export lag to 180 days, and import lag to one year, permitted any export lead but ruled out import leads (other than a 30 percent down payment on imported capital goods).

10. *Netting.* Refers to the offset of payables and receivables between related companies so that only the net balance is actually transferred. Netting may be multilateral, in which case there is a complete analysis of all intracompany liabilities and actual payments made only to the net creditors of the group. Not only does netting reduce the transfer costs associated with the movement of funds, but it also provides a mechanism for timing the clearing process so as to take advantage of anticipated shifts in exchange rates between major currencies, either by triggering clearance or postponing it. National regulation may limit a company's freedom in this regard. For example, under current French regulation netting is permitted, but it is difficult.

11. *Purchase of futures* (forward cover or a forward contract), which refers to a commitment to buy a foreign currency at a given time in the future for a stipulated amount. The cost of such a contract can be interpreted as the cost of insuring against a possible loss due to currency fluctuations. Typically, textbooks define the

cost as the difference in the exchange rate between two currencies on the date the contract is agreed upon (the spot rate) and that on the date the contract matures. A definition leading to a better management decision is that the cost of locking into a future exchange rate is the difference between the forward rate and the spot rate one anticipates for that date. In a sense, the former definition involves an accounting illusion. For example, assume that a U.S. firm purchases a machine from an English firm for a given number of pounds sterling, payable at a future date. To avoid speculating on the value of the future pound in reference to the dollar,[29] it may wish to fix the number of dollars needed to buy the pounds at that future date. The annualized cost of such a forward contract may be represented thus:

$$\frac{360}{n} \times \left[\frac{x_f - x_s}{x_s}\right]$$

where n = the number of days to maturity of the forward contract

x_f = the forward rate of exchange of pounds per dollar

x_s = the spot rate of exchange of pounds per dollar

Say the obligation is for £1,000 payable 90 days in the future, that the spot rate quoted for the British pound is $2.40 and the 90-day rate, $2.30. The *annualized* cost of a forward contract would be calculated thus:

$$\frac{360}{90} \times \frac{2.30 - 2.40}{2.30} = 4 \times \frac{-.10}{2.30} = 4(.0435) = -.1743 \text{ (or 17.40\% discount)}$$

In this case, the market is anticipating a devaluation of the pound in reference to the dollar. If the firm does not buy forward cover, and it has no receivables in pounds, it is "short" in pounds and is involved in outright speculation. It may find that when it is actually obliged to buy the £1,000 90 days later that it must do so at either a higher or lower rate than that anticipated in forward contract. If the pound 90 days out actually sells for $2.20, instead of $2.30, the firm gains $.10 per pound or $100 in our example by *not* buying a forward contract. If the actual rate 90 days in the future turns out to be $2.35 per pound, the firm will have lost $.05 per pound, or $50, by not buying a forward contract. If, on the other hand, the firm buys a forward contract, it will have lost $100 it otherwise would have gained in the first case, gained $50 it otherwise would have lost by buying the contract in the second case.

As can be noted in the example above, the U.S. firm pays 4.35 percent less for the pounds 90 days in the future than it would have if it had purchased the pounds at the time of the purchase commitment. Therefore, it gains by this amount, in our

---

[29]"Speculation in the foreign exchange market takes place when an individual or institution has an amount of assets (a future inflow) different from the amount of liabilities (a future outflow) in a given currency. If there is a change in the par value of the currency in question the value of the net holdings of the individual in that currency will change. In this case, the individual or institution has a 'net position' in that currency. This position is called 'long' if there are more assets (future inflows) than liabilities (future outflows). The net position is called 'short' if there are more liabilities (future outflows) than assets (future inflows). A net position is called *outright speculation.*" Rita M. Rodriguez and E. Eugene Carter, *International Financial Management* (Englewood Cliffs: Prentice-Hall, 1976), p. 107.

example, by \$18.11. Gains of this sort are usually taxable, in the U.S. case at a 35 percent capital gains rate. If, on the other hand, the firm were buying Deutsche marks 90 days in the future, it might well have to pay a premium. In this case, the firm incurs a cost, which is usually treated for tax purposes as a deduction from taxable income. Therefore, the net *annualized* rate on a forward contract to the company buying the contract would be represented thus:

$$\frac{360}{n} \times \frac{x_f - x_s}{x_s} (1-t)$$

where t = the effective tax rate on the forward contract gain or loss in the country in which the forward contract is sourced. (It may vary depending upon whether x_f or x_s is the larger.)

Plugging in the figures used above, we find that the actual premium to the firm is 11.35 percent, not 17.40 percent as originally calculated on an annual basis.

There is a strong market force that tends to make the cost of forward cover equal to the difference between the rates of return available in low-risk, short-term securities of the respective countries. The process that underlies this market force is as follows: If the annual rate of return on treasury bills were 8 percent in the United States and 10 percent in the United Kingdom, the cost of forward cover would tend to be a 2 percent premium for U.S. residents investing in U.K. securities and purchasing a forward contract simultaneously in order to avoid the currency fluctuation risk. If it were less, for example 1.0 percent, then U.S. residents could invest in equivalent risk securities in the United Kingdom with a 10 percent return, pay a 1.0 percent premium for a forward contract, and receive a net 9.0 percent yield as compared with an 8 percent yield on U.S. Treasury bills. The rush to take advantage of this return differential would tend to increase the cost of forward cover and/or the rate of return in the United States or decrease the rate of return in the United Kingdom. Thus, the cost of forward cover is strongly influenced by the rates of return on short-term securities in the various countries. However, in that the interest rate differentials among countries appear to be very much influenced by the policies of the respective governments, the cost of forward cover may only coincidentally reflect the actual perceived risk by the market of future currency fluctuation. So although the cost of forward cover represents the cost of insuring against loss due to foreign exchange fluctuation, it may be a poor indicator of the perceived risk of the occurrences being insured against.[30]

12. *Swaps.* A domestic firm loans dollars (possibly interest-free) to a foreign bank, which in turn makes a local currency loan to the local subsidiary of the domestic firm. After the stipulated period, the subsidiary repays the loan, and the bank repays the dollars to the corporate parent abroad. Note that the local firm gains so long as the expected local currency return on the loan invested in the business is greater than the interest on the loan from the bank. The domestic firm gains only if the cost of the swap (that is, the rate of dollar return on a comparable direct investment at free-market rates in its associated foreign firm or on an investment

---

[30]Adapted from Jose A. Lopez, "Short-Term Financial Planning in a Multinational Enterprise: A Linear Programming Solution," unpublished S.M. thesis, Sloan School of Management, M.I.T., 1972, pp. 49–51.

elsewhere, whichever is greater) is less than the gain realized by the associated foreign firm at the swap rate. (An example is given in the Merck case, which follows this chapter.)

13. *Export swap.* A domestic firm pays dollars to a foreign bank, which in turn transmits the foreign currency equivalent to a local firm, the latter being given the privilege of repaying the dollars through export proceeds accumulated over a specified time.

However, all of these devices imply some cost, either direct or implicit, in a change of business practice. When is the incurring of such cost justified? Three considerations arise: (1) how to predict a shift in parity rate with some reasonable degree of accuracy,[31] (2) how to determine the extent of a firm's net exposure to such a shift, and (3) how to determine the optimum hedging moves—that is, the extent to which a firm should shift risk, and how.

According to the rules of the International Monetary Fund (IMF) established at Bretton Woods in 1944 and continued up to the Smithsonian Agreement of December 1971, member countries[32] were not supposed to shift the parity value (defined in terms of gold) of their respective currencies more than 10 percent without prior consultation. Nor were they to permit the fluctuation of the market rate for buying and selling by more than plus or minus 2¼ percent from parity, the spread constituting the so-called band, the end points of which were the "intervention points" at which a country's central bank or exchange stabilization fund was required to start buying or selling. Up to mid-1971 IMF members attempted to maintain fixed (or pegged) exchange rates. Parity rates were changed only by government decision and by discrete amounts.[33] A few countries maintained for periods of time "floating rates" (market determined and varying), notable cases being Canada in 1970 and the United States (and its major trading partners) for a short time in 1971. Some countries tried to adjust their currencies by a "creeping peg," which refers to many frequent, small, discrete changes in the parity rate. But by 1971, the pressure on this relatively inflexible system forced a change. Coinciding with the suspension of gold convertibility of the dollar and with a 7.89 percent reduction in the gold value of the dollar, the Smithsonian Agreement of 1971 doubled the band by permitting fluctuation of plus or minus 4½ percent around parity. But in March 1973, even that rule was terminated, and since that date currencies have been "floating," some fluctuating by as much as plus

---

[31] A firm should only attempt to outguess the market if it is dealing in a currency subject to foreign exchange control and only if it feels that it has superior information. In a completely free market situation, such that the purchasing power of the two currencies is expected to maintain parity, there is no need for the firm to outguess the market, that is, to hedge.

[32] Some 115 countries including all the significant noncommunist nations other than Switzerland, which nonetheless cooperates.

[33] In fact, during this period of so-called "fixed rates" under the Bretton Woods agreement, there were more than 150 official parity changes among IMF countries, *not* including the Latin American currencies. Alan Teck, "International Business Under Floating Rates," *Columbia Journal of World Business*, vol. 11, no. 3, Fall 1976, p. 60.

Table 6.6
CURRENCY PEGS OF THE LESS DEVELOPED COUNTRIES, 1973–75

Reference pegs	Number of LDC currencies on the indicated peg		
	March–July 1973	Mid–1975	Late 1975
U.S. dollar Formal status 28 de facto status 36	64*	55*	52*
Pound sterling	11	8	6
French franc	17	13	13
South African rand	(3)*	(3)*	(3)*
Spanish peseta	1	1	1
SDRs (weighted 16-currency basket)	–	7	9†
Other weighted basket	–	9	11
Floating	3	4	5
Gold	1	–	–
Total	97	97	97

*Since the South African rand was pegged to the U.S. dollar during this period, the three LDC currencies linked to it have been included in the number of LDC currencies pegged to the U.S. dollar during the period.
†Currencies of Burma, Guinea, Iran, Jordan, Kenya, Malawi, Qatar, Tanzania and Uganda.
Source: IMF Survey, February 2, 1976, p. 35.

or minus 20 percent. In fact, IMF members employ a variety of exchange rate techniques. The currencies of many major countries are floating, but with substantial government intervention (the so-called "dirty float"). Moreover, the majority of countries have pegged their currencies in some way to other currencies, or to certain composites, such as the Special Drawing Rights (SDR)[34] or trade-weighted baskets. See Table 6.6.

In addition, a varying number of Western European countries have endeavored to keep their respective currencies within plus or minus 2¼ percent of a stated central rate, the so-called "snake." As of mid-1977, the currencies of five countries (Germany, Denmark, Belgium, Netherlands, and Luxembourg) were within the snake. Meanwhile, the currencies of the United Kingdom, Ireland, Italy, and (since March 1976) France were outside the snake and floating freely.

Forcing this greater flexibility in exchange rates were perhaps a number of factors, among them being persistent changes in the relative productivity of various national economies, thereby setting up persistent balance-of-payments pressure. Others: lack of confidence, in the United States (Watergate, Vietnam, rising unemployment, accelerating inflation, slowed economic growth

---

[34]See Appendix 1 to this chapter.

rate), a shift of liquidity from central banks to private hands,[35] growing ability of corporations to shift large amounts of funds rapidly, and more rapid dissemination of information (which means that it is virtually impossible for a central bank to intervene effectively in the market to control foreign exchange rates). Most observers are convinced that the system of floating rates is here to stay. But curiously, their advent does not seem to have had an appreciable impact on the volume of trade and investment. One explanation is that for every currency movement there is a winner and a loser. Admittedly, however, floating rates do make planning difficult. There is some indication that the impact of floating exchange rates on a firm operating internationally is to make decision-making more centralized, eliminate fixed price lists, change the currency in which bills are rendered, and to shift the sources from which markets are supplied.

The corporate treasurer obviously has a problem every time the probability of a devaluation of a currency in which the firm has a net exposed position seems significant. His problem is really three-fold: (1) how to monitor each national system important to him so as to affix a probability of a change in parity rate, and the extent of that change, with reasonable accuracy, (2) how to determine one's net exposure in a devaluation-prone currency, and (3) how to combine the probability of a devaluation and the level of one's net exposure with the cost of various hedging devices (ways of shifting the risk) so as to achieve the least cost situation given his propensity to assume risk. Consider the first problem.

In an efficient foreign exchange market, changes in relative prices of two countries correspond to changes in the exchange rate between their currencies. This phenomenon is known as the purchasing power parity theory.

The validity of the theory increases as the length of the testing period increases. Some deviations over short periods have been attributed to monetary, as well as nonmonetary, factors. The latter factors include changes in people's tastes, changes in technology, and sudden discovery of a natural resource. These nonmonetary factors affect the country's balance of payments, which in turn, puts pressure on the exchange rate. From the empirical evidence, however, we can generally state that the difference in the relative inflation rate is an approximately unbiased estimator of the change in the exchange rate.[36]

Over a very long period, the purchasing parity theory would operate even in situations where there was heavy government intervention in the exchange market. However, this long run tendency may or may not be of value to management, for the long run may fall well beyond its decision-making time horizon. The point is that it is important to hedge only when exchange markets

---

[35] For example, in 1973 the U.S. Tariff Commission estimated that private corporations controlled some $268 billion in short-term assets, which was more than the reserves of all nations put together ($152 billion).

[36]Sei Hoon Chun, "Foreign Exchange Exposure Management—A Case Study" (Cambridge, Massachusetts: S.M. thesis submitted to Alfred P. Sloan School of Management, M.I.T., 1977), p. 15.

are inefficient, that is when one or more of the following conditions is *not* met:

1. No arbitrage opportunities exist.

2. There are no capital controls or trade barriers, and no predictable interventions by governments or central banks.

3. All participants have access to all available information relevant to the exchange market.

4. Changes in the exchange rate are equal to changes in the relative inflation rates.

5. Interest rate differentials reflect the expected changes in the future spot rate.

6. The forward rate is an unbiased estimate of the expected future spot rate.

7. The forward rate discount or premium is equal to the interest rate differential.[37]

Inasmuch as all of these conditions are rarely met within the relevant time period, the corporate treasurer is left with our three problems.

A 1970 study of the literature and of current practices of U.S. corporations (the latter being based on interviews with the relevant officials in seven large banks and investment houses and 13 large internationally organized firms) came to the overall conclusion that:

Not only do scholars of the subject disagree on which are key [signals] and which are not, but so also do financial managers and bankers. It is this writer's conclusion that no approach to the problem for forecasting parity-movement yet devised, . . . is perfect for all situations, nor does there seem to be much hope that such will ever be achieved. This unfortunate circumstance is principally due to the fact that foreign exchange crises are somewhat like people in that seldom, if ever, are two exactly alike in every respect.[38]

Nonetheless, this same study concluded that "there is a certain group of phenomena of which one or more members always is a factor causing priority change." Although there is no *a priori* way of establishing which factor or factors will precipitate a parity change in a particular situation, the presence of one or more increases the probability of change. The list,[39] as stated in terms of signals of pressures toward a devaluation, follows. Contrary trends would tend to signal a revaluation.

1. Exchange market signals

    a. Increase in selling pressure in forward exchange. (A forward exchange rate, say a three-month rate, is the rate at which an exchange contract, a forward contract or futures, is negotiated for the sale and purchase of a given currency three months hence. Obviously, the actual rate may turn out to differ from the contracted rate. The advantage to the nonspeculating businessman foreseeing the need for buying or selling one currency for another is that he may thus stabilize the rate at which he will buy or sell the foreign currency, in other words

---

[37]Chun, "Foreign Exchange," p. 13.

[38]R. A. Pew, "Parity Movement Forecasting by Financial Managers," unpublished S.M. thesis, Sloan School of Management, M.I.T., June 1970, p. 86.

[39]Adapted from Pew, "Parity Movement," pp. 87–94.

"cover." The other party is betting that the actual rate, say, three months out, will be such that he can either sell the currency involved at a higher-than-spot rate, which refers to the rate prevailing at a particular time, or buy a currency at a lower rate, thereby making a profit. Thus, selling pressure on the forward exchange (when the forward rate for a currency falls in value relative to another currency) means that those dealing in exchange futures are expecting a change in the parity rate. To put it another way, "Whenever a currency is considered devaluation prone, there is a strong inducement for holders of goods and direct investors liable to be affected by a fall in prices of goods imported from the devaluing country or a fall in the converted [value of] investments in that country to hedge against possible losses by going short through forward sales of the currency to be devalued."[40] If there were no risk of devaluation, the discount or premium between a spot and forward rate would be simply the difference in the interest rates realizable in the two currencies.

b. Widening of margins between buy and sell quotations in both spot and forward transactions, which simply means that there is either a selling or buying pressure, that is, the market anticipates a shift in parity rate.

c. Widening of discrepancies between forward rates of exchange for various maturities.

d. Widening of profit margins on interest arbitrage. (Interest arbitrage refers to the movement of short-term funds between international centers as borrowers and lenders try to take advantage of differences in interest rates. If the profit margins widen, it means simply that those involved perceive a risk of parity shift and are trying to cover themselves by responding only to greater interest-rate differentials.)

e. Increase in the degree of official intervention in the exchange market (either buying or selling of a foreign currency by a central bank or exchange stabilization fund), especially indicated by a sudden arrest of a downward trend, and by continuing ability of the market to absorb a volume of exchange sales out of proportion to estimated government and commercial needs.

f. Increase in volume of transactions in the foreign exchange market, especially for weekends (when markets are closed) and other short dates, thereby demonstrating a general perception of higher risk of a parity rate change.

g. Inception of, or growth in, grey or black exchange markets. (A black market refers to illegal transactions; a grey market is illegal but is tolerated by a government even though aware of it.)

h. Depreciating tendency of the exchange rate, even without changes in the supply-demand relationship, leading to a one-way market.

i. General pessimism on the exchange market "grapevine."

j. Disequilibria between supply and demand, in respect to foreign exchange and

---

[40]Pew, "Parity Movement," p. 45. "Covering" insures against a devaluation risk on a self-liquidating transaction involving a definite amount and having a definite maturity date as in a normal purchase-and-sale agreement calling for payment of a specified amount at a specified time. Technically, "hedging" concerns nonliquidating transactions on which the risk is not of a definite amount, because the realizable value of the assets, and the effect of devaluation on their value, is uncertain.

a disinclination of the exchange rate to correct (that is, there are sellers or buyers of an exchange unable to satisfy their needs).

A phone call by the corporate financial manager to the foreign exchange department of his bank will quickly provide him with adequate information on all of these exchange market trends. The better financial newspapers such as the *Wall Street Journal, Japan Economic Journal,* and the *London Financial Times* provide enough trend warning to trigger a responsive manager to make the call.

2. National economic signals

   a. Weakening reserve position in gold and hard currencies.

   b. Introduction or tightening of trade or exchange controls.

   c. Export goods becoming less competitive in world markets because of price, technology, or taste changes.

   d. Decrease in exports or imports.

   e. Increasing or chronic balance-of-payments deficit (see Appendix 2 at the end of this chapter).

   f. Growing foreign debt or weakening ability to service foreign debt.[41]

   g. Reduced availability of foreign fund sources, especially signified by excessive interest rates on foreign borrowings.

   h. Increasing or chronic excessive government budgetary deficits.

   i. Increasing internal rate of price inflation.

   j. Disproportionate increase in volume of money in circulation or in volume of credit.

   k. Increasing occurrence of "figure fudging," indicated by discrepancies between statistics issued by different governmental agencies.

The financial manager will find the IMF monthly *International Financial Statistics* gives excellent information on all of the above except competitive position of exports (2.c.), interest rates on foreign borrowings (2.g.), and "figure fudging" (2.k.). The competitive position of exports is a condition, not a quantity, and can best be estimated from reading reports on trade in such publications as *Business International,* and the *London Financial Times,* as well as bank information services such as the FNCB Foreign Information Service, and the monthly Barclay's *Overseas Review.* "Figure fudging" is difficult and time consuming for a manager to identify, but the bank economists regularly track this down through their work with many governmental agency reports. An occasional telephone call to one or two of them will be quite adequate to keep the manager abreast of this phenomenon. Interest rates on new foreign borrowing are readily ascertained from

---

[41]"As a rule of thumb, DSR [debt-service ratio] in the 10–15 percent range is readily manageable; over 15 percent it represents a burden which is difficult to handle." Grayson, p. 8. It should be noted that many analysts overlook the level of suppliers' credits in calculating foreign debt. Normally these credits are unconsolidated and not included within officially tabulated foreign debt totals.

financial newspapers, banks, and special reports. Banks are also useful for current updates on most of the items in this national economics phenomena family.

3. Finance signals

   a. Rise in domestic interest rates relative to other countries, especially for short maturities.

   b. Reduction of foreign-owned domestic bank balances, thereby indicating a general anticipation of a devaluation.

   Both of these phenomena are covered in the monthly IMF *International Financial Statistics.* Current interest rates are also available from bankers and a host of publications, and banks are the most accessible sources of information on current changes in foreign-owned bank balances.

4. Political signals

   a. Decreasing political stability.

   b. National demoralization.

   These phenomena are conditions, not quantities, and are best gathered from personal contacts within the country in question, as well as from commentaries in published and broadcast media.

5. Production signals

   a. Increasing labor-capital disunity.

   b. Increasing wage demands and production costs.

   c. Increasing obsolescence and inefficiency of means of production.

   Other than deriving a general feel for these phenomena from reports and commentaries in the broadcast media and the press, a closer examination can be made through statistics developed by the U.S. Department of Commerce, by most foreign ministries of trade and labor, special country reports by banks, and, when noteworthy developments of trends occur, by services such as *Business International.*

   Labor-capital disunity is statistically measured by number of strikes and amount of man-hours of production lost. Production costs, including labor, are read directly from their statistics, and indirectly from product price-level statistics. Obsolescence is difficult to determine statistically except through measures of new capital investment, as is inefficiency except through higher costs.

6. Commercial signals

   a. Domestic importers and exporters respectively lengthen leads and lags on transactions denominated in foreign currencies, while foreign importers and exporters respectively shorten leads and lags on transactions determined in the domestic currency.

   b. Increased forward covering by foreigners of balances and receivables in the domestic currency, and increased hedging of their domestic currency investments.

One is hesitant even to include these commercial practice phenomena in the list, simply because they are so difficult to determine. However, they are so important and potent that even a little information about them goes a long way. The foreign exchange departments of the corporation's banks represent the most likely source of information in this area for the financial manager, outside of a review of his own company's receipts and disbursements on transactions with the country in question to spot any lead or lag tendencies.

7. International signals

    a. Adverse developments abroad which, by the domino principle, can affect the country in a variety of ways (for example, a change in the parity of the currency of an important trading partner).

    b. Adverse action by another country or other countries specifically directed at the country in question (such as trade sanctions).

The news media provide sufficient information on overt developments and actions of this nature, while banks and special services adequately cover the more subtle ones.

This list of signals of an impending change in a parity rate is fairly long, but the items on it can be monitored relatively easily for the most part, with a minimum set of information sources and an equally minimum expenditure of time. When one or more of these phenomena become apparent, it is important for the manager to determine whether they are dominating the system. He is then in a position to affix a probability of a parity change and to estimate its most likely magnitude, as well as the minimum and maximum magnitudes. The next step involves a calculation of company exposure.

Lietaer[42] developed a technique for specifying an optimal hedging strategy for a firm with a net exposure in devaluation-prone currencies; that is, currencies whose values are likely to fall relative to the currency of the investing firm, say, the U.S. dollar. Net exposure, Lietaer shows, is simply the difference between exposed assets and exposed liabilities, with exposure in each case being measured in terms of the effect of a devaluation on the dollar value, for example, on the asset or liability.

Exposed assets include accounts receivable, local currency bank deposits, and other current assets expressed in local currency. (The larger the exposed assets, the greater the devaluation loss, or the greater a negative exposure.) Exposed liabilities include local bank loans, accounts and notes payable in local currency, and local taxes payable. (The larger the exposed liabilities, the greater the devaluation gain, or the greater a positive exposure.)

---

[42]Bernard A. Lietaer, *Financial Management of Foreign Exchange: An Operational Technique to Reduce Risk* (Cambridge: M.I.T. Press, 1971). Summarized in "Managing Risks in Foreign Exchange," *Harvard Business Review*, March–April 1970, p. 127. A more complete version: "Financial Management of Devaluation Prone Currencies: An Operational Technique to Reduce Risk," unpublished S.M. thesis, Sloan School of Management,. M.I.T., 1969.

Inventories may be located any place between 100 percent positive and 100 percent negative exposure, thus

$$e = \frac{Y - X}{IW}$$

where

e = percentage of exposure of inventory
X = dollar replacement value decrease after a devaluation
Y = dollar market value decrease after a devaluation
I = book value of inventories
W = expected devaluation amount

If all inputs and outputs are imports and exports, respectively, there is no exposure; the dollar value remains unchanged (X and Y are both zero). Or, if all inputs and outputs are local and a government price freeze is equally effective or ineffective for both, exposure would likewise be zero; decrease in the dollar *replacement* value equals the decrease in the dollar *market* value (X = Y). If all inputs into inventories are local products, government price control is effective, and the output is sold abroad, the inventory would be 100 percent positively exposed, that is, abnormally high dollar profit margins are possible, and the sale of inventories after the devaluation would yield a much higher dollar profit than before devaluation. As Lietaer points out, "Obviously, only rarely will companies have inventories in any one of these extreme cases."[43] He then goes on to give an example of how to handle less extreme but more complex cases. In the situation posited in Table 6.7, it can be seen that inventories are exposed positively to the tune of 27.11 percent.

The situation is somewhat more complicated than this calculation indicates, in that the corporation is concerned with its *worldwide* net after-tax exposure in each currency, which is an algebraic sum of its exposed assets, corrected for taxes, everywhere. And since the advent of floating exchange rates, this problem is no longer subject to "back of the envelope" calculation. A few of the major international banks and a handful of consultants offer computer models that permit a company to evaluate its worldwide exposure in either accounting terms (translation exposure) or economic terms (transaction exposure). Normally, such a model requires indication of the most likely, the most optimistic, and most pessimistic forecasts in relation to currency evaluation or devaluation for each time period being evaluated. The model then indicates the expected loss or gain in each currency from the spot rates prevailing on a particular day. It may also quantify the riskiness of the exposures by indicating the

---

[43]Bernard A. Lietaer, *Financial Management of Foreign Exchange: An Operational Technique to Reduce Risk*, pp. 61–62.

Table 6.7
CALCULATING DEGREE OF INVENTORY EXPOSURES

Assumptions

1. The product is produced simultaneously for the local and export markets.
2. It has a content of imported raw materials, local raw materials, and local labor.
3. Expected devaluation of the local currency—say, the Brazilian cruzeiro—is 20 percent.
4. Export volume and price do not change after devaluation.
5. The government will succeed in freezing the price level of the product at 100 cruzeiros following devaluation.
6. The cruzeiro price of the local raw materials will increase by 5 percent.
7. After the devaluation, some (5 percent) of the imported raw materials will be replaced by cheaper local materials.
8. The average labor costs in cruzeiros will inflate by 10 percent after devaluation.
9. The book value of the inventories is the replacement value before the devaluation.

The calculation

	Before devaluation (100 Cr. = $1)				After devaluation (125 Cr. = $1)			
	Units	Price cr.	Per unit $	Total $ value	Units	Price cr.	Price $	Total $ value
Market value								
Export sales	2.0m	100	$1.0	$2.0	2.0m	125	$1.0	$2.0
Local sales	3.0m	100	1.0	3.0	3.0m	100	0.8	2.4
Total				$5.0				$4.4

$$Y = \$600,000$$

	Units	Price cr.	Per unit $	Total $ value	Units	Price cr.	Price $	Total $ value
Replacement value								
Imported raw materials	1.0	200	$2.0	$2.0	0.95	250	$2.0	$1.9
Local raw materials	0.5	200	2.0	1.0	0.55	210	1.68	0.924
Local labor (man-hours)	0.5	300	3.0	1.5	0.50	330	2.64	1.32
Total				$4.5				$4.144

$$X = \$356,000$$

$$e = \frac{Y - X}{ID} = \frac{600,000 - 356,000}{\$4,500,000 \times 20\%} = 27.11\%$$

Source: Bernard A. Lietaer, *Financial Management of Foreign Exchange: An Operational Technique to Reduce Risk* (Cambridge: M.I.T. Press, 1971), pp. 62–63. Reprinted with permission of the publisher.

maximum possible loss or gain that could be incurred at various confidence levels.[44]

Having determined the probability of a parity rate change (and of its amount) and the firm's net exposure, the final question is: What is the optimal

[44]One such model is described by Alan Teck, "International Business Under Floating Rates," *Columbia Journal of World Business*, vol. XI, no. 3, Fall 1976, pp. 68–70.

hedging policy? Lietaer describes the problem as "an attempt to find a combination of financing and hedging operations (that is, a hedging strategy) that minimizes expected costs and strategy risk and does not violate any of the operational restraints."[45] The latter includes operational requirements (such as financial requirements for each period of the planning horizon), policy decisions (such as the minimum balances of local bank loans that the firm must retain in order to keep lines of credit open, levels of various financial ratios), and legal constraints (examples: availability of swaps, forward exchange contracts, balance-sheet covenants for some loan agreements, foreign exchange controls). Strategy risk is evaluated "by a measure of dispersion of potential outcomes around the expected outcome" (variance).[46] There is no single optimal solution to the devaluation hedging problem, but, rather, an infinite strategy set from a point representing minimum risk to maximum risk, also a set from maximum cost to minimum cost. The two taken together generate an efficiency frontier. The optimum point depends upon the risk one wants to avoid (or assume) at what cost; the model makes the trade-offs explicit, but it does not determine objectively which is optimal, for that depends upon one's risk preference. Lietaer charts the data inputs required for a solution as in Figure 6.5.

Because of the diversity of strategy options in the financial area, many of which are not available or relevant in the purely domestic case, it is likely that one of the more important competitive advantages of the large firm operating internationally lies in its capacity to make more efficient use of its financial resources. A bit of indirect evidence supporting this assertion lies in a comparison of 103 wholly foreign-owned subsidiaries in the United Kingdom, with 12 quoted subsidiaries (those whose shares were listed in the London exchange) and with 1,235 British-owned public corporations.

Significantly, the quoted subsidiaries carried less debt than the wholly-owned group, especially short term debt, and their net worth was substantially larger. Also, they had on average a much larger proportion of cash and marketable securities (11.7 percent of total assets) than the wholly-owned subsidiaries (6.2 percent). Much of this can probably be attibuted to the fact they distributed relatively less of their earnings (48 percent from 1960 to 1967) than the wholly-owned group (57 percent) while their growth rate was lower and their profitability roughly the same. It seems likely that this performance in combination with a conservative dividend policy "imposed" by market conformity, led to their relatively high liquidity and low indebtedness. In other words, they had more cash than they knew what to do with. Such a situation would be much less likely to occur in a wholly-owned subsidiary where the parent company would generally increase repatriation of earnings for use elsewhere in the group if they were not needed locally.[47]

---

[45]Teck, "International Business," p. 8.

[46]Teck, "International Business," p. 9.

[47]Michael Z. Brooke and H. Lee Remmers, *The Strategy of Multinational Enterprise* (London: Longman, 1970), p. 266.

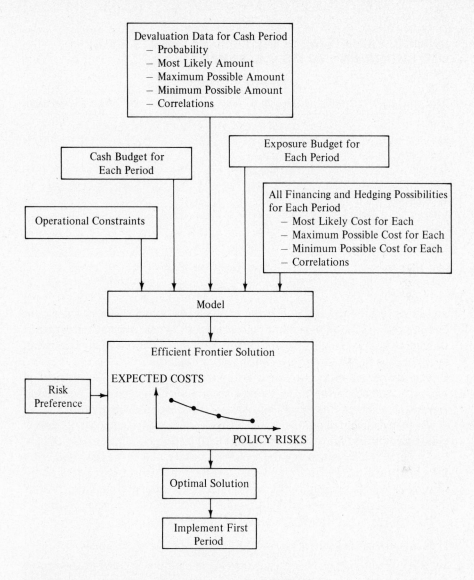

Figure 6.5
INPUTS AND OUTPUTS OF THE LIETAER MODEL

Source: Bernard A. Lietaer, *Financial Management of Foreign Exchange: An Operational Technique to Reduce Risk* (Cambridge: M.I.T. Press, 1971), p. 10. Reprinted with permission of the publisher.

Implicit in that statement is greater efficiency in the use of financial assets by those foreign firms exercising financial control.

Another study likewise points up that "wholly-owned subsidiaries do not have to worry about stock exchange consideration, or the opinions of the

Table 6.8
ANNUAL VARIATIONS IN DIVIDEND PAYMENTS BY A U.K. SUBSIDIARY TO ITS U.S. PARENT

| Year | Dividend payments (gross) | |
	Amount	Percentage of issued capital
1956	608,600	1,521.5
1957	747,800	131.2
1958–60	nil	0
1961	3,324,200	583.2
1962	1,399,400	245.5
1963	nil	0
1964	1,012,300	177.6
1965	nil	0
1966	3,596,100	630.9

Source: From Christopher Tugendhat, *The Multinationals* (New York: Random House, 1972), p. 133.

investment institution and public. Their dividends can be varied as the parent company thinks fit."[48] Not so in a public company, where normally great effort is made to follow a stable dividend policy. That the variations in dividends can be enormous in the former case is shown in Table 6.8.

The greater efficiency implied here is only realizable if management is sensitive to the benefits to be derived from a sophisticated and continuing analysis of where profits should be taken, of the most productive profit routes, of where investment decisions should be made, of the range and cost of various types and sources of financing, of the best legal instrumentalities to use, of how to minimize risk by enhancing the security of assets, and of the risks and costs associated with maintaining the value of assets in a world characterized by shifting exchange rates and differential rates of inflation and deflation. All of these considerations push in the direction of centralized financial control.

Indeed, the arguments for centralized control are strong.

1. Local executives can rarely know the liquidity position of the group.

2. They cannot analyze the exchange exposure of the group in either its component parts or as a consolidated entity.

3. The central financial office, no matter what shape it takes, draws on information from a wide number of financial institutions and can formulate a broader decision on the probable nature of financial events and protection against them.[49]

But, as this same author goes on to observe, "Centralized control must be

---

[48]Christopher Tugendhat, *The Multinationals* (New York: Random House, 1972), p. 133.

[49]Andreas Prindl, "International Money Management, the Environmental Framework," *Euromoney*, September 1971, p. 14.

weighted against the lack of whole-hearted support for rationalizing systems experienced by a number of companies when local management feels its sphere of influence is limited or its achievement down-graded."[50] More will be said on this subject in the chapter on control.

Robbins and Stobaugh[51] found that, the above comment to the contrary notwithstanding, corporations went through at least three phases in respect to centralization of financial management. Their research revealed responsibility to be very decentralized in companies relatively new to international business, but a strong tendency to centralize this function as the corporation gained experience, which is as one would expect. But they also reported a tendency for corporations to *decentralize* again as their operations grew so complex that the volume of financial transactions made it impossible for headquarters to render decisions on each transaction. At this stage, companies tended to develop guidelines within which local decisions were made, reserving only the exceptional decisions for headquarters, plus an overall monitoring function.

Discussion questions

1. When might a firm opt for profit centers based on function? On product line? On enterprise? On geographical area?

2. Why should governments agree to limit export credit generally to five years?

3. What is a Eurodollar? How are they generated and extinguished?

4. What are blocked funds? Why should they be considered as a sunk cost?

5. Under what circumstances would it be best to borrow in one country for use in another?

6. What is unadmitted insurance?

7. What are the arguments for and against a national system of foreign investment guarantees?

8. From the point of view of the ordinary international businessman, what sort of foreign exchange-rate policy is most desirable (fixed, floating, transitional floating, crawling peg, narrow, or wide band)?

9. How would you set up a monitoring system to establish probabilities for the devaluation of the Brazilian cruzeiro?

10. To what extent should a firm operating internationally centralize financial control?

11. According to the data in Table 6.9, why might the British government be concerned about these variations in dividend payments to the parent?

[50]Prindl, "International Money," p. 14.

[51]Sidney M. Robbins and Robert B. Stobaugh, *Money in the Multinational Enterprise* (New York: Basic Books, 1973).

Assignment

Select a country and assess the likelihood of a significant change in the exchange rate between its currency and the dollar within the next six months.

Recommended references

Aggarwal, Raj. *Financial Policies for the Multinational Company, the Management of Foreign Exchange*. New York: Praeger, 1976.

Baker, James C., and Thomas H. Bates. *Financing International Business Operations*. Scranton: Intext Educational Publishers, 1971.

Carlson, Sune. *International Financial Decisions*. Amsterdam: North-Holland Publishing Company, 1969.

Delaume, George R. *Legal Aspects of International Lending and Economic Development Financing*. Dobbs Ferry: Oceana Publications, 1967.

Dufey, Gunter, and Judith J. Field. *Financial Management in the International Corporation*. Ann Arbor: Institute for International Commerce, Graduate School of Business Administration, University of Michigan, 1971.

Eiteman, David K., and Arthur I. Stonehill. *International Business Finance*. Reading, Mass.: Addison-Wesley, 1973.

Enzig, Paul. *A Textbook on Foreign Exchange*. New York: St. Martin's Press, 1966.

Fatouros, A. A. *Government Guarantees to Foreign Investors*. New York: Columbia University Press, 1962.

Ferris, Paul. *The Money Men of Europe*. New York: Crowell-Collier and Macmillian, 1968.

Katz, Samuel I. "Exchange-Risk Under Fixed and Flexible Exchange Rates." *The Bulletin*, New York University Institute of Finance, nos. 83–84, June 1972.

Krefetz, Gerald, and Ruth Marossi. *Investing Abroad, A Guide to Financial Europe*. New York: Harper & Row, 1965.

Lietaer, Bernard A. *Financial Management of Foreign Exchange*. Cambridge: M.I.T. Press, 1971.

Meister, Irene W. *Managing the International Financial Function*. New York: The Conference Board, 1970.

Multinational Fiscal Incentives. Princeton: International Council for Fiscal Research, Inc., 1971.

Nehrt, Lee C., ed. *International Finance for Multinational Business*. Scranton: International Textbook Company, 1967.

Reimann, G., and Edwin F. Wigglesworth, eds. *The Challenge of International Finance*. New York: McGraw-Hill, 1966.

Rodriguez, Rita M., and E. Eugene Carter. *International Financial Management*. Englewood Cliffs: Prentice-Hall, 1976.

Wasserman, Max J., Andreas R. Prindle, Charles C. Townsend, Jr. *International Money Management*. New York: American Management Association, 1972.

Whitman, Martin van Heumann. *Government Risk-Sharing in Foreign Investment*. Princeton: Princeton University Press, 1965.

Zenoff, David B., and Jack Zwick, eds. *International Financial Management*. Englewood Cliffs: Prentice-Hall, 1969.

Appendix 1 to Chapter 6
BALANCE OF PAYMENTS AND THE INTERNATIONAL MONETARY SYSTEM

The International Monetary Fund (IMF) defines a country's balance of payments (B/P) as "a systematic record of the economic transactions during a given period between its residents and residents of the rest of the world."[52] Authoritative statements to the contrary notwithstanding, a B/P is not a *complete* accounting of all transfers of real resources and financial assets. Of the latter, perhaps; of the former, no. For example, technology or skills may be exported on the basis of a long-term contract or as a capital contribution to a foreign enterprise. But the capitalized value of that technology or skill is not recorded in the B/P. Also, capital flowing out of a country is recorded as a negative item on the B/P's accounts, but the continued ownership of the assets thus transferred, represented by shares of stock or corporate bonds, is not recorded as an asset or as a plus item. Thus, the many billions of dollars worth of United States foreign investment ($133 billion in book value at year end 1975) represented by shares of stock or corporate bonds in the hands of U.S. residents (that is, claims on assets located abroad) are not considered as part of U.S. international reserves. Yet it is possible, as in wartime Britain, that private owners of these securities could be forced to sell out and surrender the proceeds to the U.S. government. Ultimately, in the U.S. case, these foreign obligations do constitute support for the value of the U.S. dollar, which is backed ultimately by the total reservoir of goods and services and financial assets owned worldwide by the residents and public agencies of the United States.

It should also be noted that foreign borrowing by foreign subsidiaries of a nation's firms, even though guaranteed implicitly or explicitly by the parent firm, does not directly affect the B/P. Yet, unless a firm is willing to permit a foreign subsidiary to default on such obligations, this foreign borrowing does represent a potential outflow (hence, a potential negative impact on the nation's B/P) but no reserve fund to cover this possible flow is recorded.

Indeed, from some points of view the B/P appears essentially as a record of the annual cash flow (movement of liquid assets and liabilities) of a country and its residents in respect to the rest of the world, which must be equivalent to an increase or decrease of a nation's international monetary reserves. The B/P provides a measure of a nation's external liquidity.

Some have suggested that a more complete statement of the strength of a nation's currency would be of the balance statement type. In the U.S. case, for example, it would consist of (1) the value of U.S. foreign assets (direct and

---

[52]International Monetary Fund, *Balance of Payments Concepts and Definitions* (Washington, D.C.: Pamphlet Series No. 10, 1968), p. 4.

Table 6.9
U.S. RATIOS OF VARIOUS ASSETS AND LIABILITIES

	1960	1965	1970	1971	1972	1973	1974	1975
Long-term assets/liquid and short-term liabilities	2.70	3.00	2.85	2.24	2.06	2.13	1.85	1.96
Long-term liabilities to other than official agencies/total liabilities to foreigners	.47	.48	.48	.42	.41	.38	.31	.34
Long-term assets/total assets abroad	.68	.76	.81	.82	.81	.79	.74	.74
Direct investment abroad/total assets	.37	.41	.47	.46	.45	.46	.45	.44
Foreign securities*/total assets	.11	.13	.12	.13	.14	.12	.11	.12
Private long-term claims reported by banks/total assets abroad	.02	.04	.02	.02	.03	.03	.03	.03
Private long-term claims reported by nonbanking concerns/total assets	.02	.02	.02	.02	.02	.02	.02	.02
U.S. government assets abroad other than official reserves/total assets abroad	.20	.19	.19	.19	.18	.17	.14	.14
U.S. government assets, including official reserves/total assets abroad	.43	.32	.30	.27	.25	.24	.20	.19

*U.S. portfolio abroad; i.e., investments in enterprises in which the investor owns less than 10 percent of the total.

Source: Compiled from statistics published in the *Survey of Current Business*.

portfolio investment, short-term claims, private and official), less the value of comparable foreign assets in the United States, plus U.S. official reserve assets (gold, IMF drawing rights, foreign currencies). On this basis it can be shown that the net international investment position of the United States has increased on an average of $3.25 billion a year, which means an aggregate increase of 109 percent from 1960 through 1975 and of 35 percent since 1970.

However, the composition of U.S. assets and liabilities vis-à-vis the rest of the world is quite different, and the disparity has been growing. On the asset side, long-term private assets ($183.8 billion at year-end 1975, largely direct foreign investment, $133.2 billion) and U.S. government credits ($40 billion) accounted for roughly 75 percent of the total. On the liability side, private liquid and short-term claims on the United States ($52.8 billion) plus liabilities to foreign official accounts ($87.0 billion, largely liquid) constituted nearly 66 percent of the total. The largest amount of private foreign investment in the United States is in the form of portfolio holdings of U.S. corporate stocks, with an estimated market value of $36.5 billion at the end of 1975 (as contrasted with *direct* investment in the United States by foreigners of $26.7 billion). It would appear that the United States has been exchanging long-term assets for liquid and short term liabilities. The ratio declined from 3.00 in 1965 to 1.85 in 1974, but moved up slightly in 1975 to 1.96. (See Table 6.9.) It has been this declining U.S. liquidity that for some years was of greatest concern. But since 1972–73 through 1975, the indicators of U.S. liquidity have either stabilized or improved slightly (see Table 6.10).

Table 6.10

U.S. LIQUIDITY RATIOS: OUTSTANDING U.S. ASSETS ABROAD TO LIABILITIES TO FOREIGNERS, BY DEGREE OF LIQUIDITY

	1960	1965	1970	1971	1972	1973	1974	1975
Reserves/liabilities to foreign official agencies	1.63	.93	.59	.23	.21	.21	.20	.19
Liquid assets*/liabilities to foreign official agencies	1.87	1.12	.70	.28	.24	.24	.22	.21
Reserves/liquid liabilities to private foreigners† and all liabilities to foreign official agencies	.92	.52	.31	.23	.21	.21	.19	.19
Liquid assets/liquid liabilities to private foreigners† and all liabilities to foreign official agencies	1.05	.64	.39	.27	.24	.24	.23	.21
Liquid and short-term assets/liquid and short-term liabilities	1.25	.95	.68	.51	.48	.55	.65	.71
Liquid and short-term assets/liquid and short-term liabilities to private foreigners and all liabilities to foreign official agencies	.81	.62	.45	.28	.27	.30	.37	.40
Liquid and short-term assets and foreign securities‡/liquid and short-term liabilities and U.S. securities§	.84	.71	.53	.37	.36	.39	.46	.49
Long-term assets/long-term liabilities other than to official foreign agencies	3.18	3.48	3.01	2.97	2.48	2.63	3.03	2.88
Total assets/total liabilities	2.09	2.05	1.70	1.45	1.33	1.37	1.41	1.44

*Reserves plus foreign currencies and other short-term assets held by the government. Liquid claims held by banks and private nonbanking institutions are not reported separately.

†Not reported separately after 1971.

‡Portfolio investment abroad; i.e., investments in enterprises in which the investor owns less than 10 percent.

§Portfolio investment in the United States; i.e., investments in enterprises in which the investor owns less than 25 percent.

Source: Compiled from statistics published in the *Survey of Current Business,* vol. 52, no. 10, October 1972, p. 21, and vol. 56, no. 8, August 1976, p. 32. A shift in accounting categories between 1972 and 1973 makes exactly comparable calculations difficult.

A simple way of analyzing the impact of a given flow on the balance of payments is to determine the direction of the flow of cash involved. If the net flow is inward, the effect is positive; if the net flow is outward, negative. Obviously, the cash rarely flows physically; one must think in terms of the ownership (in terms of residence) of bank accounts or short-term claims—less than one year—on foreign economies or on the United States. Typical claims are commercial paper or bills for goods or services sold or letters of credit. The last refers to a bank commitment to pay an exporter upon the receipt of certain documents. The commitment rests upon the guarantee of a foreign bank in which the buyer has deposited the requisite amount of money, either an actual cash deposit or through line of credit. Commercial bills may, of course, either be sold (factored) or discounted at a bank so that the exporter may receive payment before the foreign buyer is obligated to make it.

The B/P includes several balances or imbalances. The *visible trade balance* refers to the net trade (export and import) of commodities; the *invisible trade balance*, to that of intangibles (such as tourist expenditures and receipts, fees, royalties, interest, dividends, insurance, port charges, freight). The two together represent the *current trade balance*. In addition, there are unilateral transfers (official economic assistance, military assistance, private remittances). The *capital account* includes loans and repayments, medium- and long-term investment.[53]

In United States B/P accounting, the private purchase of short-term foreign assets (for example, the discounting of commercial bills) is recorded as a negative item in that the U.S. government cannot call upon these commercial bills to meet obligations. In that the United States has played the role of a world banker because of the use of dollars as an international *transactions currency* (that is, two non-U.S. parties to a transaction often denominate their transaction in dollars) and as a *reserve currency* (because central banks have held dollars as part of their monetary reserves), it is important that the liquid position of the United States be such as to stabilize the value of the dollar. Therefore, included in the so-called above-the-line transactions are only those flows that add to or reduce the liquid assets available to the U.S. government (without recourse to the forced surrender of private assets) with which to meet the claims of its creditors, that is, foreigners owning dollars or dollar claims who may wish to swap them for gold or their own national currencies.

The balancing (or below-the-line) items, which are really a completely arbitrary notion, in a nation's balance of payments include the sale or purchase of monetary reserve assets (gold, convertible currencies, IMF drawing rights),[54] and an increase or decrease in the alien ownership of U.S. bank accounts and other liquid assets (that is, short-term claims). In the U.S. case, an increase in alien owned liquid assets includes the purchase by foreigners of most U.S. government securities, which means that a switch by foreigners from U.S. corporate bonds (the sale of which back to U.S. residents results in a cash outflow, hence contributing to a B/P deficit) to U.S. treasury bonds increases

---

[53]Medium-term is generally defined as one- to three-year commitment; long-term as anything in excess of that period or of indefinite maturity, as portfolio or direct investment. Direct investment refers to an investment made in order to participate in the management of an enterprise (for purposes of U.S. statistics, an investment equaling 10 percent or more of the equity of an enterprise or a foreign investment in the United States equaling 25 percent or more of the equity of a firm); portfolio, to other investment of long-term or indeterminate maturity.

[54]Refers to the right of a government to borrow foreign currency from the International Monetary Fund, the limit being related to the gold and the national currency deposited with the IMF. The IMF drawing rights include the special drawing rights (SDR). These SDRs, which are valued in terms of a basket of currencies (a weighted average of the market U.S. dollar value of 16 currencies), earn interest, are allocated to participating countries in proportion to their IMF quotas, and are subject to certain limits set periodically. Participating countries must accept them as legal tender in settling international accounts. Unlike the regular drawing rights, a country may utilize its SDRs when it has a B/P or a reserve need without prior consultation with the IMF and without commiting itself to either internal reform measures or a repayment schedule.

the U.S. deficit (that is, from "above the line" to "below the line") even though the purchase of the latter means a cash inflow. Other countries, however, show the switch as simply from one long-term investment to another, which means that both would appear above the line and would cancel one another. The United States has felt compelled to this practice because of its banking role; it must be in a position to refund the bonds whenever submitted in order to maintain confidence, and, hence, maintain the stability of the dollar. Finally, one comes down to errors and omissions to make the accounting balance.

In fact, the line between the current flows and the balancing flows can be drawn differently. Some options as defined by the U.S. Department of Commerce are (see also Table 6.11):

Current account balance. **The balance on goods, services, and unilateral transfers (both government and private). It measures the extent to which a country is currently earning the foreign exchange needs to carry out its international lending and investment expenditures.**

Basic balance. **The balance on current and long-term capital accounts. It measures a country's net position on current account plus nonliquid or nonvolatile capital transaction. It treats changes in private liquid assets and liabilities as financing items. This implies that all current transactions and long-term capital movements are placed above the line; all short-term capital movements, errors and omissions, and movement of gold and international monetary reserves below the line. The problem with this measure is that it rests on the assumption that short-term capital movements will fluctuate frequently and leave, over the long-run, only a small plus or minus balance. In fact, short-term capital movement is often linked directly to direct investment, current transactions, and to transactions in long-term securities. Also, since the major currencies became convertible in 1958, the fluctuation of short-term capital movements has generated a substantial negative or positive balance in the B/Ps of several major countries. The basic balance alone is not an adequate indicator of the international financial well-being of such countries.**

Liquidity balance. **Changes in official reserve assets and in liquid liabilities vis-à-vis all nonresidents. Although a broad indicator of potential pressure on a currency, it is distorted by shifts of funds held by official agencies between liquid and nonliquid categories which represent no real change in the underlying position. It should be noted that liquid liabilities comprise foreign-owned U.S. bank accounts, marketable U.S. government securities of all maturities, medium-term convertible nonmarketable government securities, short-term private money market assets. Thus, any movement of private foreign funds into U.S. bank deposits, commercial paper, or treasury bills is treated as a settlement item and not as a regular capital inflow improving the balance. In fact, such an inflow increases liquid liabilities to foreigners.**

Official balance. **Changes in official reserve assets, plus changes in liquid and certain nonliquid liabilities (for example, U.S. government securities), in the hands of foreign official agencies. A measure of the immediate market pressure on a currency. Distort-**

Table 6.11
GROUPING OF U.S. INTERNATIONAL TRANSACTIONS UNDER FIVE BALANCE-OF-PAYMENTS CONCEPTS

1	2	3	4	5
Current account balance	**Basic balance**	**Liquidity balance**	**Official balance**	**Underlying balance**
Goods and services	Goods and services	Goods and services	Goods and services	Goods and services
Remittances and pensions	Remittances and pensions	Remittances and pensions	Remittances and pensions	Remittances and pensions
U.S. government grants and capital movements	U.S. government grants and capital movements	U.S. government grants and capital movements	U.S. government grants and capital movements	U.S. government grants and capital movements
Balance on C/A	Private long-term capital, U.S. and foreign (except foreign holdings of U.S. government bonds and notes)	Private long-term capital, U.S. and foreign (except foreign holdings of U.S. government bonds and notes)	Private long-term capital, U.S. and foreign (except U.S. government bonds and notes held by foreign official monetary institutions)	Long-term capital, U.S. and foreign (except U.S. government bonds and notes held by foreign monetary institutions)
Private long-term capital, U.S. and foreign		U.S. private short-term capital	Private short-term capital, U.S. and foreign	Short-term capital, U.S. and foreign (except U.S. government notes held by foreign monetary institutions)
Private short-term capital, U.S. and foreign		Foreign commercial credits	Errors and omissions	Errors and omissions
Errors and omissions		Errors and omissions	Foreign official short-term capital (except that of official monetary institutions)	**Underlying balance**
Foreign official short-term and long-term capital	**Balance on basic transactions**	**Balance on liquidity basis**	**Balance on official reserve transactions**	Foreign monetary institutional holdings of short and long-term capital
U.S. gold, convertible currency reserves, IMF position	Private short-term capital, U.S. and foreign	Foreign private short-term capital (except commercial credits)	Foreign official monetary institutions' holdings of U.S. government bonds and notes	U.S. gold, convertible currency reserves, IMF position
	Errors and omissions	Foreign holdings of U.S. government bonds and notes	Foreign official monetary institutions' short-term capital	
	Foreign holdings of U.S. government bonds and notes	Foreign official short-term capital	U.S. gold and convertible currency reserves and IMF position	
	Foreign official short-term capital	U.S. gold and convertible currency reserves and IMF position		
	U.S. gold and convertible currency reserves and IMF position			

Note: In each case, the sum of the items above the line equals the sum of the items below the line, with the opposite sign.

Source: Adapted from Review Committee for Balance of Payments Statistics, *The Balance of Payments Statistics of the United States.*

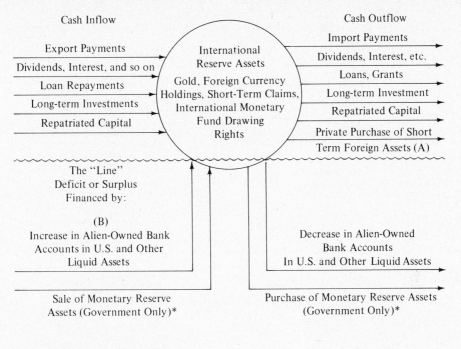

Figure 6.6
BALANCE OF PAYMENTS

*Gold, convertible currencies, IMF drawing rights (including SDRs). (1) The United States cannot call on them to meet obligations; hence, it is an "above-the-line" item. Other countries do not show this item as an inflow from the United States for it does not decrease their B/P deficit; that is, inflow of proceeds equals increase in short-term obligations. (2) Includes most U.S. government securities. A switch by foreigners from U.S. corporate bonds to U.S. Treasury bonds increases the U.S. deficit (that is, from "above the line" to "below the line"). Other countries show an outflow contributing to their B/P deficit (that is, "above the line") in both cases.

ed by some special financial transactions. Note that changes in *private* foreign liquid dollar assets are included above the line, not as a means of settling the balance.

Underlying balance. Changes in official reserve assets, less flows of short-term capital that can distort the underlying balance. A refinement of the official balance.

A useful way of analyzing significant trends in a nation's B/P is to follow one or more key ratios. The series developed by the U.S. Department of Commerce are detailed in Tables 6.8 and 6.9.

Many factors, external and internal, influence a nation's balance of payments in the sense of affecting the flows shown in Figure 6.6. A partial statement of the more important factors involved, and the interrelationships among them, is diagrammed in Figure 6.7. Bear in mind that if the pressures shown here have a persistent net *negative* effect on the flows determining a nation's balance of payments, they would force a devaluation of a nation's monetary unit; if positive, to a revaluation.

Some reasons the system cannot be quantified are as follows:

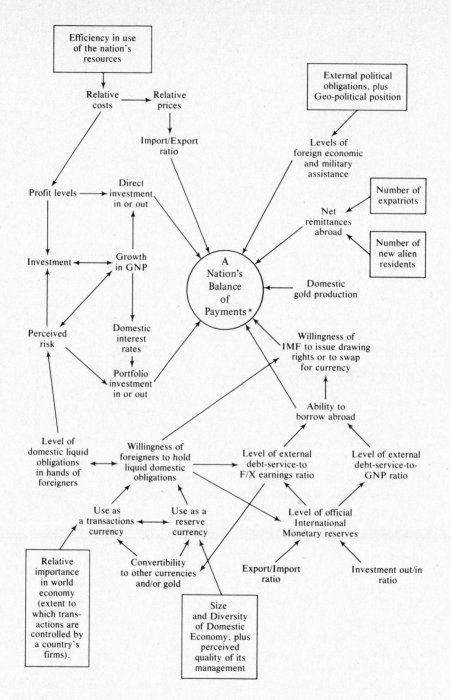

Figure 6.7
INTERRELATIONSHIP AMONG SOME FACTORS IMPACTING ON A NATION'S BALANCE OF PAYMENTS

1. The greater sensitivity of responses to perceived rates of *future* change of many variables than to present rates of change.

2. Differences in judgment as to the levels the system will tolerate before the foreign exchange rate will, in fact, change (or be changed).

3. Differences in perception of risk.

4. Differences in perception of investment opportunities.

5. Differences in political intervention (in terms of changes in interest rates, tax levels, international trade and investment incentives and impediments, and general pressures toward misallocation of domestic resources).

6. Differences in external political responses (as reflected in the same factors as five above, plus the availability of foreign credit).

7. The unpredictability of the willingness of governments to accumulate a reserve currency and to intervene in money markets so as to hold the foreign exchange rate within a specific band around parity.

8. The unpredictability of the willingness of traders to accept obligations denominated in a given currency.

The system will be kept in financial equilibrium by a system of freely floating exchange rates. The problem is that governments have been reluctant to give up control over exchange rates in that changes in the rates can produce such politically unpalatable effects as changes in domestic employment, price, and income levels, as well as change in the structure of industry as a nation's economy is forced to integrate internationally (that is, concentrate in those sectors in which the nation enjoys some comparative advantage in factor prices or an absolute advantage by reason of some geographic or climatic or topographical feature). In the process, many people may be hurt badly.

Consider what can happen in a freely floating system. If a rate falls (that is, a foreign currency unit buys more local currency), both exports and inward-bound foreign investment increase. For the former, prices in the foreign market are now relatively lower; for the latter, more can be bought for less. Both add to domestic liquidity in the first round, and are inflationary. But a government, for domestic political reasons, may be trying to stabilize prices. Or, consider the reverse case, when a rate increases because of the devaluation of

---

*Boxes indicate environmental "givens."

Note: Efficiency in the use of a nation's resources refers to its capacity to integrate the domestic economy with the international as based on comparative advantage in international trade. For example, a negative pressure on the B/P is generated any time a nation expends real resources on nonproductive activity (for example, on the military beyond a certain level) or on noncompetitive activity (such as producing goods and services that are cheaper to import because comparative advantage in factor prices lies abroad). Typically pressures producing low efficiency in resource utilization are demand for economic autarky, high sustained military expenditures, crop subsidies, wages increasing faster than productivity, wage controls, administered prices and interest rates, growth of monetary assets more rapid than growth in economic goods and services, above-average import quotas and protective tariffs (and nontariff barriers).

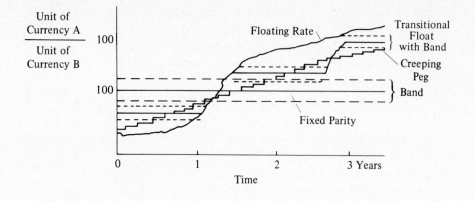

Figure 6.8
POSSIBLE PROFILE OF CHANGES IN EFFECTIVE EXCHANGE RATE BETWEEN CURRENCY A AND CURRENCY B UNDER ALTERNATIVE POLICIES

another currency due to inflation in that country. Now the prices of imported goods fall and a foreign currency unit buys less local currency. Both imports and outward-bound investment increase, and both reduce domestic liquidity and are deflationary until a new balance is struck. But a government, for purely domestic political reasons, may be trying to adhere to a policy of full employment. For such reasons most governments are restless with a truly floating exchange rate system and find some intervention compelling. Those countries in which an unusually large part of their respective GNPs is derived from international trade and investment are particularly vulnerable to a completely flexible rate system. The problem in their case is that the impact of a change of rate is immediate and massive.

One alternative to the floating rate is the "crawling peg" (sometimes called the sliding or gliding parity), which would permit nations to revalue or devalue their currencies by small amounts, say 1 or 2 percent a year, but done at weekly or monthly intervals. A second alternative is the "transitional float," which envisions a periodic floating of major currencies so as to permit them to reestablish market values and then be pegged at that new level. Some have proposed that the width of the "band" around parity be increased. This means that governments would desist from intervening over a broader band (that is, from selling foreign exchange reserves until the price of the foreign currency in terms of the local currency reached a certain upper level, or from buying foreign currency until its value in terms of domestic currency fell to a given lower level). See Figure 6.8 for a graphic presentation of these various schemes.

The so-called Bretton Woods system initiated in 1944 consisted essentially of four elements: (1) a structure of fixed exchange (parity) rates, (2) the use of gold as the measure of monetary value, (3) defense of the parity rates through official intervention if a rate approached the upper or lower limit of the approved "band"[55] (the modern equivalent of the old gold points), and (4) the establishment of the International Monetary Fund as a device for providing temporary credit while adjustment was achieved through domestic fiscal and monetary policies, and as a mechanism for changing the par values in event of a "fundamental disequilibrium."

Inherent in the system were several conflicts. First, there was possible conflict between domestic national policy objectives and those policies possibly necessary to correct an international disequilibrium (such as a politically dictated policy of full employment versus the need to deflate in order to achieve international monetary equilibrium). Second, the system provided an incentive to build up a B/P surplus with which to finance future development (a neomercantilism), in which case the deficit countries found it hard to respond effectively to the continued imbalances. Third, as the flows of international trade and investment increased, there was no guarantee as to the adequacy of world reserves with which to service those flows (the reason leading to the creation of special drawing rights). Finally, fairly rapid changes in parity rates were required as nations experienced differential growth and inflation rates, and as reserves were pulled down as a percentage of trade and investment flows.

Subsequent to Bretton Woods, specifically, since 1950, a persistent United States B/P deficit brought about an erosion in foreigners' confidence in the dollar and a consequent run down of U.S. monetary reserves as foreign-held dollars were exchanged either for U.S. gold or foreign exchange. To avoid a devaluation of the dollar, which many believe would have had far-flung consequences by reason of its wide use as both a reserve and transaction currency by non-Americans, various devices were used and facilities were developed so as to enable the United States to borrow foreign currencies from foreign central banks and to lend dollars to them on a short-term basis (the financial swap) so as to avoid "unjustified" speculative pressures on the dollar. The United States also issued long-term bonds denominated in foreign currencies, and persuaded foreign central banks to accept more uncovered dollars. (The network of cooperating central banks included those of 14 countries, plus the Bank of International Settlements.) In 1969, the special drawing rights (SDR) system was created, thereby permitting the U.S. government to swap its long-term obligations for SDRs, which foreign governments were obligated to accept. Eventually (1971), several currencies were floated against the dollar, and, after a few months, new parity rates established, and the band expanded.

It was the so-called Smithsonian Agreement of December 1971 that

---

[55]Initially, the IMF approved band was $\pm$ 1 percent of parity.

changed the International Monetary Fund rules so as to permit a $\pm$ 2¼ percent band around parity (or 4½ percent in width). Some had proposed $\pm$ 5 percent, or even $\pm$ 10 percent. Such a scheme, it was widely believed, would have permitted the market to work out temporary imbalances more easily. A combination of a broad band with transitional floats was another possibility. Such a scheme would have permitted short-term adjustment through the market as well as periodic long-term adjustment. One thing was clear: with 130-odd nations all exercising sovereignty in terms of fiscal and monetary policy and all registering different rates of change in the productivities of their economies, no system of *fixed* parity rates could remain viable forever; sooner or later intolerable strains would be placed upon the international monetary system, as in 1971–72, which forced a devaluation of the dollar in terms of major currencies (and, incidentally, an increase in the dollar price of gold).

Coincidentally, on April 24, 1972, the six initial members of the EEC agreed to a band of $\pm$ 1⅛ percent. Britain and Denmark, in anticipation of EEC membership, joined the experiment on May 1 and Norway on May 23. This band became known as the "snake within the tunnel," the tunnel being the IMF band and the snake, the narrower EEC band. Intervention action typically involved both the central bank whose currency had the highest value and the bank whose currency had the lowest value. The central bank with the highest-quoted currency purchased the weakest currency with its own currency, and the central bank with the lowest-quoted currency acted similarly. The latter absorbed its own currency from the marketplace by paying out the strongest currency held by it. This was accomplished by drawing on interbank "swap" lines. The extension of credit by one bank to another of unlimited duration was not contemplated, however, since "debtor" countries were expected to settle up after two months at the latest. In settling, debtors had to use their various reserve assets, gold, dollars, SDRs, in a ratio corresponding to the composition of their total reserves. They also use established EEC short- or medium-term credit facilities within agreed limits. Some felt that these moves were a prelude to full monetary unification within the EEC, but such was not to be, at least for the time being.

The Smithsonian Agreement notwithstanding, by January 1973 three countries had floated their currencies—Canada, the United Kingdom, and Switzerland. In addition, three others had introduced a two-tier system (France, Belgium, and Italy), which meant a fixed rate for commercial transactions, a floating rate for financial transactions. And in February 1973 there was a further 10 percent devaluation of the dollar in terms of SDRs and gold. Thereupon, the Japanese yen and Italian lira were floated. Contrary to the Smithsonian agreement, there was no agreed-upon realignment of currencies and no new central rates within the trading margin of $\pm$ 2.25 percent. Another deviation lay in the fact that there was no overall international agreement. A fragmented situation emerged. In March 1973, the six EEC members declared a joint floating ($\pm$ 2¼ percent) of their currencies against the dollar. Since that time, all currencies have been floating against one another (except those pegged to another currency), subject to varying degrees of governmental intervention, which refers to the official buying and selling of domestic currencies against foreign currencies to restrain variations in the exchange rates. Although the IMF now recognized the legitimacy of floating rates, it does impose on each member the responsibility for not manipulating exchange rates or the international monetary system in order to prevent effective balance of payments adjustments or to gain an unfair competitive advantage over other members. The fund does have the standby authority, through a majority of the total voting power of its members, to reintroduce a system based on stable but adjustable par values, in which situation each member would be required to establish a par value unless it intends to apply other arrangements. In any event, the bands surrounding such par values would be broader than before, and the fund would have the authority to change them. Finally, a member retains the right to abandon a par value without immediately establishing another unless the fund decides otherwise by a majority of its voting power.

Because of the relatively inelastic supply of gold and the pressure for its use commercially,[56] increase in gold supply constantly fell short during the 1960s of the added funds needed for international transactions and reserves. Even the massive balance-of-payments deficit registered by the United States during the decade did not push sufficient dollars into the international monetary system. In any event, as the dollars held by nonresidents increased in proportion to U.S. gold and foreign exchange reserves, the foreign holders of dollars, whether private traders or central banks, became increasingly nervous about hanging on to them. Central banks had the right to sell dollars back to the United States for gold until August 15, 1971, although not private traders. The private traders uneasy about their dollar balances used them to buy either local currency or other foreign currencies in which they had more confidence. In either event, if the relevant central banks intervened to hold the exchange rate within the band, they ended up with surplus dollars, thereby adding to their reserves and adding to local inflationary pressures in that local currency had been issued to buy the dollars. It became obvious in the mid-1960s that the international monetary system could not be based on ever larger U.S. balance-of-payments deficits.

Hence, in 1969, the special drawing right (SDR) was devised, the first international reserve asset created by decision of the international community. In the three years, 1970–72, the International Monetary Fund allocated a total

---

[56]Eighty percent of the world's supply is mined in the Union of South Africa, 80 percent of which is sold through the Zurich Gold Pool (an organization of Zurich's three largest banks) and 20 percent in London. Under international agreement, South Africa sells sufficient gold to pay for its imports and to assure an orderly market. Under the "two-tier" gold pricing system, central banks exchange gold with one another at a fixed official price and commercial buyers and sellers at a price determined by the market. Industrial use consumes about 50 percent of the gold available commercially. About a quarter of the gold sold in Zurich is said to be taken by Middle Eastern banks that have relations with those who organize gold smuggling into India.

of SDR 9.3 billion ($9.5 billion) to participating countries, which amount had not been increased as of mid-1977. The SDRs are essentially a paper money created by the IMF and allocated to members in accord to agreement among them. They may be used only for intergovernmental transactions and between the IMF and governments. Unlike the normal drawing rights a nation has against the IMF, a participant with a B/P need is able to use SDR without challenge and to acquire foreign exchange from another participant whose B/P position is relatively strong. The IMF designates which participants are to provide currency in such transactions, and the designated country is obligated to accept the SDRs as part of its reserves. A participant can also use SDRs by agreement with another participant to buy back balances of its own currency held by that participant. Such transactions result largely from settlements by central banks of obligations arising from interventions in the foreign exchange market. The fund itself accepts SDRs from participants who are repurchasing their own currencies or paying charges in the fund's general account. A participant may reduce its SDR holdings to zero at any time and is not obliged to reacquire SDRs according to any fixed schedule, although it may be designated to receive SDRs as indicated above. In any event, it is obliged over five-year periods to maintain its SDR holdings at an average of not less than 30 percent of its average allocation. A participant with holdings in excess of the amount it has been allocated earns interest on the excess holding, and a participant with holdings below its allocation pays a charge at the same rate on its net use of SDRs. The rate for interest and charges is established by a formula that employs the weighted average of short-term market rates in the United States, Germany, the United Kingdom, France, and Japan.

The SDR was initially defined in terms of grams of fine gold, which corresponded to the par value of the U.S. dollar, from the time of the Bretton Woods agreement until mid-1974. Thus, in 1970 an SDR was worth $1.00 and remained so pegged to the dollar through its two subsequent devaluations (1971 and 1973). The abandonment by the United States in 1971 of its commitment to buy and sell gold freely for dollars raised doubt about this method of evaluating the SDR. The result was that in June 1974 the fund began evaluating the SDR in terms of a basket of 16 currencies. Thus the value of the SDR was set as equivalent to 40 U.S. cents, 38 German pfennigs, 4.5 new pence (UK), 40 centimes, and so on down through the 16 currencies. The weights were broadly based on the 16 countries' share of world exports of goods and services over the 1968–72 period. (See Table 6.12 below.) The fund makes this calculation daily.

This method of evaluating the SDR has created a relatively stable value in a floating exchange rate world. The result has been that many involved in the international financial market who had been looking for some stable value have begun to denominate transactions in SDRs, thereby using the SDR as the unit of account. Also, several countries began stating their currencies in terms of SDRs. (See Table 6.13.)

Table 6.12
THE SDR: WEIGHTS AND SAMPLE VALUATION

Currency	Weights assigned to each currency in one SDR	Currency units per SDR, September 13, 1974	Currency amounts under rule 0-3	Valuation of the SDR			Currency units per SDR, September 13, 1976
				Exchange rates*	U.S. dollar equivalent		
Australian dollar	1.5	0.795866	0.0120	0.80209	0.014961		0.924144
Austrian schilling	1.0	22.3392	0.2200	17.80000	0.012360		20.5050
Belgian franc	3.5	46.7562	1.6000	38.73000	0.041312		44.6148
Canadian dollar	6.0	1.16870	0.0710	1.02410	0.072711		1.12356
Danish krone	1.5	7.42274	0.1100	6.03470	0.018228		6.95310
Deutsche mark	12.5	3.15520	0.3800	2.50940	0.151431		2.89035
French franc	7.5	5.70290	0.4400	4.92870	0.089273		5.67712
Italian lira	6.0	783.945	47.0000	840.50000	0.055919		968.653
Japanese yen	7.5	357.641	26.0000	287.45000	0.090451		331.180
Netherlands guilder	4.5	3.21297	0.1400	2.62200	0.053394		3.02088
Norwegian krone	1.5	6.57925	0.0990	5.46550	0.018114		6.29639
Pound sterling	9.0	0.511360	0.0450	1.74820	0.078669		0.659038
South African rand	1.0	0.827867	0.0082	0.86953	0.009430		1.00185
Spanish peseta	1.5	68.2939	1.1000	67.92000	0.016196		78.2411
Swedish krona	2.5	5.30424	0.1300	4.37960	0.029683		5.04460
U.S. dollar	33.0	1.18385	0.4000	1.00000	0.400000		1.152132

*Exchange rates in terms of currency units per U.S. dollar except for the pound sterling and the Canadian dollar, which are expressed as U.S. dollars per currency unit. Rate sources: London noon rates except for the yen, which is the Tokyo representative rate.
Source: IMF Survey, Fall 1976, p. 6.   Data: IMF Treasurer's Department

The so-called Second Amendment of the Fund's Articles of Agreement accepted in 1977 strengthened the SDR as an asset, thus moving it toward becoming the principal reserve asset. Although the rules governing the allocation and cancellation of SDRs remain unchanged, several characteristics of the SDR were altered for the purpose of widening the range of permitted operations and transactions. Possibly the most important extension of SDR use is the increased freedom participants have in entering into direct bilateral transactions by agreement.

A further change initiated in 1977 was the total elimination of gold as the unit of value of the SDR, likewise its role as the common denominator of the par value of currencies. There is no longer an official price of gold, members being free to deal in gold in the market and among themselves. As a consequence, obligatory payments in gold by members to the fund and the reverse were abrogated, and the fund was obliged to dispose of all the gold held by it.

It can be appreciated that an SDR is simply an IMF obligation representing the long-term bonds of the member governments whose currencies have been swapped by other governments at the IMF for SDRs. Therefore, the SDR represents a composite monetary pledge and may be used by central banks as

Table 6.13
EXCHANGE RATES, JANUARY 31, 1977
(currency units per unit listed)

Member and currency	SDR	U.S. dollar	Pound sterling	French franc	Other	Other currencies in group‡	Market rates† U.S. dollar
	Member maintains exchange rate against*						
Afghanistan (afghani)§							50.50
Algeria (dinar)§		....				‖	4.1805
Argentina (peso)§		292.50					
Australia (dollar)		....				‖	0.919963
Austria (schilling)		....				‖	17.2100
#Bahamas (dollar)§		1.00					
#Bahrain (dinar)		0.394737					
#Bangladesh (taka)§			26.70				
#Barbados (dollar)		2.00					
#Belgium (franc)§						48.6573	37.1800
Benin (franc)				50.00			
#Bolivia (peso)		20.00					
Botswana (pula)		0.869565					
Brazil (cruzeiro)§		12.52					
#Burma (kyat)	7.74289						6.7179
#Burundi (franc)		90.00					
Cambodia (riel)§							
Cameroon (franc)				50.00			
Canada (dollar)		....				‖	1.0209
Central African Empire (franc)§				50.00			
Chad (franc)				50.00			
Chile (peso)§		18.48					
#China, Republic (new Taiwan dollar)		38.00					
Colombia (peso)§		36.46					
Comoros				50.00			
Congo, People's Republic of the (franc)				50.00			
Costa Rica (colón)§		8.57					
Cyprus (pound)		....				‖	0.415541
#Denmark (krone)						7.89409	5.9300
Dominican Republic (peso)§		1.00					
Ecuador (sucre)§		25.00					
Egypt (pound)§		0.391305					
El Salvador (colón)		2.50					
Equatorial Guinea (ekuele)§					1.00††		
#Ethiopia (birr)§		2.07237					

Table 6.13

Member and currency	Member maintains exchange rate against*						Market rates†
	SDR	U.S. dollar	Pound sterling	French franc	Other	Other currencies in group‡	U.S. dollar
Fiji (dollar)						‖	0.938174
Finland (markka)						‖	3.831
France (franc)						‖	4.97575
Gabon (franc)				50.00			
Gambia, The (dalasi)			4.00				
#Germany, Federal Republic (deutsche mark)						3.15665	2.4214
Ghana (cedi)§		1.15385					
Greece (drachma)						‖	37.417
Grenada (East Caribbean dollar)		2.70					
Guatemala (quetzal)		1.00					
Guinea (syli)§	24.6853						21.365
#Guyana (dollar)§		2.55					
Haiti (gourde)		5.00					
Honduras (lempira)		2.00					
Iceland (króna)						‖	191.05
India (rupee)						‖	8.86713
Indonesia (rupiah)		415.00					
#Iran (rial)§	82.2425						70.625
#Iraq (dinar)		0.296053					
Ireland (pound)§			1.00				
#Israel (pound)						‖	8.9813
Italy (lira)						‖	882.20
Ivory Coast (franc)				50.00			
#Jamaica (dollar)		0.909091					
Japan (yen)						‖	289.30
#Jordan (dinar)	0.387755						0.334001
#Kenya (shilling)	9.66						8.38130
Korea (won)		485.00					
Kuwait (dinar)						‖	0.28964
Lao People's Dem. Republic (kip)		200.00					
Lebanon (pound)						‖	3.0075
Lesotho (rand)		0.869565					
Liberia (dollar)		1.00					
#Libyan Arab Republic (dinar)§		0.296053					
#Luxembourg (franc)§						48.6573	37.1800

Table 6.13

| Member and currency | Member maintains exchange rate against* | | | | | | Market rates† |
	SDR	U.S. dollar	Pound sterling	French franc	Other	Other currencies in group‡	U.S. dollar
Madagascar (franc)				50.00			
Malawi (kwacha)	1.05407						0.914541
Malaysia (ringgit)						‖	2.5031
Mali (franc)				100.00			
Malta (pound)						‖	0.430997
Mauritania (ouguiya)						‖	49.852
Mauritius (rupee)§	7.713759						6.69268
Mexico (peso)						‖	22.1759
Morocco (dirham)§						‖	4.5175
#Nepal (rupee)§		12.50					
#Netherlands (guilder)						3.35507	2.53400
New Zealand (dollar)						‖	1.0513
Nicaragua (córdoba)		7.00					
Niger (franc)				50.00			
Nigeria (naira)						‖	0.631153
#Norway (krone)						6.94083	5.32750
#Oman (rial Omani)		0.345395					
#Pakistan (rupee)		9.90					
Panama (balboa)		1.00					
Papua New Guinea (kina)					0.882223 ‡‡		
Paraguay (guaraní)§		126.00					
Peru (sol)§		71.05					
Philippines (peso)						‖	7.427
Portugal (escudo)						‖	32.355
Qatar (riyal)§§	4.76190						3.95917
Romania (leu)§		12.00 ‖‖					
#Rwanda (franc)		92.84					
Saudi Arabia (riyal)§§	4.28255						3.530
Senegal (franc)				50.00			
Sierra Leone (leone)			2.00				
Singapore (dollar)						‖	2.4597
#Somalia (shilling)§		6.23270					
South Africa (rand)		0.869565					
Spain (peseta)						‖	68.849
Sri Lanka (rupee)§						‖	8.69301
Sudan (pound)§		0.348242					
Swaziland (lilangeni)					1.00**		
#Sweden (krona)						5.55651	4.2695
Syrian Arab Republic (pound)		3.925					
#Tanzania (shilling)	9.66						8.38130

Table 6.13

Member and currency	Member maintains exchange rate against*						Market rates†
	SDR	U.S. dollar	Pound sterling	French franc	Other	Other currencies in group‡	U.S. dollar
#Thailand (baht)		20.00					
Togo (franc)				50.00			
Trinidad and Tobago (dollar)		2.40					
Tunisia (dinar)						‖	0.421492
Turkey (lira)§						‖	16.50
#Uganda (shilling)	9.66						8.38130
#United Arab Emirates (dirham)		3.94737					
United Kingdom (pound)§						‖	0.583362
United States (dollar)							
Upper Volta (franc)				50.00			
Uruguay (new peso)§		4.10					
Venezuela (bolívar)		4.2925					
Viet Nam, Socialist Republic (dong)	2.13087						1.84880
Western Samoa (tala)						‖	0.8700
Yemen Arab Republic (rial)		4.5625					
#Yemen, People's Dem. Republic (dinar)§		0.345395					
Yugoslavia (dinar)§						‖	18.3944
#Zaïre (zaïre)	1.00						0.867629
Zambia (kwacha)	0.921837						0.799812

*Rates other than market rates as notified to the fund.

†Latest market rates available.

‡Belgium, Denmark, Fed. Rep. of Germany, Luxembourg, The Netherlands, Norway, and Sweden maintain maximum margins of 2.25 percent for exchange rates in transactions in the official markets between their currencies and those of the other countries in this group. Rates shown are central rates expressed in terms of SDRs, as valued in accordance with Article XXI, Section 2, of the Fund Articles of Agreement.

§Member maintains multiple currency practice and/or dual exchange market.

‖ The member has notified the fund that its currency is not being maintained within specified margins in terms of another currency.

#The member is availing itself of wider margins of up to ± 2.25 percent.

**Per South African rand.

††Per Spanish peseta.

‡‡Per Australian dollar.

§§Saudi Arabia and Qatar maintain margins up to ± 7.25 percent.

‖ ‖ Rate for noncommercial transactions.

Data: IMF Treasurer's Department

Source: IMF Survey, February 21, 1977, pp. 56–57.

a reserve asset. (See footnote 49.) The day may come when all nations turn over all their official reserves (foreign exchange in excess of transaction requirements, but with the exception of gold) to the IMF for SDRs. Ultimately, gold could be virtually eliminated from the international monetary system. National currencies would then be defined wholly in terms of SDRs, a kind of composite reserve asset backed by all IMF members to the extent either that they have swapped, through the IMF, long-term indebtedness for their own or others' currencies or the IMF holds a member's currencies among its own assets. The dollar could then cease being a major reserve unit.

It should be noted that as presently constituted the larger share of the SDRs have been issued to the more developed countries in that they have the larger IMF quotas. Some have proposed that either each industrial and OPEC country that receives an SDR quota contribute a portion to the International Development Association (IDA; see Table 6.2), or that the IMF should do so directly. A third proposal is that the developed countries contribute to the IDA in their national currencies in proportion to the SDRs to which they are entitled from the IMF. Some commentators claim that since with SDRs a nation need no longer run an export surplus in order to acquire reserves, such saving of resources should benefit poor countries rather than rich countries. Such a transfer, it is said, would expand the export markets of the developed countries as a whole, and would thereby reduce the danger of conflict among those countries in search of larger margins.

The pressure to develop special facilities for the LDC problem led to the establishment, in May 1976, of a trust fund to provide developing countries with special B/P assistance. The trust fund's resources may come from profits derived from the sale of gold and from voluntary contributions and loans from the OECD and OPEC countries. Sixty-one countries were designated as eligible for assistance, which was to be given on concessional terms (.5 percent repayable over five years starting five years after disbursement) to support efforts to carry out programs of balance-of-payments adjustment. And, finally, there was the "subsidy account" created to subsidize interest payments for the purchases made by some members (12 as it turned out) under the "special oil facility." The latter refers to a temporary financial mechanism established for 1974 and 1975 through which the fund made available SDR 6.9 billion to 55 members to meet the impact of increased oil import costs. These resources were borrowed from 17 countries (including OPEC members) and final drawings made upon them in mid-1976.

Increasingly, the IMF is looked upon as the manager of the international financial system. Not only has its central authority been increased, but likewise its assets. The basic principle is that each member is given a quota, 75 percent of which must be subscribed in the country's own currency, 25 percent in currencies acceptable to the fund or in SDRs. The financial facilities of the fund available to members are summarized below in Table 6.14.

During 1977 it became known that the IMF was engaging in worldwide

Table 6.14
FINANCIAL FACILITIES OF THE FUND AND THEIR CONDITIONALITY*

Type of facility	Under regular policies†		Under temporarily widened tranches†	
	Percentage of quota available	Cumulative percentage of quota available	Percentage of quota available	Cumulative percentage of quota available
Tranche policies	25	25	25	25
Gold tranche: Condition—balance of payments need.				
First credit tranche	25	50	36.25	61.25
Program representing reasonable efforts to overcome balance of payments difficulties; performance criteria and installments not used.				
Higher credit tranches	75	125	108.75	170
Program giving substantial justification of member's efforts to overcome balance of payments difficulties; resources normally provided in the form of stand-by arrangements, which include performance criteria and drawings in installments.				
Extended facility	140	190‡	140	201.25
Medium-term program for up to three years to overcome structural balance of payments maladjustments; detailed statement of policies and measures for first and subsequent 12-month periods; resources provided in the form of extended arrangements, which include performance criteria and drawings in installments.				
Compensatory financing facility	75§	265	75	276.25
Existence of temporary export shortfall for reasons beyond the member's control; member cooperates with fund in an effort to find appropriate solutions for any balance of payments difficulties.				
Buffer stock financing facility‖	50	315	50	326.25
Existence of an international buffer stock accepted as suitable by fund; member expected to cooperate with fund as in the case of compensatory financing.				

*Members are not expected, and may not qualify, to use all of the available facilities at the same time. In addition, use of the maximum available resources under a particular facility, namely, tranche policies, is usually made in a period of years, not in one year.

†Facilities as described under regular facilities applied prior to January 20, 1976, and will probably apply again after the second amendment of the articles of agreement; the temporarily widened credut tranches, in effect from January 20, 1976 until the second amendment enters into force, provide increased access to fund resources.

‡The combined use of the extended facility and the regular credit tranches may not be above 165 percent of quota. Adding the use of the gold tranche raises the maximum to 190 percent of quota.

§Normally, not more than 50 percent of quota in any 12-month period.

‖Until the proposed second amendment enters into effect, a member with gold tranche drawing rights that purchases under the buffer stock financing facility would lose its gold tranche drawing rights *pro tanto*.

Source: IMF Survey, Fall 1976, p. 3.

Under the 1977 "second amendment," the gold tranche became a reserve tranche. A "tranche" refers to a portion of the total credit facilities available to a country.

negotiations trying to devise a fund (simply called a "facility") that would lend money to debtor nations no longer deemed creditworthy by private lenders. The target was something between $12 and $20 billion to be raised from the wealthier OPEC and non-OPEC nations. The problem had arisen because during 1974 through 1976, 71 non-oil producing countries ran cumulative current deficits in their balance of payments of $75 billion, thereby causing their total outstanding debt to swell to $157 billion. During these same years, the 13 members of OPEC registered a cumulative surplus of $169 billion. Saudi Arabia led the list with a cumulative current surplus of something over $70 billion. Of the total OPEC current surplus in 1976 of $45.8 billion, Saudi Arabia, Kuwait, and the United Arab Emirates accounted for $37.4 billion. (See Table 6.15.) These mounting LDC debts were in part due to the increased price of oil, in part to the worldwide recession that cut the demand for their exports, and in part to misconceived economic policies on their own part leading to high inflation rates and further erosion of exports. During 1974, 1975, and 1976 the critical matching of LDC needs (deficits) with "petrodollars" (surpluses), which were banked by the OPEC countries in the more developed countries, was done largely by private banks, principally the American, British, German, Swiss, and Belgian. They took the OPEC deposits and lent them to governments and other borrowers, particularly those in the LDCs with near desperate balance-of-payments problems. But private banks are limited in the extent to which they can thus "recycle" the petrodollars because of increasing concern about the ability of many of these countries to repay the loans. Hence, they needed some sort of official guarantee, and began looking more to the IMF. Not only would the IMF presumably provide credit directly to the riskiest countries and offer guarantees on bank loans to others, but it would also impose conditions on such financing that would require the recipient countries to correct faulty economic policies that might sweep them over the brink. Such external pressure has the effect in some instances of making it possible for domestic political leaders to pursue relatively unpopular fiscal and monetary policies. The IMF had already imposed such conditions on Britain, Italy, Mexico, Chile, Argentina, Egypt, Zaire, and others. It was clear by mid-1977 that the views of banking and political leaders in the United States at least favored channeling more U.S. economic assistance to the LDCs through the IMF. As one put it, "we prefer not to enter into direct confrontations with other countries in respect to their development priorities." Given the context of the comment, he obviously felt that the IMF was in a much better position to exert influence in this regard than a single foreign government which itself was vulnerable to criticism.

To measure the seriousness of the LDC debt load, one must relate it to external earning capacity, that is, exports (see Figure 6.9), although a more accurate measure of debt-carrying capacity would be the relationship of external debt (public *and private*) to exports *less essential imports*. If Figure 6.9 were adjusted in this manner, the picture would look considerably worse than it does.

The importance of the nature of the international monetary system to the

Table 6.15
HOW THE DEBTS OF THE POOR COUNTRIES HAVE GROWN . . .
(Total outstanding debt of selected developing countries, cumulative total) (Billions of dollars)

	1974	1975	1976
Latin America			
Argentina	$ 5.9	$ 6.1	$ 6.5
Brazil	17.8	24.4	30.5
Chile	3.6	4.0	4.8
Colombia	3.5	3.8	4.2
Mexico	13.2	19.6	22.7
Peru	3.1	3.9	9.7
Asia			
S. Korea	5.9	8.2	10.3
India	11.6	12.4	14.9
Pakistan	4.6	5.0	6.2
Philippines	2.6	3.2	3.9
Taiwan	2.2	3.8	4.1
Thailand	1.8	1.9	2.4
Africa			
Egypt	3.9	6.4	7.4
Tanzania	0.6	0.8	1.0
Zaire	1.5	1.9	2.1
Zambia	0.7	1.0	1.3
Total 71 less developed countries	**108.7**	**132**	**157.1**

Source: Data Bank

. . . AS THE OIL EXPORTING COUNTRIES PILE UP ANNUAL SURPLUSES.*
(Current account surpluses of selected OPEC countries) (Billions of dollars)

Iran	$12.6	$ 4.3	$ 2.6
Iraq	3.0	1.1	1.6
Kuwait	8.1	7.2	7.0
Libya	2.2	1.3	2.7
Nigeria	5.0	0.8	1.3
Qatar	1.6	1.2	1.1
Saudi Arabia	26.4	20.1	24.2
United Arab Emirates	5.6	4.9	6.2
Venezuela	5.8	3.6	1.9
Total for 13 OPEC countries	**72.2**	**41.1**	**45.8**

*1976 figures are estimated
Source: Treasury Department
The New York Times, March 28, 1977, p. 43.

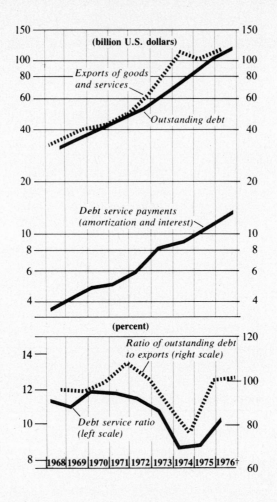

Figure 6.9
NON-OIL DEVELOPING COUNTRIES: DEBT AND DEBT SERVICE RATIOS*

*The debt and debt service figures relate only to medium and long term extenal *public or publicly guaranteed* debt, as defined in the Debt Reporting Statistics of the IBRD.
†Fund staff projections.
Data: IBRD Debtor Reporting System and Fund estimates.
Source: IMF Survey, September 20, 1976, p. 275.

international businessman is three-fold. *First,* it defines the institutional restraints upon what he can and cannot do. *Second,* it determines the degree of risk he must assume. For example, if the rate is pegged at a fixed parity, he knows that future payments and receipts will be at a given exchange rate, plus or minus the width of the band. The cost of maintaining that rate will be borne either by his government or that of its trading partner, or both. To the extent that the effective exchange rate may deviate from parity, the businessman must either assume the risk of change or cover his risk, both of which represent costs. If the rate of the relevant foreign currency shifts upward (becomes more costly), a domestic creditor (an importer on credit) and the domestic debtor (an exporter on a deferred payment basis) lose; those in a reverse position, gain. *Third*, it impacts heavily on the volume of world trade and on the capacity of nations to maintain economic growth without undue inflation. As the world economy becomes increasingly integrated by reason of increasingly liberal trade, the internal adjustment of national economies becomes more difficult and ever higher levels of international cooperation are required if inflation and unemployment (in part caused by the adjustment process) and a return to protectionism are to be averted. In the end, protectionism means lower economic growth and lower real incomes for all.

Forums for trade and monetary talks

The principal organizations and groups of countries that are discussing or are proposing to hold discussions on reforms in the world's trading and monetary system are described in brief below.

The Six. The original members of the European Economic Community (EEC), Belgium, France, Germany, Italy, Luxembourg, and the Netherlands.

The Nine. The enlarged EEC, i.e., the Six plus Denmark, Ireland, and the United Kingdom.

Group of Ten. The ten major industrial countries (the Six less Luxembourg plus Canada, Japan, Sweden, the United Kingdom, and the United States) that agreed in October 1962 to stand ready to lend their currencies to the IMF under the general arrangements to borrow. Meetings of the group of Ten finance ministers and central bank governors (and those of their deputies) have been held from time to time over the past decade to discuss the international monetary system.

Bank for International Settlements (BIS). Originally set up in 1930 to promote cooperation between European central banks and to provide additional facilities for international financial transactions. In addition, it acts as agent for the European Monetary Agreement and organizes regular meetings in Basel attended by the central bank governors of the major industrial nations. Representatives of the IMF, the OECD, and the commission of the EEC may attend these meetings.

Organization of Petroleum Exporting Countries (OPEC). Formed by the major oil producing countries to provide a forum for establishing a common oil pricing policy and resolving other matters of mutual interest.

Organization for Economic Cooperation and Development (OECD). Established in 1961 as successor to the Organization for European Economic Cooperation. Consists of 23 developed countries: the group of Ten plus Australia,

Austria, Denmark, Finland, Greece, Iceland, Ireland, Luxembourg, Norway, Portugal, Spain, Switzerland, and Turkey. Yugoslavia is an associate member. The OECD is concerned with a wide variety of economic matters.

Group of Twenty-Four. Made up of eight countries each in Africa, Asia, and Latin America deputed by the group of 77 to consider monetary matters. The 24 countries are as follows:

Algeria	Ghana	Pakistan
Argentina	Guatemala	Peru
Brazil	India	Philippines
Ceylon	Iran	Syrian Arab Republic
Colombia	Ivory Coast	Trinidad and Tobago
Egypt	Lebanon	Venezuela
Ethiopia	Mexico	Yugoslavia
Gabon	Nigeria	Zaire

Group of Seventy-seven. A group of developing countries within the United Nations Conference on Trade and Development (UNCTAD). Originally numbering 77, the Group by 1977 had 111 members. The full membership of UNCTAD, which was established under a UN General Assembly resolution of December 30, 1964, is 141 (of which 132 are members of the United Nations).

General Agreement on Tariffs and Trade (GATT). A multilateral trade treaty among governments, made up of 80 full contracting parties and one provisional member, as well as 15 other countries applying the general agreement on a *de facto* basis.

International Monetary Fund (IMF). Established in December 1945. The international organization with prime responsibility for international monetary matters. It operates on the basis of weighted voting power for its 120 members. The Fund's highest authority is the board of governors (consisting of a governor and an alternate governor appointed by each member), which normally meets once a year, but otherwise votes by mail. The general operations of the fund are the responsibility of 20 executive directors, of whom six are currently appointed by France, Germany, India, Japan, the United Kingdom, and the United States and 14 are elected by groups of members.

Recommended references

Caves, Richard E., et al. *The International Adjustment Mechanism.* Boston: Federal Reserve Bank of Boston, 1970.

Columbia Journal of World Business, vol. 11 no. 3, Fall 1976. Focus of issue is on international currency.

Grubel, Herbert G., *The International Monetary System.* Baltimore: Penguin Books, 1969.

Hein, John. *Understanding the Balance of Payments.* New York: The Conference Board, 1970.

Rodriguez, Rita M., and E. Eugene Carter. *International Financial Management.* Englewood Cliffs: Prentice-Hall, 1976.

Salant, Walter S., and Associates. *The United States Balance of Payments in 1968.* Washington, D.C.: The Brookings Institution, 1963.

Yeager, Leland B. *The International Monetary Mechanism.* New York: Holt, Rinehart and Winston, 1968.

Appendix 2 to Chapter 6
EXPORT FINANCING

As indicated in the text, debt includes short, medium, and long-term[57] export financing. Various methods are used for the debt transaction, specifically open-account, cash-against-documents, sight draft, time draft, banker's acceptance, letters of credit, consignment, factoring, and undisclosed nonrecourse financing. These are described below, arranged in order of descending risk from the point of view of the exporter. In addition are the highly specialized methods sometimes used to finance East-West trade, which were described in Chapter 1.

It should be noted that related to the export financing decision are three questions: (1) in what currency is the sale to be made? (2) where should the sale be booked (by what national subsidiary)? and (3) where is the risk to be taken (by the firm, by an external agency, or in part by both)? The risk to which we refer really breaks down into the risk of default, a foreign exchange risk, and political risk (government intervention). If the sale is to be made in a foreign currency, one must then be aware of the fact that the firm has set up a fixed foreign currency flow at some point in the future. If the export financing is denominated in another currency, one must anticipate the foreign exchange rate that will prevail at that time in order to determine the true cost of the financing.

1. Open-account (sale of unsecured credit), in which the seller ships and subsequently bills the buyer.

2. Cash-against-documents, in which cash payment is made once shipping documents have been delivered to the buyer through a commercial bank. This is a common method of payment in East-West trade.

3. Draft, which is an unconditional order written by the seller (an exporter in our case) directing the buyer (an importer) or his agent (such as a bank) to pay a specified amount of money at a specified time. Sometimes called a bill of exchange, a draft may be either a "sight draft," which is payable immediately, or a "time-draft," which is payable upon the lapse of a specified amount of time (normally,

---

[57]"Short-term" is defined generally as debt with a maturity of less than two years; "medium-term," from two to five years; "long-term," anything over five years or indeterminant. For purposes of discussing export financing, however, "short-term" refers to maturities up to 180 days; "medium-term," 181 days to five years.

Table 6.16
LETTERS OF CREDIT

	Revocable L/C	Unconfirmed irrevocable L/C	Confirmed irrevocable L/C
Who applies for L/C?	importer	importer	importer
Who is obliged to pay?	no one	issuing bank	issuing and confirming bank
Who reimburses paying bank?	issuing bank	issuing bank	issuing bank
Who reimburses issuing bank?	importer	importer	importer

Adapted from *Letters of Credit, Book 2* (Washington, D.C.: The American Bankers' Association, 1968), p. 116.

30, 90, 120, or 180 days). A time draft directed to a bank can become a *banker's acceptance* if the bank has in fact accepted the draft as a valid claim. Such a draft becomes negotiable and may be sold at an appropriate discount.

4. Letter-of-credit (L/C), which is a document issued by a bank upon request of an importer stating that it will honor drafts drawn against it by a specified party (the exporter) if the terms and conditions set forth in the L/C are satisfied. In return, the buyer promises to pay the bank the amount of the L/C, plus fees, upon mutually agreed upon terms. Once the proper documents proving shipment of the goods (bill of lading) have been delivered to a corresponding bank abroad by the exporter, payment will be made to him. The L/C is said to be a "confirmed L/C" if the corresponding bank adds its own confirmation to the L/C. In such case, if the importer does not pay his bank, both banks are nonetheless obligated to pay the exporter. In the unconfirmed case, only the bank initially issuing the L/C is liable. An L/C is said to be "revocable" if neither bank has guaranteed payment, in which case the exporter has no assurance that the L/C will not be revoked by the importer at any time prior to payment. These differences are summarized below:
An L/C becomes a "time L/C" if the exporter extends credit to the importer, which simply means that the issuing bank promises to pay only after a specified time has lapsed following the submission of shipping documents. A "transferable L/C" refers to an L/C in which some intermediary (say a trading house) is the beneficiary. As soon as the trading house finds a seller, it may request the bank to transfer the L/C to the seller.

5. Consignment, in which the seller ships the goods to a second party, but retains title. The latter simply sells the goods on behalf of the former on mutually agreed upon terms.

6. Factoring, which involves the outright sale to a bank of accounts receivable without recourse to the seller, the bank thus assuming the entire risk so long as the exporter avoids disputes relating to delivery and quality of his merchandise. The factor charges a fee for making the collections and assuming the risk. Also, cash advances to the maturity of the factored accounts carry an interest rate often somewhat above the usual rate. A variation of this latter is undisclosed, non-

recourse financing. In this case, the factor turns around and appoints the seller of the accounts receivable as the agent to complete the sale and make collections in due course on behalf of an undisclosed principal (the bank). In some instances, an exporter may induce a commercial bank to take the earlier maturities of its foreign customers' obligations (with recourse) if the exporter assumes the later maturities. In this way a firm may extend longer credit terms to its buyers.

7. Cash in advance.

In some countries, there are private firms willing to insure against insolvency, sometimes against default or delayed payment as well. An example is the Trade Indemnity Company, Ltd., which covers about one-eighth of insured British export credits.[58] Private banks and companies do not, however, insure on their own account against such noncommercial risks as war, confiscation, civil disorder, inconvertibility, and other politically decreed costs. To fill this gap, national export guarantee systems have been established, such guarantees having the effect of creating a bankable risk.[59] The U.S. system, offered jointly by the Export-Import Bank (Eximbank) and the Foreign Insurance Credit Association, is diagrammed in Figure 6.10. In mid-1971, the Eximbank and the Private Export Funding Corporation (PEFCO, in which some 40 major banks participate) concluded an agreement under which the Eximbank guarantees the principal and interest on debt obligations issued by foreign purchasers of U.S. products and services and purchased by PEFCO. PEFCO thereby acquires a portfolio of Eximbank, guaranteed paper that can be used as the basis for raising funds in the private market.

The Export-Import Bank of the United States (Eximbank) is designed to overcome deficiencies in private financial markets. Such deficiencies include the lack of adequate long-term export financing, limited knowledge of foreign markets and foreign buyers by the smaller banks and many exporters, a generally exaggerated assessment of the risk of financing foreign transactions, as well as the nonavailability of private cover for noncommercial (that is, political) risks. Major Eximbank export support programs include:

1. Fixed-rate direct credits to foreign buyers carrying long-term maturities (generally those over five years), usually in participation with private market financing.

2. Medium-term loans to foreign financial institutions to help finance U.S. exports through the Cooperative Financing Facility (CFF), generally for one to five years.

3. Discounting of medium-term export obligations that carry fixed interest rates.

4. Credit insurance and guarantees for commercial and political risks.

---

[58]Daniel Marx, Jr., "The United States Enters Export Credit Guarantee Competition," in John K. Ryans and James C. Baker, eds., *World Marketing* (New York: John Wiley & Sons, 1967), p. 171.

[59]Those with credit insurance systems include Canada, United Kingdom, France, Germany, Belgium, Austria, Hungary, Ireland, Switzerland, the Netherlands, Sweden, Denmark, Norway, Italy, Spain, Japan, Australia, India, Israel, Pakistan, Union of South Africa, United States, and Yugoslavia. A guide to export credits is published periodically by the International Export Credits Institute of New York City.

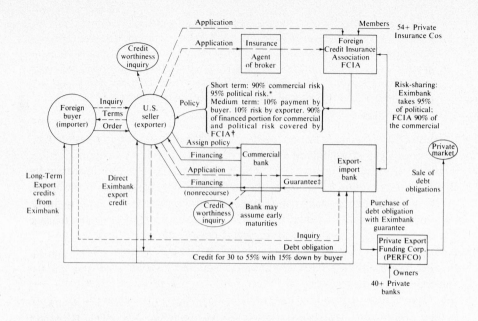

Figure 6.10

FCIA, EXIMBANK, AND PEFCO EXPORT FINANCING

*Comprehensive—all eligible exports or reasonable spread of risks. If political risk coverage alone, up to 90 percent can be covered. No cash payment by buyer required.

†On a case-by-case basis, revolving credit, whole turnover, or reasonable spread-of-risk basis.

‡Guarantees political risk for early maturities, both commercial and political for later maturities (early maturity refers to first half of installments of a one-to-three year credit or first one-and-a-half years of a three-to-five year credit, excluding the 15 percent retained by exporter). Same coverage as for FCIA medium term.

During 1976 about 11 percent of U.S. exports were officially supported. The Eximbank does not mix development aid with export financing or provide inflation indemnity coverage for changes in foreign exchange rates, or local cost financing, as do some of its foreign competitors.

Significant variations in national systems are listed below:[60]

1. Type of organization offering export credit insurance (and guaranties), preferential fixed-rate export credit, fixed-rate export credit, and direct export loans. Possible alternatives: a private company acting on behalf of a government; a governmental department; a state agency; or a government corporation—alone, or in cooperation with private banks and insurance companies. Leading export credit and export insurance agencies:

[60]For further details see Export-Import Bank of the United States, *Report to the U.S. Congress on Export Credit Competition and the Export-Import Bank of the United States* (Washington, D.C., December 1976).

Canada. Export Development Corporation (EDC) for both export credit and export credit insurance.

France. The Banque Francaise du Commerce Exterieur (BFCE) and the Bank of France for preferential fixed-rate export financing and the Compagnie Francaise d'Assurance pour le Commerce Exterieur (COFACE) for export insurance and guaranties.

Germany. Kreditanstalt fuer Wiederaufbau (KFW) for direct export loans, Ausfuhrkredit Gesellschaft (AKA) for discounting export loans, and Hermes Kreditversicherungs (Hermes) for insurance and guaranties.

Italy. Mediocredito Centrale for preferential fixed-rate export financing, Instituto Nazionale delle Assicurazioni (INA) for export insurance and guaranties.

Japan. Export Insurance Section, Ministry of International Trade and Industry, through the Export-Import Bank of Japan and "the authorized foreign exchange banks."

United Kingdom. Export Credit Guarantee Department (ECGD) for guaranties, interest rate subsidies (to the commercial banks), and refinance of part of the banks' export obligations.

United States. Export-Import Bank through private banks and insurance companies, plus the Foreign Credit Insurance Association (see Figure 6.1) for export credit guaranties, discounting of medium-term export obligations carrying fixed interest rates, fixed-rate direct credit to foreign buyers, medium-term loans to foreign financial institutions; the commercial banks for other financing; the Overseas Private Investment Corporation for guaranties of payment under service contracts, including performance bonds.

2. Categories of exports eligible for coverage: consumer goods, capital goods, services (feasibility studies, marketing, engineering, architectural, construction, management).

3. Risks that may be underwritten:

Commercial. Insolvency of the buyer, arbitrary nonacceptance by the buyer not due to the fault of the seller, buyer's failure to pay local currency deposit on due date.

Political. Cancellation of an export license (not due to fault of exporter), cancellation of a contract by a public buyer, cancellation of an import license, transport or insurance charges due to diversion of shipment caused by political events, currency inconvertibility and transfer delays, outbreak of war or civil commotion preventing delivery or payment by the buyer, requisition or expropriation or other government intervention that prevents payment.

Other. Inflation risk (exporter generally absorbs the first 6 or 7 percent and may or may not get 100 percent coverage; available in Japan, France, and United Kingdom, although the last two do not provide such coverage for exports to other EEC countries); exchange rate changes (from three to 20 percent loss per annum on contracts between two and 15 years covered by Japan; all exchange losses over 3 percent on credits of over two years' maturity, by Germany; all exchange losses over 2.25 percent per annum, by France);[61] loss from performance bond guarantee (U.K.).

4. Type of export credit policies offered: specific (by transaction, such as ordinary supplier's credit), comprehensive (covers all of a firm's export business for a specified time), selective (covers only transactions designated by the firm within the overall total), restricted (covers transactions only with certain countries), single-buyer (covers only transactions with a particular buyer), project (covers shipments to a designated project), commercial risk guarantee (covers only commercial risks), political (covers only political risks), extended (covers both political and commercial risks).

5. Types of export credit offered: fixed-rate, preferential fixed-rate (less than market rate, that is, subsidized; sometimes offered only for long-term credit, sometimes for medium-term as well), preshipment, post-shipment, short term (up to 2 years), medium term (two to five years), long term (over five years, sometimes up to 15 years), direct loan (to foreign buyer), concessionary or "mixed credits" (for certain LDCs, thus mixing developmental aid with export credit), government-to-government line of credit, local cost financing, discounting of commercial bank credit.

6. Content: local origin rules (often 80 percent or more by value must be produced in issuing country), local financing (some countries will finance the purchase of local, that is, foreign, goods and services associated with an export).

7. Terms: market interest rate, preferential rate, grace period (before repayment starts), duration (up to 15 years on some long-term loans; some countries define short-term as anything up to 18 months rather than two years).

8. Fees charged: for commitment, stand-by, management, legal.

9. Rates: may be given in a standard scale or set for each transaction (possible variables: risks covered, duration, types of goods, country of destination, credit standing of buyer).

10. Deposit requirements: such as the U.S. FCIA requirement that the buyer make a payment of 10 percent.

11. Exclusion: for example, the U.S. Eximbank is prohibited by the Trade Act of 1974 from extending export credits, export guaranties, or investment guaranties directly or indirectly to any nonmarket economy which denies its citizens freedom of emigration. Since the act does not apply to any nonmarket economy country that enjoyed most-favored-nation tariff treatment when the act was enacted, Poland is exempt. In addition, Romania was subsequently exempted from the provision when Congress approved a trade agreement with Romania in 1975.[62]

---

[61]Gains must be surrendered. Japan permits exporters of plants to certain LDCs to set aside up to 7 percent of the contract value as a nontaxable reserve against loss. If there is no loss, the reserve becomes taxable.

[62]The Johnson Debt Default Act (1934) prohibits any U.S. resident from undertaking certain financial transactions with any foreign governments in default in the payment of their obligation to the United States unless they are members of both the International Monetary Fund and the International Bank for Reconstruction and Development. Prohibited transactions include making loans (but *not* extending commercial credit) to and buying the bonds, securities, and other obligations of a proscribed government. Included are Czechoslovakia, Hungary, Poland, and the Soviet Union (but not Albania, Bulgaria, or Romania). The application of the Act to the German Democratic Republic and the People's Republic of China has not been determined; in both cases, there are defaulted obligations of predecessor governments to the U.S., but the attributability of these obligations to the present governments is uncertain.

12. Timing: the point at which an export credit guarantee may be issued. Possible variations: upon receipt of an order but prior to production or during production ("prefinancing insurance"), at time of shipment, after shipment (normal "export credit" insurance).

There is underway an effort within both the EEC and the OECD to harmonize national practice in respect to export credit, although why international competition in this area is considered bad has never been made clear. In that all national systems have some degree of government involvement, the competition is not between subsidized and nonsubsidized systems.

The 25 members of the Union d'Assureurs des Credits Internationaux ("The Berne Union"), public and private export credit institutions from 20 countries including the United States (the Export-Import Bank and the FCIA), have agreed informally to limit government-insured supplier credit five years. When a member chooses to offer longer credit terms for a certain transaction, the other members reportedly may offer similar financing to any firm in their respective countries bidding on the same contract. During 1976 several members of the Berne Union issued "unilateral declarations," which tended to bring national export credit practices closer together. A formal agreement was rendered difficult for a number of reasons, not the least of which was conflict as to whether the EEC Commission or the EEC member governments should participate in the negotiations. The U.S. Eximbank's unilateral declaration was typical (reworded slightly):

1. Cash payments will be a minimum of 15 percent of the export value.
2. Interest rates will range from 8.25 percent to 9.50 percent on direct credits with flexibility to meet competition. However, the minimum blended competitive interest rates (Exim plus private commercial) will not be less than 8 percent for credits with repayment terms over five years to highly-developed countries, 7.75 percent to intermediate countries, and 7.5 percent to developing countries (excluding insurance premium and other fees). For two-to-five year credits, the minimum blended interest rates will be 7.75 percent to the highly-developed countries and 7.25 percent to all others.
3. Maximum repayment terms will be ten years to LDCs and 8.5 years to all others. When credit authorizations to highly-developed countries have been repayment terms of more than five years, information will be given seven days in advance to the export financing agencies in other member countries.
4. If the Eximbank intends to exceed these guidelines, it will so inform other agencies seven days in advance, with an additional nine days allowed for discussion.
5. The guidelines do not apply to agricultural commodities, aircraft, and nuclear power plants. The guidelines for downpayments and maturities will not apply to satellite ground stations. Additionally, conventional power plants and steel mills will be exempt from maturity guidelines up to maximum present practices: 12 years repayment with seven days advance notice to other countries for transactions exceeding five-year repayment terms to highly-developed countries, 8.5 years to intermediate countries, and ten years to LDCs.

6. Any mixed credit that has a grant element of 25 percent or more is exempt from the guidelines. Any mixed credit having a grant element of less than 25 percent will be reported promptly to the other agencies.

Most Western European banks and financial groups are willing to extend short-term credit to Soviet bloc countries without guarantees other than those offered by the Soviet-controlled Garant Versicherungs A.G. in Vienna, Schwarzmeer und Ostsee in Hamburg, and the Black Sea and Baltic Company Ltd. in London. And many have been extending medium- and long-term credits up to 10 or 15 years, largely associated with the purchase of capital goods. Increasingly, Western governments have displayed a willingness to guarantee these credits. Credits and payments are usually channeled through the foreign trade banks of the Soviet-bloc country involved. These banks stand ready to guarantee trade notes originating in Eastern Europe. Furthermore, a whole chain of Soviet-controlled banks incorporated abroad, such as the Moscow Narodny Bank (London), the Banque Commerciale pour l'Europe du Nord (Paris), and the Wosschod Handelsbank (Zurich), are actively involved in financing East-West trade. These foreign-based institutions discount, without recourse to the Western exporter, commercial paper issued by the Eastern block foreign trade organizations and approved by the national foreign trade bank. The credit record of the East European banks is excellent. (Barter and switch trading were discussed in Section 1.9.)[63]

In 1973 ten leading U.S. insurance companies entered into an agreement with a Soviet-owned insurance company based in London that permits insurers to cover U.S. property in the Soviet Union and American exports to the Soviet Union. The agreement enabled U.S. manufacturers and exporters to buy coverage to protect themselves in event a Soviet buyer canceled an order after production had begun or in event payment was not made after shipment to the U.S.S.R.

In his study of the use of suppliers' credit in three African countries, Grayson reported frequent conflict between the objectives and practices of governmental export insurance organizations and the economic assistance organizations of the same governments, the objective of the former being the promotion of exports (even to the point of driving countries to the verge of bankruptcy) and of the latter, the sound development of the less developed trading partner. "Such lack of coordination between aid and trade," he concludes, "is characteristic of most industrialized countries." The problem is that "sizeable suppliers' credits can be accumulated within a relatively short period of time and well before the World Bank and/or the OECD's 'early warning

---

[63]See Suzanne F. Porter, *East-West Trade Financing* (Washington, D.C.: U.S. Department of Commerce, Bureau of East-West Trade, 1976).

system' would pick up the danger signals of impending foreign exchange crisis."[64]

Apart from the export credit and guarantee schemes, another area distinguishing international from uninational business is the relatively greater difficulty of determining credit worthiness of both buyers and potential associates. For U.S.-based firms, five services attempt to fill the gap: American and Foreign Credit Underwriters, Dunn & Bradstreet, Foreign Credit Interchange Bureau, The World Trade Directory (U.S. Department of Commerce), and the larger banks organized internationally. Credit worthiness of a foreign firm is a function of: (1) the firm's financial position, (2) its payment record, (3) market custom, (4) existence of exchange controls, (5) payment record of the country in which the firm is located (for comparable products or services), (6) the dynamics of the balance of payments of the country involved, and (7) accuracy of information on the foregoing points (a probability factor).

Credit terms, on the other hand, are a function of: (1) credit worthiness of the foreign firm (as determined above), (2) market custom (for a particular product or source), (3) quantity, (4) sum of money involved, (5) long-standing relationships, (6) terms granted by competitors, and (7) degree to which risk is shared or covered (by banks and/or export guarantees).

[64]Leslie E. Grayson, "The Role of Suppliers' Credits in the Industrialization of Ghana, Nigeria, and Sierra Leone," paper presented at the 13th Annual Meeting of the African Studies Association, Boston, October 21–24, 1970, mimeo., pp. 33–34.

Case J
MERCK & CO., INC. IN BRAZIL

By mid-19xx events in Brazil were worrying Mr. Leo Fernandez, vice president in charge of the Western Hemisphere, and Mr. Walter Suffern, manager of treasury operations for Merck, Sharp and Dohme, International, a division of Merck & Co., Inc. The rate at which the value of the cruzeiro had been falling, in reference to both local purchasing power and dollar equivalent, was accelerating. (See Table J.1.) As a result, the Brazilian operation was generating net losses on the parent company's books. The two men decided to visit Brazil in November to review the situation with the local Brazilian management.

The essential problem was to devise ways of insulating Merck's Brazilian company, Merck, Sharp and Dohme Industria Quimica e Farmaceutica, S.A., from the corrosive effects of inflation and falling exchange rates and to reduce the dollar investment at risk in view of the expected continued political and economic deterioration of Brazil. Messrs. Fernandez and Suffern wanted to make certain that the Brazilian management realized that the net profit showing on its books added up to a net loss insofar as the parent company was concerned. The Brazilian subsidiary was 100 percent owned by Merck and its management was American-led, U.S. nationals holding the positions of general manager, finance director, and production director.

Prior to the merger of Merck and Sharp and Dohme, both firms had exported directly to Brazil from the United States. The new enlarged firm, however,

Table J.1
EXCHANGE RATES AND PURCHASING POWER

	Exchange rate cruzeiro/$	Cost of living index	Yearly percent rise in cost of living index
8 yrs. ago	55	42	—
7 " "	76	50	19
6 " "	66	60	20
5 " "	65	73	22
4 " "	90	87	19
3 " "	138	100	15
2 " "	203	137	37
1 yr. "	205	185	35
Present yr.	318	258	40

acquired the distributor through which these products had moved in Brazil, a firm known by its initials, S.A.C.I.P.A. Later, this became the Merck, Sharp and Dohme Industria Quimica e Farmaceutica, S.A. Two years later (six years before) the parent company gave approval for the Brazilian firm to manufacture certain products—vitamins, steroids, diuretics, antibiotics (penicillin and streptomycin, that is, the "narrow-spectrum antibiotics"), and a number of pharmaceutical formulations such as tranquilizers. By the time the plant was finished three years ago, an investment of $1.8 million had been made by Merck. The property was located near Campinas, about 50 miles northwest of São Paulo.

Merck had decided to manufacture in Brazil because management believed that it was impossible to hold Merck's market position through import. Given the fact that both import duties and exchange rates grew more protective as one went up the scale from raw material to finished consumer product, important cost advantages could be realized by importing raw materials and upgrading them in products, insofar as the chemical and pharmaceutical industry was concerned. Because of the difficulty of *proving* infringement of process, Merck did not feel that it could completely prevent local competitive products from appearing behind the protective wall. If Merck itself were producing in Brazil, however, executives felt that Merck's superior research, productive capacity, and marketing skills would assure Merck an important part of the Brazilian market.

Swap transactions

Part of the problem the two men faced in analyzing the Brazilian problem was an additional $500,000 investment in the Brazilian plant for an expansion of diuretics production made in the previous year. By December of the present year, Merck had over $2 million invested in fixed assets in the Brazilian firm, divided 50–50 between equipment imported from the United States and local construction. The latter had been financed by a number of swap operations. Merck had sold dollars to the Banco do Brasil for cruzeiros, at the same time buying dollars forward at the same rate of exchange.[1] In addition there was an intercompany loan of $300,000, the U.S. parent being the creditor.

As of November of the present year, Mr. Suffern calculated the *investment at risk* in Brazil at roughly $7.5 million. He defined "investment at risk" as what Merck-U.S. would have to write off if the Brazilian company were lost. Specifically, the items included capital stock[2] and earned surplus, less markup on inventory, plus the intercompany account. Stated another way, total

---

[1] No longer possible in Brazil.
[2] Dollar value at time of investment.

Table J.2
A SWAP TRANSACTION

Transactions	Dr.		Cr.		Explanation
#1	Cr.	84,000	$	1,000	Merck-U.S. pays bank $1,000 and Merck-Brazil receives a Cr. 84,000 loan.
#2	$	1,000	Cr.	261,000	Bank sells dollars at going rate.
One year later					
#3			Cr.	87,360	Merck-Brazil repays Cr. 84,000 to the Bank plus 4 percent interest, or a total of Cr. 87,360.
	Cr.	261,000	$	1,000	Bank buys $1,000 and repays Merck-U.S. $1,000.
	$	1,000			

investment in assets,[3] less inventory markup, less local liabilities, plus intercompany account. The $7.5 million included about $3 million in swaps, the average swap rate during 1961 having been 84.1. That is, dollars had been sold for Cr. 84 and dollar futures purchased at the same rate. The average free exchange rate during 1961 had been 261:1. On the Brazilian bank's books the transactions would take place over the life of a $1,000, one year swap as illustrated in Table J.2.

The bank gains by having available for the period of the swap, say one year, cheap dollars; that is, it pays only Cr. 84 per dollar. It can then turn around and sell the dollars thus gained for Cr. 261 per dollar, thereby securing a net gain of Cr. 177,000 for the period of the swap on which it can earn interest. In addition it earns a low rate of interest (for example, 4 percent) on the Cr. 84,000 loan to Merck-Brazil. The bank pays no interest to Merck-U.S. for the use of the dollars. Any interest the bank earns, thus, is profit to the extent that it exceeds the premium the bank must pay one year hence for the dollars with which to repay Merck; that is, the gains if:

$$(x_n - x_s) \ S_s < i_b \ (x_i S_s - L) + 0.4 \ (L)$$

when

x_n = free market exchange rate at end of swap (Cr./$)
x_s = exchange rate for swap purposes (Cr./$)
S_s = dollar amount of the swap
i_b = commercial interest rate in Brazil
x_i = initial free market exchange rate (Cr./$)
L = cruzeiro loan.

For example, if the exchange rate moved up to 355:1 (from 261:1) during

---

[3]Dollar value at time of acquisition for net fixed assets.

the period of the swap, the bank would have to pay out the original Cr. 261,000, plus an added Cr. 94,000 in order to buy the $1,000 with which to repay Merck-U.S. To have broken even, the bank would have had to realize Cr. 94,000 in interest on the Cr. 177,000 and from the 4 percent charge on the cruzeiro loan to Merck-Brazil (that is, 4 percent of 84,000, or Cr. 3,360) or a return of 51.2 percent (that is, [Cr. 94,000 − Cr. 3,360]/Cr. 177,000).

Merck-Brazil profits so long as the interest on the loan (Cr. 3,360) is less than the expected cruzeiro return on the Cr. 84,000 invested in its business. Merck-Brazil gains if:

$$.04 \, (L) \, r_b \, (L),$$

when

r_b = rate of net return in cruzeiros on the cruzeiro investment in Merck-Brazil.

Built into the projected rate of cruzeiro return are assumptions as to the rate of local inflation, the degree to which that inflation is reflected in the cost of local inflation, the degree to which that inflation is reflected in the cost and prices of Merck products, and the shift in consumption of Merck products induced by the inflation.

Merck-U.S., reflecting the integrated operation, gains only if the cost of the swap in percentage terms (that is, the rate of dollar return on a direct invest-ment at free exchange rates in Merck-Brazil or on an investment elsewhere, whichever is greater) is less than the dollar gain realized by the Brazilian subsidiary at the end rate. Merck-U.S. gains only if:

$$C_s < \frac{r_b \, (L) - .04 \, (L)}{x_s},$$

when

$C_s = \dfrac{r_b \, (S_{\$} x_i)}{x_n}$ or $r_o S_{\$}$, whichever is greater

x_i = initial free exchange rate (Cr./$)

x_n = free exchange rate at end of swap period (Cr./$)

r_o = rate of return available to firm on alternative investment after tax

x_s = exchange rate for swap purposes (Cr./$)

r_b = rate of return on Brazilian investment.

Exposed assets

Although Mr. Suffern estimated a total Merck investment at risk in Brazil of $7.5 million toward the end of the present year, *net exposed assets* were substantially less. By "exposed assets" he referred to those assets vulnerable to exchange loss when converted to U.S. dollars at current exchange rates and which thereby caused exchange losses in consolidating the Brazilian financial

Table J.3
MERCK'S EXPOSED ASSETS IN BRAZIL
(October to present year)

Item	Amount in cruzeiros (millions)
Exposed Assets:	
Cash	Cr. 59
Investments (compulsory deposits on exchange purchased)	58
Accounts receivable, other, prepaid and miscellaneous	65
Accounts receivable (trade, net)	262
Inventory and exchange purchased for imports	300
Total	Cr. 744
Less: Local liabilities, accounts payable and accrued expenses	−44
Exposed assets—before hedging	Cr. 700
Deduct—swaps and local bank loans*	−460
Net Exposed Assets	Cr. 240

*Obligations to pay fixed amounts of cruzeiros in the future, that is, swaps totalling $2,802,000 repayable at 84:1 (Cr. 235.4 million) and local bank loans totalling Cr. 224.6 million.

statement into the U.S. dollar statements of Merck & Co., Inc. The level of exposed assets could be reduced by hedging operations, such as borrowing locally and/or undertaking swap transactions. In that repayment in both cases was in a fixed cruzeiro amount, exposures to inflation and exchange loss were reduced accordingly.

As of October, Messrs. Fernandez and Suffern calculated that Merck's exposed assets in Brazil came to Cr. 240 million, or about $775,000 at the then current free rate of exchange (310:1). Their calculation is shown in Table J.3.

The question in each case was, if a devaluation occurred (that is, increase in the number of cruzeiros required to buy a dollar), what effect would this have on the consolidated accounts of Merck-U.S.? Taking the October 31 current-year estimate of exposed assets, Messrs. Fernandez and Suffern pointed out to the Brazilian management that changes in the exchange rate could easily erase any net cruzeiro shown by the Brazilian company and replace them with a net loss on the books of Merck-U.S. Assuming that the relevant exchange rate at the beginning of the fiscal year (November 30 of the preceding calendar year) was 195:1 and at the end was 310:1 and using the figures provided in Table J.3, Mr. Suffern made the estimates shown in Table J.5. These estimates were for illustrative purposes only and assumed no changes in foreign currency assets and liabilities. Techniques for reflecting exchange losses in the consolidation of financial statements were more refined and exact.

Exchange gain or loss (line 11 on Table J.4) was calculated on a basis similar

Table J.4
BRAZIL—PROFIT AND LOSS ANALYSIS

Thousands $/million cr.	Two years before Cr.	Two years before $	Last year Cr.	Last year $	Current year (projected) Cr.	Current year (projected) $
1. Sales	Cr. 448	$3027	Cr. 652	$3450	Cr. 1022	$3914
2. Cost of sales	268	1812	403	2133	616	2360
3. Gross profit	180	1215	249	1317	406	1554
4. Total expenses	141	950	184	976	322	1234
5. Income before tax	39	265	65	341	84	320
6. Brazilian income tax	7	50	17	89	21	80
7. Net income (loss) before exchange	Cr. 32	$ 215	Cr. 48	$ 252	Cr. 63	$ 240
8. Less: Exchange gain (loss*)		(95)		1		(457)
9. Net income after exchange		$ 120		$ 253		$(217)
10. Less: Additional depreciation (historical rate) on fixed assets				(64)		(82)
11. Adjusted income (loss)		$ 120		$ 189		$(299)

*Loss on exposed assets in consolidation:

Exchange Rates

Beginning year	141–1	197–1	195–1
End year	197–1	195–1	310–1 (est)
Average	148–1	189–1	261–1
U.S. $ investment at risk	$8,263	$7,562	$6,230
Swaps	$5,961	$3,334	$2,802
Swap rate average	N/A	86–1	84–1

to that shown in Table J.5. Starting with the beginning of the next year, the Brazilian subsidiary was required to submit a monthly statement of exposed assets. (See Table J.6.) This report had a dual purpose: (1) to make the Brazilian management aware of the financial measures used by Merck-U.S. and (2) to provide a basis for calculating the exchange loss for the consolidated Merck P/L. Against the totals on the monthly exposed-asset report the exchange rate variation over the month was applied, thereby generating the exchange loss figure. The annual total of the monthly exchange rate losses was entered on line 8 of Table J.4. In addition, the Brazilian operation was debited the difference in the depreciation generated in cruzeiros converted at the current rate and at the rate of exchange at the time of acquisition.

It was all very well and good to analyze and draw attention to the adverse effects of Brazilian inflation and cruzeiro devaluation on the consolidated P/Ls, but the real problem was to prevent the Brazilian firm from thus setting up a drag on overall profit. This concern led to the objective of generating maximum cruzeiro profits with a minimum of exposed assets. While still in Brazil, the two men hit on a scheme of essentially calculating the marginal cost of exposed assets for each product line. Behind that approach lay an assump-

Table J.5
EXCHANGE LOSSES BASED ON EXPOSED ASSETS*

	Cr. millions	Current year			Projected next year	
		At initial rate of 195:1	At end rate of 310:1	Loss**	At end rate of 510:1	Loss†
Exposed assets						
Cash	59	303	190	113	116	74
Investments (compulsory deposits on exchange purchased)	58	297	187	110	114	73
Accounts receivable, others, prepaid and miscellaneous	65	333	210	123	127	83
Accounts receivable trade (net)	262	1344	845	499	514	331
Inventory and exchange purchased for imports	300	1538	968	570	588	380
Total	744	3815	2400	1415	1459	941
Less: local liabilities						
Accounts payable and accrued expenses	44	225	142	83	86	56
Exposed assets before bank borrowings (hedging)	700	3590	2258	1332	1373	885
Deduct swaps and bank loans	460	2359	1484	875	902	582
Net assets exposed to exchange losses	240	1231	774	457	471	303

*Figures are in thousands of dollars
**Column 3 minus column 2.
†Column 5 minus column 3.

tion that the inflation-devaluation problem would get worse rather than better. What they set out to do was to calculate the exposed assets required per unit of sales for each product line and the extent to which product price increases could compensate. The latter was important, for the Brazilian government imposed price controls on a number of Merck products because of their essential quality.

They found that accounts receivable averaged four months. Thus, at any one time one-third of annual sales was represented in accounts receivable, an exposed asset. The Brazilian firm was maintaining eight months of inventory, half of which represented dollar content. Therefore, half of the inventory was exposed, or the equivalent of four month's sales. Exchange deposit requirements were running about two months of annual sales, and miscellaneous cash and deferred charges, one month. In that accounts payable (an inflation hedge) also ran at about one month's sales, these latter two items were balanced off. Therefore, 12 units of sales required roughly ten units of exposed assets. And

Table J.6
BRAZIL—NET EXPOSED ASSETS AS OF _____

	Balance as of	± Variance from last month	± Variance from beginning of year
Month-end exchange rate			
Gross exposed assets			
Less fixed assets			
Gross exposed assets (that is, before hedging)			
Cash			
Receivables			
Inventory			
Other assets			
Less hedges			
Borrowings and credit lines			
Swap loans			
Discounted receivables			
Future exchange contracts			
Other			
Inventories imported from affiliates			
U.S. dollar assets			
Merchandise account, guaranteed rate			
Current liabilities			
Net exposed assets			
Net exposed assets ($000)			
Effect of rate fluctuation on $ value of net exposed assets at beginning of period			

these assets were declining in value at an estimated rate of 40 percent a year. Thus, the firm needed a gain or profit of four units (40 percent of 10) on the sale of 12 units in order merely to break even, or a 33 percent profit on sales. Messrs. Fernandez and Suffern roughed this out at 35 percent. Given this margin, Merck-Brazil could stay even with the expected rate of inflation and cruzeiro devaluation. In order to accomplish this dual purpose of maximizing profit margins and minimizing exposed assets, they announced the "Profit Improvement and Risk Reduction Program."

Profit improvement and risk reduction program

The two men outlined several steps to strengthen Merck's profit position in Brazil, specifically:

1. Reduce A/Rs by
   a. Cutting credit terms from 90 to 30 days.
   b. Instituting an attractive cash discount (5 percent for payment within eight days).

   c. Cutting all government A/Rs not paid within 60 days. (The average had been longer.)

2. Reduce costs by

   a. Reorienting the territory system; that is, reducing the number of towns served and the number of detail men.

   b. Eliminating all surplus personnel even if severance payments had to be made (one month's pay for each year of employment up to ten years, two months' for each year thereafter. Average employment age at this time was five years for the 750 employees then on the payroll.)

3. Reduce exposed assets by

   a. Reviewing product lines and eliminating all products with a high dollar content unless they could generate at least a 60 percent cruzeiro profit margin. (The 35 percent required to keep even with inflation plus a 25 percent profit.)

   b. Reducing inventory to four months (by placing orders before buying foreign exchange and by improving inventory control procedures in order to maintain a perfectly balanced inventory).

   c. Maximizing local debt by

     i. Using *duplicatas*, monthly billing statements acknowledged by the customer's signature, as collateral for bank advances (a *caucao* account), the cost of which was 12 percent plus bank fees or a total of about 20 percent per annum. The usual procedure was for the manufacturing firm to set up an overdraft with a commercial bank, with which the firm then deposited the *duplicatas*. The bank discounted the *duplicatas* by giving a six months' advance, the net proceeds being about 90 percent of their value. These acted as revolving collateral, with payment being credited to the account and additional advances being supported by the delivery of new *duplicatas*.

     ii. Discounting *duplicatas* with local bank.

     iii. Borrowing cruzeiro funds from U.S. and local banks operating in Brazil and from Brazilian or U.S. companies having excess cruzeiros, on the basis of a parent company guarantee when necessary, the rates varying from 17 to 30 percent depending upon duration of the loans.[4]

     iv. Selling Merck-Brazil's own notes or commercial paper through brokers on the open market at about 30 percent per annum.[5]

     v. Swaps

4. Reduce inflationary impact by

   a. Using various assumptions regarding rate of price increase for different inputs (for example, labor, packaging, dollar content, and so on) and allowable price increases, set up profit projections at various sales volumes for each product line. (Given rising local costs, currency devaluation, and relatively fixed prices,

---

[4]Includes commissions, stamp taxes, and so on.

[5]Includes discounts as well as stamp taxes, and so on.

it was reasoned that if the 35 percent profit margin could not be realized on present volume, it might be generated at a smaller volume.)

In addition, they proposed two one-shot changes to save cruzeiros or to provide cruzeiros for working capital to pay off swaps when due, or to reduce risk investment:

1. A change in the fiscal year from one ending November 30 to a terminal date of March 31. Under Brazilian law, taxes payable in any given year were based on profits made in the fiscal year ending during the preceding calendar year. For example, if the fiscal year ending November 30 of the next year were changed to January 31 of the year after that, Merck-Brazil would pay on January 31, two years out taxes on only two months' profits, that is, December and January, and 12 months prior. This would have been the maximum position. The two men felt that it would not be politic to take the maximum position, but to change the fiscal year to March 31. Thus, on March 31, two years out, Merck would pay taxes on four months (December to March of the previous year). Because some of the officers of the company were being changed simultaneously and a revaluation of assets being effected (by Cr. 650,000 to bring assets more in a line with true value, which represented a quadrupling of the capital stock, and incidentally involved the payment of a 10 percent tax), it was felt that one could justify to the Brazilian authorities this change in the fiscal year for business reasons.

2. A change in the corporate form of the Brazilian subsidiary from a *sociedade anonima* (S.A.) to a *sociedad por quotas de responsabilidade limitada*, which was a form of limited partnership. This shift meant that the Merck-Brazil was no longer obliged to pay the 30 percent tax levied on excess corporate revenue (annual increment in the excess of surplus and reserve over and above paid-in capital). Also, the *limitada* form meant much greater flexibility in managing the firm. Price Waterhouse and other similar firms were advising their U.S. clients doing business in Brazil to choose the *limitada* form.

Messrs. Fernandez and Suffern observed that in reducing personnel great care should be exercised not to demoralize the organization. All key personnel were to be assured of their tenure.

They concluded that financing the Brazilian firm by taking in Brazilian equity was out of the question because of the possible conflict in interest that would be generated. Merck-U.S. was spending about 10 percent of its sales on research. The Brazilian firm was dependent upon the parent company for both research and materials. A contractual relationship and repatriation of profit from Brazil through royalties was not an alternative, because Brazil was refusing to permit royalty payments to a foreign company owning more than 50 percent of the Brazilian company paying the royalty.

So-called export swaps were difficult out of Brazil. If, for example, the U.S. firm put up $1 million to be paid off in $1 million worth of exports by the Brazilian firm, one could not be certain that the latter could in fact export that much during the period of the swap. If it exported only $500,000 worth of products, the Brazilian authorities might call the remaining $500,000 an investment, and thus it would be locked in. Also, the firm could not use exports to any of Brazil's bilateral trade agreement partners for purposes of paying off a swap. Finally, the Banco do Brasil had the authority to regulate export prices.

Messrs. Fernandez and Suffern also concluded that Merck-U.S. could not finance Merck-Brazil by extending the latter credit for its purchases from Merck-U.S. in that Merck-Brazil was required to buy foreign exchange in advance of actually importing products.

In conclusion, the two men spelled out the immediate objective as follows: Develop and implement policies necessary to operate the subsidiary, with the key objectives being to:

1. Eliminate consolidated losses and generate a profit.

2. Have the subsidiary stand on its own feet so that it could operate on a cruzeiro cash flow basis sufficient to provide its own working capital requirements without any outside dollar financing.

3. Reduce investment at risk by paying off all maturing swaps without refinancing any part with Merck & Co., Inc. or affiliated company dollar funds.

Discussion questions

1. What is Merck's investment at risk?

2. What is Merck's net exposure?

3. What is left out of Table J.4?

4. Explain the depreciation item in Table J.4.

5. What do you think of the profit improvement program?

6. Why might the needed margin be generated on a smaller volume?

7. Why consolidate financial statements?

Chapter 7
LEGAL STRATEGY

In structuring their international operations, many firms start by determining an optimum legal strategy. Business strategies, such as sales, production, management, finance, ownership, labor, control, are made to conform. One loses sight of the fact that the firm's basic need is to determine the best strategy for generating a profit over the relevant time horizon, not to gain maximum legal security *per se*. Legal counsel should be employed in a consulting capacity, not as the final architect of a business relationship. Therefore, the relevant question one should ask is: Given a set of strategy choices in the business area, what is the best legal strategy? In the final analysis, some of the aforementioned strategy choices may have to be modified due to legal considerations, but rarely should they be determined *solely* by legal rationale.

The legal questions to be considered here can be subsumed under three general questions:

1. What should be the legal character of the party of the first part that represents the principal domestic interest vis-à-vis the foreign interest?

2. What should be the legal character of the party of the second part that represents the principal foreign interest vis-à-vis the domestic?

3. What should be the legal nature of the relationship between the two parties?

In each case, the party representing a principal may be the party itself (a domestic or foreign corporation or its branch), or its agent (possibly a wholly-owned subsidiary), or representative (a third party not controlled by the principal interest except in a limited contractual sense), or an independent contractor. Figure 7.1 illustrates this.

The range of possible legal forms is similar from country to country, but far from identical. In civil law countries (continental Europe and its former colonies, Latin America, and Japan), a corporation is considered to be a contractual relationship, and a minimum number of stockholders is required, always

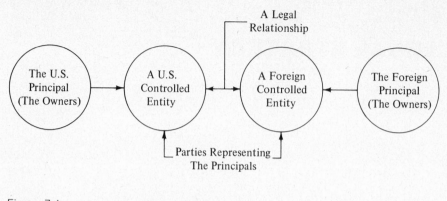

Figure 7.1
CHART OF LEGAL RELATIONSHIP

more than one. Directors do not stand in a fiduciary[1] relationship toward stockholders, but are in an agent relationship and are subject to a supervisory audit initiated by the stockholders. Hence, the stockholders are in a stronger position vis-à-vis the board than, say, in the U.S.

Major corporate control in the civil law countries rests with an executive committee or general director (or managing director) selected by and from the board. Thus, there is no distinction between officers and directors. Corporate nationality may be determined by place of actual management, rather than place of incorporation. According to the common-law concept (United Kingdom and its present and former colonies, United States), on the other hand, a corporation is a juridical person. Hence, a single person may incorporate. There is a fiduciary responsibility on the part of directors to the stockholders, and major control rests with a president elected by the directors but not necessarily from the board. Corporate nationality is often determined by place of incorporation.

Depending upon local law, alternative types of legal organization are:

1. Individual entrepreneur. Personal ownership, personal liability.

2. Branch. Legally indistinguishable from principal; liability runs to principal; often requires a capital allocation.

3. Partnership. Personal and joint liability: participation limited to named partners (individuals, partnerships, or corporations); a consortium if corporations or partnerships are the partners.

4. Limited partnership. Silent partners with liability limited to their share of quotas and full partners with unlimited liability; limited to named partners.

5. Limited partnership with shares. Same as four above except shares of silent partners are transferable.

---

[1]See Glossary.

6. Cooperative. Liability may or may not be limited; occupational limitation may be imposed on transfer of shares; profits may be distributed according to shareholders' participation in business of firm.

7. Close corporation. A limited liability company, or private corporation; participation may be limited to a given number of stockholders (often 50); transferability of shares is limited; no public issue.

8. Public corporation. Limited liability, unlimited shareholding in regard to both number and identity of shareholders; public issue possible.

9. Business trust. Organization in which one or more trustees (may be self-perpetuating) manage assets for specified purposes in which others have a beneficiary interest but no control other than that specified in the trust deed and in law. Ownership may be evidenced by transferable shares.

In 1968 a special type of legal entity was introduced in France, the Groupement d'Interêt Economique (GIE). Essentially, the GIE is a group of corporations or partnerships linked by contract, that is, a consortium. The members retain their personalities and pool whatever it suits them to pool. Their freedom of choice extends both to the purpose of the GIE and the means used, which may consist not only of contribution in cash or kind (those customary under company law), but also solely of activities and even competences in that a GIE may be created without tangible capital. Rules for operation, dissolution, and liquidation are simple, for a GIE proceeds from the will of the parties rather than from the law. Profit taxes are assessed at the member level. Formalities of incorporation are minimized; the mere drawing up of a contract and entry in the commercial register is adequate. Several thousand GIEs have been set up in France, including enterprises of all sizes and sectors. Their principal objective seems to have been related more to service activities (purchase, sale, research, transport, management, and so on) than to manufacturing.

It should be noted that although technically a branch is indivisible from the parent corporation, not infrequently local law requires that in establishing a branch the parent company provide certified copies of its articles of incorporation and by-laws, evidence of reciprocity (i.e., that the state in which the parent is domiciled permits branching by corporations of host country nationality), and of the board decision to establish the branch. The foreign corporation may also be obliged to designate or provide a responsible local represModevtive, a special power of attorney to a local counsel, and in some cases even allocate capital to the branch.

The various corporate forms are defined in commercial codes, generally at the national level, but sometimes at a lower level as in the U.S. where commercial law is a matter of state jurisdiction. In many countries there are forms not generally available in the U.S., particularly those standing between a corporation and partnership, for example, the limited partnership. In Brazil, the so-called *limitada* is very popular because it requires no minimum capital, the number of owners may be unlimited, and no publication of financial statements is required. Often in civil law countries the minimum number of incorporators is five or seven. Therefore, if a foreign firm is setting up a subsidiary, local qualifying shares are required. A problem may arise in this area because it may not be possible to transfer those qualifying shares to the parent once the subsidiary has been created. Hence, 100 percent ownership by the parent becomes impossible. Treasury stock may be very narrowly limited, if permitted at all (as in Japan). And, a corporation may not be permitted to buy its own stock and, if it does, the capital of the corporation may have to be reduced. There may also be voting limits on stock. For example, in Colombia, no one shareholder may vote more than 25 percent of the stock of a corporation, thereby requiring the holding of stock in a subsidiary by different affiliated entities, and sometimes not even that is permitted.

Some other consequences of the choice of legal form for either the first or second parties, but upon which law differs from country to country, are as follows:

1. Degree of public control exercised (audits, reports, disclosure, and so on).

2. Degree of organizational flexibility.

3. Taxation.

4. Ease of borrowing.

5. Treatment under foreign exchange control regulations.

6. Transferability of equity.

7. Ability to engage in certain types of activities (professional services, utilities, banking, mining, and so on).

8. Degree of personal liability.

9. Access to local courts (as in Japan, where a foreign company cannot be a plaintiff).

10. Types of shares or financial participation permitted (common and preferred stock, voting and nonvoting shares, voting power proportional to shares held or one vote per shareholder, bearer[2] and registered shares, cumulative and noncumulative shares,[3] convertible and nonconvertible securities, redeemable and nonredeemable shares, participating and nonparticipating preferred shares, mortgages and debentures, founders' shares such as *partes beneficiares*).

11. Paid-in requirements.

12. Minimum capital requirements.

13. Debt-equity ratio permitted.

14. Ease of dissolution, merger, and dedomiciling (i.e., moving a company's legal seat, or domicile, from one country to another).

---

[2]Reasons for bearer shares are anonymity and ease of transfer and, hence, of negotiability. For example, "Technically ... nominal shares can ... be bought [in Switzerland] by foreigners, but the owners have to be registered. The directors of a Swiss company have the right to register any person or group to whom they do not want to give voting rights. . . . Bearer shares . . . can be bought by anybody, including foreigners." Both types of shares have one vote each. Arrind V. Phatak, *Evolution of World Enterprises* (New York, American Management Association, 1971) p. 104.

[3]See Glossary.

15. Location of decision-making authority (for example, shareholders, board, officers).
16. Degree to which assets are exposed.
17. Number of shareholders required.
18. Antitrust vulnerability.
19. Basis for determining nationality (hence, the applicability of various national laws).
20. The requirement to share management in some manner with employees.
21. The requirement to share profit with employees.
22. A requirement that a given percentage of board and/or executive members be local nationals.

One other point should be made in respect to the differences in legal approach between civil law and common law countries. In the former, contracts tend to be rather lean in that many of the contractual conditions are embedded in law and need not be repeated in the contract. By contrast, contracts in common law countries often contain many pages of so-called "boiler plate," spelling out definitions, precise relationships, liabilities, and the like. One accustomed to the common law approach should be wary of a civil law contract unless one is thoroughly familiar with the relevant law.

LEGAL CHARACTER OF FIRST PARTY (THE DOMESTIC ASSOCIATE) 7.1

A business interest wishing to develop a continuing relationship with a foreign market needs to determine what legal form is best. In most cases, some will be clearly impossible. But the full range of conceivable options on the domestic side as to the legal entity lying on the international interface is as follows:

1. An individual domestic entrepreneur.
2. A domestic partnership.
3. A closely held or personal holding company.
4. The stockholders of the domestic firm.
5. Two or more domestic firms (a joint-venture agreement or consortium).
6. Principal domestic firm itself, and alone (including domestic branches and agencies).
7. A domestic subsidiary of the firm (a domestic holding company).
8. The domestic subsidiary of two or more firms (a joint holding company).
9. An associated foreign enterprise, which in turn may take any one of the forms listed above.

Major variables relevant to the choice of strategy in this area are: ownership structure of the principal firm, degree of liability risk running from the foreign enterprise, antitrust considerations, the protection of property rights, and tax law. In respect to the first two alternatives, in which an individual or partnership may be used on the international interface as agent, representative, or contractor, it should be noted that in some jurisdictions unincorporated entities cannot take credit against domestic income tax liability for foreign income taxes paid by a foreign corporation in which equity interest may be held.[4] This is the case in the United States. For a large, publicly held corporation, alternative four would be awkward. If the risk of liability is considered high, the domestic principal (as well as its stockholders) may desire to insert a domestic or foreign corporate subsidiary between itself and the principal foreign interest or to operate through a domestic representative or contractor. Possible risks to be considered in this respect are: damage suits for alleged nonperformance, personal injury, errors and omissions, and default or bankruptcy on the part of the foreign interest. On the other hand, a reputable international firm that considers itself in a foreign market to stay is unlikely to permit a foreign subsidiary, agent, or representative to destroy its image of reliability and quality, but it has been known to happen.

It should be noted that one of the problems rendering cross-national mergers difficult lies in corporate law, in that the laws of some countries are very restrictive in reference to the dissolution of a corporation. A certain percentage of the stockholders (100 percent in Belgium) may have to acquiesce. And a merger may be held to constitute dissolution and reorganization, which can be very expensive if national law treats the dissolution of a corporation and the transfer of its assets to a new merged entity as a taxable transaction tantamount to the distribution of the proceeds of a liquidation and subsequent reinvestment by the individual stockholders.

7.2   LEGAL CHARACTER OF SECOND PARTY (THE FOREIGN ASSOCIATE)

Within the limitation of local law, those alternatives listed in Section 7.1 are available. If the associated foreign business entity is completely separate from the domestic firm (party of the first part) in terms of ownership and management control, the legal character of the foreign associate is, of course, a given insofar as the domestic firm is concerned. It has no choice. The domestic firm may, however, have a choice of associating with several different foreign entities or may exert some influence on its selected associate in the direction of encouraging it to establish a subsidiary or a partnership of joint subsidiaries on the part of two or more foreign firms. Business reasons possibly making such structures optimum are: the possession of necessary services to exploit the target market by more than one foreign firm, inadequate financial re-

---

[4]They can, of course, take foreign taxes as a cost, thereby reducing taxable income.

sources in a single foreign firm, a need to isolate the projected enterprise from other involvements of the associated foreign firm in order to establish a desired equity or control position, and a need for the foreign business entity with which the domestic firm is to enter into relationship to be located in a jurisdiction different from that of the foreign principal. There is a danger, however, that the foreign subsidiary or partnership (if limited) may have no tangible assets and, hence, may carry little real liability.

The legal character of the associated foreign firm may be very important to the associate domestic firm if ownership and management control are closely related. For example, a family owned and managed corporation may slip out of family control. Also, a close corporation is legally obligated generally to disclose less of its operations. If, however, the relationship between the two firms is such that the domestic enterprise owns a controlling equity share of the foreign enterprise, a close corporation or a limited partnership with or without shares may be entirely appropriate.

CHOICE OF RELATIONSHIP BETWEEN THE TWO PARTIES   7.3

The legal relationship between associated firms on the international interface may take a number of forms, specifically:

1. Continuing communication ("understandings")
2. Agreement (cartel, conference, conscious parallelism)
3. Representation (one that acts for another vis-à-vis third parties but is liable for its own acts)
4. Distributorship (one that contracts to buy a firm's goods and services and sells to third parties)
5. Agency (one that buys nothing from the firm—its principal—but acts on its behalf as defined by agreement, with liability running to the principal)
6. Contract (management, management prerogative,[5] personnel recruitment, technical service, cooperative research, license, lease, manufacturing, purchase and sale, design, technical consulting, construction, turnkey, turnkey-plus)
7. Branch relationship (an executive agency or direct operation with a permanent place of business)
8. Partnership agreement
9. Limited partnership agreement
10. Participation in a limited partnership with shares
11. Co-ownership of a close corporation
12. Co-investment in a public corporation

---

[5]A contract in which a firm has the right to exercise managerial control over another firm in event of certain specified eventualities, such as dropping below a minimum sales volume or profit level.

The variables relevant to the selection of the optimum relationship are: degree and type of control deemed necessary, time horizon, volume of business, financial requirements, attitude of the associated foreign management, plus various legal considerations, such as antitrust, protection of property rights, and taxation. In no case should a firm enter into an international business relationship without the advice of legal counsel experienced in these matters.

Antitrust considerations

In the U.S. case, antitrust implications may arise whenever two or more firms are involved. In that U.S. antimonopoly law is probably the most developed and has the broadest application to international business transactions, the practitioner in any way involved with U.S. firms or the U.S. market must be guided to some degree by its restraints.

U.S. antitrust proceedings may be initiated either by the U.S. government or by private parties alleging injury due to the illegal acts. In the first case, possible remedies are a consent decree (essentially an out-of-court agreement by the firm to do or not do certain things) or judicial decision calling for termination or modification of the offending practices or agreements, divestiture of certain assets, compulsory licensing, creation of a competing firm, forfeiture of property, denial of trading rights, deprivation of patent protection, fine, and/or imprisonment of responsible executives. Action initiated by private parties alleging injury, often after a finding of guilty following a government-initiated case, can result in an award of treble damages. A U.S. court gets jurisdiction over a foreign party if it has assets in the U.S. (including patents), conducts any business in the U.S., or has officers present in the U.S.

Of relevance in this discussion are the foreign trade provisions in the Sherman Act (1890) and Clayton Act (1914), as amended by the Robinson-Patman Act (1936) and augmented by the Federal Trade Commission Act (1970). The first renders the following to be misdemeanors: (1) any agreement restraining commerce among the states or with foreign nations, and (2) any attempt to monopolize any part of interstate commerce or trade with foreign nations or with U.S. possessions. The Sherman Act permits various penalties to be imposed and declares that the injured private parties may recover "threefold the damages by him sustained." The Clayton Act declares as illegal (1) tying agreements (a sale or purchase conditional in some way on an agreement not to deal with a competitor) which may have the effect to "substantially lessen competition or to create a monopoly in any line of commerce" within the United States, and (2) the acquisition by one corporation engaged in commerce of stock in another corporation if the effect is "substantially to lessen competition, or to create a monopoly of any line of commerce" in any section of the country. The Robinson-Patman Act defines certain specific practices as illegal, such as price discrimination between different buyers and the paying of rebates, but the restraint must be felt within the United States, which means that discrimination among foreign buyers would be considered legal within U.S. law. In effect, such domestic practices are *per se* violations (those that are inherently illegal because the adverse effect on competition is assumed). The Federal Trade Commission Act gives the FTC authority to police unfair methods of competition in both domestic and foreign trade. The division of authority between the FTC and the Antitrust Division of the Justice Department is not clear.

Various business arrangements are exempted from attack under antitrust law either by executive decision or by statute. For example, the executive power has been used to shield U.S. oil companies that joined the Iranian Oil Consortium in 1954 and, more recently, their participation in a joint consultative board to negotiate with producer nations. In the latter case, more than 20 oil companies formed the board to deal more effectively with the producer nations. It is reported that they have obtained from the U. S. Justice Department a "letter of exemption" stating that the department has no current intention to initiate any antitrust action against them because of this activity. In the absence of legislative authority empowering Justice to make such exemptions, some experts doubt the legality of the move. The general rule, according to court decision, is that joint venturing overseas by firms competing in the domestic market implies a conspiracy to restrain trade either in the United States or in foreign commerce. Some of the statutory exemptions are:

1. Regulated industries (those under the jurisdiction of such agencies as the Federal Maritime Commission, Federal Communication Commission, Federal Power Commission, and Civil Aeronautics Board)

2. Legally exempt activities: agricultural cooperatives, export associations (Webb-Pomerene Association)[6]

3. Those to which immunity may be granted by the Executive: defense industry (Defense Production Act of 1950), small business (Small Business Mobilization Act of 1953). In the former case, approval of the Attorney General is required; in the latter, the Small Business Administration.

The following is a reasonable statement of the major risks that international firms run in respect to U.S. antitrust law and regulation. In each situation the actual degree of risk (that is, likelihood of prosecution) rests on (1) the visibility of the firms involved in terms of dominance by sector and/or geographical area, (2) sheer size of the firm, (3) the possibility of demonstrating an actual or probable restraint on U.S. trade (trade does not include investment), (4) the willingness of a foreign government to act to protect the allegedly illegal act

---

[6]The Webb-Pomerene Act (1918) authorizes joint facilities, price fixing, and allocation of orders among members. Members may be required to export through the association, but the association must engage solely in export trade (joint foreign manufacturing facilities are not covered nor is the export of capital). An association may not engage in domestic business; it may not restrain non-member exports; it may not enter into agreements with foreign companies that are illegal for independent U.S. firms. There were 28 Webb-Pomerene Associations operative as of the end of 1976.

by interposing its own law or diplomatic representation, and (5) the ability of the U.S. government to get jurisdiction over either the assets, employees, owners, or valuable commercial rights of the firms. In cases involving monopoly or attempted monopoly an important question is always, what is the relevant market, both in geographical terms and product terms? For example, are hand-held and electric razors in the same market? Is a nickel producer a potential competitor in the battery market? U.S. courts have defined the market as "the area of effective competition" which is not exactly clarifying in that all but the most essential goods and services compete for the taxpayer's disposable income, if any.

Practices that *appear* to be vulnerable in at least some circumstances, given judicial rulings are:

1. Joint venturing overseas by firms in competition within the United States, even by members of a Webb-Pomerene Association (unless it can be shown that the only effect is to reduce competition among the parties in a foreign market).

2. The acquisition of a foreign firm by a U.S. company, if that acquisition significantly reduces actual or potential competition within the United States or in U.S. foreign trade.

3. Participation by a U.S. firm in a foreign cartel that operates in such a manner as to reduce competition within the United States or in U.S. foreign trade (either importing or exporting), unless the cartel is enforced by foreign law.

4. Agreements between a U.S. firm and a foreign firm (particularly if the U.S. firm has a noncontrolling equity interest in the foreign firm) to divide markets and fix prices, that is, not to compete. (Restraint of a firm's own trade may be considered illegal.)

5. The acquisition by a foreign firm of a competing U.S. firm if, by so doing, competition within the United States or U.S. foreign trade is significantly reduced. (It appears that the acquisition of a *potential* U.S. competitor may likewise be a violation unless it can be shown that the acquiring company had no alternative feasible means of entering the U.S. market and that the acquisition is likely to lead to ultimate deconcentration of the market, the so-called "toe-hold doctrine").

6. The merger of two foreign firms, each of which has competing subsidiaries in the United States.

7. The use of technical assistance or other agreements not ancillary to a patent, copy-right, trademark, or trade secret to divide markets, force the purchase of the contractor's parts, and fix prices. (Although a simple condition not to sell the relevant products in specified markets imposed on the recipient of the technology may be all right if not for an excessive period of time, if production of the product depends on the technology, and if the agreement stands alone and is not part of a web of such agreements).

8. The use of patent pooling or cross licensing or mutual exchange of technical assistance as instruments for effectuating a general conspiracy to divide markets, if there is an effect on U.S. trade.

9. Restriction of a licensed foreign manufacturer to sell only outside the United States or to sell only in his own country.

10. Agreement with a foreign manufacturer-licensee that the U.S. licensor will not export to the home country of the licensee.

11. Imposition of a restriction on any licensee to the effect that he will not use any other trademark during the life of the agreement.

12. Discrimination between domestic and foreign sales when such discrimination is for the purpose of restraining a competitor's trade or is not based on differences in quantities purchased, cost of delivery, competitive conditions in a particular locality, or grade and quality (such as tying clauses to the effect that a second party must purchase the licensor's parts or services exclusively).

13. The merger of two or more foreign firms, or the acquisition by one foreign firm of another foreign firm, if the effect in the U.S. is to reduce competition (which would be the case if they had been competing in the U.S. prior to the merger or acquisition).

14. Imposition by the foreign owner of a U.S. patent on its U.S. licensee a requirement that he abide by certain practices that have the effect of restricting competition beyond the patent monopoly (e.g., a requirement that a particular antibiotic drug be sold only in dosage form and that prior approval must be obtained from the licensor before selling it in bulk form).

15. So-called improper payments to secure business may be in violation of the Robinson-Patman Act as an "undisclosed brokerage." (The Act was held in 1976 to cover commercial bribery, a premise that, if followed by other courts, could lead to treble damage claims by rival firms alleging that the bribes caused them to lose business.)

16. Adherence by a U.S. corporation to an international boycott that has the effect of restraining other U.S. companies from competing as subcontractors (that is, a refusal by the defendant corporation to deal with blacklisted subcontractors).

17. Selling foreign-made products in the U.S. at prices lower than the same goods are sold in the home or other markets may violate the Robinson-Patman Act, which forbids price discrimination.

18. Acquisition by a U.S. company with a foreign operation of another U.S. firm, likewise with a foreign operation, where the foreign operation of the acquired firm is a potential competitor within the U.S. of the acquiring company's foreign operation.

19. Cross-licensing so as to protect the contracting firms from external competition.

It has been observed, "On the basis of ... recent activity [by the U.S. Department of Justice], it seems reasonable to anticipate a number of suits alleging violation of section 7 [of the Clayton Act] through mergers involving foreign companies in some manner."[7] Possible anticompetitive effects of mergers involving foreign interests include (1) mergers among foreign firms owning or potentially owning a U.S. base of operations, (2) international mergers affecting U.S. commerce through imports, (3) international mergers affecting U.S. commerce through exports, and (4) foreign conglomerate mergers.

---

[7]P. L. Graham, D. H. J. Herman, and Sumner Marcus, "Section 7 of the Clayton Act and Merger Involving Foreign Interests," *Stanford Law Review*, vol. 23, no. 2, January 1971, p. 207.

Practices probably safe under U.S. law include (1) the granting of an exclusive patent or trademark license for a country (but if more than one complete, that is, nonexclusive, license is given in a country, the trademark or patent may be lost); (2) giving exclusive technical assistance or know-how agreements if not part of a larger pattern of restriction (such as a contract between two dominant companies not to provide the technology to anyone else); (3) the fixing of prices to be charged by licensees on patented products; (4) the allocation of territories and setting of prices by a parent corporation in respect to majority-owned foreign subsidiaries (or those in which the parent has enough stock to maintain effective control); and (5) joint holding by two or more firms competitive within the U.S. market on a single foreign project (a "one shot deal").

U.S. courts have held that a U.S. firm that provides technical assistance (nonproprietary technology) to a foreign company and enters into an agreement not to sell into the recipient's market (thereby restraining U.S. trade, namely its own exports) is permissible if the restraint is ancillary to the development of the technology in a new territory (otherwise the recipient would not be willing to build a plant incorporating the technology) and is otherwise reasonable.

A 1974 decision apparently upheld the right of the U.S. government to enter into voluntary restraint agreements with foreign governments or producers to limit imports of specific products into the United States causing injury to domestic industry and thereby avoid the imposition of a permanent import barrier. In a case brought by a U.S. consumer group, a court ruled that such agreements did not purport to be enforceable, either as contracts or as government actions with the force of law, and hence were not conspiracies in restraint of U.S. trade.

As the first of its kind, an agreement was signed in June 1976 by the United States and Germany providing for cooperation regarding restrictive business practices, thereby formalizing preexisting informal cooperation. The agreement provided that the antitrust authorities in the two countries assist each other in connection with antitrust investigations or proceedings, studies related to competition policy, and activities related to restrictive business practices undertaken by international organizations in which both are members. The agreement placed a positive responsibility on both to "provide the other party with any significant information which comes to the attention of its antitrust authorities and which involves restrictive business practices which, regardless of origin, have a substantial effect on the domestic or international (trade) or such other party."[8] An earlier U.S. agreement with Canada simply assures the Canadian government that it will be notified prior to prosecution

---

[8]Quoted in Michael L. Kadish, Joseph A. Vicario, Laura D. Stith, "Imports, Exports, and Related Matters," *Law and Policy in International Business*, vol. 9, no. 1, 1977, pp. 98–99.

of an antitrust case affecting Canada and be given an opportunity for its views to be heard. As of early 1977, the U.S. was in the process of negotiating agreements with the U.K., Australia, and Japan along the lines of the German accord. The U.S. purpose was to develop a series of bilateral agreements into an "international judicial agreement," which would prohibit firms from engaging in illegal border-crossing activities.[9]

Since the early 1970s both foreign and American firms may seek an informal, unofficial opinion from the U.S. Justice Department of the legality of a proposed merger or acquisition under the business review procedure. A favorable review states only the enforcement intention of the Department of Justice at the time of review and does not bar the Department from future action. In practice, no criminal actions have been brought against companies availing themselves of this procedure and which made full and accurate disclosures of all of the relevant details at the time. It is quite clear, however, that many firms do not undertake such inquiries so as to avoid drawing attention to their activities, particularly in that the business review procedure does not produce a binding opinion that would constitute a shield against subsequent prosecution.

The National Association of Manufacturers undertook in 1973 a survey of "several hundred firms with international interests." Some 70 percent of those responding ("over 100 firms") indicated that U.S. antitrust regulations and enforcement procedures had led to a decline in their international competitiveness. It was alleged that "the most important antitrust problem area is restrictions placed upon foreign joint venture formation by U.S. firms."[10] The report continued,

Uncertainty as to what will be attacked by antitrust officials and what will be upheld in court continually leads business decision-makers to turn down profitable and legal ventures because of fear of an encounter with the justice department. The business review procedure as presently structured is of little practical use to firms in doubt about antitrust law."[11]

The NAM report claimed that U.S. firms were compelled to operate abroad under stricter antitrust law than their foreign competitors due to the extraterritorial reach of the U.S. law. "American manufacturers are being placed at a competitive disadvantage vis-à-vis both state-controlled trading agencies and less-restricted foreign competitors." And more, "A standard of 'reasonableness' has not been evident in U.S. international antitrust procedures, both with respect to probable competitive effects and in light of conflicting national

---

[9]*Japan Economic Journal,* 2 July 1976, p. 2

[10]*The International Implications of U.S. Antitrust Laws* (Washington: National Association of Manufacturers, 1974), p. 12.

[11]Ibid, p. 12.

economic objectives." The NAM report concludes by urging a careful national study as to how antitrust law impinges on U.S. business competitiveness and "strong new initiatives toward international antitrust policy harmonization."[12] Even an impartial observer might be led to conclude that steps should be taken to reduce the uncertainty of U.S. antitrust law, both as to its content and its enforcement, and the elimination of the notion of *per se* violations, which renders any tests of reasonableness irrelevant. Insofar as international policy harmonization is concerned, one can already sense a certain tendency for antitrust law in the EEC, Japan, and the U.S. to converge. A number of countries, until recently critical of the long arm of U.S. antitrust law, have themselves begun to introduce laws on competition that seem vaguely familiar.

It should be kept in mind that there are two general cases in which the antimonopoly law of the U.S. type does not have a great deal of relevance. The higher a firm's fixed cost ratio, the less likely it is to be able to restrict output. Rather, there is great internal pressure to grow and, depending upon price-demand elasticities, to grow by reducing price and expanding output. Therefore a monopolist or oligopolist may behave very much as though he were in a truly competitive market. This situation also means that the government does not have to police the system as rigorously, which may be a necessary, if not sufficient, condition for the close identification of Japanese business and government. Much of Japanese industry falls into the first situation by reason of its very high fixed cost/total cost ratio due to the lifetime employment system and the typically high debt-equity ratios.

The second situation rendering the importance of antitrust regulation substantially less important is a small national market. A relatively small market makes many industries into decreasing-cost industries over the relevant range, and hence into natural monopolies. Another way of saying the same thing is that there is only room for one plant if it is to produce at anything approaching its minimum average cost. In such case, an antimonopoly law makes little sense, although price control may. Indeed, the administrative difficulty of maintaining adequate price control may constitute a pressure for pushing such enterprises into the public sector. It is of interest to note that Article 37 of the Rome Treaty requires member states to "progressively adjust any state monopolies of a commercial character in such a manner as will ensure the exclusion, at the date of expiry of the transitional period, of all discrimination between the nationals of member states in regard to conditions of supply and marketing."[13]

It appears that governments generally are becoming increasingly concerned about the anational political-economic power of the larger multinational firms. In respect to U.S. legal action against Westinghouse and two of its Japanese licensees, *Business International* observed:

---

[12]Ibid, p. 12.

[13]*European Community*, February 1971, p. 21.

Table 7.1
PERCENT SHARES OF VALUE ADDED BY LARGEST U.S. MANUFACTURING COMPANIES
(100 = Value added by all manufacturing firms)

Shares of	1947	1954	1958	1963	1967
Largest 50 firms	17	23	23	25	25
Largest 100 firms	23	30	30	33	33
Largest 150 firms	27	34	35	37	38
Largest 200 firms	30	37	38	41	42

Source: Census of Manufacturers, 1967. Reprinted in *Monthly Economic Letter* (First National City Bank), April 1972, p. 13.

One of the most ominous long-term implications of the case is the evidence of growing internationalization of antitrust efforts—and increasing extraterritorial application of antitrust laws—by governments.... As coordination, cooperation, and exchange of information among at least the developed countries' antitrust divisions increases, companies may soon be faced with something like a concerted world-wide antitrust campaign mounted against the largest international companies by a number of governments in common. [14]

An obvious reason for this governmental interest around the world is the growing concentration of world business, both at the national and international levels. But, growing concentration may mean more intense competition internationally. The automotive industry is a case in point.

There are two common measures of economic concentration. The first has to do with the shares of total activity accounted for by the 50, 100, or 200 largest firms (generally measured by corporate assets, sales, or value added in the case of manufacturing). (A recent data series is given in Table 7.1.) The second, a measure of industry or product market concentration, is the share of the value of shipments or value added by the largest firms, usually the top four, eight, 20, or 50, of the relevant market.

Quite apart from the French Groupement d'Interêt Economique, which has already been mentioned, a number of governments (for example, the Japanese, the French, and the United Kingdom) have been promoting mergers among national companies so as to put them in a better position to compete with the larger U.S.-based multinationals. According to a 1965 survey of 152 countries,[15] 1 or 2 percent of the companies in each country accounted for between 70 to 80 percent of the business conducted within their respective nations. Only 20,637 companies—less than 2 percent of the total—controlled 70 to 80 percent of all business conducted in the nonsocialist world. Outside North America, 17,137 companies accounted for this portion of the world's

---

[14]*Business International*, September 18, 1970, p. 299.

[15]By the research department of *International Management*. Reported in *International Management*, December 1965, p. 40 ff.

Table 7.2
NUMBER OF FIRMS CONTROLLING 75 PERCENT OF ALL BUSINESS (1965)

Industrialized countries

Germany	1,353	Belgium	231
United Kingdom	1,322	Spain	192
Japan	1,125	Norway	81
France	936	Greece	67
Italy	639	Ireland	44
Sweden	281	Luxembourg	19
Holland	236	Iceland	9

Latin American countries

Mexico	1,355	Chile	497
Argentina	922	Colombia	492
Venezuela	621	Uruguay	300
Peru	545	Puerto Rico	227

Source: Reprinted by special permission from the December 1965 issue of *International Management*. Copyright McGraw-Hill International Publications Limited. All rights reserved.

business; 3,500 companies within North America. Indeed, in the United States, only about 100 companies controlled 60 percent of the nation's capital assets in manufacturing, and an estimated 80 percent of the direct U.S. investment overseas as of 1967 was in the hands of 187 enterprises.[16] The number of firms accounting for about 75 percent of all business is shown by country in Table 7.2.

A more recent EEC study revealed that within the nine member countries the concentration ratios in the various industries studied (42) had risen only slightly between 1969 and 1972–73. It also revealed that the size distribution between each industry's four leading firms had remained virtually unchanged. Nonetheless, "throughout the Community, the absolute level of concentration is generally fairly high, and indeed the level would be higher if concentration were measured by reference to profits and other financial variables."[17]

Some further measures of the growing relative size of the largest corporations in 1973, the U.S. Tariff Commission estimated that private corporations controlled some $268 billion in short-term assets, substantially more than the official reserves of *all* countries combined ($152 billion). Likewise in 1973, the combined turnover (i.e., sales) of the largest 200 corporations was placed at $775 billion, or about 32.9 percent of the Gross Domestic Product of all 23

---

[16]Raymond Vernon, *Sovereignty at Bay, the Multinational Spread of U.S. Enterprises* (New York: Basic Books, 1971), p. 18

[17]*Annual Reports on Competition in OECD Member Countries* (Paris: Organization for Cooperation and Development, 1976/ no. 2), p. 160

Table 7.3
THE WORLD'S LARGEST CORPORATIONS (1974)

Rank 1974	1973	Company	Country	Sector	Turnover $ million	Net profit $ million	Staff (thousands)
1	2	Exxon (Esso)	U.S.A.	Oil	42,061.3	3,142.2	133.0
2	4	Royal Dutch/Shell Group	NL/GB	Oil	33,037.1	2,715.2	164.0
3	1	General Motors	U.S.A.	Motor Ind.	31,549.5	950.1	734.0
4	3	Ford Motor	U.S.A.	Motor Ind.	23,620.6	360.9	467.7
5	7	Texaco	U.S.A.	Oil	23,255.5	1,586.4	76.4
6	8	Mobil Oil	U.S.A.	Oil	18,929.0	1,047.4	78.1
7	15	British Petroleum	G.B.	Oil	18,269.2	1,140.1	68.0
8	14	Standard Oil (Cal.)	U.S.A.	Oil	17,191.2	970.0	39.5
9	53	National Iranian Oil	Iran	Oil	16,802.0	—	50.0
10	12	Gulf Oil	U.S.A.	Oil	16,458.0	1,065.0	52.7
11	9	Unilever	GB/NL	Food	13,666.7	362.8	357.0
12	6	General Electric	U.S.A.	Electrical goods	13,413.1	608.1	404.0
13	10	IBM	U.S.A.	Electrical goods	12,675.3	1,837.6	292.4
14	11	ITT	U.S.A.	Misc.	11,154.4	451.1	409.0
15	5	Chrysler	U.S.A.	Motor Ind.	10,971.4	—52.1	255.9
16	13	Philip's Gloeilampenfabr.	NL	Electrical goods	9,422.4	273.5	412.0
17	18	U.S. Steel	U.S.A.	Steel	9,186.4	634.9	187.5
18	26	Standard Oil (Indiana)	U.S.A.	Oil	9,085.4	970.3	47.2
19	50	Cie Française des Pétroles	F	Oil	8,908.6	294.5	27.4
20	16	Nippon Steel	Japan	Steel	8,843.6	113.1	97.8
21	43	August Thyssen-Hütte	D	Steel	8,664.0	130.0	150.9
22	27	BASF	D	Chemicals	8,497.0	201.0	111.0
23	22	Hoechst	D	Chemicals	7,821.1	205.2	178.7
24	33	Shell Oil	U.S.A.	Oil	7,633.5	620.5	32.3
25	17	Western Electric	U.S.A.	Electrical goods	7,381.7	310.6	190.0
26	41	ENI	I	Oil	7,172.8	—91.3	92.2
27	44	Continental Oil	U.S.A.	Oil	7,041.4	327.6	41.2
28	28	ICI (Imperial Chem. Ind.)	G.B.	Chemicals	6,911.8	568.0	201.0
29	29	du Pont de Nemours	U.S.A.	Chemicals	6,910.1	403.5	136.9
30	54	Atlantic Richfield	U.S.A.	Oil	6,739.7	474.6	28.8
31	25	Siemens	D	Electrical goods	6,701.7	189.1	309.0
32	19	Volkswagen	D	Motor Ind.	6,568.7	—312.6	203.7
33	21	Westinghouse Electric	U.S.A.	Electrical goods	6,466.1	28.1	199.2
34	37	Bayer	D	Chemicals	6,300.9	189.4	134.8
35	23	Daimler Benz	D	Motor Ind.	6,288.7	100.5	154.9
36	38	Montedison	I	Chemicals	6,189.8	173.6	153.2
37	20	Hitachi	Japan	Electrical goods	6,183.3	120.2	144.9
38	24	Toyota Motor	Japan	Motor Ind.	5,948.3	100.0	58.9
39	87	ELF Group	F	Oil	5,900.4	238.2	22.3
40	73	Occidental Petroleum	U.S.A.	Oil	5,719.4	280.7	34.4
41	30	Mitsubishi Heavy Ind.	Japan	Machines	5,664.8	50.1	114.1
42	31	Nestlé	CH	Food	5,603.2	250.1	138.8
43	48	Bethlehem Steel	U.S.A.	Steel	5,381.0	342.0	121.6
44	36	Renault	F	Motor Ind.	5,341.7	7.3	206.0
45	40	British Steel	G.B.	Steel	5,340.9	170.5	223.0
46	56	Union Carbide	U.S.A.	Chemicals	5,320.1	530.1	109.6
47	35	Goodyear	U.S.A.	Tires	5,256.2	157.5	154.2
48	60	British-American Tobacco	G.B.	Consumption	5,152.4	275.7	157.0
49	57	Tenneco	U.S.A.	Oil	5,001.5	321.5	61.0
50	114	Petrobrás	Brazil	Oil	4,989.7	540.6	48.8

Table 7.3 (Continued)

Rank 1974	Rank 1973	Company	Country	Sector	Turnover $ million	Net profit $ million	Staff (thousands)
51	80	Phillips Petroleum	U.S.A.	Oil	4,980.7	402.1	30.8
52	45	Internat. Harvester	U.S.A.	Machines	4,965.9	124.1	111.0
53	77	Dow Chemical	U.S.A.	Chemicals	4,938.5	557.5	53.3
54	34	Nissan Motor	Japan	Motor Ind.	4,933.6	68.6	73.3
55	58	Procter & Gamble	U.S.A.	Chemicals	4,912.3	316.7	50.0
56	39	Matsushita Electric. Ind.	Japan	Electrical goods	4,837.5	178.7	88.2
57	47	LTV	U.S.A.	Steel	4,768.0	111.7	66.0
58	85	Mannesmann	D	Steel	4,717.2	87.2	106.8
59	46	AEG-Telefunken	D	Electrical goods	4,641.3	—261.7	170.4
60	62	Pechiney Ugine Kuhlmann	F	Steel	4,623.5	154.6	105.4
61	55	Esmark	U.S.A.	Packing	4,615.7	68.1	33.5
62	42	RCA	U.S.A.	Electrical goods	4,594.3	113.3	116.0
63	51	Eastman Kodak	U.S.A.	Photo	4,583.6	629.5	124.1
64	61	Nippon Kokan	Japan	Steel	4,582.9	79.0	49.2
65	75	Ruhrkohle	D	Mines	4,529.8	—	156.1
66	63	Kraftco	U.S.A.	Food	4,471.4	94.6	50.4
67	100	Union Oil of Cal.	U.S.A.	Oil	4,419.0	288.0	15.4
68	72	Rockwell Internat.	U.S.A.	Machines	4,408.5	130.3	137.5
69	49	Fiat	I	Motor Ind.	4,358.2	0.1	188.7
70	—	Ford Motor of Canada	Canada	Motor Ind.	4,355.2	157.8	38.1
71	112	Idemitsu Kosan	Japan	Oil	4,345.1	—11.1	10.5
72	64	Saint-Gobain	F	Packing	4,344.5	146.4	146.0
73	69	Rhône-Poulenc	F	Chemicals	4,234.2	179.6	119.0
74	74	Sumitomo Metal Ind.	Japan	Steel	4,152.0	58.2	43.7
75	83	Gutehoffnungshütte	D	Machines	4,123.6	26.2	90.7
76	52	Tokyo Shibaura Electric	Japan	Electrical goods	4,116.6	48.8	119.0
77	71	Caterpillar Tractor	U.S.A.	Machines	4,082.1	229.2	80.1
78	67	Akzo	NL	Chemicals	4,009.5	141.6	105.4
79	86	ARBED	L	Steel	3,944.9	44.7	27.8
80	82	Kawasaki Steel	Japan	Steel	3,891.6	52.1	44.0
81	90	ESTEL	NL	Steel	3,799.8	120.3	77.6
82	122	Sun Oil	U.S.A.	Oil	3,799.6	377.7	27.7
83	153	Amerada Hess	U.S.A.	Oil	3,744.5	201.9	5.8
84	70	Dunlop Pirelli	GB/I	Tires	3,731.0	19.8	171.6
85	68	Boeing	U.S.A.	Aeronautics	3,730.7	72.4	74.4
86	—	Imperial Oil	Canada	Oil	3,688.1	296.5	16.1
87	76	Firestone	U.S.A.	Tires	3,674.9	154.0	120.0
88	59	British Leyland Motor	G.B.	Motor Ind.	3,644.1	—56.3	207.8
89	78	Kobe Steel	Japan	Steel	3,584.7	39.3	44.1
90	81	Xerox	U.S.A.	Electrical goods	3,576.4	331.1	101.4
91	113	Mitsubishi Chemical Ind.	Japan	Chemicals	3,563.0	52.5	18.7
92	84	Krupp-Konzern	D	Steel	3,553.0	27.4	80.9
93	91	Beatrice Foods	U.S.A.	Food	3,541.2	117.0	65.0
94	146	Petrofina	B	Oil	3,529.0	128.9	22.2
95	94	Monsanto	U.S.A.	Chemicals	3,497.9	323.2	60.9
96	89	W. R. Grace	U.S.A.	Misc.	3,472.3	130.6	74.6
97	66	Greyhound	U.S.A.	Misc.	3,458.3	58.0	54.5
98	120	United Aircraft	U.S.A.	Aeronautics	3,321.1	104.7	95.0
99	99	Borden	U.S.A.	Food	3,264.5	83.8	46.7
100	115	Reynolds Ind.	U.S.A.	Consumption	3,229.7	310.7	32.5

Source: Wirtschaftswoche, No. 35, 22 August 1975.

OECD countries. The 5,112 largest corporations in the OECD countries employed 45.9 million persons (or 22 percent of the total OECD workforce); the 260 largest, 25.1 million (or 12 percent of the total); the 100 largest, 12.2 million (6 percent). From Table 7.3 it can be calculated that corporations with annual sales over $10 billion each, of which there were 15 in 1974, generated $303 billion in sales, or 8.4 percent of the "free world" gross product. The 50 largest corporations generated $543.3 billion in sales, or 15.1 percent of the "free world" gross product. For the largest 100 corporations, comparable figures were $750 billion and 20.8 percent. The sensitivity to the great size of some of these corporations by national governments is heightened by the perception of relative size, corporate sales against gross national product. (See Table 7.4, on which the position of corporations is indicated by arrows.)

If one were to project the present trend, it appears that by 1990 or thereabouts, 60 to 80 percent of the fixed industrial assets of the nonsocialist world would be owned by perhaps 200 to 300 giant corporations. One can reasonably doubt, however, that the nation-state will permit this degree of concentration to occur, or indeed, that the economics of the situation will encourage it.

Many of the developed countries have indeed been tightening their antitrust laws, particularly in reference to takeovers by the multinationals. Canada has a Combined Investigation Act and a Restrictive Trade Practices Commission empowered to issue appropriate remedial orders where serious anticompetitive effects are found. In 1973 the Foreign Investment Review Act was passed by the Canadian Parliament, and the following year, the Foreign Investment Agency appeared. A major purpose of the latter was to block the foreign acquisition of Canadian business enterprises unless supported by significant benefit to the Canadian economy. Additionally, one purpose of the Canadian Development Corporation is to help Canadian companies withstand attempted alien takeovers. Another move is that made by Germany where the Federal Cartel Office has been given wide powers to intervene in cases of misuse of dominant position, anticompetitive mergers or similar concentration moves. The number of legalized cartels in Germany had dropped from a postwar high of 354 to 230 as of March 1976. There are many cases in which European governments have apparently prevented a merger of a national company with a foreign company, or a takeover by the latter of the former, and one can reasonably anticipate continuing European and Japanese opposition to both the mergers of multinational corporations and their acquisition of national companies. In many instances such acquisitions or mergers specifically require prior government approval. For example, Belgian law requires such approval for the acquisition by a non-EEC company of 30 percent or more of a Belgian company with assets of $2 million or more. EEC antitrust law has been interpreted recently so as to include the possibility of blocking an acquisition or merger if it can be demonstrated that misuse of dominant market position is involved (e.g., forcing the acquisition). As of 1977, the EEC Council of Ministers was actively considering a commission proposal to establish prior control of significant mergers.

Table 7.4
GROSS NATIONAL PRODUCTS, 1974
(in millions of dollars)

United States	1,259,000	→	
Japan	390,594	→	
Germany	338,831	→	
France	235,551	→	
United Kingdom	171,932	Saudi Arabia	6,817 (72)
Italy	135,195	→	
Canada	127,512	Algeria	6,695 (73)
Brazil	73,358 (72)	→	
Australia	65,984 (73)	→	
Netherlands	63,552	Ireland	6,304
India	58,164 (72)	→	
Spain	55,944 (73)	→	
Sweden	50,183	→	
Belgium	49,284	Chile	5,924
Switzerland	36,467 (73)	Libya	5,853 (73)
→		→	
Mexico	32,048 (70)	→	
Austria	29,490	Malaysia	5,456 (73)
South Africa	29,006	→	
		→	
Denmark	27,278	→	
Iran	25,728 (73)	Bangladesh	5,289 (72)
Argentina	24,789 (72)	→	
→		Peru	5,158 (72)
Venezuela	23,865		
→		→	
Finland	19,579	→	
Norway	19,546	→	
→		→	
Greece	18,770	→	
		→	
→		→	
→		Morocco	4,729 (73)
→		→	
Turkey	15,826 (72)	→	
Korea	13,221	→	
Indonesia	14,318 (73)	→	
Philippines	13,364	→	
Portugal	12,843	→	
→		→	
Nigeria	12,612 (73)	→	
Thailand	12,389	→	
New Zealand	12,281	→	
Israel	11,609	→	
→		→	
→		→	
Kuwait	10,400	→	
→		Southern Rhodesia	3,930
Colombia	9,225	→	
		→	
→		→	
→		→	
→		→	
Egypt	8,739 (73)	→	
→		→	
Pakistan	8,074 (73)	→	
→		→	
→		→	
		Tunisia	3,364
		Ecuador	3,293

Arrows indicate positions in the list of World's Largest Corporations.

In the EEC case, Articles 85 and 86 of the Rome Treaty constitute the basis for antitrust regulation. The first prohibits inter-enterprise agreements that are likely to affect trade between the member states and have as their purpose the prevention, restriction, or distortion of competition with the Common Market (in general, price fixing, restrictions on production, market-sharing, price discrimination, and tied conditions). But, such an agreement may be exempted (granted negative clearance) if (1) it has been registered with the EEC Commission, (2) it has the effect of improving production, distribution, or technology, and users receive an equitable share in the profit resulting therefrom (the so-called beneficent cartel concept), or (3) competition is not substantially reduced. Consequently, there are no *per se* violations except those defined by precedent. Article 86 has to do with the misuse of dominant position by one or more enterprises within the Common Market or within a substantial part of it. Presumably misuse of such position within a single country would not fall afoul of Article 86. Misuse seems to be established by unjustifiably high prices, price discrimination as among countries, and refusal to deal in a commodity or raw material. Where violations are established, remedies run from declaring an agreement null and void to heavy cash fines. The underlying philosophy of the EEC law in the area is to prevent the division of the community market on the one hand, and, on the other, to encourage the development of larger business units of a transnational nature so as to be more competitive with the U.S. corporate giants. The two objectives sometimes conflict.

The EEC Commission has rendered a number of decisions in the antitrust area. Although technically there are no *per se* violations, as precedence develops some practices have in fact become virtually indefensible under any set of conceivable circumstances. Some characteristic decisions follow:

1. A negative clearance was given for an agreement in which an EEC firm gave an exclusive dealership to a company outside the EEC with a prohibition against resale into the Common Market. The agreement did not perceptibly restrict competition with the EEC in that export into the EEC in this case was not possible in practice because of the customs burden involved.

2. An agreement was declared null and void in which a firm in one EEC member state granted to a firm in a second member state an exclusive national dealership and prohibited that party from selling outside its territory.

3. A negative clearance was given to an agreement between an EEC firm and a non-EEC firm which specified that the latter would not use the same trademark within the EEC as did the EEC firm.

4. An agreement was struck down in which, as partial consideration for technical services rendered, the recipient firm agreed not to use the products manufactured by the competitors of the firm providing the services, both firms being within the EEC but in different countries.

5. The provision in an agreement between a non-EEC and an EEC company in which the latter agreed not to export was declared illegal.

6. Bloc exemption has been given to exclusive bilateral distributorships between a manufacturer and a dealer whereby the latter acquires exclusive selling rights in a specified area covering one member state, but competing producers may not appoint each other as exclusive distributors.

7. A five-year exemption was given to a cooperation agreement between several medium-sized manufacturers in the same industry located in several EEC countries, as well as outside the EEC, such agreement providing for a pooling of know-how, manufacturing, and marketing.

8. A ten-year exemption was given for a specialization agreement between two large firms in two EEC member states in which each limited its freedom to invest, manufacture, handle competitive products, and market by reason of a commitment to cooperate with each other on an exclusive basis.

9. An agreement was banned in which a firm in one EEC country agreed to limit the volume of exports to the domestic market of a second EEC firm, and the latter agreed to stop selling altogether in the domestic market of the first.

10. Approval was given of agreements setting up a selective distribution system, including a limitation on the number of retailers per geographical unit.

11. An acquisition by a U.S.-based multinational firm's European subsidiary of a Dutch firm was prohibited, which would have given the U.S. firm 60 to 70 percent of the community metal-packaging market. The U.S. firm was given six months to put forward proposals to end its "unfair dominant positions" in the North European market.

12. It was found that two Dutch cartel agreements had monopolized the Dutch market to the exclusion of small firms, thereby restricting competition and creating obstacles to trade between member states. (Subsequently, both cartels were dissolved.)

13. A price-fixing agreement among a group of EEC and non-EEC firms was held to be illegal, and all members of the group were fined on the grounds that activities of subsidiaries may be imputed to their parents.

14. Collusion among a group of EEC firms to keep out international competition from their respective national markets to bolster prices and profits was ordered dissolved.

15. An agreement among three European firms to coordinate investments in the field of nuclear energy was cleared, although with continual monitoring by the commission.

16. A long-term specialization agreement relating to penicillin production by two large pharmaceutical manufacturers that would result in lower cost production by both was approved. (Reciprocal long-term supply contracts and arrangements for joint investment were involved).

17. Certain clauses in a licensing agreement between two French interests were rejected on the grounds that each new improvement patent extended the duration of the agreement by its own duration (hence, the agreement could be extended indefinitely); the licensee was required to pay royalties after expiration of the basic patent even if it did not use the improvement patent; a commitment by the licensee not to challenge the validity of the licensor's parents; a commitment by both parties

not to compete with one another; a commitment by the licensee not to sell in countries in which the licensor either licensed or assigned his patent rights to third parties; the licensor undertook not to issue a manufacturing and sales license to any other entity in France.

18. An otherwise illegal exclusive manufacturing license given by a German firm to a French firm covering expired patents was exempted on the grounds that the exclusivity would help promote technical and economic progress.

19. That a company holding a dominant market position in one area of the EEC prohibited distributors from reselling to medium or long-distance customers, charged different prices in different member states (some of which prices were deemed excessive), and refused to supply one of its major customers, was guilty of misusing its dominant position.

Although EEC law does not require a company to sell its goods at the same price throughout the community, it does require that an EEC buyer be able to buy wherever the prices are the lowest and take them back for resale to his own country. An important unresolved question is to what extent can patent rights be invoked to restrict exports within the EEC? Can a firm holding patents on a given product in two or more EEC countries limit competition among its licensees within the EEC either by contract or by legal action against third parties who buy from one licensee and reexport to another EEC country?

Charges have been made that both U.S. and EEC antitrust law has been used on occasion to keep out some foreign firms. Likewise, in both areas, antitrust law is being extended to cover more *intra*-state activities. For example, a cement cartel operating only in the Netherlands was held to be under EEC jurisdiction because its control of the Dutch market affected trade among states. Also, EEC law is being extended into the foreign commerce area even in situations where there appears to be no impact on trade among the EEC member states, but only on external trade. Major differences between the U.S. and EEC approaches include the absence of *per se* violations, the notion of a beneficent cartel, the absence of any criminal sanctions, and the process of prior notification and clearance in the EEC case. In addition, the EEC Commission has issued group exemptions covering two categories of agreements: exclusive distributor agreements and certain types of specialization agreements (joint research agreements and undertaking for other joint functions among small or medium sized firms), which means that notification of such agreements to the commission is not required. More specifically, the commission has listed eight types of specialization agreement that qualify under its group exemption:

1. Agreements whose sole object is an exchange of opinion or experience; joint market research; joint preparation of statistics and calculation models.

2. Agreements whose sole object is cooperation in accounting; joint provision of credit guarantees; joint debt-collecting associations; joint business or tax-consultancy agencies.

3. Agreements whose sole object is the joint implementation, placing and sharing out of research and development projects among the participating firms. The mere exchange of research experience and results serves for information only and does not restrict competition. It therefore need not be mentioned expressly. If, however, firms restrict their own research and development activity or the use of the results of joint work so that they do not have a free hand for R&D outside the joint projects, this can constitute an infringement of the rules of competition. Where firms do not carry out joint research work, contractual obligations or concerted practices binding them to refrain from research work of their own may result in a restraint of competition. The sharing out of sectors of research *without* an understanding providing for mutual access to the results is regarded as a case of specialization that may restrict competition. So too are undertakings to manufacture only products developed jointly. There may also be a restraint of competition if certain participating firms are excluded from the exploitation of the results, either entirely or to an extent not commensurate with their participation, or if the granting of licences to nonparticipants is expressly or tacitly excluded.

4. Agreements whose only object is the joint use of production facilities, of storage facilities, and of transport equipment. There may be a restraint of competition if the firms go beyond organizational and technical arrangements and agree on joint production.

5. Agreements whose sole object is the setting up of working partnerships for the common execution of orders, where the participating firms do not compete with each other over the work to be done, or where each of them by itself is unable to execute the orders. If, however, the absence of competition is based on concerted practices, there may be a restraint of competition. There may, however, be a restraint of competition if the firms undertake to work *solely* in the framework of an association.

6. Agreements whose sole object is joint selling arrangements or joint after-sales and repair service, provided the participating firms are not competitors over the products or services covered by the agreement.

7. Agreements whose sole object is joint advertising unless the agreement prevents the participants from themselves advertising, in which event there may be a restraint of competition.

8. Agreements whose sole object is the use of a common label to designate a certain quality, where the label is available to all competitors on the same conditions. But there may be restraint of competition if the right to use the label is linked to obligations regarding production, marketing, or price formation, for instance when the participants are obliged to manufacture or sell only products of guaranteed quality.[18]

It appears that Japanese antimonopoly law, enforced by the Fair Trade Commission (FTC), is following the general thrust of EEC law in that the actual

---

[18]Adapted from E.M.J.A. Sassen, in H. B. Thorelli, ed., *International Marketing Strategy* (Middlesex, England: Penguin Books, 1973), pp. 111–13.

impact of an act is always considered. In the Yawata-Fuji steel merger, the FTC refused to order an annulment even though the new company's share of the nation's crude production was 35.7 percent and domestic competition was significantly reduced by the merger. Rather, the FTC merely ordered the elimination of the prohibited activity, that is, a passing on of benefits. It appears to be the FTC view that the evaluation of competitiveness should be judged not only on the basis of quality and price but also on such various factors as technology, development capability, fund-raising power, market-developing capacity, management and administrative capabilities, and capability of meeting international competition.

Japanese antimonopoly law is beginning to have extraterritorial impact in that Japan's Fair Trade Commission looks with disfavor on restrictions imposed under patent license and technical assistance contracts in respect to mutual sales territories and confining the custody of patents—and improvement patents—to the contracting parties. For example, an agreement among two Japanese firms and British, German, and Swiss companies specified that the Japanese firm could not sell related products in the home markets of the other three, nor the three in Japan. The contract also provided that patent rights could not be granted by any member firm without consent of the other four. The FTC forced a lifting of the territorial sales restrictions, likewise those on the transfer of patent rights.

Japan's FTC has shown special interest of late in curbing international cartel activities and in cooperating with other governments in doing so. As evidence of undesirable international cartel activity, the FTC cites a 1972 visit to Japan of European shipbuilders to induce their Japanese counterparts to observe discretion in the building of large tankers.[19] It also cites the meeting of global aluminum smelterers, including the Japanese, to discuss production problems. The FTC fears that Japanese industries are facing the prospect of being engulfed in a growing tendency to set up international cartels that, in part, are supported by Western governments as a device to restrain Japanese competition. Japan, on its part, has encouraged the formation of *national* export cartels so as to "assure orderly exporting."

Although Japan has been identified in the minds of many with a high level of cartelization, a recent study of Japanese industry reports,

The very strong role that cartels gained in Japan during the interwar period has been diluted. Nowadays the conduct of sellers in Japanese industries is controlled partly by cartels (legal and illegal) and partly through such lesser devices as price leadership and trade-association reporting practices that are familiar in the United States. Collusive arrangements appear to be much more prevalent in Japan than in the United States.

---

[19]In 1976, the Europeans attempted to secure a commitment from the Japanese industry to limit itself to a 40 percent market share in Europe.

However, members' adherence to them is far from perfect, leaving doubts as to whether they usually effect very large restrictions of output. [20]

The most recently published figures would indicate that 985 legal cartels (i.e., exempted cartels) were operative in Japan in 1973. Some of these are ascribed to political influence. Others were associated with various government regulations, trade associations, or other cooperative arrangements to protect small enterprise, export or import cartels, with efforts to combat depression or excessive competition, and finally "rationalization" of production within certain industries.

Secretary of State Henry Kissinger observed to the UN General Assembly in 1975,

Laws against restrictive business practices must be developed, better coordinated among countries, and enforced. The United States has long been vigilant against such abuses in domestic trade, mergers, or licensing of technology. We stand by the same principles internationally. We condemn restrictive practices restraining supplies, whether by private or state-owned transnational enterprises or by the collusion of national governments. [21]

A subsequent meeting of the UN Conference on Trade and Development (UNCTAD) took up the matter of restrictive business practices with four items on the agenda: to list and agree on what conduct should be considered offensive, to explore ways of exchanging information, to develop a model antitrust law appropriate for the LDCs, and to explore whether there were antitrust principles that would be acceptable to all nations. The discussion generated few areas of agreement, but it was a first step. [22] To what, no one knew.

Closely associated with the antitrust area is the whole subject of the international protection of property rights.

Protection of property rights

The degree of protection of property rights afforded by the judicial system of a host country depends upon the ease with which the judiciary feels able to take jurisdiction, the degree to which the process is insulated from political pressure, and the time and cost of litigation. Inasmuch as systems of law vary, the U.S. businessman should not assume that what appears "reasonable" to him is in fact the law. Indeed, he may have no legal standing at all if he is not held "to be in business" in the country where he seeks to bring action. Further considerations have to do with the effect of litigation of a continuing business relationship and the ability to enforce a court award and secure assets of value

---

[20]Richard E. Caves and Masu Uekusa, *Industrial Organization in Japan* (Washington: The Brookings Institution, 1976), p. 58.

[21]Reported in Joel Davidow, "Extraterritorial Application of U.S. Antitrust Law in a Changing World," *Law and Policy in International Business*, vol. 8. no. 4, 1976, pp. 908–09.

[22]Davidow, pp. 909–10.

to the claimant. If gross denial of local justice can be shown, it is sometimes possible to bring suit in one's home courts and secure attachment of the defendant's property present in the country (for example, a shipment of goods, a vessel, or a bank account). As noted elsewhere, the *commercial* entity of a foreign government may likewise be sued in a number of countries without being blocked by the doctrine of sovereign immunity, which holds that a sovereign may not be sued without its permission. In the United States it would appear that under recent laws, the courts will undertake adjudication in cases involving the acts of a foreign government if those acts are of a commercial nature.

There is no international legal forum now available to private persons unless their cause be espoused by their respective government before the International Court of Justice. An exception is the mechanism established under the World Bank auspices in 1966, which is based on the "Convention on the Settlement of Investment Disputes between States and the Nationals of Other States," to which some 72 countries were signatories as of mid-1976 (including all of Western Europe, Japan, the United States, Yugoslavia, but none of the Sino-Soviet bloc).

If a foreign firm enters into a contract or agreement with a signatory state (or a constituent subdivision) and reference is made in that agreement to the fact that disagreements will be resolved either by arbitration or conciliation in the International Centre for the Settlement of Investment Disputes (ICSID), that agreement is considered binding and may not be unilaterally withdrawn even if the state involved subsequently withdraws from the centre. In that the centre is a member of the World Bank "family," there may be some force to reach an agreement; capricious withdrawal or refusal to enforce an award conceivably impact on a nation's credit standing. The consent may be qualified by requiring prior exhaustion of local administrative or judicial remedies. Consent may be restricted to conciliation, to arbitration, or to conciliation followed, if necessary, by arbitration. As of late 1976, no disputes submitted to the centre for arbitration had yet reached conclusion. Nonetheless, 11 national investment laws and 29 bilateral treaties had included provisions designating the ICSID as the arbitration forum. This total did not include provisions contained in private contracts not tallied by the centre. An ongoing activity of the centre has been the codification of the laws and international agreements affecting foreign investment in member LDC countries.[23]

Many firms attempt to insert into international agreements a clause subjecting them to their own laws. For U.S. firms, it should be borne in mind that domestic law may be more restrictive than foreign in several important respects; for example, in respect to licensing.

---

[23]Kathryn D. Checchi, "The World Bank Group" *Law and Policy in International Business*, vol. 9, no. 1, 1977, p. 270. See also John T. Schmidt, "Arbitration Under the Auspices of the International Centre for the Settlement of Investment Disputes (ICSID)," *Harvard International Law Journal*, vol. 17, no. 1, Winter 1976, p. 90 ff.

Vagts lists a number of areas in which U.S. law is unusually restrictive of the licensor's freedom to contract:

1. Charging royalties after expiration of the patents,

2. Insertion of a clause barring the licensee from challenging the validity of the patents licensed to him,

3. Requiring the licensee to grant back to the licensor patent rights on all improvements discovered by him, and

4. Insistence on accepting a "package" of licenses.

Vagts goes on to point out that the license is only one of several types of contracts, the interpretation of which may be more restrictive under U.S. law.

The seller of goods or equipment may be held to various types of implied warranties unknown to foreign law. An engineer may be held to a higher standard of care in giving advice or professional services; a transportation company may have to pay bigger damages for loss of life or property. American law is now more protective of certain categories of people than are many foreign laws and is less willing to allow parties in strong bargaining positions to retain the full value of the deals they have imposed.[24]

The reach of one's own judicial processes to foreign persons or corporations is problematical. The rule upheld in U.S. courts during the past two decades has been "that, given a good faith effort to obey, compliance with an American court order will be excused to the extent that it would violate foreign law."[25] But the rule is being narrowed. For example, a recent case involved an American bank that was subpoenaed by a U.S. court to produce documents held by its branch in Germany. The documents related to alleged violations of antitrust laws by several of the bank's customers. But the bank faced civil liability under German law if it obeyed the American order. The court looked at the relative weight of the national policies behind the two sets of laws, Germany banking secrecy and U.S. antitrust laws, and found that the German law was relatively weak in that a violation was merely a civil offense in contrast with the criminal sanctions behind the U.S. law. "As the antitrust laws were deemed a cornerstone of American economic regulation, the court held that American policy outweighed any countervailing German one."[26] In another case, involving the sale of foreign securities to American investors in disregard of the registration, record-keeping, and antifraud provisions of the federal securities laws, a U.S. court found that the Swiss corporation involved in the sale had accepted the stricture of U.S. law by participating in the sale of securities in the U.S. Even though compliance by the Swiss corporation with orders issued by the U.S. court to transfer both funds and associated records

---

[24]Detlev F. Vagts, "The Law and International Business," *Worldwide P&I Planning*, November–December 1970, p. 63.

[25]Keith Raffel, "Extraterritoriality—Enforcement of the United States Court Orders Conflicting with Foreign Law or Policy," *Harvard International Law Journal*, vol. 17, 1976, p. 682.

[26]Raffel, "Extraterritoriality," p. 691.

to the U.S. would entail both criminal and civil liability under Swiss banking laws, the court so ordered. The judge "considered that the equities of the situation favored the defrauded investors" over the Swiss company. (That aspect of its case was resolved when the Swiss corporation transferred funds from another source to the court's jurisdiction.)

Further difficulty may arise if one's domestic law is to be applied but it turns out that the foreign party must be sued where he resides. Requiring a court to apply a foreign law may lead it to demand proof of the relevant law, which may involve delay and expense. Also, a court may disregard the foreign law requirement if it is deemed to be contrary to its own national policy.

Of increasing importance as a device for resolving private international business disputes is arbitration. Its advantages lie in its relatively low cost and speed and in the ability of the two parties to determine ahead of time the rules or system of law that are to govern and the place of arbitration. Various arbitration organizations (most notably the American Arbitration Association and its foreign counterparts, the International Chamber of Commerce, the various commodity arbitration systems for traders in textiles, rubber, and so on) offer standard contract clauses, which set into motion a specified set of procedures once a dispute arises. The arbitration rules developed by the UN Commission on International Trade Law is a possible alternative. A typical arbitration clause in an international commercial contract might read:

The parties agree that if any controversy or claim shall arise out of the agreement or the breach thereof and either party shall request that the matter shall be settled by arbitration, the matter shall be settled exclusively by . . . the International Chamber of Commerce, Paris, France. . . . All arbitration proceedings shall be held in Paris, France, and each party agrees to comply in all respects with any award made in any such proceeding and to the entry of a judgment in any jurisdiction upon any award rendered in such proceeding. The laws of the State of Illinois, U.S.A., shall apply to and govern this agreement, its interpretation and performance.

The stipulation of Swedish law and arbitration in Sweden has become increasingly popular over recent years.

A major problem in regard to arbitration lies in the enforceability of foreign awards. U.S. bilateral commercial treaties often provide for the enforcement of arbitration agreements and awards in disputes between nationals and corporations of the respective countries, the recognized principle being that enforcement cannot be denied solely for the reason that the award was rendered in another country or that the nationality of the arbitrator was not that of the party concerned. But such clauses do not assure enforcement. Ratification by the United States of treaties or international conventions recognizing the validity of arbitration awards has been difficult because of possible conflict with state law. Nonetheless, late in 1970—as the 37th nation to do so and 12 years after the convention's inception—the United States acceded to the UN Convention on the Recognition and Enforcement of Foreign Arbitral Awards.

Adherence to this convention binds a nation to compel arbitration when the parties have so agreed and to provide judicial recourse for citizens and corporations of other adhering countries to secure recognition and enforcement of voluntary foreign arbitration agreements. U.S. participation in the convention is limited to arbitral agreements involving foreign commerce, thereby providing coverage for all commercial agreements between U.S. and foreign citizens.[27]

In a 1974 case, the U.S. Supreme Court found that arbitration could proceed in a foreign country on an alleged substantive violation of a section of the U.S. Securities Exchange Act. It found that "the need for certainty and predictability in international commerce outweighed the domestic interest in having securities issues resolved by U.S. courts."[28] The question immediately arises whether an agreement calling for international arbitration between two private parties will be considered arbitrable by U.S. courts if they arise out of international agreements, even though a violation of U.S. law may be involved, such as antitrust law. It is clear that in a purely domestic situation, the courts would not permit arbitration in such instances.

A number of countries, some of which have had an unfortunate past experience with international commercial arbitration, have banned the submission of any dispute within their respective territories to foreign arbitration. Among such countries are Saudi Arabia and the five members of the Andean Common Market. In the latter case, the ANCOM regulations specifically prohibit nonnational arbitration. Indeed, of the Latin American countries, only Ecuador and Mexico had ratified the UN Convention as of 1976, and no Latin countries had ratified the World Bank Convention on the Settlement of Investment Disputes. Regional arbitration agreements sponsored by the Inter-American Commercial Arbitration Commission have fared no better.[29]

Also worthy of mention in this context is a U.S.-Japanese effort to provide an international commercial conciliation service. With headquarters in Tokyo and New York, the Pacific Industrial Property Association offers conciliation services essentially for problems arising between U.S. and Japanese firms, but is open to others so long as one party is either American or Japanese. Its purpose is to protect industrial property rights, promote commercial progress, and to support institutions supporting the recognition of industrial property rights. Among other things, the association has developed an explicit procedure for the conciliation of disputes.

The only existing international conventions constituting enforceable international law in respect to protecting property rights internationally are those

---

[27]See Cecilia E. Cosca and Joseph J. Zimmerer, "Judicial Interpretations of Foreign Arbitral Awards Under the UN Convention," *Law and Policy in International Business*, vol. 8, 1976, p. 737 ff.

[28]See William J. Nissen, "Antitrust and Arbitration in International Commerce," *Harvard International Law Journal*, vol. 17, no. 1, Winter 1976, p. 110.

[29]See Alden F. Abbott, "Latin America and International Arbitration Conventions: The Quandary of Non-Ratification," *Harvard International Law Journal*, vol. 17, no. 1, Winter 1976, p. 131 ff.

relating to patents, trademarks, copyrights, and trade secrets.[30] Patent protection is available in approximately 120 countries; trademark protection, in 140. National laws all differ to a certain extent. U.S. patent protection is valid for 17 years; 5 to 20 years is common elsewhere. Substantial registration fees are imposed in some countries, plus an annual tax. Some countries exclude certain fields, such as chemicals and pharmaceuticals. Others may permit processes but not the products themselves to be patented (for example, Italy in the case of pharmaceuticals). Possible policies for a U.S. firm in respect to patents and trademarks are: (1) file only in the United States, (2) file in the United States and Canada, (3) file in all countries where the company manufactures, (4) file in all countries where manufacture is possible or likely. Reasons for registration abroad are threefold: as the substance for foreign investment, as a subject for licensing, or to protect a market.

Approximately 70 of the leading countries (since early 1965 including the U.S.S.R.) adhere to the International Convention for the Protection of Industrial Property ("The Paris Union" of 1883, subsequently revised six times),[31] which provides that if a patent application is filed in one member country, the applicant may file in other member countries within one year, such priority running from the date of first application. There is no protection offered prior to the original filing. A serious difficulty with this system is that the commercial value of the patent may not be ascertained within one year. The applicant can get protection if he files in a member country before his own government issues a patent (in the U.S. case, usually three to five years from the date of application), provided that there has been no publication or public use anywhere, including his home country. (In some countries only publication or public use in that country constitutes a bar to filing.) Therefore, after a patent has been issued in one country, it is no longer possible to obtain valid protection in many of the most important foreign countries, with some exceptions in Latin America. U.S. law permits the filing of a valid patent application any time within one year from publication or public use of the invention. But elsewhere, publication or public use prior to filing may act as a bar. Therefore, a firm should avoid public use or publication before U.S. filing.

Some countries require local manufacture—a "registered user"—of patented products sufficient to meet reasonable local demand, in the absence of

---

[30]To avoid the ambiguity in some of the literature on this subject, the following terminology has been adopted:

A license refers to a contractual agreement to permit another to use a functional or design invention protected by patent, a unique literary or artistic expression protected by copyright, a unique identification protected by trademark, or technology and/or skills of a secret nature. Payment is designated as a *royalty*.

A know-how or technical assistance contract refers to contractual agreement to transfer technology that is not covered by patent, copyright, trademark, or secrecy. Hence, the subject matter is considered to be in the public domain. Payment is designated as a *fee*.

[31]The most recent revision is its "Act of Stockholm" (1967). Not all of the adherents of the Paris Convention have signed all the subsequent revisions. Hence, in establishing the rules relevant to a particular country, one has to check the most recent version agreed to by that country.

which the patent may be subject to compulsory licensing if someone wants it and is willing to pay a reasonable royalty. Local manufacture is generally not required for the first three years, and indeed, under the Paris Convention compulsory licensing may not be required for the first three years. Thereafter, one often has two years to license. In Argentina, Cuba, and Venezuela, the patent owner must take steps to interest third parties in taking a license under the patent, or it becomes void.

In the U.S.S.R., legally a Soviet inventor may opt to obtain either an inventor's certificate or a patent. In the former case, the patent is assigned to the government, which thereby incurs an obligation to see that the invention is put to use. Payment to the inventor depends upon the savings realized by the invention's use up to a maximum of 20,000 rubles. If the invention is not perceived as useful, a certificate is not issued. A Soviet patent is very similar to patents elsewhere in that the owner has the exclusive right to use, sell, or license the patent to a second party. That is, Soviet industry is not permitted to use the invention unless sold or licensed to it. A foreigner obtains a patent through the U.S.S.R. Chamber of Commerce. The Stockholm Convention (1967), an amendment to the Paris Convention, gives patent status to an inventor's certificate in establishing priority of filing rights in signatory countries.

In some countries (not the U.S.) design patents are available. Generally more limited in duration than the normal patent, a design patent has to do with the appearance of an item rather than its function. Also, there are national differences in respect to the enforceability of patent rights against alleged infringers. For example, it is very difficult in the U.S. to secure a preliminary injunction to halt the production and sale of a contested product without going through a trial. In any event, a very high proportion of such infringement cases is lost. Elsewhere, as in the U.K., it may be easier to secure a preliminary injunction, for example, the Polaroid injunction against Kodak in the U.K.

Facilitating the international filing of patents are three recent international agreements, the European Patent Convention (EPC), the Community Patent Convention (CPC), and the Patent Cooperation Treaty (PCT). The first was signed in 1973 by 16 countries (the nine EEC members plus Austria, Greece, Liechtenstein, Monaco, Norway, Sweden, and Switzerland). Expected to be fully operational by 1978, the convention provides that on the basis of a single application made to the European Patent Office (EPO) in Munich, and searched by the International Patent Institute (IPI) at the Hague, a single patent may be issued for as many of the convention countries as the applicant desires. Such a patent will have the effect of national patents in the contracting states. The Community Patent Convention, signed in 1975 by the nine EEC members, is expected to come in full force in 1979. In this case, a single application to the European Patent Office will lead to a single Common Market Patent subject to EEC law. It is anticipated that community patent protection will be at least equivalent to that offered by the national laws of member countries. At the start, the use of the community patent is likely to be optional, the alternative being an EPC patent which is equivalent to *national* patents. Later, it is expected that anyone using the EPC patent route to secure patents in the EEC will be obliged to take out a community patent. The point is that one of the aims of the new EEC patent system is to abolish territorial limits for the marketing of patented goods, so that the division of the EEC into nine separate markets on the basis of patents will no longer be possible. In this way, the EEC Commission will be able "to circumvent institutionally the sanctity of valid patents as protection against the importation of infringing goods [from other member states] ... without prejudicing the right of patents to protect industrial property which is upheld by ... the Rome Treaty."[32] Both the community and the European patents are valid for 20 years from the date of filing, and both are open to nonresidents.

The Patent Cooperation Treaty had been approved on a diplomatic level by 35 countries by mid-1976. The U.S. ratified the treaty in 1975, and it was expected that the other OECD countries and the Soviet Union would follow suit, so that it could become operational by not later than 1978. The treaty makes possible a single application for designated member countries. It is not a patent system, only an application system, as is the Paris Convention system. Protection is accorded by *national* patents and lasts only so long as does the national patent. However, unlike the Paris Convention, the PCT makes possible a *single* application covering as many member states as the applicant desires, a single search and preliminary examination procedure, and provides 20 months (not 12 as under the Paris Convention) for one to determine which national patents are desired. The World Intellectual Property Organization (WIPO) in Geneva will act as the central administrative agency. As of early 1976, the International Patent Institute and at least six industrialized countries (including the U.S.) had expressed a willingness to activate their respective national patent offices as International Searching or Preliminary Examining Authorities. The idea is that the patent offices of all signatory countries will accept the search and preliminary examination report (dealing with an invention's novelty, nonobviousness, and commercial value) prepared by the authority (either the IPI or a designated national patent office) to which initial application is made. Eventually, one may be able to file through the PCT mechanism for either a community or a European patent. It is expected, nonetheless, that those needing coverage in only a few countries will do better to file individual national applications.

In ratifying the International Patent Treaty, the U.S. made two important

---

[32] *Business International,* August 31, 1973, p. 274.

reservations. First, the U.S. retained the right to reject the Preliminary Examination Reports made by other countries and to undertake its own search. Second, the U.S. did not accept the treaty's provision that information in applications should be published within 18 months from the priority date (even though no patent has been issued by that time) in that this provision conflicted with the U.S. principle that an applicant has the right to keep his invention confidential until he actually obtains patent protection.

Among the many difficulties in creating a truly international patent system has been the fact that until recently no generally accepted classification system had been developed. Since, 1968, however, a standard International Patent Classification System (IPCS) has evolved. Subject to revision every five years, the IPCS is based on 60,000 categories arranged by the principal function or field of use of a device unless it is characterized by some unique feature. Unfortunately, the U.S. Patent Office has been using a different system based on 90,000 categories arranged more on the basis of process and product. The U.S. has been participating in the IPCS working groups with the purpose of pushing towards convergence. All of Europe, Japan, and the Soviet Union have converted to the IPCS. As it now stands, the U.S. Patent Office reclassifies foreign patents into the U.S. system, and places the IPCS code on all U.S. patents issued.

Understandably, many of the LDCs have had serious second thoughts about the value of a full-fledged patent system to them given the fact that the overwhelming percentage of all patents issued are owned by individuals and corporations domiciled in the industrialized countries. Even a country such as Canada, noting that 95 percent of all patents issued in the country are based on inventions by foreigners, is becoming suspicious that the patent system may be serving as a brake on Canadian industrial development. A number of proposals have been made in Canada, including reducing the period of patent protection from 17 years to nine (with an added five years for those actively working their patents in Canada), requiring greater disclosure of information by patent holders, changing from a "first to invent" system of priority rights to a "first to file" system, and allowing imports of a patentee's product made outside Canada to be freely marketed in the country and thus discouraging noncompetitive pricing in Canada. A number of countries have declared that certain products (or processes) are not subject to patent protection, such as pharmaceuticals in the case of Italy, Brazil, and Mexico. Mexico added a number of other reserved sectors in 1976.

Major objections on the part of many LDCs to the traditional notion of a patent:

1. The guarantee of national treatment to foreign patent holders. Some have suggested that foreign-owned patents should be treated differently from locally-developed patents in respect to duration of protection and compulsory licensing requirements. The rationale advanced for the difference is threefold: R&D allocation in the industrial countries is not influenced by patent protection in the LDCs

and, hence, does not provide incentive for innovation;[33] most patents issued by the LDCs are never worked; and many patents are simply used to exclude competitors from LDC markets.

2. The nonuse of patents. Under present laws, even where compulsory licensing is enforced, it takes too long to compel licensing (one year priority for local filing, plus three years during which the compulsory licensing rule is not enforced, plus another two to three years to establish liability for not working the patent, plus perhaps another two years before a local court finally orders compulsory licensing). By that time, the life of the patent is at least half over.

3. A patentee's right to exclude imports of a nonlicensed manufacturer in respect to a patent protected locally even though there is no local production. Some have urged that such protection should be limited only to the areas of actual production.

4. The fact that no criteria are considered in issuing a patent related to the contribution of such patent protection to economic development.

5. The feeling that the covering of such essentials as pharmaceuticals and food products by patent is intolerable from a public welfare point of view.

6. The licensing of a patent by a foreign parent corporation to a local firm over which it exercises control in which case the extraction of royalties is seen as simply a device to drive down local profits and, hence, taxes.

The patent issue has entered the North-South dialogue, and the World Intellectual Property Organization has urged a number of revisions in the Paris Convention along some of the lines suggested above.[34] (In these discussions, some have argued for the abolition of patents altogether. But, if there were no patents, inventions could be kept secret—and hence, proprietary—much longer and, thus, could not be used by others as a basis for further research. Once a patent is issued, of course, patent documents describing the technology in detail are available to anyone for a nominal fee.)

In addition, the WIPO has proposed a "Transfer of Technology Patent" (TTP), which would dilute the legal protection accorded an inventor under a standard patent. For example, a U.K. firm with a product patented in the U.K. but not Brazil, would transfer the technology to a Brazilian firm that would take out a TTP in Brazil on behalf of both companies. Such a patent would prohibit imports of comparable products into Brazil, but would authorize the Brazilian firm to export anywhere. The TTP would specify that all of the know-how involved should be transferred at a maximum of 5 percent pretax sales income for a period of five years (although renewable for a second five). International firms might opt for the TTP or apply for a regular patent on their own. The WIPO has also discussed the notion of an Industrial Development

---

[33]Very clearly not the case. In the absence of patent protection in the LDCs, Kodak, for example, could have taken Polaroid's technology and built a plant, say in Brazil, and from there exported an instantaneous camera to much of the world.

[34]See Edith Penrose, "International Patenting and the Less Developed Countries," *Economic Journal*, September 1973, p. 768 ff, and Constantin Vaitsos, "The Revision of the International Patent System: Legal Considerations for a Third World Revision," *World Development*, vol. 4, no. 2, 1976, p. 85 ff.

Patent, which would simply give an exclusive right to a local firm to use technology, however it might have obtained it, for 12 years.

As the laws of many countries increasingly restrict the freedom of contract for the purchase of technology, valuable rights, and skills, one suspects that the cost of these industrial inputs goes up. At the same time, capital investment may be discouraged if it must take the form of other than a majority-owned subsidiary over which the foreign parent enjoys unambiguous control. For example, some observers feel that the relatively new Mexican industrial property law is likely to "discourage foreign investment because the government can license a patent to another party if (1) it is not exercized by the owner for a period of three years, or (2) the owner has suspended production for three months, or (3) the patent is not in the national interest as for example, the volume of product exported or the level of social benefits obtained are deemed inadequate. It is true that under the Mexican law license royalties are guaranteed, but they historically range from two to two and a half percent and only apply to the inventive part of the product and not to the entire product."[35]

From the corporate point of view, criteria for an international patent policy include imputed value (cost versus expected gain), desirability of forcing revelation of competitive information when an application is challenged, ability of other companies to make use of the information to be patented, speed of obsolescence, need to maintain secrecy (note that a patent constitutes public disclosure), location of major markets, and the danger of misdjudging them. Further decisions involved are: (1) Who makes the above decisions? (2) Who maintains surveillance for enforcement? (3) Who is responsible for paying the annual fees required in some countries?

Trade names, as distinct from trademarks, are protected in all Paris Union countries without the obligation of filing or registration, and countries of the union are obliged to provide protection against false designation of origin for nationals of member countries. Goods bearing illegal trademarks, trade names, or false origin are subject to seizure at the time of importation into countries of the union.

Use and registration of trademarks in the United States provide no protection elsewhere, although registration in the United States may be necessary as a basis for registration in some countries. Use in most foreign countries provides little or no protection except in common law countries, but even then a trademark can be lost through lack of continuous use. In the United States all trademark rights arise from use in that registration becomes possible when a mark is used in interstate commerce or when continuous use elsewhere can be demonstrated. Only in the United States, Canada, and the Philippines is use a precondition to registration; in most countries protection arises only through

---

[35]Valerius E. Herzfeld, vice-president, Business Planning and Development, Sperry Univac, in Norman B. Solomon, ed., *An International Dialogue on Technology Transfer* (Geneva: European Management Forum, Worldtech Report No. 3, August 1976), p. 28.

registration, and prior use need not be shown. Trademark protection varies from 10 to 20 years, but is subject to renewal. Barring rejection by any member state within 12 months of application, the Madrid Agreement (1891) on trademarks automatically extends trademark protection to signatory states (generally Europe, but not the United States or Scandinavia). Registration in one member state is considered to be registration in all. In that the U.S. is a member of the International Convention for the Protection of Industrial Property, the owner of a U.S. mark is given six months for filing elsewhere after the date of filing in the United States. National treatment is afforded U.S. nationals and entities in 14 Latin American countries through the General American Convention for Trademark and Commercial Protection. Also, trademark protection is often included on a reciprocal basis in friendship, commerce, and navigation treaties, some on a most-favored-nation basis. Some countries require the use of a trademark in the country within a given time after registration. Otherwise, it may be subject to cancellation.

Four important problems may arise in regard to trademarks: (1) protection in countries other than those adhering to the Paris Union may be difficult unless reciprocal protection has been written into a treaty; (2) penalties for infringement are often too light to be effective; (3) a trademark may become a generic term in the local language and hence its identity with a given make of product lost (for example, "Jilet," "Singer"); (4) occasionally someone will succeed in registering a generic term (such as salad oil, margarine). A United States management should be aware that Section 42 of the Trademark Act of 1946 prohibits importation into the United States of articles bearing marks confusingly similar to or counterfeit of trademarks registered in the Patent Office, and that Section 526 of the Tariff Act of 1930 requires the Customs Bureau to prohibit importation of foreign-made goods bearing marks registered in the Patent Office by a U.S. citizen or entity if a copy of the certificate of registration has been filed with the Treasury Department. (Curiously, however, there is no law excluding the import of articles that infringe on U.S. patents.)

Many of the British Commonwealth countries derive their trademark laws from the British Trade Marks Act of 1938 which created a statutory procedure for recording "registered users." The act defines a registered user as someone other than the owner of a trademark and who has been recorded as such, but only after scrutiny to make certain that adequate quality control will be exercized by the owner over the manufacture of the goods by the licensee. Use of a mark by a registered user is deemed use by the owner. If the licensee is not a registered user and, in fact, does not use the trademark for a certain number of years, the owner may lose his rights to the mark. In some countries, a mark may be lost if it can be demonstrated that the owner does not exercise some sort of quality control over the licensee.

Policy decisions relating to trademarks concern the option for developing local marks for each major national or regional market or for devising standard international marks. In each case, they may or may not be similar to those used in the United States market. Some United States marks cannot be used because of prior use elsewhere, such as the AMF triangle by the Australian Military Forces. General international acceptability must also be tested carefully. Development of important marks in the United States without protection elsewhere makes the firm vulnerable to extortion by pirates abroad who watch American trade literature and move quickly to secure local registration for important trademarks. Finally, there is the administrative problem as to who makes these decisions in the firm and who is responsible for maintenance of marks.

Copyrights are protected internationally under the Berne Convention of 1886 for the "protection of literary and artistic works." Adhered to by 55 countries, the convention gives automatic protection similar to that extended to local nationals in all adhering countries. Protection is the author's life plus 50 years. The U.S. is not a member. But the United States is a member of the Universal Copyright Convention of 1954, along with some 50-odd other countries, including the Soviet Union since 1974. Hence, the works of American authors first published in a UCC country are subject to copyright protection in each member country, and vice versa. Under the convention, certain formalities are eliminated for members' nationals in obtaining protection in other member states. This protection can be obtained if the owner simply inserts on the work the symbol "C" in a circle, his name, and date of first publication. Duration of copyright protection varies by country and by the nature of the protected work (books, photographs, architectural drawings). A copyright generally includes the exclusive right of translation for a specified period of time (such as ten years in Japan).

A U.S. copyright runs for 50 years after the death of the author. But, until 1982, copyright protection for U.S. citizens and any foreign national living in the United States is limited to five years for an English-language book not wholly manufactured in the United States, and there is no protection at all in such cases if more than 1,500 copies are imported into the United States. As of 1982, these protectionist provisions become inoperative. The U.S. also gives so-called "statutory protection" to unpublished works. The United States, by adhering to the Universal Copyright Convention of 1954, honors the copyright of the other signatory states.

The laws of many countries give protection to trade secrets similar to that accorded patents, but only so long as the secrecy is maintained. Companies may not choose to patent for a number of reasons, such as the time and cost involved in patenting, the difficulty of monitoring patent infringement and enforcing patent rights against alleged infringers, and the uncertainty of patent validity. It has been said that well over half of all patents issued in the U.S. are ultimately declared invalid. Coca Cola is an example of a company which has gone the trade secret route in protection of its "ingredient X." Over 20 U.S. states have laws which impose criminal sanctions against the unauthorized taking of valuable secret information. However, in a 1973 decision, a U.S. court held that valuable secrets that have not been patented, but which might have been appropriate for patent protection and which have been in commercial use over a year, cannot be protected legally even against wrongful appropriation through breach of obligation of confidence. Unlike patents, there is no statutory provision at the federal level for the protection of trade secrets. Presumably if a restriction imposed on a licensee is illegal in a patent license, it would be illegal in the case of a trade secret. Under this ruling, foreign companies are likely to think twice before licensing unpatented trade secrets in the U.S. in that their licensees cannot be held accountable for a breach of confidentiality and a licensee's employees might be hired away by a competitor. Likewise, a U.S. company is unlikely to enter into many licenses, based on trade secrets, with foreign firms if the latter know that by hiring away key employees from a U.S. firm they can capture the secrets without committing themselves to pay royalties. There is also the possibility that U.S. firms may be tempted to transfer R&D activity to foreign subsidiaries in countries with strong laws protecting trade secrets, such as Canada, Japan, and much of Europe.

In protecting trade secrets, companies rely upon employee secrecy agreements, such as nondisclosure and nonuse clauses in employment contracts. Whether a company requires all employees to sign contracts containing such clauses, or only designated categories of employees, is a matter of company policy. In some countries (France) collective labor agreements within a particular industrial sector may contain provisions prohibiting employees from committing trade secret abuses.[36]

Management problems arising out of the international patent, copyright, trademark system:

1. The need for an early evaluation of the commercial value of a patent in that the first party to apply for a patent in one Paris Union country has only one year of grace before applying for protection in other member states. He has priority against others during that year. (He can, of course, apply later if no one else has applied in the meantime, so long as publication has not occurred. The actual issuance of a patent anywhere is equivalent to publication.)

2. The need to set up a system to assure continuation of patent, trademark, or copyright validity. Payment of an annual fee may be required. In case of patents or trademarks, use may be required. In the case of a trademark, application for renewal may be required.

3. The need to set up a system to monitor important markets for infringement and to prosecute infringers.

4. The need to decide whether to develop a universal trademark or a series of national

---

[36]See *Business International,* September 27, 1974, pp. 305–06, 312; April 26, 1974, p. 132; May 3, 1974, p. 143; October 4, 1974, p. 318; October 11, 1974, pp. 325–27; also Aaron N. Wise, *Trade Secrets and Know-How Throughout the World* (New York: Clark Boardman Company, 1974).

or regional marks. If the former, the problem of avoiding legal restrictions and unpleasant connotations in every country is a formidable one requiring substantial research.

5.   The need to decide who is going to own the proprietary right—the parent company or subsidiary. If the parent, the subsidiary must be licensed to use. But such licensing of subsidiaries is not legal under all systems. If the subsidiary is 100 percent owned, the only difference is that between a dividend (posttax earnings) and a royalty (a pretax cost). But if it is a joint venture, the local partner may not take kindly to payment of a royalty (which is a cost) to the parent firm, particularly if the level of the royalty is determined by the parent. On the other hand, if a proprietary right is sold to or capitalized by a subsidiary abroad, the parent must assure itself that the right is not lost to it if ownership of the subsidiary changes hands.

6.   The need to have continuing access to legal counsel expert in international trademark, copyright, and patent law.

7.   In that prior use is not a requirement in many countries for registering a trademark and in that the U.S. is not a member of the Madrid Agreement, it may be useful for a subsidiary in one of the countries signatory to the Madrid Agreement to register the trademark. But in such cases, the subsidiary must own the trademark, which introduces the problems suggested in five above.

8.   Desirability of relying on patent protection (which constitutes publication) or on maintaining secrecy (hence, denying knowledge to competitors).

In closing, it should be noted that the distinction should be made between the *lease* of valuable rights (patents, trademarks, copyrights, commercial secrets) and their *sale.* In the latter case, ownership, and, hence, the right to use, does not terminate with the licensing agreement, which is really a sales contract. Nor can the seller restrain the right of the buyer to use the property purchased in the manner of his choice. This means that if a parent company transfers such property to a subsidiary, either by sale or investment, which is itself subsequently sold without a sell back or disinvestment of that property, the parent loses all rights. To what extent foreign and U.S. courts would recognize such a loss were the ownership of the subsidiary lost involuntarily, such as through expropriation, is not clear.

Tax law

Possibly the most complicated and important legal variable of all is taxation. National tax systems vary along important dimensions. Some of the more important are:

1.   Aggregate level. As a percentage of GNP (Denmark is among the highest with 47 percent; the United States is moderate, about 29 percent; the LDCs are generally low, an example being Turkey at 18 percent).

2.   Burden on the firm. Runs from a high in the United States and Europe (48–52 percent) to around 30 percent in many LDCs. Switzerland with its 7.2 percent tax

is the lowest of the industrialized countries. However, distributed and undistributed profits may be taxed differently, although not in the United States. Characteristically, in Continental Europe distributed profits are taxed at a lower rate, and not infrequently the shareholder can take credit against his tax liability for his pro rata share of corporate income taxes paid on his dividends. In Mexico reinvested corporate earnings are not taxed.

3. Taxation of capital gains. Runs from 35 percent in the United States down to zero percent for many European countries. Other differences relate to the definition of a capital gain and evaluation of the basis (initial value).

4. Type. Income, wealth or property, consumption or sale, transaction, value added, capital gains, dividend, withholding (a tax withheld at the source of a stream of income—interest, dividends, royalties, wages), import (import duty), export (export duty). The preeminence of certain types will determine whether the overall impact of a tax system is progressive (higher percentage imposed on the more affluent).

5. Progressiveness of corporate tax. From a flat rate regardless of income, to a three-tiered system (as in the United States) or a multiple-stepped progressive tax (often tied to a profit/capital ratio, as in several Latin American countries), sometimes called "schedular."

6. The duality of corporate taxation. The taxation of all corporate profits *and* the taxation of dividends to stockholders. Some countries tax only corporate profits (unitary); others permit the dividend recipient to take a credit for all or some of his pro rata share of the corporate tax.

7. Degree of formalization. The most formal and complex is the United States, which consists of 5,000 finely printed pages (the code itself), plus 10,000 pages of official interpretation, and thousands of pages of judicial rulings.

8. Purpose. Revenue, control, stimulation of growth, direction of economic activity. For example, in Japan, as a device to promote the export of technology, firms have been able to deduct from taxable income 70 percent of the income from know-how sales and 20 percent of the income from technical service fees. In the United States, there are tax incentives for export sales in the Western hemisphere (currently being phased out), for economic activity in U.S. possessions and in less developed countries, and for export sales generally.

9. In observance. Some tax systems are notorious for the noncompliance they enjoy, cases in point being Spain and Italy. In the latter case, the firm may be faced with the imposition of a "presumptive tax" based on the tax office's estimate of what the profit of the firm should have been. The firm then tries to negotiate it downward to what it considers to be a reasonable level. Other countries are prone to give "tax holidays" for specified periods.

10. Basis for jurisdiction. By domicile or legal situs, permanent establishment, nationality, seat of control, the conduct of an active trade or business, treaty.

11. Jurisdiction claimed. Over worldwide income (as in the U.S. case) or over local source income only (as in the case of several European countries). Some countries impose a lower tax on foreign-source income, as in the Canadian case. (Canada exempts dividends entirely if the foreign firm paying the dividend is owned at least 25 percent by the Canadian firm.)

12. In recognizing costs (i.e., defining taxable income). Transfer prices,[37] depreciation allowances, investment allowances (i.e., deduction in excess of total depreciation, investment tax credit), credits for foreign taxes paid, allocation of overhead expenses from headquarters to subsidiary. (An example: After 1958 the U.S. permitted no deduction—as a cost—against taxable income for payments made to officials or employees of a foreign government if the payment would be unlawful under U.S. law.)

13. In timing of tax. Payment to be made in the period earned or only as remitted from subsidiary to parent. (In some cases, this right of tax deferral may be lost, as in the U.S. case since 1976, by participating in an "illegal boycott" or by making "extraordinary payments" abroad. Tax deferral permits the use of "tax haven" countries, that is, the accumulation of earnings in a holding company domiciled in a country that imposes a *zero* or very low tax rate on foreign source income and on accumulated earnings.

14. Tax sparing. Recognition by a firm's parent government of a certificate issued in lieu of payment of tax by a foreign government to the firm's local subsidiary, possibly as part of a tax incentive scheme (i.e., tax holiday) to attract foreign business. The parent can use this certificate as a credit against its own tax liability (a scheme specifically rejected by the United States, but practiced by Japan and several European countries.)

15. Degree to which a tax system adheres to the principle of tax neutrality. Unless specifically intended to do otherwise, a neutral tax does not stimulate or depress particular types of income, forms of business organization, location of production, or seat of control. Internationally, there are two types of mutually inconsistent tax neutrality: (1) imposition of the same total tax burden on income received by a country's firms, whether derived abroad or domestically, (2) imposition of the same total tax burden on a country's firms as that borne by their foreign competitors.

16. Recognizing tax exemptions. For profits derived from exports (Ireland), on income generated from the export of technology and skills (Japan), on income having its origin in certain countries (Singapore in respect to neighboring Southeast Asian countries), and for certain types of business enterprise (the partnership, the Groupement d'Intérêt Economique in France).

17. Flexibility. For example, the capacity to adjust depreciation allowances to pace inflation or to adopt appropriate inventory accounting practice (last-in-first-out, LIFO, as opposed to first-in-first-out, FIFO).[38]

18. In providing tax incentives for investing in certain sectors or regions, investing more than a certain amount, or employing a certain number related to the capital invested (such as a full tax holiday, investment tax credit, accelerated depreciation, an investment allowance).

---

[37]Methods of calculation used by the U.S. taxing authorities are: arm's length or comparable uncontrolled price method, resale price (resale price less profit), cost plus reasonable profit, proportionate profit and rate of return on investment. A reallocation of income can, of course, lead to double taxation.

[38]For example, as of 1975, LIFO was not permitted in France and Sweden. See Glossary.

Table 7.5
THE FIVE METHODS OF TAXING FOREIGN SOURCE INCOME

	Exemption	Tax reduction	Crediting foreign taxes	Expensing foreign taxes	Double taxing
Taxable income abroad	$100	$100	$100	$100	$100
Foreign tax (assume 40%)	40	40	40	40	40
Dividend to parent	60	60	60	60	60
Tentative parent country tax (assume 50% in the full case, 10% in the reduced case)	0	10	50	30	50
Tax credit	0	0	40	0	0
Tax liability to parent country	0	10	10	30	50
Total tax paid	$ 40	$ 50	$ 50	$ 70	$ 90

19. Number of jurisdictions claiming taxes. For example, a firm operating a national chain of outlets in the U.S. may be subject to the income, franchise, property, license, network, sales, and use taxes in 50 states, in addition to both federal and local (county and municipal) taxes. All told, it may have to file over 1,000 tax returns and reports each year, a significant cost item.

20. In some countries (as in Mexico), a contractor can negotiate a clause in his contract to the effect that he will be reimbursed for any corporate taxes levied on him within the country. In others (as in Venezuela), such a clause is illegal; the contractor's only recourse is to anticipate the tax and include it in his fee. The more restrictive Venezuelan approach seems to be becoming more common.

There are essentially five ways of treating foreign source income for tax purposes, as demonstrated in Table 7.5.

The situation is complicated by the fact that a country may tax income at a reduced rate that is coming from certain countries, such as designated LDCs. Normally a tax credit is given only for foreign wealth and income taxes (in proportion to the dividend remitted to total taxable earnings),[39] which gives rise to a definitional problem. Does a tax on *gross* income qualify? Does a royalty on gross income—on the full value of oil received, for example—qualify? What of the oil delivered under a production sharing contract? A country also has the policy option of taxing foreign source income only when remitted (tax deferral) or when earned even though not remitted. In the latter case problems can arise if the exchange rate changes between the time the tax is assessed and the time the earnings are actually remitted. Should a further tax be extracted if the rate shifts in favor of the corporation (i.e., a devaluation of the foreign currency in reference to the parent country

---

[39]Direct credits are normally given for payment of withholding taxes imposed on interest, royalties, fees, rentals, and dividends.

Table 7.6
RESIDENCY AND DOMICILE FOR TAX PURPOSES

	Legal domicile*	
Residence	Foreign corporation (alien)	Domestic corporation† (national)
Nonresident (not engaged in business locally, no permanent establishment)	Nonresident foreign corporation‡ (nonresident alien)	Nonresident domestic corporation§ (nonresident national)
Resident (engaged in business locally, has a permanent establishment)	Resident foreign corporation‖ (resident alien)	Domestic corporation (local nationals)

*May be either where incorporated (U.S. case) or where the seat of management is located; i.e., fiscal residence of those who have final authority in all major decisions (as in the case of Germany and the U.K.).

†Even though 100 percent owned by nonresident aliens and/or foreign corporations.

‡For example, a foreign corporation that sells into the U.S. through independent representatives.

§For example, a personal holding company that does no business in the U.S. and has no permanent establishment in the U.S.

‖For example, a foreign corporation with a permanent establishment in the U.S., or conducting business in the U.S., i.e., through a branch (as opposed to an incorporated subsidiary).

currency) or a tax rebate given if the rate shifts in the opposite direction? Such a system would add enormously to the complexities surrounding taxation, but to deny such adjustments could lead to substantial inequity.

Insofar as is known, no countries require their corporations to expense foreign corporate income or wealth taxes in calculating taxable income, nor do any simply ignore foreign taxes as implied under the double taxing situation. Most countries appear either to exempt foreign source income from domestic taxation or to impose a reduced rate. The U.S. uses the tax credit system, although there have been strong pressures to apply the expensing concept. One suspects that the Japanese and Europeans would be very pleased if the U.S. Congress in its wisdom did so and thus rendered U.S. corporations noncompetitive in many parts of the world where foreign firms are virtually compelled, for economic and legal reasons, to process or manufacture locally. As it is, by not recognizing the tax-sparring principle, as do many other countries with the tax credit system, the U.S. penalizes its corporations that are encouraged by foreign governments by means of a tax holiday. To the extent that corporate earnings are remitted to the U.S. a tax holiday simply transfers earnings from the foreign treasury to the U.S. treasury. Fortunately, the U.S. still recognizes tax deferral in most cases, so that the benefits of a foreign tax holiday can be realized so long as earnings are held overseas.

To further one's understanding of international taxation, a few further definitions are in order. One needs to appreciate the importance of residency and legal domicile. Essentially, there are four possibilities, as indicated in Table 7.6.

In the U.S. case, there is a 30 percent withholding tax imposed on interest, dividends, royalties, and rents paid to nonresident foreign corporations and nonresident aliens, except as reduced by treaty. There is no federal tax imposed on sales income. A resident foreign corporation, as does a resident alien, pays full U.S. corporate (or personal income) tax on U.S.-source income. A nonresident domestic corporation (and nonresident nationals) pay full U.S. tax on world-wide income even though not remitted to the United States, with some exceptions. A domestic corporation (and a local national) pays full U.S. tax on global income. In both cases corporations can credit foreign wealth and income taxes paid, but for individuals (nonincorporated entities) such taxes are merely deductions from taxable income.

One can see that there are many definitional problems introduced here which can only be resolved by tax regulation and/or tax treaty, such as the definitions of "legal domicile," "permanent establishment," "being engaged in business," "residency," and source of income, to mention only a few.

The latter is of particular importance because of the latitude a firm may have in manipulating transactions so as to generate profit in desired locations, often in a relatively low tax area. It then is in a position to use those profits for investment purposes. Instead of having only 52 cents of the profit dollar, which would be the case if those earnings had been fully taxed in the U.S., the company may have 60 or 70 cents of the profit dollar for reinvestment purposes. Monitoring the transfer prices that give rise to the movement of profits other than through the dividend route is administratively very difficult. Hundreds of thousands of invoices and contracts would have to be studied and prices compared to "arm's length prices" which in many cases is difficult because the goods or services may be unique to a particular firm or enjoy substantial brand name price premium because of allegedly superior quality. An alternative is to allocate corporate income as many states within the U.S. do. The bulk of the income of interstate firms operating within the United States is apportioned among the states by formula based on the state's share of the firm's total economic activity, the latter being usually defined in terms of payrolls, property, and sales. Ordinarily the formula contains all three factors, but sometimes two. In the case of a three-factor formula, a particular state taxes that fraction of the firm's income equal to the average of the state's shares in the payroll, property, and sales of the firm. Some have suggested that many problems would be eliminated if the same system could be adopted internationally. Of course, unless all countries were to use the same method for measuring total and local payroll, property, and sales, the result could be either under or over taxation. By far the most troublesome problem, if the U.S. experience is any guide, lies in affixing the source of income from sales. First, what proportion of a company's income should be judged to be from sales for those goods and services produced in one country and sold in another? Secondly, what is the source of sales income, the country in which title is passed, the country of destination, the country in which the sale is negotiated? Finally, of course, each country would have to tax the corporation as a single entity on the basis of a single consolidated set of financial statements, which introduces currency translation problems.

In part to offer some needed definitions on the international level, there exists a web of bilateral tax treaties or conventions for the avoidance of double taxation with respect to taxes on income and capital. Each one varies somewhat, but characteristically a tax treaty includes provisions relating to:

1. The definition of what constitutes local source income, residency, permanent establishment, being engaged in business.

2. A mutual reduction of withholding taxes levied on dividends, interest, and royalties paid by a domestic firm to a firm located in the other country, frequently restricted to firms owned to some given percentage by the recipient firm.

3. The taxation of capital gains realized by a national or enterprise of one country within the territory of the other.

4. A reduction or elimination of taxes imposed on specific income streams originating in the other country and taxed there.

5. The allowability as costs of certain expenses such as royalties and fees paid by a foreign subsidiary to its parent, recognition of a parent country investment credit for an investment made by a qualified foreign subsidiary.

6. The rules covering the taxation of nationals of each contracting state residing or working within the other.

7. Exchange of information between the taxing authorities of the two countries and a mechanism for resolving any conflicts.

As noted, some countries tax foreign source income only when remitted (the tax deferral notion); others tax such income under certain circumstances (as the U.S., as we shall see). Under a full tax deferral system, a company can make maximum use of the tax haven holding company, which is simply a subsidiary corporation located in a country that is appealing from a tax point of view.

The ideal tax haven country also enjoys monetary stability, maintains a modern banking system, enforces banking secrecy, places no controls on the foreign exchange market, has a stable government and economy, enjoys good international communications, has a web of tax treaties that reduce withholding taxes in both directions, and has a favorable corporation law. By "favorable" is meant a law that permits the maintenance of records and offices outside the country, permits unlimited foreign stock ownership, imposes no restriction on the nationality of officers and directors, requires only the presence of a statutory representative, and permits quick and inexpensive incorporation. Popular tax haven countries include a number of Caribbean island nations, Panama, Liechtenstein, Liberia, Luxembourg, Switzerland, Monaco, and the Netherlands.[40]

---

[40]The full list of possible tax havens as of 1977: Andorra, Anguilla, Antigua, Bahamas, Barbados, Bermuda, Campione, Cayman Islands, Channel Islands, Christmas Island, Cocos (Keeling) Islands, Costa Rica, Cyprus, Gibraltar, Gilbert and Ellice, Greece, Grenada, Hong Kong, Republic of Ireland, Isle of Man, Israel, Jamaica, Jordan, Kuwait, Lebanon, Liberia, Liechtenstein, Luxembourg, Maldives, Malta, Mexico, Micronesia, Minerva, Monaco, Montserrat, Nauru, the Netherlands, the Netherlands Antilles, Nevis, New Caledonia, Norfolk Island,

For parent corporations domiciled in countries taxing only local source income or not taxing foreign source income until actually repatriated (the U.S. situation prior to 1963), the tax haven holding company can be very attractive. To the extent permitted by the taxing authorities, goods and services may be invoiced to the tax haven company at minimum prices and sold by it at maximum prices. Paying perhaps no taxes within the country of domicile, the tax haven company can accumulate virtually untaxed money for investment or to use as working capital, possibly even to loan to the parent company.

Asymmetries among national tax systems can cause difficulty. According to the General Agreement on Trade and Tariffs (GATT), indirect taxes (excise, sales, value added taxes) should be levied in the country of destination. Hence, such taxes may be rebated on exports, and such rebate is not deemed an export subsidy. And the importing country, if it also levies indirect taxes, may impose its own taxes on the imported goods. On the other hand, direct taxes (income, wealth, property, or profits taxes) should be collected, according to the GATT, in the country in which the income originates. Therefore, relief of such taxes on exports constitutes a subsidy (which is precisely what the EEC charges the U.S. with doing through the Domestic International Sales Corporation), and import duties to compensate for direct taxes not paid abroad are unacceptable. The point is that the GATT forbids export subsidies. A problem arises when a country relying heavily on indirect taxes, such as the value added tax in Europe, exports to a country relying heavily on direct taxes, such as the income tax in the U.S. In such cases, the exporting country may rebate the indirect taxes imposed on the exported goods, but the importing country may not compensate by burdening the imported goods by imposing a direct tax. Therefore, the exports enjoy a competitive advantage.

There is another asymmetry between national tax systems that can lead to a conflict of interest. If one country has a dual corporate income tax such that a higher tax is imposed on retained earnings than on distributed earnings, that country is likely to want to place a relatively high withholding tax on dividends paid to foreigners. The point is that the purpose of the dual tax is to encourage the payout of earnings to *local* shareholders, but not necessarily to *foreign* shareholders. In contrast, a country with a unitary corporate income tax, and which permits the shareholder to credit his share of the corporate tax against his own tax liability, is likely to be neutral on the issue. It makes no difference whether corporate earnings are paid to local residents or foreigners.

Indirect taxes paid abroad are always expensed, never credited against parent country tax liability. Hence, if in the course of negotiating a project abroad a corporation can trade off indirect taxes for direct taxes, it may gain even if it agrees to pay somewhat more taxes to the host country.

Panama, Pitcairn Island, Sark, St. Eustatius, St. Kitts, St. Lucia, St. Martin, St. Pierre et Miquelon, St. Vincent, Seychelles, Sealand, Singapore, South Africa, Spain, Sri Lanka, Svalbard, Tonga, Trinidad and Tobago, Tunisia, Turks and Caicos, and the Virgin Islands.

Indirect taxes are relatively low in the United States, where they constituted something like 15 percent of the total tax revenue in 1974. In Europe, the percentage is consistently higher except in the Netherlands and Belgium. And in a representative sample of 63 countries, the contribution of indirect taxes to the total averaged 37 percent.[41] Because of the importance of indirect taxes, it may be important to offer a classification for reference purposes (Table 7.7).

It should be noted that given the same rate and coverage, the amount of tax collected through a transaction tax (often called sales tax) and value added tax is the same. *But* there may be other differences:

1. Collection. In a *sales tax*, the seller (retailer) customarily charges the tax to the consumer and remits the tax to the tax collector (or the buyer remits in some cases, e.g., registered buyer system). In the case of a value added tax, a seller charges a buyer the amount of the tax, nets it against what he as a buyer has paid to others, and remits the *difference* to the tax collector.

2. Shifting. The value added tax is probably more likely to be shifted forward because a trader wishes to recapture his own tax payment. He cannot do so unless he has sales on which VAT has been charged.

3. Take occult. This relates to goods used for both production and final consumption (e.g., vehicles). With a sales tax (which is collected only at time of sale to consumer), producers' goods may be taxed twice unless a distinction can be made in terms of use (i.e., between use for production and consumption), and producers' goods are exempt from the sales tax. But if they are identified and exempted, dual-use goods (e.g. vehicles) may be certified for use as producers' goods when in fact they are going to final users—thereby evading the sales tax. This problem does not arise under the value added tax.

The most complicated tax system in the world, barring none, is that of the United States. The general principles relating to foreign source income are outlined in the appendix attached to this chapter. The reader should be forewarned not to use this outline in lieu of expert counsel. There are legions of exceptions and complications.

In fact, along with other reasons, the increasing burden of U.S. taxation on foreign source income with the elimination of tax deferral and tax credit in a number of situations, plus the cost inherent in the sheer complexity and many uncertainties in the U.S. system, has led a number of U.S. corporate executives at least to speculate upon the costs and benefits of "dedomiciling" their respective corporations. This term refers to the process of transferring ownership of most corporate assets to a parent corporation legally domiciled outside of the U.S., in which case the U.S. operation becomes a subsidiary of a foreign corporation. Although no U.S. cases of dedomiciling have been reported, Canada has lost a number of corporations. These moves followed Canada's 1971 Tax Reform Act, which contained three provisions:

---

[41]Sijbren Cnossen, "The Role and Structure of Sales and Excise Tax Systems," *Finance and Development*, vol. 12, no. 1, March 1975, p. 32.

Table 7.7
FORMS OF INDIRECT TAXES

1. **Turnover taxes** collected on sales at all or nearly all production and distribution stages; on account of their cumulative effects these taxes are also referred to as cascade taxes.

2. **Production taxes** collected on sales by producers to wholesalers, retailers, or other producers; transactions prior to the sale by the last producer are often partially exempted or taxed at reduced rates:

   a) **French-type production taxes** exempt domestically produced raw materials and intermediate goods as well as imported goods that have not been further processed;

   b) **other production taxes** exempt producer goods or apply reduced rates, while trading activities per se are excluded from the tax.

3. **Dual-stage taxes** (tandem systems) such as manufacturers'/retail taxes collected on both the sales of finished products of manufacturers to wholesalers or retailers, and on sales from retailers to final consumers.

4. **Manufacturers' taxes** collected on sales of finished products of manufacturers to wholesalers or retailers, including occasional direct sales to consumers. While capital goods are usually exempted outright, various techniques have been designed to counter the cumulative effects of the taxation of raw materials and intermediate goods:

   a) **the suspension method** permits the tax-free purchase of inputs by traders and manufacturers registered for that purpose, tax being levied when products leave the "ring" and are sold to unregistered persons;

   b) **the subtraction technique** allows for a deduction of taxable purchases from taxable sales; this can be done for

   (1) physically incorporated inputs only; or on

   (2) some other basis such as a deduction for inputs taxed at the same rate as the finished product;

   c) **the tax credit principle** provides for a credit for tax paid on purchases against tax payable on sales.

5. **Wholesale taxes** collected on sales by the last wholesaler or manufacturer to retailers, including occasional direct sales to consumers. Capital goods are usually exempted outright, while the suspension method applies to raw materials and intermediate goods.

6. **Retail/wholesale taxes** (hybrid systems) collected on the sales of retailers to final consumers and of wholesalers or manufacturers to retailers whose operations are considered too small for separate taxation. Producer goods are treated similarly as under wholesale taxes.

7. **Retail taxes** collected on sales by retailers to final consumers, including wholesalers or manufacturers selling occasionally to consumers; producer goods are generally excluded by definition.

8. **Value-added taxes** collected on sales at all or nearly all production and distribution stages, with each stage receiving a credit for tax paid on purchases from the preceding stage:

   a) **the EEC model** extends through the retail stage and provides for a credit for tax paid on all producer goods;

   b) **other types** may not cover the retail stage and sometimes do not give credit for tax paid on certain fixed assets.

Sijbren Cnossen, *Finance and Development,* vol. 12, no. 1, March 1975, p. 30.

1. The imposition of a tax on half of all capital gains, including gains realized overseas.

2. Taxation of foreign passive income (royalties, fees, and dividends) earned by a foreign subsidiary of a Canadian corporation even though not remitted.

3. Taxation of a portion of dividends (grossed-up dividends less the foreign tax credit) received from a country not having a tax treaty with Canada.

A pressure for dedomiciling other than taxation originates from the internationalization of corporate ownership, accelerated by issues of convertible Eurobonds. This development "could well trigger partial spinning off of assets to parallel parent companies in other countries where sizable segments of total corporate profits originate."[42]

A number of countries have laws permitting corporations to emigrate ("dedomicile"), and it appears that such transfers of domicile would be recognized in the U.S. Other countries accept the redomiciling of foreign corporations in time of war even though their own domestic legislation does not enable a company to emigrate (the case of the U.K.). Most of the legal transfer provisions relate to emergencies, such as war (the Swiss case). Others merely require prior approval (as Liechtenstein). The Netherlands and the Netherlands Antilles permit transfer out simply by vote of directors or shareholders. Panama permits corporations to transfer their seats abroad only if they were originally incorporated as foreign entities and subsequently transferred into Panama.

Dedomiciling was achieved by one Canadian company as follows. First it incorporated a wholly-owned Dutch subsidiary. Subsequently, the Dutch subsidiary acquired all of the Canadian company's net assets, excluding the shares held in the Dutch company, and in return issued new shares to the Canadian company. Shortly thereafter, these shares were distributed to the Canadian company's shareholders in exchange for their shares in the Canadian company. The result was that the Canadian shareholders held stock in the Dutch company, and the Dutch company owned the Canadian company, which was now its subsidiary. The value of the shareholders' equity in the Dutch company, which continued to be expressed in Canadian dollars, was equal to that of the Canadian corporation at the time of the transaction. Meanwhile, shares in the Dutch company were listed on the Toronto stock exchange, and the shares in the Canadian company delisted.

If an established U.S. corporation were to dedomicile by way of selling its assets to a foreign corporation in return for the latter's stock, whether subsequently distributed to the original shareholders or not, prior approval of the Internal Revenue Service would have to be secured. If not, the entire value of the assets thus transferred would probably be taxable as income, in that the transfer would be taking place to a controlled foreign corporation. However, if a U.S. corporation were to build up a foreign subsidiary so that it was more than 50 percent owned by non-U.S. shareholders and held assets equal to or greater than those held by the U.S. corporation directly, the situation might be substantially different. (Its assets might be built up through the sale of the subsidiary's equity in foreign markets and the establishment of parallel subsidiaries around the world, which would gradually absorb the business and assets

---

[42] *Business International,* May 11, 1973, p. 145.

of the parent company subsidiaries and, hence, redirect income.) Under those circumstances, the transaction would be a straight sale of U.S. corporate assets to a foreign corporation, part of which happened to be owned by the acquired corporation. It is difficult to see how this would constitute a taxable transaction under present law if it could be established that the transfer was undertaken for reasons other than avoidance of U.S. taxes, which should not be difficult. Failing that, there would be a possible 35 percent tax on the transfer if no gain were recognized. Indeed, one wonders if some U.S. corporations are not moving consciously in this direction. Obviously, it would be a carefully guarded secret so as not to generate adverse publicity and lead to blocking legislation. (See also note 45, p. 7.)

Discussion questions

1. Of what possible value is the establishment of a wholly-owned domestic subsidiary through which to channel the parent's foreign business (selling, buying, contracting, investing)?

2. What are the essential differences among the U.S., European Community, and Japanese antitrust laws?

3. What environmental factors may influence the formulation of national antitrust law?

4. Do you feel that U.S. antitrust law as it applies to U.S. business operating internationally is reasonable?

5. Under what circumstances should a firm opt to protect an invention by means of a patent, by secrecy?

6. Do you feel that LDCs should maintain the type of patent system characteristic of the industrial countries? Why or why not?

7. Which kind of tax neutrality do you favor in respect to the taxation of foreign source income?

8. Under what circumstances might a U.S. firm utilize a tax haven holding company?

9. What are the legal and tax consequences of operating through a foreign branch as opposed to a foreign subsidiary?

10. Do you feel that the DISC provision in U.S. law favors big business? Why or why not?

Recommended references

Antitrust Guide for International Operations. Washington: U.S. Department of Justice, 1977.

Baker, R. Palmer, et al. *Taxation of Foreign Source Income by the United States and Other Countries.* Princeton: Tax Institute of America, 1966.

Barnes, Stanley N., and S. Chesterfield Oppenheim (cochairmen), *The Attorney Gen-*

eral's National Committee to Study the Antitrust Laws. Washington: Superintendent of Documents, 1955.

Brewster, Kingman. *Antitrust and American Business Abroad.* New York: McGraw-Hill, 1958.

Costner, Thomas E., ed. *Patent Law Review—1976.* New York: Clark Boardman Company, 1977.

Duerr, Michael G. *Tax Allocations and International Business.* New York: The Conference Board, 1972.

Friedman, Wolfgang G., ed. *Legal Aspects of Foreign Investment.* Boston: Little, Brown & Company, 1959.

International Implications of U.S. Antitrust Laws. Washington: U.S. Department of Justice, 1977.

Kintner, Earl W., and Mark R. Joelson. *An International Antitrust Primer.* New York: MacMillan, 1974.

Krause, Lawrence B., and Kenneth W. Dan. *Federal Tax Treatment of Foreign Income.* Washington: The Brookings Institution, 1964.

Kroll, Arthur H., ed. *Seventh Annual Institute on International Taxation.* New York: Practicing Law Institute, 1976.

McLacklan, D. L., and D. Swan. *Competition Policy in the European Community.* London: Oxford University Press, 1967.

Musgrave, Peggy B. *United States Taxation of Foreign Source Income.* Cambridge: The Law School of Harvard University, 1969.

Richman, Peggy Brewer. *Taxation of Foreign Investment Income, an Economic Analysis.* Baltimore: Johns Hopkins Press, 1963.

United Nations. *The Impact of Multinational Corporations on Development and on International Relations, Technical Papers: Taxation.* New York: United Nations Department of Economic and Social Affairs, 1974.

United Nations. *Tax Treaties Between Developed and Developing Countries.* New York: United Nations Department of Economic and Social Affairs, 1976.

United States Income Taxation of Private Investments in Developing Countries. New York: United Nations, Department of Economic and Social Affairs, 1970.

Appendix 1 to Chapter 7

THE U.S. TAXATION OF FOREIGN INCOME

GENERAL PRINCIPLE

All income of U.S. citizens, domestic corporations, and resident aliens, regardless of source, is taxable at the full U.S. rate during the year earned. Rates: *personal*, 0–70 percent; corporations, 20 percent on the first $25,000, 22 percent on the second $25,000, 48 percent on the balance; *intercorporate dividend received deduction*, if paid by one domestic corporation to another, 85 percent exempt from taxation with the balance taxed at normal corporate rate; a 100-percent exemption when the dividend is paid by one domestic corporation to another in an affiliated group; that is, a parent and its at least 80-percent-owned domestic subsidiaries; *capital gains tax*, 35 percent; *personal holding companies* (corporations in which 50 percent or more of the value of the stock is held by five or fewer persons and at least 80 percent—60 percent in the foreign case—of its income is passive, that is, dividends, interest, royalties, and rents), which income is taxed to stockholders as personal income, 70 percent if not distributed; *nonresident aliens*, 30 percent withholding tax on U.S. source income.

EXCEPTIONS IN RESPECT TO FOREIGN SOURCE INCOME

Test: where title passes for goods, where services are performed in the case of services.

Exceptions for persons

The exclusions for U.S. citizens resident abroad were reduced by the 1976 Tax Reform Act to $15,000 from the previous range of $20,000 to $25,000, and all income above the $15,000 is taxed in the bracket that would apply if the taxpayer's entire earnings abroad had been subject to U.S. taxes.[43] Prior to 1977, the first $25,000 per year was excluded from U.S. taxation in the case of U.S. citizens who were foreign residents (after three consecutive years of residence abroad). During the first three years, the exclusion was limited to $20,000 a year, thereafter to $25,000 a year ($35,000 prior to 1965). The $20,000-a-year exclusion also applied to U.S. citizens present in foreign countries for at least 510 days during 18 consecutive months. That exclusion was reduced to $15,000 by the 1976 act for all except those working for charitable organizations, for whom it remains at $20,000. For nonresident aliens with a gross income not over $15,400 and not doing business with the United States, the rate continues to be 30 percent (or lower treaty rate) on certain U.S. income, but from 1977 on bank interest is excluded.

Exceptions for corporations

1. *Tax deduction*, which is the same as treating foreign taxes (including corporate wealth and income taxes) as expenses against taxable income of a foreign subsidiary.[44] This occurs unless the U.S. taxpayer claims a foreign tax credit. The

---

[43]Application of these provisions of the 1976 act has been deferred until 1978.

[44]In calculating taxable foreign income, no foreign bribe may be deductible. A bribe refers to a payment to a foreign government official if such payment would be illegal in the U.S. Such a bribe is considered a "deemed dividend." In that total taxable income is measured by the amount of the bribe, the foreign tax credit is reduced, since the denominator of the foreign tax credit limitation is increased. (See 2 below.)

election to deduct or credit is an annual election. Because the foreign tax credit is subject to limitations based on U.S. tax liability and upon the ratio of foreign source income and entire taxable income (worldwide) of the U.S. corporation, it may be advantageous under certain circumstances to elect to deduct all foreign taxes rather than to claim a credit. This situation arises when there is more foreign-source loss than income. For example, assume that a U.S. corporation reports $100,000 U.S.-source income, $100,000 income from country A (with a 40 percent tax), and a loss of $120,000 from country B. We assume that the U.S. tax is 50 percent.

	Deduction elected	Credit elected
U.S.-source income	$100,000	$100,000
Country A income	100,000	100,000
40% tax	40,000	40,000
Country B income (loss)	−120,000	−120,000
Taxable income in U.S.	40,000	80,000
Tentative U.S. tax	20,000	40,000
Foreign tax credit	0	0*
U.S. tax liability	20,000	40,000
Total taxes paid	60,000	80,000

*Can take no tax credit because it is limited by the ratio $\frac{-20,000}{80,000}$, which would result in a negative credit.

2. *Tax credit* for income and wealth taxes (but not for taxes on gross income or any indirect taxes) paid to foreign governments by a foreign corporation in respect to dividends or earnings remitted to a U.S. corporation owning 10 percent or more of the voting stock of the foreign corporation, or for such taxes paid by second and third tier foreign corporations if the first tier owns 10 percent or more of the voting stock of the second tier and the second owns at least 10 percent of the third, so long as the indirect ownership does not fall below 5 percent (which is simply the multiple of the percentage of ownership traceable back to the parent at all three levels). This rule embodies the "deemed paid concept." The first-tier corporation is deemed to have paid the taxes of the second and third tier corporations in proportion to ownership held. Excess taxes may be carried back two years and forward five years for credit purposes. The formula for calculating a foreign tax credit (indirect) is illustrated below. As of 1977, this method applies to foreign-source income from either developed or less developed countries earned after 1977. (Direct credit is taken for withholding taxes imposed abroad. The U.S. tax liability is reduced directly by the amount of the withholding.)

    For income received prior to 1978, from less developed country corporations (LDCC, see below) and in respect to LDCC earnings accumulated prior to 1975, the older (nongrossed up) method of calculating the foreign tax credit can be used, as illustrated below.

Limitations on the tax credit:

a) Overall limitation; that is, total credits are limited to the U.S. tax attributable to foreign source income (interest income excluded). Losses in one country are

Income	$100,000	100,000
Foreign tax (25 percent)	25,000	25,000
Profit	75,000	75,000
Reinvested profit	15,000	0
Remittance to United States	60,000	75,000
United States tax liability	$ 38,400*	$ 48,000*
Foreign tax credit	20,000†	25,000†
United States tax due	18,400	23,000
Total tax paid	$ 43,400	$ 48,000

$$*(\text{U.S. tax rate}) \times \left[\text{Remittance} + \left(\frac{\text{Remittance}}{\text{Profit}} \times \text{Foreign tax} \right) \right]$$

$$\dagger \left(\frac{\text{Remittance}}{\text{Profit}} \right) \times (\text{Foreign tax})$$

Income	$100,000	100,000
Foreign tax (25 percent)	25,000	25,000
Profit	75,000	75,000
Reinvested profit	15,000	0
Remittance to United States	60,000	75,000
United States tax liability	$ 28,800*	$ 36,000*
Foreign tax credit	15,000†	18,750†
United States tax due	13,800	17,250
Total tax paid	$ 38,800	$ 42,250

$$*(\text{U.S. tax rate}) \times (\text{Remittance})$$

$$\dagger \left(\frac{\text{Remittance}}{\text{Profit}} \right) \times \left(\frac{\text{Profit}}{\text{Income}} \times \text{Foreign tax} \right) = \left(\frac{\text{Remittance}}{\text{Income}} \right) \times \left(\text{Foreign tax} \right)$$

set off against profits in others, thereby reducing foreign income and the total tax credit permitted. The formula is as follows:

$$\frac{\text{Consolidated foreign profits and losses}}{\text{Worldwide taxable income}} \times \frac{\text{Amount of U.S.}}{\text{tax liability}} = \frac{\text{Maximum}}{\text{total credit}}$$

(Prior to 1976, a taxpayer might opt for a per-country limitation.)

b) Recapture of tax loss on U.S.-source income. When an overall loss exceeds foreign income in a given year, the excess of the losses can reduce U.S. tax on domestic source income. When this happens, the tax benefit derived from the deduction of the loss is recaptured by the U.S. when the company subsequently derives income from abroad. The recapture is accomplished by treating a portion of the later income as domestic income. The amount of foreign income treated in this way is limited to the lesser of the amount of the loss (to the extent that the loss has not been recaptured in prior taxable years) or 50 percent of the foreign taxable income for that year, or such larger percentage as the taxpayer may choose.

c) International boycott factor. A firm's operations in, or related to, countries associated in carrying out an international boycott *to* the firm's world wide operations (excluding the U.S.). Presumably, the unit of measure is taxable profits (but as of mid-1977 that was not clear). That ratio is applied to foreign tax credits, hence the limitation may be represented thus:

$$\left[1 - \frac{\text{boycott related income}}{\text{worldwide income outside U.S.}} \right] \times \frac{\text{Foreign}}{\text{tax credit}} = \frac{\text{Maximum}}{\text{permitted credit}}$$

(In addition, tax deferral is denied to such income. One of the problems is that the law seems to imply that *all* of the income of the foreign subsidiaries deriving income from business with boycotting countries may be denied tax credit or deferral treatment unless the tainted income is clearly identifiable. If, however, the income is coming to a subsidiary located in a country with which the U.S. has a tax treaty, this treatment may be contrary to the treaty.)

3. *Tax reductions*

a) Western Hemisphere Trade Corporations, the advantage to which is being phased out subsequent to 1976. The WHTC is a domestic corporation[45] whose income is (1) 95 percent or more derived from foreign sources; (2) 90 percent or more derived from the active conduct of a trade or business (dividends are not included; hence, a WHTC must operate abroad through branches); and (3) 100 percent of whose business, except incidental purchase, is done in the Western Hemisphere outside the United States. To satisfy the foreign source rules in respect to income, title to goods sold by a WHTC on behalf of its parent had to pass outside the United States. Normally, profits were divided, through transfer pricing, between parent and WHTC on a 50–50 basis. Tax was calculated thus up through 1976:

$$\frac{\text{U.S. corporate}}{\text{tax rate}} \times \left[\frac{\text{WHTC}}{\text{income}} - \left(\frac{14}{\text{U.S. corporate tax rate}} \times \frac{\text{WHTC}}{\text{income}} \right) \right],$$

which at the 48 percent rate was 34 percent. The intercorporate dividend tax of 7.2 percent (48 percent on 15 percent) increased the total tax rate to parent company to 41 percent in that dividends paid by a WHTC to its parent, even if more than 80 percent owned by the latter, were exempt from taxation only to the extent of 85 percent. Under the Tax Reform Act of 1976, the 14 point reduction in the WHTC rate became 11 percent in 1976, 8 percent in 1977, 5 percent in 1978, 2 percent in 1979, and zero percent thereafter.

b) Investment credit. For certain LDCs, on the basis of treaty, U.S. firms may receive a specified investment tax credit for qualified investments. This credit may be used as a credit against U.S. tax liability.

c) Capital gains. Taxable at 35 percent. Payment received from the transfer of intangible property, defined as patents, copyrights, trademarks, secret processes, and information in the general nature of a patentable invention, may, under certain circumstances, be considered a capital gain and not income for

---

[45]Including corporations formed in Canada or Mexico solely to comply with local law, if reported on a consolidated return.

tax purposes, whether received as a lump sum or in installments.[46] But, if the transfer is to a controlled foreign corporation (see below), the gain is taxable as ordinary income.

4. *Tax exclusions*

a) U.S. possessions corporation. A domestic corporation whose gross income is 80 percent or more derived from U.S. possessions and 50 percent or more derived from active conduct of trade or business. Taxable on world-wide income at the usual rate, but a full 48 percent foreign tax credit is given for its business and qualified investment income within the possession regardless of whether any taxes have been paid to the government of the possession. No taxes paid to a foreign country are creditable, nor is a consolidated return with the parent permitted. The special credit is effective for ten consecutive years. Tax-free distribution of earnings with or without liquidation is permitted.

b) Foreign-owned corporations (those not incorporated in the United States)

(1) Nonresident foreign corporations pay a 30 percent withholding tax on certain gross income received from U.S. sources, interest, dividends, rent, and so on. Frequently reduced to 15 percent by treaty. (See 5 below.)

(2) Resident foreign-owned corporations pay the normal U.S. tax on all income from U.S. source income. (Residency equals a permanent place of business and/or location of decision-making authority.)

5. *Tax deferral.* Note that there is no tax deferral in respect to income of foreign branches of a U.S. entity, for income is automatically consolidated during the current year. Deferral occurs only in the case of an incorporated foreign subsidiary, and then only if certain conditions are satisfied.

a) Foreign corporations (i.e., those incorporated outside the U.S.) *other than* foreign personal holding companies and U.S.-controlled foreign corporations, are not liable for any U.S. corporate income tax until earnings are repatriated to the United States *except* for income related to participation in an international boycott or to an illegal payment made abroad, in which case the tax deferral option is lost. In the case of the foreign personal holding company and the controlled foreign corporation, certain income is taxable currently to the U.S. owners whether distributed to them or not.

(1) Foreign personal holding company (a firm in which more than 50 percent of the stock is held by five or fewer U.S. citizens or residents). If 60 percent or more of the income is personal holding company income (rents, royalties, interest, dividends not earned in the active conduct of a real estate,

---

[46]To avoid the general rule that royalty income is ordinary income, and thereby open up the capital gains route, one must not be in the business of selling patents; the transfer must be of a complete and indivisible interest (that is, it must convey the exclusive right to manufacture, distribute, and sell on a national basis for the life of a patent, or, if unpatented, indefinitely; any retention of a substantial interest will defeat the purpose, but note that know-how and a patent are considered two separate pieces of property); one must hold the asset for at least six months (running from the date of patent issue or the date on which an invention was actually reduced to practice). A running royalty is permissible as a sales price for a capital asset, likewise a minimum royalty. Know-how seems to be transferable as a capital asset if there is no time limit on the transfer. A country-by-country transfer is acceptable but not a subnational transfer (for example, for northern Italy). The right of termination by the licensee is all right, but not the right of termination by the licensor.

service, banking, or insurance business), all undistributed income is taxable to the stockholders as ordinary income.

(2) Controlled foreign corporation (a foreign corporation in which at least 50 percent of the voting power is held by U.S. stockholders, each of whom holds 10 percent or more).[47] Upon liquidation, any capital gains realized by reason of earnings after 1962 are taxable as income, with the exception specified in b) below.

  (a) So-called *subpart F income* is taxed to the U.S. shareholders owning 10 percent or more of the foreign corporation, whether such income is distributed during the current year or not. Subpart F income is the total of U.S. insurance income and *foreign base company income* (FBC). The latter, in turn, is the total of (1) FBC holding company income, that is, personal holding company income (see above) received from outside the country of incorporation; (2) FBC sales income, that is, purchase of tangible property from, or sale of same to, a related entity *and* production or use of the property outside the country of incorporation (but excluding agricultural commodities not grown in the U.S. in commercially marketable quantities); (3) FBC service income, that is, services performed for or on behalf of a related entity and performance of same outside the country of incorporation;[48] (4) FBC shipping income, which is income derived from the use of aircraft or vessels in foreign commerce and directly related services; (5) funds derived from the withdrawal of income previously invested in shipping operations and in less developed countries and any increase in earnings invested in the

---

[47]Although the 1962 statute uses the voting power test of control, subsequent regulations interpreted the statutory language as referring to "actual control," whatever the percentage of formal voting power might be. Tests of control: (1) Do non-U.S. shareholders have nominal voting power disproportionate to their share of corporate earnings? (2) Do non-U.S. shareholders fail to exercise their voting power fully or independently? (3) Is the principal purpose of the arrangement to avoid classification of the corporate entity as a CFC? It appears that an affirmative answer *only* to test number three is inadequate to attack a decontrolled CFC. The mechanism by which one U.S. company successfully divested itself of a CFC is described in Howard M. Liebman, "Taxation of Foreign Source Income: Implications of CCA, Inc.," *Harvard International Law Journal,* vol. 17, no. 2, Spring 1976, pp. 335 ff.

[48]The Revenue Act of 1962 specifically provides that any gain realized by the transfer of patent rights to a controlled foreign corporation is to be taxed as ordinary income, even though such a transfer leads to a capital gain under other circumstances. If the transfer were made for stock, according to subsequent rulings, the gain was still to be treated as ordinary income, not capital gain, unless the patent rights were to be employed in the subsidiary's own manufacturing operations and there were adequate business purpose in having a separate manufacturing facility. In any event, prior IRS approval is needed, which is not forthcoming if the foreign subsidiary is going to engage in the granting of sublicenses outside of the country in which it is incorporated. However, it is clear that if the foreign subsidiary enhances the value of an invention acquired from its parent through its own R&D, then the royalties derived from licensing the improved invention to unrelated companies is not part of the subsidiary's subpart F income. Also, royalty income derived through a sublicense within the country within which the CFC is located is excluded, so likewise technical service income derived from the CFC's own licensing program regardless of where the income is derived. But, if the U.S. parent conducts a licensing program, the technical service income of the subsidiary constitutes subpart F income. If, on the other hand, the technical service is performed by the subsidiary for an unrelated party in connection with the purchase by the unrelated party of goods manufactured in the U.S. (even though by the U.S. parent), the income derived from that service by the CFC is not subpart F income. In addition, the Tax Reform Act of 1976 imposes a 35 percent excise tax on certain transfers to foreign corporations, trusts, or partnerships. The tax applies to transfers of all types of property (securities included), but only to the extent that no gain is recognized by the transferer at the time of the transfer. No tax applies when the transferer establishes that the transfer has no tax avoidance purposes.

U.S. property, that is, in tangible property in a U.S. corporation related to the parent, in the right to use U.S. patents developed in the United States, and so on, but not deposits in ordinary bank accounts nor portfolio investment in unrelated U.S. companies; and (6) income derived from illegal payments.

(b) Exclusions from subpart F income are: (1) shipping profits to the extent that they are reinvested in shipping operations; (2) income or gain from qualified investments, realized prior to 1976, in obligations of a less developed country [see b) below] corporation in which the FBC has 10 percent or more of the voting power, or in obligations of an LDC, if such gain or income is reinvested similarly in an LDC; (3) the 10–70 rule; that is, if FBC income is less than 10 percent of the income of the controlled foreign corporation, none is taxed until distributed. But if it is over 70 percent, all is taxed as subpart F income; and (4) income that is blocked by foreign currency and other restrictions (i.e., cannot legally be remitted to the U.S.)

b) Less Developed Country Corporation (LDCC). A controlled foreign corporation, 80 percent of whose gross income is derived from less developed countries and 80 percent of its assets (in value) is located similarly, or a corporation which derives 80 percent or more of its gross income from the use in foreign commerce of aircraft or vessels registered under the laws of a less developed country. In both cases the CFC must own at least 10 percent of the voting stock of a less developed corporation as defined above. Even though a controlled foreign corporation has subpart F income, earnings are not taxed until distributed to the U.S. stockholders or to a controlled foreign corporation in a developed country. After ten years, an LDC corporation may be liquidated and the proceeds returned at the capital gains tax rate. Post-1975 earnings are taxed as ordinary income. The same situation applies in the sale of stock. Note that an LDC corporation need not be incorporated in an LDC[49] and that bank accounts, even if not in less developed countries, may be included within the 80 percent of its assets located within an LDC so long as the parent company or a CFC in a developed country derives no benefit from such bank accounts, either directly or indirectly.

c) Domestic International Sales Corporations (DISC). A domestic corporation, 95 percent of whose receipts are from qualified export sales of goods and services[50] and 95 percent of whose assets are in qualified export-related forms. If manufactured with foreign components, the value added in the U.S. must equal or exceed 50 percent of fair market value. Proceeds from the sale of export assets qualify as export income, as likewise do dividends from foreign selling

---

[49]The term "less developed country" refers to any country outside the Sino-Soviet bloc and to any country or possession of the U.S. designated such by executive order, but may not include any of the Western European countries (other than Greece, Turkey, Spain, and Portugal), Australia, Canada, Hong Kong, Japan, New Zealand, Republic of South Africa.

[50]Excludes any natural resources subject to depletion other than timber unless U.S. *processing* is equal to or greater than 50 percent of the export value, and excludes one-half of the taxable income attributable to military sales made after October 2, 1975.

subsidiaries.[51] Export-related assets include service and sales facilities, inventories, working capital, and producer loans to the parent for use in modernizing or expanding export facilities.

For such corporations, tax is deferred on 50 percent of the export income exceeding 67 percent of the annual average for the 1972–75 period. (For each year after 1980, the base period moves forward one year.) The deferral lasts until such income is paid to the parent,[52] but may be deferred even so if made available as a "producers loan," which is used in the financing of export production. However, tax deferral is terminated on DISC profits that are the substance of a producer's loan if they are considered to have been invested in foreign plant or equipment. The amount considered to be so invested is the net increase in foreign assets of members of the same controlled group as the DISC acquired after the end of 1971 *less* (1) one-half of the earnings of the foreign affiliate of the corporate group, (2) the amount of debt or equity capital raised abroad by the group, (3) addition to foreign depreciation reserves, (4) the amount of stock or debt obligations of domestic members of the group issued to *unaffiliated* foreign entities after the end of 1967 to the extent that they constitute long-term foreign borrowing under the foreign direct investment control program (but less any actual foreign investment by domestic members of the group made during the period the obligations are outstanding), and (5) the liquid assets held abroad on October 13, 1971, in excess of reasonable working capital needs.[53] A parent company is permitted either (1) to price goods and service to its DISC so that it earns 4 percent on qualified export receipts plus 10 percent of its export promotion expenditures attributable to the sale or (2) to allocate to the DISC up to 50 percent of the combined taxable income of the DISC and of the parent derived from an export sale plus 10 percent of the promotional expenses attributable to the sale. A DISC may take credit for foreign taxes paid on a per-country basis.[54] No DISC benefits are applicable to income abroad derived from participation in an international boycott.

6. *Withheld tax.* A U.S. corporation must withhold a 30 percent tax on interest and dividends paid to nonresident aliens and foreign corporations not in business in the United States. The paying corporation is exempt if over 80 percent of its gross revenue is derived from foreign sources. Since 1969 the following have been treated as foreign-source income: (1) interest earned by a nonresident alien or foreign corporation on U.S. bank deposits not effectively connected with a U.S.

---

[51]That is, if the DISC owns more than 50 percent of the voting power of a foreign international sales corporation (FISC, a foreign corporation, 95 percent of whose receipts are from qualified export sales and 95 percent of whose assets are in qualified export related forms), owns less than 10 percent of the voting stock in an associated foreign corporation, or owns more than 50 percent of the voting stock of foreign corporations whose only function is to hold real property for the exclusive use of the DISC.

[52]Although the federal government may defer taxes on 50 percent of a DISC's income, the state wherein it is chartered may not. One is generally better off in those states where laws defer state corporate taxes on DISC income, as in Florida, Utah, and Delaware.

[53]DISCs have been attacked abroad as constituting a discriminatory export subsidy. At least one country, Canada, has imposed reporting duties on exporters to Canada designed to find those exporters enjoying home country tax benefits, such as DISC. It is possible that Canada may act to deny DISC's treaty-based tax exemption for corporations with no "permanent establishment" on the grounds that the DISC is tax exempt in the U.S.

[54]If the DISC income is $100,000 or more, it may defer U.S. tax on 50 percent of its export income.

business, and (2) interest received by a nonresident alien or foreign corporation from the U.S. branch of a foreign bank. This change meant that there would be no withholding on such income and, in effect, normally, it would not be taxed at all in the U.S.

Despite the non-deferrability of tax of foreign branch income, operation through foreign branches may be desirable in certain cases, for example:

a) For mining enterprises in which depletion allowances and the inclusion of intangible drilling costs as current expenses, rather than as a capital investment, are important. The U.S. provisions on these subjects do not apply to foreign corporations, even though wholly owned by U.S. nationals or by a U.S. corporation. (The depletion allowance for oil and gas was reduced in 1968 from 27½ percent to 22 percent of the gross income from the property, but not to exceed the net, and to zero for the major oil and gas producers in 1975. The 22 percent depletion was retained for producers of regulated natural gas and natural gas sold under fixed contract. Producers with no retail outlets who refine less than 50,000 barrels per day continued to enjoy the 22 percent depletion allowance on production up to 2,000 bbl per day in 1975, which subsequently phased down in annual increments of 200 bbl per day over five years, holding at 1,000 while the depletion rate phased down: 21 percent for 1981, 18 percent for 1982, 16 percent for 1983, 15 percent for 1984. Thereafter the maximum depletion allowance is 1,000 bbl per day at 15 percent or the natural gas equivalent, 6,000 cubic feet being equal to one barrel.)

b) If foreign law requires no capital allocation for a branch operation (in the sense of depositing funds or valuable securities locally) and such situation is deemed by management to minimize risk—and, hence, cost. (On the other hand, in a branch operation the host government may demand access to the records of the parent company and allocate taxable income as it deems equitable. Also, liability runs directly to the parent's assets, unless a domestic or third-country corporate buffer lies between the two.)

By using an incorporated *foreign* entity as its agent for entering into arrangements with other foreign enterprises, either through contract or investment, the U.S. principal may lose the advantages of U.S. law, such as reciprocal treaty rights between the United States and the country in which the other enterprise is incorporated in respect to reduction in withholding taxes and double taxation and in situations where regional authorities including the United States tend to limit purchasing from member states (for example, NATO). In certain cases, tax credits and the right to OPIC contracts and investment guarantees, FCIA facilities, and Export-Import Bank loans may be lost, as well as official U.S. representation on one's behalf. For example, in 1967 there was a ruling to the effect that suppliers not maintaining a regular place of business in the United States were not eligible to participate in many purchases financed by U.S. foreign economic assistance. This ruling specifies further that title must be passed within the United States from supplier to foreign buyer. However, by contract many firms have to sell through distributors and sales subsidiaries and for that reason cannot pass title at the shore line. Similar regulations can be found within the foreign economic assistance activities of other countries.

It should be noted that the so-called tax-haven holding company is attractive to the U.S. firm under at least three circumstances. These three cases are: (1) avoidance of the controlled foreign corporation classification, by placing majority ownership in the hands of non-U.S. nationals or by holding each U.S. shareholding to less than 10 percent; (2) maintenance of subpart F income at a level under 10 percent of the total taxable income of the controlled foreign corporation; (3) qualification of a foreign controlled corporation as a less-developed country corporation (which still permits 20 percent of its income and assets to be located outside of the LDCs; also U.S. bank accounts and certificates of deposit count as an LDC asset for this purpose, as long as the U.S. parent realizes no benefits, direct or indirect, from that account. If it does, it will become immediately liable to pay tax on the full amount of the alleged benefit as income).

In organizing a new corporation, its U.S. founders might incorporate the *parent* in one of the tax-haven countries, so long as it can avoid the category of a foreign personal holding company or of a controlled foreign corporation. This device is the so-called parent base company. To spin off assets of an existing U.S. parent to a foreign subsidiary requires the prior approval of the Internal Revenue Service, which is extremely hard to obtain unless one can demonstrate compelling business reasons for the spin-off. Tax avoidance is not considered a valid business reason! Apparently companies based in other countries have similar problems in initiating such a spin-off, although it has been done, as we have noted previously in the case of Canada.

Appendix 2 to Chapter 7
STANDARD ABBREVIATIONS INDICATING COMPANY LEGAL FORM

A/B	Aktiebolaget (Swedish)—public corporation	Co.Ltd.	Close corporation, frequently used in translation, for example, from Japanese
A.G.	Aktiengesellschaft (German)—public corporation	C. por A.	Compania por Acciones (Spanish)—close corporation
A/S	Aktieselskapet (Danish)—public corporation	G.I.E.	Groupement d'Intérêt Economique (France)—consortium
A/S	Aksjeselskapet (Norwegian)—corporation, public or close	G.m.b.H.	Gesellschaft mit beschrankter Haftung (German)—close corporation
A.Ş.	Anonim Şirketi (Turkish)—public corporation	G.K.	Gomei Kaisha (Japanese)—partnership
Cia.	Compania—used in place of Sociedad in some Latin American countries (for example, Venezuela)	H/B	Handelsbolaget (Swedish)—partnership
		Handelsges.	Handelsgesellschaft (German)—partnership

Inc.	Incorporated (U.S.)—corporation, public or close	S.A.	Sociedade Anonima (Portuguese)—public corporation
K.B.	Kommanditbolaget (Swedish and Norwegian)—limited partnership	S.A.	Société Anonyme (French)—public corporation
K.G.	Kommanditgesellschaft (German)—limited partnership	S.A.	Societa Anonima (Italian)—public corporation
K.K.	Kabushiki Kaisha (Japanese)—public corporation	S.Acc.	Societa Accomandita (Italian)—limited partnership
K.G.K.	Kabushiki Goshi Kaisha (Japanese)—limited partnership with shares	S.A.R.L.	Sociedade Anonima de Responsabilidade Limitada (Portuguese)—public corporation
Ltd.	Limited (U.K. and British Commonwealth)—public corporation	S.a.R.L.	Société à Responsabilité Limitée (French)—close corporation
Ltd. Inc.	Limited incorporated (U.S.)—public or close corporation; the Ltd. in the name has no legal significance and is used for prestige purposes only	S. en C.	Société en Commandite par Actions (French)—limited partnership with shares
N/V	Naamloze Vennootschap (Dutch)—public corporation	S. en C.	Société en Commandite Simple (French)—limited partnership
O/Y	Osakeyhitio (Finnish)—stock company	S. en C.	Sociedad en Comandita (Spanish)—limited partnership
O.H.G.	Offene Handelsgesellschaft (German)—partnership	S. en C.	Sociedade en Commandita (Portuguese)—limited partnership
Pt.	Perusahan terbatas (Indonesian)—public corporation	S. en N.C.	Sociedad en Nombre Colectivo (Spanish)—partnership
(private) Ltd.	Private Limited (parts of British Commonwealth) —close corporation; may be either privately or state owned, or mixed	S. en N.C.	Société en Nom Colectif (French)—close corporation
		S.p.A.	Societa per Azioni (Italian)—close corporation
Pty. Ltd.	Proprietary Limited (Australian)—close corporation, same as (private) Ltd.	S. por A.	Sociedad por Acciones (Spanish)—close corporation
S.A.	Sociedad Anonima (Spanish)—public corporation	Y.K.	Yugen Kaisha (Japanese)—close corporation

Case K
DOCKER MANUFACTURING COMPANY

The Docker Manufacturing Company was a large manufacturer of household furniture in the United States. Management was trying to decide whether or not to proceed with a Mexican venture to produce household furniture.

A Mexican customer, a firm by the name of Diaz Poirot S.A., had approached Docker a few years before to secure the Docker distributorship for all of Mexico. The president of the Mexican firm was Hugo Poirot, a man of French origin who had lived much of his life in Mexico. During many years of business association, he had impressed the Docker management very favorably. The Poirot firm, essentially a family organization, operated a large retail establishment in Mexico City, which sold only household furniture and kindred products. The Docker management had agreed to the distributorship. The Mexican market was supplied overland from Docker's Houston, Texas, plant.

Shortly after the agreement, the Mexican government had established what amounted to a prohibitive duty on imported furniture—300 percent or better in most instances. Mr. Poirot had reacted by establishing a small plant for the semimanufacture of Docker furniture. Because of the restrictions on imports, Docker had agreed to send Poirot sets of drawings and designs, frame parts, springs, and other parts not locally available and on which duties were not prohibitively high.

At this point, the Docker management had begun to consider the possibility of a Mexican manufacturing enterprise, in part because some large retailers of furniture in Mexico had been urging such a venture. They wanted a local source of Docker furniture. It was known that Mr. Poirot was very much interested in joining Docker in this undertaking, possibly as minority stockholder as well as general manager.

The upshot was that the Docker controller, Mr. Steelman, was assigned the responsibility of looking into the proposal. One of his first moves was to discuss the matter with the foreign department of the First National City Bank of New York. There he was advised to invest only enough to build and equip the plant and to borrow working capital locally. A minimum dollar investment would probably run between $500,000 and $700,000. The Docker management felt that if it went into Mexico at all it should start on a fairly small scale.

There seemed no doubt as to the existence of an adequate Mexican market. The business conducted through the Poirot firm, as well as the development of demand from other Mexican retailers, supported this conclusion. Docker's Mexican plant, as envisioned, was to produce only household furniture. Given the high transportation cost involved, the sale of such furniture depended primarily on the location of manufacture. A maximum range of really competitive distribution was perhaps indicated by the fact that within the United States Docker delivered free up to 200 miles from a plant. Though the firm would deliver in its own trucks up to 400 miles, a charge was made for anything over 200. A problem here was the return of the empty trucks.

Docker was, at this point, manufacturing between 8 and 10 percent of the upholstered living room furniture sold in the United States. It operated no retail outlets of its own. Management believed that it had achieved about as high a level of productivity as any member of the industry. Because of Docker's very large volume, maximum mechanization was permitted. None of the furniture was mass-produced in the usual sense, though certain standard elements (for example, frames) were stocked in some quantity. Otherwise, the company manufactured "custom furniture on a production basis." No furniture was produced for inventory. Labor as a percentage of gross sales ran about 34 percent. Recent financial statistics (in millions of dollars) showed:

Year	Net sales	Net income after taxes	Total assets	Current assets	Current liabilities
Present year	$63.3	$1.9	$30.1	$16.1	$3.3
One year ago	59.7	2.4	29.8	15.0	3.1
Two years ago	64.2	4.7	29.5	14.7	2.8

The company had no long-term debt. Docker was a privately held corporation, ownership residing in the Docker family. Its head offices and main plant were located in Wichita, Kansas.

Management had checked the availability in Mexico of certain hardware and materials, including lumber. There seemed to be no insurmountable technical problems.

After Mr. Steelman's conversations with the First National City Bank of New York, he discussed the matter at some length with Mr. Thompson, a member of the Chicago law firm of Thompson and Root, retained by the Docker firm. Mr. Steelman was particularly interested in learning what restrictions on foreign ownership obtained in Mexico. The Chicago law firm in turn inquired of a Mexican correspondent. The latter's reply, forwarded from Chicago, was as follows:

This will acknowledge receipt of your kind letter of the seventeenth regarding the proposed organization of a Mexican company to manufacture and sell furniture. We feel that the Mexican laws on technology and investment should receive careful study.

The first article of the 1973 Law of Registration of the Transfer of Technology and the Use and Exploitation of Patents and Trademarks created the National Registry of the Transfer of Technology under the auspices of the Minister of Industry and Commerce. The National Council of Science and Technology was designated as an "organ of consultation." Under the law, all documents, actions, contracts, or agreements (or changes in those then existing) that deal with the following matters must

be submitted to the National Registry: authorization to use trademarks; authorization to exploit patented inventions; the provision of technical expertise (as in engineering for execution of installations, rendering of technical assistance of any kind, and the provision of management and operating services). The beneficiaries of such contracts or agreements are required to register them, whether the beneficiary is a Mexican citizen, foreign resident in Mexico, or agency or subsidiary of a foreign company. Also, foreign-based technology suppliers may request registration of actions or agreements to which they are parties. Indeed, the foreign supplier is well advised to be a party to the registration. Otherwise, the Mexican purchaser is in a position to urge the registry to impose conditions favorable to him. In any event, notifications must be accomplished within 60 days of signing such agreement. Changes or cancellations likewise must be listed within 60 days of signing.

Failure to register such agreements means that the offending enterprise is not entitled to approval of its production program. Also, nonregistered agreements are null and void and, hence, unenforceable.

By law, the National Registry is required to act on appplications for registration within 90 days of submission. Failure to do so results in automatic acceptance. However, it has been practice for the registry to issue an automatic rejection if it finds itself unable to act within the 90 days, which rejection requires a resubmission and another 90 days. The registry is authorized to cancel a registration when the terms in which actions, contracts, or agreements have been registered are modified without prior registry. The registry also is empowered to verify fulfillment at any time.

In the foreword to the official translation of the law, the following paragraphs appear:

> The law is in keeping with resolutions adopted at the third UNCTAD Santiago de Chile meeting. Before the law was presented to Congress there had been a broad exchange of impressions with labor, management, and other sectors of the country, by which a consensus of opinion was obtained.
>
> The statement of motives that accompanies the law recognizes the vital importance of technology for industrial development. In consequence, the government has no desire to use this legislation as an instrument to limit the purchase of technology, but rather as a means to help Mexican entrepreneurs obtain the best technology, under the most favorable market conditions.
>
> The purpose of this law is to eliminate obstacles to Mexico's development and foreign trade; to adjust technology contracts to the guidelines of the government's industrialization policy, and to stimulate the creation of a local scientific and technological infrastructure that permits the adaptation of foreign technology to the conditions and needs of the Mexican economy.

As a complement to this law, a Center for Industrial Information is being established, also under the auspices of the Minister of Industry and Commerce. This center gathers and processes information regarding international technology supply and

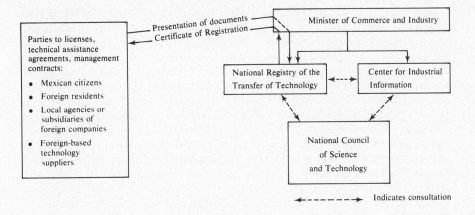

Figure K.1
MEXICO: THE ENTRY PROCESSING OF FOREIGN TECHNOLOGY

demand. It enjoys the consulting services of the country's research centers, institutions of higher learning, National Science and Technology Council, and industrial organizations. The entry processing system for foreign technology is diagrammed in Figure K.1.

The moving force behind the passage of the 1973 law on technology transfer appears to have been the Mexican government's desire to minimize the balance-of-payments drain caused by licensing and trademark agreements. Also providing justification in Mexican eyes were several cases involving payments for freely available technology, for trademarks of no commercial value, and other alleged abuses uncovered by the Ministry of the Treasury, as well as efforts by other Latin American nations—notably Argentina—to control the transfer of technology.

Interviews with officials at the National Registry for the Transfer of Technology indicate that the main problem area had concerned payments by Mexican firms to unrelated foreign technology suppliers, rather than transactions between multinational firms and their Mexican subsidiaries. Many Mexican firms apparently had felt obligated to buy highly priced foreign technology, being unable to meet the cost of developing their own technology, and hence welcomed registry pressure to renegotiate the fees of their technology agreements because of the potential savings.

Five months after the law on technology became effective, the Law for Promoting Mexican Investment and Regulating Foreign Investment appeared (May 8, 1973). It was introduced by an article that stated: "Its [law's] purpose . . . is to stimulate and regulate foreign investment in order to stimulate a just and balanced development and consolidate the country's economic independence."

The law reserves certain activities exclusively for the state (petroleum, basic petrochemicals, mining, power generation, rail transport, and radio and telephone communications); reserves other activities exclusively for Mexicans (domestic highway and air transport, radio and television, forest exploitation, gas distribution, ownership of land in border and coastal zones); permits foreign investment on a minority basis up to 49 percent in the case of exploitation and use of substances subject to ordinary concessions, up to 34 percent in case of special concessions for the exploitation of national mining reserves, up to 40 percent in secondary petrochemicals. In cases where legal provisions or regulations do not specify a given percentage, foreign owners are to be permitted to hold up to 49 percent of the capital of a Mexican firm, "provided it is not empowered, by a title, to determine the management of the business enterprise." Further, if any foreign person or entity acquires more than 25 percent of the capital, or over 49 percent of the fixed assets, of a business enterprise in Mexico, prior authorization is required. Also requiring authorization are actions by which the administration of a business enterprise is acquired by foreign investors, or by which foreign investment is empowered to determine the management of the enterprise. Hence, a minority position, if the balance of a firm's ownership is widely held, could require registration. The leasing of a business enterprise is held to be equivalent to the acquisition of assets. These authorizations are to be granted "when convenient to the country's interest" upon decision of the National Commission on Foreign Investment.

The National Commission on Foreign Investment, created by the 1973 law, is composed of representatives of the Ministries of the Interior, Foreign Affairs, Finance, Public Credit, National Patrimony, Industry and Commerce, Labor and Social Welfare, and of the Office of the Presidency. Each minister appoints undersecretaries or deputies to represent him on the board and to meet weekly with the executive secretary of the commission and two commission lawyers on an "Advisory Board." Although four of the seven secretaries are economists and three are lawyers, both the commission and the advisory board are essentially political bodies in that all of the members—the secretaries and their deputies—are appointed by the president. The present executive secretary, who is likewise appointed by the president, is Mauricio de Maria Campos, formerly the head of the Economic Section of the National Registry of the Transfer of Technology. He moved in August 1974 to initiate an Economic Analysis Section to prepare investment evaluations and recommendations for review by the advisory board and final decision by the full commission. The commission meets once a month to act on investment proposals.

Any prospective direct investor, domestic or foreign, first obtains a permit from the Ministry of Foreign Relations to establish a corporation. Prior to the 1973 law and the creation of the commission, the Ministry of Foreign Relations would itself have ruled on the acceptability of a foreign investment proposal, using essentially legal guidelines following the 1944 Decree on Foreign Investment and after consultation with the Ministry of Industry and Commerce. If the investors were purely Mexican, the permit would have been issued routinely. By 1973, however, if the investor was foreign the project was sent directly to the Foreign Investment Commission; only when the commission approved did the Ministry of Foreign Relations issue an incorporation permit. The investor then proceeded to employ a notary to draw up the incorporation papers and submitted them to a commercial court. If and when the court found the papers in order, the investor was authorized to proceed.

An additional provision was incorporated in the law relating to border zone properties; the Minister of Foreign Affairs was empowered to grant Mexican credit institutions the authority to acquire, as fiduciaries (*fideicomisos*), real property for use in industrial and tourist activities within a strip 100 kilometers (45.5 miles) deep along Mexico's borders and 50 kilometers (22.7 miles) deep along the coasts, provided that the purpose of the acquisition is to permit the use of such real property by the trust beneficiaries without constituting ownership rights over it. Such beneficiaries may be aliens or foreign-owned firms, but prior approval of the constitutions of such trusts is required by the Minister of Foreign Affairs. The National Commission on Foreign Investments determines the criteria and procedures by which these requests are decided. Such trusts may not exceed 30 years, and the fiduciary institutions that retain ownership over the real property held in trust may lease it for terms not over ten years. Real property participation certificates can be issued.

Control of acquisitions by foreign interests is thought to be justified by the Mexican government on the grounds that acquisitions merely replaced existing Mexican capital and, thus, increased foreign penetration of the Mexican economy without creating new products or new jobs. In addition, government decision makers appear to feel that current and potential profit repatriation from acquisition becomes an added drain on Mexico's foreign exchange reserves, a drain that might not materialize if acquisitions are limited.

The argument that Mexican capital thus freed by an acquisition would be available for investment in a new, more dynamic segment of the Mexican economy appears to carry little weight with Mexican officials, who feel that the chances are small that this freed capital would in fact be reinvested in Mexico. Obviously, they feel that it is more likely to find its way into the major international capital markets of Europe and the United States.

The impact of the new investment law on the growth potential of existing foreign enterprises in Mexico stems from the decision of the National Commission of Foreign Investment to consider new plant sites and new products as new investments, thereby requiring commission approval. By making product line and plant expansions subject to approval, the commission can require that Mexican partners be taken on when expansions are implemented. Such a requirement can, of course, seriously affect the plans of foreign owners to carry out expansions, especially if they are reluctant to accept Mexican partners. It should be pointed out that only the expansion is subject to Mexicanization, not the foreign investor's previously existing Mexican establishment. A degree of freedom in planning for Mexican subsidiary growth is thereby eliminated, and the foreign investor may conceivably be induced to delay or abandon plans to open a new plant or produce a new product if that expansion can only be undertaken as a joint venture with Mexican partners.

In large part, the driving force behind the commission's decision to require approval of plant and product line expansion appeared to have come from Jose Campillo-Sainz, Minister of Industry and Commerce, and a major factor in commission decisions. His prior position as head of the most powerful chambers of commerce in Mexico had given him ample exposure to the complaints of Mexican businessmen about the competition they faced from the Mexican subsidiaries of foreign firms. A new foreign-owned plant could threaten the market of a Mexican producer (or that of an existing subsidiary of a foreign firm); likewise the introduction of a new product. The political pressure existing producers could generate was reflected in the commission's policy that prior approval was needed for both new plants and products.

The experience is that normally an applicant under the law knows whether his project is acceptable or not in something like two months. The maximum time reported has been one year. Some projects must be modified and resubmitted following an initial rejection, resulting in longer periods of uncertainty.

Although the law makes no mention of any periodic review of foreign investments by the commission, any agreement entered into by foreigners without prior commission approval is considered null and void and hence unenforceable. This feature includes foreign ownership of more than 49 percent equity in a Mexican enterprise without approval, as well as any management contract or management control not backed by an approved equity holding. Violations are to be punishable by fines up to the value of the operation (confiscation) or up to U.S. $8,000 if no property is involved. Employees of the offending firm also are liable to fines of up to $8,000, and Mexican notaries and brokers who register false documents might lose their licenses; public officials, their offices. Finally, anyone assisting in evasion of the act—such as lending one's name to a dummy organization—is subject to up to nine years' imprisonment and a fine of up to $4,000. Such category of offenders presumably includes lawyers, notaries, public officials, and agents and representatives.

Under regulations promulgated on December 29, 1973, pursuant to the law, a National Registry of Foreign Investment was created under the auspices of the Ministry of Industry and Commerce and the management and supervision of the executive secretary of the National Commission of Foreign Investment.

Foreign persons or entities are required to apply for registration within one month of the date on which they subscribed or acquired corporate shares or participation in a Mexican corporation, or on which they acquired a lease or the authority to manage a Mexican corporation. Also obliged to register are Mexican corporations if one or more foreigners participate in the firm's capital, Mexican trusts in which foreigners have a participation or from which foreigners derive rights, and foreigners who own certificates representing the capital stock of Mexican corporations. Mexican corporations whose shares are quoted on the Mexican Stock Exchange and in which foreign investors have a participation are required to report such participation. Shares of a Mexican corporation negotiable abroad are to be reported by the issuing corporation. If foreigners acquire bearer shares outside Mexico, such shares are to be converted into nominal shares and registered. The director of the registry has the right to ascertain the veracity of the data submitted in registration applications and to request all necessary information. Companies obliged to register, but failing to do so, are not to be permitted to pay dividends.

The mechanism by which foreign investment applications are to be processed is diagrammed in Figure K.2.

In characteristic Latin American fashion, the modern version of the "Calvo clause" appears as Article 3 of the law:

> Foreigners who acquire properties of any kind in the Mexican Republic agree, because of such action, to consider themselves as Mexican nation-

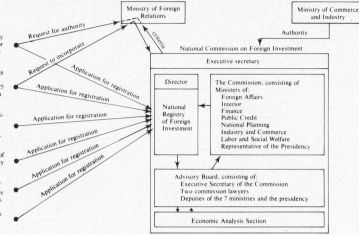

- Applications for use by foreigners of border or coastal property via a Mexican trust.

- Application for foreign investment if over 49 percent of equity or 25 percent of capital of a Mexican enterprise.*

- Application for acquisition of management rights in a Mexican majority-owned enterprise.

- Application for lease of business assets by foreigners.†

- Foreign ownership of capital stock issued by Mexican corporations.

- Mexican corporations with minority foreign interest.

Figure K.2
MEXICO: PROCESSING OF FOREIGN INVESTMENT APPLICATIONS

*Foreign interests entering in a minority position and no management rights normally need not seek commission approval.

†The term includes Mexican corporations in which a majority of the equity is owned by foreigners.

als with regard to these properties and not to invoke the protection of their governments with respect to such properties, under penalty, in case of violation, of forfeiting to the Nation the properties thus acquired.

One device to avoid Mexican control, even though surrendering majority equity interest, is to enter into an agreement under which a private bank agrees to hold the amount of stock to be Mexicanized in trust, either until an acceptable local partner is found or until the earnings record is good enough to suggest successful public sale. Under such a trust arrangement, the bank has voting rights but not dividend rights. Nor can it dispose of the stock without company concurrence. Several companies have chosen this route. Examples are International Harvester, which has turned over 51 percent equity in its tractor operation to Cia General de Aceptaciones, and Bendix Mexicana S.A., which has placed 59 percent of the equity in its vehicle brake-making subsidiary with Banco de Comercio.

The Mexican stock market remains thin and is really a viable route for spinning off equity only for companies with strong earnings records or those willing to pledge a minimum dividend regardless of profits. There have been very few new issues, one exception being an offering made in early 1973 by Kimberly Clark de Mexico. Its stock had been publicly traded previously. "The secondary offering, which lowered foreign equity to 44 percent, was snapped up in 24 hours."

Although no objective measures of impact seem to be employed by either the National Registry of the Transfer of Technology or the National Commission on

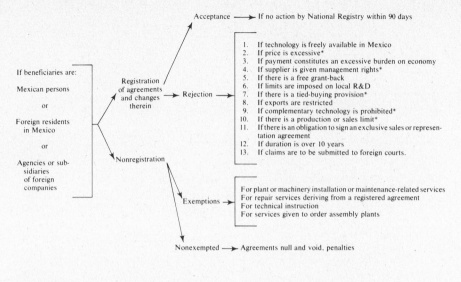

Figure K.3
MEXICO: ENTRY CONDITIONS FOR FOREIGN TECHNOLOGY

*Negotiable.

Foreign Investment, there are a number of requirements and admonitions in each case. The former are shown in Figure K.3. It should be noted that a number of these requirements are negotiable, but the general principle is that the foreign owner of the technology, proprietory right, or skill is not to be permitted to exercise any control over the management of the recipient Mexican enterprise by limiting the options of the latter. The registry is admonished by law to make no exceptions in respect to: (1) freely available technology, (2) obligations to turn over to the technology supplier ("on onerous terms or free of charge") any trademarks or improvements obtained by the importer, (3) limitations on research or technological development of the purchasing company, (4) restrictions on the export of goods and services by the technology importer "in a way contrary to the country's interest," (5) excessively long terms of enforcement (in no case, over ten years), and (6) agreement to submit disputes to the jurisdiction of foreign courts. In practice, the prohibition against registering any agreement restricting the export rights of the technology-buying firm is lifted if the foreign supplier of the technology can show that by not so limiting export rights it would run afoul of exclusive rights it had given in other countries.

The criteria used by the National Commission of Foreign Investment are embedded in the stated objectives of the law, which are, in summary form:

1. To limit foreign control over use of resources.

2. To promote national security (for example, border zone prohibitions).

3. To stimulate local ownership and control.

4. To avoid concentration of foreign ownership (by sector or region).

5. To encourage foreign investment complementary to national investment.

6. To avoid displacement of national business.

7. To produce a positive impact on the balance of payments.

8. To produce a positive impact on exports.

9. To produce a positive impact on employment and wage levels.

10. To stimulate skill transfer.

11. To stimulate use of local products in manufacturing.

12. To encourage use of foreign finance.

13. To encourage diversification.

14. To encourage regional integration (LAFTA).

15. To encourage development of less developed zones.

16. To encourage competition.

17. To encourage technology transfer.

18. To discourage inflation of prices.

19. To improve quality of products.

20. To limit external political pressure.

21. To encourage compliance with national development policy objectives.

22. To encourage respect for the country's social and cultural values.

23. To encourage that investment important in the context of the Mexican economy.

Shortly after receiving this statement, Mr. Steelman discussed the Mexican venture with Mr. Poole, a member of the public accounting firm used by Docker. Mr. Poole raised several points. First, did the Docker charter permit investment in such an undertaking? Second, was it not possible that some minority stockholder might become troublesome if L. D. Docker (the president) and Gene Docker (vice-president and treasurer) were to become stockholders in the Mexican venture as had been suggested, along with the Docker Manufacturing Company and Hugo Poirot. If at a meeting of the stockholders it were decided to limit the investment in the Mexican venture, then the two Dockers might perhaps make up the additional investment required. But in a later conversation, Mr. Thompson expressed the feeling that it would not be proper for the two Dockers to hold stock personally in the Mexican enterprise. The 15 percent interest for each, the figure mentioned, would have to be disclosed to the Securities and Exchange Commission and the other stockholders. He pointed out that when another large American company had gone into Mexico some executives had participated to the extent of 5 percent. But in that instance the SEC had ruled that no disclosure was necessary, as the participation was too small. Mr. Thompson also felt that Docker should not place Hugo Poirot under contract as manager of the Mexican plant. Contracts of employment, he held, often led to difficulties if one party or the other became dissatisfied. It was his opinion that Docker should have a repurchase agreement with Hugo Poirot for his stock interest in the Mexican company; also, that Poirot and others of the Mexican supervisory staff be bonded. These comments were duly reported by Mr. Steelman to the two Dockers.

Information on a variety of matters was supplied by the National City Bank of New York (tax and finance); Hugh Poirot (Mexican labor law and local supply); Poole & Poole Public Accountants (formation of a Mexican company, tax considerations); and Management Consultants of Syracuse, Inc. (general information on Mexican investment climate). On the basis of data so supplied, Mr. Steelman prepared the following memorandum:

Organizing a Mexican corporation

Briefly, the following furnishes an idea of the steps required in organizing a Mexican corporation. Legal counsel, particularly one with a thorough knowledge of Mexican laws, and a close acquaintance with Mexican government officials, is extremely important. The correspondent of the Thompson and Root Law Firm is Basham, Ringe & Correa of Mexico City (attorneys for many other American companies). Chase Manhattan National Bank of New York recommended Hardin & Hess of New York, who have an office in Mexico City.

In the latest *Overseas Business Report*, put out by the United States Department of Commerce, it is suggested that a corporation, or "Sociedad Anonima," is the most usual type of business organization, and the one most likely to meet the needs of United States interest. Mr. Thompson agrees to this.

Briefly, the Articles of Incorporation, which must be recorded in the Public Register of Commerce, are not too dissimilar from the requirements of many states of this country, except, perhaps they go more into the nationalities and domiciles of the natural or corporate persons who constitute the corporation.

A minimum of five members is required for the formation of a corporation, and each one of these must subscribe to at least one share of stock. It is preferable that one or more of the members have Mexican nationality.

The capital stock of a corporation must not be less than 25,000 pesos[55] and must be fully subscribed. At the time of organization, at least 20 percent of the capital stock must be paid in cash. If property is conveyed to the corporation at the time of organization in payment of capital stock, an appraisal of the value of such property is required. In such case, the shares of stock are deposited for two years, during which period they cannot be sold or transferred. (Note: It is not known whether only the shares issued for the property received must be deposited, or whether *all* the shares must be deposited. The reference to this is made because of the possibility of Hugo Poirot's conveying his plant to the new corporation in exchange for his interest.)

---

[55]The Mexican peso was floated on August 31, 1976, after having been pegged at 12.50 pesos to the U.S. dollar for 22 years. The floating resulted in a decline to a low of 28.5 pesos to the dollar. Subsequently it recovered to about 20 pesos/$U.S. in January 1977. It stood at 22.7 pesos/$U.S. as of the end of November 1977.

Shares of stock may either be bearer shares or registered shares. Shares of the same class must be of equal value and must confer equal rights. However, the Articles of Incorporation may provide for different classes of shares with special rights for each class, provided that no member is excluded from participation in earnings (does not say "equal participation").

No dividends may be paid to holders of common stock until a dividend of at least 5 percent has been paid to holders of stock having limited voting rights.

The customary officers of a corporation are the board of directors, a general manager, and an examiner. They may or may not be shareholders.

The number of directors usually is from three to five. When there are three or more directors, minority shareholders representing 25 percent of the capital stock have the right to elect one member of the board. Directors' meetings may be held either in Mexico or in a foreign country.

A general manager may be elected by the board of directors, or at a general meeting of the shareholders.

An examiner (*comisario*) must be named at the first meeting of the shareholders. He is presumed to be the direct representative of the shareholders, and he has the right of intervening in their behalf, independently of the directors, in the event that the directors should fail or refuse to comply with their duties. Minority shareholders having 25 percent of the capital stock have the right to elect an examiner to represent their interests.

Meetings of the shareholders may be either general or special, and must be held at the domicile of the corporation.

It appears that the Mexican government will favor the organization of a corporation where one or more shareholders are Mexicans. If Mexicans are shareholders, it may be well to consider the issuance of a special type of share to give the Mexican shareholders their proportionate share of earnings but retain in the American shareholders essential controls and perhaps preference as to assets in the event of liquidation.

Taxation of business enterprises

Business enterprises, whether sole proprietorships, partnerships, or corporations, are subject to a global income tax. This means all income of a business enterprise must be included in its annual tax return except dividends received from Mexican corporations and earnings of funded pension plans approved by the income tax department.

The former tax on distributable profits was repealed when the present law was enacted because it was regarded as an impediment to the reinvestment of profits in productive activities. Profits are thus taxed only when the dividends are actually paid. However, all profits of branches of foreign corporations are subject to the dividend tax mentioned above, whether or not these profits are actually remitted. Dividends paid by one Mexican corporation to another, and the issuance of stock dividends, which represent capitalization of retained earnings, are not subject to the tax.

The reinvestment of earnings is automatic, and prior authorization is not necessary to secure an exemption from taxes on retained earnings. Losses which are incurred in any one year can be charged against profits earned during the five years immediately following.

The capital gains tax is not applied on sales of real property when the property sold has been held for ten or more years. However, when capital gains are realized on real property held for a lesser period, the capital gains tax is applied at a proportionately reduced rate, that is:

Up to 2 years	100
From 2 to 4 years	80
From 4 to 6 years	60
From 6 to 8 years	40
From 8 to 10 years	20

The corporate income tax is a graduated tax with income up to 2,000 pesos being entirely exempt. Income between 2,000.01 and 3,500.00 pesos is assessed at the rate of 5 percent and income between 3,500.01 and 5,000.00 pesos is assessed at 75 pesos, plus 6 percent on the excess over 3,500.00 up to 5,000.00. Income taxes are then increased on a graduated basis to the point where the tax levied on income of 500,000 pesos and upwards is 210,000.00 pesos plus 42 percent on the amount in excess of 500,000 pesos. (See Table K.1.)

Expenditures deemed to be ordinary, necessary, and in proportion to the size of the business, plus those deductions specifically authorized by law, are allowable costs. Capital expenditures are not deductible. The principal business deductions include cost of goods sold; cost of manufacture or assembly of goods sold; wages and related payments; bad debts, when proven uncollectable or when the statute of limitations for collection has expired; rental payments for real property if used for the business; interest on borrowed capital; insurance and bond premiums if paid to Mexican insurance companies; charitable donations to government-approved recipients; and payments of royalties and technical assistance fees.

The straight-line method of depreciation and amortization, at fixed annual rates, is provided for. However, the Ministry of Finance is authorized to approve higher rates of depreciation as an industrial incentive (see tax incentives below). The maximum annual depreciation rates are:

Buildings and component parts of buildings	5%
Machinery, equipment, and other tangible property not included in the following category	10%
Transportation equipment, machinery for the construction industry, and cooperage for the wine and liquor industries	20%

Table K.1
TAX ON INCOME OF BUSINESS ENTERPRISES (MEXICAN PESOS)*

Annual taxable income		Tax calculation			Effective tax rate on lower limit
At least	Not more than	Fixed amount	Plus	On excess over	
0.01	2,000.00	—	—%	—	—%
2,000.00	3,500.00	—	5.00	2,000.00	—
3,500.00	5,000.00	75.00	6.00	3,500.00	2.14
5,000.00	8,000.00	165.00	7.00	5,000.00	3.30
8,000.00	11,000.00	375.00	8.00	8,000.00	4.69
11,000.00	14,000.00	615.00	9.00	11,000.00	5.59
14,000.00	20,000.00	885.00	10.00	14,000.00	6.32
20,000.00	26,000.00	1,485.00	11.00	20,000.00	7.43
26,000.00	32,000.00	2,145.00	13.00	26,000.00	8.25
32,000.00	38,000.00	2,925.00	16.00	32,000.00	9.14
38,000.00	50,000.00	3,885.00	18.00	38,000.00	10.22
50,000.00	62,000.00	6,045.00	19.00	50,000.00	12.09
62,000.00	74,000.00	8,325.00	20.00	62,000.00	13.43
74,000.00	86,000.00	10,725.00	21.50	74,000.00	14.49
86,000.00	100,000.00	13,305.00	22.50	86,000.00	15.47
100,000.00	150,000.00	16,455.00	24.10	100,000.00	16.46
150,000.00	200,000.00	28,505.00	26.76	150,000.00	19.00
200,000.00	300,000.00	41,885.00	29.64	200,000.00	20.94
300,000.00	400,000.00	71,525.00	34.00	300,000.00	23.84
400,000.00	500,000.00	105,525.00	38.00	400,000.00	26.38
500,000.00	—	210,000.00	42.00	500,000.00	42.00

*One peso is equal to $0.08.

Note: If the total taxable income is between 500,000.01 and 1,500,000.00 pesos, an amount equivalent to 6.65 percent of the difference between 1,500,000.00 pesos and the taxable income will be deducted from the fixed amount of 210,000.00 pesos. In accordance with the above, the income tax corresponding to the following taxable incomes would be calculated as follows:

Example 1.—Taxable income 600,000.00 pesos

Up to	$500,000.01	$210,000.00
Less:		
$1,500,000.00		
−600,000.00		
900,000.00 × 6.65% =		59,850.00
		150,150.00
	100,000.00 42%	42,000.00
	$ 600,000.00	$192,150.00

Table K.1 (Continued)

| Annual taxable income | | Tax calculation | | | Effective tax |
At least	Not more than	Fixed amount	Plus	On excess over	rate on lower limit
Example 2.—Taxable income $1,000,000.00					
Up to		$ 500,000.01			210,000.00
Less:					
	$1,500,000.00				
	1,000,000.00				
		500,000.00 × 6.65%			33,250.00
					176,750.00
				500,000.00 42%	210,000.00
				$1,000,000.00	$386,750.00
Example 3.—Taxable income 1,500,000.00 pesos					
Up to		$ 500,000.00			$210,000.00
Less:					
	$1,500,000.00				
	1,500,000.00				
		0.00			—
					210,000.00
				1,000,000.00 42%	420,000.00
				$1,500,000.00	$630,000.00

A maximum of 5 percent is allowed for amortization of intangible fixed assets and deferred charges. Types of expenditures allowed include expenses incurred in forming a company and payments for franchises, patent rights, trademarks, and literary and artistic copyrights. No deductions are allowed for amortization of goodwill.

Gross income earned in Mexico by nonresident corporations or aliens is taxed without deductions for expenses of any kind. Such income is subject to withholding by those who make such payments and includes: (1) a 20 percent withholding tax on technical service fees; (2) 10 percent on interest paid to foreign banks; (3) 20 percent on occasional commission income; (4) the progressive business tax (Table K.1) on royalties of all types.

Interest earned by foreign companies and individual incomes are taxed in accordance with the progressive rates of Table K.2 unless the loan is recognized by the Mexican treasury as of general interest, in which case a flat rate of 10 percent is applied.

Tax concession

It may be possible for Docker to secure one or more tax concessions. Under Mexico's Law of Industrial Encouragement, the Mexican government may grant tax exemptions to industries that manufacture or produce goods not

Table K.2
TAX ON INDIVIDUALS BASED ON PERSONAL
SERVICES AND/OR CAPITAL GAINS

Annual taxable income (in pesos)		Tax on lower limit (in pesos)	Plus percent on excess over lower limit
From	To		
0.01	4,800.00	0.00	Exempt
4,800.01	5,760.00	114.00	3.88
5,760.01	6,720.00	151.25	3.95
6,720.01	7,680.00	189.17	3.99
7,680.01	8,640.00	227.47	4.09
8,460.01	9,600.00	266.73	4.47
9,600.01	14,400.00	309.64	5.67
14,400.01	19,200.00	581.80	6.88
19,200.01	24,000.00	912.04	8.06
24,000.01	28,000.00	1,298.92	9.44
28,800.01	38,400.00	1,752.04	11.62
38,400.01	48,000.00	2,767.56	13.57
48,000.01	57,600.00	4,170.28	15.25
57,600.01	67,200.00	5,534.28	16.72
67,200.01	76,800.00	7,239.40	18.15
76,800.01	86,400.00	8,981.80	19.50
86,400.01	96,000.00	10,853.80	20.81
96,000.01	115,200.00	12,851.00	22.90
115,200.01	150,000.00	17,247.80	22.92
150,000.01	180,000.00	25,223.96	24.06
180,000.01	240,000.00	32,441.40	27.50
240,000.01	300,000.00	48,941.40	31.65
300,000.01	and above	67,931.40	35.00

produced in Mexico; industries that manufacture goods not produced domestically in sufficient quantity for consumer needs; industries "providing services for economically important activities"; assembly operations provided these use Mexican-produced parts that represent at least 60 percent of their products' direct cost; and industries exporting their own finished or semifinished manufactures, provided at least 60 percent of the direct production cost of such products represents Mexican manufacture.

Industries within these classifications are eligible for five-year, seven-year, or ten-year reductions in respect to, or exemptions from, the following taxes: import duties and the surcharges thereon, stamp taxes, the gross receipts tax, and the income tax. The Industrial Encouragement Law limits the income tax reduction to a maximum of 40 percent of the tax.

Among conditions frequently stipulated in the concessions granting the tax exemptions mentioned above to foreigners are those requiring that: (1) the firm have a majority Mexican capitalization; (2) foreign technicians remain in Mexico for a limited period and train Mexican replacements; and (3) payments abroad for the right to use patents, trademarks, technical assistance, and the like, whether in the form of royalties, shares in production, sales, or profits be limited to a percentage of the firm's sales, which percentage shall be determined jointly by the Ministries of Industry and Commerce and of Finance and Public Credit.

Also, the Mexican tariff provides for reductions up to 75 percent of the regular import duties for firms that import certain specified types of machinery or equipment to establish new industrial plants and expand or modernize existing plants. Prior authorization must be obtained from the Ministry of Finance for such duty reductions, and approval is not granted for the importation of types of items similar to those made in Mexico or which can be substituted by machinery produced in Mexico.

The income tax law provides for the granting of authorization to use a method of accelerated depreciation for firms which make new investments in machinery and equipment.

Firms producing manufactured goods for export may obtain subsidies from the Ministry of Finance in the form of reductions on income taxes, on the gross receipts tax, and on duties applicable to imports of raw materials and components, provided that the finished goods are in fact exported. Prior approval must be obtained from the ministry for such arrangements.

A subsidy in an amount equal to the federal portion of the gross receipts tax (1.8 percent) is granted to manufacturers in the interior on the initial sale of their goods within 20 kilometers of the U.S. border and to the free zones. The subsidy, designed to promote sales to the border areas, also includes a 25 percent reduction of railroad freight charges. Firms interested in obtaining the above benefits must be registered with the National Border Program Agency.

Under the Mexican border industrialization program, Mexican and foreign firms that establish processing plants on the Mexican side of the border are permitted duty-free importation of machinery, raw materials, and components provided all their end-products are exported. Exports made by such firms are duty free as well. The program is designed to attract foreign firms, mostly from the United States, to provide the jobs for the surplus labor located along the border areas.

Additionally, special export incentives are available in the form of import duty rebate. To qualify, the firm must utilize at least 40 percent domestic components (by value). When integration reaches the 50–59 percent level, the firm can qualify for a 67 percent rebate. When it reaches 60 percent, a 100 percent rebate is possible. Import tax rebates are also available on products sold in the northern border zone and in free zones for those manufacturers showing a cumulative increase in sales of at least 15 percent over the preceding year.

The question remained as to whether it was better to establish a new business or to purchase an existing one (for example, Hugo Poirot's company). From a tax exemption standpoint it appeared advisable to establish a new business. On the other hand, Jefferson Thompson stated that one Diaz Porfino, an influential Mexican citizen, was manufacturing furniture. It was suspected that in the event Docker opted for a new business Porfino's influence might be brought to bear, with the result that Docker's project might be deemed prejudicial to the interests of an already established manufacturer. Mr. Roberts, a second vice-president of Chase Manhattan National Bank and formerly a businessman in Mexico, stated that in his opinion it would be better to purchase an existing business. Shortly after receiving the above information from Mr. Steelman, L. D. Docker made a short visit to Mexico to look over the situation at firsthand. He came back favorably impressed with Poirot's operation and the Mexican market.

Discussion questions

1. Are you satisfied with the information presented here?
2. What relationship should Docker enter into with Hugo Poirot?
3. If you were an official of the Mexican government, would you offer a Docker enterprise in Mexico any sort of tax concession?
4. From the point of view of taxation, how should Docker set up its Mexican subsidiary or associated company?
5. Why might a minority stockholder cause trouble if L. D. and Gene Docker became stockholders in the Mexican venture?

Exercise

Assign students to assume the role of officials of the National Registry, the National Commission on Foreign Investment, and representatives of Docker. The latter should decide among themselves the design of a Mexican project and attempt to secure the necessary approvals from the Mexican authorities.

Chapter 8
CONTROL STRATEGY

Control may be defined simply as the relationships and devices designed to assure that strategy (or policy) decisions are made by designated authority in conformance with corporate goals, that tactical (or operating) decisions conform to the selected strategies, and that actual operations are in harmony.

Clearly, the administrative structure should be rationalized in terms of establishing and maintaining adequate control over the firm's activities at least cost. Administrative structure may thus be viewed as the network of channels through which authority flows, together with the feedback generated thereby. A distinct but related subject has to do with the *nature* of the flows within the system and the devices used to assure against abrupt changes in the flows.

Therefore, in considering alternative control strategies, several key questions present themselves:

1. Where should decision-making authority reside in the firm in respect to strategy choices relating to foreign markets or to global allocation of corporate resources?

2. Where should the relevant tactical decision-making authority be located?

3. By what methods should decisions be communicated?

4. By what means should operating performance be reported?

5. What measures of performance should be used (that is, conformance of strategy decisions to goals, of tactical decision to strategy, of actual operations to tactical decisions)?

6. How can decisions be enforced (that is, how can control be maintained)?

One might well ask whether there are problems in this area unique to the firm operating internationally. A listing of the differences between domestic and international control systems follows:

1. Currency differences require a more careful approach to pricing, working-capital management, and selection of funds sources, as well as great care in interpreting the meaning of overseas balance sheets and earnings statements.

2. The foreign manager may have little control over many important decisions made by the parent company, which fact may seriously affect his operating performance.

3. Economic data and historical and industry comparisons are often harder to obtain, even occasionally nonexistent, in the foreign environment, thereby making budgetary goal-setting more difficult.

4. Internal performance data for the foreign subsidiary occasionally is difficult to obtain in the form desired due to the unfamiliarity of most foreign-educated managers with management accounting techniques in the country of the parent.

5. Informal communication between foreign division manager and home office is less frequent than between domestic division manager and home office, therefore causing greater reliance on the data from the formal system.[1]

Research by Professor Skinner of the Harvard Business School has documented a strong feeling of resentment toward the home office by many overseas managers.[2] This resentment was reflected in charges of undue interference, inadequate delegation of authority, onerous reporting requirements, and lack of understanding and sympathy. On the other hand, he observed that home office executives were often frustrated "by possessing a sense of responsibility which is thwarted by having 'only paper authority' over the field operations." They are held responsible by their superiors for what goes on overseas; yet, they are unable to control the latter's daily decisions and sometimes even their policies. Though the headquarters executives may hold the ultimate power to replace the overseas executive, "this extreme action was not only distasteful but an impractical weapon because of their genuine problem in knowing enough of what went on abroad." Skinner distinguished between headquarters' "involvement" in overseas operations and the degree of "command" exercised over those operations. By the former term he refers to the functions performed by headquarters; by the latter term, to the "how" of headquarters' involvement, from nonparticipant observation to a detailed reporting system and specific orders for conformance. "Both of these elements of control can and should be tailored to the situation," he concludes. He warns against arbitrary classification of management decisions into "policy" (strategy) or "operations" (tactical). A home office may be of considerable help in resolving many overseas operating problems, and, conversely, local management may be better able to make certain policy decisions. He suggests "the probability that the interpersonal relationship will be improved by . . . an explicit defining of the role of the home office which would eliminate confusion and misunderstanding and establish a mechanism for regular review and open discussion of the role of headquarters." The difficulty of treating different countries, associated enterprises, and functions differently is admitted, and therefore the "situational viewpoint" seems required in international business.

A more recent study reports that executives stationed abroad often com-

[1]Adapted from John J. Muriel, "Evaluation and Control of Overseas Operations," in *Management Accounting*, May 1969, p. 37.

[2]Reported in C. Wickham Skinner, *American Industry in Developing Economies, the Management of International Manufacturing* (New York: Wiley & Sons, 1968).

plain that: (1) they feel out of touch with the mainstream of the company; (2) it takes an inordinate amount of time to get information from headquarters; (3) headquarters insists on making decisions that can be better made by those in the field who are closer to the situation; and (4) visits by headquarters' personnel are often "jaunts" that waste valuable time for those in the field.

On the other hand, those at corporate headquarters often complain that: (1) it takes too long to get information from the field; (2) those in foreign subsidiaries get into trouble by making decisions without consulting headquarters; (3) overseas executives become too "localized" to function at peak efficiency when they return from their international assignments; and (4) site visits abroad often waste valuable time because the overseas executives have not adequately prepared for them.[3]

One could hold plausibly that these conditions are found in all large, complex organizations. "Complaints regarding headquarters-field information barriers, and headquarters interference in local decision making, are certainly not limited to international firms."[4] The Jacques-Farris-Sirota research attempted to clarify the effect on communications of being international by hypothesizing that geographical distance was a key factor in headquarters-field relationships. Message turn-around time is magnified and reliance upon written communication becomes greater, thereby leading to less integration of the overseas executive into headquarters, a feeling of being out of touch, and a decrease in mutual trust and understanding. Resting on an in-depth, questionnaire-based study of companies in different industries, each with many foreign subsidiaries, the general conclusion was that, "By and large, communication was of similar quality between the headquarters of each company and its domestic and foreign subsidiaries."[5] Granted that the overseas executive reported making greater use of telecommunications than his domestic counterpart, and a larger cycle time for written requests to headquarters, these factors still seemed unrelated to feelings about the *quality* of communication. Again, although personal contact with headquarters personnel was less than in the domestic case, so likewise were feelings of being integrated with other personnel at headquarters (but not with top management), and no significant differences in trust and mutual understanding could be found. "Headquarters personnel were perceived, however, as having less influence on operations by the international executives than by the domestic executives," representative perhaps of the greater autonomy of overseas subsidiaries as opposed to the domestic.[6]

---

[3]F. M. Jacques, G. F. Farris, and D. Sirota, "Improving Communication in the International Firm," unpublished article, Sloan School of Management, M.I.T., 1971, p. 1; based on François M. Jacques, "Motivating Corporate Policy Implementation in Managers of Domestic and Foreign Operations," unpublished S.M. thesis, Sloan School of Management, M.I.T., 1971.

[4]Jacques, et al., "Improving Communication," p. 2.

[5]Jacques, et al., "Improving Communication," p. 3.

[6]Jacques, et al., "Improving Communication," p. 7.

In further analyzing their data, Jacques and his colleagues found that two of the four companies consistently scored significantly higher in communication for *both* foreign and domestic operations. The information received was clearer, more accurate, more timely—including their own submitted to headquarters. Characteristics of the "better-communicating" companies were (1) less control by nontop management headquarters personnel over subsidiary operations, (2) greater top management willingness to stand by decisions made in the subsidiaries that diverged from established directives, (3) a greater sense of "teamwork" with *local* colleagues, and (4) less personal contact with headquarters personnel.[7] It was then found that international executives in the better-communicating companies had had more management experience than their counterparts in the other companies, presumably most of it with the company of present employ, and had spent more time at their present location. Another characteristic of the better-communicating firms was their larger involvement in foreign markets.[8]

Inasmuch as effective communication is the key to control, one can thus derive some of the necessary, though perhaps not sufficient, conditions, as in Figure 8.1.

One problem in the Jacques study was that the accuracy of information from subsidiary to headquarters was measured in terms of perceptions on the part of transmitters and receivers. In fact, how accurately did the messages describe environmentally generated problems? To what extent were corporate decisions based on an understanding of environmental realities? It is generally agreed that the lack of systematic environmental analysis by international companies is an important deficiency.[9] Hence, the information flowing from subsidiary to headquarters, regardless of perception, may not as accurately reflect objective reality outside the firm as it does in the domestic case.

Perhaps the variable that dominates the system of corporate communications is reflected in the following observation.

The extensive management development programs that some multinational enterprises maintain appear designed to create an elite cadre of men who all know one another and who share operating experience in different types of managerial activity. The purpose of creating these elites is to foster an environment in which men who are physically distant at any one time can communicate easily and informally. If men share common experience and perceive themselves as having similar status in the hierarchy, they generally cooperate more readily than they would in other circumstances. Informal links among

---

[7]Jacques, et al., "Improving Communication," p. 8.

[8]Jacques, et al., "Improving Communication," p. 71.

[9]Confirmed by John S. Schwendiman, "Strategies and Long-Range Planning in the International Firm," unpublished Ph.D. diss., Sloan School of Management, M.I.T., 1971, p. 219; also by Daniel A. Picard, "Strategic Planning of the American Multi-National Firm in France," unpublished S.M. thesis, Sloan School of Management, M.I.T., 1971.

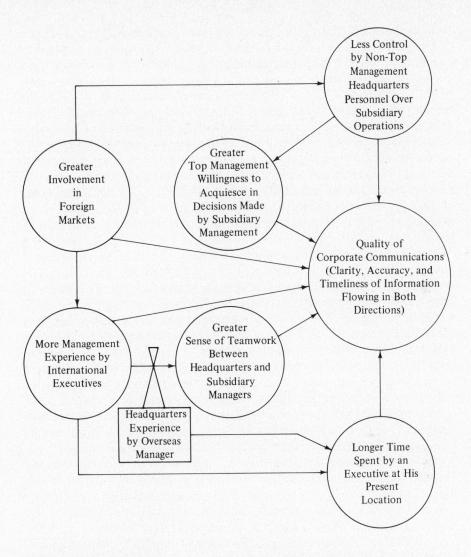

Figure 8.1
**SOME FACTORS ENHANCING INTERNATIONAL CORPORATE
COMMUNICATIONS**

*the members of the elite help to compensate for the absence of many formal reporting
relationships and reduce the demand for specialized staff.*[10]

---

[10]John M. Stopford and Louis T. Wells, Jr., "Ironing Out the New Relationships," *Worldwide P&I Planning*,
May–June 1972, p. 35. Reprinted from Stopford and Wells, *Managing the Multinational Enterprise* (New York:
Basic Books, 1972). One presumes that the authors meant to include women as well!

Some concrete examples of this sort of informal communications were reported by another researcher. In one company, foreign employers who had attended a training program at corporate headquarters often contacted friends made during that time in resolving problems; a kind of fraternity had been created by the program. In a second corporation, management had been shaken up recently by a massive reorganization (from product-line to regional). Instead of following the new official channels, much of the internal business communications moved through informal links based on personal relationships developed within the *former* organizational structure. Within another corporation was found a large informal network based upon common university experience and membership in the same college fraternity. Many of the links, obviously, are unlikely to appear within an internationally oriented business unless there is opportunity for the face-to-face association of executives from the various regions.[11]

It follows that companies in which the tenure of the relevant managers is relatively long and in which they are promoted by seniority (that is, an age group moves up together) would, all else being equal, lead to the most effective international communication network. The Japanese system, in which there are few intercompany transfers of top managers and in which there are personal ties of long standing, suggests itself. Indeed, the impression one gets is that the international communication network within an established Japanese corporation is so tightly drawn that it is virtually impossible for new managers to be introduced into the system effectively, whether they be Japanese or non-Japanese. Although apparently verifiable by no empirical research done to date, a plausible hypothesis is that as Japanese firms nationalize the managements of their foreign subsidiaries the communications problem will be exceedingly difficult. As much as the local and Japanese management try to have it otherwise, one suspects that the local manager will have a feeling of facing a tightly knit monolithic structure into which he is denied any real access. His frustration is very likely to lead to an erosion of communication and of effective control. This situation suggests why the Japanese have developed the trading company approach, which is discussed in a later section.

As Brandt and Hulbert point out, "Exchange of information between home office and subsidiary management plays a crucial role in coordinating and controlling multinational operations."[12] On the basis of an empirical study of the communications systems used by 63 multinational corporations with subsidiaries in Brazil, the researchers attempted to identify those characteristics of a communication system associated with better understanding between headquarters and field, as perceived by field managers,

---

[11]Gijsbert G. Sandberg, "The Organization of Multinational Corporations," unpublished S.M. thesis, Sloan School of Management, M.I.T., 1972, pp. 51–55.

[12]William K. Brandt and James M. Hulbert, "Patterns of Communications in the Multinational Corporation: An Empirical Study," *Journal of International Business Studies*, vol. 7, no. 1, Spring 1976, p. 57.

and to draw comparisons between European, Japanese, and U.S.-based corporations. Among their findings: (1) U.S. companies report to headquarters more frequently than do their Japanese and European counterparts, which appeared to prefer "management by exception" (that is, responding only when they identify a problem or opportunity); (2) U.S.-based companies are far more inclined to hold regular management meetings on a regional or worldwide basis; (3) U.S. companies rely much more on personal visits between the chief executive of the subsidiary and his home-office superior.[13]

These differences raise questions about the impact of these differences in communications flows. Relying on research dealing with communications, Brandt and Hulbert identify a number of possibly relevant variables:

Company demographics

1. Firms with more extensive experience outside their home markets should have fewer problems with intrafirm communication.
2. Capital-intensive subsidiaries should be better understood by headquarters.
3. The greater the physical and cultural distance, the less understanding is there at headquarters.
4. The larger the subsidiary's business, the better it is understood by headquarters.
5. The longer the subsidiary's history, the greater the home office understanding.

Organizational structure

1. The greater the organizational complexity in terms of product lines, the more difficult is communication between subsidiary and headquarters.
2. The more levels there are in organizational hierarchy between subsidiary and headquarters, the less the understanding at headquarters.

Reporting procedures

1. More reports from subsidiary to headquarters, and regular responses, should lead to more understanding.
2. Excessive demands for information from the subsidiary can lead to frustration and demoralization of the subsidiary and clog communications with superficial, redundant, and inaccurate information, thus leading to less understanding at headquarters.

Shared experience

1. The more the personal contact between subsidiary and headquarters, the greater the understanding at headquarters.
2. The more direct overseas experience or knowledge about the subsidiary's operation on the part of headquarters personnel, the greater the latter's understanding.

---

[13]Brandt and Hulbert, "Patterns of Communications," pp. 58–60.

3. The longer the chief subsidiary executive holds office, the better his communication with headquarters is likely to be.

Brandt and Hulbert found that the nationality of the parent company had the strongest influence on the level of perceived understanding at headquarters. Chief excutives of Japanese subsidiaries, it was revealed, perceived that their home offices were much less knowledgeable about Brazilian problems when compared with the perceptions of American and of European subsidiary chief executives. It was felt that the relative newness of the Japanese firms in Brazil was at least part of the explanation.[14] They also found positive correlation between the capital-intensity of the subsidiary and better perceived understanding by home-office management. Likewise, the amount of Brazilian experience by the home office superior and the chief subsidiary executive's tenure with the company correlated positively with understanding. The complexity of subsidiary operations correlated negatively. But "neither the size of worldwide sales nor the extent of multinational experience, as measured by proportion of sales outside the home-country market had any effect on perceptions of home office understanding."[15] The authors also observed:

Although the number of reports sent monthly from subsidiary to home office had no effect on the criterion variable [that is, perceived headquarters understanding], the use of these reports at home office had a strong impact. The more these reports were read and evaluated, the greater the perceived understanding. In contrast, more reports from home office to subsidiary reduced home-office understanding. Whether this reflects real misunderstanding by home office or the [subsidiary] COE's reaction against the barrage of home-office reports cannot be determined. It is clear, however, that merely increasing the information flow without regard to quality will not improve the relationships. In many firms some type of special "international information system" was urgently needed to coordinate and control the constant flow of communication.[16]

The final conclusions: "Home offices clearly need to give more thought and planning to their information systems," and, "Our findings suggest it is easier to build bridges when home-office personnel have first-hand knowledge of the subsidiary's operations, which may well require more than brief visits."[17]

Toyne has pointed out that "the success of a firm depends to a large extent on its ability to organize a cohesive management group who can mobilize the firm's physical resources and exploit opportunities to the firm's advantage." The degree of managerial cohesiveness, almost by definition, impacts heavily upon a firm's capacity to control effectively. In an empirically-based study in Mexico, Toyne sought to ascertain whether differences existed between "the managerial belief and need patterns" of Mexican managers of U.S. subsidiaries, Mexican managers of Mexican firms, and American managers of Mexican subsidiaries. Secondly, he sought to find out what influence industry and

---

[14]Brandt and Hulbert, "Patterns of Communications," pp. 62–63.

[15]Brandt and Hulbert, "Patterns of Communications," p. 63.

[16]Brandt and Hulbert, "Patterns of Communications," p. 63.

[17]Brandt and Hulbert, "Patterns of Communications," pp. 63–64.

company characteristics had "on the degree of change experienced in these belief and need patterns." A third objective was to ascertain if "sociological and behavioral trait differences might influence the degree of change experienced in the managerial belief and need patterns of the Mexican subsidiary managers because of their exposure to the organization culture of foreign subsidiary operations."[18] But, in fact, only a partial change of beliefs was found in their case.

The overall conclusion of the study was summarized thus:

The extent that managerial beliefs and needs are transferable is dependent on industry, company, and personal attributes. MNCs and host countries are therefore capable of moderating, not controlling, this transfer process. Grouping foreign subsidiaries by industry and company attributes would enable MNCs to determine how policies and practices at the local level need to be modified to enhance the organization, coordination and control of their global operations.[19]

The company and industry attributes to which reference is made include capital intensity, R&D intensity, and marketing intensity. Personal attributes include education, age, exposure to foreign environments, and managerial position. In other words, all of these factors may impact on the ability of the parent corporation to control effectively a subsidiary's operations.

LOCATION OF AUTHORITY FOR STRATEGY SELECTION 8.1

The locale of such authority relating to overseas operations generally depends on:

1. the relative importance of foreign and domestic markets as perceived by management,
2. volume of business and degree of diversity of product,
3. the structure of the firm, such as degree of divisional autonomy, division size, basis for divisional organization (region, function, product, customer, or process),
4. the location of personal interest and expertness within the firm vis-à-vis foreign markets,
5. multinationality of ownership,
6. multinationality of top corporate management personnel,
7. the nature of the planning process.

The degree to which control is centralized[20] is probably related to:

---

[18]Brian Toyne, "Host Country Managers of Multinational Firms: An Evaluation of Variables Affecting Their Managerial Thinking Patterns," *Journal of International Business Studies*, vol. 7, no. 1, Spring 1976, pp. 39–40.

[19]Toyne, "Host Country Managers," p. 53.

[20]Degree of centralization may be defined in terms of the number of organizational levels between the chief executive and the heads of the foreign units, the implementation of profit centers, the existence of formal task descriptions with authority specifications, the perceived degree of autonomy given to foreign units by headquarters' managers, and the degree of standardized information transmission.

1. extent to which divisions are integrated (that is, the amount of selling to, and procuring from, each other),

2. amount of personnel exchange and intersubsidiary financing,

3. the degree of divisional autonomy in regard to *domestic* strategy (in sales, supply, management, labor, and finance),

4. personal interest and expertise on the corporate level in regard to foreign markets,

5. the level of external political pressure to relinquish control,

6. ownership structure (for example, if ownership is in the hands of a family, the family stockholders may exercise close surveillance over strategy choice in regard to ownership, management, and finance, thereby forcing corporate headquarters to retain control in these areas).

This latter point leads to the conclusion that corporate goals are relevant. If the principal goal is power maximization, extreme centralization may be optimum; if market share maximization, extreme decentralization; if profit maximization, more moderate decentralization; if rate-of-return maximization, somewhat more centralized control. If one holds other factors constant, the priority of corporate goals could perhaps be implied by the level of centralization. No one seems to have researched this interesting hypothesis.

A 1968 study of 153 European affiliates of U.S. companies[21] concluded that there was no general pattern regarding the degree of control exercised by corporate headquarters, even among corporations of the same size and industry. The general conclusions of the study were as follows:[22]

1. Companies in certain industries tend toward centralized control (for example, drug manufacturers because they require product consistency; photographic equipment manufacturers because of product uniformity and little variation among local markets; oil processors because worldwide coordination of exploration, production, processing, shipping, and storage is required).

2. Manufacturing subsidiaries are more tightly controlled generally than marketing units.

3. Finance tends to be centrally controlled in virtually all cases; also very commonly controlled are accounting procedures, sales reporting, personnel policy (particularly executive appointments and compensation), sources of supply, quality control, trademark and name, and advertising.

4. Subsidiaries with a wide range of products with a variety of markets tend to be more autonomous than affiliates with uniform products and markets.

5. Companies with a few large subsidiaries in a region tend to exercise less control than those with many small units.

6. Distant subsidiaries tend to have greater autonomy, particularly if located in

---

[21]Robert J. Alsegg, *Control Relationships between American Corporations and Their European Subsidiaries* (New York: American Management Association, 1971).
[22]Alsegg, *Control Relationships*, pp. 7–8, summarized.

countries with unfamiliar socioeconomic conditions, unstable political conditions, and stringent legal requirements.

7. Joint ventures have considerable local autonomy.

8. Newly acquired subsidiaries that continue to manufacture their old product lines under their former management tend to have greater autonomy.

9. Controls are seldom constant; during early stages the control may be very loose but tighten as the foreign operation grows—up to a point.

"Of the 127 companies whose European subsidiaries and other units . . . [included in the study] . . . approximately 40 percent imposed strict control, 40 percent had loose control, and 20 percent had control that was intermediate, flexible, and undeterminable, or in the process of being changed."[23] Nonetheless, a trend toward stricter control generally was perceived by the author. Reasons given for the trend are: (1) development of jet transportation and transatlantic telephone and telex; (2) growth of the European subsidiaries since World War II; (3) the development of the Common Market; (4) the unsatisfactory performance of many subsidiaries.[24]

The same study concluded that strict control is imposed only so long as required, is determined in large measure by management confidence,[25] and depends on the subsidiary's success and the control methods used. Major problems occur because of headquarters' lack of knowledge about conditions abroad, disregard of human factors, delays in decisions from headquarters, cumbersome reporting systems, the lack of knowledge about immediate situations, disregard of local managers' recommendations, and poorly qualified subsidiary managers (particularly for companies with newly established subsidiaries and those which are highly centralized and thus have difficulty in attracting competent overseas managers).[26]

The more important of these relationships are summarized in Figure 8.2.

Even though greater or lesser participation by the foreign units is possible, in virtually all cases some strategy choices are likely to be retained by corporate headquarters, specifically:

1. What to produce, where, and with what inputs, for sale where, and under what conditions?

2. What R&D to undertake, where, and on what scale?

3. The recruitment, development, and assignment of individuals carrying high-level skills, including managerial, and, hence, their remuneration.

[23]Alsegg, *Control Relationships*, p. 8.

[24]Alsegg, *Control Relationships*, p. 9.

[25]Supported by I. A. Litvak, C. J. Maule, and R. D. Robinson, *Dual Loyalty: Canadian/U.S. Business Arrangements* (Toronto: McGraw-Hill Company of Canada, Limited, 1971).

[26]Alsegg, *Control Relationships*, pp. 11–13.

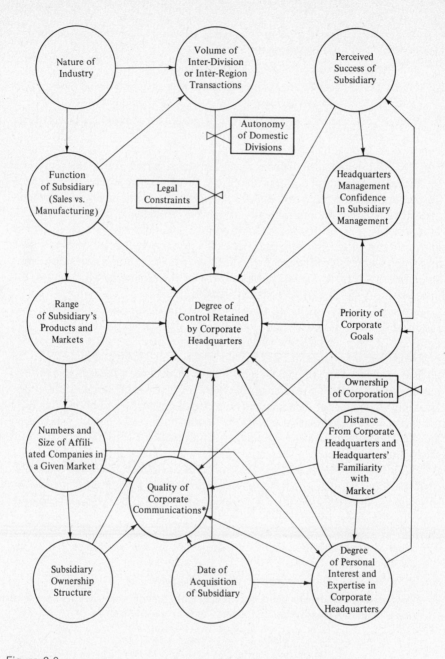

Figure 8.2
**MAJOR FACTORS RELATING TO DEGREE OF CONTROL
RETAINED BY CORPORATE HEADQUARTERS**

*See Figure 8.1.

Table 8.1
DEGREE OF LOCAL MANAGEMENT AUTONOMY CLASSIFIED ACCORDING TO TYPE OF LOCAL MARKETING DECISION*

Degree of local management autonomy	Local marketing decision			
	Product design	Advertising approach	Retail price	Distribution outlets per 1,000 population
Primary authority rested with local management	30%	86%	74%	61%
Local management shared authority with other levels in organization	15%	8%	20%	38%
Decision primarily imposed upon local management	55%	6%	6%	1%
	100%	100%	100%	100%
N (Marketing programs observed)	N = 86	N = 84†	N = 84†	N = 86

*For Western European affiliates of 9 US-based manufacturers.

†Classification information not available in two cases.

Source: R. J. Aylmer, "Global Marketing in the Multinational Corporation," in H. B. Thorelli, ed., *International Marketing Strategy* (Middlesex: Penguin Books, 1973), p. 303.

4. The negotiation of working conditions with labor (now that international labor organizations are appearing).

5. The incurring of large-scale financial commitment.

6. Intrasubsidiary movements of goods, services, and people.

7. The reporting of profits and losses.

Strategy decisions relating to the development and servicing of foreign markets may be made in the domestic operating divisions; in a domestically oriented corporate headquarters assisted by staff office specializing in exports; in an international division; in a regional, product, or functional headquarters; or in a transnational corporate headquarters.

Of recent years there has been some empirical research as to the international centralization of control over certain functions imposed by corporations. For example, in the marketing area, Aylmer found considerable dispersion. (See Table 8.1.) As can be seen, local management was primarily responsible for 86 percent of the advertising decisions, 74 percent of the pricing decisions, and 61 percent of the channel decisions. But product design was quite another matter.

Aylmer went on to develop data that strongly suggested that the most important firm characteristics influencing location of marketing authority were the relative importance of the firm's international operations and the relative importance of the affiliate's position within the firm. The higher the firm's international sales as a percentage of total sales, the greater was the tendency for marketing decisions to be centrally controlled. Also, the greater the relative importance of an affiliate in terms of percentage of total sales, the less likely was it that decisions were imposed by headquarters.[27]

There would appear to be mounting evidence that money management tends to be highly centralized in many corporations operating internationally, possibly spurred by the floating of exchange rates among major trading currencies since 1973. As Prindl pointed out, the arguments for centralized control are strong:

1. Local executives can rarely know the liquidity position of the group.
2. They cannot analyze the exchange exposure of the group in either its component parts or as a consolidated entity.
3. The central financial office, no matter what shape it takes, draws on formation from a wide number of financial institutions and can formulate a broader decision on the probable nature of financial events and protection against them.[28]

Prindl goes on to caution, "Centralized control must be weighed against the lack of whole-hearted support for rationalizing systems experienced by a number of companies when local management feels its sphere of influence is limited or its achievement down-graded."[29] The solution, he suggests, is to make certain that local finance managers are judged within the constraints placed upon them, and that they know it. He concludes, "Most multinational corporations impose a direct and centralized [financial] control over their international affiliates."[30]

The findings of a 1974 study of perceived changes in the degree of control exercised by nine large U.S.-based corporations over their foreign subsidiaries, all of which had at least three overseas subsidiaries that contributed at least 20 percent of total sales, were surprising. Classifying these changes, as perceived by headquarters' managers, the results are shown below in Table 8.2. In each case, the respondent was asked to specify the change in control over the past ten years.

It should be noted that the labor negotiation function remained primarily in subsidiary hands and investment decisions in parent company hands.

Typically, control of certain legal, ownership, financial, and R&D strategies is retained at the corporate level regardless of type of firm. In the final analysis, corporate control over strategy should be maintained only in those functional areas in which a suboptimization problem is likely to arise as between the division (whether international, regional, product, or functional) and the entire corporate family, or as between subsidiary and division. Such problems may appear when important economies of scale arise in the joint utilization of

[27]R. J. Aylmer, "Global Marketing in the Multinational Corporations," in H. B. Thorelli, ed., *International Marketing Strategy* (Middlesex, England: Penguin Books, 1973), pp. 305–9.
[28]Andreas Prindl, "International Money Management, the Environmental Framework," *Euromoney*, September 1971, p. 14.
[29]Prindl, "International Money," p. 14.
[30]Prindl, "International Money," p. 14.

Table 8.2
TRENDS IN CONTROL EXERCISED BY THE PARENT, BY FUNCTIONAL AREA*

	More subsidiary control	Unchanged			More U.S. control
	1	2	3	4	5
Personnel policy decisions	5	2	2	0	0
Labor negotiations	1	1	6	1	0
Manufacturing operations	5	3	1	0	0
Sourcing (two no comments)	5	0	2	0	0
Financial reporting	0	1	3	0	5
Investment decisions (one no comment)	0	1	7	0	0

*Scaled

Source: Constructed from data in Ernst L. Ranft, ''Foreign Wholly Owned Subsidiaries: How Independent Are They?'' (Cambridge: unpublished Masters thesis, Alfred P. Sloan School of Management, M.I.T., 1974).

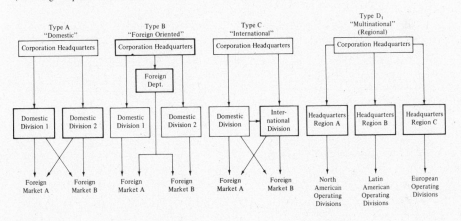

Figure 8.3
TYPES OF FIRMS BY LOCATION OF AUTHORITY OVER ASSOCIATED FOREIGN ENTERPRISE

Note: Heavily lined boxes indicate source of effective line authority in respect to foreign operations.

scarce resources, including high-cost specialized personnel. Even in the latter situation, however, specialized personnel at the corporate level may be used only in an advisory capacity to division or subsidiary managements in determining strategy.

Variations in corporate structure are outlined in Figure 8.3. Bear in mind here that we are really concerned with the reality of the decision-making structure rather than any empty organizational or legal shell.

In types A, B, and C, the domestic divisions may be defined by geographical area (New England, Midwest, and the like), product, function, process (for example, mining, smelting, refining, shipping), or customer (government, in-

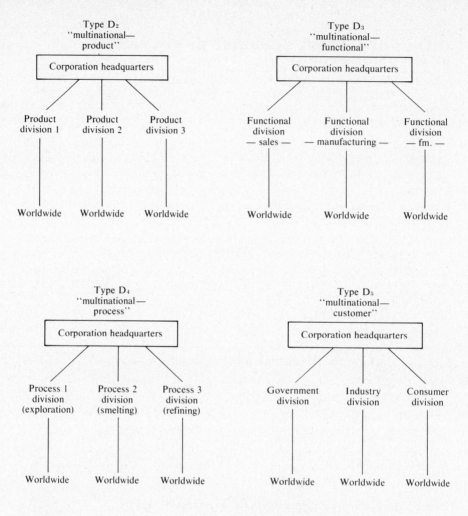

Figure 8.4
VARIATIONS OF THE MULTINATIONAL CORPORATION

dustry, consumer). In type C, the international division is, by definition, regional. In type D (only one form of which is diagrammed in Figure 8.3) the first layer of organization under corporate headquarters, whatever called (headquarters, division, group, or coordinating committee), may likewise be defined by geographical area, product, function, process, or customer (as indicated in Figure 8.4). Hence, D_1 is a regionally organized multinational firm. **Henceforth, let it be noted that in this text, the terms foreign-orientation, international, multinational, and transnational are not used interchangeably.**

Also possible are Types E and F, firms, which, insofar as the flow of authority goes, look the same as Type D. Type E, the "transnational" firm, becomes such when its members develop loyalty to the firm of a sort that transcends national identity, thus eliminating covert or psychologically based national bias in decision making and making possible an optimum allocation of corporate resources insofar as the impact of national law on corporate decisions permits. Corporate headquarters itself becomes multinational in terms of personnel. Indeed, key decision-makers may, in fact, no longer reside in the parent country. A firm owned and managed multinationally (that is, by nationals of different countries) becomes, almost by definition, transnational. Several international corporate mergers within Europe have given rise to true transnational firms.[31] Figures 8.5a and 8.5b detail the structure of some of them. Temporary transnational ventures are likewise to be found in Europe, such as those related to the Atlantic, Hawk, Main Battle Tank, Concorde, and Nadge projects. This last is diagrammed in Figure 8.6. A major problem associated with this type of transnational venture lies in the fact of their temporary nature. Managers assigned to the ventures anticipate returning to their parent firms and, hence, are in a position of great role conflict.[32]

A further word about the definition of the multinational corporation is in order. The multinational corporation (MNC), technically defined, is characterized by four factors:

1. Ownership and management of a parent corporation essentially by the nationals of one country.

2. An integrated international production system (that is, centralized control production).

3. Equity-based control (that is, the centralized control is based preeminently on ownership except where local law blocks alien ownership).

4. A legal domicile within the country with which the preponderance of parent company owners and managers identify.

If one changes any one of these four dimensions, a different type of enterprise emerges, from which one can expect different behavior.

For example, if one postulates ownership and management of the parent corporation by the nationals of more than one country to a significant degree, one has a *transnational corporation*. (Figure 8.7.) If the corporation is not managing an integrated international production system, then it is simply an *international holding company* of some sort, possibly based on financial linkages and some vaguely defined policy guidelines, characteristics of the international corporation. If its control is not equity based, but rather rests on

---

[31]Discussed in detail in Paul Goldberg, "Transnational Firms in Europe," unpublished Ph.D. diss., Sloan School of Management, M.I.T., 1971.

[32]For details see Milton S. Hochmuth, "The Effect of Structure and Strategy, the Government Sponsored Multinational Joint Ventures," unpublished D.B.A. diss., Harvard Graduate School of Business Administration, 1972.

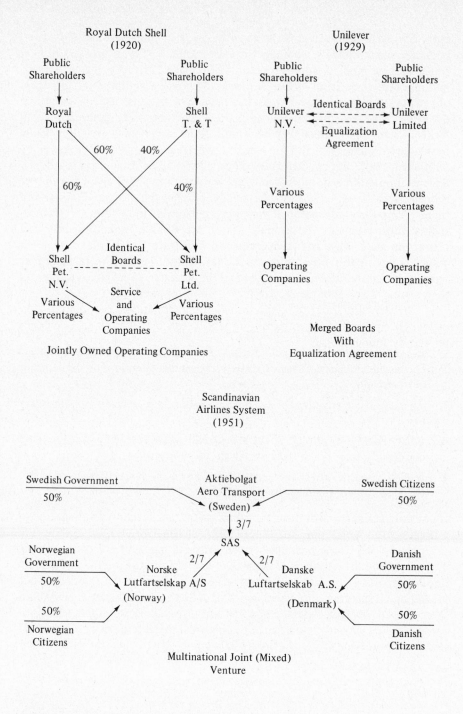

Figure 8.5a
THE PRE-EEC TRANSNATIONAL FIRMS

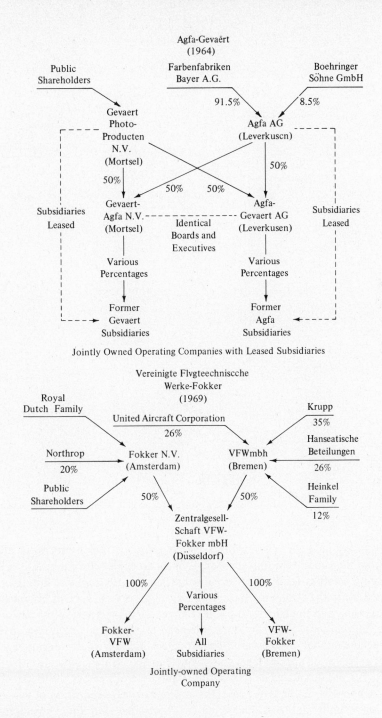

Jointly Owned Operating Companies with Leased Subsidiaries

Jointly-owned Operating
Company

Figure 8.5b
THE POST-EEC TRANSNATIONAL FIRMS

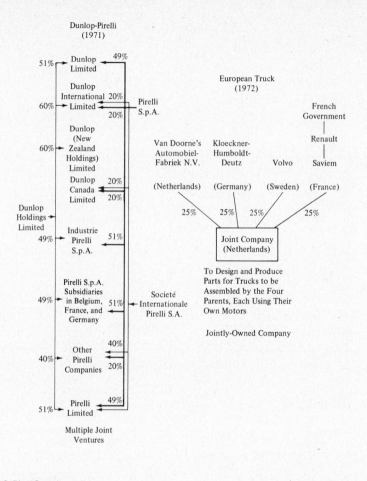

Figure 8.5b (Continued)

contracts, we have an *international service company*, which can range all the way from the general trading companies of Japan, which are essentially selling marketing services (and other services ancillary to that central function; see Figure 8.8), to the company marketing a specific service, such as engineering, construction, and the like. And if one changes the fourth part of the definition of the multinational either by domiciling the parent corporation in a country with which neither owners nor top managers identify or by permitting the parent corporation special legal status under international convention (so that legally it is not domiciled in any nation-state), one either has the *dedomiciled multinational* or, in the latter case, the *supranational corporation* of which we have only public (International Bank for Reconstruction and Development) and quasipublic (International Telecommunications Satellite System, or Intelsat) examples. (See Figure 8.9.) Another, the Agro-Industrial Development

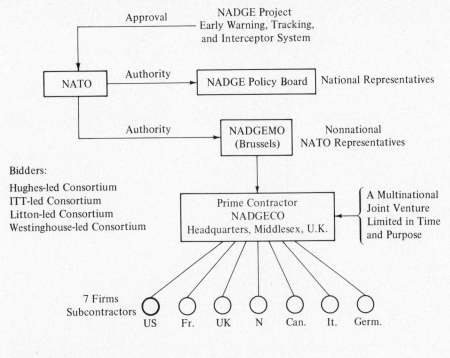

Figure 8.6
A TRANSNATIONAL VENTURE OF A TEMPORARY NATURE

Note: Conditions—fixed price; prime contractor responsible for system integration; and B/P provision (2 percent margin), national contribution equal to local spending ±2 percent.

Corporation, was urged for the Middle East at one time, but dropped. (See Figure 8.10.)[33]

One of the difficulties with so much research in the international business area (including the Harvard-based multinational study), is that it has not seen the nature of the international enterprise itself as an important variable. For example, much data has been collected on "multinational corporations" which in fact includes information on many firms that are not multinational as defined above. Only rarely is such data classified by type of corporation. One might derive data for corporations with or without international divisions, but it is exceedingly important to distinguish between those corporations that have had an international division in the past and dissolved it in favor of a true multinational structure and those firms which have never evolved far enough beyond export to have created an international division. And, in some in-

[33]Not too dissimilar from the international community development corporation proposed by John Vafai, "The International Community Development Corporation," *Columbia Journal of Transnational Law*, vol. 10, no. 2, Fall 1971, pp. 364 ff.

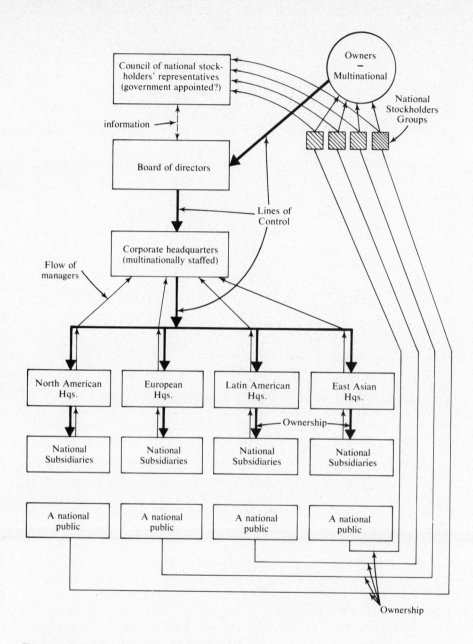

Figure 8.7
A TRANSNATIONAL CORPORATE MODEL

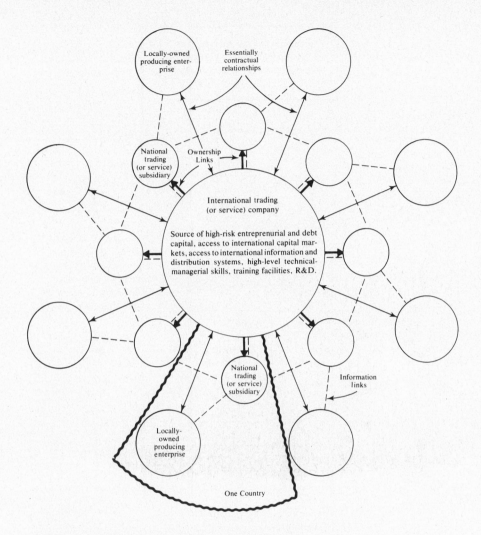

Figure 8.8
AN INTERNATIONAL SERVICE COMPANY, OR TRANSNATIONAL-MULTINATIONAL ASSOCIATION MODEL

Note: If the international company is owned and managed essentially by local nationals, it is a *multinational* association; if owned largely by the associated firms and managed at least in part by them, it is a transnational association.

stances an international division is retained *after* multinationalization, simply as a staff-support, planning, and/or integrative unit.

The taxonomy of international corporate form has been further compounded by the United Nations' insistence on using the term "transnational" to cover all firms operating internationally. Given the definitions used here and

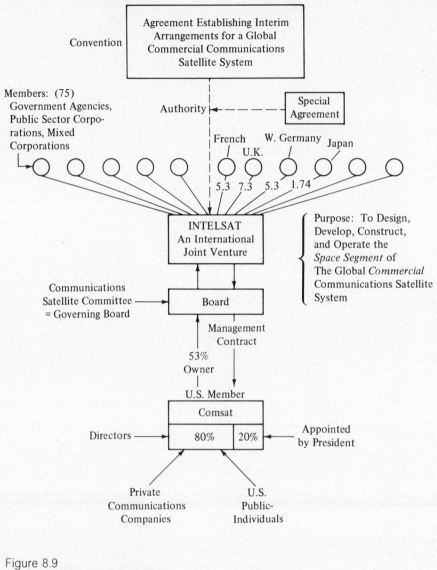

Figure 8.9
STRUCTURE OF INTELSAT

elsewhere in the more technical literature, the term "transnational" as used by the United Nations includes export-oriented, international, multinational, and transnational firms, plus international service companies, international holding companies, and dedomiciled multinationals. The point is that each type of corporation gives rise to different public policy issues. For example, if the multinational is in greatest conflict with host country governments, one might

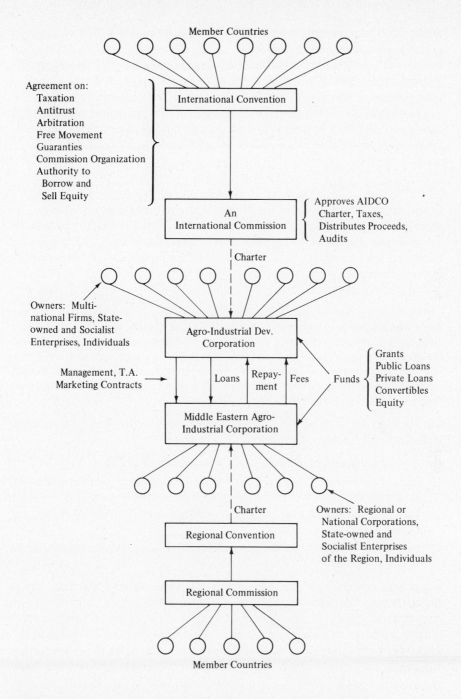

Member Countries

Agreement on:
Taxation
Antitrust
Arbitration
Free Movement
Guaranties
Commission Organization
Authority to
Borrow and
Sell Equity

International Convention

An
International Commission

Approves AIDCO
Charter, Taxes,
Distributes Proceeds,
Audits

Charter

Owners: Multi-
national Firms, State-
owned and Socialist
Enterprises, Individuals

Agro-Industrial Dev.
Corporation

Management, T.A.
Marketing Contracts

Loans   Repay-   Fees
ment

Funds

Grants
Public Loans
Private Loans
Convertibles
Equity

Middle Eastern Agro-
Industrial Corporation

Charter

Owners: Regional or
National Corporations,
State-owned and
Socialist Enterprises
of the Region, Individuals

Regional Convention

Regional Commission

Member Countries

Figure 8.10

AIDCO (AGRO-INDUSTRIAL DEVELOPMENT CORPORATION)

argue that the transnationals are likely to be in greatest conflict with *parent country governments*. It is important to make these definitional distinctions because it seems very likely that they impact on corporate behavior (for example, the degree of national bias in decision making) and, hence, on public policy issues. Curiously, there has been virtually no research as to how the internationalization of the firm, and subsequently its multinationalization and transnationalization, impact on the nature and quality of corporate decisions. However, national differences in corporate behavior may be suggestive.

Evolution of the firm

In speaking of the evolution of the firm in its international dimension, one must superimpose two related but distinct processes. There is, first, the pattern of geographical dispersion of corporate resources and, second, the pattern of functional and organizational development as the perceived corporate market internationalizes.

Carlson observed:

> *As long as the survival of a firm is not threatened, its primary objective is to grow. Its immediate goal is to increase its sales, with the qualification that it can at the same time reach a certain profit level, a certain level of financial stability, etc. If these conditions cannot be fulfilled in its present operations, it starts to search for new alternative activities. But since new alternatives generally seem more uncertain than old ones, we assume that this search will be directed to alternatives which are as similar as possible to those with which it is already familiar.* [34]

Carlson goes on to point out that the uncertainty the firm feels during such a search is due to four factors:

1. Lack of knowledge of the existence of possible new alternatives.
2. Lack of knowledge of the conditions, internal or external to the firm, which will determine the consequences of a new alternative.
3. Lack of knowledge of what consequences these conditions, even when they are known, may have for the firm.
4. Lack of knowledge of how these consequences may be expressed in relevant terms of goal fulfillment. [35]

It has been noted frequently that uncertainty increases with the time which elapses between decision and outcome and with the degree of unfamiliarity in respect to the place of that outcome, that is, its "degree of foreignness." Carlson adds the uncertainty associated with what he dubs "frontier problems," such as the variety of laws and regulations relating to the cross-border movement of goods, money, and people. Export experience reduces both

[34]Sune Carlson, *How Foreign Is Foreign Trade?* (Uppsala, Sweden: Acta Universitatis Upsaliensis, 1975), pp. 6–7.

[35]Carlson, *How Foreign*, p. 7. Carlson makes attribution to E. Hornell and J. E. Vahlnes, "Information vid etableringsbeslut," in Jan Johanson, ed., *Exportstrategiska problem* (Stockholm, 1972), p. 96.

elements of this uncertainty over time, and hence usually precedes any major commitment of corporate assets to the purchase of fixed assets abroad. In any event, the accumulation of the new information sufficient to reduce uncertainty bears a cost. The information must be collected, transmitted, and interpreted.

Carlson uses the notion of "cultural distance," which he defines in terms of the difference between home country and foreign market in respect to level of development, education, business language, everyday language, cultural distance, and extent of the connection between the two countries. Various Swedish studies reported by Carlson, his own included, seem to establish that buying preferences of Swedish firms correlate negatively with cultural distance, so likewise the degree of corporate commitment in exploiting foreign markets although once a firm has progressed to the point of establishing a sales *subsidiary* in a particular country, it seems to be more influenced by size of market than by cultural distance. Finally, another Swedish study reported by Carlson concluded that Swedish firms "start to establish subsidiaries in culturally nearby countries before they do so further away, but there seems to be a certain difference in the chronological order as between different periods, different branches of industry, and different sized firms. Firms that produced technology-intensive products seemed to be more influenced by cultural distance than other firms, and small firms were more influenced than large firms."[36] These studies support the observation that historically U.S. firms very frequently moved assets first into Canada, then into the United Kingdom and other English-speaking countries, even before the firm became either multinational or international in structure. And it was often true that these first investments came about as the result of some personal relationship or interest at the top, not as the result of a global scanning process.

If the evolution of administrative structure is viewed alongside growth of foreign sales of the firm (*in relation to domestic sales*), types A, B, C, and D tend to follow one another in time for a given firm. (See Table 8.3.)

In type A, each domestic division handles its own foreign sales, which arise initially in response to largely unsolicited orders from overseas. If the potential foreign market is indeed small, if divisions are organized on a product basis, and if divisions are relatively autonomous and large, type A may be optimal. One problem is that the foreign market potential from the point of view of each division may be seen as relatively small, in which event no one in the firm develops sufficient interest to examine the potential of various foreign markets and to combine corporate resources for full exploitation. Nor are experts employed who are capable of realizing such foreign-market potential, nor the specialists capable of facilitating product movement into such markets (such as documenters, linguists, freight forwarders, customs expeditors, credit and insurance negotiators, foreign exchange transactors).

---

[36]Carlson, *How Foreign*, pp. 14–19.

Table 8.3

CHARACTERISTIC BUSINESS PATTERNS OF FIRMS AT VARIOUS EVOLUTIONARY LEVELS
(foreign activity as a percent of the corporate total)

	Foreign Sales	Foreign Mfg.	Foreign Assets in Mfg.	Foreign Profits
A. Domestic (no specialized export effort)	0–10%	0	0	0–15%
B. Export (specialized export effort)	10–20	0–5	0–5	15–20
C. International (Export bias eliminated, emphasis on foreign market entry by any strategy)	20–40	5–30	5–20	20–40
D. Multinational (Discontinuity between domestic and foreign decisions minimal)	40–60	30–60	30–50	40–70
E. Transnational (Elimination of all national bias in decision-making except that legally imposed)	60–80	60–100	50–90	70–95

In part out of realization of this deficiency, the firm may move to type B, in which case authority for foreign market development is centralized in corporate headquarters within a foreign or export department. (An intermediate step may be the employment of an independent combination export managing firm; see Section 1.5.) Strategy determination follows. The ease with which this move may be made is very largely a function of the perceived relative profitability of the foreign business by top corporate management. That is, if profits derived on foreign sales are greater than average, the attention of the chief executive is attracted. The export or foreign department is likely to appear first as a staff office, but subsequently gains more and more line authority in respect to overseas activities, thereby causing friction with the operating divisions. Also, the foreign department may have difficulty in inducing the product divisions to fill export orders promptly or at all. Meanwhile, sooner or later top management will perceive that the optimum entry strategy in respect to one or more foreign markets is through licensing or direct investment, not exports. A decision-making process that is not functionally biased (biased in favor of exporting as against licensing or direct investment) requires individuals whose careers do not rest on a record of successful export and who have some knowledge of production as well as sales in the foreign context.

These sources of frictions, plus the need for line control over foreign operations by qualified people, push a firm to introduce a type C structure, the characteristic hallmark of which is the international division.

Ideally an international division[37] should be so organized and staffed as to facilitate a functionally and geographically bias-free search for the most profitable opportunities abroad (whether via exporting, importing, licensing, selling technical assistance or managerial services, making direct investments in manufacturing, joint-venturing, or providing debt capital). It should also have the capacity to recruit corporate resources to take advantage of perceived opportunities, to start up operations overseas, and to control overseas operations. In each function, specialized skills are required in such areas as negotiation, law, finance, marketing, personnel, accounting, R&D, and line management with manufacturing competence. Note that virtually all the *technical* skills required for establishing and maintaining a manufacturing facility are embedded in the domestic divisions, and embodied in people with little or no foreign experience and typically with an exaggerated notion as to the superiority of their own nationality, national business system, and technical competency.

As the foreign part of a firm's business achieves a significant percentage of the total, certain frictions are likely to develop within the firm. The international division may find it difficult to attract competent operating personnel from the domestic manufacturing divisions, to induce corporate staff departments to develop the relevant expertness and interest (say, in legal and financial matters), or to stimulate R&D in reference to product and processes so as to be more responsive to differing market environments. The domestic divisions may assign their least competent, most expendable personnel to overseas projects. If a division manager is being evaluated on his profit and loss, why should he do otherwise unless participation in the overseas project somehow contributes to division profit?

This last consideration has on occasion induced a system of interdepartmental administrative credit memos. The international division negotiates with a domestic division for certain technical assistance and personnel, say, for plant construction, start-up, and training of foreign personnel. For such assistance, the domestic division might be awarded a contract (for example, with a minimum fee plus a percentage of the gross sales of the foreign activity and/or a participation in net earnings). But, over time, such a system can create an onerous and costly internal accounting problem, and profit expectations may not be realized (indeed, a particular operation may not be seen as

---

[37]Whether an international division is set up as a domestic incorporated subsidiary is irrelevant to our discussion unless one assumes that managers are fooled by a "legal illusion," so that the "international corporation" somehow has greater prestige and, hence, command over corporate resources. Somehow, setting up a separate corporation seems to insulate what is initially a relatively weak division from the internal politics of the corporation. It may be given its own capital and be permitted to reinvest earnings without referral to the corporate investment center. As an IBM executive observed, separate corporate identity gives greater autonomy, facilitates overseas expansion, and provides a better arm's-length relationship. Technically, all of this could be achieved, of course, with a division set-up.

a profit center at all later on). In any event, the R&D and staff problems remain, as well as those inherent in the ethnocentric attitude of many of the managers and technicians. The result is that there is a demonstrable tendency for an international division eventually to start building up its own staff. It can do so more easily, of course, if it is physically separated from corporate headquarters, which in fact is often the case for U.S. corporations headquartered outside of New York City in that international divisions are often located in the city.

The type C structure, thus, tends to create divided loyalties (international versus domestic) and to isolate virtually all interest and expertness in foreign operations within the international division. Even in the formation of the international division, those with special knowledge or interest in international business were probably pulled out of corporate headquarters and the operating divisions. The upshot is that overseas projects are likely not to be given the same attention as comparable domestic projects by the corporate staff or on the strategy decision-making level. And risk attached to overseas projects tends to be exaggerated. All of these problems are compounded if the international division is located physically apart from corporate headquarters. The influence of the internationally oriented managers on the rest of the firm may thus be reduced as their division becomes isolated and physically removed from corporate headquarters.

Characteristically, a type C firm (international) initially tends to expand its overseas operations rapidly. If the international division is relatively isolated from corporate headquarters, and if it is perceived by top management as a distinct organization, a discontinuity in decision making may appear, which facilitates this rapid growth. A certain capital budget may be established for the division, which means that so long as it does not attempt to capture *more* corporate resources, decisions relative to overseas expansion can be made very largely on the division level. And for a time, there may be an understanding that the division earnings can be retained for investment. Given this new willingness to commit resources through a wider band of strategies to develop important overseas markets, the firm is very likely to enjoy a sudden spurt in overseas business. This pressure for expansion, plus division management's desire to prove itself (but a desire restrained by a lack of foreign environmental expertness in the division) may well lead to a willingness to enter into joint ventures and contractual arrangements.[38] At this point, there is little awareness of the possible advantages to setting up integrated production and marketing systems regionally or globally. Indeed, the company has usually not developed foreign markets sufficiently at this point so as to make integration across

---

[38] It has been suggested that the relatively high propensity for joint venturing on the part of Japanese firms is due at least in part to the fact that relatively more Japanese firms investing abroad are *new* international corporations than is true of the U.S. case.

borders an attractive proposition. Hence, there is little pressure for centralized control except over purely technical and financial matters.

However, as the system builds, as market penetration goes deeper, and as foreign environmental expertise builds up in division headquarters (that is, control capability), control over production and marketing is very likely to become more centralized. A corollary is that an increasing number of U.S. nationals are dispatched abroad to manage foreign manufacturing and marketing subsidiaries. And an effort begins to buy up the local equity held in the corporation's far-flung enterprises, so that the newly centralized control can be exercised with less resistance. The advantages in exercising some flexibility in transfer pricing become apparent, which provides further reason to avoid joint venturing wherever possible. (The movement of profit by means other than dividends is awkward if one has minority partners.) We now have what might be dubbed "the mature international corporation," one that is ripe for evolution into the multinational phase. But until that move is made, a distinction remains. Decisions relating to the allocation of corporate resources overseas continue to be made largely in the international division. If it wants to grow at a rate faster than retained earnings permit, the division faces a challenge from internal corporate politics. Its demand for a greater allocation of the corporate pie is likely to face the opposition of equally ambitious domestic division managers, who probably outscore the international division management in terms of numbers and seniority within the corporation.

In a study of 12 major Japanese companies, Kobayashi described Japanese corporate decision-making processes relative to the commitment of assets to overseas markets. Despite the previously-described unique features of Japanese management, Kobayashi's 12 corporations can be classified according to the scheme offered here. In fact, in his concluding remarks, he observes:

Systems for decision-making in connection with overseas investments vary from one company to another, depending upon (1) the kind of industry or business in which one engages, (2) the size of the business activities, (3) the degree of commitment to overseas activities and also (4) the degree of diversification . . . (in product) lines. However, in my survey, I have found that among the companies [which] . . . made a start [in] . . . overseas activities earlier than others, there gradually emerge organizations which are almost identical, at least in form, to the Western version of the International Division system. [39]

But of possible significance, only one of the 12 had apparently moved beyond the international phase by melting the functions of the international division into the rest of the corporation, thereby transforming itself into a true multinational. Kobayashi also emphasized the "culture unfamiliarity and information gap" on the part of the managements he studied. [40]

---

[39]Noritake Kobayashi, "Decision Making for Direct Foreign Investments by Japanese Companies," unpublished typed manuscript, 1976, p. 41.

[40]Kobayashi, "Decision Making," p. 32.

The international division is possibly optimum if (1) sales outside the United States remain a small part of the total corporate sales (and are significantly less than sales of one of the larger domestic divisions), (2) the firm has activities in a very limited number of countries, (3) there are few internationally experienced executives within the firm, (4) the firm has few product lines, or (5) the products are of such a nature that the environmental influences on sales and production strategy vary little if at all from one national market to another. The last is likely to be more true of capital-intensive, technologically complex products sold to a sophisticated market.

But if any of these conditions fails to be satisfied, pressures are very likely to develop within the firm pushing it toward the multinational form or type D structure.[41] And, over time, as foreign markets continue to grow, one or more of these conditions will, in most cases, fail to be satisfied. The level of foreign sales, which is roughly equal to those of one of the larger domestic divisions, may be the critical level psychologically in bringing about a change in corporate structure. It will then be perceived by top corporate management that the international division lacks the leverage within the corporation to sell overseas projects and to recruit adequate corporate resources to service the expanding foreign market opportunities.

As one U.S. executive observed:

We [UNIVAC Division, Sperry-Rand International Corporation] abolished the international division because it was quickly apparent that it was a Parkinson's Law appendage which jealously guarded its authority and prerogative—thus very effectively shielding the international operations from all good ideas in the domestic group.[42]

Another U.S. executive made somewhat the same point when he said:

While undue influence from the domestic organization is to be avoided, so should the international organization refrain from becoming too exclusive or remote and beyond the comprehension of the other management personnel. There is a considerable tendency on the part of international executives to guard closely the activities of their divisions or operations. In doing so, they divorce themselves from the rest of the organization. Cooperation between domestic and international divisions becomes more difficult and any desire on the part of domestic personnel to become more familiar with the international operations gradually dies.[43]

Still another: "If we split the company strictly between foreign and domestic

---

[41]Note that the definition of multinational used here differs from the common use of the word, which is to designate a firm with foreign manufacturing operations. The definition used in the Harvard Business School multinational corporation research project was those corporations among *Fortune's* 1967 list of the 500 largest U.S. firms (those with receipts in excess of $100 million) that had manufacturing subsidiaries in six or more countries, or had, at one time, such subsidiaries being at least 25 percent owned. Obviously, some international corporations were included since 82 of the 187 corporations satisfying the Harvard definition were operating overseas through international divisions. Raymond Vernon, *Sovereignty at Bay, the Multinational Spread of U.S. Enterprise* (New York: Basic Books, 1971), pp. 11 and 128.

[42]Gordon Smith (vice-president, UNIVAC Division, Sperry-Rand), "How Sperry-Rand Increased Revenues in Europe by 63%," *International Management*, September 1964, p. 41.

[43]Richard J. DoBettis (assistant to the president, Eriez Manufacturing), "The International Division—Growth Patterns Vary," *International Trade Review*, March 1964, p. 12.

business, we would have ended up with two general staffs. And if people grew up in only one area of the company, we would have lost the advantage of being able to interchange them freely."[44] The disappearance of the international division continues on the part of the more mature international firms. The Harvard study of 187 "multinational" corporations revealed that "57 of the 72 enterprises that adopted [an international division] at some point in their development had given it up by 1968."[45]

But not everyone agrees. Professor Schollhammer reports, on the basis of a study of 12 large chemical pharmaceutical companies (two French, three German, two Swiss, two English, three U.S.), that he could find no evidence that the firms had changed their respective structures or intended to do so. He concluded, "The experience of the 12 companies refutes the idea that with an increasing magnitude of the international business activities a firm would shift its organizational structure from a domestic orientation to an international division approach, and, finally, to a global approach."[46] The problem may be that Schollhammer's time span was too short. Also, the experience of 12 firms in one industry hardly constitutes a general refutation. It may be, however, that there are at least two intervening variables of significance between a firm's perception that its market is internationalizing and its structural response, specifically, the levels of the technologies and cultures involved. If one is dealing with a relatively static technology in relatively advanced societies, the firm may drop the international division structure more slowly in favor of some form of global management than if it were involved with a more dynamic technology in less developed countries. In the latter case, an international division would probably be unable to compete effectively for corporate skills in exploiting the rapidly changing technology internationally, nor would it be able to exert sufficient pressure to effect environmentally inspired product and process changes.

In any event, the ease with which the transformation from international to multinational can be made obviously varies enormously, and is a relevant variable. Great size, a prior domestic *regional* organization, a strong corporate headquarters, and personal interest and expertness in key places obviously facilitate matters greatly.[47]

In the case of the regionally-organized multinational, a useful bit of research would be the identification of the location of the regional headquarters of firms, the reasons for the choice, and the magnitude of the benefits flowing to the host country. One knows that Brussels is a common choice for the Euro-

[44]William Blackie (president of Caterpillar Tractor), in "CAT Bounds Ahead in Foreign Markets," *International Management*, October 1966, p. 59.

[45]Vernon, *Sovereignty at Bay*, p. 126.

[46]Hans Schollhammer. "Organization Structures of Multinational Corporations," *Academy of Management Journal*, September 1971, p. 345.

[47]For a classic case of this evolutionary process, see R. D. Robinson. *Cases in International Business* (New York: Holt, Rinehart and Winston, 1962), p. 7. See also Cedric L. Suzman, "Whatever Happened to the Export Manager?" *Worldwide P&I Planning*, November-December 1968, pp. 16 ff.

pean headquarters of U.S.-based multinationals, in part because of the need to interface with the EEC bureaucracy. We also know that many U.S. multinationals have located their Latin American headquarters in Coral Gables, Florida, in part because of the ease of communicating with Central and South America from that point. Also, one suspects that as a group of corporate regional headquarters becomes situated in a particular site, for whatever reason, others are attracted. And, of course, the greater the number, the more pressure can be exerted on telecommunications and airline companies to improve services. Elsewhere the pattern is not so recognizable. In Southeast Asia, a number of countries are competing for corporate regional headquarters by offering relief from certain taxes and work permit requirements for foreign personnel. The Philippines and Malaysia have offered special facilities. In France, there is a special official at the Finance Ministry charged with welcoming foreign headquarters. Materials promoting the selection of France as the site for European regional headquarters have been circulated, and residence permits for headquarters' employees have been expedited.

Business International has reported that some MNCs have recently (1976) moved their regional executives into corporate headquarters. The reasons given: need to improve communication between regional staff and upper corporate management at headquarters, the realization that technically intraregional communication is no better than between the United States and the region (telex, telephone), and reduced cost. It was estimated that a company might realize a 30 to 50 percent saving by having regional executives in the United States.[48] One cannot help but speculate that the physical presence of foreign regional management in the U.S. headquarters will facilitate the upward mobility of foreign managers into top corporate management, thereby facilitating the transformation into a transnational.

As was the case of the international corporation before it, the multinational corporation has built into it the seeds its own destruction. It is not in stable equilibrium either with itself or with the environment. Point one: although corporate personnel are given multinational responsibilities, characteristically many have had little international experience and no relevant technical-professional training. Point two: being members of a corporate headquarters peopled almost entirely with fellow nationals, the executives with new global responsibilities possess a set of values and a world perception that is very likely to bias their decision making. Although they may possess a *willingness* to allocate corporate resources optimally on a global basis, in fact, they are *psychologically* and *legally* incapable of doing so. Point three: given the nonavailability of headquarters personnel equipped to operate effectively overseas, and the lower cost of employing *local* national managers abroad rather than home country expatriates, plus the rapid rate of expansion often characteristic of the multina-

---

[48] *Business International*, July 30, 1976, p. 247.

tional stage, the firm employs largely local nationals to manage its new foreign facilities. It may also continue to enter into a number of joint ventures, which are often legally required in the LDCs. Hence, it may lack the capacity to maintain really effective central control. It depends upon how "mature" the international divisions had become prior to the transformation into a multinational.

Although perhaps initially inclined for these reasons to permit substantial autonomy to their associated foreign firms, the multinationals, as they mature and gain international experience at the center eventually begin to accelerate the centralization process. The benefits to be derived from integrating the worldwide movement of corporate resources become increasingly apparent as the contribution to corporate profits from overseas activity mounts and as the skill to effect such integration appears in corporate headquarters. They then begin to try to capture control at the center and to buy up whatever partially owned affiliates remain.

Louis Wells has demonstrated that a firm's propensity to enter joint ventures seems to lessen as its products become more mature (that is, as its technology becomes static), particularly if the firm pursues the strategy of devoting resources to marketing techniques to create product differentiation or a strategy of allocating resources to R&D in order to generate new products to serve *traditional* needs and customers. On the contrary, a firm seems to demonstrate a somewhat lower joint venture entry ratio if it pursues a strategy of allocating resources to R&D for generating products diversified as to function and customers or a strategy of retaining control over raw material sources. His research also suggests that relatively small firms and late entrants to foreign markets have a greater propensity to enter joint ventures than larger firms and earlier entrants.[49] These findings tend to support the evolutionary model developed here.

In any event, the capture of control at corporate headquarters is very likely to generate powerful internal conflicts. On the one hand, we have competent and now experienced, local national managers moving upward toward their respective national subsidiary ceilings in terms of promotion. On the other hand is the fact of increasingly centralized control within the multinational corporate headquarters. The local manager may respond by pushing for greater autonomy of his own operation, which is often signaled by a breakdown in communication between subsidiary and headquarters, an exaggerated importance given to environmental factors in decision making, and continued inability of the firm to maintain effective control. Or, the local manager may leave the employ of the firm. Host governments tend to support the local manager's

[49]John M. Stopford and Louis T. Wells, Jr., *Managing the Multinational Enterprise: Organization of the Firm and Ownership* (New York: Basic Books, 1972). See also Lawrence Franko, "Strategy Choice and Multinational Corporate Tolerance for Joint Ventures with Foreign Partners" (Boston: Harvard Graduate School of Business Administration, unpublished D.B.A. diss., 1969).

desire for greater autonomy, for the increased external control over the allocation of domestic resources sooner or later becomes politically unacceptable.[50]
The environmental factor thus, in fact, becomes blown up; so likewise, the loss
of key manpower.

*The mergers in Western Europe—often triggered off by the impact of the Americans—
have been accompanied by an obsessive interest in managerial education, corporate
reorganization, and the activities of management consultants. These efforts have often
appeared faintly laughable, or even sinister to Europeans. But they have helped to make
European-owned industry more competitive, and they have been reinforced by the extremely valuable training ground provided by the American-owned companies in
Europe. There is a constant drain from these concerns of able men fretting at the strict
controls under which they have to operate and the knowledge that, in most American-
owned companies, they cannot rise above the management of the subsidiary of their own
country. And no European company now feels secure without its quota of men trained
by Ford or Proctor & Gamble.[51]*

Eventually, the multinational headquarters perceives the cost inherent in the
communications breakdown, loss of control, mounting political pressures, and
possible loss of key foreign managerial personnel. As it does so, nationality
barriers are removed, and foreign nationals are likely to begin appearing in
responsible managerial spots outside their respective national subsidiaries, first
in regional headquarters if there are such, then in corporate headquarters
itself.[52] This is where the model begins to diverge from the Japanese, because
it is almost inconceivable that non-Japanese managers could work effectively
at high levels within the corporate headquarters of a Japanese corporation,
particularly when one considers the system of permanent employment and
relatively permanent work groups still characteristic of large Japanese
corporations. How can the non-Japanese manager be thrust into such a
situation horizontally and be expected to relate effectively? Commenting
somewhat along the same line, Tecoz (Chairman of the Investment Bank of
Zurich) observed:

European corporations have long ago understood the importance and efficiency of

---

[50]An example is the move in June 1972 by the Province of Ontario to require that all companies incorporated
in Ontario must have Canadian directors by October 1, 1973, and hold most of their board meetings in Canada
with Canadian directors the majority at every meeting. The measure is explicitly designed to stem U.S. control
of Ontario plants.

[51]Nicholas Faith, *The Infiltrators, the European Business Invasion of America* (New York: E. P. Dutton & Co.,
1972), p. 35.

[52]A number of non-U.S. nationals are now showing up in top executive positions within U.S. corporate
headquarters. Unfortunately, this critical subject has not been adequately researched, so one can project no
figures. A study based on 1965 data reported less than 1 percent of the executives in 150 New York-based
internationally active firms were non-U.S. nationals. (Kenneth Simmonds, "Multinational? Well Not Quite,"
Columbia Journal of World Business, Fall 1966, pp. 115–22.) The situation may have changed significantly
since then, particularly in regard to European headquarters personnel. Also, U.S. entry barriers have been
relaxed. (See Section 4.1.) It may be revealing that a survey of 1,029 directors conducted in the course of the
Harvard study of multinational corporations turned up 19 foreigners, of whom 14 were either Canadian or
British (Vernon, *Sovereignty at Bay*, p. 146), but that was some years ago.

having on their boards nationals of the countries where they export, or manufacture for that matter.

U.S. companies were completely closed to non-U.S. board members until some years ago, but they now have begun to open up.

But Japanese corporations seem to stay very reluctant [to participate] in that evolution.[53]

Returning to our non-Japanese model, one should note that several forces combine over time to multinationalize the *ownership* of the multinational corporation. Among these for the U.S.-based multinational are the attraction of swapping U.S. parent company stock for foreign assets, the foreign sale of debentures convertible to parent company stock, and the listing of parent company stock on foreign stock exchanges. For the European-based multinationals, the relatively small size of the local capital market pushes in the direction of multinational ownership, including the appeal of cross-border mergers and/or repeated joint venturing among multinationals. In fact, as already noted (Figures 8.5a and 8.5b), a number of European transnationals have appeared. In addition, there have been several thousand common undertakings by European firms of different nationalities,[54] which, over time, look very much like transnational enterprises. One also suspects that repeated participation in transnational ventures of a temporary nature (see Figure 8.6) could lead to more permanent association.

Both in the more and less developed countries one may be compelled to recognize host society demands—often translated into political pressures—for a share in the profit derived from its market. It is even conceivable that an LDC government, rather than compelling the spinoff of ownership in the local subsidiary, might opt to trade MNC access to local market and resources in return for *parent* company stock of equivalent value, plus some sort of representation at the top level of the corporation. Although not yet actually proposed, the idea has been discussed among some LDC decision-makers.

The degree to which ownership has been in fact multinationalized is another inadequately researched subject for which we have no empirically based trend line. The Harvard multinational corporate study found, "The stock ownership of U.S.-controlled multinational enterprises is overwhelmingly in the hands of U.S. nationals. Only a very few of the outstanding shares of the parent firm— something in the order of 2 or 3 percent—are owned by foreigners."[55] Some have speculated, however, that the many billions of dollars in the hands of foreign central banks might constitute a pressure on these governments to

---

[53]*The Japan Economic Journal*, vol. 12, no. 583, February 26, 1974, p. 4.

[54]Christopher Tugendhat, *The Multinationals* (New York: Random House, 1972), p. 78.

[55]Vernon, *Sovereignty at Bay*, p. 145. One problem is, of course, the definition of multinational. (See p. 666, n. 41.) Also, there is considerable difficulty in tracing ownership. Finally, the Harvard data are perhaps ten years out of date.

induce American-owned subsidiaries to sell a substantial part of their common stock to host country residents. It was reported by early 1972 that one central bank had already committed $100 million for the purchase of U.S. common stocks.[56] As of the end of 1975, foreigners owned $26.7 billion in U.S. corporate stocks and $9.8 billion in U.S. corporate bonds. In any case, substantial local ownership of foreign subsidiaries may induce such a conflict of interest as to push the mature multinational firm to swap its own stock for the local equity in its associated overseas enterprises.

Many firms are undoubtedly now in this transitional state between the multinational firm and the truly transnational firm. The latter is simply a corporation that has lost its national identity except insofar as legal restraints may impact upon its decisions and operations. It is owned and managed by the nationals of more than one country. It is possibly true that in the long run a necessary, if not sufficient, condition for maximum corporate growth is multinational ownership and management at all levels. Thus, the transnational corporations may grow more rapidly than the multinational.

Likewise supporting this line of argument is the possibility that in the transnational case technology would move more easily; there would be a reduced fear of losing *national* control. Also, the R&D effort of a truly transnational firm would possibly be less culturally biased; there should be a greater readiness to address R&D directly to the problems suggested within specific markets.

Transnationals with annual gross sales of upward of $50 billion may soon not be uncommon. It has been predicted that there will be some 300 such corporations by 1985 controlling a very large part of the fixed industrial assets of the free world.[57] But, in fact, will they? Their sheer size, and absence of all national loyalty inherent in their multinational ownership and management, may bring such corporations onto a collision course with the nation-state. Indeed, there is considerable evidence that even though governments may be promoting or permitting *national* mergers and industrial concentrations, increasingly they are resisting mergers and arrangements among the giant multinationals and transnationals. As noted elsewhere, it is U.S. antitrust policy to prevent mergers, wherever they take place or whatever the nationality of the merging companies, if the effect of the merger would be to reduce competition significantly within the United States or within the foreign trade of the United States. The European community seems to be setting precedent barring the further acquisition of important national companies by large multinationals or transnationals. The Japanese have been restrictive in this regard for some time, and one sees no reason that they should shift direction. But to achieve effective political control of such giant multinational and transnational firms requires new international institutions, particularly in

---

[56]Alan Greenspan. *New York Times*, 13 March 1972, p. 53.

[57]Howard Perlmutter, "Geocentric Giants to Rule Business World," *Business Abroad*, April 1969, p. 9.

regard to the *dedomiciled* multinationals and transnationals because of their greater growth potential and absence of national loyalty or bias. No national government, or even an international regional agency such as the EEC, can claim the right to determine the law under which a multinationally owned and multinationally managed corporation, with resources strewn around the world, should operate. This rationale will be particularly relevant to corporations operating beyond the reach of any national sovereignty—the deep ocean bed, arctic regions, space, and icebergs. In the final analysis what one faces is the management of global resources.

Therefore, the next stage in the evolutionary process may be the appearance of the supranational firm. Such entities must necessarily rest on special inter-governmental agreements or treaties, which in each case provide the legal basis for a governing body. One can expect two further near-term developments: (1) the emergence of a European corporation chartered and controlled—if not taxed—under an EEC law and (2) the appearance of an international seabed authority which would charter, control, and possibly tax corporations operating on the bed of the deep sea. Various proposals have been made for a *general* international convention, under which some sort of commission would be created for the chartering, controlling, and taxing of corporations satisfying certain conditions in respect to multinationality of ownership and management, but this seems far off.

It would appear that during the past 20 years or so the real value of world-wide sales of the large corporations has been increasing about 10 percent a year, while the real GNP of the nation-states has been growing at the most by 5 percent. It has been pointed out that if one assumes a 20 percent growth rate for a firm with present sales (1970) of a billion dollars, and a 6 percent world growth rate, by the year 2035 the firm's sales would exceed the world's GNP![58] For the large firms, continued rapid growth is obviously a short-run phenomenon. And, once the limit has been reached, then it will not be the large firms that will be growing, but the smaller ones. It is entirely possible that many of the super-firms of the near future will break up because they will be unable to attract resources (particularly skilled people).

But in the meantime, the size of these multinationals and transnationals is likely to be viewed by nation-states as politically intolerable. The degree to which economic power may become concentrated in the hands of decision-makers virtually unreachable by any government could render it impossible for any single nation-states, or even regional groupings, to regulate these firms. The common interest of nation-states almost compels them to participate in an effort to harmonize national policy in regard to antitrust, taxation, corporate law, and restraint on resource allocation.

The common interest becomes irresistibly compelling if one adds the

---

[58]Richard N. Farmer, "Where Does Business Go from Here?" *Economic and Business Bulletin*, Temple University, vol. 23, no. 1, Fall 1970, p. 24.

mounting pressure to internationalize political decision making as we approach the finite limits of our global environment. Obviously, the rate of resource usage, energy consumption, atmospheric and oceanic pollution can only be resolved on a global basis. Finally, there is no evidence leading one to believe that the giant multinational or transnational corporation will voluntarily incorporate any mechanism rendering it socially responsible other than through the market place, which even within the United States is perceived as inadequate in respect to the protection of consumer, investor, worker, and the general welfare. It would appear that either the nation-states in concert will dominate the giant multinationals and transnationals or the reverse will occur. Bear in mind that the former implies an international convention creating a body of basic law and a representative body with adequate resources to control these corporations. The international corporate law may specify, for example, that national shareholders will be represented in the corporate board by a government appointee approved by those shareholders. Given such a system of international law and control, the possibility of a truly supranational corporation appears.

If nations find it impossible to collaborate to this degree, they are very likely to act to restrain further transnational corporate growth, first by forbidding further mergers and acquisitions and, if this is seen as an inadequate impediment to further growth, then by expropriating local assets. Most vulnerable, of course, would be integrated plants in mature industries that serve primarily the local market and that belong to transnational corporations in which there is little or no local equity involvement.

Or, it may just be that the pattern apparently emerging in Japan and elsewhere for some of the reasons already suggested will prove so profitable that the large North American and Western European-based multinationals and transnationals will be induced to change their structure. What seems to be developing in Japan is the multinational *association*, more commonly known as the general trading company. (See Figure 8.8.) At the center is a Japanese-owned and managed corporation, which is linked internationally by a web of contractual relations with largely locally owned and managed associated firms. The center supplies capital-intensive, scarce resources, such as new technology (that is, research and development plus the training of local nationals), management and managerial training, international marketing services, purchase and sale contracts, debt capital, and possibly initial high-risk (entrepreneurial) equity that is later withdrawn. The associated, eventually largely locally owned and managed, firms produce. Such an association becomes transnational if the central corporation is owned by the associated foreign firms.

There are many pressures combining to push multinationals to evolve more in the direction of the international association than into transnationals. *First,* many managements are learning—in part through experience in East-West trade, which is necessarily limited to contract in most cases—that the sale or lease of capital-intensive inputs (particularly technology and high-level skills) can be very lucrative, more so than the return on direct investment. Not only may the rate of return on corporate assets committed be heightened, but the risk of costly adverse political acts may be significantly reduced. The corporation has few fixed assets in place subject to expropriation. In most cases, payment for services provided under contract parallels the delivery of those services. Hence, the corporation has greater flexibility; it can walk away from an unpleasant (costly) situation more easily than if it had fixed assets in place for which it hoped to earn a return through dividends spread over several years. *Second,* experience shows that most host countries under balance of payments pressure are inclined to make foreign exchange available for the payment of fees, royalties, imported goods, and interest before permitting the remittance of earnings in the form of dividends. The host country can easily perceive the *quid pro quo* in the sale or lease of a particular item or service for a specified price. It can see the value of that for which payment is made. Not so in the case of a dividend, particularly if the investment has been in place for any period of time. Increasingly, the host country may see those remittances as representing "unearned" foreign profit derived from the local market, local labor, locally available technology (transferred technology), and local capital (reinvested earnings). Under exchange pressure, dividends are invariably the first to suffer. *Third,* the contract route also permits a systematic periodic renegotiation as the benefit-cost ratios shift, which, for instance, would be signalled when another firm is prepared to provide comparable inputs at less cost. Increasingly are the LDCs unwilling to accept alien ownership of a local enterprise without a specific date for withdrawal of that ownership. Hence, even ownership is taking on the coloration of a contractual relationship. *Fourth,* in part for these reasons, plus the gathering worldwide movement toward public sector enterprises, profit-sharing enterprises, and management-sharing (employee participation) enterprises also suggest that this pattern may indeed be the wave of the future, that the multinational and transnational corporation as presently conceived will prove to be relatively short-lived transitional forms. The point is that the degree of international integration, hence centralized control, required for multinationals and transnationals may become unrealistic in view of mounting pressures for *local* control.[59]

Briefly, management of an integrated international *marketing* system may prove to be the most profitable and least risky form of international business. In fact, there is some evidence that it is the most rapidly growing. Although figures in this area are slippery, it would appear that the average growth of the

---

[59]Another point should be made. As trade liberalization moves forward, international economic integration accelerates. As this happens, the need to move national resources constantly into new sectors and uses requires state leadership and influence (if not control) over the flow of internal resources. Unless the state itself moves into production, such state intervention means ever closer government-business relations, including government-backed guarantee of continuous employment for displaced workers. One thus moves in the direction of the corporate state, which implies greater emphasis on public control and enforces pressure for *local* control courses.

multinationals and transnationals is in the 10 percent range, of the large general trading companies, 20 to 30 percent. A more refined monitoring of the rates of growth of various types of international business activity is needed as a guide to the future.

One is thus driven to the conclusion that either a mechanism is created for providing international political control over the giant transnational firms, which could constitute an important next step on the long road to effective world government, or the Japanese model of multinational associations is very likely to dominate. As these associations become transnational in nature, at which point the Japanese may find themselves at a disadvantage, the need for some form of international political control will again arise. Such control is also dictated by the environmental problem and the global resource allocation process such implies. So, following either route, the pressure of world business is likely one day to force the nation-states into a posture of cooperation thus far unknown.

It can be seen that we have been discussing the locale and structural-psychological restraints on decision making. To summarize:

1. In type A (domestic) firms, there is no particular interest or expertness engaged in searching for and developing foreign markets. Decision making is prejudiced against any commitment to overseas activity and is entirely responsive to external pressures, not to an internally generated search process.

2. In type B (foreign-oriented) firms, international interest and expertness are limited to a staff department and are restricted to searching for and developing *export markets only*, but decisions are made in the domestic divisions and domestically oriented staff departments, hence, such decisions are strongly *biased nationally*.

3. In type C (international) firms, interest and expertness are in an international division, but with functional expertness remaining in the domestic divisions and domestically oriented staff departments. Decisions are less biased in terms of the type of foreign market entry strategy that will be considered, but are still heavily biased nationally. Initially, the capacity to exercise centralized control over foreign operations is weak and the pressure to grow rapidly high. Hence, a joint venturing and contracting strategy may be adopted. But in time, pressure toward increased control and centralization emerge and key positions overseas are filled with home country nationals.

4. In type D (multinational) firms, international interest and expertise are located throughout the firm, but top corporate managers are still home country nationals and initially lack international experience and expertness. There is, nonetheless, an effort to make decisions less nationally biased, but an inability to effect a true centralization of control persists in headquarters, particularly if local equity participation continues to be permitted. As the firm grows locally, political pressures develop to compel greater local control and, hence, subsidiary autonomy. In the meantime, as the firm gathers more environmental expertise in headquarters and perceives more clearly the advantages of greater integration, it will attempt to reestablish central control over its foreign operations, including the buying-up of local equity. Conflict with host governments tends to increase.

5. In type E (transnational) firms, which are owned and managed multinationally, decision making is centralized but free of national bias except as legally imposed. The firm loses loyalty to a single nation, thereby putting it on a collision course with its parent government.

6. In type F (supranational) firms, management is free structurally, psychologically and legally to allocate resources on a global basis in conformance with corporate goals insofar as they do not conflict with the international political regime controlling the corporation.

The point is made that if a firm's foreign market is perceived as growing relative to the domestic, all of these types are unstable except the last. Pressures in the system either propel a firm to the next level or push it back. An alternative to the supranational corporation, if the legal basis fails to materialize, might be the multinational or transnational association. The center might or might not be owned and managed multinationally. But if it is, it is thereby differentiated from a multinational association and becomes transnational.

It will be noted that Perlmutter's three-type classification system, with some modification, identifies the characteristic behavior of the international, multinational, and *transitional* multinational firm. (See Table 8.4.) Its shortcoming is that it falls short of describing a dynamic system in that it does not specify the pressures pushing a firm from one orientation to another; nor does it go far enough. It fails to specify the distinctive orientation of the truly transnational and supranational firms. Neither does it refer to the interrelationship between orientation and structure, nor to the interrelationship between these two aspects and the priority of control centers.

Internal structure

As already noted, whatever the type of corporation, a division, a "group," or a "headquarters" may be identified with a product-line, a function (sales, production, finance), a region, a process (for example, exploration, refining, concentrating, smelting, shipping), or a class of customer (government or an industry). Coordination within a large organization may be necessary along more than one of these dimensions. For a firm expanding internationally a very real question is, which one of these linkages should be given priority and represent the primary chain-of-command line? Which are the staff lines? Or, different line authority may be delegated along different dimensions, which brings one to the subject of the matrix (or grid) organization. Forgetting the customer and process-based organizational structures (which are unusual), the possible combinations are shown in Figure 8.11. Figure 8.12 shows a two-dimensional matrix management.

In U.S.-based firms, one is more likely to find the product divisions in the vertical position; the functional, in the horizontal. The latter are most frequently called "coordinating committees" or "groups." European firms are more

Table 8.4
THREE TYPES OF HEADQUARTERS ORIENTATION TOWARD SUBSIDIARIES IN AN INTERNATIONAL ENTERPRISE— THE PERLMUTTER MODEL ADAPTED

Organization design	Ethnocentric (international)	Polycentric (multinational)	Geocentric (transitional multinational)
Complexity of organization	Complex in home country, simple in subsidiaries	Varied and independent	Increasingly complex and interdependent
Authority; decision-making	High in headquarters	Relatively low in headquarters	Aim for a collaborative approach between headquarters and subsidiaries
Evaluation and control	Home standards applied for persons and performance	Determined locally	Find standards that are universal and local
Rewards and punishments; incentives	High in headquarters, low in subsidiaries	Wide variation; can be high or low rewards for subsidiary performance	International and local executives rewarded for reaching local and worldwide objectives
Communication; information flow	High volume to subsidiaries of orders, commands, advice	Little to and from headquarters. Little between subsidiaries	Both ways and between subsidiaries. Heads of subsidiaries part of management team
Identification	Nationality of owner	Nationality of host country	Truly international company but identifying with national interests*
Perpetuation (recruiting, staffing, development)	Recruit and develop people of home country for key positions everywhere in the world	Develop people of local nationality for key positions in their own country	Develop best men everywhere in the world for key positions everywhere in the world

*If this term were to read "truly international company not identifying with the interest of any single nation except as legally imposed," then this column would describe the orientation of the true transnational firm.

Source: Adapted from Howard V. Perlmutter, "The Tortuous Evolution of the Multinational Corporation," *Columbia Journal of World Business,* January–February 1969, p. 12.

likely to give priority to the functional division or possibly to make both the product and functional divisions vertical.[60] The foreign trade organizations of

[60]See Andrew J. Lombard, "How European Companies Organize Their International Operations," *European Business,* July 1969, pp. 37–48. See also John S. Schwendiman, *Strategic and Long-Range Planning in the International Firm* (Cambridge: M.I.T., Alfred P. Sloan School of Management, 1971).

First Level	Product P		Area A		Function F	
Second Level	Function PF	Area PA	Function AF	Product AP	Product FP	Area FA
Third Level	Area PFA	Function PAF	Product AFP	Function APF	Area FPA	Product FAP

Figure 8.11
POSSIBLE TYPES OF MATRIX MANAGEMENT

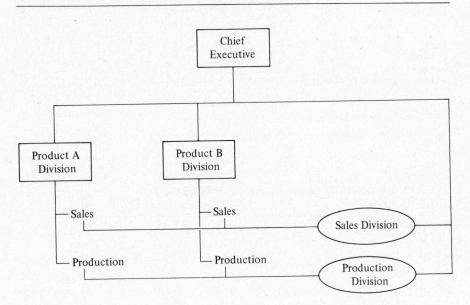

Figure 8.12
A TWO-DIMENSIONAL MATRIX MANAGEMENT OF THE PF TYPE

Soviet bloc countries are almost invariably organized on a product-line basis.

The three-dimensional matrix management can be diagrammed most easily as in Figure 8.13. We assume the APF variety, which is possibly the most common for the big U.S.-based multinationals. The Harvard "multinational" corporation study revealed that of the 72 corporations without an international division, 24 percent were organized regionally, 41 percent by product division, and 35 percent had a mixed structure. This last category included three enter-

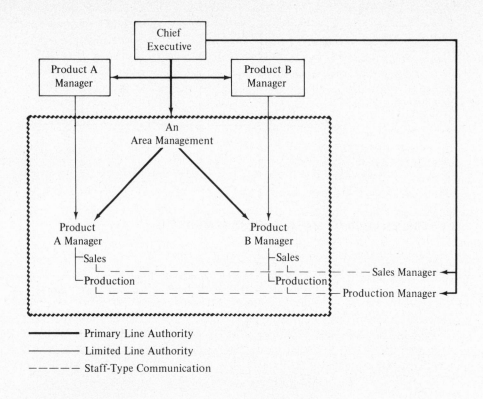

Figure 8.13
**A THREE-DIMENSIONAL MATRIX MANAGEMENT
OF THE APF TYPE**

prises "organized on the principle that every operating unit would report both to a product division and to an area division simultaneously [matrix management] and 22 organized partially on a product division and partially on an area division breakdown."[61]

The obvious next question is, under what circumstances should a firm with international operations opt for one form or another, say for a PAF, an APF, or an FAP? Which are apparently the most common? Key questions here have to do with specifying the most important similarities and dissimilarities. For example:

1. Is each differentiated *region* essentially homogeneous in respect to functions and products and significantly different from other regions along one or more important dimensions? If so, a regional structure is suggested.

---

[61]Vernon, *Sovereignty at Bay*, p. 128.

Probable firm characteristics:[62] Those with products or manufacturing processes significantly influenced by environmental factors (such as taste, law, factor mix, access, internal movement, politics, income, population size) that differ markedly from one definable region to another (definable in such terms as access and internal market integration, trade and investment impediments, homogeneity in taste and factor mix, relevant law, political pressures). Tends to be true generally for low-technology, mature, consumer-oriented products not closely related to one another and in respect to which political pressure for local control is likely to develop. Another probable characteristic is a substantial economy of scale in production (meaning that plants will be large and that intraregional sales of component parts and final products are significant). Large-scale interregional sales or resource transfers are unlikely because of the environmental influence.

2. Does each differentiated *product line* possess essentially the same characteristics insofar as function and region are concerned but remain significantly different from other product lines? If so, the product division approach is suggested.

Probable firm characteristics: Those with products or manufacturing processes relatively little influenced by environmental factors (a standard product using a single technology with little factor substitutability possible, as in parts of the chemical industry) or influenced by factors not differing *consistently* from one definable region to another. Tends to be true for firms with several relatively high technology, new, capital intensive products that are not closely related. (Hence, interdivisional transactions will be few, but movement of a given product among regions will be great. Also, servicing on a regional or global basis—rather than on a national one—is probably most economic.)

3. Is each differentiated function essentially similar for different products and geographical areas? If so, a functional structure is suggested.

Probable firm characteristics: Those with a single or a few closely related products manufactured in the same plants, sold through the same channels to the same customers regardless of geographical area. Thus, environmental factors are minimal in respect to both product and manufacturing process, but may impact significantly on function.

In a study of European-based multinationals, Lorange concluded, "It seems as if the greater the diversity among the product lines and the greater the rate of change of products in the line, the greater the pressure towards a geographically dominated structure."[63] He speculates that possibly such a structure is better able to cope with production scheduling problems and those associated with the frequent introduction of new products. In contrast, Stopford, in a study of 170 companies out of *Fortune's* list of 500, concluded that worldwide

---

[62]The term "probable" is used here for, insofar as can be ascertained, this subject has not been researched in any systematic way. The Harvard study of the "multinational" corporation did find that the enterprise characteristic most closely linked with the choice between a regional or product-based organization was the "width of its product line": the broader the line, the more likely the firm is to be organized on a product basis. (Vernon, *Sovereignty at Bay*, p. 127.)

[63]Peter Lorange. "Formal Planning Systems: Design Considerations for Multinationals," unpublished typed manuscript, December 1973, p. 16.

product divisions were characteristic of companies with a relatively high percentage of sales outside the major product line; area divisions, of companies with a relatively low percentage of sales outside the major product line.[64]

From a number of observations, it is quite clear that some U.S.-based multinationals are now following the European model in that they "have abandoned the notion that concentration on one variable should dominate the organization."[65] Characteristically, according to the Stopford and Wells study, U.S. firms opting for a true matrix type organization (that is, equality of variables) use product and geographical area. This is in contrast to the product and functional matrix structure characteristic of at least some European multinationals. Understandably, firms have been moving slowly in relinquishing the time honored notion of unity of command in favor of shared responsibility. But there are many pressures that may push a management in this direction. Some of the pressure sources are: (1) different product lines may share common facilities in smaller national markets, but not in others; (2) in different regions similar problems appear, which are related in that what happens in country A (both politically and managerially) may serve as a model to country B (three obvious examples: investment entry contracts, labor negotiations, a firm's political involvement); and (3) functions may vary widely from product to product in some countries, not at all in others. As a firm develops a full matrix management, the demands on the individual manager increase. He must now respond to different reporting requirements and act more as an integrator. Even greater training, maturity, and experience are possibly required.

Host-government pressures tend to push a corporation with multiple entities within a country to establish a national management for purposes of interfacing with the government. If such a headquarters is not in place, the government may face a number of relatively small enterprises; it has no ready way of communicating effectively with corporate headquarters. Recent research in Canada indicates that U.S. conglomerates with multiple and unrelated operations in Canada tend to be less sensitive to Canadian national interests.[66] Figure 8.14 portrays a viable solution. In fact, it is now clear that at least some governments will hold all of the local subsidiaries of a single foreign parent collectively responsible for liabilities of any one of them.

A similar situation arises whenever two or more countries enter into a continuing economic or political relationship such as a free trade area or common market. For a variety of reasons it may be highly desirable to have a regional headquarters to interface with the new regional institutions as

---

[64]Stopford and Wells, *Managing the Multinational.*
[65]Stopford and Wells, *Managing the Multinational*, p. 32.
[66]Litvak, Maule, and Robinson, *Dual Loyalty.*

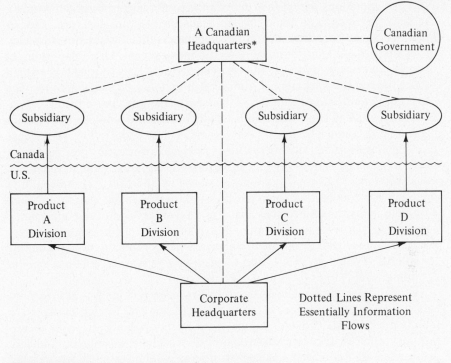

Figure 8.14
THE NATIONAL HEADQUARTERS CONCEPT

*Is not necessarily an incorporated operating entity.

lobbyist, negotiator, and as transmitter of information to corporate headquarters. It may also become virtually mandatory that the firm rationalize production and other functions on a regional basis to take advantage of special regional arrangements such as specialization agreements (in the Central American Common Market), complimentarity agreements (in the Latin American Free Trade Area), special financial institutions whose resources are available only to regionally oriented projects, and intraregional tariffs and other concessions.

It is all very well to speak of "decision-making authority," but in fact to what decisions does one refer? A comprehensive control strategy calls for distinguishing the level and the location on that level of each set of strategy alternatives discussed in the preceding chapters.

For example, at what level is policy in regard to management remuneration (Section 4.3) to be set and where on that level? If the firm were of type A, and each division were free to select its own policy in this regard, the level of strategy decision would be the domestic division—but where in that division?

If foreign operations were placed under an export or international department, the department director might, in fact, make the relevant decisions. Bear in mind that at the same time a corporate personnel officer may set down policy in regard to the remuneration of domestic management. Discordant policies between domestic and foreign and between divisions may thus emerge, which render the transfer of personnel from foreign to domestic assignment (or vice versa) or interdivisional transfer of overseas personnel very difficult.

Ideally, strategy choices should be made for both the foreign and domestic markets at the same level by officers working in close cooperation. The relegation of policy decisions relating to foreign markets to domestic divisions is very likely to generate serious conflict in virtually every area, from substance of sales (Section 1.1) to choice of legal relationships (Section 7.2). Indeed, it is precisely this conflict that generates pressure toward a type B structure once corporate management becomes aware of the conflict and of the importance of resolving it in order to effect an optimum allocation of corporate resources. An international staff department emerges, which eventually becomes an international division (type C), due to previously discussed conflicts on the operating level.

In the truly internationally oriented firm, management tends to realize more clearly that strategy choices between the domestic and foreign markets are closely interrelated. The international division set-up, however, tends to isolate such choices. In a type D structure, each regional headquarters ideally possesses a staff competent to deal with strategy choices left open to it by corporate headquarters. For example, the latter may well set strategy in relation to source of product (Section 1.9), intracompany competition (Section 1.10), and intercompany competition (Section 1.11), and leave other decisions in the sales strategy set to regional headquarters. In turn, the latter may leave choice of channels within a foreign market (Section 1.6) to the national operating subsidiaries or branches concerned. The type D structure probably facilitates this type of delegation, but the system is only feasible if the regional headquarters, one or more of which deal with the domestic market, handle a volume of business large enough to justify hiring comparable staff experts.

Corporate planning

But in all of these cases, optimum decision making is unlikely unless corporate goals have been spelled out and communicated, and a continuing planning process institutionalized so as to make the goals operational.

Corporate planning has been defined as follows:

Corporate planning is the process of developing objectives for the corporation and its subparts as well as developing and evaluating alternative courses of action to reach these objectives; doing this on the basis of a systematic evaluation of external threats and opportunities and internal audits of strengths and weaknesses.[67]

In contrast, Steiner suggested a planning typology:

1. *Strategic planning.* Conducted by the highest levels of management and concerned with the development of fundamental goals and the major policies for deployment of corporate resources to meet those goals.

2. *Intermediate- or long-range planning.* Takes the overall strategies and defines action programs and steps for the accomplishment of the strategic objectives over a relevant (four to five year, perhaps longer) time period.

3. *Tactical planning.* The programming of activities through one or two year or shorter time period budgets.

4. *Planning studies.* Initiated at the request of top management to provide background for strategic and long-range planning.[68]

On the basis of in-depth study of European and U.S. corporate strategic and long-range planning, the 1971 Schwendiman study[69] reached several significant conclusions. Using Figure 8.15 as the baseline, Schwendiman concluded that only about half of the companies investigated,[70] both in Europe and the United States, even began to come close to the overall planning ideal suggested in that figure. Extension of planning to cover overseas activities, Schwendiman found, was relatively new. A weak point in all of the firms was environmental analysis.

Headquarters' capability and proficiency was poor in analyzing political, economic, and social factors around the world. This arose, I suspect, because of a feeling that a continuing headquarters environmental assessment was really not needed with people "on the spot." But what if a venture is proposed for an area with no one "on the spot"? A common answer: an outside consultant or in-company task force was assigned to investigate the environment. However, these are "one-shot" approaches; follow-up is difficult. Even in companies with decentralized operations, top management should have some basis for evaluating proposals rather than relying completely on analysis from "on the spot company people" who may have prejudices or a distorted perspective.[71]

Schwendiman also reported that many companies seemed to lack an in-depth analysis of internal strengths and weaknesses as compared with their competitors. He suggests the possibility "that organizations as well as individu-

---

[67]K. A. Ringbakk, "Organized Corporate Planning Systems: An Empirical Study of Planning Practices and Experiences in American Big Business," unpublished Ph.D. diss., University of Wisconsin, 1968, p. 31.

[68]Adapted from George A. Steiner and Warren M. Cannon, *Multinational Corporate Planning* (New York: Crowell-Collier and MacMillan, 1966), pp. 11–16, by John S. Schwendiman, *Strategic and Long-Range Planning in the International Firm*, p. 19.

[69]John S. Schwendiman, summarized in "International Strategic Planning: Still in Its Infancy?" *Worldwide P&I Planning*, September-October 1971, pp. 52–61.

[70]Twenty-five large internationals and multinationals—10 European-based, 12 U.S.-based—in three industries, the automative, electrical equipment, and chemical.

[71]John S. Schwendiman, "International Strategic Planning," pp. 53–54.

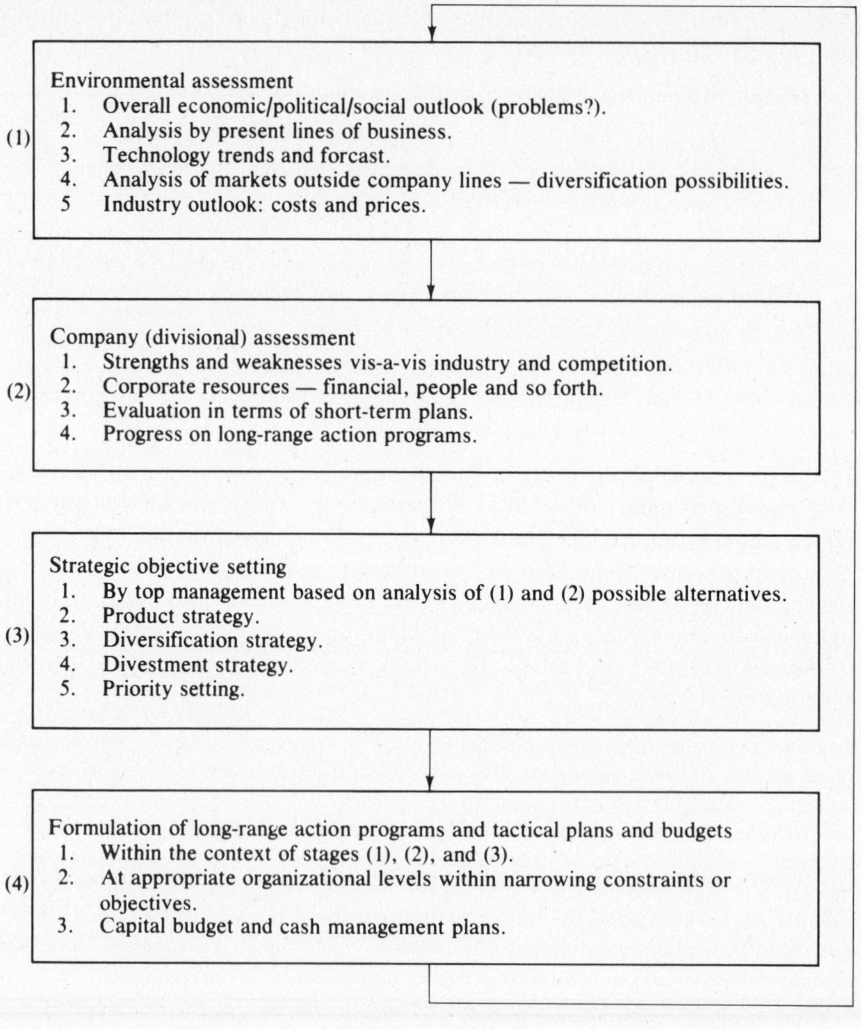

```
┌──────────────────────────────────────────────────────────────┐
│      Environmental assessment                                  │
│      1.  Overall economic/political/social outlook (problems?).│
│ (1)  2.  Analysis by present lines of business.                │
│      3.  Technology trends and forcast.                        │
│      4.  Analysis of markets outside company lines — diversifi-│
│          cation possibilities.                                 │
│      5   Industry outlook: costs and prices.                   │
└──────────────────────────────────────────────────────────────┘

┌──────────────────────────────────────────────────────────────┐
│      Company (divisional) assessment                           │
│      1.  Strengths and weaknesses vis-a-vis industry and com-  │
│          petition.                                             │
│ (2)  2.  Corporate resources — financial, people and so forth. │
│      3.  Evaluation in terms of short-term plans.              │
│      4.  Progress on long-range action programs.               │
└──────────────────────────────────────────────────────────────┘

┌──────────────────────────────────────────────────────────────┐
│      Strategic objective setting                               │
│      1.  By top management based on analysis of (1) and (2)    │
│          possible alternatives.                                │
│ (3)  2.  Product strategy.                                     │
│      3.  Diversification strategy.                             │
│      4.  Divestment strategy.                                  │
│      5.  Priority setting.                                     │
└──────────────────────────────────────────────────────────────┘

┌──────────────────────────────────────────────────────────────┐
│      Formulation of long-range action programs and tactical    │
│      plans and budgets                                         │
│      1.  Within the context of stages (1), (2), and (3).       │
│ (4)  2.  At appropriate organizational levels within narrowing │
│          constraints or objectives.                            │
│      3.  Capital budget and cash management plans.             │
└──────────────────────────────────────────────────────────────┘
```

Figure 8.15
AN IDEAL CORPORATE PLANNING PROCESS

Source: John S. Schwendiman, *Strategic and Long-Range Planning in the International Firm* (Cambridge: Massachusetts Institute of Technology, Alfred P. Sloan School of Management, 1971), p. 83.

als tend to be 'satisficing' may explain the rather limited efforts at environmental and internal company assessment in the sample companies."[72] Going on, he emphasized that formalized corporate planning is unlikely to be meaningful

[72]John S. Schwendiman, *Strategic and Long-Range Planning*, p. 243.

unless it has the enthusiastic participation of top management. Some of the most frequently mentioned international planning problems are (1) gaining top level support in articulating and communicating corporate goals, (2) lack of strategic integration of plans and operations (as between domestic and international and among various international subunits), (3) gaining a personal commitment to planning at all management levels, and (4) the adequacy and economy of information flows—including that related to contingencies such as an inaccurate projection of sales or costs.[73] It is obvious that commitment to long-run planning requires an incentive scheme built on something more than short-run performance.

One might suspect that the effectiveness of long-range planning in the Japanese firm would be significantly greater than in the characteristic European or U.S.-based firms. The permanent employment and lock-step promotion of managers in Japanese firms may make possible a longer-term evaluation before one is singled out for special reward. This changes the entire personal time-dimension of decision making. However, there is one bit of evidence suggesting that the Japanese are less satisfied with long-range planning than managers in other companies, including the United States.[74]

Lorange writes, "Strategic planning in a multinational corporation has a two-fold task: to identify the strategic options most relevant to the corporation and to 'narrow down' these options into the one best plan."[75] He goes on:

The broad definition of the strategic planning tasks given above has several implications. In order to be able to identify the most relevant strategic options, the corporation needs to adapt *continuously to the environment. Also, in order to narrow down the strategic options into the one best plan, the corporation must be able to* integrate *its many diverse activities.*[76]

He then proceeds to relate the nature and cost of the planning function to the structure of the multinational corporation. Admitting that other structures are possible, he chooses to deal with four, all being variations on what have been labeled here as product and regionally-organized multinationals. In fact, of course, very few multinationals, if any, would be organized exclusively by product or region. As Lorange points out:

Complete domination of corporate structure by one dimension can prove to be inefficient. For instance, there might be considerable duplication of effort in having the product divisions operate their own separate organizations in one country. When evolving from such a product structure, the matrix structure might be described as consisting of a leading *product dimension and a* grown *area dimension.*

---

[73]Summarized from John S. Schwendiman, *Strategic and Long-Range Planning*, pp. 234–37.

[74]George A. Steiner and Hans Schollhammer, "Pitfalls in Multi-National Long-Range Planning," *Long-Range Planning*, April 1975, p. 9.

[75]Peter Lorange, "A Framework for Strategic Planning in Multinational Corporations," *Long-Range Planning*, June 1976, p. 30.

[76]Lorange, "Framework," p. 30.

Table 8.5
SUMMARY OF THE INTEGRATION AND ADAPTATION PLANNING TASKS OF THE MULTINATIONAL CORPORATIONS IN OUR TAXONOMY

Taxonomy of corporations	Adaptation	Integration
Worldwide product divisions	Along area dimension	Along product dimension
Product leading/area grown matrix	Primarily along area dimension; some along product dimension	Primarily along product dimension; some along area dimension
Area leading/product grown matrix	Primarily along product dimension; some along area dimension	Primarily along area dimension; some along product dimension
Geographical area divisions	Along product dimension	Along area dimension

Source: Peter Lorange, "A Framework for Strategic Planning in Multinational Corporations," *Long-Range Planning,* June 1976, p. 34.

Alternatively, when evolving out of an area-dominated structure, the matrix structure would have a leading area dimension and a grown product dimension. [77]

Consequently, Lorange sees the structure of a multinational lying along a continuum from product-oriented on one extreme, through product-leading/area-grown and area-leading/product-grown, to area-oriented on the other. He argues that the way in which the corporation is organized defines its integration and adaptation tasks, as in Table 8.5.

Following the Lorange argument further, the planning function is broken down into three phases:

1. Objective setting—Reexamine the fundamental assumptions for being in business; consider whether the rationale for the firm's policies are still valid; in short, analyze where the firm stands relative to the environment

2. Planning—Follow up the major issues for adaption developed in phase one

3. Budgeting—Prepare more detailed budgets within the framework set out in the plans.

It is pointed out that integration plays a minor role in the objective setting phase, a somewhat more important role in the planning phase, and dominates in the budgeting phase.[78] In that in each of the corporate types there will be different roles for the product and area dimensions with respect to performing the adaptive and integrative tasks, the relative importance of these tasks shifts as one goes forward with the planning function; that is, through the narrowing-down process. The implication of this is that "interaction among executives of the two dimensions of the matrix structure does not have to take place all through the narrowing-down process, but only during the middle

[77]Lorange, "Framework," p. 31.
[78]Lorange, "Framework," p. 35.

stage; i.e., the planning stage."[79] The consequence of this realization should be a considerable cost saving in the planning process in that full-blown interaction between the dimensions at each stage of the process need not take place.[80]

On the basis of a questionnaire sent to companies in six countries (United States, Canada, United Kingdom, Italy, Australia, and Japan), which elicited 460 useable responses, Steiner and Schollhammer attempted to identify those pitfalls in long-range planning that companies around the world feel are the most important. The result is shown in Table 8.6. Other conclusions from their study: (1) more companies are satisfied with their planning systems than are dissatisfied; (2) those companies with greater formality and greater documentation are the most satisfied; (3) divisionalized companies are more satisfied than those not organized into divisions; (4) companies with the longest experience with planning are the most satisfied. A few national characteristics were of some interest. The Japanese seemed to be somewhat less satisfied with the reported planning system and in all other aspects seemed to be the reverse.[81]

Unless consistent incentives are built into the system to participate and support planning activity, subsidiary managers, particularly in the international area, may feed in wholly inadequate or misleading data, and do so quite deliberately. In this manner they can shield themselves to a degree from overly centralized control and loss of subsidiary autonomy. For this reason, really effective international long-range planning may be limited to the transnational corporations.

If a normative rule can be laid down at all it is that control should be decentralized to the extent possible within the constraints of perceived managerial ability and the achievement of corporate goals. At the same time, it should be noted that national or even regional managers over time are likely to become emotionally attached to their respective areas. If so, reporting and decision making may become heavily biased, so much so that the firm will find it difficult to cut its losses and retire from a hopeless situation. At the same time, it is quite clear that centralized control cannot be effective in the absence of both the necessary functional competence and adequate understanding of the environment involved. The final word may be that of Gianluig Gabetti, president of Olivetti Underwood: "If a multinational firm is not centralized, at least for control and coordination, all the advantages of its worldwide association are lost."[82]

---

[79]Lorange, "Framework," p. 36.

[80]Lorange, "Framework," p. 36.

[81]George A. Steiner and Hans Schollhammer, "Pitfalls in Multi-National Long-Range Planning," *Long-Range Planning*, April 1975, pp. 2 ff.

[82]As reported in *Business Abroad*, September 1969, p. 16.

Table 8.6

THE TEN MOST IMPORTANT LONG-RANGE PLANNING PITFALLS TO BE AVOIDED AS RANKED BY RESPONDENTS

Pitfall number (see appendix A)	Description of Pitfall	Total sample	U.S.A.	Canada	England	Italy	Australia	Japan
1	Top management's assumption that it can delegate the planning function to a planner.	1	2	1	1	1	8	4
24	Top management becomes so engrossed in current problems that it spends insufficient time on long-range planning and the process becomes discredited among other managers and staff.	2	1	2	8	2	1	1
28	Failure to develop company goals suitable as a basis for formulating long-range plans.	3	3	3	2	6	3	3
11	Failure to create a climate in the company that is congenial and not resistant to planning.	4	4		3	5	9	7
42	Failure of top management to review with departmental and divisional heads the long-range plans they have developed.	5	8			10	2	2
26	Failure to assure the necessary involvement in the planning process of major line personnel.	6	5	10	9		7	9
15	Assuming that corporate comprehensive planning is something separate from the entire management process.	7	6	4	10	4		
16	Failure to make sure that top management and major line officers really understand the nature of long-range planning and what it will accomplish for them and the company.	8	10	5			6	10
12	Failure to locate the corporate planner at a high enough level in the managerial hierarchy.	9	9		6	7		
47	Failure to use plans as standards for measuring managerial performance.	10	7					
27	Too much centralization of long-range planning in the central headquarters so that divisions feel little responsibility for developing effective plans.			6	4			

No.	Pitfall					
43	Forgetting that the fundamental purpose of planning is to make better current decisions.	5				7
13	Failure to make sure that the planning staff has the necessary qualities of leadership, technical expertise, and personality to discharge properly its responsibilities in making the planning system effective.		5			8
14	Forgetting that planning is a political, a social, and an organizational, as well as a rational process.					9
10	Failure to develop a clear understanding of the long-range planning procedure before the process is actually undertaken.	8			5	
18	Assuming that plans can be made by staff planners for line managers to implement.				7	
31	Failure to make realistic plans (e.g., due to overoptimism and/or overcautiousness).					
45	Top management's consistently rejecting the formal planning mechanism by making intuitive decisions that conflict with the formal plans.			3		
8	Assuming that a formal system can be introduced into a company without a careful and perhaps "agonizing appraisal" of current managerial practices and decision-making processes.		4	8		
37	Doing long-range planning periodically and forgetting it in-between cycles.		10	9		
39	Failure of top management, and/or the planning staff, to give departments and divisions sufficient information and guidance (e.g., top management interests, environmental projections, etc.).	6				

Source: George A. Steiner and Hans Schollhammer, "Pitfalls in Multi-National Long-Range Planning," *Long Range Planning,* April 1975, p. 4.

8.2   LOCATION OF TACTICAL DECISION-MAKING AUTHORITY

Operating of tactical decision-making authority may or may not be separated out from that authority making strategy choices. The larger the firm, the more compelling separation becomes, particularly in the international case. In the firm driving toward optimum penetration of foreign markets, the pressure for localizing tactical decision-making authority becomes almost compelling due to the myriad of cultural variables relevant to such decisions. It is one thing for an international division or regional or corporate headquarters to specify, for example, that the strategy in regard to choice of channels shall be overseas agencies. It is quite another to ascertain the identity of the agents to be used. A management remuneration policy is one thing; how much to pay Mr. X in Brazil is another. So it goes.

Experienced firms operating internationally tend to push all tactical decision-making authority down to the local (national) level unless there is compelling reason for retaining it at divisional, regional, or even corporate level. Some compelling reasons are tax and antitrust considerations, a high degree of integration between different national enterprises (in respect to sales, supply, finance, management), feedback effects (such as in labor negotiations and in relations with domestic customers), and political implications to which the parent government is sensitive (for example, U.S. trade restrictions with the Soviet bloc or Cuba). A word of caution should be entered here. It is not at all clear that the formulation of corporate goals should occur at one corporate level, long-range planning on another, strategy selection on another, and tactical decision-making on still another. Corporate headquarters is often in a position, by reason of greater breadth of information and a higher level of technical competence, to assist in tactical decision-making, just as local subsidiary managers may be helpful in strategy determination because of their greater environmental knowledge.

8.3   METHODS OF COMMUNICATING DECISIONS

Possible choices in this area are training indoctrination, a company journal, conferences, personal visits by decision-making personnel or their representatives, written SOPs, and budgets. Obviously, these choices are not mutually exclusive. To be considered in determining strategy in this regard are such factors as cost, the number of entities and people involved, and the extent to which decision-making authority is retained by higher headquarters.

Experienced managements offer a few guidelines:

1. All decisions made by a level higher than that implementing the decision, however the decision may be communicated initially, should be committed to writing.

(Exceptions: those felt to be politically and/or legally vulnerable.) Given the pitfalls of inter-cultural communication, this rule is more important than in comparable domestic situations.

2. Visits by decision-making authorities or their representatives should be on a regular periodic basis, not occasioned exclusively by crisis situations.

3. Periodic conferences of key personnel of similar function from both domestic and foreign operations are of great utility in developing universally valid strategies and in the delegation of tactical decisions to lower levels.

4. Management training and development assumes greater importance for foreign operations because of the differences in cultural backgrounds, in the meaning of management, in the status of managers, and in sources of management recruitment as one moves from one national society to another. Such training facilitates both the decentralization of decision-making authority and improvement in the quality and effectiveness of those decisions made at higher organizational levels.

5. Periodic rotation of overseas managers to regional or corporate headquarters may be one of the most effective ways of communicating overall corporate goals and the rationale for corporate strategy, including the degree of control retained at each level.

MEANS OF REPORTING PERFORMANCE   8.4

Reports of performance should flow in a reverse pattern to decisions. The more decentralized the latter, the less the volume of the former. To require unnecessary reports is costly, particularly for those moving across language barriers, cultural frontiers, and great distances. Every report requirement should be carefully justified.

The range of possible reports is similar to that of a purely domestic operation, but certain difficulties arise peculiar to the foreign case. One of these is time lag, which may seriously reduce the value of a given report. For that reason the means of reporting may have to be changed. Essentially, there are six ways to communicate internationally other than by travel, all varying considerably in cost, namely, mail, telephone, cable, telex, leased channel, and computer conferencing. Which one is optimum in a specific situation depends on message frequency, average length, destination, urgency, and ease of personal communication. The various firms engaged in international communications supply analysts to assist individual firms in making optimum choices.

It has been suggested that a number of firms become over-enthusiastic about the advantage of telex and waste money by misusing it in sending short messages that could go more cheaply by telegram or cable. For a given location, one should obtain the minimum telex charges to each country, also the cable cost per word to the same destinations. If one then divides the minimum telex fee by the cable cost per word, the result is the break-even point between telex and cable costs, expressed in the number of words.[83]

Another problem peculiar to foreign operations in establishing report strategy lies in securing reports that contain information that may be properly evaluated; that is, compared with domestic and other national data. Some of the complicating factors are differential inflation rates, shifting exchange rates, imprecise statistical services, and different legal and accounting requirements.

8.5 EVALUATION OF PERFORMANCE

Possible measures of overseas management performance, as in the domestic case, include (1) conformance to decisions by higher authority, (2) local profit, (3) contribution to consolidated profit, (4) rate of return on investment, (5) dollar volume, (6) cash flows, (7) physical volumes, (8) efficiency (input-output ratios, such as annual added value per employee, or per man-hour), (9) dollar flows, and (10) market share.

For operations in countries with price levels changing at rates different from those in the parent country, and from changes in local currency/foreign exchange rates, reports of two, three, four, five, and six above are exceedingly hard to evaluate, for international comparisons are rarely valid. (See also Section 6.4.) In each case relevant factors not under the control of local management may be involved, such factors as price controls, control over the revaluation of assets,[84] depreciation allowances, exchange rates prevailing at the time at which profits are remitted, costs assessed by associated firms (such as the parent company) against the foreign operation (for example, price of materials, foreign wages and other benefits paid on behalf of nonnational personnel, general overhead charges), the availability of local debt financing, and local currency evaluation of foreign-source assets invested. The problem is essentially that of sorting out current profit and loss from liquidation of assets and investment.

Also subject to national differences, and hence not easily judged on the basis of standard measures, are input-output ratios (where product and process design differ due to market requirements, different relative factor costs, and varying plant sizes), physical volume (for similar reasons), and conformance to decisions by higher authority (because of communications and legal obstacles and behavioral differences).

In assessing associated foreign enterprises, many firms look only at *growth* (in terms of physical volume of sales in respect to the total market, such as market share in physical terms) and at *net convertible currency* flow. The latter includes all convertible currency investments, all expenditures made on behalf

---

[83]For a specific example, see *Business Asia*, July 9, 1971, p. 222.

[84]Whatever is legally permitted, the real value of assets is equal to the present value of the stream of future earnings.

of the overseas firm (those that would not occur in the absence of the foreign operation) whether by the parent firm or a third-country enterprise, all cash remitted to the parent (dividends, royalties, fees, interest) or otherwise made available, and all income earned by the parent firm by reason of the foreign enterprise (such as profits on sales to the latter, remittances by third-country firms by reason of supply from or sales to the firm in question, taxes saved for reinvestment purposes, profits on purchases from the foreign enterprise).

Any sort of financial control and evaluation system obviously rests on a flow of accounting information, on which basis comparisons are made (either with other operating units, historical results, a budget, or competitors). In a recent survey of 30 U.S. companies, 18 (60 percent) reported "some formal effort to standardize their accounting practices throughout the company." Without such standardization the degree of comparability as to merit comparison with the performance of other units would not be present. (The same study noted a tendency for somewhat fewer reports and less detailed reports to be required of foreign affiliates than of domestic operating units.)[85] But recent developments have made such standardization within a company difficult.

The extensive currency adjustments that took place after 1971 led the U.S. accounting industry, through its Financial Accounting Standards Board (FASB)[86] to set forth binding rules in respect to the disclosure of the effect of foreign currency translation on consolidated or foreign financial statements. These regulations specify the information that listed U.S. companies must divulge on their balance sheets and profit and loss statements.

It should be noted that there are two general methods of translating financial statements from one currency to another: monetary/nonmonetary and current/noncurrent (or temporal). The first refers to the system under which financial items (cash, receivables, payables) are translated at the year-end foreign exchange rates; all other items, at historic rates (those at the time of the initial transaction). The current/noncurrent (temporal) method refers to the translation of current assets and current liabilities at year-end foreign exchange rate; the translation of all long-term items at historic rates. In 1974, a *Business International* survey of 200 U.S. firms revealed that 60 percent employed some form of the monetary/nonmonetary method; 39 percent the current/noncurrent method.[87] Another report suggests that the ratio was more on the order of 80 percent and 20 percent.[88]

In October 1975, the FASB issued its controversial standard number 8, which spelled out how U.S. corporations should account for the translation of foreign currency transactions and foreign currency financial statements. The

[85]J. M. McInnes, "Financial Control Systems for Multinational Operation: An Empirical Investigation," *Journal of International Business Studies*, Fall 1971, pp. 13, 17.

[86]Replaced the Accounting Principles Board in 1972.

[87]*Business International*, May 31, 1974, p. 174.

[88]Patricia Harrigan, "The Double Sand-bag in Foreign Exchange Accounting," *Euromoney*, June 1976.

rules required that all of the effects of currency fluctuations in foreign assets, liabilities, and transactions be included currently, that is, quarterly. Previously, it had been permissible to defer unrealized translation gains, which could then be offset by subsequent unrealized translation losses. It was now required that all translation gains and losses be reported, whether realized or unrealized. And of course many, in fact, would never be realized. The choice of translation systems was, hence, closed; all U.S. firms were required to use the temporal method. All assets and liabilities that would be realized currently or in the future must be translated at the current exchange rate (end-of-quarter) and all assets and liabilities reported in the past (inventories and fixed assets) at the historical rates of exchange. Let it be noted that, in general, the gains or losses resulting from the translation of locally-denominated assets and liabilities do not result in taxable gains or loss in the United States. Expert opinion holds that,

The ultimate tax treatment of gains and losses resulting from the payment or realization of foreign assets and liabilities of U.S. corporations is unclear and is presently a very controversial area of taxation.[89]

The result of standard number 8 was that reported corporate earnings began bouncing around in that the accounting changes introduced left companies exposed to translation losses or gains whenever exchange rates shifted which, under a floating rate system, they do constantly. Previously, most companies had offset the impact of currency fluctuations on such exposed assets or liabilities by reporting gains or losses only at year-end, and by using reserves to level out such gains and losses over several years. Standard number 8 required quarterly statements, and ruled out reserves. But corporations in many other countries continue to have the options now prohibited for U.S. corporations.

The only way in which a U.S. company can now prevent its earnings from fluctuating wildly is to keep assets and liabilities in balance in each of the "risk currencies." Thus, assets in the form of plant and equipment in, for example, Italian lira, should be matched by equivalent loans or bank borrowings. "In this way gains on assets are cancelled out by losses on liabilities and vice versa. So there is no net gain or loss to be translated."[90] But, in the meantime, the company incurs costs that it would not otherwise have.

Standard U.S. accounting practice has been for U.S.-based parent firms (1) to state foreign fixed assets at their value when purchased, with perhaps a note specifying estimated current value (current dollar value should equal present discounted value of future dollar flow), (2) to use LIFO inventory accounting (which means that the flow of goods out of inventory should approximate current prices, but inventory value should become less realistic),

---

[89] *FASB 8* (New York: Coopers & Lybrand, 1976).

[90] *International Accounting & Financial Report,* January 17, 1977, p. 5.

(3) to state *current* assets and liabilities at the current exchange rate, and
(4) to show long-term liabilities at the exchange rate on the date incurred.

These rules do not solve the problem of multiple exchange rates or the classification of assets and liabilities. For example, was depreciation of fixed assets to be reported on a historic or current basis? In either case, a special replacement allowance or investment fund would be required. Another relevant query: How were costs calculated for a *dollar* profit-and-loss report? Some firms used a monthly average of exchange rates.

Such accounting difficulties as these rendered consolidated accounts exceedingly difficult to set up. At best, extensive notes were required. The introduction of standard number 8 may have simplified the translation problem, and hence consolidation, but the extent to which the resulting reports reflect reality is another matter.

Conceptually, a firm has the choice of consolidating either all of its overseas holdings, only those firms in which it has more than 50 percent ownership, only 100 percent-owned subsidiaries, only 100 percent-owned subsidiaries in financially-stable countries, or none. In the U.S. case it has been most common to consolidate all subsidiary holdings, with limited exception, but it has not been required, as in the United Kingdom, Canada, and Denmark. In fact, in the U.S. case, a firm is not permitted to consolidate its interest in a company in which it owns 50 percent or less, even though exercising effective control. However, the stockholders of the parent company must receive the statements of unconsolidated subsidiaries.[91]

Responding to pressures for international harmonization, the International Accounting Standards Commission was founded in June 1973, its constituency being 18 associations of accountants in ten countries, including the American Institute of Certified Public Accountants in the United States, plus 23 associate members in 18 additional countries. Its purpose was to formulate and publish accounting standards and to promote their worldwide acceptance. As of April 1977, it had published 11 standards and had proposed four others. In addition, the European Commission has been active in trying to effect greater harmony among accounting practices and laws within the nine member states. It should be noted that one of the impacts of the harmonization of financial reporting would be to ease the task of controlling corporations with global spread. One of the difficulties is that U.S. accounting practice is irreconcilably different from all others, most of whom use current foreign exchange rates for consolidation purposes and defer some items in respect to current income. In contrast, the United States, as noted, accounts for certain items at historical rates, some at the current rate, but all must be taken into current income.

What we have really been talking about is comparability of financial statements of companies located in different countries. To the extent that they are

---

[91]*A Survey in 46 Countries of Accounting Principles and Reporting Practices* (New York: Price Waterhouse, 1975).

not comparable, these statements cannot be used as the basis for allocating corporate resources or for evaluating the profit or loss of a particular enterprise against the profit and loss of those located elsewhere. The many different legal requiements causing variations in accounting principles and practices from country to country often compel a firm to maintain multiple financial reporting systems. As an example, Price Waterhouse reports the major differences between the United States and Brazil on this score in Table 8.7.

A firm may thus have to set up accounting procedures so as to satisfy (1) host country tax authorities; (2) parent country tax authorities, who may have different notions as to appropriate transfer prices, overhead allocation, depreciation allowances; (3) a banking institution, which may want to ascertain a corporation's global debt/equity position or return on investment; (4) internal control requirements in that the company's own allocation of cost and profits, rates of depreciation and obsolescence, changes in reserve funds set up to cover a variety of contingencies, and the exchange rates used for conversion purposes in that such rules imposed by host and parent country may, within the context of the firm, diverge from reality.

8.6   ENFORCEMENT OF DECISIONS (MAINTENANCE OF CONTROL)

A control system is purely informational unless sufficient pressure can be built up to make the operational feedback conform, within a given range, to that anticipated by the initiators of the inputs—the decision-makers. How does one bring this about when the system operates across international frontiers? Important restraints on effectiveness in this case include those provided by the legal structure of the countries involved, national interest as perceived by political leaders, and the quality of communications. The latter subject has been dealt with in Section 4.1 and more briefly in the introduction to this chapter.

Basic methods of enforcement include (1) legal pressure, (2) business pressure, (3) persuasion, and (4) mutual benefit.

Legal pressure can operate only if one has a legal claim through guarantee, contract, financial obligation, or ownership. Even then pressure may not be effective if important political considerations or national sensitivities are involved. (See also Section 6.8.) *Business pressure* can be generated provided an affiliated enterprise stands in an important sales, supply, management, or financial position in relation to the parent firm. Importance must be rated in terms of both criticalness and uniqueness of that input.

If the foreign firm is substantially independent financially (that is, it generates its own operating funds), is not tied by contract to the parent firm, and is not selling to or buying from the parent, control by the parent management may be exceedingly difficult even though technically it "owns" the foreign firm. In this case, the parent firm may be understandably reluctant to com-

Table 8.7
ACCOUNTING PRINCIPLES AND PRACTICES IN BRAZIL THAT ARE DIFFERENT FROM THOSE GENERALLY ACCEPTED IN THE UNITED STATES

Accounting	Explanation of differences
Overconservatism	1. Overconservatism is practiced often through unwarranted general provisions for doubtful accounts receivable.
Price level changes	2. Partial price level accounting is required by law. An adjustment must be or may be made on the basis of indices for restatement of fixed assets and accumulated depreciation, intangibles and accumulated amortization, certain investments, and foreign currency accounts. The net effect of these adjustments must be recorded in a variety of ways, some as charges to income, reduction of deficits, adjustment of foreign currency liabilities, reduction of accumulated depreciation, and credits to capital surplus accounts.
Price level changes	3. Tax regulations allow, and accounting practice permits, a provision for maintenance of working capital (presently limited to 20 percent of taxable income) representing erosion of working capital through inflation.
Exchange losses	4. The cost of fixed assets is increased by exchange losses arising on foreign currency liabilities incurred for the purchase of such assets.
Contingency reserves	5. General provisions (and subsequent reversals) are often used to shift income between periods.
Surplus entries	6. Unrestricted retained earnings are often decreased directly by special charges for directors' fees (participations) without passing through income.
Investments	7. Adjustments to the initial valuation of permanent investments may not be made even though there is evidence of a permanent decline in value.
Accounts payable	8. Known liabilities or losses generally are provided for only when they are deductible for tax purposes.
Income taxes	9. If accounting per books differs from tax accounting, the tax effect of the difference is (a) never disclosed in footnotes, and (b) never recorded as a deferred charge or credit.
Income taxes	10. Income taxes are often charged against results of operations only as and when paid (on a cash basis) rather than being based on the current income (accrual method).

Disclosure	Explanation of differences
Change in accounting methods	11. The monetary effect of a change in accounting practices is seldom disclosed.
Subsequent events	12. Subsequent events are seldom disclosed.
Consolidation of financial statements	13. In the case of a parent company having subsidiaries, consolidated (or group) accounts are not included in the statutory financial statements. Further, the parent's equity in subsidiaries, carried at cost, is not disclosed.
Rental commitments	14. Material rental commitments on long-term leases (say, over one year) are seldom disclosed.
Contingent liabilities	15. Contingent liabilities are not disclosed.
Retained earnings	16. Restrictions on retained earnings are seldom disclosed.
Retained earnings	17. Cumulative dividends in arrears are not always disclosed.

Source: George C. Watt, ed., *Guide for the Reader of Foreign Financial Statements* (New York: Price Waterhouse & Co., 1971), pp. 10–13.

pound the problem by installing a management dominated by local nationals. The crucial element here is personal loyalty to the firm, the ability of the parent firm to *persuade* local management to abide by its decisions. Threat will be ineffective.

In the final analysis, persuasion is only effective if the party being persuaded feels it to be in his interest to be persuaded. If the parent management finds it imposssible to so frame a decision flowing to a foreign enterprise so as to embody *mutual benefit* in a positive sense, implicit or explicit, then the control structure is threatened with collapse. Something is wrong. Reported response may still appear to comply but not actual behavior. And to the extent that the foreign enterprise involves the public interest, the mutuality of benefit must likewise encompass the national interests of the host country, as perceived by its authorities, if effective control is to be maintained. In all cases, a relevant query is: How important is the particular type of control the parent firm is trying to retain (important in terms of profit maximization for the parent firm)? International business relations are much more sensitive to unneeded controls than are comparable domestic relations.

In the ability to resolve the control problem and strike a mutually acceptable balance may lie the essential quality of good international management. To achieve such balance requires extraordinary flexibility, for each situation is unique, demanding a unique solution. The balance must be a constantly shifting one, as the capability of management and the size and nature of one's business changes, if the cold war between headquarters and the field is to be kept within tolerable limits. Extraordinary sensitivity to the full range of the relevant variables, and the ability to weigh each with some degree of accuracy, is demanded. This capacity is the mark of the effective international manager.

Discussion questions

1. Why might one anticipate a trend toward stricter control by U.S.-based firms over their European subsidiaries? Would you expect this to be a worldwide phenomenon? Why or why not?

2. Why might corporate goals be important in determining the degree of control retained by corporate headquarters over foreign subsidiaries?

3. Give examples of types of firms (other than those cited in the text) that might best organize internationally on a regional basis, product basis, functional basis, process basis, customer basis.

4. As foreign sales grow, why does the export department in a firm tend to disappear?

5. Why does an international division represent an unstable structure in the face of increasing foreign sales?

6. What frictions are likely to develop within a multinational corporation?

7. How is the centralized control within an international firm different from that in a transitional multinational or truly transnational firm?

8. How is the apparent difference in ownership strategy between Japanese and U.S.-based corporations possibly related to the forms into which these corporations may ultimately evolve?

9. Why might the Japanese find it difficult to develop transnational associations?

10 Under what circumstances will local subsidiary managers tend to exaggerate environmental differences?

11. Why is it more difficult to evaluate the performance of overseas managers than domestic managers?

12. What are the implications of some of the accounting principles and practices in Brazil that are different from those generally accepted in the United States?

13. In your own words explain Figures 8.2 and 8.3.

14. How would your relate the organizational-control evolution of international business over the next several decades to the environmental variables listed on pages 745 and 746?

Recommended references

Alsegg, Robert J. *Control Relationships between American Corporations and Their European Subsidiaries.* New York: American Management Society, 1971.

Berg, K. B., G. G. Mueller, and L. M. Walker, eds. *Readings in International Accounting.* Boston: Houghton Mifflin Company, 1969.

Chorafas, Dimetris N. *The Communication Barrier in International Management.* New York: American Management Association, 1969.

Goldberg, Paul M. *The Evolution of Transnational Companies in Europe.* Cambridge: Alfred P. Sloan School of Management, Massachusetts Institute of Technology, unpublished Ph.D. dissertation, 1971, soon to be published by the M.I.T. Press.

Litvak, A. K., C. Maule, and R. D. Robinson. *Dual Loyalty, Canadian-U.S. Business Relationships.* Toronto: McGraw-Hill, 1971.

Professional Accounting in 25 Countries. New York: American Institute of Certified Public Accountants, 1964.

Skinner, C. Wickham. *American Industry in Developing Economies, the Management of International Manufacturing.* New York: John Wiley & Sons, 1968.

Steiner, George A., and Warren M. Cannon. *Multinational Corporate Planning.* New York: Crowell-Collier and MacMillan, Inc., 1966.

A Survey in 46 Countries, Accounting Principles and Reporting Practices. New York: Price Waterhouse, 1975.

Watt, George C., ed. *Guide for the Reader of Foreign Financial Statements.* New York: Price Waterhouse, 1971.

Case L

AGCHEM CORPORATION[1]

Background. By 1935, James E. Frost, then 41 years old, was one of the outstanding salesmen of a large chemical company in the United States. As a student, he had been well trained at Purdue University in the characteristics and uses of various agricultural chemical materials. For some years, he had worked primarily in the field of agricultural fertilizers and, through this experience, had become well acquainted with the large farm interests and distributors of agricultural supplies throughout the country. He was technically competent, and kept himself well-informed regarding new scientific developments.

As he saw middle age approaching, Frost decided that, to make the best use of his experience, abilities, and friendships, he would start his own company. With a relatively small amount of capital ($10,000), largely from family savings, he set up the James E. Frost Company in the fall of 1935. To avoid pointblank competition with the well-established agricultural chemical firms, he conceived of his company as essentially a service organization to assist large scale farms with special problems in maintaining soil fertility. He purchased fertilizer components in bulk from the big producers, whom he knew well, and formulated fertilizer mixtures to individual specifications, which were then sold on contract to the agricultural users. He was, in effect, offering his customers expert technical advice, plus the convenience of providing custom-formulated materials to meet specific needs. Early in 1936, he added parasiticides, which also were formulated to specific requirements, with most of this business also arising from special problem situations.

By early 1940, the company was still small but reasonably successful and, because of Frost's conservative business policies, was financially quite sound. Since Frost was primarily in the consulting or service type of business, his overhead and labor costs were low. He employed one technically-trained salesman, Joseph F. Wagner, a man who had been employed formerly in a large chemical company. It was an ideal business for him, he felt, since he liked the idea of operating as a "one man band."

However, Frost began to see quite intense competition in his field—the custom-formulated fertilizer and parasiticide business—coming from the large chemical fertilizer producers, so in mid-1940, he decided that the future of the company would depend primarily on its ability to supply those needs his

---

[1]Original case prepared by John A. Purinton, Jr., Lecturer in Business Administration, for use in class discussions. Copyright by the Sponsors of the Graduate School of Business Administration, University of Virginia, Revised by Richard D. Robinson for classroom use at the Alfred P. Sloan School of Management, Massachusetts Institute of Technology. Reproduced with permission.

competitors could not supply. To accomplish this, he set up a small research organization primarily to study unusual agricultural problems. He felt that, with more intensive cultivation of land and with the continual appearance of new diseases and infestations of agricultural crops, the future was wide open. He also established a small chemical plant to manufacture those materials he expected to result from his company's research, but which could not be purchased economically elsewhere. Since the Frost family owned substantially all of the stock in the company, he was in a fortunately flexible position to do all of this. His son, John L., had joined the firm upon graduation from Purdue in 1939, where he had taken an S.M. in chemistry.

Growth from the war. Before he could really get started, World War II changed the company's course abruptly. Confident of his limited, but competent, technical staff, primarily hired to carry out his research plans, and wanting to use the small plant, located in Atlanta, Georgia, which he had been able to put together, he sought government contracts for chemical materials for military and related purposes. These were not difficult to obtain. Meanwhile, John L. had gone into military service where he remained for three years, spending two of the three in Southeast Asia.

From then on the business, like so many others during those years, expanded rapidly. With defense plant money and priorities for equipment and materials (which followed from military contracts), Frost found himself operating production facilities far larger than he could otherwise have anticipated.

Following the war, he was able promptly to resolve the problem of government money and to retain ownership of the expanded plant. In a few months he had reconstructed his small but growing organization, which had been somewhat scattered during the war years. All of his former key employees returned to him and these were supplemented by other selected men as they were released from the military services, including his son.

Subsequently, James E. Frost was killed in an automobile accident. His son, John L. Frost, then 31 years old, succeeded him as president and chief executive officer. John Frost had always supported the policies of his father, but went even further in his dedication to the policy that the future of the company depended upon aggressive research. He decided that the company should veer away from its present course—that it should no longer limit itself to the formulation and distribution of agricultural chemicals from components available on the open market. Instead, he plunged headlong into a research program to develop new and patentable products that could be marketed as the company's own specialties. He was pleased with his key research man, Dr. George Nutting, whose practical vision and technical competence justified his appointment as director of research. Along with changing the company purposes, Frost also felt it desirable to change the company "image" with its current and potential customers, and so adopted a new name, "The Agchem Corporation."

By the late 1950s Agchem had succeeded in developing several new patented agricultural chemicals to combat plant diseases, a few of which were truly outstanding research achievements. These had resulted from some lucky research "breaks," to be sure, but were primarily due to the caliber of the research staff and the excellence of its administration. It so happened that, as the research program was unfolding, the company's interests pointed largely toward fungicides, since that seemed to be the field in which they were achieving their greatest successes. It also developed that these fungicides were of particular interest in tropical and subtropical agriculture. As volume increased, the manufacturing plant and staff, under Mr. Michael Stone as director of production, were strengthened. Financial administration was consolidated under Mr. George Pashko, who was hired from the company's accounting firm.

Export beginnings. Realizing that the market for the new products was by no means restricted to the United States, John Frost cultivated and established distributors in Southern Europe, Africa, and the Middle East. In general, he was wise in his choice of distributor organizations, and soon was supplying increasing amounts of his products to these areas. By 1958 he had extended his distribution to the Pacific area with distributors in Australia, Thailand, Hong Kong, Japan, the Philippines, and Malaya.

Because of his interest in the export field, in each instance Frost had made the initial contact and consummated the operating agreement himself, sometimes in person, but usually by correspondence. Essentially, he was chief executive officer, domestic sales manager, and foreign sales manager.

Frost soon found out that expansion of the organization for international operations was essential, since he could not spread himself so thinly. His research, financial, and production problems were in the capable hands of Nutting, Pashko, and Stone. He did not want to give up the domestic sales function; he had grown up with it, enjoyed his business friendships, and really did not feel that anyone else could handle the job as well as he. He, therefore, decided to look for a foreign sales manager to develop his current "mail order" distributor business overseas, feeling that a large untapped opportunity was there. Such a person would also take much of the load off his shoulders.

In analyzing the job, Frost was well aware of its limitations in attracting a top-flight operator in international business. He felt that he could afford to pay between $18,000 and $20,000 a year, but no more. After all, Frost himself had done the job for several years and how could he justify paying as much as $30,000 for an assistant! What he thought he really wanted was a young person who could grow in stature with the overseas business. However, he did have to have a person with some international experience. As he saw it, the salary he could offer was not big enough to interest the "headhunters" in finding his man. So he advertised in the *Wall Street Journal* and one or two other business publications. The returns were motley. The preponderance was from job jumpers, malcontents, and incompetents. Out of 30 inquiries, one struck a spark.

Richard Merlin had graduated four years previously with an M.B.A. degree from Wharton and since that time had been employed in the foreign sales division of a large chemical manufacturer. A year and one-half in the home office had given him a good exposure to international organizational operations, which was followed by overseas travel. His reason for leaving was that he was "stuck" in an established hierarchy of young executives and he wanted a position where he could rise or fall on his own abilities. He was eager and alert, and fortunately his wife did not object too strenuously to his travel assignments. She was even looking forward to accompanying him on some of his trips, should this prove practical.

Merlin joined Agchem in January 1959 at age 27, and took over quite rapidly. He quickly grasped an understanding of the relationships with the distributors and developed an easy, confident rapport with them.

The research division continued to be successful in developing new agricultural chemical specialities, primarily in the field of parasiticides. In general, these were useful in all agricultural climates, although some of the more interesting newer developments were of particular value in tropical and subtropical areas. Because of this speciality business, Agchem was able to increase business volume with all of its distributor relationships and to add new distributors throughout the world.

The international company. Visualizing that they would soon be in international operations in a relatively big way, in the fall of 1960, Frost and Merlin established an international subsidiary (wholly owned), Agchem International, Inc., incorporated in the United States. Merlin was made president.

Because it was impossible for Merlin himself to manage the international company at home and to travel sufficiently to maintain sales and service contacts with all distributors, an area manager, James Bollen, was appointed for Western Europe and the Middle East, with an office in Paris. Shortly after, a similar area manager, Harry Kelly, was appointed for the Pacific area with an office in Hawaii. Later in 1961, Mr. Malcolm Warner was selected as area manager for Latin America with an office in Miami. Since both Kelly and Warner traveled as much as nine months a year, it was decided that their families should live in American surroundings rather than be isolated in a foreign community during his extended journeys away from home.

From their first association, Merlin and Frost recognized the "handwriting on the wall." Because of the intensifying nationalistic feelings of foreign countries and the increasing shortage of dollar exchange, the distributor relationships were already running into trouble. Also, they recognized the rising scientific and technical competition from companies in France, Germany, and Italy, some of which were already manufacturing and selling. They therefore concluded that the only way in which to progress in the international field was to establish production facilities strategically located throughout the world. This was to be done on a small scale in the beginning, on a minimum of capital investment, with the expectation that expansion could be handled through use of offshore profits not subject to United States corporate income tax. In order to set up the mechanisms for doing this, they decided to establish a foreign base company, a device encouraged by the tax laws of the United States. Incorporation of such a company under the laws of a tax-haven country involved very little expense—legal costs, a small office, a bronze plaque on the door, and a part-time employee to handle the bookkeeping (who was accustomed to performing the same services for others). On advice of their lawyers, they chose the Republic of Panama as the tax-haven country, and set up Agchem, S.A. in Panama City in June 1961 as a wholly-owned subsidiary of Agchem International.

The international company (Agchem International, Inc.) was primarily an organization for marketing and developing new operating relationships overseas. Since it relied on the line and staff functions of the parent company in many areas, all of the divisions of the parent company became involved in overseas operations. These included:

Planning section (under Mr. Chadwick)
Sales department (under Mr. Wagner)
Production department (under Mr. Stone)
Quality control (a separate department reporting to Mr. Moir)
Personnel (a separate department reporting to Mr. Taylor)
Research and development (under Dr. Nutting)
Financial section (under Mr. Pashko)

These assignments were not formalized; they had just grown over the years. Fortunately the cooperation between Merlin (and his staff) and the other areas of the organization had been excellent and there had been no suggestion of duplicating any of these functional responsibilities in the international company. Probably because of the interest of Frost himself in overseas business and the personality of Merlin, the parent company's personnel were becoming increasingly internationally minded. However, communications and control were conducted rather informally, usually on a specific situation basis, and this had resulted in some confusion and lack of information where needed.

Overseas expansion

Present overseas operations included:

Distributors:

Argentina	India
Australia	Italy
Brazil	Japan
Canada	Mexico
Chile	New Zealand
Colombia	South Africa
Formosa	Spain
Germany	Sweden
Greece	Thailand
Hong Kong	Turkey

Some of these were quite active. Others had withered to almost nothing because of governmental restrictions and lack of foreign exchange.

Processing affiliates: *England.* A wholly owned subsidiary (except for a few shares owned by the president and general manager) had been formed in 1969. The active chemical components were processed, on a contract basis, by an English chemical company that blended these components into finished products and packed them for shipment. All operations followed the processes specified by the parent company, including the methods of quality control. In effect, this subsidiary was primarily a marketing and distributing organization that also served at times as liaison between the parent company and the processing contractor. In addition to the "home market," finished products were exported to established distributors in countries in the sterling area and elsewhere where pounds, but not dollars, were available. It was envisioned that the English company would serve as a distribution base for other EFTA areas. The president and general manager was Walter Starbuck, who had been a close friend of James F. Frost. Starbuck, an English national, had come to know Frost when they both attended a summer seminar in New York back in the early '30s. Later, the Frosts and Starbucks had traveled around the world together.

France. A licensing agreement had been established in 1970 with Produits Chimiques, S.A., a firm that manufactured finished products (from basic raw materials purchased in France) following the processes and control of Agchem. These were sold to distributors in France and in other EEC countries. Produits Chimiques was ranked as one of the largest producers of key inorganic chemicals, ranging from sulphuric acid, fertilizers and insecticides to dyestuffs and ferro alloys. It had plants and two research centers and employed 3,000 people (not counting recently acquired Compagnie du Rhône and separately held subsidiaries). Produits Chimiques S.A. listed ten French chemical companies in which it participated as of last year whose principal activities covered a spectrum of chemical products.

Its sales were:

Three years ago	$30 million
Two years ago	$38
One year ago	$35
Last year	$45

Products manufactured under Agchem's license amounted to about 5 percent of its sales last year.

Agchem in Thailand. The distributor in Thailand was K. Sumi & Company. This company was owned and operated by Kassem Sumi, a relatively wealthy businessman and a politician in Bangkok. His interests were rather diverse, but his major enterprise was K. Sumi & Company. This company was primarily involved in agricultural chemicals, importing from various manufacturers throughout the world and distributing in Thailand. Apart from the profit motive, Sumi was very much interested in developing the agriculture of the country and improving its performance.

In 1974, Sumi had visited the United States, primarily to learn what he could about new developments in the agricultural chemical field. It so happened that, about that time, a new and obscure disease was infesting many of the rice paddies, reducing yields drastically. He was particularly anxious to see what could be done toward controlling it. Having heard about Agchem through friends in the trade, he called on Frost.

After a few days of discussion, Frost had appointed Sumi as his distributor in Thailand. He did not anticipate much volume, at least in the beginning, since the use of Agchem's products would involve considerable field study to determine their effectiveness before routine use could be anticipated. Frost agreed to supply initial quantities of two products, Fungo-D and Fungo-X, free of charge, to initiate these trials.

Sumi returned to Thailand and immediately set up his studies. Within a relatively short while, his work, in cooperation with local growers, demonstrated that both products (particularly Fungo-D) were effective in controlling the rice disease problem. He soon began to receive commercial orders, especially from the more progressive producers who wanted to extend the scope of their early experimental trials. Volume was small at first, but at least Agchem's exports to Thailand were under way.

After this promising start, Frost's interest was whetted and Kelly made several trips to Bangkok to be of what help he could toward furthering the progress made. Agchem was currently selling in Thailand slightly over $150,-000 per year of the two products, Fungo-D and Fungo-X. While use of these specialized chemicals was by no means universal in Thailand, there was every promise that their application would be extended as additional growers gained experience with them.

In June, 1978, Frost received the following letter from Sumi:

"My dear good friend, Mr. Frost:

"As always it pleases me to address you my very good friend, but this time it is not without misgivings. After the progress we have made, and the future which we can anticipate, I must relate to you sad situations which are developing in Thailand. Our country is old but is now seeing the birth of new industrial ambitions. These are affecting the policies of our government leaders, and I must in all candor say rightfully so.

"In informal discussions with several of these persons, I have been advised that the policy of developing manufacturing industry in Thailand has not only been adopted by the government, but will be pursued with utmost vigor and rigidity. To accomplish these purposes, it is their intention to restrict manufacture of imported products of all kinds, even to the point of temporary hardship to our country, in order to force the beginning of manufacture here.

"In addition, the foreign exchange situation is stringent, particularly in the hard currencies of the world. Our country cannot continue to import at its present rate from the major industrial nations such as the United States. Specifically, the government has told me that, in order to continue to supply Fungo-D and Fungo-X, it will be necessary to complete at least partial manufacture in Thailand. I explained that this would be difficult because of the highly technical nature of the manufacturing methods, but these officials insisted that steps be taken toward producing the products here. Because of the technical problems involved, they finally agreed to permit importation from the United States of intermediate chemical components provided the final steps of the synthesis be completed in Thailand.

"I humbly appreciate the difficulties involved, but I have no choice except to propose that the manufacture of Fungo-D and Fungo-X, at least in the last stages, be done in our country.

"While we have not discussed this unexpected possibility before, I am prepared to consider the formation of a new company in Bangkok for this purpose. I would suggest that we think of a company jointly owned by Agchem Corporation and K. Sumi & Company, with approximately equal holdings. I am prepared to supply the funds for buildings, working capital, etc., and would propose that Agchem's investment primarily be in imported equipment and technological knowledge. The new company would, of course, require Agchem's processes which I would protect with the same concern as I would my own property. The technical advice of Mr. Stone and his staff would, I am sure, enable us to start manufacture in a satisfactory way.

"The selling prices of the intermediate chemicals cannot be exorbitant, but should be adequate to yield the parent Agchem a profit on these sales. In addition, the government has assured me that it will permit the new company to return to you, in dollars, Agchem's share of the profits made here. This is a special concession because of the importance of the products to our agricultural future. In frankness, I cannot assure you that this policy will stand forever, but the business people in our government are quite stable and I think it is a good chance to take.

"I would like, Mr. Frost, if you could come to Bangkok yourself and appraise the situation with your own eyes. In the meantime, I am forced to restrict our future orders for Fungo-D and Fungo-X. The government is permitting me to import 40 percent of last year's purchases over the next eight months with the understanding that, by that time, we shall have completed our plans for manufacture in Thailand.

"Since this will be your first visit to our beautiful country, we are happily anticipating greeting you at the airport. Until that time, I remain, as always, your humble servant.

"Most sincerely yours,"

It was impossible for Frost to make the trip to Thailand; the pressures of the growing business had curtailed his foreign travel considerably and he felt that Sumi's business did not justify the investment of his time. He wrote Kelly immediately, instructing him to go to Bangkok at his earliest opportunity to size up the situation.

Subsequently, Kelly spent two weeks in Bangkok and found that what Sumi had said was true. He had always liked Sumi himself, and had reason to believe that his complete confidence in him was well deserved. Kelly also studied the possible future market for Agchem's products, and concluded that, if supplies were available, the volumes would increase steadily over the next five years or more.

Kelly returned forthwith to the parent company and reported to Frost his findings. It was his recommendation that Sumi's proposal be accepted and he estimated that the initial total capital expenditure would not exceed $800,000. All the Thailand government was requiring was completion of the final chemical steps; these were reasonably simple reactions and the necessary equipment was not too complicated or costly. He suggested that a 50–50 venture be considered.

After a week of further investigation and deliberation, Frost decided to go ahead. He called all persons involved into his office, announced his decision, and instructed each to take the action necessary to expedite the project.

Subsequently, in late August, 1978, Frost had held a meeting of his major executives in his office. These included Stone (production), Dr. Nutting (research & development), Pashko (financial), Merlin (international), Wagner (sales), and Chadwick (planning). He opened the meeting with these comments:

"Our venture with Sumi seems to be going along nicely, but it has caused me to do a lot of thinking lately. Each of you has pitched in and done his part and done it well. In fact, we are just about on schedule, which is good when one considers the difficulties in accomplishing things in distant countries. We should be in production within six months.

"But it seems to me that we are just about at a turning point in our international business. All of us realize that, although our foreign volume was largely built up through distributor relationships, these all cannot last. While some of them are doing well, others are blocked by conditions beyond their control. It is inevitable that our major international growth will not come from distributors. Recognizing this, we set up our operations in England and France, and these were wise moves. They have just about got their feet on the ground now and we can look forward to increasing activities in Europe.

"Our Sumi venture is a different kind of thing, with new problems involved. It has brought home to me the fact that, as we get deeper and deeper into international operations, we are not handling these in the way we should.

"Our foreign business started very modestly, as is usually the case, and primarily through distributors. This was principally a marketing function which Dick and his staff have handled capably. With England and France, we face new problems—problems that are much more complicated. They involve almost all the functional aspects of our domestic business. When problems heretofore have come up in your individual areas, they have been tossed directly at you and each of you has fielded the ball well. As our international activities have grown gradually, responsibilities have been handled informally and very often directly between the source of the problem and the one of you who had to put out the fire. This has worked satisfactorily, so far, with a few exceptions here and there. Now, I visualize that we will add several more operating ventures of various types throughout the world over the next few years. As this grows, our present way of doing things is bound to fall apart at the seams.

"What I am concerned about now is communications and control. These are bound to involve paperwork, which we don't like and which we will desperately try to keep at a minimum. But still, we must know what is going on in our overseas installations. We must let them know our policies and practices—what we want to accomplish and how we want it accomplished—and hold them accountable for reasonable performance. In turn, we must let them know what is going on here in so far as it affects them—such as new marketing developments, new research angles, new process improvements, and all those kinds of things. At the same time, communications should be brought to the attention of all those involved in responsibility here at the home office, as well as in the field, such as Jim Bollen and Harry Kelly. We cannot operate a plant in Bangkok as we do here, but we do want to bring to them the best of our skills, which we have developed through intelligence, improvements, and hard work.

"Well, how is all of this going to be done? Frankly, I don't know, and that is why you are here. I do know this—before we find ourselves fumbling about, we should set up a well thought out plan of how we should run things.

"The new Sumi venture gives us an opportunity to do this. We are starting from scratch, and no fixed habits have developed that will have to be modified. If we can come up with a good operating plan or system, it not only will serve our purposes in Thailand, but can serve as a pattern for future ventures. It might even be adapted to France and England, where these habits already have been formed to a great extent.

"So far we have made no attempt to duplicate functional responsibilities in the international company, other than in the marketing area. For one thing, the expense involved in having a separate research director, director of production, and treasurer would not be justified economically. But more important than that, I want *all* of us to think internationally. Because of the importance of the future overseas business to our company, we must *all* be concerned with international affairs. Dick Merlin agrees with me. So, we will continue to utilize the line and staff functions of the parent company in connection with international problems. What we want to do now is to systematize this.

"I would like each of you to give this your serious thought over the next few days. Then put down on paper what you think we should do. Each of you will naturally look in his own area of responsibility very carefully, but think of the problems from the standpoint of the overall.

"First, we should define what routine and reoccurring reports should be instituted, to whom they should go, and how often.

"Second, when nonroutine communications come up, we should have it well understood who, other than the sender or the receiver, should receive copies.

"Possibly you may have some additional ideas, such as developing manuals of operations. If you think these are advisable, don't attempt to write the manual now, but merely indicate what it should accomplish.

"Consider all the mechanisms of control and communication we should use. We possibly should think of a standing committee, or committees, to review our international problems. This may sound more formal than we are accustomed to, but it might be a proper idea.

"How often should our people visit Bangkok, and who? Who from Bangkok should visit us here, and how often?

"In setting up your systems, don't forget the people you will be dealing with. Sumi will be president of the joint company, and in addition to overall responsibilities will, at least in the beginning, oversee all research field trials. There will be a plant manager, a secretary-treasurer, and a sales manager. These will be the main functions in Bangkok. Of course, Harry Kelly will do most of our direct contact work with the Thailand company; but, remember he travels about nine or ten months out of a year.

"Just to try to pinpoint my own thoughts, I have made some notations of each department's responsibilities that might be involved in international operations. I have had these notes typed up and here is a copy for each of you. I don't say that the list is complete, but at least it will serve as a starter.

"Can we meet Friday morning of next week to dig into this? I think we should plan to spend at least a half a day on it, because if things don't fall into place readily, it is going to take some time. I would also point out that the domestic U.S. market seems to have tightened up somewhat over the past three or four years."

Discussion questions

1. What signals are there that Agchem has problems?

2. Should Agchem reorganize itself? If so, how?*

Appendix to Case L
FROST'S NOTES

Responsibilities of domestic divisions in foreign operations

Sales department:
Sales methods and training
Sales forecasting methods
Market development
Sales expense control
Promotion and advertising

Production division:
Processing equipment
Processing techniques
Cost reproduction and control
Maintenance methods
Plant design and construction
Production control and scheduling (of export items)
Warehousing and shipping methods

Research & development division:
New product development
New product uses
Field studies of product performance
Engineering design of specialized equipment and apparatus
Process improvement (pilot plant)

Financial department:
Taxation
Accounting methods and control
Credit practices
Development of cost information
Inventory control
Purchasing specifications and pricing
Office procedures and order processing

---

*Note: the case may be used as the basis of a simulated meeting of the relevant executives or for an extended exercise in long-range planning.

Legal (with outside counsel):
Patents
Trademarks
Licensing
Contracts and agreements
Litigations (if any)

Personnel department:
Methods for evaluating and selecting new employees
Training methods
Fringe benefit programs

Planning:
Short-run and long-run plans
Profitability of products
Coordination of production and sales

Additional data on company and personnel: Agchem Products. The company was producing a range of chemicals, facilities for which were acquired during and after World War II. Although developed for temperate climates, Agchem products were well suited to the needs of tropical and semi-tropical agriculture.

In order of their sales values they were, (1) products for farm use including herbicides, insecticides, fungicides, fumigants and fertilizers, (2) plastics, (3) surfactants.

The farm chemical area was the company's strongest and it accounted for 70 percent of sales. Among the products were sodium alpha alpha dichoropropionate, a herbicide; "Tzetran," a fungicide sold as "bug killer"; "Quelene," which controlled tropical cattle grubs and "Agchem-On," which had extensive use for weed control in rubber, banana, and sugar plantations.

Sales of farm chemicals increased over the years despite the fact that the company experienced increased competition both from new and foreign producers. Movement of new products into trade was relatively slow and efforts toward refinement in market planning and testing were underway.

During the war, the company had secured a contract to manufacture various kinds of plasticizers. A plasticizer is a chemical that is compounded with a polymer to produce a plastic. The function of a plasticizer is to impart certain characteristics to the final product such as greater flexibility, heat resistance, or light stability. Although a number of different plasticizers for different applications were being produced, the phthalate plasticizer is used to illustrate the business.

The required raw materials, phthalic anhydride and higher alcohols, were bought from other manufacturers and the converted product, phthalate plasticizer, sold to large plastic manufacturers who combined it with, say, polyvinyl chloride resin in the ratio of 40:100 to make a plastic compound. The end uses of the plastic varied from cable coverings to applications in explosives.

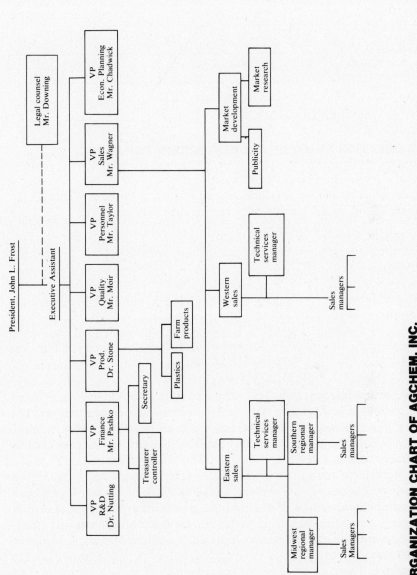

Figure L.1
PRESENT ORGANIZATION CHART OF AGCHEM, INC.

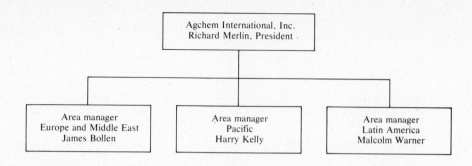

Figure L.2
ORGANIZATION CHART OF AGCHEM INTERNATIONAL, INC.

Later on, after the war, Agchem started producing all the products on the diagram below, except alcohol, plus various other plastics.

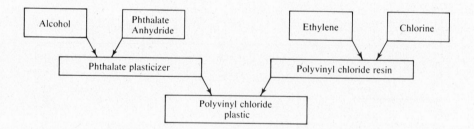

Several new plastics reached the advanced stage of development and many more were born in Agchem's research laboratories. The competition was becoming very intense. Nonetheless, there was an increase in sales volume, although partially offset by price declines. The sales for plastics amounted to 25 percent of total sales.

Surfactants, or surface active chemicals, were chemicals which reduce the surface tension of a liquid, thereby changing its wetting, emulsifying, and suspending characteristics. It was used in a great number of industries such as detergents, paints, plastics, pharmaceuticals, textiles, and cosmetics. The largest users were soap and detergent companies. It accounted for about 5 percent of total sales.

Research. There were 110 people engaged in research within the firm. The major share of the research budget (6 percent of sales) was devoted to the improvement of existing products and processes, work which was considered a vital necessity if the company were to maintain its competitive position in the industry in terms of efficiency, product quality and ability to tap new markets. The sales position in weed killers, polyethylenes and other products

Table L.1
CONDENSED TEN YEAR STATEMENT OF *FINANCIAL CONDITION*, AGCHEM, INC. AND SUBSIDIARY COMPANIES*

	Last year	1 yr. ago	2 yrs. ago	3 yrs. ago	4 yrs. ago	5 yrs. ago	6 yrs. ago	7 yrs. ago	8 yrs. ago	9 yrs. ago
Current assets										
Cash and marketable securities	$ 2.24	$ 2.32	$ 1.52	$ 3.62	$ 5.38	$ 6.51	$10.12	$ 5.63	$ 2.38	$ 2.17
Receivables (less reserves)	4.30	5.34	4.27	3.86	3.21	3.00	2.49	2.18	2.14	1.51
Inventories	7.99	7.31	6.94	5.23	3.82	4.14	3.72	3.84	2.44	1.70
Total current assets	$14.53	$14.97	$12.73	$12.71	$12.41	$13.65	$16.33	$11.65	$ 6.96	$ 5.38
Current liabilities										
Notes payable	$ 1.58	$ 2.78	$ 2.85		$ 1.60	$ 2.50	$ 5.00	$ 2.50	$ 2.09	$ 1.24
Accounts payable and accruals	3.83	3.75	3.60	$ 2.96	2.43	2.16	2.33	2.24	3.35	.86
Taxes on income	.34	1.90	2.08	2.58	1.91	1.48	2.62	4.94		
Total current liabilities	$ 5.75	$ 8.43	$ 8.53	$ 5.54	$ 5.94	$ 6.14	$ 9.95	$ 9.68	$ 5.55	$ 2.12
Working capital (A)	$ 8.78	$ 6.54	$ 4.19	$ 7.17	$ 7.47	$ 7.51	$ 6.38	$ 1.37	$ 1.51	$ 3.17
Property (at cost)	$51.92	$53.29	$43.95	$36.49	$31.35	$32.37	$30.10	$25.92	$19.23	$14.98
Depreciation, amortization, and depletion	23.72	26.44	21.12	17.67	14.71	11.45	8.65	6.43	5.21	4.38
Net property (B)	$28.20	$26.86	$22.83	$18.82	$16.64	$20.92	$21.45	$19.49	$14.02	$10.60
Other assets (C)	$ 1.03	$ 1.13	$ 1.04	$ .79	$ .92	$ .68	$ .67	$ .59	$ .39	$ .39
Investment (A) plus (B) plus (C)	$38.01	$34.53	$28.08	$26.78	$28.02	$29.05	$28.49	$22.25	$15.91	$14.17
Long-term indebtedness	13.73	8.12	6.63	7.99	12.15	13.90	13.98	9.11	4.85	5.45
Reserves	.11	.70	.09	.08	.05	.06	.04	.05	.09	.08
Total	$13.84	$ 8.82	$ 6.72	$ 8.07	$12.20	$13.46	$14.02	$ 9.16	$ 4.94	$ 5.53
Stockholders' equity	$24.17	$25.84	$21.36	$18.72	$15.82	$15.15	$14.47	$12.40	$10.97	$ 8.63

*Figures are for year ending December 31. Amounts are expressed in millions of dollars.

Table L.2
CONDENSED TEN YEAR STATEMENT OF EARNINGS, AGCHEM, INC. AND SUBSIDIARY COMPANIES*

	Last year	1 yr. ago	2 yrs. ago	3 yrs. ago	4 yrs. ago	5 yrs. ago	6 yrs. ago	7 yrs. ago	8 yrs. ago	9 yrs. ago
Sales and other revenue										
Net sales	$31.27	$31.80	$31.39	$28.27	$23.54	$21.42	$21.52	$20.36	$16.98	$11.04
Other revenue	.41	.45	.35	.21	.41	.41	.46	.36	.29	.26
Total	$31.68	$32.25	$31.74	$28.48	$23.95	$21.83	$21.98	$20.72	$17.27	$11.30
Costs and other charges										
Cost of sales	$20.60	$20.34	$18.82	$15.85	$13.70	$13.04	$12.80	$11.85	$ 9.35	$ 6.54
Depreciation, amortization, and depletion	4.14	4.12	4.04	3.70	3.65	3.23	2.60	1.64	1.12	1.02
Selling and administrative expenses	3.34	3.34	2.91	2.46	2.12	1.85	1.43	1.34	.97	.80
Pension and profit-sharing plans	.47	.45	.38	.31	.27	.25	.21	.19	.16	.14
Interest expense	.49	.55	.27	.29	.43	.53	.48	.16	.08	.09
Other income charges	.34	.05	.07	.16	.08	.04	.14	.08	.11	.06
Taxes on income	1.27	1.72	2.58	2.73	1.80	1.22	2.54	3.69	3.45	.98
Total	$30.65	$30.57	$29.07	$25.50	$21.97	$20.16	$20.20	$18.95	$15.24	$ 9.63
Earnings for the year	$ 1.03	$ 1.68	$ 2.67	$ 2.98	$ 1.98	$ 1.67	$ 1.78	$ 1.77	$ 2.03	$ 1.73
Other statistics										
Wages paid	$ 8.75	$ 9.16	$ 8.27	$ 7.02	$ 5.88	$ 5.72	$ 5.24	$ 4.76	$ 3.70	$ 2.76
Number of employees at year end (thousands)	1.30	1.33	1.36	1.26	1.13	1.09	1.07	1.02	.84	.70

*Figures are for year ending December 31. Amounts expressed in millions of dollars.

was dependent on a continuous flow of new ideas applied to process and product improvement.

Agchem also aimed at a broader product line, and new product research was mostly directly related to the continuing long-term profitability of the business.

It was observed that a new product with unique utility and properly protected by patents could be expected to yield a far more attractive rate of return than an older product, which might be broadly established in the industry on a competitive basis.

During the last year, Agchem had been awarded 13 United States patents, double the average of the previous years. Approximately $3.5 million of last year's sales revenue was derived from products introduced within the last two years.

International Operations. International operations, those beyond the U.S. and Canada, were characterized by strong increases in market demand for Agchem chemicals and byproducts. International activities (including Canada) accounted for over 20 percent of sales income, and profit yield continued to be relatively high. Much of the success in building this international business resulted from know-how and capabilities developed in the home markets.

The present policy was to enter international markets through exports. When it was believed that local production would result in substantial sales increases at acceptable profit levels, Agchem would consider establishing plants in or near major consumption areas.

Last year's exports were distributed as follows:

To Europe and Middle East	50 percent	$3,520 million
To Latin America	20	1,440
To Pacific and S. Africa	10	710
To Canada	20	1,384
Total		$7,054

Management. A brief note follows on the backgrounds of some of the men, on their position and duties, plus a description of them based on a collection of quotes made by their colleagues.

Mr. John L. Frost, now 62 years old and the majority stockholder, had received his A.B. from Stanford. Until quite recently he had handled the sales side of the company—both domestic and international—in addition to the presidency. He actively concerned himself with company planning and with major investment and product decisions.

"Mr. Frost considers the company in a highly personal manner, which, among our small executive group, makes for a very warm, intimate feeling. His weakest point is a tendency to permit details of secondary importance to occupy his time. But he has a gift for making people enthusiastic. He is a wonderful morale builder."

Dr. George Nutting received his Doctor of Science degree in chemical engineering from the University of California and joined Agchem in 1945 as works chemist. By 1955 he was in charge of all the research and development.

"George is a chemical engineer of outstanding ability and a genius in his speciality—the planning and design of chemical process and plant. If one could say that one man works harder among this group of managers, George could merit this compliment. At the same time he tends to become too attached to his own people and projects. He can be moody and unpleasantly stubborn on occasions."

Dr. Michael Stone received his Ph.D. in chemical engineering at the University of Berlin, Germany, and joined the company in 1950. He was named vice president, production, in 1957.

"Michael is probably the best liked man in the plant. The workers trust him and come to him with their problems, which is a great help to us all. As a consequence, he has been shifting more and more from the technical and production managerial function to that of personnel welfare."

Mr. Kenneth Downing received both his A.B. degree and his law degree from Harvard, and upon graduation joined the firm of Davidson, Levin and Wheeler, an Atlanta law firm that had served Agchem from the founding of the company. Downing considered himself a specialist in corporate matters.

"Ken is a man with exceptional intellect and perception. He can quickly grasp new situations, adapt his thinking, organize to meet problems and see a program through. He is also a brilliant negotiator. He is, however, young and tends to be a bit emotional in his work."

Mr. George Pashko, an M.B.A. from Columbia in accounting and finance, had worked with Parks, Siegel and Co., Agchem's local auditing firm. He was hired away from them in 1954 and later became the financial VP for Agchem. He was 42 at the time.

"George has demonstrated his ability to plan business activities comprehensively and realistically. He has a great deal of drive, flexibility and the capacity to see the shape of things to come as contrasted with a tendency merely to extrapolate present trends."

Mr. Peter Chadwick, a British national, did his "Tripos" in economics at Cambridge University and later joined the firm of Mansfield and Wouk, a U.S. firm of business consultants. He was hired in 1965 from them to head the planning division of the company. He was a personal friend of Mr. Frost, whom he met in England.

"Peter is known and accepted in the industry. He has a wide acquaintance with men in other companies and with bankers and leaders or planners in other industries. He has the ability to lead and stimulate subordinates and associates and can effectively chair meetings of management groups."

Mr. Joseph F. Wagner attended Purdue University, from which he received his A.B. in liberal arts. He was hired by Mr. James E. Frost in 1946, and subsequently rose in the ranks of the company to become vice president for sales at the age of 52. His wife and Mr. Frost's wife are sisters.

"Joe is an easy going person who loves to travel and meet people. His interests are mainly in the arts and literature, and he is considered something of an authority on Albert Camus. He works by instinct, and his intuition is usually right. He is highly respected by all."

Mr. James Bollen, a graduate of Cambridge University and Harvard Business School, had worked for I.C.I. in France as Assistant Sales Manager for France before being hired by Agchem as area manager for Europe and the Middle East. Mr. Peter Chadwick and Mr. Bollen had been colleagues at Trinity College.

"Jim has a lot of personal charm. He speaks fluent French, Swedish, and Italian. He has a lot of drive and seems to get his way by convincing others quite easily."

Mr. Harry Kelly received his A.B. from Yale and continued there at the law school. Later he joined the U.S. State Department and was stationed in Japan. He left the foreign service because he wanted his children to be brought up at home in the States and he with them. He was working as a consultant with Mansfield and Wouk, before being hired by Agchem in early 1960 as area manager for the Pacific. He wanted to go back to the Far East then as his children were at college.

"Harry is a very likeable person, and in every sense of the word a diplomat. He is very quick in his thinking. He loves the Far East and is fond of traveling."

Mr. Malcolm Warner graduated from M.I.T. with a bachelor's degree in chemical engineering. He later worked five years for a very large chemical company in New York as an assistant to the sales manager for Latin America. His wife was from a very wealthy, aristocratic Argentinian family that had many business and political affiliations. Mr. Frost had met him at a cocktail party given by the Argentinian consul general in New York and had been very much impressed by his credentials and contacts. Mr. Frost spoke to him about Agchem and after a few months and many meetings with him, he was appointed Agchem's area manager for Latin America.

"One cannot afford to own a yacht and a plane and live the way Malcolm does on his salary. He does not need to work for a living, but he enjoys doing so and loves the challenge presented in his work. He is our star salesman. Since he took over as area manager, our sales have gone up 100-fold in his area. He is very fond of Mr. Frost and is an amiable person, though now and then he tends to be arrogant, but that too suits his dynamic personality."

Mr. Robert Moir graduated from the University of California with an S.M. in chemical engineering. He worked for a large Los Angeles chemical company in their quality control department. He was hired in 1961 by Agchem to head the new quality control department.

"Bob is a brilliant young man. He is very demanding and is conscientious, which earns him the respect of all his colleagues and subordinates. He is quite a sportsman—loves sailing, scuba diving, and golf and is excellent at all three."

Mr. Walter Taylor attended college for a time, but was forced to leave after a year when his father died and his mother was left a dependent widow. For a time they had lived very shabbily, but finally he worked his way up to the job of personnel manager for a small paint manufacturing company with 400 employees in Atlanta. He was hired by Mr. Frost to assist in personnel matters at Agchem in 1958. Mr. Frost had known Mr. Taylor for a number of years in that they were both active in the same church. Frost, hearing many good things about Taylor, decided to promote him to head Agchem's personnel department. That was some ten years ago.

"Walter is a gentleman. He is liked by all at the plant and he himself takes a very keen personal interest in them. The company has had a long record of no strikes and very low accident rate as compared to the industry and he is largely responsible for it."

Plant location and headquarters:
Headquarters: Atlanta, Georgia
Plants: Atlanta, Los Angeles, Houston, and Chicago
Sales office: Throughout the United States (eight in all)
Bankers: Citizens Southern Bank (Atlanta)
Lawyers: Davidson, Levin and Wheeler (Atlanta)
Auditors: Parks, Siegel and Company (Atlanta)

Chapter 9
PUBLIC AFFAIRS STRATEGY

The public affairs function explains corporate strategy to the corporation's many constituencies, attempts to create a more favorable political-social-economic climate, and reports the response, present and anticipated, to management. It also presses for appropriate adjustment in corporate strategy so as to render the corporation more harmonious with its many-faceted environment at home and abroad.

Only in the last half dozen years have corporations realized that they are in fact major actors in the formulation of both national and international public policy. As major forces in the allocation of the world's resources, corporations have a responsibility to indicate to the political sector how political decisions are likely to impact upon the national and global allocation systems in interaction with ongoing economic and social-psychological processes. Such corporate representation is only now being accepted as a legitimate corporate function, just as labor and other common interest organizations, but possibly less so in the U.S. than in Europe and Japan. The organizational analogue of this corporate realization is the appearance of new staff departments in the larger corporations, variously known as public affairs, external affairs, government relations, or public policy.

Let it be noted that this function is quite distinct from the traditional public relations function, which is really part of corporate marketing in that it is focused on improving the corporate image vis-à-vis the public, that is, the consumer, and thereby enhancing the acceptance of the firm's products. Public affairs, in contrast, represents—on the one hand—the corporate attempt to influence the social-political-legal (and indirectly, the economic) environment in which the firm operates so as to render the environment more congenial to the realization of corporate objectives, however these may be defined. On the other hand, public affairs is concerned with analyzing the implications of environmental changes for corporate strategy. In short, public affairs has to do with affecting a convergence between corporate strategy, political decision, and social change. At some point, a compromise tolerable to all major actors must be struck that is responsive to on-going social processes.

Public relations and public affairs functions may well be in conflict when the corporation publicly eschews a public effort to alter some aspect of its environment, which, for the moment at any rate, is unpopular with a significant number of consumers. A case in point was the intense effort launched by a few U.S. corporations in 1977 to convince Congress not to enact legislation in respect to the Arab boycott, which, it was alleged, would so damage the competitive position of U.S. firms in Arab markets as to virtually deliver those markets to Japanese and European competitors. At the same time, possibly many millions of Americans—consumers—were deeply offended by the Arab boycott. Whether they should have been was quite another matter; they obviously were.

Boddewyn suggests that external affairs and government relations are not identical and offers the following definition:

External Affairs is concerned with enlisting the support and negating the opposition of nonmarket units (public and private organizations, looser collectivities, and individuals) in the firm's environment. More specifically, this function deals with: (1) government in its multiple roles of legitimizer, regulator, and promoter; (2) business, trade, labor, and professional associations as well as other firms in their pressure-group, private-regulator, and legitimizing roles; (3) the intellectual, moral, and scientific communities as legitimizers and opinion-makers, (4) public opinion at large as voter and general legitimizer; and (5) the firm's stockholders and employees as legitimizers. These units constitute the "nonmarket environment" of the firm as distinguished from the "markets" for its commercial inputs and outputs.[1]

In other words, government is only one element in the firm's nonmarket environment, albeit of considerable importance. One can argue for the phrase "public affairs" rather than "external affairs" in that among the actors in the nonmarket environment with which the corporation must relate positively are *internal* to the corporation, its stockholders, and employees (including managers), not in their immediate economic roles but in their broader, societal roles. But one can hardly call them external to the corporation, whatever their roles. Hence we use the term public affairs, as do many corporations.

In setting public affairs strategy, the corporation faces two basic options.

1. It can seek a low profile (passive strategy) or a high profile (active strategy).
2. It can pursue its strategy alone or in concert with other corporations or through nonbusiness intermediary institutions.

9.1 CHOICE OF PROFILE

Many corporations, although possibly a declining number, opt to pursue a neutral, or at least a hidden (covert), strategy in respect to efforts to change

---

[1] Jean J. Boddewyn, "The External Affairs of Transnational Firms: A Research Note," *Management International Review*, 1976, vol. 16, no. 3, pp. 47–48.

their social, political, economic, or legal environments. For example, in the debates preceding the controversial Tax Reform Act of 1976 and the anti-boycott legislation of 1977, few U.S. corporations were willing to take a public position. Apparently, many were so sensitive to the intense criticism in the U.S. of "multinational corporations" generally that they either assumed their overt opposition to the proposed legislation would be counterproductive, or they were intimidated by highly organized public pressure groups. One of the reasons for the antimultinational climate in the U.S. is undoubtedly the revelations of past covert attempts by certain corporations to alter their political environments overseas, most notably the ITT-CIA scandal in Chile allegedly involving an attempt to overthrow the national government, the United Brands effort to alter a tax law in Honduras by large payments to influential individuals, and the Lockheed effort to influence Japanese government military purchasing through multimillion dollar "commissons."[2]

One of the characteristics of the U.S. scene is the intense four-way adversary relationship between business, labor, government, and consumer, which some observers believe is building costs into the U.S. economy and thereby rendering U.S. business less competitive in world markets. These costs take many forms, but of overriding importance is possibly the element of uncertainty thereby introduced into business strategy. European and Japanese executives may be concerned about the relatively high fixed costs their more cooperative social and corporate structures imply, plus an alleged reduction in incentive. But, GNP growth rates, unemployment levels, and relative rates of innovation, insofar as they can be measured, would seem to indicate a relative loss of U.S. competitiveness. The cost of the cops and robbers game being played out by U.S. politicians, business executives, labor leaders, and consumer groups, all cheered on by the academic community, may prove to be exceedingly costly. It is a demonstrable fact that many corporations are so intimidated that they are unwilling, or unable, to communicate effectively with the political sector or with the public other than through the market. Suffice it to say that a high profile public affairs strategy is very likely to be counterproductive unless the corporation has creditability with the target audience.

CHOICE OF MODE   9.2

A corporation may choose to pursue a public affairs strategy identified directly with itself, to identify with the collective efforts of other firms, or to operate through nonbusiness intermediaries. Primarily, the choice depends upon the relative creditability of the corporation and the skills it can bring to bear.

---

[2]More recently one might note the revelation that the Bell Helicopter Company was training Uganda pilots in Texas, despite the public denunciation of Idi Amin's regime.

Lacking creditability, it may gain by joining other firms in whatever the enterprise might be. And, if business generally lacks creditability, as in the U.S. and many LDCs, a better strategy may be to support nonbusiness intermediaries that seem to be working toward constructive ends from the corporate point of view. Examples would be universities, research institutes, and public media.

Apart from their many trade associations,[3] firms operating internationally out of the U.S. have only recently begun to fashion collective and representative organizations to research important international trade and investment issues and speak out with some authority and creditability. Among these are the Emergency Committee for American Trade (ECAT), which is a lobby for freer international trade and investment composed of the leaders of 66 of the largest American firms and banks with international interests, and the Trade Action Coordinating Committee, which is a forum of about 100 representatives of national associations, law firms, and corporations committed to working for international trade expansion. Of regional concern is the American Association of Latin America (AACCLA), whose membership represents an estimated $20 billion U.S. direct investment in Latin America. Other U.S. organizations active in presenting corporate views on international issues are the U.S. Committee of the International Chamber of Commerce and the National Council for United States-China Trade. Another important international business forum in the U.S. is the National Foreign Trade Council. Possibly the most highly organized of any national business community is that of Japan. Quasi-official industry associations linked to the Ministry of International Trade and Investment appear to be consulted before the Japanese government makes any moves in the international trade and investment area, so much so that a U.S. businessman in negotiating with Japanese executives is never quite sure whether he is negotiating with a private firm or the government.

At the international level is the Trilateral Commission, which was organized in 1973 upon the urging of David Rockefeller. Consisting of 180 prominent persons from Western Europe, Japan, and the U.S. (largely businessmen), its purpose is to promote "the habit of working together" on political, economic, and security issues in the three regions and to "seek to devise and disseminate proposals of general benefit" to both the public and governments.[4] Also operating at the international level is the Comité Internationale de l'Organisation Scientifique (CIOS), which is a confederation of national management and business organizations providing an international forum for discussion of issues and a vehicle for the establishment of common positions. At the secondary level are three associated regional federations, the Pan-American Committee of CIOS (PACCIOS), the Asian Association of

---

[3] *National Trade & Professional Associations of the United States and Canada* (Washington: Columbia Books, Inc., 1977).

[4] *New York Times*, 24 October 1973, p. 4.

Management Organizations of CIOS (AMMOCIOS), and the Conseil l'Européen de CIOS (CECIOS).

In the category of nonbusiness intermediaries stands the Conference Board, an independent, nonprofit business research organization headquartered in New York, whose purpose is to promote prosperity and security by assisting in the effective operation and sound development of voluntary productive enterprise. The board has more than 4,000 associates and serves some 40,000 individuals throughout the world by means of its continuing research in matters of interest to business firms. Somewhat similar organizations exist elsewhere, such as the Nomura Research Institute of Japan. By reason of the apparent objective professional quality of much of their work, their reports enjoy a relatively high level of creditability.

The skills required for an effective public affairs function become apparent when one lists the vehicles for effecting strategy in this area. The list includes: (1) the ability to scan the corporate environment so as to be able to order the priorities of public issues pressing upon it; (2) the capacity to derive some measure of cost effectiveness of a public affairs effort in respect to a given issue (will the gain in a changed environment be worth the alienation of individuals and interests, not to mention the expenditure of corporate resources?); (3) a high level of communications skill; (4) the capacity to negotiate with public authorities so as to match corporate strategy with the perceived public interest. Obviously, the common denominator is environmental analysis, which in turn rests upon a carefully designed and accurate information system, plus concern for socio-political processes impacting on the market well after the usual time-horizon for normal business decisions and which can only be quantified approximately. It should be noted that the more dynamic is the environment, the greater the uncertainty, and the higher the rate by which future earnings should be discounted. The result is a very short time-horizon for most business decisions. In the contemporary world, long-term business planning can usually be no longer than five years if it is to have any impact on current decisions. And corporate executives are normally evaluated upon *annual* performance. But the public affairs executive must be thinking in much longer terms. To have an impact on corporate activity he must be a very senior and influential person with direct access to the corporate president and board of directors and have an assured tenure. And in his task he must be assisted by political and social analysts. For the first time corporations are beginning to employ political scientists, cultural anthropologists, and sociologists, not only economists.

Some of the vehicles for effecting corporate public affairs strategy include (1) participating in, or supporting, surveys and other research designed to prove the costs or benefits of a particular public policy or legislative proposal (subsidized research); (2) presenting views to various public bodies and influential individuals (lobbying); (3) buying space in publications or air time to argue a point of view on a public issue, either in its own words or those of some scholar or well-known public figure ("advocacy advertising"); (4) donations of funds to nonprofit organizations known to be sympathetic to one or more corporate policy positions or that are working to improve some environmental factor considered important to the corporation or that are believed will improve the intellectual inputs to corporate policy formulation ("charitable contributions"); (5) negotiating with public and private bodies so as to improve the conditions under which the corporation acts; (6) the restructuring of the corporation so as to be more reflective of major environmental changes (such as the placing of public interest members on corporate boards); (7) the volunteering of corporate skills to help resolve public problems; and (8) the payment of funds (or other material benefits) to public officials or others to achieve a change of policy advantageous to the corporation ("bribes").

The last is a device to be used only under the most extreme, desperate circumstances, for it must be assumed that the details will become known publicly sooner or later, probably sooner. Disclosure only takes one disgruntled knowledgeable employee, one honest official, or one astute and courageous journalist. Anticipation of the impact of ultimate disclosure must be a factor in the decision.

The problem of "illegal payments" is a complicated one, which may best be analyzed in terms of initiating pressures, forms of payment, objective of the payment, mode, and impact within the parent country (see Figure 9.1). The corporation may be under pressure to make such a payment either by reason of competitive pressure or pressure from its parent government in order to gain some political or military advantage. The payment may be made either directly or through an intermediary. It may end as a personal gain for the beneficiary public official (government, political, labor, or other influential public personage) or for some social purpose, such as a project, the benefits of which accrue largely to society. And it may be in the form of money or some service rendered gratis or below market price, such as an "inspection trip" to corporate headquarters. The specific object of the payment may be to expedite the achievement of a legal objective (such as moving goods through customs), to create a competitive bias in favor of the donor (as in government purchasing or in prohibiting import of competing goods or services), to achieve an objective illegal under local law, to influence national economic policy, to influence political outcomes, to achieve an objective illegal under parent country law (such as evasion of U.S. export controls, antitrust law, taxes, etc.), or to further parent country policy objectives. Obviously, these are not all mutually exclusive categories. The mode of payment may be either overt or covert. And the payment may have no impact on the parent country; it may impact negatively (for example, the loss of business by other parent country firms, the undermining of parent country foreign policy through contributions to a political party known to be hostile to parent country interests, the stimulation of demands for military equipment contrary to parent country interests, or the commitment of an act illegal under parent country law); or the payment may have a positive impact in the parent country. Examples of the latter would include a gain in employment and profits for U.S. business generally through subcontractors and others, improvement of the U.S. balance of payments, or support of U.S. policy. Examples of the last would be gaining access to critically needed raw materials, undermining an unfriendly government, or inducing the acceptance of U.S. products (e.g., U.S. weapons systems).

As can be perceived from these comments, and from Figure 9.1, what is generally considered to be reprehensible (at least in the U.S.) is a direct payment generated by competitive pressures for the personal gain of a government official for any purpose other than to further U.S. policy objectives, particularly if it is covert and produces a negative impact in the U.S. Overt action might still be reprehensible if illegal under U.S. law, such as corporate support of foreign political groups (which may be perfectly legal under foreign law, as in Canada), or if producing a negative impact in the U.S. But there are many grey areas. What of corporate sponsorship of a visit by host government officials to the parent country in an effort to improve the host country political image and hence influence national policy of the parent country? Which is precisely what Mobil apparently did in 1969 when it sponsored a visit of a Nigerian government official to the U.S. in order to try to offset pro-Biafran sentiment in the U.S.[5] What of making corporate facilities available to a parent government effort to overthrow the host country government? What of payments to labor leaders? What of the distribution in Ecuador by Texas-Gulf of pamphlets prepared by the U.S. Information Agency extolling the benefits of private oil distribution?[6] We have now probably crossed the line of what is doubtful to what is fully acceptable. Even more clearly acceptable was the building of school buildings in Mexico financed by Ford dealers.[7] We have now moved into the area of charitable donations or philanthropy, the motive of which may well be to influence national economic policy and/or political outcomes more favorable to the donor company.

Let us look closely at philanthropy in the corporate context, for this is an important tool of the public affairs manager. Philanthropy has to do with making corporate resources available to activities that do not enter into the production and/or sales function within the business planning horizon and is not legally required. Philanthropic expenditures are discretionary in the sense that corporate managers do not expect them to impact on either costs, sales, or profits within the planning period. Such definition, however, does not provide an easy categorization of many corporate expenditures. For example, on-site feeding of employees may well be a *business* expense, not philanthropy, if a direct impact on productivity and absenteeism is expected. Support of research in respect to increasing yields on local farms, on the other hand, is probably philanthropy unless the firm itself is in the agro-business sector and

---

[5] *New York Times*, 29 January 1969.
[6] *New York Times*, 22 March 1972.
[7] *New York Times*, 22 August 1971.

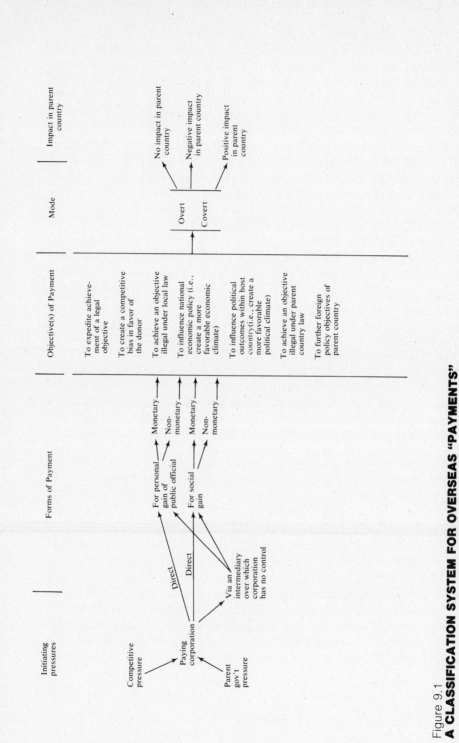

Figure 9.1
A CLASSIFICATION SYSTEM FOR OVERSEAS "PAYMENTS"

stands to benefit in some direct, short-term way. But is support for a technical institute engaged in research in a specific sector philanthropy? No easy answer is possible.

It would seem that corporate philanthropy is nonetheless generally perceived by the donors, and, indeed, it must be internally justified on this basis, as supporting corporate goals. So, what we are talking about is the expenditure of corporate resources for activities the donors believe will impact on corporate goals *in the longer run*. To say that the corporate goal is maximum profit is not adequate, for it begs several questions, specifically:

1. Maximum profit over what time horizon (which quickly gets one into consideration of perceived risks and discount rates)?

2. Maximum profit for whom?—management, labor, owners, customers, government?

It can be argued that valid non-business giving would satisfy corporate goals if:

1. It is seen as *cost-reducing* over time (e.g., improving the relevant infrastructure, improving employee productivity or stability). In a very real sense such expenditures may be viewed as corporate payment for society's expenditures from which the corporation derives benefit, such as the use of manpower trained with public and private resources external to the firm.

2. It is seen as *risk-reducing* over time (e.g., improvement of the corporate image; support of the development of a climate compatible with long-term corporate survival, thereby reducing the probability of discontinuous change disruptive of either market or production or of the probability of wrong assumptions about the path of change of relevant environmental variables).

But corporate philanthropy is possibly not valid if it merely satisfies the personal desires of owners, managers, and/or employees. Many believe that the corporation is not the appropriate vehicle for generalizing the social priorities of such groups, which is exactly what it does if it uses its resources in support of activities unrelated to corporate objectives. If corporate resources are devoted to nonmarket-related purposes, one is on very slippery ground in the absence of some general consensus, which is best reached through *political* processes, not corporate.

One of the problems is that there is no clear consensus as to how to resolve some of the basic issues we face, even if one tries to justify corporate philanthropy on the basis that it supports either national interest or world welfare. The satisfaction of national interest in a world in which there is obvious need for global management of food, energy, exhaustible resources, and exploitation of space and the deep sea, begs a number of questions. In fact, it is not even clear that U.S. foreign policy, for example, is really responsive to its own long-term national interests. On the one hand, it would appear that it is U.S. foreign policy to support the development of the LDCs. Yet, recent tax legislation has the effect of increasing the cost of U.S. capital to the LDCs and significantly slowing the flow of U.S. capital and technology into the LDCs. And where does world welfare lie when one is called upon to support the notion of self-dependency in a world increasingly interdependent in reality? Much emphasis has been placed by some upon the need for diverting resources in support of the poorest of the poor. Yet we know that we live in a world of finite resources. The point is that it seems unsupportable for corporations to make decisions on these issues in the absence of some sort of political consensus, which is precisely what a corporation does when it justifies corporate philanthropy on this basis. In fact, it is not at all clear that, given the apparent successes of the People's Republic of China, world welfare is best served even by supporting traditional capitalist values in some parts of the world. How does one define world welfare? It would be presumptuous for a corporation to do so.

There would even seem to be reasonable limits to what might otherwise be considered as perfectly valid corporate philanthropy. Two tests might be suggested: the willingness of the corporate donor to make public both the fact of its philanthropy and its true motivation. Furthermore, corporate survival should not be viewed necessarily in terms of continued ownership of fixed assets, but rather, on the maintenance of a reasonable stream of earnings whether derived from direct investment, the sales of production inputs through contract (i.e., management skills, technology and associated skills, finance, capital goods, or other materials), or from providing access to international marketing and information networks. If otherwise valid corporate philanthropy is open and truly conceived as an effort to protect a profitable relationship with a given market—not merely in defense of a single ownership and control strategy—then it has claim to legitimacy. Otherwise, the validity of the act is brought into question for it cannot be said to be truly risk-reducing in the long run. Obviously, any philanthropic act that runs counter to the basic interest of the host society compounds political risk, even though those interests may not yet be explicitly articulated. Therefore, corporate donations to support research designed to provide better understanding of the underlying dynamics of societies in which the corporation does business is of signal importance, but that research is of little value to the corporation unless it has access to that research and uses it in its decision-making.

Other than payments to government officials and corporate philanthropy, a frequent device used by the public affairs department is what has come to be known as advocacy advertising. Research by Sethi would challenge the effectiveness of most such advertising in the U.S. He concludes,

No amount of advocacy advertising will help unless there is a recognition that some of the criticism directed against business institutions is indeed valid. There must be a demonstrated willingness to change where current methods of operation and standards of performance fall short of societal expectations. Business must take steps to put its own house in order. Generalized statements of self-righteousness are ineffective in presenting one's case. Nor does it help to explain away wrongdoing; e.g., illegal political payoffs and bribes at home and abroad, in terms of the "rotten apple theory" when such behavior is persistent and widespread, and equally well reported in the news media.

The cause of business is poorly served when corporate spokesmen concentrate their fire on critics; e.g., labor radical groups, government bureaucrats, and environmentalists, and refuse to speak out against business practices that are illegal or considered socially irresponsible.[8]

If this be a valid assessment of advocacy advertising within the U.S., consider the case of a large alien enterprise in a foreign country, particularly in an LDC with an antiforeign business prejudice. The classic case of the misuse of advocacy advertising was the newspaper campaign of International Petroleum Corporation (a subsidiary of Exxon, then Esso) in Peru that labeled certain statements of high-level Peruvian government officials as untrue. Whether their statements were true or not was irrelevant. The point is that those designing the advertisements displayed a curious inability to project themselves into the shoes of the ordinary Peruvian and predict his reaction. The response, of course, was increased pressure for the expropriation of the IPC properties in Peru. It brings to mind those Americans who fully expected that a Gringo-sponsored invasion of Cuba would spark a popular Cuban uprising against the Castro regime! A positive public response rests on a long record of behavior generally perceived to be beneficial in some sense by the majority of the relevant public, or—at the very least—not perceived to be harmful or deceitful.

The point is that advocacy advertising, whatever its cultural setting, should not be seen as a public relations effort, but as public *affairs* function, which means that it represents an honest effort to spell out the ramifications of certain political or social acts on employment, incomes, productivity, prices, sales, or investment. And it should only be used if the public creditability of the corporation is relatively high.

Another device available to those responsible for the public affairs function is negotiating with public bodies to produce satisfactory environmental conditions. Corporate executives, the U.S. included, seem to have been remarkably weak in this area. The hallmark of the effective negotiator is the capacity to project oneself vicariously into the shoes of the people on the other side of the bargaining table so as to understand the pressures to which they are responding. If one starts from the position of assumed superiority in wisdom and integrity, as do many business leaders (which is apparent in the sarcasm with which many refer to political leaders and others, not to mention the extraordi-

---

[8]S. Prakash Sethi, "Advocacy Advertizing as a Strategy of Corporate Response to Societal Pressures: the American Experiences," paper presented to a seminar on marketing and public policy, Cergy, France, September 30–October 1, 1976, mimeo., pp. 27–28.

nary incomes many receive), it is very difficult to bring off successful negotiation.

Another common pitfall is insensitivity to the face-saving need on the part of the other side, a need not unique to the much-maligned oriental, nor to the politician! Although manifest in different ways, virtually everyone other than a masochist endeavors to save face. Any negotiating ploy that forces another into a losing situation, or into a position that will subject him or her to ridicule or public condemnation, is bound to set up a countervailing force. The battle may be won, but not the war. A corollary is that face-destroying rudeness or anger in a negotiation are inexcusable and probably self-defeating unless carefully calculated in advance. It should be realized that there are always several possible explanations for the behavior one witnesses until it is probed.

For example, a negotiation became bogged down in Turkey some years ago. The Turkish government had summarily reneged on an agreement with a U.S. firm, on which basis the company had invested substantial resources. The U.S. management immediately jumped to the conclusion that this act, plus the obstinance exhibited by the principal Turkish negotiator, was generated either by ignorance or the desire for personal gain through some sort of illegal payment. What was not adequately appreciated was the fact that the Turkish negotiator was very nationalistic in the sense of a commitment to get the best deal for his country, that he had a very limited staff for evaluating the technical and economic soundness of the proposed project, that the law made him *personally* responsible for the feasibility of the project under negotiation, that he had quite sincere doubts about the price, and that he had no prior experience with the U.S. company. The company president rushed into the situation and requested an audience with the Turkish prime minister. In so doing, he was making several assumptions: (1) that his company's position was thoroughly defensible, (2) that the Turkish negotiator was acting without the knowledge and support of the prime minister, (3) that the Turkish negotiator was not acting in good faith. Fortunately, he became conscious of these assumptions prior to the appointment with the prime minister and gained a postponement on the grounds of illness. It later developed that there were some technical errors in the company's proposal, that the price could be scaled down, that the Turkish negotiator had acted with the support of the prime minister, and that the negotiator was scrupulously honest. Had the company president gone to the prime minister and impugned either the integrity or competence of the Turkish negotiator, the company would have been in serious trouble. The matter was resolved amiably with the submission of a somewhat different proposal, with full credit being given to the astuteness of the Turkish negotiator. In fact, the changes made were not really material, but the Turks were convinced by this act that the proposal was sound and properly priced. Face had been saved.

An experienced negotiator speculates very carefully, before he responds, as to all of the possible explanations for the behavior exhibited by the other party and then devises ways to probe the system to ascertain the most likely explanation. Such an analysis presupposes adequate insight into the social-political system in which the other negotiating party is operating. For example, if a negotiator is unsure of his technical ability to evaluate a particular proposal, he may delay negotiations until he can build up a personal relationship with the other party, thereby creating an element of personal trust and confidence. In some societies, this personal relationship is a prelude to striking any bargain.

In a complex international business negotiation, experienced negotiators report the wisdom of an informal negotiation preceding or paralleling the formal sessions. For example, the informal negotiation might take place between lawyers, between engineers, or between accountants from each side for the purpose of reaching a one-to-one agreement before bringing up specific technical subjects for formal negotiation. Others caution about the possibility of a negotiation being spoiled by "bad actors"; that is, those who insist on passing judgment on matters outside the areas of their own competence. The worst sin is for a negotiating team to enter negotiations without a consistent position among team members on all important issues, and without fall back positions having been defined. But falling back to a lesser position in one area should always be contingent upon successful negotiation in another. Otherwise, one is the victim of the "ratchet effect," as point after point is bargained away.

A very useful device in preparing for an important negotiation is a simulated negotiation in which members of one's own company are assigned to represent the other side in as vigorous a fashion as possible. It is revealing to note how unprepared many corporate representatives are to state the conditions they seek in terms of the interests of the other party. Take the typical LDC case, in which a foreign company is trying to negotiate satisfactory conditions for entry. Whatever it proposes should be justified in terms of the political-economic priorities of the host country, whether they be foreign exchange conservation, export promotion, employment and income generation, income distribution, technology transfer, or control transfer, to mention a few. This means that the corporate negotiators should be fully familiar with micro and macroeconomic theory, the various theories of economic development, with international trade and investment theory, with the local development plans, and with the political realities of the local scene, as well as the technical aspects of the proposal. Very few corporate negotiating teams bring these skills to the negotiating table. As the level of sophistication of host LDC government negotiators increases, corporate negotiators are frequently outgunned. One only has to read some of the more recent agreements between the Indonesian government and incoming foreign companies.[9]

The same charge could be made in respect to the testimony of many high-level U.S. corporate executives before congressional committees. Many of

---

[9]It should be noted that the Georgetown Law Center (Washington, D.C.) and the UN Centre on Transnational Corporations have been running training seminars for government negotiators.

their statements are obviously self-serving and full of illogic and partial truths. Such statements continue to undermine the public credibility of the entire business community.

One further observation is made by experienced and successful negotiators. Once a negotiation has deteriorated into acrimony and personal hostility, change the negotiators. Bring in a new team. Particularly is this true on the interface between a large alien corporation and a LDC government.[10] And, one might add, to strike an agreement that will remain viable, the corporate negotiators must be able to anticipate the impacts of that agreement and to assess the probability of unfavorable political impact which may force a subsequent change in the bargain. At this stage, scenario writing is a useful technique.

It follows that an important part of the public affairs function is the monitoring of the corporate impact on various measures of public welfare, such measures depending upon the political priorities of the countries involved, both parent and host.

In the U.S. case, coming high on the list should be the ratio of imports (from foreign subsidiaries, associated firms, licensees, and technology contractors) to exports (from the corporation's domestic operations), given the fact that the larger U.S. corporations are under constant attack from labor on the grounds that by investing and contracting overseas they are "exporting jobs."[11] Another sensitive issue in the U.S. case is the matter of illegal payments overseas. Recent revelations by corporations at the behest of the Securities and Exchange Commission have excited public attention, and by mid-1977 it seemed distinctly possible that certain corporate acts overseas would be made criminal offenses under U.S. law. Already, under the 1976 Tax Reform Act, they could lead to denial of tax deferral and the crediting of foreign wealth and income taxes against U.S. tax liability. Not only had many large corporations begun to monitor very closely any questionable payments made overseas by their personnel, but some had issued explicit guidelines on the issue. The relevant IBM statement read:

IBM will not make contributions or payments to political parties or candidates. Nor will IBM bribe or make payoffs to government officials, civil servants or anyone. This is a single worldwide policy. If you ever are approached for what you believe is a questionable payment, report the circumstances to your manager as soon as possible.

In many countries political contributions by corporations are illegal. In other countries they are legal, but IBM will not make them in either case. Nor will IBM provide things other than direct cash payments which may be considered contributions. For example, if you want to campaign for a political candidate, the company will give you reasonable

---

[10]Some of these same points are made by John Fayerweather and Ashok Kapoor, *Strategy Negotiation for the International Corporation* (Cambridge: Ballinger Publishing Company, 1976)

[11]An example is *Union Carbide's International Investment Benefits the U.S. Economy,* a 35-page study by the Union Carbide Corporation, first issued in October, 1972, and updated November, 1975.

amounts of time off from work without pay, commensurate with your duties. IBM encourages people to be involved in politics, but on their own time and at their own expense. If IBM were to pay you while you were campaigning, your salary could be considered a contribution to the candidate or party you were supporting.[12]

Issued in several languages, the booklet containing this statement is distributed to all IBM employees in decision-making positions, and annually they are requested to sign a statement to the effect that they have read and understood it. It should be emphasized that such a rule may place the individual manager in a difficult dilemma if he is being judged purely on annual sales or profit achievement. And, the more competitive the situation, the tighter is the dilemma, and possibly the less effective is the corporate guideline.

What should be realized is that "large scale payments by multinational corporations do not represent an aberration to be analyzed in terms of a decline in morality (business or general) or comparative ethical or legal systems." Kobrin, the author of this observation, goes on to point out that such payments "are a manifestation of three interrelated and more general issues that in turn are a function of developments in technology as applied to production and communication." These are:

1. The concentration of economic and thus political power in the modern corporation; the fact that business has "gained a power not sensitively subject to control by the market."[13]

2. The emergence of significant nongovernmental transnational political actors.

3. The presence of powerful actors within a given nation-state that are responsive to external forces and not entirely under the control of the host government. (This last point, perhaps, should be subsumed under the first two.)[14]

He concludes, "The basic issue is that of changes that are necessary in both socioeconomic and political institutions to cope with the major changes that have taken place in the nature of productive enterprise,"[15] to wit its size, internationalization, and politicalization.

Many U.S. corporations have also felt obliged to respond to various pressures from stockholders, employees, consumers, and others by examining with care their policies in the Republic of South Africa.[16] The relevant political question is whether the continued presence of the corporation is supportive or subversive of apartheid. Of direct concern to a corporation's decision-makers is the probability of majority black government, when, and the pursuit of corporate policies believed most likely to preserve corporate interests through

---

[12] *IBM Business Conduct Guidelines* (undated), p. 10.

[13] V. O. Key, Jr., *Politics, Parties and Pressure Groups* (New York: Crowell Company, 1964, 5th ed.), p. 25.

[14] Stephen J. Kobrin, "Morality, Political Power and Illegal Payments by Multinational Corporations," *Columbia Journal of World Business*, Winter 1976, p. 109.

[15] Kobrin, "Morality," p. 110.

[16] The U.K. government, in 1976, began requiring U.K.-based corporations operating in South Africa to report their policies regarding black employees.

such a transition. It could be argued that, even if the withdrawal of U.S. corporations from South Africa might greatly enhance the probability of revolutionary change, the use of foreign corporations to trigger a revolution is not a valid use of corporations, whether one favors the revolution or not. However, as representatives of U.S. society—and, hence, to a certain extent of U.S. values—U.S. corporate executives undoubtedly feel obliged to push the advancement of their black employees in South Africa to the limit of the law, possibly beyond. To do so requires careful monitoring of the changing legal-political climate of South Africa and of the performance of affiliated firms there. Indeed, given the increased concern in the U.S. with human rights everywhere, any U.S.-based corporation fails at its peril to monitor this dimension of its operations in countries under attack from the point of view of alleged violations of human rights, whether it be South Africa, Chile, the Soviet Union, or Uganda.

Other areas of particular concern to the public affairs officer of a U.S.-based corporation in respect to response within the U.S. are the participation in any international boycotts by foreign affiliates and any major environmental pollution caused by a foreign affiliate (particularly atmospheric and oceanic). The first is now illegal and the second, destructive of a corporation's creditability at home.

When one considers the matters to be monitored abroad in response to anticipated political pressures in *host* countries, the list lengthens considerably. A public affairs department should be measuring on a *continuing* basis for each country in which it operates, the impact of corporate activities on balance of trade, balance of payments, net domestic product, employment, and income distribution (overall, geographically, sectorally, private-public, and by important groups—tribe, ethnic, political, and the like). In addition, the corporation is wise if periodically it employs expert independent analysts to examine the overall political vulnerability of the corporation in each country wherein are located important corporate assets. A key measure of the failure of the public affairs function is the number of times the corporation is faced with an unanticipated political event. The other key measure is the ability of the public affairs department to suggest financially feasible strategies that permit the corporation to survive what would otherwise prove to be a costly change in the political environment.

In respect to tracking changes, the attitudes of elites around the world may prove relevant. Several recent studies have been made. In 1970, Fayerweather surveyed four leadership groups in Britain and France, specifically, national legislators, permanent government officials, heads of business firms, and labor union leaders. The key points emerging from the survey were, in the author's own words,

In ranking criteria for judging the value of foreign firms, the leaders place economic impact first, with effect on control of national affairs close behind, and influence on way of life significantly lower.

With the exception of the labor leaders, the elite group express an overall favorable judgment of the value of foreign investment.

On major areas of impact, however, the assessments differ. Briefly the attitudes run as follows:

1. Effect on control of national affairs—quite adverse
2. Economic impact—partly adverse, partly favorable
3. Influence on national way of life—moderately favorable

Labor union leaders have substantially more adverse attitudes toward foreign firms than the other three elite groups.

On most points the elite attitudes in Britain and France were quite similar—a striking contrast to the distinctly more negative official policies in France in recent years.[17]

A survey of U.S. public opinion vis-à-vis "multinational corporations" conducted in early 1975 revealed an ambivalence about the benefits derived from the foreign operations of U.S.-based firms.[18] Chief benefits listed: added earnings to shareholders, increased jobs, support of U.S. foreign policy, lower domestic prices, expansion of international trade. Chief disadvantages: loss of jobs in the United States, loss of investment capital, loss of tax revenue. Almost 30 percent of the U.S. public strongly objected to the expansion of foreign-owned business in the United States, the reason given most frequently being objection to the control of U.S. industry or economy by foreign business. But once the presence of a foreign-owned business was accepted in the United States, 60 percent of the public felt that it did not matter where its home base was. But, over half of the public preferred a product made by a U.S.-controlled firm, although this bias fell with age. Of the 18–29 groups, only 34 percent cared.

A conclusion reached was that there was "no great indignation in the United States about the behavior of its MNCs abroad"[19] other than in the labor establishment, which was "massively critical." Earlier studies had revealed that the "American leadership community," despite many reservations, were "for the MNC as a useful and powerful form of corporate structure."[20] On the basis of such public opinion polls, the polling firm issued a series of so-called "early warnings" to its business clientele. The link between public opinion and political action, however, was not specified. Presumably it would differ from country to country.

Major findings of a 1975–76 Conference Board study of the attitudes of the

---

[17]John Fayerweather, "Attitudes of British and French Elite Groups Toward Foreign Companies," *MSU Business Topics*, Winter 1972, p. 44 ff.

[18]*The American Public Looks at the Multinational Corporation* (New York: Louis Harris and Associates, 1975, mimeo.), pp. 3–4.

[19]*The American Public Looks at the Multinational Corporation*, p. 20.

[20]Ibid., p. 27.

relevant elite in Canada and Italy[21] regarding the behavior of U.S. corporations in the two countries was summarized thusly:

(1) For developed countries like Canada and Italy, many of the alleged multinational defects so dear to the hearts of MNC critics (and often to those who do research on and write about MNCs) are not widely identified as problems at all. The payment of taxes, product quality, transfer pricing, trade and distribution practices, personnel policies, health and safety practices, land use, training of employees, reinvestment of earnings, and repatriation of profits are not primary concerns of host-country elites.

(2) In these countries, elites are generally confident of their ability to ensure that multinational enterprises will conform to the country's legal and administrative requirements. In fact, enforcement is rarely necessary. Where good corporate citizenship refers to strict adherence to a host-country's laws, the affiliates of American MNCs rarely fall below prevailing national standards, and they are frequently exemplars.

(3) In both Italy and Canada, the most frequent criticisms directed at American MNCs have less to do with the MNC as such than with the failures or excesses of governments. Canadians and Italians attack their own governments' inability to develop adequate and efficient regulatory frameworks for MNCs. They also attack the actions of the U.S. government—mainly the extraterritorial application of U.S. law on and through foreign affiliates of U.S. corporations. In fact, in Canada, many feel that U.S. extraterritoriality is the single most serious impediment U.S. firms face in their dealings.

(4) Staffing local affiliate managerial positions with nationals of host countries often creates as many problems as it may solve. In any case, this strategy is not the answer to some very basic feelings about autonomy expressed by Canadians and Italians, including the managers of U.S.-MNC affiliates.

(5) Company codes of conduct, translated into indigenous languages and diffused to the general public of host countries, can be self-defeating. In any event, they are not likely to cut much ice with the critics of U.S. corporate affiliates. Nor are they likely to be emulated by the MNCs of other countries with which U.S. affiliates abroad are forced to compete.

(6) The classic arguments against the decentralization of R and D will find fewer and fewer sympathetic listeners abroad. The question of technology transfer and of assisting host countries to develop their own technologies will be one of the most insistently pressing issues in the years ahead.

(7) Far from lamenting the political involvements and contributions of some American MNC affiliates. Canadian and Italian elites criticize even more the failure of U.S. MNCs in their countries to become more deeply integrated locally, and to develop more acute sensitivity to local feelings, mores, usages.

---

[21]Based on "focused interviews" of between 75 and 100 of "proximate decision-makers," that is, those "so intimately involved in the making of public policy making that their acts of commission or omission can be shown to have a direct impact on the determination and execution of such policies." The phrase includes legislators, cabinet members, highest level public administrators, judges, leading trade unionists and industrialists, mass media leaders, intellectual leaders, interest-group leaders, and strategically placed regional and local personalities of influence. Joseph LaPalombara and Stephen Blank, *Multinational Corporations and National Elites: A Study in Tensions* (New York: The Conference Board, 1976), p. 120.

(8) In both Italy and Canada, elites by and large believe that the further economic development of their countries is dependent upon continued inputs of foreign, and especially American, capital. This view is shared by leading Communist officials in Italy and by many nationalists in Canada.

(9) In both countries, however, it is clear that increasing demands will be made on MNCs to provide greater benefits to host countries, and that conditions governing the activities of MNCs will not be as liberal as in the past.

(10) Most responsible critics of MNC's in these countries do not want them to be forced out, nor do they fail to understand that MNC operations are dependent in the end upon their profitability. What they question, however, is the capacity of the MNC to adapt to changing situations in which the nature of the firm's costs and benefits and how these should be assessed may well be different than in the past.[22]

Another recent study of opinion leaders in Chile and Venezuela emphasized the dissonance between perception and reality. In this case, the perceptions were those of government officials, labor leaders, local business leaders, intellectuals, and students, in all 300 for each country. Some of the conclusions falling out of this study:

1. The differences between perception, expectation and reality were greater in Venezuela than in Chile.

2. There was much more of a consensus in Chile.

3. The Chileans exhibited a more favorable attitude toward foreign business.

4. Several issues emerged as important in both countries: availability of training, lack of opportunity for advancement in foreign companies, level of expenditure on local R&D, and level of public service activity.

5. U.S. firms were viewed in both countries as doing better than national firms in exports, and in R&D expenditures, but generally they were not regarded as beneficial to the nation as national or mixed firms. The reasons: economic, political and technological dependency; loss of control; and a belief that the foreign company benefited more than the host country.[23]

On this last point the authors add that even though the elites charge U.S. companies with extracting excessive profits, their perception of what constitutes a reasonable rate of return came very close to that actually reported. The authors assume that the difference between reality and perception is significant. But one might challenge the realism of the reported rates of return. Were the reported rates of return accurate? Had all transfer prices been recorded at arm's length? Any public affairs effort to bring reality and perception closer together is unlikely to succeed so long as there exists suspicion as to what constitutes reality.

---

[22]LaPalombara and Blank, *Multinational Corporations*, pp. 2–3.

[23]Nancy S. Truit and David H. Blake, *Opinion Leaders and Private Investment, An Attitude Survey in Chile and Venezuela* (New York: Fund For Multinational Management Education, 1976.)

One of the most difficult public affairs tasks is the assessment of political risk, by which phrase is meant determining the probability of a political event that impacts on the firm to its disadvantage. Typical impacts: imposition of an unexpected cost (such as a tax), loss of some degree of management control (such as inability to lay off employees), blockage of earnings (such as the imposition of foreign exchange controls), loss of assets (expropriation), physical loss (such as destruction of assets due to violence, kidnapping of personnel). In fact, all could be subsumed under unanticipated increase in cost resulting from nonmarket forces. The point is that discontinuous political change does not translate into political risk for the corporation unless that change impacts on cost.

As the probability of one or more of these events increases, the public affairs analyst should be responsible for alerting management and suggesting ways of either influencing the anticipated political event so as to be less onerous (costly) and/or shifting the burden of such politically induced costs to an external agency and/or adjusting corporate strategy so as to minimize that cost.

The sophisticated corporate analyst does not assume a linkage between sudden political change and corporate well-being. Hence, aggregate measures suggesting a political discontinuity, say a coup, are an inadequate guide to corporate behavior. One needs to interpret that coup in terms of impacts on the corporation of the sort listed above. Hence, it is suggested here that political risk is a function of (1) pressures within the surrounding political system, (2) the capacity of that system to adjust so as to keep these pressures within tolerable limits, (3) the degree of leverage possessed by the firm (market advantage), and (4) responsiveness of corporate strategy. What may constitute very high political risk for one firm may mean zero risk for another.

The art in political risk assessment comes in sensing the level of pressure a given political system will tolerate. At what point will discontinuous structural changes be forced? Obviously, the more rigid the system, the more likely such changes will occur in the face of a given level of pressure. The relevant questions are: What is the nature of the critical pressures? What are the measures of a system's rigidity?

One can only list some of the critical pressures without specifying any generalizable measures, for each national society is highly idiosyncratic in that all of these pressures interrelate and interact, both among themselves and with other dimensions of the social-economic-political environment. Included on the list of important indicators of pressures would be:

1. Increasing wealth and income disparity, particularly if identified with ethnic, religious, and/or regional groupings and if consumption differences are visible.

2. Deprivation of status (economic or social) of a formerly important group (for example, military officers) or a large number of individuals, particularly if concentrated geographically.

3. Large-scale and accelerating rural-urban movement, particularly if led by a large unattached young male population.

4. Loss of land rights by a significant segment of the rural population to large town-dwelling landlords, particularly if they are of different ethnic, religious, or tribal identity.

5. Mounting external debt, dwindling domestic reserves, deteriorating credit position, and increasing scarcity of essential imports, particularly if involving imports to which a significant part of the population has become accustomed.

6. Accelerating inflation without serious effort to equalize its impact among various groups and economic classes.

7. Inability of the government to maintain law and order in important areas.

8. Mounting corruption at high levels of government, which may be indicative of a shortening time horizon on the part of leaders.

9. Declining real incomes after a long period of growth.

10. The presence of persistent, organized, violent (actual or potential) opposition under charismatic leadership—labor, religious, political.

But the capability of a political system to tolerate such pressures, even at high levels, lies in its capacity to respond by introducing an appropriate adjustment mechanism. A competitive political system with multiple power centers and a long record of more or less peaceful adjustment is possibly best able to respond effectively to pressures. But one should not be misled by labels. A single party system, in which there are multiple factions held together by a strong charismatic leader, may be highly representative and responsive. Competition and representation simply take place at a different level under different labels.

Until very recently, there has been extraordinary contrast between economic and political inputs to corporate decisions. The latter have been treated either as constants or random variables, almost never subject to rigorous analysis by expert analysts, as have been economic inputs. In contrast with economic analysis, virtually everyone claims the skills and insights needed for political analysis. All one need do is to read the *New York Times* or comparable paper. If political turbulence is reported, the political risk discount figure becomes infinitely high. Of course, the political crisis may be wholly irrelevant to the business climate. We thus derive our first trap for the unwary, the "crisis syndrome." Of particular danger is the second trap, the "old hands syndrome," those who know because they were there. A classic case was the old China hands, principally missionaries and businessmen, who scoffed at the notion that the communists could ever take over in China. But this suggests a very serious problem in establishing an effective political intelligence system, for long-established local managers may well insist on having the last word. Yet, they are very unlikely to be sensitive to new political currents which do not intrude into the social gatherings of the more affluent part of the society. We thus introduce the third trap, the "well groomed syndrome." Apparently no manager of a subsidiary of a U.S. firm in pre-Castro Cuba had any notion that the "bearded unwashed in the hills" were about to take over the country. They were not well groomed, respectable members of society, hence, not worthy of attention. The result was that not a *single* U.S. firm bothered to take out a U.S. government guarantee against expropriation of its Cuban assets. It is almost certain that a skilled political scientist specializing in Caribbean affairs would have specified a probability of something more than zero of a Castro-led takeover. It is also clear that the corporate interest in political intelligence tends to be relatively high at the point of entry (that is, investment decision) into a country, but thereafter is somewhat reduced. We thus introduce the fourth trap, the "entry syndrome." What some firms are now doing is to maintain an *ongoing* "profile" for each country in which it has significant operations. These profiles are maintained by trained political analysts, whether in the firm or external to it, with input from local management but not final evaluation. One alarm signal may be triggered by a significant difference between the assessment by local management and an independent political analyst.

Let us assume that a high probability of political discontinuity is specified for a country. This fact may not translate into political risk for the firm if its leverage is great, that is, if it is perceived as the sole purveyor of essential goods and services at a given price or if the internal corporate balance of transfers (incoming capital, technology, and skills set off against outgoing fees, royalties, and dividends) is still very much in favor of the host country. What is often missed by corporate executives is that a firm's leverage is very likely to be reduced over time. A case in point was the International Petroleum Company in Peru. Initially, it was investing foreign savings, technology, and skills, for which there was no other source at comparable price. And it was producing essentially for external markets to which it had low cost access. Over time the flow of new capital dwindled to a trickle. The essential technology had been transferred and local skills, developed. And what was not available locally could be purchased from a variety of independent service organizations. Finally, the local market was absorbing virtually the entire production. Obviously, the firm had lost most of its initial leverage, and its political vulnerability was greatly enhanced as a result. Still, IPC might have survived if it had anticipated political events in Peru and, sensitive to its loss of leverage, had adjusted its strategy from one of ownership and control to that of a seller of services—technology, technical skills, marketing, management, and international financing—and a buyer of product.

Hence, political risk analysis must proceed on all four levels—political pressures, the capacity of the political system to adjust, corporate leverage, and the responsiveness of corporate strategy. This point is lost by those professing to reduce political risk to a pure numbers game. In fact, there is some evidence that at least some corporations have dropped the idea of expressing political risk in a single number that can be used for discounting purposes. Not only is there a tendency for financial analysts and others to "overinterpret" such numbers, but it is conceptually invalid to use a single number in that political risk varies depending upon corporate response. There is no single political risk factor, hence, no single discount rate. As one corporate public affairs analyst commented, "We are responding to government initiative and are negotiating. We are more concerned about contract terms." In other words, his corporation was more interested in negotiating—that is, selecting strategy—in order to reduce or eliminate political risk.

We have been speaking here of relatively short-term environmental changes. Public affairs should also be concerning itself with plotting the probable course of much longer term social-political-economic processes likely to impact on the corporation. A possible list:

1. The appearance of socially responsible governments in the LDCs (that is, more honestly responsive to the interests of their own societies)

2. The broadening dispersion of high-level technical and managerial skills

3. The widening disparity in per capita well being between poorest and richest nations.

4. The growing inequality of incomes within certain countries.

5. The rising demand for environmental and consumer protection in the more developed countries.

6. The growing appeal of the Japanese, Cuban, and Chinese "models" of development.

7. Worldwide shortages of certain commodities, given present price structures (e.g., energy, food, and the like)

8. The appeal of the OPEC model of cartelization among commodity-producing nations

9. Shift in liquid assets to commodity-producing countries, initially the oil producers

10. Growth of employee participation in decision making

11. Increasing entry of women into the labor force and resulting change in family structure.

12. Aging population in industrialized countries

13. Declining relative importance of the U.S. economy vis-à-vis the world economy (in terms of total production, international trade, innovation).

14. The increasing internationalization of production (that is, increasing integration of national economies).

15. Internationalization of organized labor

16. Regionalization of markets

17. Possible worldwide slowdown in technological innovation.

Possible derivatives of these underlying forces are:

1. Persistent worldwide inflation.

2. A floating exchange rate system

3. Loss of faith in the market allocation process and increased pressure for government intervention.

4. Slowdown in the application of new commercial technology.

5. Accelerating shift of manufacturing from the more developed countries to the less developed countries.

6. Increasing nationalistic identity.

7. Shift of economic power toward the LDCs.

8. Reduced implicit political-economic threat of the U.S.

9. Increasing economic interdependency.

10. Multinationalization of ownership and management of many large corporations.

11. International agreements relating to the control of large corporations operating internationally.

This last point needs expansion, for corporate public affairs analysts are becoming increasingly concerned with the possibility of such agreements. Given the many efforts to put together a set of guidelines for international corporate behavior, it is apparent that at least some bodies have concluded that the nation-state is an inadequate vehicle for controlling the larger corporations operating internationally. The upshot is that at least five codes have been proposed: by the Organization for Economic Cooperation and Development,[24] by the International Chamber of Commerce,[25] by the Council of Europe,[26] by the Nonaligned Countries,[27] and by ten Latin American and Caribbean nations.[28] In addition, the five-nation Andean Common Market has articulated a *regional* code (Decisions 24), and both the EEC and the Association of South East Asian Nations have been discussing codes, so likewise various international labor bodies. One should also note the codes Japan and Sweden have urged upon their corporations operating overseas. Finally, the United Nations, as a result of a report issued by the UN Commission on Transnational Corporations in 1974[29] gave birth to the UN Centre for Transnational

---

[24] *International Investment and Multinational Enterprises* (Paris: Organization for Economic Cooperation and Development, 1976).

[25] *Guidelines for International Investment* (Paris: International Chamber of Commerce, 1972).

[26] *Resolution 639*, Parliamentary Assembly, Council of Europe, Strasburg, 1976.

[27] "Draft Statute for the Treatment of Foreign Investment, Transnational Corporations and the Transfer of Technology" (Lima: Conference of Ministers for Foreign Affairs of Non-Aligned Countries, 25–29 August 1975).

[28] *Commission on Transnational Corporations, Report on the Second Session*, Supplement No. 5 (United Nations: Economic and Social Council, 1976), pp. 17–34.

[29] Bear in mind that in the UN usage the term "transnational" applies to any corporation operating internationally (international, multinational, transnational, multinational and transnational associations, and international service companies).

Corporations the next year. U.S. policy on the subject was enunciated in 1975 by the then Secretary of State Henry Kissinger,

The United States believes that the time has come for the international community to articulate standards of conduct for both enterprises and governments. The U.N. Commission on Transnational Corporations, and other governmental bodies, have begun such an effort. We must reach agreement on balanced principles. These should apply to transnational enterprises in their relations with governments, and to governments in their relations with enterprises, and with other governments.[30]

For a code to be really effective, several conditions might be suggested:

1. It must apply to both the behavior of corporations and the behavior of states.

2. It must not penalize those corporations attempting to abide by the code.

3. It must not impact so as to penalize the smaller corporations or reward the large.

4. It must not introduce added costs so as to reduce aggregate flows of private capital, technology, and skills from the more developed to the less developed countries.

5. The code must be stated in sufficient detail as to be operational.

All of the codes thus far proposed fail to satisfy one or more of these conditions. Although several satisfy condition one, those corporations trying to conform would be penalized. Their strategy selection would seem to be more restricted than those corporations choosing to ignore the guidelines. And there is no explicit reward for the "good behaviors" other than enhanced public image which, in the LDCs, may not be widely perceived as a particularly valuable attribute. Until it becomes quite clear that host governments are more protective of the rights of alien corporations demonstrating sensitivity to local interests—which the guidelines purport to encourage—than of others, then the good behaviors derive no benefit. Do host governments in fact differentiate in terms of ownership policies, availability of local resources, and profit remittance permits? There seems to be precious little evidence that they do. Each new governmental intervention in the market, whether on a national or international level, tends to reward the large corporation that can afford the specialized staff or counsel to plot its course through—or around—the regulation. A small firm cannot. Also, the addition of further restrictions, assuming that the code becomes effective, translates into more entry barriers, reduced competition, and increased costs of desired transfers of capital, skills, and technology. The exact reverse is needed, that is, an improvement of markets. None of the improved codes really propose measures to do that. Finally, none of the codes are in sufficient detail as to be operational and, indeed, if they were, they would undoubtedly conflict with one or more national codes. Even a stricture that a corporation not tolerate any discrimination on the basis of race, ethnic origin, or political activity introduces a problem. What does a corporation do about

---

[30]September 1, 1975.

the laws and regulations in Malaysia, Indonesia, and the Philippines regarding the Chinese? What of similar rules in respect to the whites in Zambia and elsewhere, or in respect to the blacks in South Africa and Rhodesia? What of enforced political discrimination in communist countries? Business is required by law to discriminate. Should it be forced to withdraw wherever it is required to do so? Or take the area of restrictive business practices and competitive policy. Is an agreement between a corporation and a government to keep out all competition a restrictive business practice? Apparently the overall purpose of these codes is to render it difficult for an alien corporation to relocate in another country because its present host insists that it behave differently in some way. But in order for a code to be effective on this basis *enforcement at the national level* is required. Given the very different intensity of national needs for infusions of foreign capital, skills, and technology, it is difficult to see how such a code could be effective. Again the bad behavior—this time a country's—would be rewarded. In fact, countries would have to avoid the prohibited practices as well as corporations.

Because of these and other difficulties inherent in the idea of an international code as presently conceived, one is driven to the conclusion that eventually a very different approach will evolve. This different approach would rest on several premises, specifically:

1. That corporations behaving in what has been politically determined as a socially acceptable manner should be rewarded.

2. That the principal area of conflict among nations generated by international business should be addressed—the division of taxable income.

3. That there be some measure of effective *international* control over unilateral breach of agreement between host government and alien corporation.

4. That each country should specify upon the entry of an alien corporation the behavior it expects.[31]

It should be noted that the principal problems perceived by host governments in dealing with alien business is the lack of public information regarding corporate activities, the alleged use of corporations to further *parent* government policy objectives (including the extraterritorial application of parent government law), conflict over the allocation of taxable income, and the inability (or unwillingness) of many governments to enforce their own laws.

Some observers have suggested that corporations satisfying certain conditions should be registered with an international agency. The conditions: multinational activity at some specified level, a corporate commitment to disclose specified information about its activities, and a corporate commitment to adhere to a set of operating principles. The international agency most frequently suggested in this context is the International Bank for Reconstruction and Development, perhaps in the form of a functionally enlarged International

---

[31]Many are now doing so. See Richard D. Robinson, *National Control of the Entry of Foreign Business* (New York: Prager, 1976).

Centre for the Settlement of Investment Disputes (ICSID). Both corporation and nation-state might feel restrained from treating an agency under such auspices in a cavalier fashion.

As a reward, a "registered corporation" would be given special status by countries signatory to the convention establishing the international agency. This might take the form of

1. Taxing only local-source income, such income to be determined objectively by calculating the average of local assets/global assets, local sales/global sales, local employment/global employment ratios. (The international agency would establish the accounting rules and receive global operating statements.);[32]

2. Permitting the registration of a corporation's shares on local stock exchanges (that is, acceptance of an internationally-accepted disclosure statement);

3. A host government and corporate commitment to submit differences to international arbitration before the ICSID;

4. Exemption by a corporation's parent government of the corporation from withholding taxes on dividends, interest, and royalties paid to individuals or corporations domiciled in other signatory countries;

5. A World Bank-backed guarantee against loss due to uncompensated expropriation and unilateral breach of contract by signatory nations;

6. Exemption by signatory governments of requirements for performance bonds or guaranties;

7. Otherwise, a commitment by host governments to treat corporations as national corporations.

Further rules that might render such a convention more attractive:

1. Registered corporations could only merge with one another or acquire one another on the basis of prior clearance by the international agency. (Signatory nations would have to agree to give such clearance legal status under national law.)

2. Any member state could bring charges against a registered corporation before the ICSID on the grounds that it was not living up to its commitments made upon entry or subsequently. A finding of guilty could result in revocation of registered status.

3. Likewise, a corporation could bring charges against a member state before the ICSID on the grounds that the state was not living up to its commitments made upon entry or subsequently. A finding of guilt could lead to an order to pay damages.

4. Failure to maintain strict political neutrality on the part of foreign controlled and/or owned enterprises, foreign personnel, and contractors in host countries could void all governmental guarantees that may be offered.

Political neutrality might be defined as nonintervention in partisan politics except

---

[32]At the very least, signatory countries should recognize the tax sparing principle for registered corporations domiciled within their jurisdictions.

as a corporation might attempt to influence policies by means of *public* statements or to the extent commonly tolerated for a local corporation. Any *covert* activity of a political nature on behalf of another government could be deemed a per se violation of neutrality.

5. Failure to adhere to all local laws on the part of foreign-owned and/or controlled enterprises and contractors would be a bar to recovery in event of expropriation or unilateral breach of contract by the host government, even without effective, prompt, and adequate compensation (unless the law be discriminating or of an *ex post facto* nature, that is, a host nation violation of agreed-upon entry conditions).

6. A host government commitment to recognize foreign ownership (upon control) of tangible and intangible rights, and/or management control of same, for 20 years (unless a shorter period is agreed upon at the time of entry). These rights should be inalienable during such period if (1) the rights are established locally in accord with local law and upon the consent of a signatory government, and (2) the foreign investor and/or contractor adheres to the entry conditions *unless* adherence is made impossible either by the host government or by a change of circumstances beyond the control of the foreign interest involved.

In speculating upon the reality and utility of such an international control system, it is possibly useful to bear in mind that in all probability international business of the future will consist primarily of international federations of locally owned firms, to which the central organization will sell research findings, technical assistance, venture capital, debt capital, and access to international marketing and information systems. The central organization itself is very likely to be owned by nationals of many different states. As ownership and operation broaden geographically, the rationale that would require the central body to register as a legal entity under the laws of any *one* national state appreciably weakens, and the argument for the recognition of private, internationally chartered corporations becomes compelling.

One can predict with some confidence that in the last decades of the 20th century international business will constitute a powerful pressure in the direction of *internationalizing* the process of political socialization, through the institutional relationships it creates and the flow of communication inherent in them. Even communist societies may be included, for the private ownership of the actual machines of production is not a necessary prerequisite for this relationship. In many countries joint public-private ownership of large sectors of production has already occurred, and in some of these situations private foreign enterprise is participating.

It is relevant to point out that a number of foreseeable technical developments will likewise push in the direction of international, rather than national, development. Reference is made to such innovations as deep-sea mining, weather control, supersonic transport flight, worldwide television networks, use of outer space, and arctic exploitation, not to mention the pressing need for the global management of the environment, of exhaustible resources, and of food and water. A prophetic study on this subject some years ago concluded,

Current concepts of national sovereignty are not well suited to the orderly regulation of these advances nor to their development for maximum utility with minimum conflict. Policy planners will find it increasingly necessary to explore new types of supranational organization. [33]

International business leaders are now transcending national frontiers in their willingness to undertake anything, anywhere, in association with anybody, so long as it promises a reasonable long-run return. By legally elevating the transmission of those business services suggested here to the international level, the business organizations involved would be, at least in part, insulated from use by nationalist political authorities to further the ambitions of any state against another. One can sense that there indeed exists an international business community, the members of which have ceased being emotionally committed to the perpetuation of particular cultures and value systems. This community has members in both the more developed and less developed worlds, and in the "capitalist" and the "communist."

The significance of this development may be enormous. Political scientist Hans J. Morganthau once wrote, "When the national state will have been replaced by another mode of organization, foreign policy must then protect the interest in survival of that new organization." He then suggested that such organization would come into existence only by conquest or by "consent based upon the mutual recognition of the national interests of the nations concerned." It is suggested here that there is perhaps another route that has been largely overlooked—specifically, the expansion of internationally constituted private groups (that is, business) whose mutual interests are contrary to the continued existence of national sovereignty as presently constituted. Already these groups have significant impact on national foreign policy. It is conceivable that they will of themselves create a supranational interest possessed of not insignificant power. "Foreign policy must then protect the interest in survival of that new organization." [34]

The distinguishing characteristic of the international business approach to international relations is that it envisages institutional, functional, nonpolitical, multinational relationships that are conducive to the weaving of an ever larger fabric of common interest and loyalty, thereby eroding the concept of national sovereignty and conflicting national interests. In the end it is possible even to imagine the appearance of privately owned supranational corporations, registered, controlled, and taxed by an international organization, [35] perhaps—as suggested earlier—by some agency of the International Bank for

[33]*Possible Nonmilitary Scientific Developments and their Potential Impact on Foreign Policy Problems of the United States* (prepared by the Stanford Research Institute, for the Committee on Foreign Relations, Senate, 86th Congress, 1st Session, September 1959), p. 1.

[34]Morganthau's comment on these ideas, "What you say about the problem of national sovereignty is entirely correct." (Personal letter.)

[35]Insofar as is known by the author, this idea was first suggested by Eugene Staley in his *War and the Private Investor* (New York: Doubleday & Company, 1935).

Reconstruction and Development. But there is a very long road to travel. International business needs a theory, a unifying purpose, and internationally skilled managements to give it reality. It is hoped that this text contributes to bringing that reality closer.

Discussion questions

1. What are the functions of a corporate public affairs department? (Prepare a directive outlining the department's function.)

2. How would you control illegal corporate payments overseas?

3. Do you find the definition of "political neutrality" and "legality" suggested on pages 749–50 to be operational?

4. Do you feel that there is sufficient inducement in the proposed international convention for a less developed country to participate?

5. As a responsible executive of a large, U.S.-based corporation, how would you testify before the U.S. Senate Foreign Relations Committee if a proposal such as that suggested here were under serious consideration?

6. Assignment: Assess the probability of a sudden political change in a specific country.

Recommended references

Behrman, Jack N. *National Interests and the Multinational Enterprises.* Englewood Cliffs, New Jersey: Prentice-Hall, Inc. 1970.

————.*U.S. International Business and Governments.* New York: McGraw-Hill, 1971.

Fayerweather, John, and Ashok Kapour. *Strategy Negotiations for The International Corporation.* Cambridge, Massachusetts: Ballinger, 1976.

Goldberg, Paul M. and Charles P. Kindleberger. "Toward a GATT for Investment: A Proposal for Supervision of the International Corporation." *Law and Policy in International Business,* vol. 2, no. 2, Summer 1970 pp. 295 ff.

Herlihy, Edward D., and Theodore A. Levine, "Corporate Crisis: The Overseas Payment Problem," *Law and Policy in International Business,* vol. 8, no. 3, 1976, pp. 547–629.

Robinson, Richard D. "A Program for International Business." In *Private Foreign Investment,* Hearings Before the Subcommittee on Foreign Trade Policy of the Committee on Ways, House of Representatives, 85th Congress, Second Session, December 1958. Washington: U.S. Government Printing Office, 1959, p. 543 ff.

————.*National Control of Foreign Business Entry.* New York: Praeger, 1976.

Sauvant, Karl P., and Farid G. Lavipour, eds. *Controlling Multinational Enterprise.* Boulder, Colorado: Westview Press, 1976.

Case M
THE BETA CORPORATION[1]

The Beta Corporation, a U.S.-based manufacturer of industrial control products started its international operations in the mid-1960s. The importance of the activities abroad increased rapidly, thereby motivating top management to look for executives with international business experience. The company also adopted an organization based on area divisions. By early 1977 it had manufacturing facilities operating in Europe and Southeast Asia. Export, marketing, and the distribution of subsidiaries' products in 14 countries of Latin America, Europe and the Middle East were also part of the Beta International network. A number of these subsidiaries were also assembling some of the products.

While headquarters' management knew that in some of its subsidiaries sporadic payments to government officials and civil servants were made, and that these could undoubtedly be considered bribes by some standards, management had not paid much attention to these practices. It had dismissed any discussion of the subject by noting that this was the way in which business was done in these countries, and everyone had to do it in order to survive.

Recently, however, attention had been focused by the media and the public on scandals involving major MNCs. This situation made some people in Beta's management wonder if it would not be a good idea to start being more cautious.

Parallel to this development, Beta's general manager in San Sebastian, where the firm had one of its Latin American distribution facilities, was approached by a prominent government official. He suggested that in exchange for a "donation" he would see that the proper government agency would make a long term, low interest loan to Beta to start some kind of assembling and manufacturing facility in San Sebastian, and that the "appropriate" tariff barriers would be erected to protect this operation.

Activities of this sort were not uncommon in San Sebastian, nor for that matter to Beta's subsidiary there, which many times had given donations to "influence" sales to government enterprises, labor negotiations, custom clearances, etc. This time, however, the scale of the "project" was such that management decided that a meeting with the relevant people in Beta's San Sebastian operations was necessary. Attending the meeting in New York were the public affairs manager from corporate headquarters; the general manager, industrial relations manager, the sales manager, and the purchasing manager from the San Sebastian subsidiary; the Latin America area manager; the Latin

---

[1]This case was prepared by Moise Naim, Alfred P. Sloan School of Management, M.I.T., 1977.

American sales manager; and the Middle Eastern area manager. It was expected that, as a result of this meeting, the public affairs manager would urge upon top corporate management a specific policy establishing clear criteria on how personnel should deal with "bribes" and "donations"-related issues.

Assignment: A simulated meeting in which members of the class represent the eight corporate executives, at the end of which the public affairs manager should enunciate the policy to be recommended to top corporate management.

LIST OF ACRONYMS USED IN THE TEXT

Note standard abbreviations indicating company legal form at the end of Chapter 8.

AACCLA	Asian Association of Chambers of Commerce of Latin America	ANZAC	Australian-New Zealand (free trade area)
AAMOCIOS	Asian Association of Management Organizations of CIOS	APF	Area-product-function (organization type)
		A/R	Account receivable
AATUF	All African Trade Union Federation	ARO	Asian Regional Organization
ACP	Asian-Caribbean-Pacific (countries associated with the EEC through the Lomé Convention)	ASEAN	Association of South East Asian Nations
		ASP	American selling price
ADB	Asian Development Bank	ATUC	African Trade Union Federation
ADELA	Atlantic Community Development Group for Latin American	AUCCTU	Central Council of Trade Unions (Soviet Union)
ADR	American depository receipt	BAFA	Bundesanstalt fur Arbeit (Federal Institute for Labor, Germany)
AFL-CIO	American Federation of Labor-Congress of Industrial Organizations	BASF	Badische Anilin
		BENELUX	Belgium-Netherlands-Luxembourg (customs union)
A.I.D.	Agency for International Development (U.S.)	BFCE	Banque Française du Commerce Extérieur (France)
AIDCO	Agro-industrial complex		
AIEC	Association of Iron Ore Exporting Countries	BLEU	Belgium Luxembourg Economic Union
AKA	Ausfuhrkredit Gesellschaft (Germany)	BOAL	Basic Organization of Associated Labor (Yugoslavia)
ANCOM	Andean Common Market		
ANRPC	Association of Natural Rubber Producing Countries	B/P	Balance of payments
		BTN	Brussels Tariff Nomenclature

C/A	Capital account (in balance of payments accounting)
CACM	Central American Common Market
CARE	Cooperative for American Relief Everywhere
CARIFTA	Caribbean Free Trade Area
CCCE	Caisse Centrale de Cooperation Economique (France)
CCM	Caribbean Common Market
CD	Certificate of Deposit
CDC	Commonwealth Development Corporation (U.K.)
CDR	Continental depository receipt
CECIOS	Conseil l'Européen de CIOS
CEDEAO	Economic Community of West African States
CEI	Centre d'Etudes Industrielles (Geneva)
CEM	Combination export manager
CEO	Chief executive officer
CENEL	European Standards Coordinating Committee
CESCA	Economic and Social Community of Central America
CFA	Communauté Financière Africaine
CFC	Controlled foreign corporation (U.S.)
CIA	Central Intelligence Agency (U.S.)
CIDC	Community Industrial Development Contract
c.i.f.	const., insurance, freight
CIOS	Comité Internationale de l'Organisation Scientifique
CIPEC	Council of Copper Exporting Countries
CISL	Confederazine Italiano Sindicati Lavoratori (Italian Confederation of Trade Unions)
CMEA	Council for Mutual Ecnomic Assistance (East European)
COCOM	Coordinating Committee (for export control)
COFACE	Compagnie Française d'Assurance pour le Commerce Extérieur (France)
COMECON	Council for Mutual Economic Assistance (East European)
COPANT	Pan American Standards Commission
CP	Commercial paper
CPC	Community Patent Convention
CSA	Commonwealth Sugar Agreement
CXT	Common external tariff
DATAR	Industrial Development Agency (France)
DC	Developed country
DEG	Deutsche Entwicklungsgesellschaft (German export finance)
DGB	Deutscher Gewerkschaftsbund (West German Trade Union Confederation)
DISC	Domestic International Sales Corporation (U.S.)
DM	Deutschemark
DSR	Debt/service ratio
EAC	East African Community
ECAT	Emergency Committee for American Trade
ECGD	Export Credit Guarantee Department (U.K.)
ECLA	European Committee for Latin America
ECSC	European Coal and Steel Community

EDA	Economic Development Administration (U.S.)	f.o.b.	Free on board
EDC	Export Development Corporation (U.K.)	FTC	Fair Trade Commission (Japan)
EEC	European Economic Community	FTO	Foreign trade organization
EFTA	European Free Trade Association	F/X	Foreign exchange
EIB	European Investment Bank	GATT	General Agreement on Tariffs and Trade
EMC	Export management company	GIE	Groupement d'Intérêt Economique (France)
EPC	European Patent Convention	GNP	Gross national product
EPO	European Patent Office	IATA	International Air Transport Association
ERISA	Employment Retirement Security Act (U.S.)	IBA	International Bauxite Association
ESAN	Escuela de Administracion de Negocios para Graduados (Peru)	IBM	International Business Machines Corporation
		IBRD	International Bank for Reconstruction and Development (World Bank)
ESF	European Social Fund	ICATO	International Conference of Arab Trade Unions
Exim	Export-Import Bank (U.S.)	ICCC	International Customs Corporation Council
FAP	Function-area-product (organization type)	ICF	International Federation of Chemical and General Workers' Union
f.a.s.	Free along side		
FASB	Financial Accounting Standards Board (U.S.)	ICFTU	International Confederation of Free Trade Unions
FBC	Foreign base company		
FCN	Friendship, commerce, and navigation (treaties)	ICIC	International Standard Industrial Classification
FCIA	Foreign Credit Insurance Association (U.S.)	ICSID	International Centre for the Settlement of Investment Disputes
FIET	International Federation of Commercial, Clerical and Technical Employees	IDA	International Development Association
FIFO	First in, first out (inventory accounting)	IDB	Inter-American Development Bank
FIRA	Foreign Investment Review Agency (Canada)	IDR	International depository receipt
FISC	Foreign international sales corporation (U.S.)	IEC	International Electrotechnical Commission
FMO	Financiengs Maatschappig Voor Ontwickelingslanden (Netherlands)	IFC	International Finance Corporation

IFU	Industrialization Fund for Developing Countries (Denmark)	ITT	International Telephone and Telegraph Corporation
IFCTU	International Federation of Christian Trade Unions	J-V	Joint venture
		KFW	Kreditanstalt fuer Wiederaufbau (Germany)
IFPCW	International Federation of Petroleum and Chemical Workers	L/C	Letter of credit
		LDC	Less developed country
ILO	International Labour Organization	LDCC	Less developed country corporation (U.S.)
		LIB	London International Bank Rate
IMEDE	Institute pour l'Etude des Methodes de Direction de l'Enterprise (Lausanne)	LIFO	Last in, first out (inventory accounting)
		LTA	Long term arrangement (or agreement)
IMF	International Metalworkers' Federation	MFN	Most favored nation
		MNC	Multinational corporation
		MTN	Multilateral trade negotiations
IMF	International Monetary Fund	MV	Marginal value
INA	Instituto Nazionale delle Assicurazioni (Italy)	NAM	National Association of Manufacturers (U.S.)
INCAE	Instituto Centroamericano de Administracio de Expresas (Nicaragua)	NATO	North Atlantic Treaty Organization
		NNP	Net national product
		n.o.s.	Not otherwise specified
ISA	International Sugar Agreement	NTB	Non-tariff barrier
INSEAD	Institute Européen d'Administration des Affaires (Fountainebleau)	OAS	Organization of American States
		OAU	Organization of African Unity
INTELSAT	International Telecommunications Satellite System	OCAM	Organisation Commune Africaine Malgache et Mauricienne
IPC	International Petroleum Company	OCEF	Overseas Economic Fund (Japan)
IPCS	International Patent Classification System	OECD	Organization for Economic Cooperation and Development
IPI	International Patent Institute	OMA	Orderly marketing agreement (or arrangement)
ISO	International Standardization Organization	OPEC	Organization of Petroleum Exporting Countries
ITF	International Transport Workers' Federation	OPIC	Overseas Private Investment Corporation (U.S.)
ITS	International Trade Secretariat		

ORIT	Inter-American Regional Organization of Workers
PACCIOS	Pan-American Committee of CIOS
PAF	Product-area-function (organization type)
PCT	Patent Cooperation Treaty
PEFCO	Private Export Funding Corporation (U.S.)
PICA	Private Investment Cooperation for Asia
P/L	Profit and loss statement
RCD	Regional Cooperation for Development
R&D	Research and Development
SBA	Small Business Administration
SDR	Special drawing rights
SEC	Securities and Exchange Commission (U.S.)
SELA	Latin American Economic System
SIC	Standard Industrial Classification
SITC	Standard International Trade Classification
TA	Technical assistance
TATS	Thematic apperception tests
TSUS	Tariff Schedule of the U.S.
T/T	Transfer of technology (patent)
TUC	Trade Union Congress (U.K.)
UAE	United Arab Emirates
UAW	United Auto Workers (U.S.)
UBEC	Union of Banana Exporting Countries
UCC	Universal Copyright Convention
UDEAC	Union Douanière Economique de l'Afrique Centrale
U.K.	United Kingdom
UN	United Nations
UNCTAD	United Nations Conference for Trade and Development
UNIDO	United Nations Industrial Development Organization
UNDP	United Nations Development Program
UNITAR	United Nations Institute for Training and Research
VAD	Special shares issued to labor (Netherlands)
VAT	Value added tax
VRA	Voluntary restraint arrangement
WCL	World Confederation of Labor
WFTU	World Federation of Free Trade Unions
WHTC	Western Hemisphere Trade Corporation (U.S.)
WIPO	World Intellectual Property Organization

GLOSSARY

Asymmetric economic relationship The relationship existing between two nations or other entities that are significantly unequal in the wealth or resources they command and are parties to an economic transaction or transactions (as in the flow of trade and investment).

Capital intensity The capital required per unit of output. Capital intensity is often stated in terms of capital invested per employee. This is a poor measure, principally because it ignores different rates of capital exhaustion or use. A better measure is depreciation of capital equipment, capital maintenance expenditures, plus interest and dividends (cost of capital) per unit of time (say, one year) per unit of value added (say, millions of dollars).

Capital intensive Processes or products in which the capital per man-hour of labor needed to produce a unit of output is relatively high.

Complementarity agreements Agreements among two or more countries to establish free trade for specific products such that either each participating country manufactures different products within the same product line, exchanges them, and assembles them into the final product, or each country performs a different step in the production process.

Conscious parallelism A situation in which two or more firms, although not explicitly agreeing to fix prices, restrain production, etc., are in fact doing so by monitoring each other's activities.

Contract manufacturing The employment by one firm of an essentially unrelated firm to manufacture specified products for delivery back to itself.

Cumulation In reference to stock shares, a preferred stock which, if the specified dividend is missed in any period, must be paid arrears before any dividend may be paid on common stock.

Convertible currency One of the major trading currencies or a currency freely convertible into them; that is, one for which there is a relatively free market

Deblockage list A list of goods that may be exported, the foreign currency proceeds of which (in whole or in part) may be retained by the exporter for purpose of reimbursing himself for funds that otherwise would have to be held in local currency.

Debt leverage The ratio of debt to equity, at market prices. The leverage refers to the extent a decrease or increase in borrowing by a firm influences the rate of return on equity.

Discontinuities Events or trends that do not represent a simple extension of the past, but appear in the nature of abrupt changes.

Draw down A reduction in the total credit available to a firm by reason of its borrowing or otherwise incurring obligations (such as gurantees).

Economy of scale A reduction in per unit cost by increasing the size of an operation. Large economies of scale imply that reasonable efficiency can be obtained only by large scale production.

Factor complementarity Production factors which, taken in concert, make production feasible without a significant redundancy in the supply of any one. If country X possesses a supply of resources which, when combined with the capital and skills of country Y, yield a marketable, competitively priced product, the two countries enjoy factor complementarity.

Factor mix The relative abundance—and therefore relative cost—of the factors of production (labor, capital, management, entrepreneurship).

Fiduciary One who holds in trust property to which another has beneficial title. Distinguished from an agent who has entire charge of a principal's property and authority to use it on his own authority without consulting his principal, merely turning over net profit periodically to the principal.

Foreign direct investment International investment in the equity (that is, ownership) of an enterprise with the intent of exercising some management control and responsibility. Statistically, acquisition of anything in excess of 10 percent of the voting stock of a company is frequently deemed to be FDI; anything less than that, a portfolio investment. The U.S. uses 10 percent for outgoing investment, 25 percent for incoming. Of course, one might not secure managerial control with 10 percent of the equity. On the other hand, one might secure control with less. It depends upon the spread of the balance of the ownership.

Hedging operations The purchase of assets whose value to the owner is expected to remain substantially unchanged whether certain events take place or not. Risk of loss is thereby reduced or eliminated. Frequently used in reference to protecting oneself against loss due to price inflation (by buying assets whose value will increase with inflation and selling those that will not) or to currency devaluation (by buying "forward," that is, buying a given number of desired currency units to be delivered at some time in the future).

Income-demand elasticity The degree of sensitivity of demand for a given good or service to changes in the income of consumers, often expressed as percentage of change in demand over percentage of change in income.

Indent merchant A commission agent who receives orders or "indents" from foreign buyers for the purchase of specified goods and services.

Integrated distributor One who performs all the necessary marketing functions up to the final consumer.

Integration *In reference to a nation*, the degree to which citizens identify with the nation, perform specialized functions, and are mutually dependent upon one another within a single social-economic system. *In reference to a national market*, the degree to which the population sells and buys in a market so organized that goods and services can move easily throughout the society. *In reference to a firm*, the extent to which the firm internalizes processing from the raw material to the final consumer good (vertical integration), or the extent to which the firm manufactures complementary or associated goods and services (horizontal integration—for example, the production of component parts for automobiles as opposed to assembly of components produced by others). *In reference to local integration*, the degree to which a foreign owned firm subcontracts locally for the purchase of services, products, and skills from locally owned enterprise.

Labor input The amount of labor used in the production of a good or service.

Labor intensity The man-hours of labor required per unit of output.

Linkage In the international marketing sense, the creation of demand in a second national market by reason of either the movement of the product or the foreign customer, or both, into that market.

Lumpiness of investment Where economies of scale are significant, once the capacity of a plant is reached a large investment is needed to produce one more unit.

Marginal cost The added cost incurred by reason of the last unit produced.

Marginal utility The value to the user or beneficiary (for example, the host society in the case of foreign investment) of the last unit produced or made available.

Market gravity The geographical center of the purchasing power of a market.

Maslow's Hierarchy of Needs A widely used classification of human needs, developed by Abraham Maslow, into three levels: *first level*, intrinsic or physiological (safety, food, shelter); *second level*, extrinsic or social (affiliation, belonging, social esteem, prestige, status); *third level*, self-actualization (self-esteem, competence, power, achievement). It is assumed that some degree of satisfaction of a lower need is necessary before a higher need becomes motivating.

Multinational option The strategy of acquiring and allocating resources without regard to national boundaries except when they affect either cost or return. This policy relates both to the source of capital and management and to the sale of goods and services.

Nonrecourse financing Financing in which the creditor assumes full responsibility for collecting from a third party in the sense of waiving his right to claim reimbursement from the debtor in the event that the third party defaults.

Participation In reference to stock shares, a preferred stock that participates beyond the fixed rate with the common stock in the distribution of earnings.

Portfolio investment An investment in which there is no intent to exercise management control or responsibility. Statistically, very frequently anything less than a 10 percent holding of voting stock is considered portfolio. See *Foreign Direct Investment*. Portfolio, however, may be in the form of either debt or equity.

Pre-emption In reference to stock shares, the right of first refusal in relation to the issue of additional stock by a company.

Preference A share of stock with a claim on profits before distribution to common stockholders, possibly upon assets at time of liquidation as well. May or may not be voting. May or may not have a right to participate in management. May be entitled only to a fixed dividend or may participate in the dividend distributed to common shareholders, whichever is the higher.

Price-demand elasticity The extent to which demand for a given good or service changes as price changes, often expressed as percentage of change in demand over percentage of change in price.

Risk The probability of a predictable outcome actually occurring; for example, that an individual will die at the age of 75. Another way of stating risk is that it is the likely variability of returns on a project, the measure of which is variance. See *Uncertainty*.

Sinking fund The aggregate of sums of money, set apart usually at fixed intervals, and deposited or invested to extinguish a debt, or for other purposes.

Specialization agreements Agreements among two or more countries permitting the establishment of specified industries in each of the participating countries to serve all on a preferential basis. Sometimes called "industries of integration."

Spill-over In the international market sense, the creation of demand in one country by reason of promotion in another.

Suboptimization problem The problem created by the tendency of each component of an entity to maximize its own satisfaction without regard for the welfare of the entire entity. (For example, a company division that maximizes its own profit by charging other divisions unduly high prices for its products, thereby reducing the latters' sales and profits to the extent that the combined profit is less than it otherwise would have been.)

Sunk cost A cost already incurred and which does not represent an asset that can be sold for a currency of use of the owner.

Theory X One of a dichotomous management classification system, developed by Douglas MacGregor, that is equated with the "classical" management theory. It assumes that efficiency is measured solely in terms of productivity, that human beings act "rationally," that coordination will not be achieved unless directed from above, that people prefer the security of a definite task and do not value the freedom of determining their own approach to problems (that is, they prefer to be directed and will not cooperate unless a pattern is planned formally for them), that the activities of a group should be viewed on an objective and impersonal basis, that workers are motivated by economic needs and therefore incentives should be in terms of monetary rewards, that people do not like to work and close supervision and accountability should be emphasized, that authority has its source at the top of a hierarchy and is delegated downward, that managerial functions in varied types of activities have universal characteristics and can be performed in a given manner regardless of environment and the qualities of the personnel involved.

Theory Y An alternative set of assumptions (often associated with "modern" or "participative" management) for a normative theory of management derived from Maslow's need hierarchy. Underlying assumptions are that the expenditure of physical and mental work is natural (that it may be either a source of satisfaction or of punishment, depending upon circumstances), that man will exercise self-direction and self-control in the service of an objective to which he is committed, that commitment to an objective is a function of the reward associated with its achievement (the most significant being ego satisfaction and self-actualization needs), that the average human being learns under proper conditions to accept *and* to seek responsibility, that the capacity to exercise a relatively high degree of imagination and creativity in the solution of organizational problems is widely distributed in the population, that under conditions of modern industrial life the intellectual potentiality of the average human being is only partially being utilized.

Tie-in buying and selling Compulsory purchase or sale between two or more firms of certain goods and services. The element of compulsion comes from making an opposite flow of desired goods and services contingent upon the tie-in contract, or by so limiting the supply of capital and skills to an associated firm that it must purchase the missing links from the other.

Transfer price The price at which a firm sells a good or service from one division of the firm to another, or from one subsidiary to another.

Turn-key operation The construction, under contract, of a project up to the point of operation, at which time it is turned over to the owner.

Turn-key plus A turn-key contract plus the provision of certain other inputs likewise under contract, such as management training, technical assistance and training, financial assistance, etc.

Uncertainty The probability of an unpredictable outcome's occurring; that is, one for which there is no actuarial basis. In such case, one might use a normal distribution curve based on minimum and maximum estimates. An example would be the size of an untested market. See *Risk*.

INDEX